The AstroTwins'
2026
Horoscope

Copyright © 2025 by Tali & Ophira Edut (The AstroTwins)
Published by Mediarology, Inc. All rights reserved.
Reproduction without permission is strictly prohibited.

Astrostyle • www.astrostyle.com
Authors: Tali Edut, Ophira Edut

Managing Editor: Lisa M. Sundry
Copy Editor: Amy Anthony
Contributing Editor: Felicia Bender, Helena Woods
Research Editors: Jennifer Karnik, James Kerti
Stevie Goldstein, Stephanie Gailing, Tasha Beg

Cover Illustration © 2025 by Bodil Jane
Book Design: Yvette L. Robinson
Interior Illustrations: Yvette L. Robinson, Will Dudley

TABLE OF CONTENTS

INTRODUCTION

- 3 How To Use This Book
- 4 Year of the Unbridled Spirit
- 7 2026 Global Highlights
- 20 2026 Tarot Card & Crystal

HOROSCOPES
FORECASTS FOR THE 12 ZODIAC SIGNS

- 21 Aries
- 56 Taurus
- 88 Gemini
- 119 Cancer
- 152 Leo
- 184 Virgo
- 215 Libra
- 246 Scorpio
- 278 Sagittarius
- 309 Capricorn
- 341 Aquarius
- 372 Pisces

2026 ALMANAC
THE ASTROTWINS' GLOBAL PREDICTIONS FOR THE YEAR AHEAD

- 582 2026 Global Almanac

MONTHLY HOTSPOTS
MOON TABLES & 2026'S KEY DATES

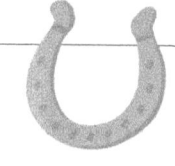

- 405 January
- 418 February
- 429 March
- 441 April
- 452 May
- 464 June
- 475 July
- 486 August
- 497 September
- 507 October
- 518 November
- 527 December

THE STARS IN 2026
TRANSIT TABLES & THEMES

- 539 The Sun in 2026
- 542 The Moon in 2026
- 548 Eclipses in 2026
- 552 The Inner Planets in 2026
- 559 The Outer Planets in 2026
- 567 Retrogrades in 2026
- 570 2026 Ephemeris
- 640 The Year of the Fire Horse
- 643 Numerology: 1 Universal Year

HOW TO USE THIS BOOK

Welcome! We created this guide to help you navigate 2026 with clarity, confidence and a little cosmic magic. Life is beautifully complex. Why not use the stars to plan your moves and make the best decisions possible? Here's how to get the most out of your 2026 Horoscope book all year long:

1. YEARLY HOROSCOPES
Start big-picture. Read the Yearly Overview and Top 5 Themes for your sign. These reveal the major trends shaping your 2026 forecast. Plus, tarot and crystal of the year, numerology and Chinese astrology.

2. MONTHLY HOROSCOPES
Drill down to the details with in-depth monthly forecasts for your sign. Follow the key astrological moments—new and full moons, eclipses, retrogrades and more—with an overview that will help you plan each month.

3. DAILY HOTSPOTS & CALENDAR PAGES
Where is the moon today? Is Mercury retrograde? Find out what's in the stars 365 days of the year. Plan and write notes in the daily calendar pages, each with a word of the day you can use as a guiding mantra. Read hotspot forecasts for every important moment of the year, from retrogrades to eclipses to planetary transits.

4. TRANSIT TABLES
Want a quick cosmic reference? Our at-a-glance tables track the Sun, moon and all the planets as they move through the zodiac. For advanced stargazers, monthly ephemeris pages provide deeper data.

WELCOME TO 2026

the Year of the Unbridled Spirit

A MESSAGE FROM THE ASTROTWINS

You are a spiritual being having a human experience.

This could be the universal truth that restores us all to our senses in 2026.

Spirit, the animating force within, comes alive under this year's cosmic influences. It transcends our human foibles and our glaringly divergent political ideologies. Spirit is the base note of our essence. It's the core of who we are, the spark of light that follows us in—and out—of our human form. And in the year ahead, it's the part of ourselves that must fly free.

Welcome to the Year of the Unbridled Spirit.

When we say "spirit" we're not talking about religion. We're not even talking about spirituality, at least in the sense of a ritual practice. By all means, enjoy your sabbath services, your sage wands and your samsaras. But don't confuse these connective actions with the concept of spirit itself.

To remember that we are spirit is to go beyond the tactile, material plane. To acknowledge spirit is to embrace universality. You are spirit. I am spirit. We are all spirit. This is a oneness that connects us all. And it's stupefyingly simple.

So why does it feel like divisiveness has become an Olympian sport? Politicians, news outlets, podcasters, corporations, religious leaders and autocrats all seem to be vying for the gold in tearing people apart. For communities living on the margins, this isn't exactly new material. Yet, the level of cruel aggression toward the "other" seems to have no bottom.

As astrologers, one of the most common questions we heard in 2025 was, "When is it going to get better?" There's an overriding despair among conscientious people as inhumane behavior seems to be roundly celebrated among the powers that be.

Looking at the forces shaping 2026, our answer is this: *When humanity starts to focus on what unites us instead of what divides us.*

Fortunately, there are plenty of cosmic forces converging to support that mission! What, you thought we'd leave you with no hope? Never that! In fact, the answer may be as simple as a lyrics from the Spice Girl's song, "2 Become 1."

Set your spirit free
It's the only way to be

This saccharine pop single was released on December 16, 1998, one of the last times that karmic Saturn was at 0° Aries, the very first degree of the zodiac. (And yes, that has a lot to do with 2026, thankyouverymuch, Cynical Spice.)

On February 20, 2026, earthbound Saturn greets spiritual Neptune at 0° Aries, AKA "the Aries point," an event that hasn't taken place in thousands of years! Saturn and Neptune HAVE synced up in Aries a few times in the CE era, making exact conjunctions in the Ram's realm in 1703, 1380 and 1051—but never at 0°, the very beginning of the zodiac.

This is quite the odd-couple mashup! Saturn is the boundary hound, Neptune is the boundary dissolver. (What's real, anyway? Who wants to microdose?) For much of 2025, Saturn and Neptune traveled together in close proximity through the very last degree of the zodiac, 29° Pisces, and the very first, 0° Aries.

As they make an exact conjunction at 0° Aries this February 20, humanity has the opportunity for an incredible reset. Zero is the number of infinite possibilities; nothing and everything all at once. Here come lessons in embracing duality: Saturn is the body, Neptune is the spirit. Can we be both embodied and transcendent at once? Is it possible to celebrate our differences while also remaining vigilantly aware that we are spiritual beings having a human experience?

This may seem like a tall order in the age of continuous scrolling and "AI Everything." Being present in our human bodies, aware of our feelings and engaged in the "right here, right now" of the 3D world? A mere three decades ago, that was second nature. In 2026, it may feel like a Herculean effort to rebuild a muscle, especially while alchemical Pluto in Aquarius trines futurist Uranus in Gemini, pulling us into new scientific frontiers.

We are indeed in novel terrain here. Numerology echoes this: 2026 is a 1 Universal Year (2 + 0 + 2 + 6 = 10, 1 + 0 = 1), kicking off a fresh, nine-year cycle. Tear up the old scripts because they just aren't relevant. A 1 Universal Year demands action, just like the influence of Aries, the fiery first sign of the zodiac.

Before we can figure out what's next, we might need a moment to recover from the narcotizing effects of the 9 Universal Year. (2025, we won't miss you.) Better make it a power nap! On February 17, the Aquarius new moon and solar eclipse ushers in the Year of the Fire Horse.

This is NOT giving "Daddy, I want a pony" vibes. Quite the opposite! The last Fire Horse year was 1966, which brought us the first lunar landing, the founding of NOW (National Organization of Women), ATM machines, Star Trek, counterculture, Civil Rights movements and Vietnam War protests. According to lore, girls born during a Fire Horse year would grow up to kill their husbands. While we're certainly not condoning such things, the increased patriarchal oppression has certainly lit a match of rage among women.

Fire Horses—if there were such a thing in the 3D world—would be, yes, unbridled, running free across open planes with their manes whipping in the wind. We wish this feeling of unfettered liberation for you in 2026, even if it means letting go of the reins to which you've clutched so tightly.

You are a spiritual being having a human experience.

Let's race to the horizon without trampling each other in the process.

GROUNDED IN LOVE,
TALI & OPHI

2026
Global Highlights

WHAT'S IN THE STARS FOR ALL OF US?

As we zoom into the second half of the decade, most of the generation-shaping outer planets have shifted into fire and air signs. This dynamic, innovative and yang-heavy energy marks a major pivot from the first half of the 2020s, which we jokingly named The Boring Twenties. From 2020 to 2024, the outer planets (Jupiter, Saturn, Uranus, Neptune and Pluto) cycled through long tours of material-minded and nostalgic earth and water signs.

After this yin kickoff to the 2020s, the collective energy accelerated in 2025—The Year of The Divine Pendulum, as we declared it. Planets swung back and forth between their old (earth, water) and new (fire, air) positions in the zodiac. Disruptions and uncertainty spread.

Major Planetary Movements of 2026

Jupiter in Cancer:
June 9, 2025 – June 30, 2026

Jupiter in Leo:
June 30, 2026 – July 26, 2027

Saturn in Aries:
February 13, 2026 – April 12, 2028

Uranus in Gemini:
April 25, 2026 – May 22, 2033

Neptune in Aries:
January 26, 2026 – March 23, 2039

North Node Aquarius/South Node Leo:
July 26, 2026 – March 26, 2028

A surge of momentum arrives in 2026, which we've named The Year of the Unbridled Spirit. We have little choice but to gallop along with the whiplash-inducing progress that's remixing life as we know it, even as the guardrails become increasingly hard to locate.

The big question: Can we sail into the future without destroying THIS planet? Ensuring that technological development remains ethical and doesn't outpace human capacity will be essential as the 2020s go from "snore" to "roar."

JUPITER IN CANCER: IRON FIST IN THE VELVET GLOVE
JUNE 9, 2025 TO JUNE 30, 2026

Until this June 30, 2026, Jupiter travels through Cancer, the zodiac's "divine mother" sign. This passage, which began on June 9, 2025, is the red-spotted planet's first visit here since June 2013 to July 2014. But don't mistake this watery brand of nurturing as soft or passive. Jupiter is exalted in Cancer, its most free-flowing position in the zodiac. With this "power-top" pose in effect, we're seeing feminine might expressed in all its forms: political, protective and occasionally, punishing.

Women step into command. Since this transit began, women leaders have appeared on Jupiter's global stage. Japan welcomed its first female prime minister, Sanae Takaichi. Nepal's interim P.M. Sushila Karki was appointed after a Gen-Z-led revolution and will remain in power until (and possibly after) the March 5, 2026 election. Venezuela's opposition leader, María Corina Machado, became the first Latina to win the Nobel Peace Prize, controversially devoting her award to Donald Trump.

In the U.S., philanthropists like Mackenzie Scott and Melinda Gates redirected billions toward women's education and global health. And in October 2025, *Town & Country* magazine published an article touting "The Return of the All-Girls School." Meanwhile, polarizing figures like Kristi Noem, Erika Kirk, Pam Bondi and Karoline Leavitt embodied the Iron Woman archetype—wielding and weaponizing conservative values in a post-Roe v. Wade world.

The shadow side of protection emerges. Jupiter in Cancer magnifies national identity, evident in the "America first" rhetoric. The same energy that rallies communities can also fuel xenophobia and isolationism. Immigration policies have turned into violent raids and arrests by mercenary agents. Debates about "who belongs" dominate headlines across continents. Government control is sweeping through the U.K. as British prime minister Keir Starmer attempts to mandate a digital I.D. which can track citizens' residency but also their private purchases.

Baby boxes. As abortion rights are eradicated in a growing number of red U.S. states, a new trend is spreading. Women who bring babies to term and don't want to keep the baby can now anonymously "surrender" their newborns. Baby boxes—temperature-controlled bassinets installed outside of fire stations and hospitals—are a supposedly "safe" way for mothers in 18 states (at this writing) to drop off their infants to be put into the adoption system.

No, this is not a dystopian sci-fi movie. Never mind that the cost to install one of these contraptions is around $16,000, but there is no followup step to support the mother with any psychological and emotional trauma she may experience from the ordeal. (To stay current on laws, advocacy and protections for women's reproductive rights, visit the Center for Reproductive Rights at reproductiverights.org.)

Food insecurity. Jupiter in Cancer beams the spotlight onto our access to nourishment. The 2025 Global Report on Food Crises estimated that 295 million people around the globe faced acute hunger at the end of 2024, which was the sixth consecutive annual increase. War and natural disasters in places like Gaza, Sudan and Yemen created catastrophic levels of starvation. The United States' government shutdown of late 2025 imperiled benefits like the Supplemental Nutrition Assistance Program (SNAP) and Head Start programs that serve breakfast to kids. Food pantries have seen record long lines and the question remains: Will humanity keep allowing this to happen in 2026? While Jupiter is retrograde from November 11, 2025 to March 10, 2026, this crisis could reach a peak.

Pop culture reflects the duality. Outspoken Jupiter in Cancer has brought a wave of truth-telling and revelations to the pop zeitgeist. In October 2025, *British Vogue* published an article titled "Is Having a Boyfriend Embarrassing Now?" revealing how the #couplegoals of the early 2020s have become cringe-y in the decade's latter half. The feminine archetype swings from saint to shadow as girl groups dominate the airwaves. The animated blockbuster K-Pop Demon Hunters literalized the battle between "good girls" and "dark angels." Lily Allen returned to the scene with a post-divorce burn of her ex. Women artists, creators, writers and filmmakers will continue to be the voice of resistance in 2026.

JUPITER IN LEO: BIG LOVE, LOUD POWER
JUNE 30, 2026 TO JULY 26, 2027

Curtains up! Starting June 30, the world shifts from Cancer's protective shell to regal Leo's gilded throne. For the first time since August 2014, Jupiter blazes through the Lion's den, flipping on our creativity and self-expression. After a year of nesting and hunkering into groups, Leo's heart-led courage and performative energy sweeps in and steals the spotlight.

The gold rush returns. Every prior Jupiter-in-Leo era has been gilded—literally. In 1717, when Jupiter was in Leo, Britain adopted the Gold Standard when Sir Isaac Newton—who was in charge of the Royal Mint—accidentally caused silver coins to go out of circulation. Then, when Jupiter was in Leo in September 1931, Britain historically abandoned the gold standard in a period of economic collapse. On July 1, 1944, days after Jupiter completed a lap through Leo, the historic Bretton Woods Conference established that the U.S. dollar could be converted to gold at a fixed rate, which lasted until 1971. The 1967 "gold pool" collapse (a month after Jupiter left Leo) paved the way for free-market pricing; 1979's Jupiter-in-Leo session brought a gold boom. In 2025, gold reached its highest price since 1979, surpassing $4,000 an ounce for the first time ever. With the U.S. dollar on shaky ground, those who hold gold (and silver) in their portfolios could make a fortune in the second half of 2026. But with gambler Jupiter's track record, the golden bubble could also burst.

Celebrity becomes diplomacy. Jupiter in Leo magnifies fame, and this time it's geopolitical. The 1956 "Wedding of the Century" between Grace Kelly and Prince Rainier and the 1991 moment when Queen Elizabeth addressed the U.S. Congress both happened under this Jupiter transit. In 2026-27, royal marriages, political power couples and cultural figureheads may dominate the headlines. Prince Harry could resume royal duties, and we may see Prince William ascend to the role of King.

Kids count! Leo is the sign that rules childhood, and young people could capture the cultural imagination. From nine-year-old Jackie Cooper's 1931 Oscar nod to the birth of the Nickelodeon Kids' Choice Awards in 1991, Jupiter in Leo has always spotlighted youth. This year, Gen Alpha kids, some now in their teens, could step forward as creators, demanding visibility. The "child star" archetype could morph into the "child activist" with a demand for social and environmental justice and better options for education and future standard of living.

Art meets rebellion. Each Jupiter-in-Leo cycle coincides with an artistic renaissance. In 1860, Manet's Spanish Singer broke conventions and opened the door to modernism; in 1967, the Summer of Love exploded with color, sound and social change. As this transit unfolds alongside Uranus in Gemini and Pluto in Aquarius—the same trio active during the Enlightenment—the arts again become the language of revolution. Hybrid media, immersive performance and radical theater blur the line between entertainment and resistance.

Overexposed! Leo's brilliance can lead to fame fatigue and narcissism. In 2002, "Bennifer" became the first widely-used portmanteau as Leo-on-Leo couple Ben Affleck and Jennifer Lopez captivated the world with their OTT relationship and pink-diamond engagement ring drama. A huge leak of nude celebrity photos, coined "The Fappening," was released by hackers during Jupiter's 2014 tour of Leo. As Trump plans a UFC fight in the White House "Club Rose Garden" for his 80th birthday on June 14—a couple weeks before Jupiter moves into Leo—the writing might just be on the cold, cement wall.

SATURN & NEPTUNE IN ARIES: THE DAWN OF NEW THOUGHT

SATURN IN ARIES: FEBRUARY 13, 2026 TO APRIL 12, 2028
NEPTUNE IN ARIES: JANUARY 26, 2026 TO MARCH 23, 2039

Historical moment alert! On February 20, Saturn and Neptune unite at 0° Aries, the very first degree of the zodiac and the birthplace of beginnings. This duo aligns every 35-36 years, but only in Aries every 300-ish years. It's been over a thousand years since Saturn and Neptune connected at The Aries Point (0° Aries), making this conjunction a truly epochal reset.

Prior to this, Neptune was taking an odyssey through its home sign of spiritual Pisces, a voyage that began April 4, 2011. Saturn joined Neptune in this watery realm on March 7, 2023. These cycles brought the esoteric into the mainstream: yoga retreats, meditation apps, psychedelic healing, astrology and Tarot (served on YouTube and TikTok). Conversation around mental health, trauma and emotional wellness entered the global zeitgeist.

Both Neptune and Saturn took brief journeys through Aries in 2025, moving our dreams from a passive to an active state. On January 26, Neptune plants itself in Aries until March 2039. Saturn returns to Aries on February 13 and sets up residence for two years. Whatever's been bubbling in our psyches since 2011 is ready to take shape.

War wounds. At its fiercest, Aries is the sign of war. With Saturn's authoritarian influence and Neptune's ideological spell, battles could intensify and spread in 2026. This energetic current could feel extremely turbulent in Q1, with Saturn and Neptune at a close degree of Aries. With Western powers openly vying to dominate South America at this writing, attacks on Venezuela and other socialist and communist regimes could bring a violent transfer of power. Neptune was at 0° Aries during the opening of the Civil War in 1861, remaining in the Ram's realm through 1872, a time that spanned much of the Reconstruction era as well.

Holy rollers! Saturn rules systems, governments and the material world. Neptune governs dreams, spirituality and illusion. When they merge in Aries, beliefs solidify into institutions. What humanity builds now—both literally and ideologically—will define the next 36-year cycle of thought. Saturn's institutional stance along with Neptune's hypnotic effect could give faith leaders unchecked power over their disciples in the first half of 2026. Megachurches and politicized faith organizations like Turning Point USA and The Heritage Foundation could be handed more power. Schisms between Jews and Muslims continue to be politicized around the globe. We predict this will fade by late July when the lunar North Node moves into democratic Aquarius (more on that below).

Corporatized wellness trends. While Saturn and Neptune toured Pisces from 2023 to early 2026, "plant medicine" went mainstream, leading to early decriminalization of psychedelics in a handful of states. We expect this trend to continue with big pharma getting in on the "shroom boom." Aries rules both sharp objects AND superhuman strength. Botox and GLP-1s will be joined by other injectables that turn back the clock and enhance human capacity. Neural implants are not far behind, especially since Aries rules the head and the brain.

New school of thought. Novelty-seeking Aries loves to learn about the latest and greatest thing. Get ready for waves of stimulating thought along with structures to support it. In 1051 C.E., during another Saturn-Neptune conjunction in Aries, movable type was taking hold in China, allowing print media to blossom. In 1380, Italian scholar Petrarch's revival of classical texts helped ignite the Renaissance and humanism. The last Saturn-Neptune conjunction in Aries brought us the coffee house in 1703. This became the first "third space," where ordinary citizens exchanged ideas that shaped modern democracy. With Generative AI now disrupting the landscape, humans are learning and discovering at quantum speed.

URANUS IN GEMINI: DIGITIZE ME
APRIL 25, 2026 TO MAY 22, 2033

On April 25, Uranus, the planet of disruption and innovation, heads into Gemini until 2033. It also wraps up a seven-year tour of Taurus which began in May 2018. As the first earth sign, Taurus governs our material values, the money we earn and how we work for the food on our table. There's no doubt about it, the past seven years have brought radical shifts. The economy has been turbulent, surging during the pandemic's lower interest rates then devolving into chaos with global tariffs and rising cost of goods. Uranus in Taurus brought us cryptocurrency, creator economies, quiet-quitting and remote work.

Now, the focus shifts. Uranus heads into air-sign Gemini, bringing radical change to the way we communicate, cooperate and interact. We got a taste of this cycle from June 7 to November 7, 2025. Starting April 25, 2026, the side-spinning planet settles back into the sign of the Twins until May 22, 2033.

Quantum leaps in innovation. When radical Uranus last toured Gemini from 1941 to 1949, humanity split the atom, launched television and entered the nuclear age. Over the next seven years, the push for digital everything could bring us to the crossroads of personal convenience and governmental control. Quantum computing, chip manufacturing, robotics, generative AI—some will adapt and others may rebel, sequestering into small, analog communities like the Luddites, artisans who rebelled against the industrial loom from 1811-16 when Uranus was in Sagittarius (Gemini's opposite sign).

The AI "arms" race. In 2026, nations and corporations alike are sprinting to dominate AI infrastructure with ethical oversight severely lagging. Tech titans cast themselves as visionaries: Peter Thiel famously declared that anyone who regulates AI is "the antichrist," while others promise "productivity without the tax of human labor." Drones and robotics are replacing vast swaths of skilled human labor forces leaving citizens vulnerable to government dependency and control.

Surveillance and simulation become indistinguishable. Deepfakes, digital dupes and AI-generated voices distort reality in real time. Propaganda is being pushed through paid creators. The psychological toll is measurable and could get worse. Clinicians have documented "AI psychosis," the disorienting inability to discern truth from fabrication. Chatbots trained for mental health support have sparked scandals after offering suicide assistance. With the U.S. midterm elections taking place in 2026, digital interference and manipulation with vote count could become a threat to a legitimate election.

Independent media fights for freedom. As public trust in legacy media collapses due to conservative billionaire ownership, independent journalists may have a heyday similar to the 1860s Uranus-in-Gemini "muckrakers" who exposed corruption during The Gilded Age. Creators may decentralize their work through the blockchain, micro-subscriptions and new social media networks. Truth becomes peer-to-peer again—a digital echo of Uranus's last tour through Gemini, when radio and television first liberated (and manipulated) mass consciousness.

NORTH NODE IN AQUARIUS / SOUTH NODE IN LEO: CROWD VS. CROWN
JULY 26, 2026 TO MARCH 26, 2028

For the first time in nearly two decades, the lunar nodes shift into Aquarius (North) and Leo (South), pulling humanity between collective progress and individual pride. Aquarius calls us toward innovation, equality and interdependence. Leo traffics in personal power, performance and prestige. The tension between "we" and "me" defines this 18-month cycle.

Power to the people. The North Node in Aquarius amplifies collective action and shared governance. Each time this axis returns, society reinvents itself—the New Deal of the 1930s, the Civil Rights blueprint of the 1950s, the fall of the Berlin Wall in 1989. Expect a surge of decentralized movements: cooperatives, union alliances and global campaigns for digital rights.

Celebrity politicians. With the U.S. midterm elections taking place from April to November 2026, the political landscape demands attention, especially with democracy at stake. The next great influencers may be organizers of "the people," including politicians with a celebrity flair such as AOC and Gavin Newsom. With the South Node in Leo, Hollywood celebrities are likely to step forward to support global change.

iOStarpower. With Jupiter blazing alongside the South Node in Leo from June 30, 2026 to July 26, 2027, human creative potential burns bright, but there may be no escaping AI as a tool for expression. Technology becomes both muse and rival, helping artists write screenplays, compose scores and render actors with lifelike realism. Hollywood will be pushed to explore what remains uniquely human about performance. New genres may emerge in both the acoustic and digital spaces.

Future frequency. Aquarius governs progress, technology and the collective mind. Despite authoritarian and corporate efforts to thwart "the people," underground movements could swell into paradigm shifts. Advancements are ahead in clean energy, cooperative digital economies and micro-communities that adopt a people-first ethos. The ideals of the Internet's early promise—freedom, equality and open access—may resurface as younger generations reclaim unexpected aspects of the digital sphere from corporate monopolies. The attention economy may shift in startling ways, weakening the "broligarchy" as users rebel by leaving their platforms.

CHIRON IN TAURUS — HEALING WHAT WE VALUE
JUNE 19 TO SEPTEMBER 17, 2026

For the first time since 1983, "wounded healer" Chiron dips into Taurus, briefly leaving warmongering Aries, where it's been since 2018. This short preview of a longer cycle (beginning in April 2027) turns our collective attention toward healing material insecurity and redefining worth. Taurus rules our values, the economy, food and the ways we nourish and sustain ourselves on a day-to-day basis. The shadow side of Taurus can be material greed and resource-hoarding. Will we learn from the past and make the right choices?

This land is my land. In the wake of 2025's tariff-fueled Farmageddon, which left crops rotting on fields and bankrupt land stewards grappling for recovery, this Chiron cycle could bring a wakeup call and a shift. Financial recovery, food systems and the body-earth connection all come into focus. Jimmy Carter, the peanut-farmer-turned President, was in office for much of Chiron's last tour of Taurus from 1976 to 1983. In addition to expanding the national park services, he brokered the historic peace treaty between Egypt and Israel, The Camp David Accords. Could Chiron in Taurus bring the two-state solution between Israel and Palestine? While this is unlikely to happen in 2026, there may be historic turns when Chiron embarks on its longer journey through Taurus after April 2027.

Critical climate moments.
Beginning in 1930, insufficient rainfall in the Great Plains set the stage for a long drought. As the decade wore on, record-breaking heatwaves and dust storms devastated crops. On the brink of Chiron's move into Taurus, AI data centers are buying up farmland and gobbling up water resources, setting the stage for a man-made version of these conditions.

Financial reckonings. Chiron was in Taurus from 1926 to 1934, a period when the Roaring Twenties opulence crashed with the Stock Market in 1929 and led to worldwide economic devastation, including the Great Depression. It was a confluence of factors that threw society into this preventable peril, from climate catastrophe (drought) to power struggles between Wall Street and the Federal Reserve, to anti-immigrant sentiment and tariffs that shut down global trade. This is an eerie echo of what is happening today with Trump's tariffs and the ICE raids.

The 1930 Smoot-Hawley Tariff Act, fueled by protectionist attitudes and the scapegoating of immigrants, effectively halted global trade. Chiron's tour of Taurus in the 1970s dovetailed with the 1979 Oil Crisis when the Iranian Revolution brought a steep rise in oil prices and destabilized the global economy. Will the 2026 administration continue to tear apart international relations with punishing tariffs on foreign trade partners?

Rumblings of economic trouble are in the air as interest rates remain high, fueling fears of stagflation. The Federal Reserve quietly lent billions of dollars to U.S. banks in November 2025. Meanwhile, the stock market hedges its bets on AI, potentially creating a bubble. As Chiron does a short lap through Taurus mid-2026, technologized nations may be pushed to explore new ways of supporting citizens such as a Universal Basic Income that subsidizes everything from food to health care. This controversial solution may create a form of tech feudalism, turning Silicon Valley CEOs into modern day lords doling out resources to everyday people as if they were peasants on a fief. What stipulations will be placed upon people who accept this money—and who will set those rules?

Impacts on the labor force. At the bottom of the Great Depression, America faced a 25 percent unemployment rate: One in four Americans were jobless, many losing their homes and life savings. In fall 2025, companies including Amazon, Microsoft and UPS laid off tens of thousands of workers. Chiron's return to Taurus reminds us: We don't have to repeat our mistakes. In 2026, Chiron's preview parade through Taurus could reveal early breakthroughs in sustainable agriculture and give us a glimpse of the economic crossroads ahead while there's still time to make better choices.

OTHER NOTABLE TRANSITS

LUNAR NODES IN PISCES/VIRGO — THE SYSTEMS AND THE SOUL
JANUARY 11, 2025 TO JULY 26, 2026

As 2026 opens, the lunar nodes continue their 19-month passage through Pisces (North) and Virgo (South). The North Node in Pisces urges compassion, imagination and collective healing, while the South Node in Virgo tests bureaucratic and medical systems built for efficiency over empathy. This axis continues to shape global discussions around health care, policy and public service. Spiritual warfare and faith-based bureaucrats may hypnotize the masses as humanity grapples with both losses and gains in compassion.

YEAR OF THE FIRE HORSE — THE REBEL RETURNS
FEBRUARY 17, 2026 TO FEBRUARY 6, 2027

The fiery, untamed Horse gallops back into the Chinese zodiac for the first time since 1966, this time beginning with the fanfare of an Aquarius solar (new moon) eclipse—which is also an annular "ring of fire" eclipse. (Talk about celestial symbology!) Fire Horse years are notorious for upheaval, independence and iconoclasts who refuse to be bridled. In 1966, it marked the height of counterculture movements and revolutionary art. In 2026, the same defiant spirit reignites. Renegade creators, whistleblowers and reformers rise to challenge institutions and rewrite what freedom means in a hyper-connected world.

VENUS TURNS RETROGRADE THIS FALL
OCTOBER 3 TO NOVEMBER 13, 2026

Don't lose the key to those fur-lined toys during cuffing season 2026! Love planet Venus turns retrograde from October 3 to November 13, backing up through two of the most relationship-oriented signs: Scorpio until October 25 and then Libra until November 13. Spicy situations could go from "five chilis" to ice cold as past information surfaces or attractions cool unceremoniously. Don't be too quick to ghost! Venus retrograde could also churn up unhealthy attachments to narcissists, toxic exes and other types that fall into the "trauma-informed" category. If you're planning a wedding or romantic ceremony during this cycle, we recommend getting the licensing done before October 3 or after November 13. Or plan on renewing vows in 2027: Venus turns retrograde every 18 months so you're in the clear next year. Look back to fall 2018 for clues of what might come up, which was the last time Venus reversed through Scorpio and Libra.

FOUR ECLIPSES
FEBRUARY 17: ANNULAR SOLAR ECLIPSE IN AQUARIUS
MARCH 3: TOTAL LUNAR ECLIPSE IN VIRGO
AUGUST 12: TOTAL SOLAR ECLIPSE IN LEO
AUGUST 28: PARTIAL LUNAR ECLIPSE IN PISCES

A new series of eclipses begins this year, striking the Aquarius/Leo axis and revving up issues of the people versus the privileged. Simultaneously, we also round out a set of Virgo/Pisces eclipses that have been rocking our material and spiritual worlds since October 2023. On February 17, a "ring of fire" solar eclipse in Aquarius kicks off The Year of the Fire Horse and brings a blaze of civic engagement. Two weeks later, on March 3, a total lunar eclipse in Virgo could reveal breaches in policy and ethics. (The Epstein Files or maybe The Tesla Files—get ready.) The second eclipse corridor arrives in August with a Total Solar Eclipse with the new moon in Leo on August 12, an event that last occurred with The Great American Eclipse on August 21, 2017, and will occur again over Luxor, Egypt on August 2, 2027, when the sky will darken for over six minutes. New leaders could emerge along with huge celebrity moments. A partial lunar eclipse arrives on August 28 with the Pisces full moon sending buried information bubbling to the surface.

MERCURY'S TRIO OF RETROGRADES ARE IN WATER SIGNS

FEBRUARY 26--MARCH 20 (PISCES)

JUNE 29-JULY 23 (CANCER)

OCTOBER 24-NOVEMBER 13 (SCORPIO)

Water, water everywhere! Mercury will be retrograde in all three water signs this year: Pisces, Cancer and Scorpio. Deep feelings won't be crowded out by the spate of outer planets in (far less sensitive) fire and air signs. These moments are a hidden blessing, allowing us to tap into the deeper corners of our hearts, souls and psyches. Nostalgia reigns!

Want more global astrology?
Head to page 582 for our 2026 Astrological Almanac. This special section contains a series of articles about worldwide trends and predictions according to the stars. What do relationships look like in the Age of Aquarius? Will there be a civil war in 2026? What is the economic forecast for the year ahead? Plus: 2026 forecasts in Human Design, Astrocartography, Numerology and Chinese (Lunar) Astrology.

Tune in to our weekly podcast, **AstroTwins Radio,** *where we discuss headline news through the lens of astrology:* **astrostyle.com/podcast**

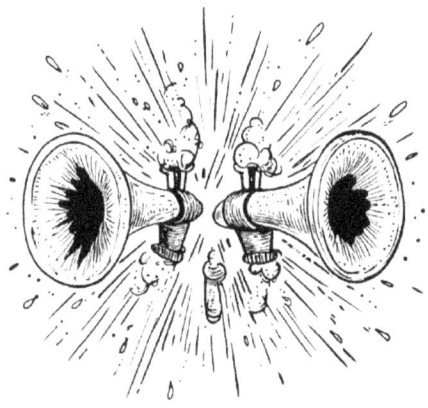

PLANETARY KEY

ZODIAC SIGNS

♈	ARIES
♉	TAURUS
♊	GEMINI
♋	CANCER
♌	LEO
♍	VIRGO
♎	LIBRA
♏	SCORPIO
♐	SAGITTARIUS
♑	CAPRICORN
♒	AQUARIUS
♓	PISCES

PLANETS

☉	SUN
☽	MOON
♂	MARS
☿	MERCURY
♀	VENUS
♄	SATURN
♃	JUPITER
♆	NEPTUNE
♅	URANUS
♇	PLUTO

MOONS

FM	FULL MOON
NM	NEW MOON
LE	LUNAR ECLIPSE
SE	SOLAR ECLIPSE

TAROT CARD OF THE YEAR

THE CHARIOT
Willpower, Action, Control, Determination

All aboard! After a year of pausing and processing, the wheels are turning again. The Chariot charges in as the Tarot card of 2026, urging you to move forward with purposeful determination. Enough ruminating on the past. In 2026, progress requires direct action—along with courage and control. The road ahead may twist and turn, with a few challenging obstacles along the way. Keep your hands on the wheel until you arrive triumphantly at your destination.

CRYSTAL OF THE YEAR

CARNELIAN
Motivation, Vitality, Courage

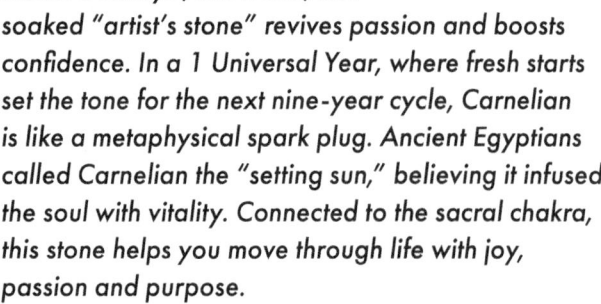

Deep orange Carnelian blazes in as 2026's crystal of the year, radiating energy that gets your imagination firing on all cylinders. A true creative catalyst, this warm, sun-soaked "artist's stone" revives passion and boosts confidence. In a 1 Universal Year, where fresh starts set the tone for the next nine-year cycle, Carnelian is like a metaphysical spark plug. Ancient Egyptians called Carnelian the "setting sun," believing it infused the soul with vitality. Connected to the sacral chakra, this stone helps you move through life with joy, passion and purpose.

ARIES
IN 2026

| ALL THE PLANETS IN ARIES IN 2026 | YOUR 2026 HOROSCOPE | TOP 5 THEMES FOR ARIES IN 2026 | LOVE HOROSCOPE + LUCKY DATES | MONEY HOROSCOPE + LUCKY DATES |

Aries in 2026

Your year of:
METAMORPHOSIS, CREATIVE LEADERSHIP, COOPERATION

THIS IS YOUR CHRYSALIS YEAR, ARIES.

The restless spark that once had you saying yes to "everything, everywhere all at once" is shifting into a fixed focus. You're learning that progress doesn't come from doing more, but from opting in to what truly matters. Projects with heart and purpose rise to the top, while home and relationships give you the roots to grow with confidence. By December, you'll notice the shift: less rushing, more resonance. This year isn't about speed—it's about building a life that feels like a custom fit for you.

THE PLANETS IN Aries

THE SUN MAR 20–APR 19	Happy birthday season! With the Sun in your sign, you're clear to take chances, chase fresh adventures, and command the spotlight.
NEW MOON APR 17 7:52PM, 27°29'	Happy bonus New Year! Set your intentions for the next six months, then take a brave step forward. Your fans await!
FULL MOON SEP 26 12:49PM; 3°37'	Manifestation moment! Your work of the past six months bears fruit. Celebrate your progress and harvest the rewards.
MERCURY APRIL 14–MAY 2	Hold court! When charismatic Mercury zips through your sign, your social status soars. Work the room, make connections—but keep your commitments realistic to avoid overpromising.
VENUS MARCH 6–30	Love is in the air! When the galactic glamazon struts through your sign, your powers of seduction skyrocket. Irresistible charm, luxe tastes and flirtatious vibes abound—just keep an eye on your budget.
MARS APRIL 9–MAY 18	Motivation is off the charts when energetic Mars blazes through your sign every couple of years. You're bold, driven and unstoppable—but watch that combative streak and ease up on the intensity.
SATURN FEB 13–DEC 31 RETROGRADE IN ARIES: JUL 26–DEC 10	Welcome to cosmic boot camp! Discipline and focus are demanded as you stabilize the foundation of your life. Saturn visits your sign every 29.5 years for a 3-year visit. It ain't easy, but the growth will be epic!
CHIRON JAN 1–JUN 19 SEP 17–DEC 31 RETROGRADE IN ARIES: JAN 1–2; SEP 17–DEC 31	The wounded-healer comet holds the key to turning pain into prescient gifts. Since it moved into Aries on April 17, 2018, you've journeyed through a dark night of the soul. This cycle is winding down in 2026 and 2027. Prepare to emerge a sage!
NEPTUNE JAN 26–DEC 31 RETROGRADE IN ARIES: JUL 7–DEC 12	This 14-year cycle (until March 23, 2039!) is shifting your identity, spiritual self-discovery and enhanced connection to the ethereal realm. Prioritize deep healing. Get involved in charitable work. Take your dreams seriously.

Aries in 2026
HIGHLIGHTS

DREAMS BECOME YOUR REALITY AS SPIRITUAL NEPTUNE FLOWS INTO ARIES FOR 14 YEARS

Starting January 26, soulful Neptune settles into Aries for its first extended tour since 1862–1875. You got a taste of this identity-shifting cycle from March 30 to October 22 of 2025. Now, Neptune sets sail through your sign for fourteen years, until March 23, 2039. A deeply spiritual chapter unfolds—one some people will never experience in their lives since Neptune takes 165 years to cycle through the zodiac. Your life purpose fuses with higher callings, artistic visions and mystical ideals.

STRATEGIC SATURN PARKS IN ARIES FOR TWO YEARS, PUTS STRUCTURE BEHIND YOUR DREAMS

On February 13, Saturn kicks off a no-nonsense mission in your sign, staying until April 12, 2028. You got a short preview of this cycle last year, when the ringed taskmaster visited Aries from May 24 to September 1. The coming two years may feel like cosmic boot camp at times: challenging but transformational. Take heart! When Saturn visits your sign every 29.5 years, it imbues you with grit and discipline. Show up, suit up and build a legacy-level goal.

HEAL FROM THE INSIDE OUT: LUNAR NODES IN VIRGO AND PISCES UNTIL JULY 26

Let's get (meta)physical! For the first half of the year, the North Node in Pisces and South Node in Virgo activate your health and healing axis, guiding you through an inside-out glow up. This cycle has been underway since January 11, 2025, teaching you to release perfectionism while you prioritize self-care. Mindfulness, meditation and gentle movement practices keep you balanced. Let thy food be thy medicine.

GET YOUR HOUSE IN ORDER BEFORE JULY: JUPITER IN COZY CANCER

Lucky Jupiter turns home into your launchpad in the first half of 2026, as it completes its yearlong tour through Cancer and your domestic fourth house (June 9, 2025 to June 30, 2026). With the adventurous planet here, you could launch a business from your living room, take an ancestral pilgrimage to explore your roots, or relocate to a zip code that aligns with your long-term vision. Wherever you hang your hat, make sure it fuels your future.

YOUR RULER, MAKE-IT-HAPPEN MARS, VISITS YOUR SIGN FOR THE FIRST TIME IN TWO YEARS

From April 9 to May 18, fiery Mars powers through Aries, pumping you full of energy, confidence and unstoppable drive. This biennial rocket boost is prime time to launch epic projects, take strategic risks and unapologetically step forth as the trailblazer you were born to be.

WELCOME TO THE INNOVATION STATION: DISRUPTOR URANUS IN GEMINI

Welcome to the Innovation Station! Starting April 25, Uranus kicks off a seven-year tour through Gemini, firing up your third house of communication and ideas. Your thoughts travel far—and fast—whether you're launching a podcast, tapping into AI, or becoming a group chat legend. While this cycle wages on until 2033, think ahead, speak up and don't be afraid to shake up the conversation.

WOUNDED HEALER CHIRON MOVES BRIEFLY OUT OF YOUR SIGN—SWEET RELIEF!

Since 2018, soothsayer Chiron's been on a soulful excavation in Aries, rebuilding your confidence from the inside out. From June 19 to September 17, the "wounded healer" takes a breather in Taurus, giving you space to integrate the lessons of this eight-year internal evolution. As you celebrate how much you've grown, others will notice! You may be tapped as a mentor, guide or healer for someone struggling with a situation that you've overcome.

PLAYTIME AND PLEASURE ABOUND WHEN LUCKY JUPITER CIRCLES INTO LEO ON JUNE 30

Lights, camera, Aries! Maximizer Jupiter blazes into Leo on June 30, blessing you with undisputed main character energy. Love, creativity and full-throttle self-expression take center stage for the next 13 months. Whether you're showing off your talents, falling in love (again) or welcoming a new addition to your life, this cycle is all about joy and expansion. And since Jupiter rules travel, don't be surprised if romance finds you far from home—or through someone with a very different background. Your passport to passion and purpose is officially stamped!

TEAMWORK MAKES YOUR DREAM WORK WHEN THE NORTH NODE ENTERS AQUARIUS ON JULY 26

Pillar of the community? Captain of the dream team? For the first time in nearly two decades, the lunar North Node heads into Aquarius this July 26, energizing your eleventh house of groups, technology and future visions for 20 months. Join forces with like-minded souls for an impact-driven mission. Lean into innovation to build something for the collective good. Meanwhile, the Leo South Node reveals new ways to shine as an individual while sharing the spotlight with an ensemble cast. finds you far from home—

or through someone with a very different background. Your passport to passion and purpose is officially stamped!

MERCURY RETROGRADES: SLOW DOWN TO POWER UP

Mercury turns retrograde three times in 2026, Aries, pressing pause so you can regroup in important areas of your life. From February 26 to March 20, the messenger planet rewinds through your twelfth house of rest and reflection. Use this stretch to catch up on unfinished projects, recharge, and clear out old baggage. June 29 to July 23, Mercury pivots in your fourth house of home and family. A domestic matter may need rethinking, or a relative could resurface with unfinished business. The final cycle, October 24 to November 13, falls in your eighth house of intimacy and shared resources. With Venus also retrograde in Libra, relationship dynamics could get a full review. Money matters, trust issues, or joint commitments may need renegotiation before you move ahead.

OLD FLAMES, NEW STANDARDS: VENUS RETROGRADE 2026

From October 3 to November 13, Venus retrogrades through Scorpio and Libra, stirring up intense themes in relationships, money, and self-worth. Old flames could reappear, unresolved dynamics resurface, or you may feel restless in your closest bonds. Instead of rushing decisions, use this pause to recalibrate your standards. And here's the kicker: Venus retraces this same patch of sky every 8 years (minus 2°), flashing you back to fall 2018. Think about who you were dating, what you were creating, or how you were defining your standards then. The story resurfaces—not to repeat, but to show how far you've evolved.

Love

ARIES 2026 FORECAST

What love goals are you ready to architect, Aries? As January dawns, lovebirds Venus and Mars sync up in ambitious Capricorn, bringing that vision into form. What's the ideal structure for your relationship? What qualities are non-negotiable for you to find in a mate? What would you love to build together with your partner this year? Spell it all out, but leave a little room for experimentation. With Venus and Mars getting frisky in Aquarius from January 23 to February 10, romance could pivot in an unconventional direction. You might discover a new kink or hot-blooded turn-on before the Year of the Fire Horse begins on February 17.

Echoing this dichotomy, a pair of "odd couple" planets are cruising into your sign in Q1. First up is dreamy, romanticizing Neptune, the dissolver of boundaries, who begins a 13-year cruise through Aries this January 26. Two weeks later, on February 13, traditional Saturn begins its two-year trek through Aries. Like a heavy counterweight, Saturn wants everything defined, including boundaries.

In every part of your life, including love, you'll navigate this interesting paradox. How can you blur lines just enough to keep things exciting and mysterious—but sharpen them enough to prevent you from cascading into an anxious attachment spiral? While Neptune wears rose-colored glasses, Saturn sniffs out red flags. There CAN be a "best of both worlds" scenario here, but it might take a little while for you to adjust to these dueling energies.

While we are always fans of clear communication, this might be one year where sharing unprocessed thoughts with a love interest could go south. Neptune in Aries is bound to stir up illusions and fears of "losing yourself" while Saturn can treat every interested party like a prime suspect. Your inner saboteur will be active this year, Aries. Investing in a wise objective sounding board, like a coach, mentor or therapist, can be the relationship insurance you didn't know you needed.

On a proactive note, the Saturn-Neptune duet makes 2026 a great year for "auramaxxing." This TikTok trend has been around for a while and essentially boils down to paying conscious attention to the energy you exude so that your presence becomes an even-more-attractive force. What we love so much about this concept is that it starts with self-care: improving your sleep, starting a meditation practice, getting your hormone levels checked (time for HRT?). Then it taps into that pure self-expression that Aries live for, like dabbing on a signature scent and picking a palette that becomes unrecognizably yours. For decades our Aries Aunt Betsy has always left us awestruck with her artfully chosen purple nails, shoes and accessories.

Speaking of color, those bright yellow daffodils have nothing on you this spring. You're in full bloom from March 6 to 30, as Venus sashays into Aries and boosts your magnetism to supernova levels. And what a relief! The love planet will NOT be retrograde in Aries, as was the case last year (March 1 to 27, 2025). Nope, Aries, there's nothing short-circuiting your spring awakening this year. Dress up, dazzle and just be your spitfire self. Summer lovin' can happen so fast! On June 30, Jupiter's grand entrance into Leo cuts the ribbon on 13 months of explosive passion and exciting progress! Whether you're searching for a soulmate, gearing up for parenthood or planning a wedding, romance is front and center in the second half of 2026. Love boldly and co-author a relationship adventure that would make a Hollywood producer want to buy the movie rights. Yes, that will take some imagination and possibly a major change of scenery if you've been stuck in a rut. Find someone who can hold this visionary energy or you could spiral out into nonstop drama.

Adding to the lionhearted vibes? The karmic South Node slips into Leo on July 26, ushering in 20 months of soulful romantic exploration. A meant-to-be match could arise, even a twin flame, someone who feels like a familiar from another lifetime. Embrace the chance to make up for lost time, if only to close the loop and move on elsewhere. Highlight August 12 on your calendar! A potent solar (new moon) eclipse in Leo charges up your fifth house of romance, passion and fame. This heart-opening event could spark a new love or reveal passionate chemistry that's been hiding in plain sight.

The deepest relationship shifts may arrive between October 3 and November 13 when Venus spins retrograde. This time around, the planet of amour backs up through Scorpio and Libra—and your eighth house of eroticism and intimacy, then your seventh house of commitments. There's no dodging the love lessons of this cycle, Aries. If you hit any blockades, trust, vulnerability and transparency are a must. Strip off the mask! Demand that anyone who wants to love you do the same. Scary as this can feel, you'll never build a rock-solid bond if you hide behind a curated image.

Feeling nostalgic? Old lovers could pop back into the plotline. Or you may finally heal a heartache you've been carrying quietly for too long. Venus retrograde is NOT the time to make any sudden moves. While you or your S.O. might need a little more space, this six-week period can evoke positive transformation if you both pull back and do your respective "inner work."

Venus turns direct on November 13 and returns to sultry Scorpio on December 4 for the rest of the year, pulling you into some of the deepest emotional waters imaginable. Casual connections? What are those? Relationships that don't hold emotional weight could dissolve, clearing space for meaningful connections to flow in. Power dynamics in relationships will also be exposed with Venus in this investigative sign—and might just set the stage for some spicy role playing. The only question is, Aries, who's on top?

Money & Career

ARIES 2026 FORECAST

Authority figure? Role model? Imagineer? 2026 is a year of major leadership upgrades—and that's saying something for you, o' fearless one! On February 13, structured Saturn parks in your sign for its first full year since the late 90s, launching a two-year cycle of professional mastery. Whether you're elevating your skills or literally designing your future from the ground up, be patient. Methodical Saturn's learning curve can be steep, but it's for your own good. The ringed taskmaster demands integrity, but it also rewards consistency and discipline.

Not that it will be all work, no play! Glamorous Neptune swan-dives into Aries for a 13-year tour starting January 26, infusing your professional path with creative, spiritual and idealistic flair. Forget about simply working for a paycheck. This mission- and impact-driven cycle is here to help you align your outer ambitions with your inner calling. Aries who work in an artistic, healing or humanitarian field could rise to the top of your game while Neptune's on this journey until 2039. No matter what you do, start adding more soul to your goals ASAP.

You'll have major momentum from April 9 to May 18, so don't waste a second of that time! For the first time in two years, go-getter Mars—your red-hot ruling planet—powers through Aries and puts some muscle in your hustle! Here's your cosmic green light to launch, pitch and take action.

On April 25, innovative Uranus zips into Gemini where it will charge up your communication zone until 2033! This seven-year cycle positions you as a vocal force and disruptor in your field. Your work may become far more mobile, whether you're literally on the go, working remotely between multiple locations or running around town all day. Your channels could explode with innovative new projects—from viral content to digital ventures to brilliant writing.

Got a talent to monetize? Don't wait to be discovered! Abundant Jupiter swings into Leo on June 30, igniting your fifth house of fame and self-expression until July 26, 2027. This cycle only comes around every 12-13 years. (The last time was July 16, 2014 to August 11, 2015.) Proactively claim your space and make some noise promoting your work on social media and anywhere you can grab a spotlight. This is another boon for Aries artists, musicians and performers of all stripes. Get thee to a stage!

On July 26, the North Node shifts into Aquarius, activating your visionary eleventh house and pointing your path toward cutting-edge industries, social impact work and digital platforms. Impact-driven industries like solar and renewables could call your name. Some Aries might even find their way into politics during this 20-month cycle, which wages on until March 26, 2028. Whether you're launching a startup, joining a cause-driven team or building a global network, 2026 is about aligning your career with the future—and helping shape it.

If you've felt stuck in outdated roles, 2026 offers multiple chances to pivot. A Virgo lunar eclipse in March and a Pisces lunar eclipse in August spotlight your work-life balance, calling for smarter systems and deeper purpose. The bottom line is this: Don't just work hard, Aries, work meaningfully!

TOP 5 THEMES FOR Aries in 2026

1	2	3	4	5
BUILD YOUR DREAM SELF	FIND YOUR TRUE HOME	REFRAME THE NARRATIVE	LEAD THE REVOLUTION	REDEFINE INTIMACY

1 BUILD YOUR DREAM SELF

NEPTUNE IN ARIES
JANUARY 26, 2026–MARCH 23, 2039

SATURN IN ARIES
FEBRUARY 13, 2026–APRIL 12, 2028

What happens when the planet of hard data meets the planet of pure fantasy—in your sign, no less? You're about to get a masterclass in that, Aries. An ultra-rare convergence of boundary-hound Saturn and boundary-dissolver Neptune is officially underway. For the next two years, they combine their disparate energies in your first house of identity, image and self-actualization. And what a weird ride it will be.

Bottom line, these two planetary powerhouses couldn't be more different. Saturn builds walls. Neptune dissolves them. Saturn demands structure, responsibility and realism. Neptune whispers of dreams, intuition and spiritual surrender. Because they move at such different speeds through the zodiac, they only sync up in the same sign every 35 to 40 years. And the last time they joined hands in Aries? Well, that was way back in 1702. Suffice it to say, this is a rare gift—and one to navigate with care and curiosity.

You got a brief taste of this duo last year. Fluid Neptune drifted into Aries from March 30 to October 22, 2025. Directional Saturn helped right that ship during its brief visit to your sign, from May 24 to September 1. Now, both are embarking on longer treks through Aries. Neptune settles into Aries for the long haul on January 26, beginning a 13-year journey through your psyche and persona. Saturn follows close behind on February 13, initiating a two-year boot camp in self-mastery. Where will this lead you? You're going to have to take it one step at a time.

February 20 is a landmark moment. For the first time since 1989, Saturn and Neptune make an exact conjunction. This time around, they team up at 0º Aries, their only direct hit during their shared journey through your sign. It's a pivotal point in your personal evolution as the universe fuses your soul's highest calling (Neptune) with the discipline to actually live it out (Saturn).

But how to balance these bizarre energies? Escape-artist Neptune wants you to run off with the band, like Aries Kate Hudson in Almost Famous; to dissolve into your art and mystical pursuits. But, nope! Taskmaster Saturn will have none of that—well, not unless you're a Ram with a plan. How do you plan to pay your bills, feed yourself and take care of your responsibilities? There's no wiggling out of the pragmatic stuff under Saturn's watch.

While Saturn's temperance can feel soul-crushing at first, rein in any selfish or careless impulses. You've grown so much over the past years by making tough choices in the name of evolution. Saturn won't let you undo all that progress, even if you do wind up with a raging case of FOMO.

There's plenty of fun to be had this year, don't worry! But what if you could enjoy it without leaving a trail of destruction in your wake? That's what we mean by the best of both worlds. They don't call Saturn the planet of adulting for nothing.

The trick is not choosing one over the other, but learning to let them inform each other. Like water, you can move through both liquid and solid states. Structured Saturn gives Neptune a container to pour all its dreams into. Spiritual Neptune gives stoic Saturn's plans a richer meaning. Starting in 2026, your wildest imaginings could go from "wouldn't it be crazy if" notions to an actual blueprint—one that may eventually put money in the bank.

Since the first house rules your personal image, this conjunction may spark a radical redefinition of self. Shed old labels, Aries, and stop forcing yourself to keep plodding along through an identity that you've outgrown. For many Rams, 2026 is a year to wipe the canvas clean. You can expect to feel both terrified and exhilarated by the unscripted road ahead. It's normal to feel lost in the fog during a Neptune transit, and this one will leave you questioning everything. Thankfully, Saturn is right there helping you rebuild on solid ground.

If you don't know who you are anymore, consider it a good sign. That's the first step toward becoming who you are meant to be next. Human beings (even you, daring Aries) struggle with the concept of uncertainty. This year, one of your biggest accomplishments may be sitting through tough feelings—WITHOUT rushing to make a move, fix the problem or react emotionally.

In the process, you'll confront fears around loneliness, visibility or not being "enough." But again, that's where the growth happens. When you stop chasing external validation and start aligning with your inner compass, everything shifts. Your presence becomes magnetic, your words carry weight and your identity feels grounded in something real.

Know this, Aries: With Saturn pushing through your sign for two years, you're going to feel like you're enrolled in boot camp some days. Responsibilities pile up, decisions carry weight and your youthful zest takes a backseat to new levels of adulting. Get ready to push yourself harder than you knew was humanly possible. Fortunately, this cycle only comes around every 29.5 years—and when it ends on April 12, 2028, you'll feel stronger and more bulletproof than ever.

There's an added challenge to contend with because Saturn is "in fall" in Aries, one of the toughest positions in the zodiac for this planet. Your impulsive, risk-taking nature doesn't jibe with Saturn's slow, methodical pace. But herein lies a golden opportunity to master a more mindful approach to life—particularly the way you manage time, which is ruled by Lord Kronos (Saturn's other name). This cycle might lower your risk tolerance but hey, Aries, maybe living on the edge IS overrated.

If you're willing to earn your stripes, you'll cash in big time. A promotion, a powerful role or an influential platform could all be in the cards. Saturn is the planet of authority. What will it take to command respect? Over the coming two years, you could return to school for a certification, work with a master coach or teacher or pivot into a more aligned field. Aries who resist structure may feel utterly blocked. Those who lean into Saturn's merit-based "curriculum" will mature into elevated positions slowly but surely.

Neptune's long stay in your sign will continue to blur boundaries—between self and soul, between what you desire and what the world needs from you. At times, you may feel like a stranger in your own skin, unsure whether you're evolving or disappearing. That's Neptune's fog, and it's normal. But you don't have to lose yourself in the mist.

When those identity questions arise, anchor into your body. You're a fire sign, Aries—you need physicality to reconnect with your power. Movement is medicine in 2026. Go for long walks, dance in your living room, lift something heavy, or stretch it out on a mat. Grounding rituals like breathwork, cold plunges or even a quick burst of jumping jacks can bring you back to center when your head is in the clouds. Let your body remind you of who you are when your mind forgets.

2 FIND YOUR TRUE HOME

JUPITER IN CANCER
JUNE 9, 2025–JUNE 30, 2026

Riddle us this, Aries: How DOES a firebrand like you "settle down"? Ever since indie-spirited Jupiter dropped anchor in family-friendly Cancer on June 9, 2025, you've been on a mission to find a little patch of peace. Surprise, surprise. It's less about hanging your hat in a cozy location and more about creating a deep sense of home within yourself. Dive into this discovery! What will it take for you to feel safe and supported? How can you nurture yourself, even when no one else is around to ladle up chicken soup for your soul? You could find yourself experimenting with all types of self-care while Jupiter knits and pearls its way through Cancer and your fourth house of roots and emotional security until June 30, 2026. Good on you, Ram!

If your instinct has always been radical independence, Jupiter asks you to try something revolutionary: radical self-intimacy. Can you sit with your most uncomfortable emotions without immediately springing into action or numbing out? Mindfulness practices like body scans, somatic breathwork, or simply placing your hand on your heart when you feel triggered can be deeply healing. Name and claim your feelings—even if you're barraged with a multipack of 'em all at once. It IS possible to be melancholy, turned-on and angry all at once.

For many Aries, this is a pivotal year to reconnect to your inner child and heal old wounds that may be quietly shaping your adult choices. Do you bolt when things get too close? Freeze when faced with change? Feel like you always have to fend for yourself? This is your invitation to rewrite old scripts. Therapy tools like Internal Family Systems, EMDR or Family Constellation work could be transformational. These modalities help you identify the younger parts of yourself that still fear abandonment, rejection or loss—and learn to parent them, instead of abandoning yourself in stressful moments.

No matter how optimal (or not) your childhood was, there's always a lot to unpack when it comes to our pasts. While Jupiter travels through maternal Cancer, "mommy issues" (we all have 'em to some degree) could feel raw and inflamed. Since Jupiter's already been in this part of your chart since June 9, 2025, there's a chance you're well on your way to healing these core wounds. All this while learning new ways to mother yourself, like cooking healthy meals, getting to bed at a good time and keeping yourself out of harm's way. Yes, even when a friend shows up on a shiny new motorcycle and invites you to go riding in the rain.

All this maternal energy may evoke your own overwhelming desire to nurture. Even if you've been an army of one for years, you could feel a sudden urge to conceive, adopt or expand your family—whether that's through children, step-kids or even a furry companion. If the longing is there but the timing isn't quite right, this could be the year to freeze your eggs or begin preparing your body for pregnancy by adopting healthier eating.

Aries parents may have startling epiphanies about generational patterns that you are unconsciously repeating and want to break. We don't have to tell you, Ram, that the way you show up for your kids can be radically different from how you were raised. Regardless, it's easy to slip into hard-wired habits. This year, make it your mission to be attuned, emotionally present and compassionate in all your interactions, especially with the little ones in your life.

Again, that includes your inner child! Speak kindly and lovingly to yourself and make space for all your feelings. No, they aren't all facts, Ram. But they are valid. Notice how your patience deepens for your innermost circle as you embrace self-compassion.

On that note, your idea of what and who constitutes "family" could go through a radical change this year. In a perfect world, those people would be your own kith and kin, but we know life doesn't always serve a traditional script. This year, you could find your people—a chosen family of friends who share your values and unflinchingly have your back. Unconventional living situations are on the table, too, so tap into your own definition of comfort and safety. Your "white picket fence" fantasy might involve a portable tiny home, a communal farm or a pied-a-terre in Mexico City.

You've always marched to your own beat, Ram, so why not do the same when it comes to your personal life and space? If you know it would be best for your mental health, for example, to move away from your childhood hometown, liberating Jupiter basically packs your bags and rents you a U-Haul. With the globe-trotting planet influencing your domestic zone, you could feel called to move—perhaps to a different region, or even a new country. Even if you're not looking to buy property, you might build an ADU, turn your apartment into a business hub, or lean into free-spirited Jupiter's vibe and spend the first half of 2026 as a digital nomad.

Unexpected abundance could arrive through real estate or family assets. Although interest rates are less than desirable in the U.S., you might profit from a home sale, inherit property or invest in a fixer-upper or international residence that appreciates quickly. If you've been holding on to land or a house that no longer feels aligned, selling it now could free you up—both emotionally and financially—to create the lifestyle you actually want. Just be sure to anchor big decisions in a sense of long-term stability, not impulsive urgency. The right move now could set you up for generational wealth.

JUPITER IN LEO
JUNE 30, 2026–JULY 26, 2027

All hail the royal Ram! If you flew under the radar for the first half of 2026, that solitary cycle comes to an abrupt halt on June 30. That's when bountiful Jupiter ascends to Leo's throne, rolling out a long red carpet in your fifth house of fame, luxury, romance and fertility. Your Gilded Age has officially begun—and you'll enjoy your fair share of standing ovations between now and July 26, 2027.

Spotlights, glam squads, red-velvet ropes? Yes, Aries, you're the zodiac's Most Influential now. But don't mistake this for a hollow brush with celebrity. While you may live for the applause (applause) like Aries Lady Gaga, your sign is more of an artiste than a fame monster. Even if you can't quite explain your vision yet, dive into development full stop during the second half of 2026.

Planetary PSA: The muse doesn't do random fly-bys. She shows up when you call her in. Want her to stick around? Roll up your sleeves and be her creative partner. Yes, this will require some dedicated intention. Is there enough whitespace in your busy calendar for you to actually download inspiration, much less get your hands in the clay? Some scheduling changes may be in order, Aries, even if that means pressing pause on a few beloved extracurriculars so as to make time for your percolating passions.

Even if you never considered yourself artistic, we all have gifts to share with the world. The fifth house rules self-expression in all its forms, from dance to fashion to performance to party-planning. In Leo, liberating Jupiter urges you to let your hair down and play. Without the pressure to create a masterpiece, you might tap a rich vein of gold within your own imagination.

Already busy honing your craft? How about turning it into a source of income? Enterprising Jupiter in Leo can inspire you to platform yourself after June 30. The camera loves an Aries and there's no one better than you to sell your brand. If you're too shy or modest for that, no worries. There are plenty of clever ways to reach your audience. One Aries we know stacks her fingers with rings to hawk her treasure trove of crystals live on Instagram. With only her hands and the gems in the frame, she's mastered the art of lighting and sells out her collection within hours. But don't resist the stage if it IS calling. Aries performers may have a peak season in the second half of the year. Get thee to an audition! Find yourself an agent or start livestreaming on your own YouTube channel.

If motivating the masses is your jam, join a speaker's bureau or start positioning yourself as an expert with LinkedIn posts and Substacks. Show up at conferences where you can rub elbows with people who might hire you to rev up the room—your sign's specialty!

Been rocking the same style for years now? Nothing wrong with having a signature look, Aries, but with Jupiter jazzing up your fifth house of self-expression, your outer aesthetic becomes a powerful extension of your inner fire. You could overhaul your wardrobe, radically change your hair or splash your personal brand with a rainbow of new colors. Jupiter in Leo can inspire iconic shifts, whether you're going from minimalist to maximalist or vice versa. Let your style tell the story of who you're becoming, not who you used to be.

Romance will be cinematic—and hedonistic—under Jupiter's unfettered hand. Whether you're swiping or swooning, this yearlong chapter could be one of the most exciting and memorable times you've had in forever. Well, provided that you don't go chasing after destructive forms of drama—a legit risk while the red-spotted planet gets rowdy in theatrical Leo. Follow your bliss without putting yourself at risk and you could hit a delicious high note.

If you're just getting out into the dating pool again, go big with the grand gestures, spontaneous sexcapades and dress-up dates. Part of the fun now is sharing adventures, especially while others eye you with envy. Yes, this is a total 180 from the first half of the year, but you'll be in your flamboyant element. People will watch you one way or another now. Might as well give them something to talk about.

Coupled? This transit pours gold dust over your bond. Travel to a new port of call, build something beautiful together, or say yes to a next big leap—be it engagement, cohabitation or parenthood. While Jupiter in Cancer revved up your nurturing side, Jupiter in Leo can bring major developments in the fertility department. You may feel even MORE excited to start a family, freeze eggs or adopt that Labradoodle.

If you're already a parent, your kids will be central to your joy and inspiration. Leo is the sign that rules childlike wonder. There's no better way to tap into that then to see it through the eyes of your own offspring. Prioritize their passions, get involved in their worlds, and let them teach you a thing or two about fun and fearlessness.

3 REFRAME THE NARRATIVE

URANUS IN GEMINI
APRIL 25, 2026 – MAY 22, 2033

New crew, new view! A major mindset shift is underway this year when innovative Uranus makes landfall in Gemini and your third house of communication, ideas and kindred spirits. If you've held a stubbornly fixed perspective, get ready, Aries. An unlikely source could come along and turn your entire worldview upside down.

You already got a taste of this in the second half of 2025, when Uranus made a four-month sprint into Gemini from July 7 to November 7, its first landfall here since 1941-49. On April 25, 2026, Uranus will plug back into Gemini's grid, electrifying your intellect until May 22, 2033.

If your social life has hit a plateau, a powerful pivot could soon be underway. Don't go looking for friends in familiar places, though. With changemaker Uranus in your neighborhood and local activity house for the next seven years, you'll meet your next bestie or creative collaborator in an unlikely place. Swap your espresso martini bar for a community garden project. Head out to Trivia Night instead of hunkering at home bingeing a series alone. Ask ChatGPT to spin up a social itinerary (Uranus rules technology) with some wild-card recs.

Uranus is the planet of activism and progress, and its new post in Gemini could inspire you to explore local politics. No such ambitions? Raise your hand for an opening on the school board, the PTA or a nonprofit's event planning committee. Could you make an impact by organizing fun events that stimulate the economy in your district and bring interesting people together? Think: a vintage shop hop, a brunch crawl, a pop-up gallery for area artists.

The third house rules siblings and neighbors, and you could team up with yours, perhaps for a cause. You might discover new ways of communicating with a brother or sister, or a friend who feels as close as one, evolving out of outworn childhood rivalries. If you're always trying to fix or coach each other, independent Uranus helps you respect one another's autonomous adult choices. Agree to disagree—and don't be afraid of your differences!

Aries, you're a strong individual and you like to leave your mark. But is your message hitting? On that note, does it even reflect your current values and beliefs? You've just emerged from eight years of Uranus in Taurus and your second house of self-worth. Many of your priorities have shifted along with your confidence.

In 2026, you're ripe for a rebrand. From your social media feeds to your LinkedIn bio to the way you engage in conversations, your style of self-expression is changing. You might decide to launch a podcast or an independent platform where you can freely share your views. Just make an effort to temper your edge, especially if you're the type of Aries who can be blunt or brusque.

Uranus is the planet of rebellion, and it can fuel natural impulsivity, tempting you to fire off regrettable one-liners. Find the sweet spot between irreverence and impact, Aries. You can still ask pointed questions that challenge the status quo without being divisive or disrespectful.

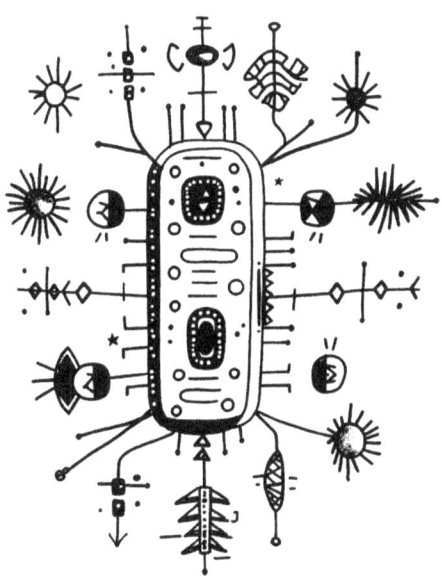

4 LEAD THE REVOLUTION

LUNAR NODES IN LEO AND AQUARIUS
NORTH NODE IN AQUARIUS, SOUTH NODE IN LEO JULY 26, 2026–MARCH 26, 2028

Even the most renegade Aries know that the strength of a mission relies on its leadership AND its teamwork. Both realms of your life get an epic burst of momentum this July 26. As the lunar North Node heads into Aquarius for the first time since 2007-09, you could find yourself ensconced in your own League of Legends. Meanwhile, the karmic South Node dons Leo's crown, helping you find new ways to shine, even while you're part of an ensemble cast.

Collaborative ventures are rich with destiny-driven potential during this 20-month evolutionary cycle, which wages on until March 26, 2028. That's saying something in a year that's also pumping up your personal passions. But no compromising your core values allowed when it comes to joining forces! Seek out groups that allow your unicorn-level individuality to shine.

The utopian ideal? A collective that embraces and accepts each other's autonomy but also abides by a set of democratic agreements. You're not looking for anarchy now; more like high-vibe self-governance. If you can't find a space like that, Aries, maybe it's time to create one yourself, especially in a time when so many social resources are in flux. The Leo South Node is traveling alongside kingmaker Jupiter in the lion's den for the first year of this journey, which will put your trailblazing brand of leadership to good use. Who knows? You could spearhead an experimental community of tiny homes that run on renewable energy or repurpose a building with a group of friends. That might seem like a huge leap, but by the time this 20-month cycle is through, some sort of sharing model may feel like a natural next step in your life path.

The eleventh house is the technology and innovation sector. With the Aquarius North Node plugged into its grid, you could find yourself drawn to a cutting-edge and impact-driven industry. Open your mind to all of it, Aries: AI, robotics, biotech, regenerative energy and tech (search "mycoremediation"). Even if you're just in the spec phase, don't dismiss your sci-fi ideas. You could be taking them to the bank when the North Node crests into Capricorn and your tenth house of professional gains on March 26, 2028.

Alas, there's no ducking the limelight with both Jupiter and the karmic South Node settling onto the throne of Leo and your regal, romantic fifth house. Check your front-facing materials. Do you need new profile pics, a sleek pitch deck, a social media or YouTube strategy? This nodal journey can take you from low-key genius to viral creator, especially if you share your wisdom. Give your design a mid-year review to make sure the graphics sing with sophistication. Learn some SEO tricks or hire someone who knows them to make sure your content gets the visibility it deserves.

Warning: The South Node can trigger a few bouts of imposter syndrome. Let's be honest, Aries. You like to command respect! But no matter how much you learn, there will always be someone who knows more or questions your authority. Stepping forward as a voice or leader doesn't mean being omniscient. Be honest about any limitations or bandwidth concerns. If you don't have a quick response, you can always say, "Let me get back to you on that."

There's a fated quality to any romantic developments that happen under the Leo South Node. During this 20-month cycle, you could encounter a soulmate who fits with the lifestyle you want to lead—and lock in an official status. Coupled Rams could actualize a long-held dream that's only lived (up 'til now) on your bucket list, like building your dream kitchen or moving to Portugal. This fertile South Node cycle could bring a walk down the aisle, an addition to the family or another co-created project that puts your name on the map.

If you've reached the end of your shared journey, this 18-month cycle will be tide turning. You just can't fake it where the South Node is concerned. But here's some good news: The undeniably passionate energy of the Leo South Node can support a quicker turnaround, helping you find a more suitable love without prolonging the agony. Even if there are hurt feelings, it doesn't have to turn into a catty smear campaign. In 2026, you have an option to sidestep the drama, especially since the Aquarius North Node is rising high in your progressive, experimental eleventh house. A split doesn't have to create a yawning chasm. Rewrite the rules so they suit your unique situation. You may have no choice but to get creative if children or co-ownership of a thriving company is part of the package. Keep things as harmonious as you can.

The concept of "relationship anarchy" applies broadly for Rams in 2026. Buck against convention and roll your eyes at "what the neighbors have to say." Their judgment speaks volumes about them—not you. And, you never know: As you proudly live life by your own design, you might set a trend that THEY wind up following.

5 REDEFINE INTIMACY

VENUS RETROGRADE IN SCORPIO AND LIBRA
VENUS RETROGRADE IN SCORPIO: OCTOBER 3–25
VENUS RETROGRADE IN LIBRA: OCTOBER 25–NOVEMBER 13

Cuffing season rolls in with a complex plotline this year—and a few spicy mysteries to unravel. From October 3 to November 13, Venus slips into her six-week retrograde, an unavoidable cycle that comes around every 18 months.

Intensifying matters even more? This time around, the love planet steals back through the zodiac's most relationship-oriented signs, Scorpio and Libra. This is a very different experience than the last time Venus flipped in reverse—which took place in Aries and Pisces from March 1 to April 12, 2025. You won't be in the direct line of fire this time around, which is a relief. Still, dynamics could get sticky in all types of partnerships, and you won't just be able to lie low until the storm passes. Nope, Aries, if you want to keep your closest bonds intact, you have to engage in the process.

That could look a lot of different ways, but the one thing any retrograde demands is a willingness to take an honest inventory of your buried feelings. Looking outside of yourself for solutions just won't deliver the data, epiphanies or improved connections you're hoping for. That's actually an empowering reality to accept. After all, the only person you can really control is yourself. During this six-week cycle, your jaw could hit the ground as you realize

how making subtle changes—in everything from the way you seduce, make suggestions and set up your day-to-day life—can have a seismic effect on the people you love the most.

Starting with subtle cues is actually a smart move, because from October 3 to 25, Venus will be retrograde in scintillating Scorpio and your alchemical eighth house. Even when we are silent, we are still "signaling" to the people around us with our body language and facial responses. Aries are often so busy interacting with their own thoughts that you are unaware of the cues you're sending out. How many times have you heard people say, "I thought you were mad at me" or "I had no idea you were actually so friendly." All you were doing was trying to process the sensory stimulation of the room. You had no idea that you were scowling with RBF or looking right through someone who was waving you over.

Try this on: Venus retrograde in both Scorpio and gracious Libra will invite you to be... inviting. A sly little smile, relaxed posture and open gaze? It doesn't take much more than that for you to be utterly magnetic. A slow scan of the room to take in the people there? You'll see more eager, friendly faces than you imagine. If social anxiety makes that hard, consider designing a few relaxation rituals before you meet a date or sit down with your S.O. to have a hard conversation. (Anything from box breathing to self-pleasuring is on that menu.)

Have you been selectively sharing yourself with the one (or the people) you love? If it's trust and intimacy you're after, it's time to pry open your chamber of secrets. Maybe you've been hiding an erotic desire or shaming yourself for an experience from your past. The trouble is, NOT expressing your truth is making your lover feel like a stranger.

The veil-lifting influence of Venus retrograde can pave the way for serious soul baring. Isn't it better that this information comes straight from the source (you)? Invariably, anyone you partner with—for long-term business or personal purposes—will discover the truth. If you can't be 100% authentic with your innermost VIPs, then how "real" is a relationship ever going to be?

It might be your partner who surfaces a buried secret during this retrograde. Discoveries like these are never easy to process, but here's the cold truth. Many a relationship has grown stronger after a potentially shattering revelation. If you learn something jarring, you don't have to bail; but definitely don't suppress your feelings. By the time November 13 rolls around, make it your mission to dig deep enough to discover whether or not you can move through this together—or begin to now.

The Venus Cazimi on October 23 could be a hugely eye-opening moment. That's the day during each Venus retrograde where the love planet unites at the same degree as the Sun and disappears from the sky for about a week. Some Rams may decide to wipe the slate clean, starting over with a new approach to dating and love—or a new chapter in an existing relationship. If it is indeed time to break up, this moment can help you release some of your painful abandonment fears and the attachments that are keeping you stuck in the wrong thing.

Stormy feelings become easier to process after October 25, as Venus slips back into Libra for the rest of the reverse commute, until November 13. In your seventh house of peace, love and harmony, you might discover ways that YOU have been picking fights to keep things "interesting." Try a new tack for getting your adrenaline rush, one that isn't destructive to your most important bonds. Take a fall class together, plan a long-weekend getaway, scan the cultural calendar for bands you both love and get tickets.

Conversely, your efforts to "rise above" things you consider petty and dramatic could have left the people you adore feeling stifled, stonewalled even. Boundaries are one thing, Aries. But if you've declared certain subjects off limits or refuse to "go there," you could wind up creating a climate of secrecy instead of one that is grounded in transparency. If you struggle to navigate these charged conversations, let a couple's or family therapist help facilitate the dialogue.

Whether it feels like a bodice-ripper or a moment for ripping your heart out of your chest, this Venus retrograde CAN help you deepen intimacy. If you rushed into a relationship without reviewing practical considerations (like, say, incompatible life paths or totally different financial values) you may have to tap the brakes.

Retrogrades stir up the past and things could heat up with an ex—or the one who got away before your connection had a chance to gain momentum. Even when Venus isn't retrograde, situations fraught with history should be entered with care. And with the ardent planet off course, you want to keep your eyes wide open. It's all too easy to don the proverbial sex goggles with Venus slipping back through Scorpio or to get overtaken by someone's love-bombing gestures so that you ignore red flags.

The old chestnut is true that only time will tell. And during a retrograde, the clock is basically winding backwards, prolonging your ability to get a clear read on how to proceed. Once Venus turns direct on November 13, you can slowly make sense of any partnership developments that transpire in early fall. Plus, with Venus powering through Libra and Scorpio for the remainder of the year, you'll have the rest of 2026 to put any "Will we or won't we?" situations through a proper stress test.

2026
ARIES

12 MONTH OVERVIEW

January   MONTHLY HOROSCOPE

Destiny meets discipline this January as planets parade through Capricorn and Aquarius. With the Sun in the Sea Goat's realm until the 19th, you've got legacy on your mind. What structures will support your build? Get those in place—especially at home during the Cancer full moon on the 3rd. Your career takes off at a gallop with the Capricorn new moon on the 18th. Set benchmarks to build out over the next six months, but don't sideline your love goals in the process. Cosmic canoodlers Venus and Mars travel side-by-side through traditional Capricorn until the 17th, then unite again in experimental, idealistic Aquarius after January 23rd. From the bedroom to the boardroom, align yourself with people who share your "anything is possible" outlook. If it's been lonely at the top, that all changes once the Sun shifts into collaborative Aquarius for a month on the 19th. Join forces and optimize your tech so you can work smarter, not harder. On the 2nd, wounded healer Chiron ends a five-month retrograde in Aries, mitigating stress in your personal life. The true curtain-raiser arrives on January 26, when mystical Neptune re-enters your sign until 2039. After a sneak preview in 2025, this 13-year cycle paves the way for a spiritual rebirth. Over the next decade-plus, your identity will be shaped by dreams, ideals and a soulful brand of courage.

February   MONTHLY HOROSCOPE

The more is the mightier for Rams in February! With the Sun in team-spirited Aquarius until the 18th, lean into collaboration and network with intention. There's no better time to rally support for a shared mission, but forget about fading into the background. The Leo full moon thrusts you into the spotlight on the 1st, opening the month with a rush of passion, creativity and stage presence. On February 17, the new moon in Aquarius arrives as a powerful solar eclipse—the first one to land in this sign since July 2018! The Year of the Fire Horse begins the same day. Team efforts could take off at a gallop, but also bring sudden changes amongst the ranks. Romantically, February moves from social to soulful. Venus is in Aquarius until February 10, making for easy clicks with people you meet via mutual friends or apps. After the 10th, Venus' move into Pisces can bring a dreamy, nostalgic (and sometimes sacrificial) vibe to relationships. Mark your calendar: Saturn re-enters Aries on February 13, launching a two-year chapter of unflinching self-development. You had a sneak peek in 2025—now the real work begins. Will it feel like boot camp some days? Yes, but you'll also rise into a new level of expertise and authority. Valentine's Day arrives just one day after Saturn's shift, with a Capricorn moon calling for tradition. Opt for meaningful over flashy this year. Slow down and reflect once

Mercury turns retrograde in Pisces from February 26 to March 20. Before your birthday begins, protect your peace and carve out space to rejuvenate.

March MONTHLY HOROSCOPE

March lures you into deep, reflective waters as the Sun, Mercury retrograde, Mars plus a Pisces new moon (on the 18th) flow into your transitional twelfth house throughout the month. Let yourself drift, dream and detox as needed. But pay attention to the physical realm on the 3rd! A total lunar (full moon) eclipse in Virgo slams your sixth house of wellness and work. If you're burning the candle at both ends, drastic change is in order. Replace unsustainable systems with stress-busting ones, even if that means hiring people to support you. Commit to routines that support your body AND your peace of mind. Take some time off if you can this month. On the 2nd, Mars, your ruler, slips into Pisces for a six-week sabbatical, helping you channel your prodigious energy into spiritual or creative work. Love is one area of life that won't slow down, not once Venus enters Aries on March 6. Charm, confidence and magnetism? You're bringing all three to the romance game. Does your home feel like your castle? Domestic discord lifts after the 10th, as Jupiter ends a four-month retrograde in Cancer and your sensitive fourth house. Whether you're upgrading your living situation or healing a family rift, make way for the new! Ready to expand your base? Global Jupiter paves the way for an international move or a home-based business that has international reach. Then, it's liftoff. The Sun enters Aries on March 20—the Spring Equinox—and your solar new year begins. Mercury stations direct the same day, ending three foggy weeks of confusion. You're officially back, Aries, launching into a new chapter with full rizz and firepower!

April MONTHLY HOROSCOPE

Aries season is in full swing with the Sun blazing through your sign until April 19. This is your annual power surge, a time for exponential growth and the unapologetic pursuit of novelty. Go big with your personal ambitions, Ram, but first, a checkpoint: On the 1st, the Libra full moon shines in your partnership corner. Joining forces can be a double-edged sword for your indie-spirited sign. You love when people fan the flames of your wild ideas, but if they clip your wings? Dealbreaker. Some adjustments to your tag-teams may be in order. That autonomous urge grows even stronger after the 9th, when your ruler, firebrand Mars, zooms into Aries, pumping your confidence and drive to full strength. Pour yourself into your passions while this cycle blazes on until May

18—just make sure you don't steamroll people who "get in your way." On the 17th, the year's only new moon in Aries could inspire you to makeover an area of your life so you represent like a 2026 Ram. With so much personal activity, you'll be relieved to hear this: Love cruises along on autopilot while Venus idles in sensual Taurus until the 24th. Enjoy the slow buildup with a new romantic interest or sink into the comfort of sharing daily routines with a rock-solid mate. Once Taurus season begins on April 19, the pace slows enough for you to gain traction and start monetizing your ideas. Back up all your supersized visions with clear action steps and begin your build. Disruptive Uranus makes a huge shift on April 25, wrapping a seven-year tour through tactile Taurus and buzzing into intellectual Gemini and your communicative, cooperative third house until May 22, 2033. Get ready for mental lightning strikes, paradigm shifts and exciting developments in your social life.

May MONTHLY HOROSCOPE

Excitable Mars (your ruler) races through your sign until the 18th keeping you fired up and in active pursuit of your goals. Simultaneously, the Taurus Sun steadies your aim as it hunkers down in your practical magic zone until May 20. The key to locking in gains this month? Organize your vision into a plan or a system. There IS a method to your madness, Aries, and it could be one you monetize this month. Pay attention to promising investments that appear near the Scorpio full moon on May 1! Joint ventures could come together beautifully, both in the boardroom and the bedroom. Under this "all or nothing" full moon, you may be ready to release an outdated partnership or go full-on with someone unexpectedly. Team dynamics could shift on May 6, when Pluto spins into its annual retrograde (in Aquarius and your eleventh house of community) until October 15. Mother's Day, May 10, coincides with a communal quarter moon in Aquarius. Make it a group celebration or do something fun and experimental. Ready to increase your earnings? Be proactive! Supermoon season begins with the new moon in Taurus on May 16, revving up your second house of money and values and helping you drum up big ideas for saving and manifesting. In love, you may struggle to settle down as Venus in curious Gemini gives you a wandering eye until the 18th. Coupled Rams: Put more playdates on the books to stave off boredom. The vibes get committed and cozy once Venus AND her copilot Mars switch signs on the 18th. Venus nestles into Cancer while Mars gets cuddly in tactile Taurus. May wraps with a Sagittarius full moon on the 31st. This rare blue moon spreads its wings in your wise and worldly ninth house offering a fresh perspective on life—and a solid reason to roam!

June MONTHLY HOROSCOPE

Brainstorms become monsoons while the Sun buzzes through clever, curious Gemini until June 21. The world wants to hear your unique perspective, which could have the makings of a podcast, Substack or a new turn as a creator. Whatever's on deck, you'll have ample discipline for the mission, thanks to motivator Mars hunkered down in Taurus until June 28. And you might not go it alone! The June 14 Gemini new moon—the second supermoon in a three-part series—could catapult a promising collab into motion. Test the waters with a one-time project to see how your styles mesh. Some soul-deep relief is on its way this June 19 when "wounded healer" Chiron exits your sign and moves into Taurus until September 17. This karmic asteroid has been in Aries since April 17, 2018, dragging you through a profound (and sometimes painful!) round of shadow work. This three-month reprieve brings an opportunity for you to synthesize your lessons—and figure out what's really valuable to you. Better news still? After April 14, 2027, you won't host Chiron again for nearly 50 years. There's no dodging deeper feelings after June 21, as the Sun slips into tender-hearted Cancer for a month. It's also Father's Day AND the summer solstice, shining a light on your lineage. What do you want to celebrate about your upbringing? What generational patterns are you ready to break? Reflect to protect. Romantically, you may feel like keeping your cards closer to your vest while Venus tours Cancer until the 13th. But once the love planet struts into passionate Leo, you're holding nothing back. That goes quadruple on June 30! Bighearted, joyful Jupiter wraps a 12-month tour through Cancer and joins Venus (the other radiant "benefic" of the skies) in the Lion's den for thirteen fame-fueling months. Passion hits a high note between now and July 26, 2027—and oh, the places you'll go to get your fix! The month ends on an ambitious high note with the Capricorn full moon on June 29. Make your mark, but aim carefully. Mercury turns retrograde in Cancer the same day, stirring up three weeks when your privacy is as important to guard as your public image.

July MONTHLY HOROSCOPE

Grab a thick beach read and your oversized sunnies—and bring your journal, too. Not only is the Sun tucked away in Cancer until the 22nd, but Mercury will be retrograde in the Crab's castle until July 23. You have lots of introspecting to do, Aries! Clear your calendar for inner circle VIPs. There's no better time to reunite with beloved relatives and old friends, and the new supermoon in Cancer could reboot a sentimental connection on the 14th. Just avoid the toxic branches of your family tree. On the 7th, therapeutic

Neptune turns retrograde in Aries, throwing you into five months of soulful self-inquiry. Since 2026 began, you may have rushed headlong into a new identity. Now, you may wish to reclaim some parts of the "old you" that are worth keeping. And don't worry, you're not going to turn into a total hermit. Energizer Mars spends all month in curious, loquacious Gemini so the invites keep rolling in. Once Leo season sparks up on the 22nd, you'll be ready to strut down the summer catwalk and celebrate life. Festivals, outdoor concerts, cookouts and day trips—with convivial Venus in Virgo from July 9 on, you won't mind playing entertainment director for your squad. With Mercury finally wrapping its retrograde on July 23, you can feel safe booking that block of tickets. Impact-driven Aries, take note: Your community spirit gets a karmic reboot on July 26 when the lunar North Node heads into Aquarius for 20 visionary months. This cycle, which hasn't occurred in nearly two decades, makes everything you do feel impact driven. Technology, politics and humanitarian work could figure in. Don't rush to formalize a plan though. Saturn turns retrograde in Aries the same day, giving you five months to research, study and sharpen your skills. July 29 is another banner moment. As the Sun and Jupiter form their annual conjunction in Leo, you could be thrust into the spotlight. This "Day of Miracles" could serve as a milestone moment for love, fame and creativity. Simultaneously, the Aquarius full moon lights up your eleventh house of community and collaboration. A team project may come full circle, or you could find yourself reconnecting with a group that shares your vision for the future.

August MONTHLY HOROSCOPE

Get ready for a month of cosmic course corrections and world-rocking epiphanies. Chiron spins retrograde in Taurus on August 3, riling up old insecurities around money, stability and trust. Don't confuse your net worth with your self-worth, Aries. Surround yourself with encouraging people who cheer you on. Home becomes a hub of activity after the 11th, as excitable Mars moves into Cancer. As much as you love a visitor, protecting your peace becomes top priority. Set clear boundaries with loved ones who don't always recognize your need for space. Eclipse season begins on the 12th, with the total solar (new moon) eclipse in Leo—the first one in this sign since January 2019. This lunation will crack your heart wide open, but whoa! You might be surprised by what you discover in there, like brewing resentment or a crescendoing crush for someone you never thought of like "that" before. Eclipses can bring sudden pivots and opportunities that spring up out of the blue. In your fifth house of fame and recognition, there's no telling what spotlight could swing your way. Be ready for your close-up at any moment—and don't doubt yourself! With Venus gliding through Libra from the 6th on, you'll be ready to swill a few shots of love potion. Attractions deepen into something more meaningful—and you may reconnect with someone who truly gets you. Work and wellness are in the spotlight when Virgo season kicks off on the 22nd. Minimize stress while maxing out on healthy habits like clean eating, soul-nourishing workouts and daily meditations. On the 28th, a partial lunar (full moon) eclipse in Pisces and your twelfth house of closure and surrender could pull an outmoded situation from your grasp. Let it go, Ram, trusting that it will either come back in a better form or make space for something more ideal. August ends with a rare and grounding gift. On the 31st, lucky Jupiter in Leo forms a harmonious trine to Saturn in Aries. This is the first of two magical alignments (the second comes April 2027), blending expansion with structure, vision with responsibility. If you've been working hard on a creative goal or romantic relationship, your hustle could transform into lasting success!

September MONTHLY HOROSCOPE

3, 2, 1, streamline! With the Sun on an efficiency tear through Virgo until the 22nd, September's your month to get organized! Streamline your workflow and bump self-care to the top of the priority list. Regular workouts, healthy meals, serene sleep—these are the things that bring work-life balance. As Mars buzzes through domestic Cancer until the 27th, upgrade home life habits, like keeping the fridge stocked with healthy food and powering down devices an hour before bed. On the 10th, the Virgo new moon could bring job-related news, like a promotion or a fresh set of responsibilities. Techie Uranus torques into retrograde, also on the 10th. Use this five-month backspin through Gemini and your mobile third house to refine your digital footprint and get up to speed with the modern world. (Solar power! EVs! Generative AI!) Reskilling or a specialized training may be part of the game plan. Leave some room in your schedule for one-on-ones. Venus is pedaling through the most partnership-powered signs—Libra, until the 10th, then Scorpio—shifting your focus from "me" to "we." This is a buffer period before Venus turns retrograde for six weeks on October 3. Inject as much goodwill as possible to fortify your bonds. This will act as an insurance policy against next month's misunderstandings. Libra season begins with the equinox on the 22nd, bringing attractive "opposites" into your life. Collaborations feel inspired during this four-week cycle, so test the waters! A healing chapter is winding down this month, too. On September 17, soothsayer Chiron slips back into Aries until April 2027. This is the "wounded healer" asteroid's final run (for another 49 years) through your sign, completing a profound journey that began in 2018. You've grown from the inside out—and this fall, you start to see just how far you've come. On

September 26, the year's only full moon in Aries spotlights YOU—a peak moment for broadcasting personal initiatives. Promote yourself with pride!

October MONTHLY HOROSCOPE

The love rollercoaster takes you on a dizzying ride this month, so make sure your belt is securely fastened! On October 3, ardent Venus pivots retrograde, backing up through sultry, possessive Scorpio until the 25th, then slinking back through romanticizing Libra until November 13. Who do you love? How do you love? This introspective, six-week cycle is a powerful time to put outdated love stories to bed. Misunderstandings may crop up regularly, causing you to retreat in silence and hurt. Fortunately, the life-giving Sun is beaming into Libra until the 23rd—and with a new moon in Libra on the 10th, you will have support with diplomatic discussions about your feelings. It also helps that your red-hot ruler, Mars, spends October in passionate Leo, lending creativity to your romantic and artistic game. The catch? Drama could escalate at lightning speed if you heap too much pressure onto the situation. On October 23, the Sun slinks into seductive Scorpio and your eighth house of intimacy and transformation—which is also the same day as the Venus Cazimi, a rare and powerful moment where Venus aligns with the Sun. This is the heart of the retrograde and a turning point for love. Venus disappears from the evening sky and returns a week later as a morning star, twinkling just before dawn. Now the question becomes: What new energies do you want to wake up in your love life, Aries? Figuring that out could take more introspection because Mercury joins Venus in retrograde on the 24th, backing up through Scorpio until November 13. Don't rush to conclusions this month because feelings fluctuate hourly. On the other end of the spectrum, deep-diving Pluto FINISHES its retrograde on October 15 and powers forward through Aquarius and your eleventh house of friendships and future plans. A stalled group initiative starts to gain traction, especially if you put your powerful energy back into the mix. The month wraps with a grounding full moon in Taurus on October 26. Work and money situations could stabilize at last. For full "woosah," scale back and simplify unnecessary complexities.

November MONTHLY HOROSCOPE

Surface-level moves won't cut it this November, not while the Scorpio Sun submerges in your investigative, seductive eighth house until November 22. Dig until you strike gold. With Mercury retrograde in Scorpio and backspinning Venus slinking through Libra—both until the 13th—this is a month of profound transformation. Patience will be required, but stay the course through difficult interactions. On the 9th, the Scorpio new moon reboots desire and sex appeal and could bring a relationship milestone. (Venus retrograde, be damned!) Mars, your ruler, is in fiery Leo until the 25th, keeping interactions warm and spontaneous. Don't fan any flames that could lead to a dumpster fire, like, say, trying to be "friends" with a toxic ex only to wind up in bed. (Again.) Coupled Aries may need to renegotiate some relationship rules, but wait until after Venus turns direct on the 13th to hammer anything out. Sagittarius season begins November 22, delivering a fierce wave of wanderlust. Between now and December 21, you'll want to travel, speak your truth and rush ahead into the next epic odyssey. Temper those urges for a couple days! After Mercury turns direct on the 13th, the coast will be clear(er) to book the flight or publish your tell-all post. Kindred spirits pop up with the full supermoon in Gemini on the 24th, bringing a buzzy rush to your social life. Even better? A healthy, wealthy holiday season is in store as your ruler, Mars, parks in Virgo on November 25 for the rest of the year. Roll up your sleeves so you can finish the year strong.

December MONTHLY HOROSCOPE

Sagittarius season is in full swing this December, enticing you to stretch outside your comfort zone and revive your adventurous spirit. But where to roam next? Two outer planets—strategic Saturn and visionary Neptune—wrap up five month retrogrades in Aries on the 10th and 12th, respectively. The fog lifts, revealing a clear path forward. And thanks to motivator Mars powering through your administrative sixth house all month, your planning powers are in rare form. Book the tickets, secure the location, get it all set in stone. Love sizzles with seduction and intensity after the 4th, as Venus heads back into Scorpio for a post-retrograde pass. Desire deepens, but a few trust issues could arise. Don't rush the getting-to-know-you phase or sweep a potential sticking point under the rug. Intimacy is worth the investment of time and energy. While you're busy gearing up for the holidays, hedonistic Jupiter turns retrograde in Leo on December 12. If your celebrations are ballooning into a daunting production, scale back and focus on a few truly meaningful aspects. Home for the holidays? Maybe or maybe not. Opportunity could DM you from afar during the Sagittarius new moon on the 8th and may bring a spontaneous travel plan to life. No matter where you deck the halls, the December 23 Cancer full moon—the final supermoon of 2026—warms the hearth of your cozy, domestic fourth house, casting a sentimental glow over Christmas. And talk about ending the year on a magnanimous note! On the 31st, the Capricorn Sun trines your red-hot ruler Mars in Virgo. You'll feel pumped to provide for your people and explore ways to make the world a richer place.

TAURUS IN 2026

| ALL THE PLANETS IN TAURUS IN 2026 | YOUR 2026 HOROSCOPE | TOP 5 THEMES FOR TAURUS IN 2026 | LOVE HOROSCOPE + LUCKY DATES | MONEY HOROSCOPE + LUCKY DATES |

Taurus in 2026

Your year of:
COMMUNITY, GROUNDING, SPIRITUAL EVOLUTION

STABILITY, AT LAST!

You're ready to reset your foundation, Taurus—one brick at a time. After years of change and uncertainty, you can breathe a little easier and start creating the kind of life that feels solid underfoot. Work and finances take on greater importance, but avoid quick fixes. 2026 calls for steady growth. Opt in to projects that stand the test of time. Make choices that bring pride as well as peace of mind. Relationships echo this theme, too: Loyalty and consistency feel like the true luxuries of 2026. By December, you'll see the reward of your patience—a structure that supports you, and roots deep enough to keep growing.

THE PLANETS IN Taurus

THE SUN APR 19–MAY 20	Happy birthday season! With the Sun in your sign, you're clear to take chances, chase fresh adventures, and command the spotlight.
NEW MOON, SUPERMOON MAY 16 4:01 PM; 25°58′	Hello, bonus New Year! Set personal intentions under this accelerating new supermoon. Then dive into action!
FULL MOON OCT 26 12:12 AM, 2°46′	Manifestation moment! Your work of the past six months bears fruit. Celebrate your progress and harvest the rewards.
MERCURY MAY 2–17	Hold court! When charismatic Mercury zips through your sign, your social status soars. Work the room, make connections—but keep your commitments realistic to avoid overpromising.
VENUS MAR 30–APR 24	Love is in the air! When the galactic glamazon struts through your sign, your powers of seduction skyrocket. Irresistible charm, luxe tastes and flirtatious vibes abound—just keep an eye on your budget
MARS MAY 18–JUN 28	Motivation is off the charts when energetic Mars blazes through your sign every couple of years. You're bold, driven and unstoppable—but watch that combative streak and ease up on the intensity.
CHIRON JUN 19–SEP 17 **RETROGRADE IN TAURUS:** AUG 3–SEP 17	The wounded-healer comet holds the key to turning pain into prescient gifts. And when it visits your sign for a cycle every 49 years, you may journey through a dark night of the soul to emerge a sage. This is the first year of seven that you'll host Chiron, so get ready for some powerful epiphanies as you examine your past.
URANUS JAN 1–APR 25 **RETROGRADE IN TAURUS:** JAN 1–FEB 3	Life feels like a sci-fi movie when Uranus visits your sign (for seven years) every 84 years. Ungrounding and chaotic as it's been, you've made incredible life changes since this cycle began in 2018. You're in the final stretch of this transit: Uranus leaves your sign on April 25 restoring the stability your sign prefers.

Taurus in 2026 HIGHLIGHTS

CUE THE SLOW CLAP: URANUS FINALLY LEAVES YOUR SIGN AFTER SEVEN YEARS OF SHAKE-UPS

Take a good look at you now! This April 25, disruptor Uranus finally sidespins OUT of Taurus, ending a cycle that's been rewiring your identity since May 15, 2018. Life has felt stranger than fiction for the past seven years. Maybe you traded your corporate job for the gig economy, stopped cutting (or dying) your hair or thumbed your nose at "society." However the cosmic chaos agent affected you, you're not the same Bull you were last decade. And fortunately, you sign won't host Uranus again for another 84 years. As of April 25, Uranus plugs into Gemini until 2033, spotlighting your finances, values and skills. Think beyond "budgeting"—this is about aligning money with meaning. You got a preview of the Uranus-in-Gemini cycle in 2025, from July 7 to November 7. Economic developments that began then could pick up again now.

SATURN AND NEPTUNE STIR YOUR INNER WORLD

Let go, so you can grow. Starting January 26, soulful Neptune moves into Aries for a 14-year stay, with Saturn joining on February 13 for a two-year tour. Together they activate your twelfth house of rest, healing and closure. Saturn says: Get disciplined about your downtime. Neptune thins the veil and helps you access deeper parts of your psyche. This could look like finally committing to therapy, meditating before bed, or turning your Sunday scroll into a sound bath. It's not indulgence—it's spiritual maintenance. By clearing old baggage, you create space for new inspiration.

JUPITER IN CANCER SIGNAL BOOSTS YOUR VOICE UNTIL JUNE 30

Until the summer, Jupiter lights up Cancer and your third house of communication, siblings and short trips. Your words have reach, so pitch the story, start the podcast or post that thought piece. Even a group chat idea could snowball into a local initiative. This is also a sweet window to reconnect with siblings and explore your region. Sometimes the best adventures are just a train ride away.

GROUND YOUR GOALS: NEW AND FULL MOONS IN TAURUS

Circle May 16, the Taurus new moon, for your annual reset on personal intentions and self-expression. This one's a supermoon, giving extra weight to the goals you set and the commitments you make to yourself. Watch for results or big revelations around the Taurus full moon on October 26, which highlights how far you've come. Whether it's a personal milestone, a creative breakthrough or simply a stronger sense of self, these lunations spotlight your growth and remind you to keep building on solid ground.

MARS FUELS YOUR AMBITION FROM MAY 18 TO JUNE 28

For the first time in over two years, firecracker Mars barrels through Taurus from May 18 to June 28, igniting your confidence and drive. This biennial boost makes you magnetic—and maybe a little impatient. Channel it wisely: Pitch yourself for a dream gig, tackle a fitness goal or plan an eye-popping rebrand. But don't bulldoze people in your rush. Strength paired with strategy will carry you farther.

CHIRON BRIEFLY DIPS INTO TAURUS—HELLO, HEALING PREVIEW

Since 2018, Chiron has been tucked into Aries, healing your hidden fears from your therapeutic twelfth house. From June 19 to September 17, the wounded healer asteroid makes a rare visit to Taurus, stirring themes of self-worth and identity. This is your sneak preview of a profound metamorphosis that begins again in April 2027. If you've wrestled with imposter syndrome, this summer may bring a breakthrough. Coaching, journaling or even mentorship could help you shed deep-seated fear and shame so you can fully shine as a contributor to the world.

PERIPATETIC JUPITER GETS COZY IN YOUR HOME ZONE AFTER JUNE 30

On June 30, worldly Jupiter wraps a yearlong journey through Cancer and your communication zone and sets up shop in Leo and your domestic fourth house, where it stays until July 2027. Home becomes your anchor AND your launch pad. Some Bulls will move, expand their families or dive into a renovation project. Others may reconnect with ancestry or root themselves more deeply in a community. Turn your space into a sanctuary that inspires you and supports your most enterprising ideas.

MERCURY'S 2026 RETROGRADES: RETHINK, RECONNECT, REBALANCE

Mercury turns retrograde three times in 2026, Taurus, calling for reflection and course correction in key areas of your life. From February 26 to March 20, the rewind runs through your eleventh house of friendships and future plans. An old collaborator could circle back, or you may rethink your role in a group or project. The June 29 to July 23 retrograde in your third house could scramble communication—double-check travel, tech and contracts, and be patient with misunderstandings. The final cycle, October 24 to November 13, lands in your seventh house of partnerships—and this one doubles down with Venus also retrograde in Libra. Expect a blast from the past in love, or the need to renegotiate the terms of a key union. Each retrograde reminds you to pause, recalibrate and strengthen the connections that truly count.

DESTINY SHIFTS: THE LUNAR NODES CHANGE SIGNS MIDYEAR

Creative projects, love life and friendships are getting a karmic upgrade until July 26, as the South Node in Virgo and North Node in Pisces highlight your fifth and eleventh houses. Let go of perfectionism in romance and embrace collaborations that fuel your dreams. Then the Nodes shift into Aquarius and Leo for 20 months, spotlighting career versus home. Get ready to balance public power with private truth. Maybe you're launching something big at work while redesigning your living space behind the scenes. Work-life balance is more than just an elusive goal now, it's a destiny worth discovering.

VENUS RETROGRADE CALLS FOR REVIEWS THIS FALL

From October 3 to November 13, Venus—your ruling planet—retrogrades through Scorpio and Libra, spotlighting relationships, routines and work-life balance. You may reconnect with an old partner or reexamine dynamics that no longer feel equal. Professionally, collaborations could stall, giving you space to renegotiate terms. Venus returns to the same retrograde territory every 8 years (minus 2°), so this cycle echoes back to fall 2018. Look for parallels in love, money or daily rhythm. This is your chance to reframe those choices with more grounded self-worth.

Love

TAURUS 2026 FORECAST

You sail into 2026 with Venus and Mars on a pleasure cruise through Capricorn and your worldly, adventurous ninth house until January 17. Others might be in the mood to hibernate, but not you! Roll the dice on a romantic proposition. Bulls might date long-distance or cross-culturally. Coupled? Plunk down a deposit on a baecation or sign up for a workshop together in Q1. Novelty fuels connection early this year.

There will be plenty of opportunities to explore close to home, too. Expansive Jupiter sails through Cancer and your neighborly third house until June 30. This is prime time to meet someone while you're out and about through friends, events or casual encounters. That's a good excuse to join the indoor pickleball league or IRL Artist's Way group.

On March 3, a total lunar eclipse lands in Virgo, activating your fifth house of romance. This could bring a surprise pregnancy, a passionate attraction or a plot twist that forces you to renegotiate an aspect of your relationship. Dealing is healing, Bull, so don't resist. No matter what shakes out, you'll have no trouble refilling your love tanks when your ruler, ardent Venus, makes her annual visit to Taurus from March 30 to April 24. This is your peak season for attraction! You're radiating confidence and magnetism, helping you draw in new admirers or wake up your slumbering libido.

This is all fun and games, and you'll enjoy every minute of it. But starting April 25, you'll also be ready to settle into somewhat of a consistent groove. Chaotic Uranus exits your sign after seven disruptive years, closing a cycle of shakeups and experiments. It's possible that your entire romantic landscape has shifted since 2018. Either way, you're entering a new era where you can integrate your growth into a steady (and sensual!) rhythm.

Set intentions for how you want to show up in partnerships this May 16, the day of the new supermoon in Taurus. Passionate Mars blazes through your sign from May 18 to June 28, amping up your charisma and libido. Sparks could ignite quickly, whether through fast-burning chemistry or by consciously creating connection. Try "kinesthetic dates" where you ditch the mobile devices and use your hands for more than swiping a cold screen. (We'll leave the "how" up to you.)

There will be lots of motivation to explore your erotic nature, too. Black Moon Lilith, representing the exiled shadow and untamed desire, moves through Sagittarius and your intimate eighth house until September 14. Time to work through shame or patriarchal programming that prevents you from fully embodying your desires.

A few more karmic lessons arrive this summer as wounded healer Chiron briefly visits Taurus (June 19 to September 17), previewing a longer stay in 2027. If old heartaches resurface, take time to process them with supportive healers and therapists. This is your chance to alchemize pain into wisdom and claim a more empowered vision of love. Venus will retrograde this year from October 3 to November 13, beginning in Scorpio and your partnership house. No matter how smoothly things have been sailing, power struggles may erupt. An ex could resurface or a current bond may need recalibration.

With Mercury also retrograde in Scorpio from October 24 to November 13, words can sting, so choose them carefully. Venus finishes its retrograde in Libra, spotlighting your sixth house of service, reminding you that sustainable love rests on consistent acts of care. Your ultimate 2026 assignment? Upgrade your "love toolbox" with both wisdom and play. Drop rigid checklists and tune in to how someone makes you feel. The more you experiment with new practices, the more magnetic and enduring your connections become.

Money & Career

TAURUS 2026 FORECAST

Destiny meets disruption—and pays dividends! Until July 26, the fateful North Node is plugged into Pisces and your eleventh house of innovation and collaboration. You're building a new kind of wealth this year, one rooted in connection, community and creativity. It's all about who you know, Taurus, so get out and circulate among the industry cognoscenti.

With this futuristic sector getting pinged, you could be drawn to emerging industries, digital projects or a cause that taps your idealism. That's not necessarily a new trend. The North Node has been in Pisces since January 11, 2025, so it's possible you're already riding this wave.

Those big ideas you have are only half the equation. How are you marketing yourself? Across the zodiac gameboard, the lunar South Node is plugged into Virgo and your front-facing fifth house until July 26. Even if you're gainfully employed, AI shakeups are fully underway. Make sure the world knows that you're indispensable by polishing up your personal brand. Whether on LinkedIn or a personal site or feed, catalog your accomplishments and share your expertise through posts and conversation-starters. A leadership role may be calling, one that blends artistic flair with practical results.

There's still a bit of uncertainty to work through early this year. Disruptive Uranus is finishing its seven-year shake-up in Taurus, a cycle that began back in May 2018. Expect one final growth spurt before the planet of change leaves your sign for good on April 25—not to return for another 80 years. The past several years have stretched your identity in every direction, pushing you to embrace flexibility and innovation. You've outgrown the old ways of doing business—and life.

On April 25, Uranus zips into Gemini and your second house of income and self-worth (where it will stay until 2033) and the money revolution begins. An unconventional source of revenue could open up through digital ventures, side hustles or ideas so ahead of the curve that only a few thought leaders understand WTH you're talking about. Stay curious and adaptable. Your values may evolve right along with your earning power.

Meanwhile, powerhouse Pluto spends its second full year in Aquarius, activating your tenth house of career and public standing. Hello, influencer. This 19-year cycle pushes you to transform how you

lead, work and succeed—possibly by breaking away from hierarchical systems that no longer fit. Taurus entrepreneurs could rise to prominence; others may take on higher-level roles that come with real authority. When the North Node joins Pluto in Aquarius on July 26, your professional destiny kicks into high gear. Visibility surges, and with it, a chance to make a lasting mark on your industry while this cycle lasts until March 2028.

Before you start decorating a corner office on your Pinterest vision board, imagine a home set-up, too. On June 30, abundant Jupiter settles into Leo and your domestic fourth house for a thirteen-month stay, shifting some focus toward family, real estate and emotional security.

The best opportunities now may stem from your roots—perhaps a family business, a home-based enterprise or a job in the hospitality sector. With the karmic South Node joining Leo on July 26, building your nest egg takes priority. You could invest in property or finally start flowing funds into a retirement account like an IRA or 401(k).

This year demands that you balance your pragmatic side with your pioneering one. In 2026, you're building stability on your own terms, through innovation, integrity and courage. Don't cling to old formulas for success, Taurus. Reinvention IS your revenue stream in 2026.

TOP 5 THEMES FOR Taurus in 2026

1	2	3	4	5
RETREAT TO RECHARGE	ACT LOCALLY	CREATE SECURITY	BUILD YOUR LEGACY	REDEFINE DEVOTION

1 RETREAT TO RECHARGE

NEPTUNE IN ARIES
JANUARY 26, 2026–MARCH 23, 2039

SATURN IN ARIES
FEBRUARY 13, 2026–APRIL 12, 2028

Off-grid, offline or just off those draining feeds! One way or another, Taurus, you will feel the urge to step back from human-made chaos in 2026. In the very beginning of the year, two of the most impactful outer planets—Saturn and Neptune—begin longer tours through Aries and your twelfth house of endings, healing and soul-level surrender. On February 20, they form an exact conjunction at 0° Aries—a once-in-a-lifetime cosmic convergence that hasn't happened in this sign since 1702. Let that sink in.

The twelfth house is NOT overly concerned with the tangible results or 10-year plans a Taurus tends to be obsessed with. Its core focus is the unseen realm. As the final house of the zodiac, it brings vivid dreams but also dissolutions. And along with those come grief, forgiveness and the quiet unraveling of who you used to be.

In short, you're stepping into a sacred "in between" phase. The weirdest part? This journey will be concierged by two VERY different planets: Saturn the rigid accountability hound and Neptune the planet of fantasy, surrender and spiritual connection. This is definitely astrological odd couple vibes! As they row together through the esoteric waters of your twelfth house, healing becomes your most vital pursuit.

Intense as that sounds, you're already somewhat prepared. In 2025, Saturn did a quick preview tour through Aries from May 24 to September 1. Neptune also completed a short lap in the Ram's realm from March 30 to October 22. In 2026, both planets commit to their longer cycles through Aries and your twelfth house: Neptune for a mystical 13 years starting January 26, and Saturn for a concentrated two-year stay as of February 13.

This pairing is rare, especially in such a non-material sector of your chart. Saturn and Neptune only connect like this every 35-40 years—and like we said, this hasn't happened in Aries since the early 1700s! For your earthbound, goal-oriented sign, it's going to feel like a radical shift to your way of life. You may start craving solitude instead of nonstop family time. Rather than grinding like a workhorse, you want to step back from the external hustle and simplify your commitments. No, you don't have to go full sabbatical (unless you want to). But don't be surprised if you require more frequent retreats from the grind in the year ahead. Living part-time in a quieter location is also on deck as a possibility. Hey, you're an earth sign! Every Taurus would do well to embrace a "farm era" at some point in life. Define it as you will. How about a monthlong artist's residency among chickens and fruit trees while you finish your screenplay?

Even if your outer life looks the same, your inner universe is set to undergo a change. The exact Saturn-Neptune conjunction on February 20 could spark a breakdown-to-breakthrough moment; a release of something you've been carrying for years—maybe even lifetimes. There's no avoiding any emotional wounds you've kept in the vault. You're due for an ancestral healing or a spiritual reorientation. And don't worry, Bull. You're so ready for this.

Head's up: This process may feel foggy one moment (Neptune), crystal clear the next (Saturn). Neptune's influence can feel like walking through mist. You sense transformation is happening, but can't quite grasp the granular details. Simultaneously, Saturn brings structure to this process. There's no better time to start a regular spiritual practice that quiets your monkey mind. Yoga, meditation, breathwork, therapy: You're here for it all. Clear clutter from your physical space to support mental clarity. Set strict boundaries around activities (and vampiric people) that drain your energy.

This transit may bring a reckoning with any self-sabotaging habits. Have you been numbing with food, booze, work or endless distractions? Saturn's not here to punish— but it WILL hold you accountable. Meanwhile, Neptune gently guides you to unpack emotions and find the root cause. What's the childhood wound driving the unhealthy habit or the longing behind the over-functioning? You can't outrun your own shadow now—but you can finally integrate it.

Artistically, this cycle could provoke a renaissance. The twelfth house is profoundly creative and imaginative Neptune's presence can awaken a longing to make music, paint, write or express something you can't even name yet. Meanwhile Saturn's disciplined influence brings those visions out of your head and into form. Get ready to build a lasting body of work.

Since the twelfth house is the zone of compassion and charity, you may also feel called to support others. Proceed carefully. This transit can blur the line between energizing generosity and unhealthy sacrifice. Avoid slipping into rescuer mode or taking on pain that isn't yours. If you find yourself in the role of a caretaker, it's imperative that you get yourself support—perhaps from a free CoDA (Codependents Anonymous) group or a grief circle. Remember that healthy detachment is a sacred act of love, too. As much as you want to take away other people's hurt, find ways to do so that don't injure YOU. By the time Saturn exits Aries on April 12, 2028, you'll have emerged from a cocoon of profound internal transformation. And when Neptune moves on in 2039? You might not recognize the person you were before. Not because you lost yourself—but because you finally learned to meet yourself beyond the roles, titles and old stories. Moreover, both planets will head into Taurus once they finish their tours through Aries. The inner work you do may dredge up some old feelings, but you're priming the canvas for your own renewal.

Your best bet in 2026? Take the long view, Taurus. This isn't a year for speed—it's one for soulful awakenings. Let go of what's no longer yours to carry. Empty your arms so they can hold something new. The outer world may not understand your reflective turn, but as you surrender to that inner calling, your spirit will flourish.

2 ACT LOCALLY

JUPITER IN CANCER
JUNE 9, 2025–JUNE 30, 2026

Pack your day bag and grab your mobile charger! For the first half of 2026, you're the zodiac's resident superconnector. Unless you're hosting a fete, you might not be home as much as your cozy sign prefers.

The reason for this? You're entering 2026 midway through Jupiter's yearlong tour of Cancer. This cycle (which only comes around every 12-13 years) has been charging up your buzzy, communicative third house since June 9, 2025. And until June 30, 2026, you'll keep playing "local entertainment director" for the people you adore.

No need to invest in a (second) Louis Vuitton rolling suitcase. In your locally grown third house, Jupiter brings the fun to your own doorstep—or an Uber ride away. From the specialty coffeeshop that remembers your macchiato order before you get to the counter to the fitness studio with your favorite Pilates fusion class, find your hubs close to home. Jupiter (AKA Zeus) is the god of gods, which means wherever this planet goes, it shines a light on leadership opportunities. Some Bulls will hear the call to get involved in local politics. This could be the year that you run for office or a board seat, or put more energy

into supporting a candidate for the midterm elections. Any sort of community advocacy work is favored now. Find a way to get involved in supporting vulnerable members of your area. Jupiter is in nurturing Cancer, so that might involve volunteering at a food bank or women's shelter, tutoring kids or becoming a Big Brother/Big Sister.
With so many options swirling around, it's essential that you keep an eye on your calendar. "More is more" Jupiter loves to say "yes" to every invite, but your energy is finite. Be intentional to avoid double-booking yourself into exhaustion.

Who else is on a similar mission? Since the third house rules platonic partnerships, teaming up with like-minded people multiplies your impact—and your enjoyment. Projects you work on in early 2026 don't have to be a "forever" thing, and probably shouldn't be in most cases. You need variety. Test the waters with one-off collabs that don't tie you down for eternity. Fresh faces and fresh ideas are what keep you inspired. Don't underestimate your power to organize the masses! As the third house rules peers and siblings, your inner circle could become your creative team.

Speaking of local influence, Jupiter is the zodiac's entrepreneur. If you have an idea for a neighborhood business, you might beta-test it with a pop-up shop. Rent a booth at a fair or take on a fractional role that lets you juggle a few different clients. If you're passionate about a product, you could rack up serious commission through affiliate sales. In need of a little reskilling? Erudite Jupiter loves to expand your mind. The winter will fly by if you immerse yourself in a workshop, community class or certification program. From a practical trade to a quirky hobby, anything you learn now could quickly come in handy—and very likely add to your income streams.

Got a message to trumpet to the world? An empowering story to tell? Worldly Jupiter hands you a much-bigger mic, so find a way to platform yourself. Your words can travel far and wide under the red-spotted planet's influence. Share your perspective, whether that's through writing, podcasting or motivating people with regular social media posts. Your message could become the thread that connects and uplifts the masses!

JUPITER IN LEO
JUNE 30, 2026–JULY 26, 2027

Simmering down seems like a fine idea starting June 30. Ahhh. After thirteen busy months, Jupiter trades Cancer's PTA president vibe for Leo's luxuriating repose. Now, the bountiful planet turns its attention to your domestic fourth

house, giving you thirteen months to make sure your home feels like your castle.

Plot twist: How you define "home" could be up for reinterpretation! Expansive Jupiter last toured Leo from July 16, 2014 until August 11, 2015. Scroll back on your timeline. Did you make any major changes to your living sitch back then?

Either way, all options are on the marble slab table now. Lucky Jupiter could drop a too-good-to-ignore real estate listing in your lap during this cycle. It could be anything from a dream rental in the heart of the city or a vacation property for sale. Bulls in the home-selling market could make a mint. Some of you might even get your real estate license.

Staying put? Enterprising Jupiter could inspire a major upgrade. Maybe it's finally time to add that chef's kitchen or build an ADU as a rental unit for extra income. Home-based businesses can thrive while the red-spotted titan hustles through this part of your chart. Not ready for any major housing updates in 2026? That's okay, too. Simply reimagining how and where you feel most rooted can send a powerful message to the universe. Any efforts to make your space feel more well-appointed and relaxing will do.

Bottom line: Your roots could grow in unexpected places after June 30. Since Jupiter is the freedom-loving jetsetter of the skies, it will be hard to resist the temptation of exploring a new corner of the globe. Not merely as a traveler, but as a potential resident or "adopted" member of the community who visits regularly. Visit friends in other cities or rent an Airbnb for a week to see how the locals live elsewhere.

Family relationships could see a huge growth spurt in the second half of 2026. But this won't come at the expense of transparency. With Jupiter dousing your fourth house with truth serum, difficult—but necessary—conversations might bubble up. Seize the moment and air out old tensions, possibly with the support of a family therapist. The goal is to create open dialogue—not to hurl blame like a wrecking ball in an antiques shop. Lead with curiosity and compassion, even when you have to get real. That's how you'll break generational patterns and get the branches of your family tree reaching for the sun together.

Who are the most regal and creative women you know? The fourth house is the feminine realm of the zodiac wheel. With live-out-loud Jupiter in this Leo-governed part of your chart, these are the people to surround yourself with. Not only will their courage empower you to be bolder, but they can broaden your horizons in every direction. Bring on the sister acts!

3 CREATE SECURITY

URANUS IN GEMINI
APRIL 25, 2026 – MAY 22, 2033

Who are you, Taurus—really? A decade ago, you'd answer that in a snap. That, however, was before radical changemaker Uranus blew through your sign for nearly eight years, giving your entire identity an extreme makeover. Uranus only visits each sign every 84 years (its prior trip through Taurus was from 1934-42), so yes, it's as big a deal as it sounds!

If you look back to May 15, 2018, when Uranus first made landfall in Taurus, you might not even recognize yourself. From your appearance to your lifestyle to your priorities, Uranus lifted the rug out from under you and took you on a magic carpet ride. Through this quest, you (hopefully) unearthed the most experimental, edgy and individualistic parts of yourself.

There might be no better example than Taurus-Taurus duo Megan Fox and Machine Gun Kelly, who went from being self-proclaimed "twin flames" to exes (erasing all of their "achingly beautiful" Instagram red carpet moments, much to the public's chagrin) to uncoupled co-parents between 2022 and 2025 while Uranus spun through their shared sign. None of these identifiers are typically found on the traditional Taurean relationship checklist, and may not be again. But that's the power of liberated, progressive, IDGAF Uranus. You, Taurus, became the unlikely disrupter of norms and conventions—and we thank you for adding to the legacy.

On the political front, Taurus Cory Booker made history with Uranus in Taurus by delivering a 25-hour speech on the Senate floor that lasted from March 31 to April 1, 2025—the longest in history. This act of resistance against what Booker believed to be an abuse of government power was a live demonstration of Uranus' anti-establishment "power to the people" footprint. Viva la resistance!

Wild as this journey has been, the adventure is winding down—and let's be honest, your security-seeking sign might be equal parts wistful and relieved. Uranus is in "fall" in Taurus, meaning it's one of its weakened placements. The planet of change is not at ease in steady, traditional Taurus, which created a constant tension.

Sure, you got "comfortable being uncomfortable," but as an earth sign, you can't live in limbo forever. Good news: This April 25, Uranus begins a new seven-year era as it exits your sign and moves into Gemini, not returning to Taurus until 2102.

So...here we are. Taurus 2.0 is hard-launched and it's time to build!! Between now and 2033, while Uranus visits Gemini, you'll add plot, themes and supporting cast members to the bold new biopic that your reality has become. And while it will be great to have some predictability, we really recommend that you make growth one of your enduring habits. Fend off stagnation at all costs. Check in with your plans, question assumptions and make sure you're not lapsing into a routine just because it's easy and familiar.

Ask yourself: What kind of lifestyle do you need to keep growing? As Uranus advances into Gemini and your second house of money, daily routines and values, it could take a few experiments to pinpoint your new priorities. (You had a brief sneak preview from July 7-November 7, 2025, when Uranus did a short stint in Gemini before backing into Taurus again.)

The key? Try new approaches rather than stubbornly clinging to habits and regimens. You might change your diet, noticing the connection between mood and food, and calibrating as you go. (Bonus: Liberator Uranus in Gemini can free you from cravings and vices.) If you've been a night owl, you could shock everyone by turning into a morning person, rising with the sun to exercise or write your novel.

As the natural ruler of the zodiac's second house, it will be interesting to host Uranus on your home turf. Consider this the "surge protector" for Uranus' electrifying energy. All those currents now have a safe place to ground, and you can channel all that power into something concrete. The second house rules money, security and financial foundations. With Uranus charging this sector, everything that falls into those categories will be up for review and inspection, from your career trajectory to your investment strategy.

Do you tend to get a little casual about things like insurance, taxes and savings? In Gemini, Uranus will bring ingenious solutions, but it will also settle down and take these matters a lot more seriously. Don't be afraid to use technology and modernized systems, which futurist Uranus rules. It's time to take all those brilliant ideas and find a way to monetize some of them! With digital native Uranus playing banker, you might even decide to add some cryptocurrency or tech stocks to your portfolio.

The bottom line? Uranus is here to bring fresh opportunities for you to showcase your talents and make a living doing so! Direct Uranus' flow of "mad genius" energy toward things that feed your bank account and bring lasting security.

4 BUILD YOUR LEGACY

LUNAR NODES IN LEO AND AQUARIUS
NORTH NODE IN AQUARIUS, SOUTH NODE IN LEO JULY 26, 2026–MARCH 26, 2028

Money, power and recognition—yes, please! This July 26, 2026, the lunar nodes shift signs, and you'll be feeling the full effect. The North Node soars into Aquarius until March 26, 2028, supercharging your tenth house of career and public image. Across the zodiac wheel, the karmic South Node settles into Leo, anchoring in your fourth house of home, family and security. Over the next 20 months, your mission is clear: Balance your soaring ambitions with the roots that keep you grounded.

Since January 11, 2025, while the North Node was in Pisces and your eleventh house of community, you've been cultivating networks and friendships. By now, you've learned who belongs in your circle—and who doesn't. That groundwork becomes the launchpad for your professional ascent in the second half of 2026. With the North Node blazing through Aquarius, opportunities for leadership and visibility arrive suddenly, and in some cases, dramatically. Prepare to be noticed for your brilliance, persistence and ability to blend traditional Taurus determination with fresh, innovative ideas.

No more hiding in the background: This is your time to step into the public eye. The Aquarius North Node favors big visions and futuristic thinking. What's that industry-disrupting concept you've toyed with? A sustainable brand, a new venture in tech, a creative project with long-term potential? Not for nothing, but you DO share a sign with Sophia Amoruso, Mark Zuckerberg and Sam Altman, all people who, for better and for worse, shook up fashion, social practices and AI. Draft a plan. Start sketching. Find collaborators who believe in your vision. The next 20 months are ripe for taking your most forward-thinking ideas and giving them form.

If you're firmly planted in a company or organization, don't underestimate your power to reshape things as an insider. You may be the one pushing for innovative strategies, introducing cutting-edge tools or spearheading an initiative that aligns with both profit and purpose. Will you encounter resistance? Likely. But your steady, earthy energy helps others trust the process. Keep your eye on the long game, and recognition could follow in the form of promotions, awards or industry clout.

Meanwhile, the South Node in Leo calls your attention back to home and family. As your public status expands, you'll need to make sure you have ample support in your personal life. Some Bulls may relocate, renovate or restructure their living space to support new professional demands. Others may need firmer boundaries with relatives—or even to address old family patterns that have been swept under the rug for too long. Healing this dynamic, even if it ruffles feathers, will bring you greater stability.

This isn't all heavy lifting, though. The South Node's journey through Leo can help you deepen family ties or establish new traditions that make your personal life feel richer. Sunday dinners, cozy rituals with kids or simple time to nest can keep you balanced while your career heats up. Single? Gatherings at home—or introductions through family and friends—could lead to some of the most meaningful connections you've had in years.

By the time this nodal cycle wraps in 2028, Taurus, you'll have solidified a stronger foundation at home while claiming your rightful place in the world. Think of it as laying down bedrock beneath your feet even as you climb to new, dazzling heights.

5 REDEFINE DEVOTION

VENUS RETROGRADE IN SCORPIO AND LIBRA
VENUS RETROGRADE IN SCORPIO: OCTOBER 3–25
VENUS RETROGRADE IN LIBRA: OCTOBER 25–NOVEMBER 13

Like it or not, every relationship comes with a certain amount of baggage, Taurus. Some you tuck away in deep storage and some seems to roll with you like a Louis Vuitton carry-on. But this October 3, you could reach your tipping point. Suddenly, it feels impossible to take another step forward without unpacking what's weighing you down in your closest connections. As your ruling planet, ardent Venus, turns retrograde until November 13, you'll have a prime opportunity to do just that.

This unavoidable backspin happens every 18 months, but in 2026, Venus divides her retrograde between two intense signs, making the cycle especially nuanced. From October 3 to 25, the love planet slips back through sultry Scorpio and your partnership sector, putting your closest relationships under the microscope. Then, from October 25 to November 13, Venus drifts into balanced Libra and your sixth house of work, health and daily routines, calling for a reality check on how you're managing your energy and financial resources.

Dealing with love and money, two of the most triggering topics for most people, might sound like a tall order for fall, Taurus. The good news is, you can handle it in phases. While Venus retrogrades through Scorpio (October 3–25), focus on recalibrating your romantic and business partnerships. Interdependence is a noble goal, a state where you and the people in your life cooperate beautifully while also honoring each other's autonomy.

But you need to do a gut check this October: Have you crossed into unhealthy codependence, enabling others to drain your energy and dump their responsibilities on you? Maybe it's not THAT extreme, but more that you feel a certain person is leaning a little too heavily on you.

Conversely, a partner could be siphoning your time or energy with endless vent sessions, last-minute "favors" or constant crises. You know you need to articulate firm boundaries but may fear it will spiral into a huge drama. And with Venus, the planet of peace and diplomacy, in reverse, it's a legitimate concern. A simple, "I can't take that on right now," spoken calmly, can be as powerful as slamming a door. The less confrontational you can be in your delivery, the better the results.

You can always wait until the retrograde is over on November 13 to schedule these essential heart-to-hearts. In the meanwhile, gather some savvy sounding boards who can help you finesse your delivery. Clear AND kind is the goal.

Nonetheless, your notorious Taurus temper could be riled by little irritations between October 3 and November 13. But before you throw in the towel over a deeply lopsided chore chart or a forgotten anniversary, give yourself space to cool off. Venus retrograde can heighten sensitivity, making you more prone to overreading situations. If larger issues need addressing, consider bringing in a neutral third party like a couples' counselor or objective coach.

Dating? This is a time for your most discerning eye. Don't brush off red flags with a "let's wait and see." Retrogrades are optimal times for investigating those little triggers—whether it's a "roommate" situation that doesn't add up (...is that actually his wife?)

or someone whose conspirituality reposts on Insta don't match up with their sensible IRL persona.

And yes, retrogrades rule the past. With Venus slipping back through your partnership zone from October 3 to 25, you're more at risk that most signs for an encounter with a former flame. If the sweet-but-unreliable ex reappears with promises of a different ending this time, keep at least one eyebrow raised. Unless they've done significant inner work, you can't just blame it on bad timing. Plus, Venus retrograde clouds judgment. As hard as it is to restrain yourself in the face of such attractive temptation, let time (and their actions) reveal the truth before you commit. The real question isn't just about chemistry, Taurus—it's about whether your lifestyles can sync without constant friction.

From October 25 to November 13, Venus retreats into balanced, beauty-loving Libra and your meticulous sixth house, putting your wellness and workflow in the spotlight. If your self-care rituals have slipped, now's your moment to bring them back. You can't pour from an empty cup and still be your best for others. Watch for scope creep at work, too: meetings that eat into personal time, colleagues expecting instant replies or your own tendency to "just handle it" rather than delegate. Protect your bandwidth and your boundaries.

Health-wise, you may be pondering a more rigorous approach to exercise and eating—but watch out for this! Decadent Venus wants wellness to feel like self-care, not punishment. You might return to a regimen you once loved, that yin yoga series or dance class. Pull up some Mediterranean diet recipes or read up on intuitive eating. This is the perfect time to tune into your body's deeper signals and wisdom.

Trouble is, the service-driven sixth house also governs obligations, so you may feel bogged down by daily demands. Still, Bull, you need to find time for yourself! If possible, outsource chores or delegate lower-priority work so you can invest in what truly moves the needle. Just be selective about who you trust with sensitive details like your accounts or private information. By November 13, you'll have a sharper sense of who—and what—is worth your time, energy and heart. And that, Taurus, is worth every ounce of effort you put in this season.

2026 TAURUS

12 MONTH OVERVIEW

January MONTHLY HOROSCOPE

Adventure and ambition fuel your January, Taurus! With the Sun trekking through Capricorn until the 19th, your ninth house of expansion is wide open. Set some stretch goals then jump right into action: Book the trip, sign up for the masterclass, pitch the edgy idea because, why not? The Cancer full moon on the 3rd rustles your communication zone, making it impossible for you NOT to speak your truth. Now's the time to share your wisdom, reconnect with inspiring allies or finally hit "send" on that message you saved to Drafts. On the 18th, the Capricorn new moon greenlights a big dream which could involve travel, study or connecting with people around the globe. Map out the vision and give it a six-month runway. Lovebirds Venus and Mars cuddle close in Capricorn until the 17th, then realign in Aquarius after the 23rd, energizing your tenth house of success. Translation? Choose collaborators who match your ambition—and your vision. Career momentum surges when the Sun shifts into Aquarius on the 19th. Could your systems (and your tech) use an upgrade? Do what it takes to stay current and at the top of your game. With communal Aquarius energy in the mix, connect with forward-thinkers who can help you rise. The month is charged with inner work, too. On the 2nd, Chiron, the wounded healer asteroid, pivots direct in Aries, helping you drop a hidden worry you've carried too long. And on the 26th, dreamweaver Neptune drifts back into Aries for a 13-year stay. Your spiritual life is about to become the compass for everything else you build. Tap in!

February MONTHLY HOROSCOPE

Step up, Taurus! February is a peak month for your career as the commanding Sun powers through Aquarius and your ambitious tenth house until the 18th. Set your sights high and go all in. The Leo full moon on the 1st spotlights your home zone, bringing a domestic matter to a head. This could be the final push to move, renovate or resolve tension with a relative. On February 17, the Aquarius new moon arrives as a sweeping solar eclipse—the first in this sign since 2018—just as the Year of the Fire Horse begins. A career opportunity could gallop in, but you'll need to grab the reins. Until February 10, magnetic Venus boosts your influence in professional circles. Then your ruling planet drifts into dreamy Pisces and your eleventh house, turning friendships and social networks into fertile ground for both love and collaboration. On February 13, stern Saturn re-enters Aries, starting a two-year cycle of healing. Some days may feel like spiritual boot camp, but the growth you'll gain will be profound. Valentine's Day follows with the practical Capricorn moon, favoring depth over flash. As Pisces season begins on the 18th, your eleventh house of community and future visions lights up, inspiring you to reconnect with your wider network. This is your reminder that you don't have to do it all alone—friends, colleagues, and collaborators are ready to support you. Mercury's retrograde here from February 26 to March 20 may jumble logistics, but it also offers a chance to revisit old alliances, revive stalled projects, or reconnect with groups that still hold meaning. Use this cycle to clarify your long-term vision and gather inspiration. By the time the messenger planet buzzes forward, you'll know exactly which relationships and projects deserve your energy for the next chapter.

March MONTHLY HOROSCOPE

March pulls your attention toward community and collaboration as the Sun, Mercury retrograde, driven Mars and a Pisces new moon (on the 18th) activate your eleventh house of teamwork and future vision. Who are your allies and how can you strengthen those ties? Focus on the ones who elevate your vision and give back as much as they receive. On the 3rd, the total lunar (full moon) eclipse in Virgo lights up your fifth house of romance, creativity and self-expression. If you've been playing it too safe, this lunation could push you to take a risk—whether in love, artistry or the pursuit of joy. A passion project you've been working on could reach a dazzling finale within two weeks of the eclipse. On the 2nd, go-getter Mars enters Pisces for a six-week stay, fueling group efforts and urging you to align with kindred spirits. No more going it alone, Bull! Love takes a sultry turn once Venus slips into Aries on March 6, stirring hidden desires in your twelfth house. A private romance could take shape, or you may feel the pull of nostalgia drawing you back to the past. Your mind is abuzz starting March 10 as upbeat Jupiter ends a four-month retrograde and powers ahead in Cancer and your third house. Sibling bonds and communication issues smooth out. Opportunities to write, teach and contribute locally begin flowing again. Expand your reach with a project that connects across neighborhoods. Jupiter's momentum can help

you spread your message far and wide. In between all this buzzy activity, open up some whitespace in your calendar after March 20. Aries season begins with the spring equinox. As the Sun nestles in your twelfth house of closure and release for four weeks— and Mercury turns direct the same day—clear the decks and recharge before you forge ahead full-speed. A new chapter begins with Taurus season next month, and you'll want to greet it with a lighter load.

April MONTHLY HOROSCOPE

Rest and recharge, Bull. As the Sun moves through Aries and your twelfth house of healing and closure until the 19th, your energy may flag a bit. Don't fight it. This is your annual prep cycle before your birthday season begins. What can you release so you can start fresh? Start by decluttering your environment then dig into the emotional part of the work. Those tears, they are your gift. The Libra full moon on the 1st lights up your sixth house of work and wellness, urging you to clean up your routines. If you've been burning out or overcommitting, put better systems in place. Balance is key, so find rhythms that actually support you. That reflective vibe intensifies after April 9, when Mars storms into Aries and your twelfth house for six weeks. Old baggage may resurface, but face what's been weighing on you so you can let it go for good. On the 17th, the year's only new moon in Aries pokes that same twelfth house, making it the perfect moment to close a chapter that's been done and dusted for a while. Energy returns with a vengeance once the Sun enters Taurus on the 19th. Your solar new year begins, and with it comes confidence, magnetism and momentum. Love should feel steady and sensual all month, thanks to your romantic ruler, Venus, cruising through Taurus until the 24th. Whether you're savoring routines with a partner or enjoying a slow-building attraction, simple pleasures mean the most now. Then comes the ginormous shift—one that will be a HUGE relief for your sign! On the 25th, disruptive Uranus ends its seven-year tour of Taurus and blasts into Gemini until 2033. After nearly a decade of shake-ups, chaos and radical reinventions, you can get yourself back into a steady groove. With your second house of self-worth and value illuminated, you could carve out a prominent space as a role model in this unscripted era. Share your practical magic with the masses and watch your popularity soar!

May MONTHLY HOROSCOPE

Birthday season is here, Taurus! The radiant Sun beams through your sign until May 20, infusing you with vitality and magnetic presence. On May 1, the alchemical full moon in Scorpio shines in your seventh house of partnerships, bringing a relationship to a decisive turning point. You may solidify a commitment or close the chapter on one, creating space for new partnerships to flow in. Transformational Pluto pivots retrograde in Aquarius and your tenth house of career from May 6 through October

15. Reset power dynamics in your professional life, but stay humble. The quarter moon in Aquarius on May 10 makes Mother's Day ideal for an original celebration with an upscale twist. Splurge a little on the matriarchs in your life! Your annual reset arrives with the Taurus new supermoon on the 16th. Set intentions for love, prosperity and personal growth and watch them unfold over the coming half year. When the Sun moves into Gemini on May 20, financial opportunities and questions of self-worth come into focus. Set smart money goals for the weeks ahead. Until May 18, magnetic Venus tours Gemini and your twelfth house, favoring private romance, closure work and quiet, creative retreats. On the 18th, affectionate Venus glides into Cancer and your eleventh house of friendships while fiery Mars powers into Taurus and your first house—a combo that draws supportive allies as your confidence surges. Sparks can fly through friends or community events. Say yes to any "random" invite that intrigues you. The month ends with the Sagittarius blue full moon lighting your eighth house of intimacy and shared resources on the 31st. Wise investments could pay off handsomely, so get ready to reap the rewards.

June MONTHLY HOROSCOPE

June is your money month, Taurus, as the Sun blazes through curious Gemini and your second house of income and values until June 21. Your ideas could quickly turn profitable, especially with motivator Mars powering through Taurus until the 28th, giving you grit and stamina. The June 14 Gemini new moon—the second supermoon in a rare three-part series—lands in your financial zone, sparking fresh opportunities to grow your income. A notable shift arrives on the 19th when "wounded healer" Chiron dips into Taurus for a three-month preview tour—the first time this asteroid has visited your sign since the early 1980s. Since April 2018, Chiron has been pressing on your subconscious twelfth house, stirring old wounds and hidden fears. Now, this short summer stay opens the door to transform those tender spots into healing gifts and to experiment with new ways of honoring your worth. On April 14, 2027, Chiron will return to Taurus for a full seven-year stay, guiding you through a deeper journey of restoration, resilience and self-discovery. On June 21, the Sun shifts into Cancer, your expressive third house, just as Father's Day and the summer solstice arrive. Intellectual exchanges are lively and inspiring. Circulate locally or set up residence in a second city. You need to find your kindred spirits! In love, Venus lingers in Cancer until the 13th, favoring heartfelt talks and tender exchanges. Once she struts into Leo, your private fourth house, passion heats up behind closed doors. On June 30, jubilant Jupiter gets cozy in Leo's den, marking the start of a thirteen-month cycle that blesses your domestic life—love, nesting and family bonds all expand. The month ends on June 29 with the Capricorn full moon in your ninth house of travel and expansion. Mercury turns retrograde in Cancer (for three weeks) the same day, so double-check logistics before making any public announcements or booking that redeye!

July MONTHLY HOROSCOPE

Iced lattes in hand and your favorite notebook nearby, you're buzzing with ideas this July, Taurus. The Sun lingers in Cancer and your quick-thinking third house until the 22nd, while Mercury retrograde here until the 23rd stirs up déjà-vu through old friends, neighborhood connections and half-finished projects. The Cancer new moon (a supermoon) on the 14th could help you formalize a creative partnership or cement someone's BFF status. On July 7, mystical Neptune pivots retrograde in Aries, beginning five months of soul-searching behind the scenes. Then, on the 26th, taskmaster Saturn follows suit in Aries, doubling down on this call for inner work. Mentors or healers from your past could reappear with guidance to support your growth. Not that you should ignore practical concerns: Motivator Mars charges through Gemini and your second house all month, fueling smart money moves and investments in skills that pay dividends later. (Just keep an eye on impulse splurges.) Once Leo season kicks in on the 22nd, your focus shifts to home and family. Make your space a summer sanctuary, host a cozy gathering or simply revel in your roots. Venus in Virgo from the 9th adds a playful vibe, bringing romance and creativity through festivals, weekend getaways or a fling that feels like pure summer fun. Mercury stations direct on the 23rd, smoothing out crossed wires in your inner circle. Then comes the headline: On July 26, the destiny-driven North Node enters Aquarius and your tenth house of career for the first time in nearly two decades. Until March 2028, your public path takes on fated weight—think legacy, leadership and visibility. The same day, Saturn retrogrades in Aries, reminding you that inner work and discipline are the ballast for those ambitions. July wraps with fireworks on the 29th as the Sun and Jupiter unite in Leo for their annual "Day of Miracles," lighting up your home and family sector with joy, luck and maybe even a real estate win. Simultaneously, the Aquarius full moon crowns you with career recognition. Private joys meet public triumphs, helping you end the month feeling like you "have it all."

August MONTHLY HOROSCOPE

August pulls you inward, Taurus, but also primes you for a brand-new chapter. On the 3rd, healer-feeler Chiron turns retrograde in Taurus and your first house of identity. Old wounds around belonging may resurface but only to fortify your independence and help you rewrite your personal narrative. With the Leo Sun simmering in your domestic zone until the 22nd, that may include working through some old childhood pain. By the 11th, Mars races into Cancer and your third house, filling your days with buzzing group chats, neighborhood happenings and back-to-back invites. But protect your bandwidth: Not every coffee date request deserves a yes. Eclipse season sparks on the 12th with a total solar eclipse in Leo—the first here since 2019—shaking up your fourth house of home. A surprise move, renovation or family shift could flip the script quickly. Stay nimble and you could land somewhere better than you'd imagined. On the 6th, your ruler Venus slips into Libra, sprinkling everyday life with beauty. Think upgraded skincare rituals, playlists that set the mood or turning meal prep into a social event. Virgo season begins on the 22nd, spotlighting love, creativity and self-expression for four decadent weeks. Host a late-summer dinner party, show off a passion project or slip away for a romantic getaway. The Pisces lunar eclipse on the 28th beams into your eleventh house of community, nudging you to release a draining group dynamic so you can magnetize allies who get your vision. August closes with rare cosmic support as Jupiter in Leo forms a stabilizing trine with Saturn in Aries on the 31st. A dream tied to home, family or your inner foundation could finally click into place, grounding you in a way that feels both luxe and lasting.

September MONTHLY HOROSCOPE

Joy is the master plan this September, as the Virgo Sun brightens your festive, romantic and fame-fueling fifth house through the 22nd. Mix soul-fueling activities in with your "back to school" vibes: a late-summer gallery crawl, an indie film festival, glamorous dinner dates. Sizzling Mars keeps on grooving through Cancer and your third house until the 27th bringing heat to your conversational exchanges. Don't let brilliance languish in the group chat. Meet up IRL with people who help keep your genius ideas flowing. On the 10th, the year's only new moon in Virgo gets a creative mission in motion. Pay attention to the people you meet today—there may be romantic or artistic potential brewing. The same day, sidewinding Uranus pivots retrograde, backing up through Gemini and your second house of money and values. Use this five-month backspin to refine your financial strategy and upskill as needed to greet the needs of the current economy. Your ruler Venus lingers in Libra until the 10th, elevating daily rituals, then slinks into Scorpio and your partnership zone. Top off your love tanks any way you can, Taurus—even if that means wining and dining yourself. If you're in a relationship, put extra effort into bonding and keeping things on an equal playing field. You'll need the reserves! On October 3, Venus turns retrograde for six weeks, which could bring a bit of a love drought. Libra season begins with the fall equinox on the 22nd, calling for balance around workflow and wellness. Streamline routines, upgrade systems and make sure your schedule supports—not sabotages—your goals. On the 17th, wounded healer asteroid Chiron backs into Aries and your twelfth house until April 2027, closing a long healing loop that began in 2018. Therapy breakthroughs, retreats or simply learning to rest without guilt are all part of the curriculum. A transitional point arrives on the 26th with the full moon in Aries. No more clutching on to things that are draining you, Bull. Let go so you can grow.

October MONTHLY HOROSCOPE

Relationship audit time! On October 3, Venus—your cosmic ruler—turns retrograde, rewinding through Scorpio and your partnership zone until the 25th, then moonwalking into Libra and your sixth house of habits until November 13. Love, collaboration, even your daily flow, could hit speed bumps. But are these really detours or are they the signs pointing you to a better route? Which bonds deserve the long haul, and where have you been doing all the heavy lifting? A few boundary tweaks or schedule resets could change the whole dynamic. The Sun beams through Libra until the 23rd, spotlighting your sixth house of wellness and productivity. The Libra new moon on the 10th is your green light to refresh routines. Swap your morning doomscroll for meditation, try reformer Pilates, invest in noise-canceling headphones that help you focus. Meanwhile, Mars charges through Leo and your fourth house all month, stoking action (and maybe some drama) at home. Redecorating spree? Impromptu family gathering? That DIY project you swore you'd finish? Go for it. The catch? Sparks fly easily, but so do tempers, so do your best to deescalate tension under your roof. October 15 brings a turning point as Pluto powers forward in Aquarius and your ambitious tenth house after a five-month retrograde. A stalled pitch, promotion or leadership role could finally pick up pace. Then, on the 23rd, the Sun dives into Scorpio and your relationship sector—the same day Venus retrograde aligns with the Sun in a rare Cazimi. You'll see exactly who (or what) deserves your devotion. Head's up: Mercury joins the retrograde parade on the 24th, backing up through Scorpio and your relationship zone until November 13. Misunderstandings are inevitable, so spell things out clearly and resist the urge to overreact. And under the Taurus full moon on the 26th, it's all about you. Step out of the noise, recharge and claim the spotlight. Spa day? Solo getaway? Yes, please.

November MONTHLY HOROSCOPE

Lift the veil, Taurus. With the Scorpio Sun investigating your partnership zone until the 22nd, relationships of all stripes demand transparency. From business deals to budding romances, this is a month for trust-building. Expect challenges along the way. Mercury retrograde in Scorpio and Venus retrograde in Libra—both until the 13th—could slow negotiations and stir misunderstandings, especially around shared resources. Spell out responsibilities clearly and put agreements in writing. On the 9th, the Scorpio new moon resets your relationship landscape. Doors open to a new commitment or a fresh chapter in an existing bond. (Retrograde hiccups, be damned!) Close to home, Mars powers through fiery Leo until the 25th, warming your hearth. Family dynamics will be both exciting and stressful, so do your best to keep things calm at Chateau Toro. Ideally, wait until after the retrogrades wrap on the 13th to tackle any renovations or radically change your living situation. It's officially sexy season for you on the 22nd, when the Sun streams into Sagittarius and your seductive, wealth-building eighth house. Don ye now your sultry apparel and your power suit, too. What (and who!) you invest in could pay off handsomely. The full supermoon in Gemini on the 24th spotlights your money zone. Your hard work of the past six months could bring a payoff, along with a reminder to keep managing your cash with your savvy Taurus pragmatism. The spotlight swings your way on the 25th when firecracker Mars shifts into Virgo and your fifth house of fame, romance and creative expression for the rest of the year. Shine your light and fearlessly promote your talents. You'll give that Rockefeller Center tree a run for its lumens!

December

MONTHLY HOROSCOPE

Sagittarius season is on until the 21st, swilling the intense waters of your eighth house of intimacy, power and wealth. Bonding awaits, but how close do you want to get? The Sagittarius new moon on the 8th could ignite a promising merger for romance or finance. As you explore your emotional edges, two outer planets—no-nonsense Saturn and fluid Neptune—end five-month retrogrades in Aries on the 10th and 12th, respectively, lifting the fog on private matters and helping you set the right boundaries. With motivator Mars charging through Virgo and your festive fifth house all month, put your planning powers to good use and organize the fun: glamorous soirées, fundraising events, seasonal frolicking. Romance ignites after the 4th, when Venus makes a sultry return to Scorpio and your partnership zone. A whirlwind attraction could sweep you off your feet or you could finally stabilize upheaval that began when Venus turned retrograde this past October 3. On the 12th, maximizer Jupiter slips into a four-month retrograde in Leo and your home zone. If holiday prep is spiraling into a Broadway-scale production, trim it back. Twinkle lights, a lovingly cooked meal and cozy fireside gatherings are the vibe! Wider vistas call after the 21st when Capricorn season kicks off with the winter solstice. Holiday travel plans could upgrade quickly. Don't let stubborn worries stop you from being spontaneous. Your words hit with impact during the Cancer full supermoon on the 23rd, perfect for penning those holiday cards and sweet DMs. Ring in the New Year in adventurous spirits! A thrilling Sun-Mars trine on the 31st could direct your attention to novel experiences and distant lands, whether you're celebrating abroad or planning an international adventure for early 2027.

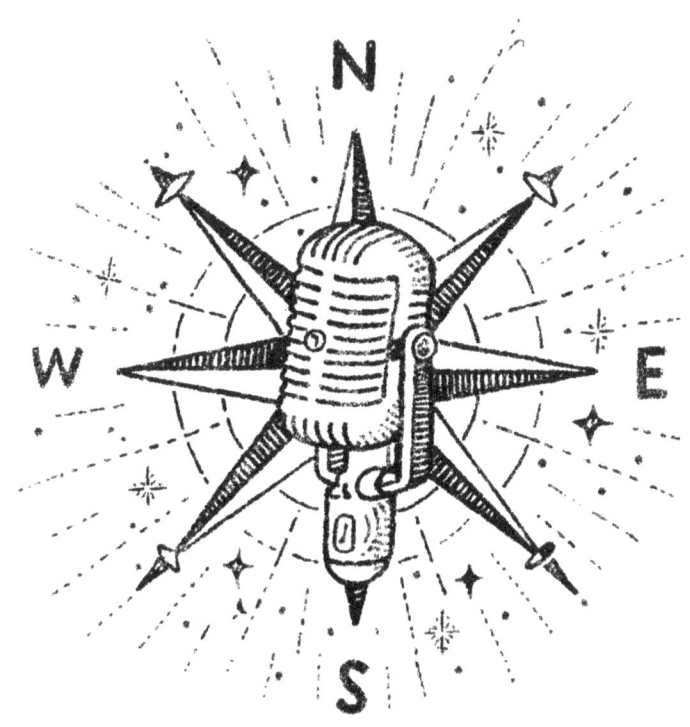

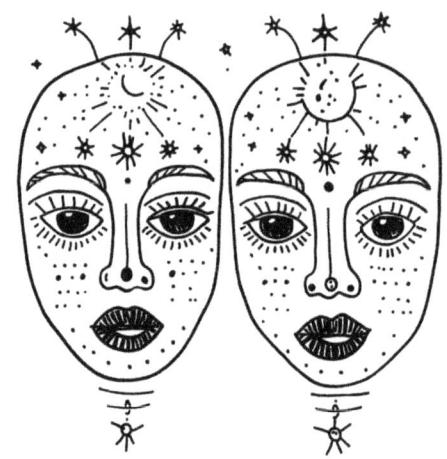

GEMINI IN 2026

| ALL THE PLANETS IN GEMINI IN 2026 | YOUR 2026 HOROSCOPE | TOP 5 THEMES FOR GEMINI IN 2026 | LOVE HOROSCOPE + LUCKY DATES | MONEY HOROSCOPE + LUCKY DATES |

Gemini in 2026

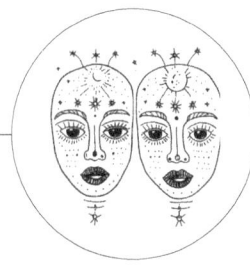

Your year of:
REINVENTION, EXPERIMENTATION, VOCAL EXPRESSION

WHO DO YOU THINK YOU ARE, GEMINI?

Don't rush to answer. In 2026, you're on the cusp of a metamorphosis—and curiosity is your best guide. Follow the pull to explore new roles, cutting-edge ideas and identities, even as old patterns slip quietly away. Will every experiment stick? Of course not. But the ones that do will change everything. Guard against scattering your brilliance across half-finished pursuits. The real magic comes through collaborations (think octuplets, not twins), which act as turning points and door openings you couldn't have imagined alone. By December, you'll see how much has settled into place: Ideas that once felt fleeting now carry weight, ready to propel you into even bigger adventures.

THE PLANETS IN *Gemini*

♊

THE SUN
MAY 20–JUN 21

Happy birthday season! With the Sun in your sign, you're clear to take chances, chase fresh adventures, and command the spotlight.

NEW MOON, SUPERMOON
JUN 14
10:54PM; 24°03'

Hello, bonus New Year! Set personal intentions under this accelerating new supermoon. Then dive into action!

FULL MOON, SUPERMOON
NOV 24
9:53AM, 2°20'

Manifestation moment! Your work of the past six months bears fruit. Celebrate your progress and harvest the extra-bountiful rewards the supermoon brings.

MERCURY
MAY 17–JUN 1

Hold court! When charismatic Mercury zips through your sign, your social status soars. Work the room, make connections—but keep your commitments realistic to avoid overpromising.

VENUS
APR 24–MAY 18

Love is in the air! When the galactic glamazon struts through your sign, your powers of seduction skyrocket. Irresistible charm, luxe tastes and flirtatious vibes abound—just keep an eye on your budget.

MARS
JUN 28–AUG 11

Motivation is off the charts when energetic Mars blazes through your sign every couple of years. You're bold, driven, and unstoppable—but watch that combative streak and ease up on the intensity.

URANUS
APR 25–DEC 31

RETROGRADE IN GEMINI:
SEP 10–DEC 31

Life feels like a sci-fi movie when Uranus visits your sign (for seven years) every 84 years. This cycle (that extends to August 3, 2032!) may at times feel ungrounding and chaotic, but you'll make incredible life changes along the way.

Gemini in 2026
HIGHLIGHTS

WELCOME TO YOUR REINVENTION ERA:
URANUS ELECTRIFIES GEMINI FOR SEVEN YEARS

Sound the cosmic airhorns, Gemini—on April 25, Uranus the revolutionary disruptor returns to your sign for its first long-haul stay since 1941-49. This seven-year cycle launches a personal revolution, shaking up everything from your identity to your creative expression. You got a teaser from July 7 to November 7, 2025, when the side-spinning planet briefly plugged into your sign, but now the future is fully here as Uranus rocks Gemini from April 25, 2026 to May 22, 2033. Expect lifestyle revamps, sudden pivots and a more authentic YOU emerging for all the world to see.

VISIONARY TEAMWORK: SATURN AND NEPTUNE ALIGN YOUR FUTURE CREW

Normies or non-conformists? Rigid Saturn and artsy Neptune continue their joint tour of Aries and your eleventh house of community, as of February 13 and January 26, respectively. Saturn lays the foundation for serious goals, helping you define who belongs on your dream team. Neptune infuses your groups with inspiration and compassion. The result? A soul-aligned network that helps you take your boldest visions from concept to reality. Let the casting commence!

MONEY MATTERS TAKE FOCUS: JUPITER IN CANCER UNTIL JUNE 30

How fat is your (crypto) wallet? Until midyear, lucky Jupiter activates your second house of income and values. Financial opportunities may roll in, but so do questions about worth. Are you being paid enough for your talents? Are you investing in what truly matters? This is your chance to stabilize, build security and align your money moves with your deeper purpose.

MARS POWERS THROUGH GEMINI:
YOUR ROCKET FUEL FROM JUNE 28 TO AUGUST 11

From June 28 to August 11, energizer Mars charges through your sign, pumping you with confidence, drive and undeniable magnetism. This biennial boost is prime time to launch projects, make bold asks and turn heads everywhere you go. Just pace yourself—Mars can scatter your energy as easily as it fires it up. Focus is your secret weapon.

MERCURY RETROGRADES: REVISIONS ON THE ROAD AHEAD

Mercury turns retrograde three times in 2026, Gemini, putting the brakes on your plans so you can make key adjustments. From February 26 to March 20, the backspin is in your tenth house of career and long-term goals. Expect delays at work or the return of an old opportunity you're now ready to handle differently. From June 29 to July 23, Mercury reverses in your second house of money and security. Review your budget, renegotiate rates or revisit financial decisions before committing to anything new. The final retrograde, October 24 to November 13, lands in your sixth house of health, habits and daily routines. With Venus also retrograde in Libra, you may reconnect with old coworkers, refine your wellness practices, or rework a project to bring more balance and creativity into your everyday life.

SPEAK YOUR TRUTH: NEW AND FULL MOONS IN GEMINI

Circle June 14, the Gemini new moon, your annual reset for personal goals and identity. This one's a supermoon, encouraging you to set audacious goals. These could manifest with a major milestone near the Gemini full moon, also a supermoon, on November 24. Either way, the spotlight swings to the progress you've made, revealing the results of your self-authorized moves.

STORYTELLING MAGIC: JUPITER MOVES INTO LEO AFTER JUNE 30

Your message could move the masses this year, Twin, so find your platform! On June 30, worldly, candid Jupiter blazes into Leo for a 13-month stay, lighting up your third house of communication. Choose your métier: mediamaking, teaching, keynoting or getting involved in local action groups. Weave in personal narrative and let your stories be heard. And it goes both ways. If you have a stage, use it to amplify other voices, too.

HEALING IN PROGRESS: CHIRON BRIEFLY DETOURS INTO TAURUS

Since 2018, Chiron has been working through Aries, surfacing wounds around belonging and friendships. From June 19 to September 17, the wounded healer comet slips into Taurus and your twelfth house of healing and transition. This is a brief preview of a longer, seven-year cycle that begins in April 2027. Begin unpacking fear, shame and generational trauma. Not easy stuff, Gemini, but you're ready to peel back those deeper layers of pain and turn them into power! When Chiron circles back to Aries for one final lap this September, you'll be ready to integrate some early lessons into your collaborations with others.

DESTINY AT THE CROSSROADS: NODES SHIFT MIDYEAR

Until July 26, the South Node in Virgo and North Node in Pisces highlight your push-pull between home and career. The challenge has been how best to balance your private foundations with your public ambition. Then mid-summer, the Nodes shift into Aquarius (North) and Leo (South), sparking a 20-month cycle around community and creativity. You'll be asked to balance old obligations to groups that drain you while stepping more fully into your personal passions. This is your cosmic invitation to expand your influence further than ever before while maintaining valuable ties within your local community.

LOVE AND CREATIVITY UNDER REVIEW: VENUS RETROGRADE THIS FALL

From October 3 to November 13, ardent Venus retrogrades through Scorpio and Libra, tossing curveballs into romance, creativity and your daily grind. Old flames, forgotten projects or unfinished artistic work may resurface. Don't rush ahead. First, reflect on what truly lights you up. Venus follows an 8-year retrograde rhythm (minus 2°), so fall 2026 connects back to fall 2018. Think about what you were creating, who you were dating and how you were spending your energy then. Now, you get to edit that story with a wiser lens.

Love

GEMINI 2026 FORECAST

The year begins with a sultry twist as Venus and Mars cruise together through Capricorn and your seduction zone until January 17. Normally, you like to keep things light and breezy (you've been known to bail before dessert is served). But early this year, it might be you who is lingering over tiramisu—or nibbling that whipped-cream-frosted dessert off a lover behind closed doors.

Don't lock yourself down too tightly, however. Venus and Mars both head into Aquarius and your liberated ninth house after January 23 and you'll chafe at anyone trying to possess you. On February 17 the solar (new moon) eclipse in Aquarius kicks off the Year of the Fire Horse. You don't exactly need permission to run wild, but this lunation gives you cosmic clearance. The Fire Horse's free spirit matches your own—in fact Horse is associated with Gemini across the Eastern-Western zodiac. As you gallop into this lunar year, remember that your most potent connections come when you're exploring, learning and laughing your way through life.

Then comes the headline moment: Uranus enters Gemini on April 25, beginning a seven-year cycle of radical reinvention. Translation? You're about to remix everything—your identity, your style, your relationships. Partners will need to adjust to your new rhythm, so be patient! You might find that unconventional arrangements suit you best. Your challenge, trickster Twin, is to avoid bolting the second things feel too predictable. There will be many days this year when a steady partner who can be your rock will be just what the love doctor ordered.

Venus turns you into the zodiac's heartthrob when she tours Gemini from April 24 to May 18. Romance gets a playful glow-up and you'll feel magnetic, flirtatious and ready to socialize. If you're in a relationship, get out and mingle as a pair. You might even host a party or three together. Lusty Mars joins the party June 28 to August 11, fueling passion and desire. This summer could be one for the steamiest pages of your diary and confessional brunches. You know how you love a story worth retelling.

You may encounter a few of your dating demons this year, however. Black Moon Lilith—a point in the sky that is associated with our shadow work, suppressed desire and empowerment—is moving through Sagittarius and Capricorn, the two signs that rule your relationship zones. Hidden feelings around equality, power or boundaries could disrupt your romantic reveries. Worse: it's a little too easy to project your frustrations onto partners. You may indeed need to cut someone loose, but make sure you aren't playing the victim. It takes two to tango, even if your only "sin" was ignoring red flags because the sex was so damn hot.

Revelations also come in hot this year, so just stay open to them! They are an essential compass in your journey toward romantic fulfillment. You have two supermoons in your sign which will amplify epiphanies. The June 14 new supermoon in Gemini could be the launchpad for a new stage of dating and relating. The November 24 full supermoon brings clarity around family, children or next-stage commitments.

Fall could bring a few hiccups—as well as some delicious do-overs. Ardent Venus spins retrograde in Scorpio and Libra from October 3 to November 13. An ex could resurface or unfinished romantic business might return, especially while the love planet moonwalks through Libra from October 25 to November 13. Mercury retrograde piles on (October 24 to November 13), so don't let your tongue, texts—or your imagination—run away with you. If a calm discussion isn't possible, don't force the issue. This retrograde could also bring some surprises, like a pregnancy, engagement or another romantic milestone that might catch you off guard.

By year's end, you'll have rewritten your own love story in radical Gemini fashion. Commitment doesn't mean confinement. Freedom doesn't mean flight risk. Your 2026 mission? Experiment with new ways of loving while remembering that flexibility is your ultimate superpower.

Money & Career

GEMINI 2026 FORECAST

Fractional executive? Changemaking consultant? Industry disruptor? However you label it, 2026 is the year your work life takes a quantum leap. Lucky Jupiter spends the first half of the year in Cancer, expanding your second house of income and values until June 30. Money could flow in from multiple sources, and you might finally land a steady gig or client that gives you both stability and breathing room. But freedom is still the ultimate currency, Gemini. You're craving a work life that's flexible, mobile and fully aligned with your evolving priorities. Jupiter here can help you build wealth—but it also challenges you to define what "security" really means.

The cosmic winds shift on June 30. Abundant Jupiter struts into Leo for a thirteen-month tour of your third house of communication, ideas and short-term projects. The entrepreneurial spark is undeniable! This cycle favors pitching, publishing and partnerships—especially with people who share your curiosity and creative drive. You could find yourself juggling multiple gigs, consulting roles or educational pursuits. Learn first, leap second: With Jupiter's enthusiasm on high, it's easy to overcommit. Give yourself space to test and recalibrate before locking into any one path.

Your identity—and your ambitions—are also in flux as Uranus, planet of disruption and innovation, settles into Gemini on April 25 for a seven-year stay. You got a taste of this energy in 2025, and now the revolution is official. After seven years of Uranus stirring up your twelfth house of endings and transitions, you've likely closed some long chapters and cleared outdated patterns. This new cycle electrifies your sense of self and how you approach work. Expect sudden pivots, brilliant breakthroughs and the courage to do things your way—even if your methodology surprises everyone else.

On February 13, Saturn and Neptune join forces in Aries and your eleventh house of groups and innovation, beginning a two-year collaboration that blends structure with spirituality. The creative dreamer and the disciplined builder unite, urging you to find your tribe of forward-thinkers. If your old circles feel stagnant, branch out. New organizations, networks or causes could provide both inspiration and opportunity. Metaphysical meets methodical under this transit—your "woo" is backed by strategy. Whether you're coding, coaching or crafting a collective, this is where vision turns tangible.

Then, on July 26, the North Node joins the cosmic chorus, moving into Aquarius and your ninth house of entrepreneurship, education and expansion for a 20-month stay. Think globally! You might start a business, return to school or develop your own teaching platform. Long-distance clients, international ventures or travel for work could open new frontiers. A lunar eclipse in Pisces on August 28 activates your career zone, bringing a project to culmination—or forcing a fast pivot that catapults you toward something more aligned.

After years of searching, the path is clearing. The stars aren't asking you to choose one lane, they're challenging you to design a new one. In 2026, your greatest asset is your originality.

TOP 5 THEMES FOR Gemini in 2026

1	2	3	4	5
BUILD A PURPOSEFUL POSSE	TURN IDEAS INTO INCOME	DARE TO EVOLVE	EXPLORE NEW WORLDS	LOVE ON YOUR OWN TERMS

1 BUILD A PURPOSEFUL POSSE

NEPTUNE IN ARIES
JANUARY 26, 2026–MARCH 23, 2039

SATURN IN ARIES
FEBRUARY 13, 2026–APRIL 12, 2028

Light and breezy interactions? You're all about those, Gemini. But when you have a team by your side, you are literally unstoppable. The community spirit washes over you straightaway this 2026 and you are so here for it! On January 26, spiritual Neptune launches a 13-year tour through Aries and your collaborative eleventh house. Just weeks later, on February 13, stalwart Saturn follows suit, hunkering down in the Ram's realm for two years. Time to mingle meaningfully and build a network that feels like scaffolding for your most visionary life plans.

This may feel like a social whirlwind at first. Fluid Neptune weaves dreams, dissolves boundaries and inspires soulful connection. Parts of your circle may come undone, especially if you've known for a while that it was time to let go of these unhealthy (and possibly unholy) alliances. Meanwhile, Saturn sets hard limits and insists on integrity. It demands that you put in the work to earn people's trust.

Together, they challenge you to curate your crowd and show up with purpose. Who are you building with—and what kind of future are you authoring together? When these two powerhouse planets make an exact conjunction on February 20—their first in Aries since 1702—your casual connections could crystallize into something serious, maybe even movement-making.

You already got a taste of this shift in 2025. Neptune's brief tour through Aries from March 30 to October 22 may have stirred an urge to get involved with causes or communities that mirror your values. While Saturn dipped into Aries from May 24 to September 1, it began organizing that chaos, prompting questions like: Who actually deserves my time and energy?

The Saturn-Neptune conjunction this February 20 marks a defining moment—not just for you, but for the collective circles you're part of. This is "get intentional" energy. You're no longer content to flit between friend groups or float from project to project. You want to root down and create something real.

But don't rush. Neptune's influence is visionary but foggy; Saturn's is structured but slow. Your job is to balance the "Wouldn't it be crazy if?" dream with the "Here's how it's going down" plan. The "why" behind your connections matters mightily in 2026. You might be drawn to activist circles, spiritual communities or tech ventures with heart—and a vision for social impact or climate regeneration.

Just be mindful of burnout and martyrdom. There's a lot of world to "save" but you can't do it all. Find ways to contribute meaningfully to a slice of it that truly speaks to you. And do your independent research before getting swept along by a cause celebre! Neptune can make you susceptible to charismatic guru figures who SEEM to be knowledgeable but are actually spewing conspiracy theories. While there's nothing wrong with having a wise teacher (Saturn's all about that!), be wary of anyone who whips you into a frenzied state then introduces a radical agenda. Revolutions can happen without emotional dysregulation, Gemini.

Saturn in Aries could bring a leadership test. You may be tapped to step up as community organizer, guide a team or mentor others. Charm alone won't win this campaign. Saturn demands strategy, boundaries and a clear sense of mission. Your usual social ease may meet resistance as Saturn insists you define your standards. Not everyone gets access to the Gemini VIP room in 2026. That's not snobbery, it's discernment.

And yes, some friendships may fade during this cycle. But the ones that remain will be unshakeable. On a deeper level, Neptune in your eleventh house can stir a longing to belong—truly, deeply, and not just superficially. But beware the illusion of connection. Someone may seem aligned with your values, only to reveal flakiness or fuzzy motives later. Vet your allies, even (and especially) if you get the insta-besties vibe. Nevertheless, the creative and collaborative potential here is massive. If you've got a visionary idea—an impact-driven start-up, a conscious content platform, a community-based initiative—2026 could be the year it begins to crystallize. That's especially true if you're willing to commit (while pacing yourself) and bring others into the process who complement your strengths.

By the time Saturn exits Aries in 2028, you'll look back on 2026 as the year you stopped scattering your energy and started building something bigger than yourself—something that could truly ripple out into the world. This isn't about abandoning levity, Gemini. It's about learning that seriousness isn't a threat to your joy—it's the structure that gives it staying power.

2 TURN IDEAS INTO INCOME

JUPITER IN CANCER
JUNE 9, 2026–JUNE 30, 2026

Stay on your grind, Gemini! It's about to bring a windfall! For the first half of 2026, rainmaker Jupiter keeps pouring its abundant energy into Cancer and your money-earning second house. This cycle, which only comes around every 12-13 years, began on June 9, 2025. Since then, you've likely made some progress around work and financial stability.

Good news! You have until June 30, 2026 to keep tapping this cash-positive energy. Spend the first couple months of the year getting all your ducks in a row. Once Jupiter ends its retrograde on March 10, it's all systems go.

Jupiter is the planet of "more" but in 2026, you want to apply that to your income column rather than your expenses. More financial resources, more valuable connections on LinkedIn and IRL, more bang for your buck. Optimistic Jupiter also buoys your faith in what's possible—and yes, Gemini, "more" is available to you than you've even allowed yourself to envision. Your whole definition of what work looks like could shift in the first half of 2026, if it hasn't already. Remote work with a global client list or even a stable desk job—however you earn your bread, the key is figuring out how to manage lifestyle costs so that you're not drowning in bills.

No one's saying you have to become a total ascetic here—the second house is both sensible AND sensual. Just tighten your Gucci chain belt and indulge responsibly. Create a budget for thoughtful splurges like a well-planned vacation, courses that help you upskill for the AI revolution, a few investment pieces for your wardrobe and dinner out once or twice a week (instead of nightly). Put $100 a week into a savings account and watch it add up fast.

Let's be honest: You're a social butterfly whose life can get pricey if you try to keep up with cash-flush friends who are more, erm, liberal with their disposable income. So you need to craft a way that feels good to YOU when you inform them that their favorite bon vivant is putting a temporary moratorium on indiscriminate spending.

Instead of saying, "I can't afford that right now," which implies a scarcity mindset, try saying, "I'm saving up for some important investments." Then, get creative with your hangouts. No one can find—or dream up—a low-cost entertainment option quite like you. Game and craft nights, concerts in the park, hot girl walks, pay-what-you-can museum days, full moon tarot rituals—that's just skimming the surface. And with your considerable network, don't be surprised if friends with VIP connections comp you in as a plus-one for all sorts of things.

Speaking of your network, the second house is the zone of values. With philosophical Jupiter here, you may find yourself longing for the company of people who share your ethics. Variety is the spice of a Gemini's life. And this is why you have so many friends who think (and possibly vote) differently than you. But when it comes to your inner circle, Jupiter in Cancer wants you to tighten up the radius. Don't get locked in an echo chamber, but do find at least one activity where you connect regularly with people who support your spiritual ideals.

The way you do your work also matters! Jupiter in maternal Cancer can help you find an income path that feels nourishing rather than draining. Home-based options should be considered, but if that feels too isolating, this could be a great year to join a coworking space.

And, uh, are you getting paid what you're worth? Your rates could be due for an increase, especially if your paycheck hasn't risen in accord with inflation, your advancing skills and cost of living. Research competitive salaries while Jupiter is retrograde until March 10 and get your professional profile up to industry standard.

Work-related travel could still be on your docket, especially if you've laid the groundwork during last year's Jupiter-in-Gemini cycle. Keep your passport handy and your mind open. Why NOT raise your hand to be the company delegate who opens the London office or moves to Mumbai for six months?

Do watch for burnout. Jupiter doesn't have an off switch and in your second house, you could wind up working around the clock if you don't put things like dinner, fitness and friend time on your calendar. Anything you can do to sanctify your sleep is recommended. Hang the darkening curtains, turn your binaural beats app to the nighttime setting and (this is the hard one) stop the screens an hour before you tuck in. Your mind and body will thank you!

JUPITER IN LEO
JUNE 30, 2026–JULY 26, 2027

Curiosity is catnip for a Gemini, so here's some news that will make you purr. On June 30, Jupiter struts into a far more playful part of your chart: Leo and your social, experimental, communicative third house. After months of practical, slow-and-steady energy, life is about to pick up speed in the best possible way.

With adventurous Jupiter buzzing here until July 26, 2027, you can officially claim your spot as mayor or queen of whatever scene you choose to be part of. Yes, Gem, you're back in your element—literally, since the third house is naturally linked to your dynamic sign, the third in the zodiac.

So many interests, so little time! To avoid scattering your focus, here's a pro tip: Think globally and act locally. Jupiter is the worldwide traveler, but the third house rules hometown happenings. Sounds like a paradox, but not if you bring your wanderlust closer to home. Journeys in the second half of the year won't require frequent flyer miles or EV charging stations. Just get yourself to a community where you can thrive—ideally IRL, but if that's not an option, find a virtual one where you are one of the peas in a pod full of inspired innovators.

For some Twins, this may involve bi-city living. If you're not ready to invest in a full-on pied-a-terre, how about an apartment swap or petsitting gig? See what it's like to live like a resident in a town that has always felt resonant with your spirit. Short trips are the domain of the third house. When you DO need to get away here and there, long weekends, even staycations, can do the trick. You'll probably prefer a culturally active metropolis—with plenty of glamorous outfit debut opportunities—to a remote cabin in the woods during this people-centric cycle. But if you're joining a group retreat or renting an A-frame in Idyllwild with six of your besties, you can tick all the Jupiter-in-Leo boxes.

Or just get out and wander with a wide open mind! Jupiter in Leo could make your own neighborhood feel like a treasure hunt. Turn down a new block and you could stumble upon the perfect café for writing your screenplay. Talk to strangers (not like we have to nudge you here). You could score an invite to a meaningful community group or start to dabble in local politics. If a seat on a governing board is not your jam, that's okay. Fellow citizens need a vocal person like you at that town hall.

Still, Gemini, you might want to start shopping for mobile recording equipment. Your facile mind knows just the right questions to ask as you engage people with wit and wisdom. Why not conduct some of these "interviews" on air? Mediamaking Jupiter thrives in the third house of messaging. Your hot takes will be scorching under Jupiter in Leo's fire. And if you back them up with research and facts, you could become an influential voice in the zeitgeist.

3 DARE TO EVOLVE

URANUS IN GEMINI
APRIL 25, 2026 – MAY 22, 2033

The only constant is change, Gemini. At least, that's what you're likely to experience as metamorphic Uranus blazes a dynamic, disruptive trail through your sign this April 25, hanging out as the resident radical until 2033.

This the first time Uranus has visited Gemini since 1941-49, aside from a brief sneak preview from July 7-November 7, 2025. As the celestial shock jock electrifies your first house of self, identity and appearance, you may not recognize the person you see in the mirror soon enough!

That's been a recurring theme for the past couple years. You already hosted expansive Jupiter in Gemini from May 25, 2024 to June 9, 2025. A month later, Uranus came along to continue the shakeups. If you're one of the secretly controlling Geminis, this has probably been a bit anxiety-producing for you. Luckily, as the zodiac's mutable air sign, change is in Gemini's astrological DNA. You're able to adapt, even shape-shift, even if you don't initially resist.

If you're the type of Gemini who thrives in uncertainty and chaos, congratulations! With the side-spinning planet now unstuck from heavy Taurus and your hazy twelfth house (where it's been since mid-2018), life will move at warp speed. Finally, the rest of the world might be able to keep up with your lightning-fast brain! Uranus, after all, is the planet of genius and innovation. Go ahead, keep your brain set to "mad scientist" and blaze new trails. Who needs chatbots and augmented reality glasses when you have the mind of a Gemini?

An idea that's been germinating recently—or maybe gestating in your imagination for the past eight years—could begin sprouting into something real. As Uranus moves into Gemini, those percolating projects could start to take tangible shape.

Even better? You could be in a great emotional place, one that allows you to "hold space" for new levels of abundance. While Uranus was in Taurus, you could have processed some of the inner blocks that were standing in your way—whether you were ready to or not. The past eight years have been a period of profound inner growth, marked by soulful lessons, grief, losses and divine inspiration.

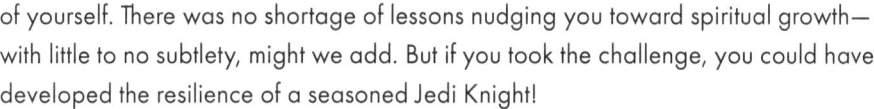

That's all well and good, but not without setbacks. Hard launching your projects into the world may have felt like a frustrating series of power surges and power outages. Just when you got close, an obstacle popped up, forcing you to do deep inner work or confront a "hidden enemy" who was reflecting a shadow part of yourself. There was no shortage of lessons nudging you toward spiritual growth— with little to no subtlety, might we add. But if you took the challenge, you could have developed the resilience of a seasoned Jedi Knight!

Whatever the case, you now have a solid seven years to harness Uranus' power. Go ahead, put your trailblazing idea out there before you're "ready." Audition for a starring role. This phase is about daring and experimentation. Mild caution, though: Don't get too attached to any one fixed direction too quickly. Uranus is the planet of the unexpected, and you may find yourself making pivots and unplanned detours on a regular basis this year. Try before you buy—at least, when it comes to something long-term and binding.

Luckily, that's kind of your M.O. already, Gemini. We're not saying you can't stick with anything—because you certainly can. However, you're a carpe diem sign who doesn't hesitate to shift gears when a better opportunity presents itself. As long as you protect yourself with proper due diligence (and yes, checking in with your gut and your guides can be part of that!), there's no reason not to try. No regrets, right?

What will the long-term impact of Uranus in Gemini be? That will unfold between now and 2033. By the time Uranus moves on to Cancer next decade, your identity, appearance, career path and relationship style could be in a wonderfully wild and individualized place. That will be the result of the new chances you start taking in 2026, as you begin to feel more free and open than you have in your life. Sure, you may fancy yourself the punk rock rebel, answering to no one. But what about your secret fears and anxieties? As a sign that has a closet Type A streak, get ready to release some of that control—and discover what happens when the cosmic disrupter takes up residence in your life.

4 EXPLORE NEW WORLDS

LUNAR NODES IN LEO AND AQUARIUS
NORTH NODE IN AQUARIUS, SOUTH NODE IN LEO JULY 26, 2026–MARCH 26, 2028

Pack your cosmic carry-on, Gemini—you're about to embark on the adventure of a lifetime. On July 26, 2026, the North Node sails into Aquarius until March 26, 2028, supercharging your ninth house of travel, learning and cross-cultural exploration. Simultaneously, the karmic South Node lands in Leo and your third house of local ties and everyday interactions. For the next 20 months, your growth comes from stretching beyond the familiar and opening your mind to new horizons.

Since January 11, 2025, the North Node has been in Pisces, illuminating your tenth house of career while the South Node in Virgo pulled focus to home and family. Since then, you've been learning how to balance your professional climb with your private foundations. Now, as the nodes shift, the emphasis pivots: Your destiny is calling you outward, urging you to broaden your world through bold leaps and visionary pursuits.

This is your chance to study, publish or connect with global communities. Book that long-dreamed-of trip, enroll in a certificate or degree program or pitch an idea to an international collaborator. The Aquarius North Node lives for innovation and original experiences. Don't just trek around monuments and museums. Engage with the culture of each location. As you do, new cultures, philosophies, and even technologies, can reshape the way you see yourself and your place in the world.

Not every adventure requires a passport, either. The ninth house rules spiritual and intellectual expansion. You might dive into an immersive training, join a mastermind group or explore new philosophies with people who challenge your thinking. Your quicksilver curiosity finds fuel in fresh dialogues and ideas.

Romantically, this cycle could write a love story with an international flair. A cross-cultural connection may ignite through travel, study or a shared spiritual pursuit. Long-distance dating isn't off the table either—you may find yourself falling for someone whose zip code, accent or perspective feels wildly different from your own. And yes, it's absolutely worth the exploration. The South Node in Leo, however, cautions you not to get stuck on surface-level sparks or charming banter. Words are easy; you need someone who expands your worldview and grows alongside your restless spirit.

Meanwhile, the South Node in Leo reminds you not to get bogged down in neighborhood squabbles, gossip or endless chit-chat. While you'll always be plugged into your local scene, the lesson now is to distinguish between busywork and meaningful communication. Daily interactions can be rich, but only if they support your larger vision.

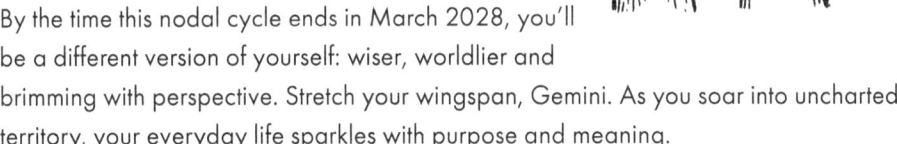

Partnerships may evolve, too, as you collaborate with people who share your thirst for growth. Just make sure expectations are spelled out clearly. The South Node in Leo could blur lines, especially with siblings, friends or peers, so write down agreements and keep boundaries crisp.

By the time this nodal cycle ends in March 2028, you'll be a different version of yourself: wiser, worldlier and brimming with perspective. Stretch your wingspan, Gemini. As you soar into uncharted territory, your everyday life sparkles with purpose and meaning.

5
LOVE ON YOUR OWN TERMS

VENUS RETROGRADE IN SCORPIO AND LIBRA
VENUS RETROGRADE IN SCORPIO: OCTOBER 3–25
VENUS RETROGRADE IN LIBRA: OCTOBER 25–NOVEMBER 13

Fall 2026 could be a season of profound self-inquiry, Gemini—especially when it comes to how you give, receive and experience love. Starting October 3, Venus, planet of romance, beauty and harmony, slips into a six-week retrograde. This unavoidable cycle comes around every 18 months, slowing the action and forcing a deeper look at the state of your unions.

This year, the love planet splits the backspin between two very different arenas of your chart, so you'll be navigating a shift in focus halfway through. From October 3 to 25, Venus rewinds through focused Scorpio and your industrious sixth house. Then, from October 25 to November 13, she drifts back into luxurious Libra and your passionate, pleasure-driven fifth house. Business in the front, party in the back? Something like that, Gemini, but you might be fine-tuning your approach to work, love and celebration before you can pop any corks.

While in no-nonsense Scorpio from October 3 to 25, Venus wants more self-nourishment, less overextending. It's hard for you to say no to your people, Twin, out of love and sheer FOMO. But you need to be more intentional about your energy for the sake of both your health and your productivity. Open up that calendar app and scan for non-essential "obligations" that are zapping your energy. Create whitespace that you will not fill in with any scheduled activities.

Venus is the planet of beauty and harmony and in sensual Scorpio and your sixth house of health, bring more joy into your self-care rituals. Meal-prep while listening to inspiring podcasts and your favorite playlists. Give your workspace an aesthetic upgrade. There's no reason your crystal collection can't live right there next to your laptop, Twin. That's what we call a savvy "charging station."

What NOT to do? Force yourself into any extreme boot camps, fasts or cleanses. Book a risky cosmetic procedure or push yourself to go to a party when you're feeling under the weather. Taking sketchy chances in the Venus-ruled areas of life is inadvisable any day of the year, but that goes quadruple until after November 13.

In love, patience will serve you well. If you're dating, keep things light and exploratory rather than rushing to make things Instagram official or define labels. Retrogrades can distort perception, so give yourself even more time than you think you need to see people's outlines clearly. Partnered Gems, this is your cue to practice restraint when tensions rise. Instead of firing off a reactive text or letting a small annoyance spiral into an epic showdown, take a beat—literally. Step away, move your body, write it out or breathe through it before re-engaging.

Still, you may finally have to admit to yourself that a certain relationship is not ticking all your boxes on the practical plane. Don't kid yourself about these issues resolving over time. Different values or approaches to time and money? These things have a tendency to balloon as you become more entwined. In some cases, you might have to make the bittersweet decision to part ways for the sake of your mental and emotional well-being. On October 25, Venus slips back into her ruling sign, romantic, poetic Libra and finishes out the retrograde in your passionate fifth house. This can be a bit of a double whammy in some respects, so keep the guardrails up! It's all too easy to get carried away between now and November 13, projecting soulmate status onto someone who has not actualized their potential.

It's fine to flirt, play and turn heads even while Venus is in reverse. (Not that we could stop a Gemini anyway!) Being admired is a turn-on. Just be warned that flattery can distort your boundaries this fall.

Since Venus retrograde has a tendency to call in lovers-past, you might hear from an ex or three between October 25 to November 13. If you don't want them returning, it's wise to mute their social profiles and DM threads now. Simply thinking about them can send out a loud call across the quantum field, inviting them back from the ether. Nostalgia aside, if you know they haven't "done their work," it's best to leave them in your permanent archives.

If you're happily coupled, nostalgia is the vibe this fall. Get tickets for a retro band you both "live for." Plan a vacation to a favorite spot to put some sparkle back into your connection. While you might know each other intimately, don't assume that there's nothing left to learn. Take a workshop in an area that neither of you has ever explored before and you could see new dimensions of each other emerge. Spicy!

By the time Venus corrects course on November 13, you'll have a clearer sense of who belongs in your orbit. Fortunately, it's easier for you than most others to remain on the fence about people. You have full cosmic permission to revel in that uncertainty this fall. As long as you aren't giving others false hope, it's a savvy place to stand.

2026 GEMINI

12 MONTH OVERVIEW

January MONTHLY HOROSCOPE

January's mission? Find meaningful ways to make (and spend) your money. With the Sun powering through Capricorn until the 19th, your eighth house of shared resources is in the spotlight. Time to get clear: Where do you want to merge, and where do you need firmer fiscal boundaries? The Cancer full moon beams into your value-driven second house on the 3rd spotlighting your savings goals. If you have enough tucked away, treat yourself to an investment piece—a quality item that you'll use (and enjoy!) every damn day. By the Capricorn new moon on the 18th, you'll be ready to map out a legit 2026 budget for yourself. Lovebirds Venus and Mars hold court in Capricorn until the 17th, turning up the passion in your most intimate ties, then sync again in Aquarius after the 23rd. Romance thrives when you lead with curiosity. Who excites both your mind and your heart? Follow that thread. The Sun zips into Aquarius on the 19th, activating your worldly ninth house. It's time to expand in every way! Plan travel, publish your ideas or dive into studies that stretch your perspective. But this month isn't only about growth—it's about reparations, too. On the 2nd, soothsayer asteroid Chiron pivots direct in Aries, smoothing out friendship drama and reminding you who really belongs in your corner. Then on the 26th, dreamweaver Neptune drifts back into Aries for a 13-year stay. Your community is about to evolve, Gemini. Get to work building your soul squad and let your ideals shape your connections.

February MONTHLY HOROSCOPE

Eyes on the horizon, Gemini! The radiant Sun blazes through Aquarius and your adventurous ninth house until the 18th, urging you to dream without limits. Where are you ready to stretch? Now's the time to take a few calculated leaps. The Leo full moon lights up your cooperative third house on the 1st, connecting you to kindred spirits and bringing a peak moment for a partnership. Then, on February 17, the Aquarius new moon arrives as a sweeping solar eclipse, the first here since 2018, just as the Year of the Fire Horse kicks off. An entrepreneurial venture, travel or academic opportunity could launch at lightning speed. Until February 10, Venus sizzles in Aquarius, which could bring spicy long-distance encounters and cross-cultural connections. Then Venus moves into Pisces and your tenth house, amplifying professional allure. Mentors appear, career doors open—and romance sparks in high-powered settings. Structured Saturn re-enters Aries on the 13th, beginning a two-year cycle in your community sector. Friendships and alliances will be tested for staying power. Don't ignore the red flags OR the green ones! Valentine's Day arrives with the grounded Capricorn moon, favoring depth over dazzle. As Pisces season begins on the 18th, your tenth house of career takes center stage, nudging you to align with goals that truly excite you. Mercury retrograde here from February 26 to March 20 could delay launches, but it also gives you time to refine your message, strengthen your pitch, and reconnect with mentors or opportunities from the past. Think of it as edit mode—polish now, publish later.

March MONTHLY HOROSCOPE

Your ambitions are front and center this March as the Sun, Mercury retrograde, can-do Mars and a Pisces new moon (on the 18th) light up your tenth house of career and public image. Where do you want to make your mark, Twin? Zero in on one clear goal and give it your full attention. Pay attention to the 3rd, when a total lunar (full moon) eclipse in Virgo strikes your fourth house of home and family. Domestic dynamics could reach a breaking point, especially if work-life balance has been off. A move, renovation or important family decision could come to a head. On the 2nd, Mars shifts into Pisces for a six-week stay, fueling your drive to succeed and pushing you into the spotlight. Channel this energy into professional projects that need your disruptive ideas and stamina. Love gets cozier after March 6, when Venus enters Aries and your eleventh house of friendships. Romance could blossom with someone from your circle, or a casual connection could turn unexpectedly flirty. On the 10th, abundant Jupiter ends a four-month retrograde in Cancer and your second house of money and security. Financial flow improves and opportunities to stabilize income or grow a project finally pick up speed. Could you expand your earning power through a raise, new client or creative revenue stream? Explore! The Sun sails into Aries and your eleventh house on March 20—the spring equinox—charging up your social life and group collaborations. Your ruler, Mercury, stations direct the same day, clearing three weeks of crossed wires. Teamwork becomes smoother, and your plans regain momentum. Let's go!

April MONTHLY HOROSCOPE

Rally the troops, Twin! With the radiant Sun powering through Aries and your collaborative eleventh house until the 19th, this is your time to network, pitch bold ideas and build momentum around group goals. Where do you need more joy in your life? Start by surrounding yourself with friends who fan your flames and projects that make you feel alive. The Libra full moon on the 1st beams into your fifth house of love, creativity and play, reminding you to put passion first. A romance could turn a corner or a creative project might debut to rave reviews. After April 9, fiery Mars storms into Aries for a six-week stay, revving up team efforts and pushing you to mobilize around a cause. On the 17th, the year's only new moon in Aries ignites your eleventh house, opening doors for fresh alliances and future-focused ventures. When the Sun drifts into Taurus on the 19th, your twelfth house of rest and release takes over, calling for solitude and reflection. Tie up loose ends, recharge your batteries and make space for the new cycle ahead. Love, meanwhile, hums along in the background while Venus luxuriates in Taurus until the 24th, favoring private moments and even a reconnection with someone from your past. Then comes the thunderclap: On the 25th, electric Uranus rockets into Gemini for the first time in 84 years, ending its seven-year tour of Taurus. This is a once-in-a-lifetime reinvention cycle. With your first house of identity illuminated until 2033, you're stepping into a radical new era of self-expression. Expect breakthroughs in how you show up in the world, flashes of brilliance and a revolution in your personal style. It's all about YOU!

May MONTHLY HOROSCOPE

You're in a reflective stretch, Gemini, as the Taurus Sun drifts through your twelfth house until May 20. Recharge, tie up loose ends and quietly prepare for the fresh energy of your birthday season. The Scorpio full moon on May 1 beams into your sixth house of health and routines, bringing a project or habit to completion. If something isn't sustainable, this lunation gives you the courage to change it. Alchemical Pluto turns retrograde on the 6th, backing up through Aquarius until October 15. Personal growth experiences may involve shadow work—along with travel, study and other boundary-pushing experiences. Embrace the challenge! Mother's Day arrives with a quarter moon in Aquarius, calling for adventure. Celebrate with a cultural experience or a day trip (or weekend getaway!) that broadens your horizons. On the 16th, the new supermoon in Taurus lands in your twelfth house, helping you close out a chapter and restore your spirit. Just in the nick of time! Gemini season begins on May 20. As the Sun bursts into your first house, it supercharges your energy. A personal reboot is underway: Set exhilarating intentions for your next spin around the Sun. Magnetic Venus graces Gemini and your first house until the 18th, boosting your allure and drawing admirers a-plenty. (Hello, thirst trap.) Then, Venus shifts into Cancer and your traditional second house while fiery Mars hunkers in your fantasy-fueled twelfth house for the rest of the month. Romance could feel both irresistible and complicated after May 18. Take things slowly to see where they land. On the 31st, the year's only Sagittarius full moon arrives as a rare blue moon. A key bond may reach a defining milestone, giving you the green light to move ahead—or pivot in a totally new direction.

June MONTHLY HOROSCOPE

Birthday season is in full swing, Gemini, as the radiant Sun powers through your first house of identity and fresh starts until June 21. Novelty is key: Have fun experimenting with your style and fresh social activities. The June 14 new moon—the second supermoon in a rare three-part series—lands in Gemini and reboots your operating system. Set midyear resolutions that focus on personal growth and experiential learning. Simultaneously, motivator Mars in Taurus fuels your twelfth house until June 28, helping you clear baggage and quietly wrap up old business that's interfering with new plans. Relief arrives June 19 when "wounded healer" Chiron slips into Taurus for a three-month preview of its longer 2027-2034 stay. Since 2018, Chiron has pressed on your community zone, testing friendships and alliances. This summer, the focus shifts inward, as you heal through solitude and reflection. On June 21, the Sun enters Cancer, activating your second house of money and security, just in time for the solstice and Father's Day. Invest in what truly sustains you—both financially and emotionally. In love, Venus lingers in Cancer until the 13th, favoring cozy dates and heartfelt exchanges. Once she struts into Leo, your third house, romance takes a playful, conversational turn. On June 30, can't-stop-won't-stop Jupiter races into Leo for thirteen months. Think locally, act globally. Popularity soars and your ideas and messages could move the masses worldwide! The month closes with the June 29 full moon in Capricorn. In your sultry eighth house of intimacy and shared resources, you could radar in on a trusted plus-one who can go the distance. An investment could pay off handsomely, too. One caveat: Mercury retrograde in Cancer begins the same day, so cover all your bases before signing on to any lasting deals over the next three weeks.

July
MONTHLY HOROSCOPE

Your birthday glow-up is still in effect, Gemini, but the spotlight shifts to your values this month. The Sun cruises through Cancer and your second house of money and priorities until the 22nd, while Mercury retrograde here until the 23rd forces a rethink of what—and who—is truly worth your energy. Rethread your budget, renegotiate a deal or revive a skill that can bring in extra income. The Cancer new moon (a supermoon) on the 14th could bring a payout, an "aha" moment about your earning potential or even a long-overdue raise. On July 7, mystical Neptune begins its retrograde in Aries, pulling you into five months of reflection around your networks and collective visions. Then, on the 26th, Saturn also backspins through Aries, helping you make wise choices about which communities to engage with. Look at your group chats, professional circles, even your "personal brand" of activism: Are they aligned with your long game? Firebrand Mars, meanwhile, turbocharges Gemini all month, giving you undeniable magnetism and momentum. Your temper may flare, so channel this energy toward a meaningful personal goal. On the 22nd, Leo season shifts the vibe to curiosity and creative play. Short trips, cultural events or even a late-summer class could recharge your mind. Venus in Virgo from the 9th turns home into your style lab. Immerse yourself in DIY projects and host a potluck or dinner party. Once your ruler Mercury stations direct on the 23rd, you can make some decisive money moves. Big news! On the 26th, the lunar North Node moves into Aquarius and your ninth house of publishing, travel and global platforms for the first time in nearly 20 years. Through March 2028, your destiny is tied to amplifying your voice, whether via thought leadership, media (a podcast or a Substack?) or just living with your passport within reach. July ends with fireworks: On the 29th, the Sun and Jupiter unite in Leo for the annual "Day of Miracles," sparking major buzz for your ideas. Simultaneously, the Aquarius full moon beams into your ninth house, sealing the deal on an opportunity that takes you further than you thought possible.

August MONTHLY HOROSCOPE

August has you rethinking what really matters, Gemini—and the Leo Sun keeps your mind active through the 22nd. On the 3rd, Chiron turns retrograde in Taurus and your twelfth house of closure and healing, surfacing old doubts or memories you thought you'd shelved. Rather than dodge them, let these echoes point to what still needs release. Meditation, journaling, or even a quiet digital detox, could bring clarity you didn't realize you needed. By the 11th, Mars fuels Cancer and your second house of money and values, motivating you to hustle smarter. Pursue projects that feel both profitable and purposeful—but keep your spending savvy. (Skip the TikTok hauls in favor of timeless classics.) Eclipse season kicks off on the 12th with a total solar eclipse in Leo—the first here since 2019—energizing your third house of ideas and communication. A podcast, writing project or viral post could suddenly put your voice on the map. Venus enters Libra on the 6th, setting your fifth house of creativity and love ablaze. Expect sparks to fly—romantic, artistic, or both—as you dive into live music, playful dates and late-summer flings. Virgo season grounds you on the 22nd as the Sun shifts into your fourth house of home and family. Nest, redecorate or reconnect with your roots before fall demands take over. On the 28th, the Pisces lunar eclipse beams into your tenth house of career, fast-tracking a leadership role or high-profile project that reshapes your trajectory. August wraps with rare cosmic synergy on the 31st: Jupiter in Leo forms a fire trine with Saturn in Aries, blending vision with discipline. A big idea you've been nurturing could solidify into something lasting—especially if you team up with the right collaborators.

September MONTHLY HOROSCOPE

Your favorite question this September might be, "Want to come over?" With the Virgo Sun activating your fourth house of home until the 22nd, you'll find joy in nesting, entertaining and creating a hub for the people you adore. Whether you're hosting a little soirée, tackling a décor refresh or carving out more family time, this grounded energy helps you put down roots. Meanwhile, go-getter Mars is heating up Cancer and your second house of money until the 27th, sharpening your hustle and reminding you not to undersell your talents. Take initiative with projects that showcase your skills and don't be shy about asking for what you're worth. On the 10th, the year's only new moon in Virgo lands in your domestic zone, opening the door for a fresh start with family, living situations or even a new home base. Pay attention to who shows up around this date: An ally could become key to building long-term stability. That same day, Uranus pivots retrograde in Gemini and your first house of identity. Over the next five months, take time to integrate the changes you've made to your look, lifestyle and POV since this spring. Venus lingers in Libra until the 10th, bringing sparks to romance and creative ventures before it slides into Scorpio and your wellness sector. Balance pleasure with mindful routines to keep your energy high. Head's up: From October 3 to November 13, Venus will turn retrograde, so systems you put in place NOW with work, self-care and close relationships will create a helpful buffer then. The fall equinox on the 22nd ushers in Libra season. Balance work with play and lean into artistic pursuits. On the 17th, Chiron (the wounded healer asteroid) backs into Aries and your eleventh house of friendships, helping you mend group dynamics and strengthen community ties. And by the Aries full moon on the 26th, it's time to release social obligations that drain instead of inspire. Align with the people and projects that truly elevate you, Gemini.

October MONTHLY HOROSCOPE

Press pause and recalibrate, Twin. On October 3, Venus turns retrograde, backing through Scorpio and your sixth house of routines until the 25th, then moonwalking into Libra and your fifth house of fun and creativity until November 13. From the boardroom to the bedroom, things could feel wobbly. But are these hiccups really setbacks—or cosmic cues to remix your approach? What habits are producing positive results and which ones are draining your joy? Recalibrate. The Sun beams through Libra until the 23rd, spotlighting your fifth house of romance and self-expression. The Libra new moon on the 10th could reignite your cultural curiosity. Take a photography workshop, invest in a museum membership, put your name on the open-mic list. Meanwhile, Mars struts through Leo and your chatty third house all month, supercharging your voice and ideas. Expect a flood of invites, from panel discussions to political fundraisers. The twist? Your quick wit could spark admiration—or friction—depending on your delivery. The Sun sashays into Scorpio and your wellness sector on the 23rd, the same day Venus retrograde meets el Sol in a rare Cazimi. You may see, with zero uncertainty, exactly which relationships (and relationship dynamics) are healthy and which ones need a serious update. October 15 brings momentum as Pluto ends its retrograde in Aquarius and your ninth house of travel and expansion. A course, media project or international trip that's been on hold could finally gather steam. But start by doing some research. Mercury turns retrograde in Scorpio on the 24th, tangling schedules and muddling details until November 13. End the month with a sweet sabbatical under the Taurus full moon on the 26th. Book a sound bath, slip away on a retreat or simply unplug for a weekend. Your system needs a full reset.

November MONTHLY HOROSCOPE

Polish the gears, Gemini. With the Scorpio Sun fine-tuning your sixth house of health and daily routines until the 22nd, this is not the month for winging it. Mercury retrograde in Scorpio and Venus retrograde in Libra—both until the 13th—could gum up schedules and tangle plans, but don't scrap your goals. Use this time to overhaul unsustainable systems and create manageable routines that you can maintain for longer than a 30-day challenge. On the 9th, the Scorpio new moon brings a refreshing reset. What will keep you centered: a reformer Pilates package, a meal-delivery service, calming herbal supplements that support your sleep? Invest in your wellbeing. Socially, November is abuzz as red-hot Mars in Leo electrifies your third house of communication through the 25th. Stimulate your mind with thought-provoking panels, podcasts and workshops. You'll have opinions—lots of them—and your words land with impact. Easy, though! Don't scorch the group chat with a sarcastic zinger that hits below the belt. Duos get dynamic when the Sun enters Sagittarius and your seventh house of partnerships on the 22nd. Flip on the searchlight and find an "attractive opposite" who complements you beautifully. The full supermoon in Gemini on the 24th is your day to shine like a solo star. Push your independent ideas and projects into the zeitgeist. (You might just go viral.) On November 25, Mars decamps into Virgo and your domestic fourth house for the rest of the year. Your plate could quickly fill with family responsibilities, home repairs and hosting duties—and, yes, the return of household drama if boundaries slip. Avoid overgiving, Twin. Your space is a sanctuary, not ground zero for demanding (or toxic) branches of the family tree.

December MONTHLY HOROSCOPE

Who deserves a front-row seat in your world? Sagittarius season is on until the 21st, spotlighting your seventh house of partnerships, balance and dynamic duos. The Sagittarius new moon on the 8th could usher in a fresh partnership—romantic, creative or business. Two is your magic number early this month, but you might expand that to three or more after the 10th. Solid Saturn and idealistic Neptune wrap up five-month retrogrades in Aries, on the 10th and 12th, respectively, clearing the haze around friendships and group projects. Alliances that once felt fuzzy will come into focus, helping you see who's in it for the long game. With motivator Mars powering through Virgo and your domestic fourth house all month, pour energy into home improvements, seasonal hosting and long-overdue cozy time. But watch out for stress coming from toxic members of the family tree and don't feel bad about keeping them OFF your guest list. Venus swings back into Scorpio and your wellness zone on the 4th. Sparks could fly in everyday settings: a yoga class, the office, even a holiday market—possibly with someone you met before the October 3 to November 13 retrograde. If your social calendar is ballooning into a logistical nightmare, scale back after the 12th when expansive Jupiter turns retrograde in Leo for four months. Choose quality over quantity: intimate dinner parties, thoughtful catch-ups, handwritten notes. Your need for privacy intensifies once Capricorn season begins with the winter solstice on the 21st. This is the sultriest season of the year for you, so snuggle up to someone trust—and lust—worthy. Money flows in with the Cancer full supermoon on the 23rd, a reward for your hard work! A Sun-Mars trine closes the year with a soulful vibe this NYE. Huddle up for an intimate celebration and ring in 2027 with the people you love the most.

Read your extended monthly forecast for life, love, money and career! astrostyle.com

CANCER IN 2026

| ALL THE PLANETS IN CANCER IN 2026 | YOUR 2026 HOROSCOPE | TOP 5 THEMES FOR CANCER IN 2026 | LOVE HOROSCOPE + LUCKY DATES | MONEY HOROSCOPE + LUCKY DATES |

Cancer in 2026

Your year of:
VISIBILITY, BREAKTHROUGHS, FINANCIAL EMPOWERMENT

WHERE DO YOU FEEL MOST AT HOME, CANCER?

The answer may surprise you in 2026. This year asks you to rethink what "comfort" and "belonging" truly mean. Is it the people around you, the walls that surround you or the feeling you carry wherever you go? As your roots shift, so do your ambitions. You'll crave stability but also the freedom to expand beyond old roles. And get ready for a surge of visibility as you settle into energizing environments! By December, you'll find yourself shining in new ways, with a stronger sense of both place and purpose.

THE PLANETS IN *Cancer*

THE SUN JUN 21–JUL 22	Happy birthday season! With the Sun in your sign, you're clear to take chances, chase fresh adventures, and command the spotlight.
NEW MOON, SUPERMOON JUL 14 5:44AM, 21°59'	Hello, bonus New Year! Set personal intentions under this accelerating new supermoon. Then dive into action!
FULL MOON #1 JAN 3 5:03AM, 13°02' **FULL MOON #2, SUPERMOON** DEC 23 (8:28PM, 2°14')	You'll host not one but TWO full moons in your sign this year, and one is a potent supermoon! As with all full moons: Ready, set, manifest! Your work of the prior six months bears fruit, and it's time to harvest the bountiful rewards.
MERCURY JUN 1–AUG 9 **RETROGRADE IN CANCER:** JUN 29-JUL 23	Hold court! When charismatic Mercury zips through your sign, your social status soars. Work the room, make connections. Keep your commitments realistic to avoid overpromising—especially during the retrograde, which could scramble signals or resurface old drama.
VENUS MAY 18–JUN 13	Love is in the air! When the galactic glamazon struts through your sign, your powers of seduction skyrocket. Irresistible charm, luxe tastes and flirtatious vibes abound—just keep an eye on your budget.
MARS AUG 11–SEP 27	Motivation is off the charts when energetic Mars blazes through your sign every couple of years. You're bold, driven, and unstoppable—but watch that combative streak and ease up on the intensity.
JUPITER JAN 1–JUN 30 **RETROGRADE IN CANCER:** JAN 1–MAR 10	How lucky can you get? Bountiful Jupiter visits your sign once every 10–12 years, blessing you with extra fortune. Everything's exciting…and extra! Take calculated risks but avoid gambles, particularly during the retrograde.

Cancer in 2026 HIGHLIGHTS

SHINE ON: JUPITER IN CANCER MAKES YOU IMPOSSIBLE TO MISS

Keep launching yourself into the zeitgeist, Cancer! Lucky, adventurous Jupiter is in your sign until June 30, completing an expansive cycle that began on June 9, 2025. This gift only comes once every 12-13 years, so don't squander the glow-up. With confidence, visibility and self-expression amplified, you owe it to yourself (and the world) to share your brilliance. Test-drive a project, pitch your ideas or go public with a personal rebrand. Invest in headshots, update your LinkedIn. If you're shy about self-promotion, look for an agent. The world is watching—and ready to cheer you on.

CAREER DREAMS GET SCAFFOLDING: SATURN AND NEPTUNE IN ARIES

Ready to put some discipline behind your dreams? (Yes. You. Are.) Pro-level Saturn and imaginative Neptune are teaming up in Aries to help you build the scaffolding to support your dreams. Saturn sets boundaries and calls for strategy, while Neptune urges you to infuse your work with artistry. A passion project could morph into a side hustle—or even a full-time path—if you give it structure. Want to pivot careers or add a new service? Take the certification course, update your portfolio or reach out to a mentor. Legacy-level work doesn't happen overnight, but this is your start. Already at the top of your game? Leadership is your calling!

FRIEND AUDIT: URANUS EXITS TAURUS, ENTERS GEMINI

On April 25, Uranus wraps up its seven-year shakeup of your friendship and community sector. Some circles dissolved, others surprised you, but you're walking into 2026 with a clearer sense of who deserves a spot in the Cancer Crew. This spring, the side-spinning planet moves into Gemini, shaking up your twelfth house of spirituality, healing and behind-the-scenes projects until 2033. Outdated connections fall away creating space for more soul-nourishing bonds. Your subconscious is rich with innovative ideas, which may arrive during meditation, therapy or even in your dreams. Step away from the noise so you can hear your own inner guidance. A digital detox may be part of the plan: Less screens, more spirituality.

MERCURY RETROGRADES: PRESS PAUSE, FIND YOUR FLOW

Mercury turns retrograde three times in 2026, slowing things down so you can realign. From February 26 to March 20, the backspin stirs your ninth house of travel, education and big-picture goals. Travel plans could hit snags or an old plan for school, media or a global venture may resurface. June 29 to July 23, Mercury reverses in your first house of identity. Expect delays or second thoughts around personal initiatives, image shifts or how you're presenting yourself. Finally, from October 24 to November 13, Mercury spins backward in your fifth house of love, creativity and self-expression. With Venus also retrograde in Libra, past romances could resurface, or you may revisit an old artistic project. Take your time. These forced timeouts are designed to help you refine what truly inspires you.

BOOKMARK YOUR MILESTONES: THREE POWERFUL MOONS IN CANCER

Your sign takes center stage in 2026 with not one but two full moons and a supercharged new moon. The first arrives on January 3, spotlighting how far you've come since your last birthday and asking you to recommit to promises you've left hanging. Then, on July 14, the Cancer new moon—a high-energy supermoon—offers a rare and potent reset. Set intentions that stretch into the future and back them with a ritual that makes them tangible: a journal entry, a vision board, even a date on your calendar to check your progress. Finally, the year closes on December 23 with a Cancer full supermoon, the last lunation of 2026. This dramatic bookend illuminates your growth and shows you what's ripened. Think of these three moons as cosmic milestones marking the chapters of your personal evolution.

MARS IN CANCER FIRES YOU UP: AUGUST 11 TO SEPTEMBER 27

Ain't no stopping you now! From August 11 to September 27, fiery Mars charges through Cancer, pumping you with confidence and courage. You'll feel braver about asserting yourself—whether that means renegotiating your salary, exiting a draining group chat or taking the lead in a passion project. Your magnetism is undeniable. Just watch for mood swings. When emotions run hot, so does your temper. Balance intensity with grounding practices: sauna sweats, boxing classes or even an old-school rage-clean of your kitchen.

DESTINY CHECK-IN: NODES SHIFT MIDYEAR

Until July 26, the North Node in Pisces pushes you to broaden your worldview while the South Node in Virgo challenges you to release perfectionism in day-to-day life. Translation? Stop over-editing emails and start booking classes, trips and experiences that broaden your horizons. Mid-summer, the Nodes pivot into Aquarius and Leo, spotlighting money, intimacy and shared resources. Put agreements in writing! Growth comes through deeper trust, smarter financial strategies and learning to collaborate without losing ground.

LOVE UNDER REVIEW: VENUS RETROGRADE THIS FALL

From October 3 to November 13, Venus rewinds through Scorpio and Libra, first spotlighting your fifth house of romance, creativity and self-expression, then moving into your fourth house of home and family. Old flames may resurface or you could find yourself revisiting past passions—an artistic project, a playful hobby or even a style of love you once craved. This retrograde also invites you to reflect on how your upbringing, home base and family patterns shape the way you give and receive love. Venus repeats her retrograde cycle every 8 years (minus 2°), flashing you back to fall 2018. What stories around love, belonging or creativity were unfolding then? Now you get to revisit those themes with stronger boundaries and deeper self-knowledge. Use this time to heal old love scripts and reimagine both romance and home as spaces of true comfort.

Love

CANCER 2026 FORECAST

Love takes center stage right from the start of 2026, as ardent Venus and lusty Mars float together through your relationship zones (Capricorn and Aquarius) until February 10. Take advantage of the winter hibernation vibes to create the sort of closeness your sign loves: Cook dinners together, cozy up in bed to watch movies and read side by side. This is also prime time for a couples' getaway, ideally to a Crab's other favorite location besides home—the beach.

Single Cancers, make the effort to bundle up for brunches, cultural events and lowkey gatherings. Someone with legit romantic potential could appear. Better still? In Q1, you'll be ready to strike while the iron's hot, especially once the Year of the Fire Horse gallops in with a sultry eighth house solar eclipse on February 17.

And don't worry! This is not a year when you'll lose yourself in love. Independent Jupiter, which first powered into Cancer on June 9, 2025, lingers in your sign until June 30, making you magnetic and self-possessed. You won't have to tamp down any "clingy Crab" vibes this year. If anything, it will be YOU who's requesting greater autonomy. (Which, incidentally, WILL make your heart grow fonder in 2026.) Consciously planning date nights could be necessary to make sure you aren't two ships passing in the night.

Enjoy Jupiter's confidence boost and shine on your own terms instead of bending to fit a partner's mold. The red-spotted planet can turn you into quite the risk taker. Roll the dice on a relationship that feels bigger and more expansive than you've ever imagined. Coupled Crabs could push the envelope in spicy ways before June 30, even carving out an unconventional arrangement that suits your needs.

Your powers of attraction are in peak form while Venus tours Cancer from May 18 to June 13. You're feeling irresistible and unafraid to flaunt it. So, do! Passionate Mars sweeps through Cancer for its biennial visit from August 11 to September 27, dialing up your sensuality—and just in time! With Jupiter leaving your sign and heading into Leo from June 30, 2026 to July 26, 2027, you may be ready to pull someone close again and actually keep them there. By the second half of the year, you're primed to attract a partner who wants to build something real—or, if coupled, to design structures that feel nourishing and sustainable.

But no skipping the shadow work. With transformational Pluto in Aquarius all year (and until 2044), your eighth house of intimacy, eroticism and trust is undergoing a slow but deep renovation. Black Moon Lilith lands in Capricorn on September 14, stirring your relationship house for nine months. Lilith reveals both our wounds and empowered truths around our sexuality. Brace yourself. Bottled-up anger could surface, especially if you've made too many concessions in love.

Now for the tricky part: Can you "retrain" your S.O. to embrace an equitable dynamic without boiling in resentment? If you have a willing mate, this process could deepen your bond exponentially—but it requires you to own up to your part in this role-playing, too. Speaking of which, you might want to choose a safe word. Some Cancers could find erotic freedom this year through exploring a fetish or BDSM.

Romance goes retro this fall as Venus spins retrograde from October 3 to November 13. On the plus side, this nostalgic cycle can regenerate some of the sparks that brought you to your partner in the first place. But it can also herald the return of an ex, possibly "the one that got away." Proceed with caution and keep a firm no-contact rule around anyone who earned the title of "toxic" in the past. With Venus backing up through Scorpio until October 25, you could weather a few surprises, such as a pregnancy or a dramatic confession you wish you didn't hear. Hopefully it won't rock the boat too hard for you. Mercury will also be retrograde (in Scorpio) from October 24 to November 13, forcing you to discuss topics that can feel dramatic and risky, but will ultimately be freeing.

By year's end, you'll have tested and strengthened your relationship foundations. Single Cancers, this year proves just how much you bring to the table. Call in someone who recognizes that. Crabs in relationships will get a master class in balancing closeness with independence so both of you thrive. Practice emotional honesty without rushing to fix everything. Sometimes just naming the truth is the most intimate act of all.

Money & Career

CANCER 2026 FORECAST

It's not just what you do, Cancer—it's WHY you do it. In 2026, purpose becomes your bottom line as the stars push you to merge passion with prosperity. Abundant Jupiter is camped out in Cancer until June 30, amplifying your personal brand and opening doors to opportunity. You've been under this expansion spell since June 9, 2025, and the momentum is only growing. Whether you're heading back to school with a new focus, striking out on your own or innovating from inside an organization, freedom and exploration are nonnegotiable. Learning, teaching, publishing or media ventures could soar now. Your ideas deserve a bigger audience. Broadcast them!

On April 25, changemaker Uranus zips into Gemini and your twelfth house of spirituality, imagination and behind-the-scenes work, where it will stay until 2033. Creative breakthroughs may arrive through dreams, intuition or divine downloads. You could be drawn to projects that feel more soulful than status-driven, or to industries tied to healing, psychology or consciousness. Let your imagination run wild—but don't ghost reality entirely. Your most original ideas need structure to thrive, not just stardust.

Luckily, the universe delivers just that. On February 13, Saturn and Neptune unite forces in Aries and your tenth house of career and achievement, beginning a two-year stretch that blends discipline with vision. You're being primed for greater authority—and possibly a major leadership role in the not-too-distant future. Some Cancers could land a coveted executive position or oversee a high-profile initiative. Others may secure a corporate or "whale" client that anchors their portfolio. Saturn brings the mastery; Neptune adds the magic. Lead with integrity and purpose and you'll inspire others to follow.

The real financial fireworks start midyear. When Jupiter blasts into Leo on June 30, your second house of income and values lights up for the first time in over a decade. Ideas turn into tangible results and confidence becomes your biggest asset. It's time to monetize what you've learned over the past year, build a sustainable revenue stream and invest in tools that support your growth. After a season of dreaming big, you're ready to produce something that lasts.

Then comes another powerful shift: On July 26, the lunar nodes change signs. The destiny-driven North Node moves into Aquarius and your eighth house of wealth, investments and joint ventures, activating a 20-month cycle that lasts until March 2028. Money could come through partnerships, inheritances or smart long-term plays like compounding interest or cryptocurrency. This is your crash course in financial empowerment.

Across the sky, the South Node teams up with Jupiter in Leo, reminding you that how you earn matters as much as what you earn. Align your income with your values and refuse to sell your soul for a paycheck.

In 2026, the stars ask you to merge heart and hustle, vision and structure. The more you anchor your dreams in strategy, the higher—and steadier—you'll rise.

TOP 5 THEMES FOR Cancer in 2026

1	2	3	4	5
LEAD WITH PURPOSE	SHINE WITHOUT APOLOGY	UNLEASH YOUR CREATIVE SUPERPOWERS	MERGE WITH MEANING	RETHINK ROMANCE

1 LEAD WITH PURPOSE

NEPTUNE IN ARIES
JANUARY 26, 2026–MARCH 23, 2039

SATURN IN ARIES
FEBRUARY 13, 2026–APRIL 12, 2028

No pressure, Cancer, but as you set your 2026 resolutions, you might want to start thinking about your higher purpose. Two potent outer planets—Saturn and Neptune—are heading into Aries this year, kicking off long passages through your tenth house of legacies, goals and public prestige. As these planets shine like jewels at the crown of your chart, you can't help but get noticed. This could be one of the most defining eras of your life!

Here's where things get interesting. Hazy Neptune is the planet of dreams, ideals and transcendent creativity. Realistic Saturn is the no-nonsense builder, obsessed with structure, timing and integrity. Together, they represent the tension—and the magic—between vision and execution. And when they converge in your tenth house of long-term goals? Big things are possible—as long as you're willing to do the work AND refuse to waver from your dream.

Highlight February 20 in neon. That's the day that Saturn and Neptune unite in the sky for an ultra-rare conjunction. Because they move at such different speeds through the sky, this only occurs every 35 to 40 years. And a Saturn-Neptune conjunction in Aries? Well, that hasn't happened since 1702!

While this feels truly historical (and it is, Cancer), you already got a little taste of what's ahead back in 2025. From March 30 to October 22, Neptune floated into Aries for a short stay, softening your ambitions and teasing a more heart-led approach to success. Saturn joined Neptune in Aries from May 24 to September 1, 2025, reminding you that integrity and consistency were still part of the deal.

This year, the real ascent begins! Neptune returns for a 13-year residency on January 26, and Saturn settles in for a two-year run starting February 13. This duo's exact alignment on February 20 kicks off a profound reckoning: What is your purpose—and how will you live it out with the work you do in the world? Aries rules your tenth house of success. While this zone is typically associated with professional gains, it can also cover other sorts of game-changing goals, especially ones that impact people who depend on you for resources—kids, parents, employees.

Before you do any grandiose maneuvering, give your life an audit. Some changes may be in order. Maybe you realize that your title, company affiliation or professional goals no longer align with your deeper values. Or, you might see your long-nurtured passions finally take shape in the public eye. Whether you're

climbing a traditional ladder or building your own platform from scratch, this is the year to get clear on what kind of impact you want to make—and what you're willing to trade to get there. With visionary Jupiter in your sign until June 30, you have a leg-up with this, especially since you'll be more open to taking risks.

Meanwhile, compassionate Neptune's presence will elevate your work with meaning and artistry. You may feel called to do more mission-driven work, get involved in social impact or healing, or shift toward industries where empathy and vision are essential. The shadow side? It's a little too easy to let others overshadow you because you're trying to be "fair" or "nice." Be mindful not to fall into the trap of working for validation or sacrificing your well-deserved fame to please others.

Meanwhile, Saturn offers you the structure and accountability to make real progress—but only if you're willing to commit to a disciplined growth process. And that may require you to be very un-Cancerian. Instead of letting emotions guide your choices, you'll need to define your boundaries, guard your time, and get crystal clear on your priorities. As you learn to say "no," you'll stop being swept up by distractions. And surprise! As you learn to set firmer expectations with your team, they'll respect you as much as they adore you.

Make no mistakes, Cancer. This duo will test your resilience. Saturn in Aries forms a challenging square to your Cancer Sun, which could bring moments of doubt, burnout or pressure to prove yourself. But trust in this: every challenge is also a training ground. This year, you're being asked to stretch into a new level of leadership, confidence and visibility. That may look like raising your rates, applying for a next-level position, pitching a bold idea or finally going public with a passion project.

If you've been freelancing or floating, you might crave more stability. Think: a traditional job with a consistent schedule. And if you've been quietly plotting a pivot, this is your green light to map out your transition strategy. Saturn favors long-term planning. If you need to reskill, consider working with a coach, returning to school or investing in professional development that expands your credentials.

Whatever your path, 2026 will challenge you to show up with full integrity. Not perfection, not polish—just real, rooted commitment to what you stand for. As Neptune guides your intuition and Saturn sharpens your focus, you'll discover that the most successful version of you isn't performative; it's a soul-powered leader who knows exactly what they came to planet Earth to do.

2 SHINE WITHOUT APOLOGY

JUPITER IN CANCER
JUNE 9, 2026–JUNE 30, 2026

Keep the volume raised on your self-expression! You are fully immersed in your Baddie Era as 2026 begins, and ain't no stopping you now. This NYD, Jupiter is near the halfway mark of its rare, 13-month journey through Cancer that began on June 9, 2025. The larger-than-life planet only visits your sign once every 12 years—and until June 30, it keeps on lighting up your first house of self-sovereignty and fresh starts.

There's extra magic here, too: Jupiter is exalted in Cancer, which means this boundlessly generous planet feels right at home in your nurturing sign. But here's the twist. Instead of draining your resources supporting everyone else, it's time to invest in YOU. This is your personal permission slip to think bigger, act bolder and tune in to YOUR desires first.

This isn't selfish, Cancer. As you grow, you'll have much more to share with the ones you love. Let Jupiter pour cosmic Miracle-Gro on your passions and initiatives. By the time this cycle ends on June 30, you'll be a garden in full bloom. And if you want to go back to playing Best Supporting Castmate then, the role will be waiting for you.

But hey, there's a chance you might not feel like reprising that part again. As Jupiter in Cancer expands your horizons, you could soar into a whole new realm of possibilities. The first half of 2026 could find you applying to a degree program or executive role, relocating to a new corner of the globe or completely redoing your life so that you have greater freedom to pursue what brings you joy. Have you mastered a subject? Brainy Jupiter could inspire you to develop your own curriculum to pass on your knowledge. Don't be shy about charging a premium for your wisdom—people will find it surprising if you DON'T.

As a cardinal water sign, you have mixed feelings about the spotlight. You certainly know how to command it when it swings your way. But oh, the vulnerability hangovers you can feel after you've stepped off stage. Swill a shot from Jupiter's cup of courage and wage a PR campaign on your own behalf. There's no hiding behind your shell in the first half of the year! Your passion project could land you on a podcast, or you could be invited to share your expertise at a conference. If you're feeling called to put yourself out there with a personal brand, blog or social media platform, this Jupiter cycle can help you grow your audience organically.

It's also fine to have ZERO ideas about what's next for you, Cancer. You're standing on the starting block of a fresh 12-year cycle. No matter what, this will be some sort of reset. If you're uncertain about your path forward, then slow your roll. You don't have to be certain now! It's uncomfortable for your security-seeking sign, we know. But let yourself dabble. Not every idea will be a keeper. The boutique coaching firm? Try working with one client and see how you like it. The organic lavender farm in Provence? A good excuse for a vacation.

While you're beta-testing interests, you don't have to stand still. Robust Jupiter in your sign can bring a surge of vitality. Reconnect to your body through regular movement and nutrition. Your next big idea could flow in while you're doing planks in a HIIT circuit class or biking along a beautiful trail.

Freedom is paramount for Crabs in the first half of 2026, but don't confuse that with trying to do everything by yourself. As you stretch your wings, empower your team, family and collaborators to trust in their own independent strengths. Stop micromanaging and reposition yourself as the supportive leader who holds space for everyone to rise.

While we usually don't have to warn your cautious sign of this, be mindful not to slip into overexposure. As the planet of authenticity, Jupiter won't let you hide your genuine self. But bloviating can also drive up obnoxious behavior, like rare moments of spotlight-hogging, zealous preaching or competing with people who should be allies in your industry.

Careful, too, of a tendency to enjoy "too much of a good thing." As a sign that loves their food and drink, you could go overboard with the treats. Sloppy, teary confessionals are not a good look at the office picnic—and friends have better things to do with their time than help you stagger home after a "rosé all day" Saturday. Although Jupiter is technically a lucky planet, get ready for the mirror to be held up here and there. If you're not thrilled with certain things you see, bless the mess. This is the cue you need to clean it up and emerge stronger, wiser and more in command of your life.

Your biggest challenge, Cancer, may be accepting just how much you deserve the good things that life has to offer. People around the globe ARE going through hell, but your suffering won't make their situation better. Keep yourself strong, vital and on top of your game and you'll be able to help more folks than you can imagine.

JUPITER IN LEO
JUNE 30, 2026–JULY 26, 2027

Ready to slow things down and savor your expansion, Cancer? Mid-2026 invites you to hop off the wildly exhilarating (and sometimes exhausting) ride you've been on while Jupiter was turbo-charging your sign. Starting June 30, the planet of abundance shifts into Leo and your second house of finances, security and self-worth for the first time since summer 2015. This "slow and steady" transit helps you integrate all the growth you've experienced since June 9, 2025—and build a rock-solid foundation for your next big leap.

Think of this as your moment to stack some cash and anchor the genius ideas you've dreamed up while Jupiter blazed through Cancer. For the coming thirteen months, the focus turns to making your money work for you in ways that feel nourishing, not draining—the Cancerian recipe for success!

And with Jupiter in Leo until July 26, 2027, you could save up for some luxury experiences. This is definitely an elevated vibe, but also a responsible one. Instead of "Roman orgy," think of the Roman emperor Marcus Aurelius, the stoic philosopher who wrote, "Perfection of character is this: to live each day as if it were your last, without frenzy, without apathy, without pretense." Small, well-thought-out pleasures can make life sing: a colorful Le Creuset enamel pot, a perfectly tailored blazer, a velvet headboard.

Yes, you can still dust off your crown and place it squarely on your noggin. Jupiter in luxe Leo wants you to claim your value—and show it off with the regal confidence this sign demands. Calculated risks could pay off beautifully as long as you're backing them with strategy instead of wishful thinking. Run the numbers, source the right people and materials, and pace yourself for sustainable growth.

It's also the perfect time to do a salary review. Are you earning what you're capable of commanding? We suggest taking inventory of your skill set to see if there are gaps you could close with a fresh certification or training. This doesn't have to be a full-on university degree, although it could be. Even a short-term course may do the trick. Investing in your development will help you stay relevant in this rapidly changing, enigmatic world.

With globe-trotting Jupiter in this realm, work-related travel could be on the table, but you'll need equal amounts of downtime to refuel between any trips. The second half of 2026 could find you representing your company at conferences or making regular visits to an overseas office. Guard your calendar from getting overstuffed. Jupiter in the industrious second house can turn you into a workaholic if you're not careful. The potential for financial growth is sky-high, but so is the risk of burnout. Aim for a balanced regimen of hustle and hibernation.

Plus, you don't want to miss out on another bountiful gift of Jupiter in the second house— the boundless connection to sensuality. Since this zone of your chart is ruled by decadent Leo, you have an incredible opportunity to remember just what makes being in a human body so delicious. Sights, sounds, tastes, those nerve endings in your hands, feet and other organs.

For the record, you probably WON'T maximize this by swiping on a cold, hard screen. Get your paws on living organisms. Plant a garden, adopt a furry pet, drop into a ceramics studio, take a massage workshop (and get them regularly).

Purposely unplug when you can, and especially before bed. Sleep sanctification is a must if you want to get a solid night of rest. In addition to making your bedroom feel like a spa (soft sheets, aromatherapy mister, pillow spray, cooling eye mask), swap your evening scrolling for an old-school paperback.

While you're at it, keep your phone out of reach during family dinners. Not every moment needs to be photographed and cataloged for public review. Let yourself truly take in the experience. Being 100% present and engaged will burn the memory into your subconscious in ways that no digital image can.

This level of presence will heighten every relationship in your life. Don't be surprised if romance blossoms along with your windowsill herb garden. Jupiter in heart-opening Leo can reconnect us all to the desire to love and be loved. For you, Cancer, that recipe is sweet and simple in the second half of 2026: morning coffee, evening strolls, comfortable coexistence. And bring on the old-fashioned courtship rituals! A hand-lettered sonnet and a tied bouquet could make you swoon.

3 UNLEASH YOU

URANUS IN GEMINI
APRIL 25, 2026 – MAY 22, 2033

Wake up or hit snooze? You may be doing a bit of both this spring. While expansive Jupiter in Cancer is boosting your visibility until June 30, another outer planet draws you back into the reflective depths. On April 25, trailblazing Uranus will settle into Gemini for a seven-year stretch, electrifying your twelfth house of introspection, closure and healing all the way through May 22, 2033.

You had a small taste of this from July 7 to November 7, 2025, when Uranus dipped into Gemini for a four-month sneak preview—its first visit to this sign since 1941-49. If your dreams were vivid or your intuition channeled "hits" at fiber optic speed, well, that was a warmup. Your pipeline to the divine is ready to receive some fascinating downloads! Your job for the rest of this decade? Stay in your highest vibration and surround yourself with people who elevate and amplify your best qualities.

This is especially important because the twelfth house rules hidden agendas and even secret enemies. They may not have nefarious intentions; these could simply be people who siphon your energy and drain you. Perhaps they demand excessive caretaking, monopolize your attention and refuse to uphold their share of responsibilities, leaving you to be the "adult in the room." It's a role many Cancers can unconsciously lapse into—but Uranus is here to yank you out of those patterns and rewire your emotional circuitry!

Before you start rattling off a list of resentments, Crab, remember that the mirror goes both ways. Is there a part of you that's secretly playing the child, longing to be rescued or taken care of by others? You may even be giving that nurturing energy to others in the hopes that you'll receive it in return. Self-sufficient Uranus will pull the plug on that, too.

This cycle helps you become authentic and transparent instead of masking those parts of yourself.

Want to free yourself from the prison of pretending, Cancer? Tell the truth. It's better to just openly admit, "I have a needy streak, I confess! But I'm working on it," or, "I hate asking for affection, but dammit, I crave it 24/7!" than to set up some elaborate scenario where you cosplay a stone-cold stoic while your inner child withers of neglect. We know, we know—easier said than done for your self-protective sign. But with Uranus in Gemini, magic will happen when you turn your sensitivities into your strengths.

Are you just so done with a chapter of your life, a toxic person or a self-sabotaging pattern? Good! Metamorphic Uranus could prompt a radical release of anything that no longer serves you. Heads up: It could happen fast! Uranus acts on impulse, and its presence in your twelfth house of transitions can evoke a cold turkey, rip-the-bandage-off approach.

We're not saying that's the best way. In fact, you'll need to keep your Spidey senses alert for false gurus and people promising instant results. The twelfth house can be deceptive, and with Uranus here, you could encounter some fascinating but fraudulent characters. Did you really "manifest" them—or are they preying on people's insecurities? Research anyone and anything thoroughly before you get on board.

We know that may sound contradictory after we told you to be open and real. Hear us out. In many ways, hosting boldfaced Uranus in your mysterious twelfth house is a paradox, one you'll learn to navigate between now and 2033. The key? Screen all contenders before you drop the drawbridge. Make sure they come in peace, not with a shady agenda! Once they clear security and get inside the castle gates, THEN your mission is to be honest about your emotions, hesitations and old patterns. Stay vigilant for the first signs that you might be projecting your own baggage onto people, or repeating a trauma cycle from childhood by going into a repetitive role. Avoid the traps by identifying them!

If you're not familiar with the Karpman Drama Triangle, it's a psychological model that describes patterns of unhealthy relationships where people cycle through three roles: Victim, Rescuer and Persecutor. Like everyone else, you've surely played each of them at various moments. Uranus is the liberator—so free yourself, Cancer.

You might also distance yourself from anyone who drags you down with their negativity. A scientifically-proven phenomenon known as "emotional contagion" showed that being around someone in a bad mood is actually contagious—and that's a viral vibe you don't want to catch. Radical thought: You don't have to listen to people complain, especially if they're not willing to do anything to change it. A brief vent is one thing, a chronic kvetch is another. Uranus in Gemini helps you retire from the thankless role of unpaid therapist, life coach and rescuer (cue that trauma triangle again).

Do your part, too. By being upfront about your desires, needs and limits instead of being indirect, you can stop skittering into situations with a sideways crabwalk. We promise, it will clear up so many of the misunderstandings you've endured.

Spaciousness will also be a sanity-saver while Uranus is in Gemini. Breaking patterns, some of them wired deep in your neural network, takes time. One of your first tasks should be clearing your schedule of obligations that drain you, waste your time or no longer feel like a fit. Unsubscribe!

Fill that white space up with gorgeous, sensual things that help you luxuriate like a divine creature. (Sounds enticing, right?) With Uranus in this wildly creative zone, your imagination will be on overdrive, producing more than a few genius moments. Head to the recording studio or find a dance class where you can channel your emotions into inspired movement. With Uranus in your fantasy zone, turn your bedroom into a den of delights. Invite any consensual playmates in and explore a few of the scenarios that tantalize all parties involved (yes, safe words might be needed!).

The twelfth house is the zodiac's day spa, so why not make your day-to-day life feel like you've taken up residency at Canyon Ranch? Set up a meditation cave, a journaling practice, an art studio. Perhaps you'll even lead an online workshop or get certified in the healing arts, leading retreats and meeting fascinating people. But first: Treat yourself. Book regular massages—or learn to give (and receive!) them with a romantic partner. The twelfth house is also associated with Pisces, ruler of the feet. From reflexology to luxe pedicures to standing barefoot on the ground, you can literally plug into the Uranian energy grid and receive divine inspiration. Talk about a "sole-to-soul" connection!

Sleep will be of utmost importance now, too, as the twelfth house governs the subconscious and we connect to ours best through shuteye. Erratic Uranus can disrupt your sleep patterns at first, so tap into technology and innovation (Uranus' domain) with a sleep tracker, hypnosis or a wearable device that sends vibrating waves and haptic feedback to support your desired emotional state. Avoiding electronic devices and screens at night isn't exactly new advice, but it's guidance you might want to take more seriously now, as your emotional field will be especially porous before bedtime.

Have you grappled with addiction, or hit an impasse in talk therapy? Go a layer deeper with hypnosis or a past-life regression. In the coming years, you might explore the trauma-healing power of plant medicine and psychedelics, which fall in the realm of the otherworldly twelfth house. If that's still a bridge too far for you, join a spiritual community or tap into the power of community service and volunteer work. The compassionate twelfth house is also the sector of charity and selfless giving (reminder: to the TRULY needy, not the greedy!). When you feel helpless or grief-wracked about the state of the world, being part of an impactful community can remind you of your agency.

Embrace the surreal life and enjoy the ride. Futurist Uranus is giving you a glimpse of your powers, beckoning you to honor your creativity and compassion as superpowers—and to use them to change the world for the better. Don't deprive the planet of your gifts by tucking them away, Cancer!

Think of that symbolic Crab shell as a reversible jacket. Sometimes, you need to wear your armor on the outside, and other times, you can turn it inside-out and lead with that fluffy, fleece-y, cozy part of yourself, knowing that there's a protective layer shielding your most delicate parts.

4 MERGE WITH MEANING

LUNAR NODES IN LEO AND AQUARIUS
NORTH NODE IN AQUARIUS, SOUTH NODE IN LEO JULY 26, 2026–MARCH 26, 2028

Soul-deep transformation ahead! On July 26, 2026, the fateful North Node shifts into Aquarius and your eighth house of intimacy, shared resources and rebirth, where it remains until March 26, 2028. Across the wheel, the South Node settles into Leo and your second house of money, possessions and self-worth. For the next 20 months, your challenge will be balancing your desire for independence and security with the growth that comes from merging forces—emotionally, financially and spiritually.

Since January 11, 2025, the North Node has been traveling through Pisces and your ninth house of expansion, pushing you to broaden your horizons through study, travel or worldview shifts, while the South Node in Virgo kept you tethered to day-to-day tasks and details. That was the wide-angle lens; now the cosmic camera zooms in on the hidden depths of trust, intimacy and transformation.

The Aquarius North Node invites you into deeper bonds, whether through love, business or family ties. Joint financial ventures, investments or inheritance matters could surface, along with conversations about commitment and long-term stability. On the personal front, this cycle encourages vulnerability: Can you trust someone enough to share your heart, your resources and maybe even your secrets? That's something to really, REALLY think through carefully now. By the same token, you may need to shed a few defenses (or at least lower your walls a smidge). Every reward requires a little bit of risk, after all.

Meanwhile, the Leo South Node challenges you to examine your relationship with money and possessions. Have you been clinging too tightly to "what's mine" as a way to feel secure? This 20-month cycle asks you to loosen your crab claws. True stability won't come from stockpiling; it comes from learning interdependence and trusting in shared power.

Cancers in relationships may face pivotal talks about money, intimacy and future plans. Are you pooling resources fairly? Are both partners contributing in ways that feel balanced? If issues around trust or control have been simmering, they'll boil to the surface now. In some cases, outside support—from a therapist, financial adviser, or mediator—could help navigate the terrain.

Single? The North Node's presence in your eighth house adds a karmic quality to romance. Connections formed now could feel magnetic and fated, with the power to completely reshape your path. But there's a test: Passion alone isn't enough. This is about building bonds rooted in honesty, trust and mutual transformation.

Professionally, you might be drawn into managing other people's resources, stepping into roles that demand both discretion and emotional intelligence. The eighth house rules "other people's money," so loans, joint ventures or even angel investors could enter the picture. If debts are an issue, this cycle helps you face them directly and create empowering repayment strategies. You're ready to tackle this and get to the root of the issue. What's driving this, Cancer, and what will it take to make a real change?

This nodal journey can be intense at times, but you are well-equipped to weather it. By the end of it, you'll have a radically deeper understanding of what it means to share your life with others, in every sense of the word. Intimacy, power and trust are your soul's curriculum. Learn them well, and you'll emerge stronger, freer and more authentically yourself than ever.

5 RETHINK ROMANCE

VENUS RETROGRADE IN SCORPIO AND LIBRA
VENUS RETROGRADE IN SCORPIO: OCTOBER 3–25
VENUS RETROGRADE IN LIBRA: OCTOBER 25–NOVEMBER 13

Thought you'd sit out this cuffing season? Not so fast, Crab. The spirit of sentimental romance could drift back into your world starting October 3, as ardent Venus spins into a memory-steeped six-week retrograde. If you suddenly can't stop thinking about "the one that got away" or wish you could recapture that first-spark magic with your live-in partner, brace yourself. This cosmic love rewind runs until November 13, and Cupid's arrows may be tipped with déjà vu.

Romantic Venus only turns retrograde every 18 months, but this year's cycle could stir your tender heart in ways you haven't felt in ages. From October 3 to 25, the love planet moves backward through sultry, magnetic Scorpio and your passionate fifth house, reigniting dormant fireworks or tempting you to light them yourself. Then, from October 25 to November 13, Venus slips into gracious Libra and your nurturing, domestic fourth house, turning your attention toward home and family. Is it time to move in together, swap keys or relocate somewhere your love life can truly flourish? These questions could take over your thoughts during this reflective stretch.

Before you make any bold leaps, pause and reflect. Have you been looking for love in places that don't truly suit your soulful nature—or avoiding it altogether to protect your precious independence? Cancer, you can be deeply content in your own cozy bubble… maybe too content. Venus retrograde in penetrating Scorpio could draw in someone who understands your need for both closeness and breathing room in equal measure.

Coupled Crabs may revisit long-buried issues or (eesh) even feel a flicker of attraction to someone outside the relationship. If you're sharing more intimate confidences or playful banter with a friend or coworker than with your partner, it's worth a closer look. That kind of emotional outsourcing can be exciting at first, but it's no substitute for the nourishing intimacy you crave at home.

Your challenge? Use this retrograde to address what's missing. Did you become too accommodating and lose your spark? Are household duties or financial responsibilities uneven? While you can't recreate the rush of "new relationship energy," you can cultivate a deeper, more lasting passion by trying new activities together. During Venus' magnetic Scorpio leg (October 3 to 25), channel your sensual side—dress up for no reason, book a luxurious spa day or invest in weekly self-care rituals. Confidence is irresistibly attractive, and it will make you feel just as radiant as you look. But think before you ink, dye or inject! Bigger beauty moves—like a dramatic hair color or bold tattoo—are best postponed until after November 13.

If you're still healing from heartbreak, these six weeks are a gift. Give yourself full permission to process before diving back into the dating pool. Once Venus moves into Libra from October 25 to November 13, your emotions may ride closer to the surface. Use that heightened sensitivity to release old wounds and lighten your emotional load.

On the family front, the Libra phase of the backspin, from October 25 to November 13, could demand more of your time and attention. Don't skip fall family gatherings or sidestep loved ones. You'll pay an emotional price if your inner circle feels overlooked. Your support network thrives on mutual care and presence, which means YOU get to ask for their help, too!

So, how can your inner circle make YOUR life easier, Cancer? That's not a question your caretaking sign remembers to ask very often, because you may fear being a "burden" to your squad. The opposite is true. Allowing people to return your kindnesses actually keeps the relationship on an even keel. People want to give back to you, but because you often look like you've got it all together, they might not have a clue that you need anything. This Venus retrograde could push you to a point where you have to buckle and reach out. Consider it a blessing in disguise. You're not meant to handle all those obligations by yourself!

And if you're tempted to refresh your living space during Venus' homeward retreat? Stick to changes that can easily be undone. Rearrange furniture, browse Pinterest, collect swatches—but hold off on major investments or renovations. That leather club chair or trending paint color could feel "so wrong!" in six weeks. Wait until the astrological aesthete turns direct mid-November to make design choices that legitimately feel like your vibe.

2026
CANCER

12 MONTH OVERVIEW

January MONTHLY HOROSCOPE

Relationships are front and center this January, Cancer, just in time for hygge season. With the Sun in Capricorn until the 19th, your seventh house of partnerships takes the spotlight. Who are the people you want to huddle with in 2026? Early this month, you may need to clarify commitments and sign agreements in the case of business relationships. Meanwhile, invite more balance into your closest ties. On the 3rd, the full moon in Cancer puts you in the hot seat: Are you honoring your own needs, too? Carve out some sacred alone time to putter, make art and not have to tend to a single soul. Your favorite people are back in the spotlight by the Capricorn new moon on the 18th. What bonds do you want to strengthen over the next six months? This lunar lift could reveal a few solid candidates for a collaboration. Lovebirds Venus and Mars travel side by side in Capricorn until the 17th, then in Aquarius after the 23rd, fueling intimacy and trust. Merging resources may be on the table, which can make you feel simultaneously safe and a little uncomfortably vulnerable. Try not to retreat out of fear. Seductive vibes heat up on the 19th, as the Sun moves into Aquarius and your mysterious, erotic eighth house. The fun happens behind closed doors now, Cancer. While partnerships are surging, your inner world needs attention, too. On the 2nd, wounded healer asteroid Chiron turns direct in Aries, easing career strain. Then on the 26th, mystical Neptune returns to Aries for a 13-year cycle, urging you to weave imagination into your ambitions. Over the next decade-plus, your professional path will be guided by purpose as much as achievement. Let's go!

February MONTHLY HOROSCOPE

Peer beyond the veil, Cancer! February pulls you into the realm of intimacy, power and transformation as the penetrating Sun moves through Aquarius and your eighth house until the 18th. What passions are worth pursuing, and where are you giving more than you're getting? Desire should be a two-way street, so lean into equal exchanges and keep your power playfully balanced. The decadent Leo full moon on the 1st lights up your second house of money and values, bringing a financial matter or self-worth issue to a climax. Then, on February 17, the Aquarius new moon arrives as a transformative solar eclipse—the first here since 2018—just as the Year of the Fire Horse kicks off. A joint venture, loan, or soul-bonded relationship could shift suddenly, opening the door to a whole new level of intensity. Until February 10, Venus simmers in Aquarius, drawing in support and heightening attraction in your private life. Afterward, she sails into Pisces and your adventurous ninth house, sparking romance through travel, study, or cross-cultural intrigue. Disciplined Saturn re-enters Aries on the 13th, launching a two-year career cycle that demands structure and resilience. Yes, the pressure builds—but so does your prestige. Valentine's Day follows with the pragmatic Capricorn moon, encouraging gestures that are sensual and sincere rather than flashy. And keep watch: Mercury turns retrograde in Pisces on February 26, tangling travel and enterprising plans until March 20. Build in buffer time, confirm every detail, and protect your bandwidth so passion— not paperwork—remains your priority.

March MONTHLY HOROSCOPE

You, a homebody? Not this March, while the radiant Sun, Mercury retrograde, impassioned Mars, and a Pisces new moon (on the 18th) charge through your ninth house of growth, expansion and adventure. Where do you feel called to stretch beyond your comfort zone? Say yes to the growth experiences that scare you a little, possibly ones that you've turned down in the past. On the 3rd, a total lunar (full moon) eclipse in Virgo lights up your third house of communication, forcing you to clarify your message. A contract, deal or important conversation could reach a dramatic turning point and you'll need to be on top of your negotiating game. On the 2nd, Mars moves into Pisces for a six-week stay, fueling wanderlust and a hunger for new knowledge. Take action on a travel plan, dive into study or publish your ideas. Love takes on a bold, public glow once Venus enters Aries on March 6, heating up your tenth house of career. A workplace romance could spark, or your professional magnetism may attract admirers. Lucky Jupiter ends a four-month retrograde on the 10th, powering forward through Cancer and your first house of identity. Confidence returns and plans you've been refining since last year finally gather steam. Are you ready to relaunch yourself in a bigger way? The Sun enters Aries on March 20—the spring equinox—igniting your tenth house of success and visibility. Mercury stations direct the same day, untangling three weeks of confusion. Career momentum builds quickly now, and the spotlight swings squarely onto you. Step into it, Cancer—you've been preparing for this!

April MONTHLY HOROSCOPE

Career momentum is building, Crab! The brilliant Sun blazes through Aries and your tenth house of public image until the 19th, urging you to step into visibility and claim your place as a leader. Where do you want to make your mark? Aim high and commit—this is your moment to push something important over the finish line. On April 1, the Libra full moon beams into your domestic fourth house, bringing family dynamics or home matters to a climax. A move, renovation or conversation with a relative could reach resolution. After the 9th, fiery Mars storms into Aries for a six-week stay, giving you extra grit to succeed but also testing your patience with authority figures. Channel that surge into your own ambitions instead of power struggles. The new moon in Aries on the 17th drops fresh opportunities in your career zone, planting seeds for advancement that could unfold over the months ahead. Then, on the 19th, the steady Taurus Sun shifts into your eleventh house of teamwork and community, encouraging you to plug into your networks and collaborate with allies who inspire you. Love flows easily while Venus lounges in Taurus until the 24th, making it a sweet time to bond with friends who feel like family—or maybe even meet a romantic interest through your social circle. The real headline, though, arrives on the 25th, when rebellious Uranus ends its seven-year tour of Taurus and rockets into Gemini until 2033. With your twelfth house now electrified, breakthroughs will come through healing, intuition and your inner world. Expect flashes of insight, the unraveling of old baggage and a radical reimagining of how you nurture your spiritual self.

May

MONTHLY HOROSCOPE

Who are the people in your posse? Your social circle could swell this month, as the luminous Sun powers through Taurus and your eleventh house of community and collaboration until May 20. Surround yourself with allies who uplift your vision! On the 1st, the full moon in Scorpio revs up your fifth house of romance and creativity. Take your walk of fame—and give your most ardent fan some undivided attention. Transformational Pluto turns retrograde in Aquarius on the 6th, backing up through your eighth house of intimacy and shared resources until October 15. Break out the magnifying glass: It's time to review financial agreements and emotional entanglements to be sure everything's on the level. With a quarter moon in Aquarius on the 10th, Mother's Day could inspire a healing ritual that celebrates the depth and power of your bond. On May 16, the new Taurus supermoon lands in your eleventh house, amplifying your role in groups and planting seeds for meaningful collaborations. The Sun enters Gemini on May 20, moving into your twelfth house and urging you to slow down. Wrap up loose ends before your birthday season arrives. Until May 18, magnetic Venus moves through Gemini and your twelfth house, heightening private passions and hidden connections. Then, on the 18th, affectionate Venus enters Cancer while fiery Mars charges into Taurus and your social eleventh house. Confidence swells so get out and mingle! Romance could spark at a group event, possibly with someone already in your circle. The month closes with the Sagittarius full blue moon in your sixth house of health and routines this May 31. A work project may reach completion, or a lifestyle habit could get a decisive upgrade. Keep choosing what nourishes you!

June MONTHLY HOROSCOPE

June is your runway to a fresh cycle, Cancer, as the Sun simmers in Gemini and your twelfth house of rest and release until the 21st. Tie up loose ends and clear space for your season ahead. On the 14th, the Gemini new moon—the second supermoon in a rare three-part series—lands in this same reflective zone, doubling down on your need for closure. Forgiveness can be freeing now (even with no contact) if you begin to let go of anger that has run its course. Motivator Mars in Taurus energizes your eleventh house until June 28, fueling team projects and group alliances. Lean into friendships that inspire and uplift. A pivotal shift comes June 19 when "wounded healer" Chiron enters Taurus for a three-month preview of its 2027-2034 stay. Since 2018, this asteroid has challenged your career path, helping you tackle insecurities around achievement. This summer, the healing work shifts to your networks, encouraging you to choose collaborators who respect your vision. On June 21, the Sun blazes into Cancer, your first house of identity, just in time for the solstice and Father's Day. Confidence and magnetism return and you're back in your element! In love, Venus lingers in Cancer until the 13th, amplifying your allure and sweetening romance. When she moves into Leo and your second house, healthy routines—and lots of affection—are essential RDAs. On June 30, you wave goodbye to jubilant Jupiter as it wraps a thirteen-month tour through your sign. This expansive cycle stretched your horizons and reshaped your identity. Now comes the real magic: turning that growth into stability. As Jupiter shifts into Leo, you're poised to monetize your talents, solidify your confidence and build prosperity through values that truly feel aligned. The month ends with the Capricorn full moon on the 29th in your seventh house of partnerships. A relationship could reach a turning point, but head's up! Mercury turns retrograde in Cancer the same day making the next few weeks an imperative time to check in with yourself and guard your independence like a hawk.

July MONTHLY HOROSCOPE

The Sun beams alongside Mercury retrograde in Cancer until the 22nd, making this a reflective birthday season. As you blow out the candles, you're ready to revive some archived parts of your identity. Let nostalgia be the basis for your "rebrand" in the year ahead. The Cancer new moon (a supermoon) on the 14th delivers a personal milestone moment. Step into the limelight and share your gifts publicly. On July 7, mystical Neptune turns retrograde in Aries, beginning five months of career soul-searching. Taskmaster Saturn follows suit on the 26th, doubling down with a reality check. If your professional path has been built on other people's expectations, redirect toward goals that feed your soul. Meanwhile, Mars powers through Gemini and your twelfth house all month, turning your imagination into overdrive. Solitude fuels your best ideas, so slip off when you can. Leo season kicks off on the 22nd and you're ready to monetize some of these new (and old) ideas. Rework your budget and explore income streams that align with your talents. Got a rainy-day stash? Invest in something that brings lasting comfort. Venus glides into Virgo on the 9th, adding sparkle to your everyday exchanges. Text threads and casual conversations could lead to collaborations worth pursuing. Once Mercury stations direct on the 23rd, you'll be ready to leap ahead with a personal quest. A major shift comes on the 26th, when the lunar North Node slips into Aquarius and your mystical eighth house for the first time in nearly two decades. Until March 2028, you could swing way out of your comfort zone in the name of exploring intimacy, wealth-building investments and spiritual relationships. Bonus: Leaning into these deeper connections can feel incredibly sexy. July ends with fireworks on the 29th: The Sun and Jupiter unite in Leo for their annual "Day of Miracles," spotlighting your second house of money and self-worth. Simultaneously, the Aquarius full moon lands in your eighth house, illuminating a financial milestone or a moment of deep personal transformation. Translation? Your value is rising, Cancer—and when you own it, the world adjusts accordingly.

August MONTHLY HOROSCOPE

Who truly deserves a seat at your table, Cancer? August begins with a friendship audit as the Leo Sun shimmers in your self-worth zone until the 22nd. On the 3rd, Chiron pivots retrograde in Taurus and your eleventh house of community, exposing group dynamics that no longer feel nourishing. If certain alliances drain you, step back and reinvest in the connections that actually lift you up and align with your evolving interests. On the 11th, Mars rockets into Cancer, flooding you with momentum and drive until September 27. This biennial cycle is your cosmic green light to initiate daring moves, from launching a passion project to championing a cause. Step into spaces with your full confidence. People are ready to follow your lead. Eclipse season kicks off on the 12th with a total solar eclipse in Leo—the first here since 2019—spotlighting your second house of money and self-worth. A raise, luxe purchase or an epiphany about what you truly value could land suddenly, setting the tone for a new era of abundance. Venus enters Libra on the 6th, bringing harmony to your home life: Perfect timing for revamping your space, hosting dinner parties or bonding with loved ones through late-summer rituals. When Virgo season begins on the 22nd, your words carry extra weight. Pitch ideas, start that food blog or sign up for a class that expands your skills. The Pisces lunar eclipse on the 28th lights up your ninth house of travel and wisdom, pushing you past familiar borders. A trip, a workshop, or even a spiritual download could shift your perspective in dramatic ways. August closes with finesse on the 31st as Jupiter in Leo harmonizes with Saturn in Aries, blending big goals with steady strategy. Ambition meets patience here, Cancer, giving you proof that your efforts can translate into lasting success.

September MONTHLY HOROSCOPE

September is buzzing with conversations and connection! With the Virgo Sun illuminating your convivial third house until the 22nd, your calendar fills with neighborhood hangouts and impromptu ideas that actually turn into plans. Whether you're pitching an idea, streaming your latest hot take or writing poetry, your voice carries weight now. Meanwhile, lusty Mars keeps charging through your sign until the 27th, giving you a magnetic presence. Channel that energy into passion projects and personal goals before it slips away. On the 10th, the year's only new moon in Virgo lands in your communication zone, sparking new opportunities for writing, teaching or mediamaking. Someone you meet through a networking event or on a group text could turn out to be a key collaborator before 2026 is through. Also that day, disruptor Uranus pivots retrograde in Gemini and your twelfth house of closure and healing. Over the next five months, give yourself permission to shed baggage and tie up loose ends. Until the 10th, Venus lounges in Libra and your domestic sector, making nights in feel like the sweetest luxury. Then it glides into Scorpio and your playful fifth house, turning the dial up on creativity, romance and fun. Dive into a DIY project, host a dinner party with a theme or swipe right with curiosity. Just know that from October 3 to November 13, Venus will be retrograde, which may disrupt your romantic groove a bit. Build momentum now so you have a cushion later. The fall equinox on the 22nd ushers in Libra season, pulling your focus back to home and family. On the 17th, Chiron slips into Aries and your career-driven tenth house, highlighting the need to heal old patterns around leadership and ambition. And by the Aries full moon on the 26th, your professional path reaches a crossroads. Recognition may arrive—or you might decide to shift lanes into work that feels more aligned with your soul.

October MONTHLY HOROSCOPE

Take time to rediscover your innate rhythm this month, Cancer. On October 3, Venus turns retrograde, rewinding through Scorpio and your fifth house of love and creativity until the 25th, then backtracking into Libra and your domestic fourth house until November 13. Romance may wobble, artistic projects could stall and family dynamics might feel testy. Rather than panic, treat this as a tune-up: Which connections still excite you? Where has joy slipped into routine? Until the 23rd, the Sun travels through Libra, lighting up your home sector. The Libra new moon on the 10th revs up nesting instincts—whether it's redecorating with richer colors, hosting a cozy dinner party or scouting neighborhoods that feel more "you." Meanwhile, Mars barrels through Leo and your second house of money all month. You're motivated to earn, but watch those impulse buys. Splurges could erase your progress in a single click. On October 15, Pluto powers forward in Aquarius and your eighth house, reviving momentum with shared resources or intimacy. Then on the 23rd, the Sun shifts into Scorpio and your playful fifth house—the same day Venus retrograde fuses with the Sun in a rare Cazimi. Suddenly, what felt murky in love or creativity snaps into focus. Is it a fairy tale or a lesson? You'll soon see. Not that you should rush to act upon anything. The next day, Mercury also turns retrograde in Scorpio, so expect crossed wires in dating or artistic collabs. The Taurus full moon on the 26th brings glowing results to community efforts. A group project could wrap successfully. You might decide to move on from here and invest your energy in activities that truly inspire you.

November MONTHLY HOROSCOPE

No hiding in the wings this November, Cancer! With the Scorpio Sun parading through your fifth house of passion, play and fame until the 22nd, you'll cast your spell on center stage. But here's the paradox: Mercury retrograde in Scorpio and Venus retrograde in Libra—both until the 13th—may cloak your charisma in mystery. Tease, tantalize, but don't be so enigmatic that you lose your audience. On the 9th, the Scorpio new moon invites you to reset the stage: Unveil a creative project, plan a glamorous night out or turn a love affair in an exciting new direction. Financially, November hums with activity as Mars in Leo powers through your second house of income and stability until the 25th. Motivation to grow your earnings runs strong, but temper those retail therapy impulses.

Overindulgence could cancel out progress if you aren't mindful. On the 22nd, the Sun grapevines into Sagittarius, kicking off your annual (somewhat ill-timed) wellness kick. Who says you can't be healthy during the holiday season? Enjoy your treats along with roasted veggies, lean protein and vitamin-rich fresh foods. Make daily exercise non-negotiable: Even a 20-minute HIIT workout in the living room will do! Ready to release some baggage? The Gemini full supermoon on the 24th lands in your twelfth house of endings, supporting you with the "let it go, let it flow" mission. This lunar lift could also spotlight a sage mentor whose wisdom helps you finish the year strong. Go-getter Mars buzzes into Virgo on the 25th, activating your third house of communication for the rest of the year. Your voice will be strong and dynamic. Use it to whip up neighborhood goodwill and push an important message out into the public.

December MONTHLY HOROSCOPE

You don't have to skip the cookie tray to stay on track, Cancer! But 'tis your zodiac season for salubrious self-care. The Sagittarius Sun spotlights your sixth house of wellness, organization and daily rhythm until the 21st. Routines get a reboot from the new moon in Sag on the 8th: Try a new fitness class, streamline your morning ritual, cut out a draining distraction (those DM alerts). Two outer planets—strategic Saturn and visionary Neptune—wrap up five-month retrogrades in Aries on the 10th and 12th, respectively, lifting the fog around career ambitions and long-term plans. A benchmark that felt out of reach suddenly looks possible. Better still? Support could come in from well-heeled VIP contacts. With motivator Mars buzzing through Virgo all month, you're quite the culture vulture. Circulate at holiday markets, neighborhood gatherings and productions of The Nutcracker. You never know who you might meet! Chemistry bubbles after the 4th when Venus makes a post-retrograde return to Scorpio. Dress up and hit the town, solo or power-coupled! On the 12th, abundant Jupiter pivots retrograde in Leo for four months. If your seasonal spending is creeping into splurge territory, rein it in. Homemade gifts, cozy potlucks and quality time are treasures, too! After the 21st, Capricorn season and the solstice spotlight your seventh house of partnerships, strengthening romantic and business ties. The Cancer full supermoon on the 23rd—the year's last supermoon—puts YOU in the spotlight. Make the toast, take the selfie, own the room. Popularity soars this NYE as a radiant Sun-Mars trine makes you the name on everyone's invite list. Go where the fascinating people are: Conversations pop, ideas spark and your words could open doors as 2027 begins.

Read your extended monthly forecast for life, love, money and career! astrostyle.com

LEO IN 2026

| ALL THE PLANETS IN LEO IN 2026 | YOUR 2026 HOROSCOPE | TOP 5 THEMES FOR LEO IN 2026 | LOVE HOROSCOPE + LUCKY DATES | MONEY HOROSCOPE + LUCKY DATES |

Leo in 2026

Your year of:
GLOBAL EXPANSION, INDEPENDENCE, INTERNAL RECALIBRATION

STEP UP AND CLAIM CENTER STAGE, LEO!

But don't ignore the influence you have behind the scenes as well. In 2026, opportunities arrive that push you beyond your usual sphere of influence. The call has been sounded: Share your voice with a wider audience. People are clamoring for your gifts. Projects with reach and resonance come into focus, while your natural charisma attracts allies who want to amplify your vision. Love feels passionate and expansive, too, leading to connections that broaden your world. By year's end, you'll see how far your light can travel when you choose opportunities that truly match your potential.

THE PLANETS IN Leo

THE SUN JUL 22–AUG 22	Happy birthday season! With the Sun in your sign, you're clear to take chances, chase fresh adventures, and command the spotlight.
NEW MOON, TOTAL SOLAR ECLIPSE AUG 12 1:37PM, 20°02'	Happy bonus New Year! The first eclipse in your sign since 2019 rockets you into a new league. Set intentions with care, considering every possible angle.
FULL MOON FEB 1 5:09PM; 13°04'	Manifestation moment! Your work of the past six months bears fruit. Celebrate your progress and harvest the rewards.
MERCURY AUG 9–25	Hold court! When charismatic Mercury zips through your sign, your social status soars. Work the room, make connections—but keep your commitments realistic to avoid overpromising.
VENUS JUN 13–JUL 9	Love is in the air! When the galactic glamazon struts through your sign, your powers of seduction skyrocket. Irresistible charm, luxe tastes and flirtatious vibes abound—just keep an eye on your budget.
MARS SEP 27–NOV 25	Motivation is off the charts when energetic Mars blazes through your sign every couple of years. You're bold, driven, and unstoppable—but watch that combative streak and ease up on the intensity.
JUPITER JUN 30–DEC 31 RETROGRADE IN LEO: DEC 12–31	How lucky can you get? Bountiful Jupiter visits your sign once every 10–12 years, blessing you with extra fortune. Everything's exciting…and extra! Take calculated risks but avoid gambles, particularly during the retrograde.
SOUTH NODE JUL 26–DEC 31	Life feels both surreal and karmic when the lunar South Node backs up through your sign (for 18 months) every 18.5 years. Surrender to the vision quest and prepare to let go of unworkable habits. This will all make sense when the cycle ends.

Leo in 2026
HIGHLIGHTS

EXPAND YOUR WORLDVIEW: SATURN AND NEPTUNE IN ARIES
Your horizons are broadening in beautiful ways! Dreamy Neptune and grounded Saturn float back into Aries (January 26 and February 13, respectively), buffering your ninth house of higher learning, global adventures and wisdom. Saturn wants you to study, commit and put structure around your worldview for the next two years. Neptune calls for visioning through an imaginative and spiritual lens between now and 2039. Maybe you're writing a book, planning a pilgrimage or finally turning in that grad school application. Travel could also be transformative—an ancestry trip, a semester abroad or even a digital nomad chapter.

REINVENT YOUR NETWORK: URANUS SHIFTS INTO GEMINI FOR SEVEN YEARS
On April 25, Uranus ends its seven-year shake-up of your career zone and heads into Gemini until 2033. Now the focus is on your eleventh house of teamwork and tech. Get ready for some fresh energy: inventive alliances, group projects that take off unexpectedly and a stronger pull toward activism or community work. Here's where you step out of the solo spotlight and co-create with like-minded people. Use your influence to signal-boost people whose work you admire. Emerging industries are calling your name, from AI to renewable energy to space travel. Future-casting is your superpower—start sharing those big ideas.

MERCURY RETROGRADES: RESET AND REALIGN
Mercury turns retrograde three times in 2026, asking you to take stock of your inner world and closest bonds. From February 26 to March 20, the backspin runs through your eighth house of intimacy, shared resources and long-term investments. Old entanglements may need review, in love or finance. You could reconnect with someone from your past. From June 29 to July 23, Mercury reverses in your twelfth house of release. Hidden feelings could surface. Use this time to wrap up unfinished business. The final cycle, October 24 to November 13, lands in your fourth house of home and family. With Venus also retrograde in this zone, some of your closest relationships will require rebalancing. You could revisit plans for a move or renovation. Each cycle gives you the chance to reset and clear space before stepping into what's next.

GLOW-UP INCOMING: JUPITER ARRIVES IN LEO JUNE 30
Spotlight's on YOU, Leo. On June 30, Jupiter enters your sign for the first time since 2014, launching a 13-month cycle of growth, joy and unapologetic self-expression. This is your cosmic glow-up era, so don't shy away from increased visibility! Invest in your presentation because—yes—the world is watching. Refresh your branding, update your wardrobe, revamp your social feeds. Whether you're going viral or going deep, make yourself accessible to the people who matter most.

IDENTITY DETOX: THE NODES SHIFT INTO LEO AND AQUARIUS
On July 26, the karmic South Node enters Leo for the first time since 2008, kicking off a 20-month cycle of self-reinvention. Translation? Time to shed outdated versions of yourself and release the need to pivot to meet other people's "requirements." Across the zodiac wheel, the fateful North Node in Aquarius pulls you toward partnership and collaboration. The lesson: You don't have to carry the spotlight alone. This cycle, which last occurred from 2007-09, is a chance to practice vulnerability, share the stage and find power in "we."

MARK YOUR CALENDAR: NEW AND FULL MOONS IN LEO
Look how far you've come! February 1 delivers a Leo full moon, spotlighting your growth. This is a peak manifestation moment, so shoot your shot. On August 12, the first Leo eclipse since 2019 arrives with the new moon—and it's a total solar eclipse! Unanticipated opportunities could flood in, ones you may need to leap on fast! Read every bit of fine print to make sure you fully understand the assignment. This lunation could spark a reinvention that catapults you into a next-level version of yourself. Use these cosmic checkpoints like milestones: Launch the brand, throw the event or make a bold declaration about who you are becoming.

MARS IN LEO FROM SEPTEMBER 27 TO NOVEMBER 25
Get ready for a confidence surge! From September 27 to November 25, firebrand Mars storms through Leo, fueling passion, charisma and creative drive. You'll feel unstoppable, whether you're pitching, performing or pursuing romance. Just be mindful of ego clashes. Your passion can attract as much friction as applause. Channel that extra energy into personal goals, creative projects or any group effort that is crying out for leadership.

LOVE AND LEGACY CHECK: VENUS RETROGRADE THIS FALL

Where do you feel at home? From October 3 to November 13, Venus retrogrades through your home and local community zones. You might question whether you've been chasing the right applause or find yourself rethinking personal alliances. An old family dynamic could resurface. Venus retrogrades repeat every 8 years (minus 2°), so fall 2026 links back to fall 2018. Look for echoes in communication roles and relationship priorities, as well as how you give and receive comfort. This time, the question is: What does connection feel like on YOUR terms? Romantically, this cycle could redirect your shared goals or pull you back to a "type" that you haven't pursued in a while.

Love
LEO 2026 FORECAST

Is it all a dream? Limitless Jupiter's on a pleasure cruise through Cancer and your hazy twelfth house until June 30, blurring the line between fantasy fodder and "legit relationship." Don't freak out if your romantic future feels foggy in the first half of the year. You could be closing a chapter, processing old heartbreak or simply giving things space to evolve organically. Don't force the "happily ever after," Leo. Solo time can actually help you spot the habits and patterns that have kept you stuck. Retreat into your velvet den in January, whether you're solo or coupled, to do this inner work.

You won't be by yourself all the time though! From January 23 to February 10, cosmic lovebirds Venus and Mars sync in Aquarius and your relationship house, giving both new and established unions a cosmic boost. Single? Keep your eyes open: Someone with long-term potential could show up when you least expect it. On February 17 the Aquarius solar eclipse kicks off the Year of the Fire Horse, fanning those flames. A karmic connection could reveal itself ("Have we met in another lifetime?") or you could have an epiphany that reawakens chemistry in a current bond.

Venus and Mars both do time in Pisces and your seductive eighth house in Q1. From February 10 to March 6, Venus paddles through these sultry waters, so plan for a private celebration this Valentine's Day. With bodice-ripping Mars here from March 2 to April 9, you could get a head start on your 2026 spring awakening. Give the quiet ones a chance to woo you.

Do you know the difference between love and obsession, Leo? Shadowdancer Lilith, the "black moon" that governs erotic empowerment—along with a host of swirling feelings from shame to exile—travels through Sagittarius and your passionate fifth house until September 14. This year, you may confront your relationship with romance itself. Are you addicted to the chase, the chemistry, the adrenaline? Lilith pushes you to balance excitement with consistency. Lean into the slow, consistent burn.

Summer is when things really start to shift. Venus makes her annual visit to Leo from June 13 to July 9, boosting your confidence and magnetism. On June 30, Jupiter enters Leo for the first time since 2014, launching a 13-month cycle of expansion in love and life. What you needed in the past might not do it for you once the red-spotted planet circles into your first house of identity. You're on an epic growth trajectory between now and July 26, 2027. Open your world to people who can grow with you. If they can't keep up, they might get left behind.

A show-stopping moment comes near the August 12 solar eclipse in Leo, the first in your sign since 2019. Expect big realizations about the kind of love that sustains you, whether that means deepening a bond, redefining your "type" or bravely stepping away from an old script.

The North Node shifts into Aquarius and your relationship house on July 26, opening a 20-month window for destiny-driven connections. But with the karmic South Node riding shotgun through Leo, relationships will be a giant mirror, too. Release old patterns, like making love a performance. Being adored feels great, but this time it's about co-starring in a story where both leads shine.

Cuffing season could be hotter than ever, thanks to randy Mars charging through Leo from September 27 to November 25. You'll have no reservations about pursuing exactly what and who you desire. The only catch? Venus will be retrograde (in Scorpio and Libra) from October 3 to November 13, which could throw off your "picker." An ex could creep back into your life or you could find your moods changing hourly—one minute you cling, the next you want miles between you and a certain someone. Don't rush into ultimatums! There will be mixed messages and possibly a few red flags to investigate this fall.

By year's end, you'll have danced through healing, passion and honest self-reflection. Your 2026 love assignment is to create a vision of partnership that balances your hunger for excitement with your need for stability. When you stop chasing admiration and start honoring your own truth, you'll draw in the kind of love that lasts long after the curtain falls.

Money & Career

LEO 2026 FORECAST

After years of professional plot twists, you're ready to write a steadier—and more satisfying—chapter. On February 13, Saturn and Neptune will both have left Pisces, where they've been churning up confusion in your eighth house of joint finances, power and long-term commitments. Since 2023, this demanded deep work: managing shared resources, rethinking debt or weathering uncertainty around business or creative partnerships. You've been forced to develop endurance and discernment.

For the next two years, structured Saturn and imaginative Neptune team up in Aries, a fellow fire sign, energizing your worldly, enterprising ninth house. Bring on the growth opportunities! You could expand your reach through teaching, travel or media making. (Time to publish that book?) Disciplined Saturn rewards those who commit to mastery. Formal training or a credential could pay off. Spiritual Neptune inspires you to do something meaningful with what you know, perhaps blending your expertise into a course, book or consulting niche. Work involving international markets, media or education could take off.

Career turbulence eases, too. On April 25, chaotic Uranus finally exits Taurus and your professional tenth house, wrapping up a seven-year cycle of reinvention that began in 2018. You may have had to pivot repeatedly since then—not always by choice. Frustrating as it's been, those experiments taught you what truly fits.

Late April, Uranus moves on to Gemini, plugging into your eleventh house of networks and innovation until 2033. Seek out collectives, tech-savvy teams or cause-driven projects where you can both lead and learn. One strategic alliance could have long-term potential for profit.

By midyear, you'll feel unmistakable tailwinds. On June 30, abundant Jupiter soars into Leo for the first time since 2013-14, launching a 13-month cycle of confidence and visibility. You're motivated to stand on your own two feet again—maybe by reviving a personal brand, pitching original work or stepping into a leadership role that lets you direct the vision.

Tired of a boss breathing down your neck? This is an excellent period for self-employment, passion projects and roles that require charisma and creativity. Circle August 12, when a new-moon solar eclipse in Leo could bring an epic breakthrough that validates all the groundwork you've laid. On July 26, the karmic South Node moves into Leo, insisting that anything you pursue feel like "soul work." Stop chasing approval and start sharing your original ideas. That's how you'll attract the opportunities that are legit win-wins.

Across the aisle, the fateful North Node slides into Aquarius and your partnership house for this 20-month cycle. Even as you assert your independence, your next level will depend on the alliances you build. Whether that's an agent, mentor, co-founder or trusted collaborator, choose people whose strengths complement yours.

After several demanding years, 2026 restores your faith in what you do and in how brightly you can shine when the timing and team are right. Lead with vision and integrity, Leo, and you'll build influence that lasts.

TOP 5 THEMES FOR *Leo* in 2026

1	2	3	4	5
EXPAND YOUR REACH	IGNITE YOUR NEXT ERA	CURATE YOUR CREW	POWER UP YOUR PARTNERSHIPS	REDEFINE HOME & HEART

1 EXPAND YOUR REACH

NEPTUNE IN ARIES
JANUARY 26, 2026–MARCH 23, 2039

SATURN IN ARIES
FEBRUARY 13, 2026–APRIL 12, 2028

What happens when the planet of ambition meets the planet of imagination—in daredevil Aries, no less? You're about to get a masterclass in that, Leo. In 2026, a rare convergence of structure-loving Saturn and vision-driven Neptune is setting off sparks in your ninth house of travel, truth-seeking and global exploration. And what a wild journey it promises to be.

Saturn and Neptune are quite the odd couple, which makes this even wonkier. In some ways, these planets couldn't be more opposite! Saturn builds walls; Neptune dissolves boundaries. Saturn demands discipline, logistics and realistic follow-through. Neptune whispers of expansive vision, spiritual adventures and soulful quests. Because they move at such different speeds, they only team up in the sky every 35 to 40 years. Even more impressive? The last Saturn-Neptune conjunction in Aries was way back in 1702! This is a rare cosmic gift, but one to navigate with intrepid curiosity AND steady footing.

You got a sneak peek of this dynamic duo in 2025. Dreamy Neptune drifted through Aries from March 30 to October 22 while stabilizing Saturn popped in from May 24 to September 1. Now, both begin their long-haul tours through your ninth house. Neptune leads on January 26, launching a 13-year odyssey through your global dreams; Saturn follows on February 13, ushering in a two-year boot camp in vision-grounding strategy.

But how to balance this bizarre duo? Free-spirited Neptune wants you leaping onto the TED stage in Bali, dancing 'til dawn in Ibiza, and launching an impact-driven entrepreneurial venture. Sounds good, Leo, but, um, how do you plan to pull it all off? That's where Saturn comes in and helps you design your roadmap—if one is actually possible. There's a 50/50 chance of that, so don't give up OR rush in capriciously.

February 20 marks a major milestone. That day, Saturn and Neptune make their only EXACT conjunction of this cycle, teaming up at 0° Aries. Treat this day like a personal vision quest. This is a pivotal moment where your soul's calling (Neptune) meets the discipline to make it a reality (Saturn). Marked progress could occur near this date. More likely, plans will begin to take shape. Quiet your mind because you could finally get the download for what you want to pursue next.

Saturn's restrictions may feel frustrating at first, especially for a Leo craving freedom and adventure. They're actually your ballast. While Neptune in Aries blesses you with G-force breaking imagination, Saturn won't let you float away without an anchor. Starting in 2026, your most expansive ideas aren't just fantasies—they become structured projects that you can eventually take to the bank.

Get ready for a radical expansion in your worldview. With these heavy-hitting planets in your global ninth house, you could gain a new level of compassion (Neptune) for suffering nations. Saturn supports you with cultivating an effective way to give back— and can also remind you of the importance of self-care when you're deeply invested in humanistic causes. Balance is key, Leo. Travel may be part of the picture, or perhaps you'll link your home base with a sister city in another part of the world.

What you learn along the way could spark a personal philosophy reset. You may be both terrified and exhilarated by what you discover. Foggy moments are part of the process; that's Neptune's gift. But Saturn is right there helping you catalog each insight into a meaningful framework.

If you don't know exactly where you're headed? That's okay, Leo. Sometimes you have to get lost in order to find yourself. Your hardest lesson may not be producing results, but rather learning to sit with uncertainty without jumping into action hero mode.
In the process, you may confront fears about your platform, voice or global impact. But that's where the growth hides. When you stay aligned with your highest convictions— even as they evolve—you become magnetic in ways you can't predict. It helps that both Saturn and Neptune in Aries are forming a miracle-making 120-degree angle, a trine, to your Leo Sun. This fire-sign mashup adds fuel to your endeavors. Play your cards right and you could become the hottest thing in town—or on TikTok.

Know this, Leo: As Saturn pushes through your ninth house, you might feel like you're in cosmic grad school—information overload one day, itinerary chaos the next. Once Saturn moves on to Taurus on April 12, 2028, you'll be more grounded, wise and globally influential than ever.

There's an added twist: Saturn is "in fall" in Aries, a difficult position for the ringed planet in the sky. You may chafe at structure as you crave freedom. Careful not to self-sabotage in a moment of boredom or rebellion. If you're willing to earn your stripes—drafting plans, booking retreats, securing mentors—you're on track to build not just a journey, but a legacy. That book, course or cultural mission you've always dreamed of bringing to life? Thanks to this rare cosmic pairing, 2026 might be the year it begins in earnest. Neptune in your ninth house will continue to expand your horizons—spiritually, culturally, academically—through 2039. At times, you may feel disoriented or unsure if you're exploring or escaping. That's Neptune's fog, and it's part of the process. But you don't have to get lost in it. Some grounded friends will be essential accessories.

When uncertainty threatens to capsize you, anchor into your physicality. Turn on a playlist and dance until you sweat, ease into gentle yoga, or take a long bike ride along a favorite trail. Let your body remind you who you are! These rituals bring you back to your center while you're racing toward the horizon.

2 IGNITE YOUR NEXT ERA

JUPITER IN CANCER
JUNE 9, 2026–JUNE 30, 2026

Should you invest in the Coachella VIP Access pass...or just head straight to the sacred medicine ceremony in Joshua Tree? The answer may surprise you in the first half of 2026. With philosophical Jupiter on sabbatical in your spiritual twelfth house until June 30, your soul is craving a quieter vibe. And while we would never deny your festive (and festival-loving!) sign an opportunity to dress like a Carnival queen and dance under the stars, your desire to be in the center of the action won't kick in until mid-summer. Sit with that.

The reason for this low-key kickoff to 2026? You're midway through Jupiter's thirteen-month tour of Cancer, which rules the twelfth and final house of your solar chart. This is a quiet time for the normally live-out-loud planet as it gathers steam for its return to YOUR sign from June 30, 2026 to July 26, 2027.

Goal No. 1: Fight against FOMO, Leo! We know that's a daunting task for your fun-loving sign, but we promise you, there's magic in stillness. By NOT leaping into action, you create space for heretofore unimagined possibilities to arise. Jupiter in the twelfth house makes miracles. It can turn your life into a spun-gold story arc that feels like a modern-day fairy tale. Don't be so busy that you miss the moment!

Not that you have to be passive with this process. There's no time like the first half of 2026 to start a mindfulness practice—yoga, journaling, meditation, breathwork, even a sauna and cold-plunge contrast regimen. Get out into wide-open spaces. Let the breezes tangle your mane, professional blowouts be damned! This is a rare opportunity to recharge and process all the big feelings that have piled up in your psyche. Since Jupiter has been in Cancer since June 9, 2025, there's a solid chance you're already steeped in this stoic cycle. Keep going with it.

Now for the REALLY hard part. You need to loosen your grip on trying to control every last detail and hand over the wheel to your spiritual side. Life may still feel fluid—almost like you're drifting through a lucid dream. Keep your off-duty schedule light and open-ended instead of locking into anything stressful, high-pressure or permanently binding. Because you're a fixed sign that loves a stable plan, this constant ebb and flow can stir up some anxiety. Again, that's where mindfulness practices really come in handy!

The twelfth house is a space of transition, so try not to get too attached to how anything should play out. Just when you think you've locked onto the thing, it could slip right through your fingers like water. If you feel ready to close a chapter—maybe a relationship you've outgrown, a job that no longer lights you up, or a place you're ready to leave behind—Jupiter in Cancer gives you the courage to carve a fresh path forward. Some of these endings could happen swiftly but others will feel like a gentler drift. If you're still dreaming up what your next phase looks like, give yourself grace to move at your own pace. Clarity could come in with a resounding "yes!" once Jupiter strides into your sign from June 30, 2026 through July 26, 2027.

Before then, be ready for old emotions to bubble to the surface. You might feel raw after everything you've held in—but you'll feel wildly alive, too, even if you're laughing through tears. Your natural compassion could hit peak levels, but warning, Leo! Giving too much could drain your already tapped-out reserves. This is the time to make self-compassion your first priority—and read a few books on the subject. The common advice applies: Strap on your own oxygen mask before you assist other "passengers."

Permission granted to book a healing retreat, work with a trauma-informed therapist—maybe one who specializes in hypnosis or EMDR. And while your creativity is this vivid, let the muse lead you. Channel your pain, your healing and your breakthroughs to pour into cathartic works of art.

Soulmate alert! We've seen Jupiter in the twelfth house deliver some seriously meant-to-be connections—especially for those who open themselves up to the full spectrum of their emotions. Boundaries can dissolve during this cycle, which is not always a bad thing. Teary-eyed confessions of love (sweet love) could happen anywhere from your DMs to the wedding altar in the first half of the year—especially after Jupiter wraps its four-month retrograde on March 10. If you've been a little TOO guarded of your heart, this Jupiter cycle might just melt it.

Forgiveness is a huge theme of the twelfth house. Certain grudges may be ready for release, especially if they're poisoning your experience of life. People are gonna people, Leo, that's just life. If you've been holding loved ones at arm's length, ask yourself: Have they truly done harm or have I created an impossible standard? In some cases, it's best to remain estranged. In others, you may regain a capacity for acceptance; one that brings everyone serenity.

Much of your growth will be invisible to the outside world in early 2026, but what matters is that you can sense it happening. It's a lot like seeds germinating in the dark soil. While you may not see obvious results until mid-summer, Jupiter is working its magic behind the scenes. You don't need the whole world watching now. Capture events in your mind or a private album. You can make your big announcements (or not) once Jupiter blasts into your sign this June 30.

In the meanwhile, guard your peace from outside critics—and even well-meaning loved ones whose advice resonates with THEM, not you. Developing the virtue of patience will carry you far in life. Come June 30, you'll reap the rewards of your delayed gratification!

JUPITER IN LEO
JUNE 30, 2026 – JULY 26, 2027

Roar and soar, Leo—no flying chariot required! On June 30, larger-than-life Jupiter bursts into your sign, launching you into an electrifying reinvention tour that lasts until July 26, 2027. Shake off the heavy vibes of the past thirteen months! The house lights dim and the curtain raises as Jupiter in Leo trumpets your return to center stage.

Jupiter only swings through your sign every 12–13 years, so this is a major moment—dare we say, a full-on comeback for some Lions! Flip back to your calendar and see what was happening during that last visit, from July 16, 2014 until August 11, 2015. What milestones or adventures did you live out back then? While this transit won't be a carbon copy, similar themes of self-expansion, courage and fierce reinvention could resurface.

And here's some glitter to sprinkle on top: In Leo, Jupiter feels completely emboldened to be fabulous! Anything "matte" or "mid" are no longer viable options. More is more is more in the second half of 2026. Leo is ruled by the radiant Sun, so you're already a born energizer. And when the planet of abundance arrives in your sign? Your goddess-given brilliance gets amplified to superstar levels.

Are you the humblebragging type of Leo? We suggest you stop downplaying your gifts immediately. When you're fully lit up, you inspire everyone around you to shine. No more hiding in the wings as the Executive Producer in someone else's drama. Your own storyline is ready for a fresh narrative arc. The ensemble cast WILL form around you, but first, take time to identify your chosen role. You're not meant to be caretaking when Jupiter is in your sign. That doesn't mean you have to abandon your people. But here's a chance to empower them to build up their skills. Step back and watch them grow—even if you have to restrain yourself from rushing to soothe when they throw a world-class tantrum.

As the ruler of higher education and big ideas, Jupiter in Leo could nudge you back toward a degree or specialized training. Already a master of your craft? Disseminate your wisdom to the world. Design a course, launch a podcast or build a brand around your expertise. And please, Leo, don't be modest about your rates. With the planet of abundance in your corner, you are well-positioned to create a premium offer and rake in the big bucks.

With your independent streak blazing, you may trade your 9-5 for contract work or claim a more sovereign leadership role within an existing gig. (Think: Intrapreneurship.) Careful, however, that you don't pile so much on your plate that you wind up bogged down. True Leo leadership is magnetic. You inspire loyalty and greatness by empowering the people around you. Practice lifting up your pride—in every area of life. Hold up the mirror so they see their best selves reflected back. That's the kind of win-win your regal heart can stand behind.

Still, this is YOUR time to shine. In short, Leo, it won't take much to draw all eyes your way—and possibly go viral—after June 30. And if you DO enact a little strategic PR to prime the pump? The floodgates will open, so make sure you're ready to serve your hungry fans. Since Jupiter doesn't have an off switch, it's wise to time your big reveals strategically.

Jupiter's global touch might send you chasing the sun across oceans. Whether you do it virtually or via travel, casting a wide net will bring in a bounty. Some Leos could make an international move in the second half of 2026—or possibly purchase property in an area far from home base. In truth, you might not spend as much time in your den after June 30. (So how about a tiny home that travels with you?) No matter your GPS coordinates, you can't keep your power caged up now. Get out there and let the world celebrate you in your full Leo glory!

3 CURATE YOUR CREW

URANUS IN GEMINI
APRIL 25, 2026 – MAY 22, 2033

Lions are communal creatures, and this April 25, your "pride" is about to go wide. Radical disruptor Uranus makes landfall in Gemini and your eleventh house of groups, friendships and technology until May 22, 2033. Fascinating new figures could enter your world, the kind of people you might have considered "fringe" before. Maybe your paths never naturally crossed, but this year—and for the rest of the decade—you find yourselves unlikely colleagues or collaborators.

You had a sneak peek at this brand-new energy from July 7-November 7, 2024 when Uranus took a short test flight through the Gemini skies for four months. There may have been a shakeup in your social circle or an exciting invitation to join a new crew. If you found yourself drawn to emerging ideas or social movements, welcome to the Uranus in Gemini era. The side-spinning planet hasn't been in this sign since 1941-49.

For the next seven years, electrifying Uranus will supercharge your connections. On the plus side? Your inner event planner will be in heaven. From rooftop hangouts to grassroots rallies, you'll find every excuse to gather your crew for something meaningful, outrageous—or quite likely both.

Are you feeling stir-crazy from hanging out with the same handful of people? As much as you might hate to admit it, your steadfast squad could be feeling basic, conventional and stuck at a personal development plateau. Warning signs? You're talking about the same topics (rarely going deep), gossiping and not welcoming fresh ideas and faces into the fold.

Get ready, Leo: Uranus in Gemini will give your inner circle a cosmic remix. With quirky Uranus stirring the pot, you'll attract rebels, visionaries and avant-garde thinkers. Some of them might be too "extra" for your longtime friends, and don't feel pressured to blend your worlds. It's okay to keep certain friendships separate if that makes the dynamics smoother, especially if these new bonds are still developing. What matters most is that you feel uplifted by the kindred spirit connection—not that they're bridal party contenders or laugh at the inside jokes you share with your siblings or college roommates. Experiment, Leo! An important new part of you is emerging, and it's being reflected and amplified by the trailblazers you meet.

As the planet of disruption, Uranus brings radical self-expression. In this placement, it empowers you to champion bold ideas, then build momentum with kindred spirits who share your passion for progress. The eleventh house is the domain of activism and altruism—so you could easily find yourself joining a cause or even leading one. But here's the twist: This isn't about molding yourself to fit someone else's mission. It's about standing strong in your truth—and inviting others to rise alongside you. Authenticity is your most magnetic trait now.

Teamwork remains crucial, but the format is changing. Leo, it's time to step off the pedestal and stand shoulder-to-shoulder with your peers. You're a natural-born leader, yes—but this Uranian cycle calls for a more collaborative approach. Let others take the wheel, even if they drive a little wonky at first. Don't feel like you have to "fake it 'til you make it" or figure things out for everyone. Quite the opposite! For the rest of the decade and into the next one, leadership is about listening—and really hearing—what other people want. Descend from the throne and get in the trenches with "the people."

Uranus invites you to release the idea that you, or anyone else, knows best. There may be a few messy moments, but tame your compulsion to step in, take over and micromanage. Opt for curiosity instead of control. Uranus in your democratic eleventh house thrives when everyone participates and has a voice. You'll accomplish more in a respectful space where people can "agree to disagree" while still building a common agenda. With Uranus in the political eleventh house, you might even run for office, channeling your heart-led creativity into healing our divided world.

On a personal level, have you been overly accommodating or caretaking—at your own expense? Uranus is the planet of detachment, and 2026 could reveal where you've gotten a little too involved in other people's affairs. Disentangle thyself, Leo. If you've been the unofficial therapist among your friends and coworkers, gently but firmly step back. Nurture people's growth when it's appropriate (i.e., where you're a mentor, teacher or adult figure). For everyone else? Cheer them on—and let go. You've earned the right to relax, knowing the vision is in capable (if learning) hands. Now, pass that baton…and maybe a mimosa, too.

4 POWER UP YOUR PARTNERSHIPS

LUNAR NODES IN LEO AND AQUARIUS
NORTH NODE IN AQUARIUS, SOUTH NODE IN LEO JULY 26, 2026–MARCH 26, 2028

Relationships become your karmic classroom this July 26, so settle in for some epic soul growth. With the lunar North Node moving into Aquarius and your seventh house of partnerships until March 26, 2028, shining as your most fabulous self is not the main point. How do you show up when working with others, Leo, especially when no one else is watching? (Or so you think…)

This is a refreshing change of pace after the last nodal cycle. Since January 11, 2025, the Pisces North Node has kept your nose to the grindstone. With a focus on work, wellness and efficiency, you haven't had as much time to "people" as your outgoing sign prefers. Starting July 26, collaboration is your curriculum. Instead of proving your strength by leading alone, earn it by sharing power, practicing compromise and going farther in the art of teamwork than you ever have. This might be a stretch goal, but it's also a relief! Stop carrying everything yourself and start inviting others to contribute. Ask for input. Let people support you. Say yes when partnership opportunities arise instead of assuming you'll be better off solo.

At the same time, the South Node lands in Leo and your first house of identity. That alone can be game changing, but this 20-month cycle packs an extra oomph. Expansive Jupiter (also in Leo) rides shotgun to the South Node until summer 2027. You will naturally draw attention and attract opportunities to shine during this cycle, but the challenge is not to let recognition turn into a distraction. Yes, you'll command attention, but your greatest victories now come from amplifying others, too. When applause arrives, share it generously.

Also: Tamp down that competitive side, Leo. You've collected all the gold stars—that's not a problem for you. But what's the point of having a stellar outcome if you alienate your collaborators along the way? Impeccable Lioness Martha Stewart has taken many public hits for prioritizing her sky-high standards over her kitchen-side manners with her team. While we're not suggesting you water down your performance, the experience of getting to the curtain call matters big time. Sharpen your listening. Open your mind. Let others have a say. You WILL be pleasantly surprised.

In love, lean into commitment and honesty. Single Lions: Seek partners who challenge you to grow rather than simply adoring you from afar. In a relationship? Strengthen the foundation by setting mutual goals and regular checkpoints along the way. Don't simply expect devotion or stand on ceremony. Earn it by showing up consistently and listening as carefully as you speak. Small actions will carry more weight than dramatic gestures.

Professionally, partnerships hold the key to your progress after July 26. Seek out people who balance your skills, not simply mirror them. Align with colleagues who stretch you into new territory, even if they initially test your patience. During this cycle, expect to sign contracts, pitch joint projects or co-create ventures. Your instinct may be to protect your independence, but the North Node in your opposite sign demands that you see the power in "we." With careful negotiation, you'll feel solid about moving ahead. And by investing in alliances, you'll achieve results you could never reach on your own.

Socially, step into the role of helper as much as leader. Instead of organizing every bridal shower, vacation planning and family reunion, how about empowering someone else to play entertainment director? The more space you make for others to bring their visions to life, the more people will trust you with their energy and ideas.

Meanwhile, the South Node highlights old hang-ups about identity. You may find yourself fixating on how others perceive you, but the lesson is to move past surface-level concerns. Authenticity matters more than appearances. Jupiter amplifies whatever you project, so focus on showing up with honesty and integrity. When you operate from a place of rock-solid realness, your natural magnetism becomes impossible to resist.

By the end of this cycle in March 2028, you will have mastered the balance between independence and interdependence. Your challenge is simple but profound: Keep showing up as your vibrant, fiery self while allowing others to stand beside you. True leadership now comes not from dazzling alone but from creating constellations of brilliance.

5 REDEFINE HOME AND HEART

VENUS RETROGRADE IN SCORPIO AND LIBRA
VENUS RETROGRADE IN SCORPIO: OCTOBER 3–25
VENUS RETROGRADE IN LIBRA: OCTOBER 25–NOVEMBER 13

While your summer may be consumed by independent activities, slide back into the group chat this fall. As convivial Venus turns retrograde this October 3, you may feel a pull to reconnect with the people who know you best. Start the outreach with family and your oldest, dearest friends. Until October 25, Venus reverses through intimate Scorpio and your fourth house of kith and kin. Then, for the remainder of the retrograde (until November 13), she slips back into lighthearted Libra and your neighborly, social third house, igniting a networking spree with people from your past.

Before you so much as drop a hand-heart emoji in a thread, others could beat you to the punch. Relatives you haven't heard from in ages could suddenly pop into your DMs, or you might stumble across an old photo that inspires you to text your college suitemates about meeting up for a Zoom brunch. Follow those instincts, Leo. Nostalgic reunions can be surprisingly heartwarming, and potentially rich with opportunity, under this retrograde.

If you're planning an autumn getaway, let Venus guide your decisions. While, yes, you COULD go luxe with a resort that has five-star spa services, that's not the vibe as the cosmic design star is simmering in Scorpio from October 3 to 25. You're likely to have a better time tucked into a cozy Airbnb with a sun-drenched, modern kitchen and a fireplace for late-night chats. You might also decide that your own den is the best place to host. Frankly, Venus retrograde can severely shorten your patience for noisy crowds. Roll out the welcome mat selectively! Invite supportive besties and the healthy branches of your family tree to the Leo Lair for home-cooked feasts and streaming marathons.

If you're trying to mend fences with a relative or longtime friend, peacekeeping Venus CAN help, but that comes with a bit of a flag. During the retrograde, you may want to do your own private processing to make sure your "side of the street" is as tidy as possible before you call anyone else out for their misdeeds. Can't hold it in until after November 13? Keep conversations as low-stakes and gradual as possible. Venus retrograde isn't the time for dramatic gestures. Start with a phone call, then build up to an in-person hang on neutral turf.

A few minor adjustments can shift things miraculously. For example, how do you greet your partner after you've both had a long day? Do you flood them with dramatic updates, pout or hand them a "honey-do" list? What if, instead, you took some time to quietly journal, creating a little transition time for the two of you to unwind. If you're feeling especially generous, you might even pick up a little snack to share or pour a couple mocktails or tea. Nostalgia is always a smart strategy during Venus retrograde, so see what happens if you revive a few of those sweet gestures you made in the early days of your relationship. You'll probably enjoy them as much as your S.O.

Single Lions, have you been too quick to write off the sweet person "next door"? Venus in reverse might lift the veil, revealing someone's deeper potential. The best partners for you aren't always the flashiest or most obvious contenders. This retrograde is a chance to slow down, get curious and give the genuinely kind, emotionally available types a second look. People who stand by you when the spotlight dims are the real hidden gems!

If you share space with anyone, the first leg of the retrograde (through October 25) may spark conversations about space—both emotional and physical. Does everyone have room to relax, recharge and be creative without tripping over each other? If not, get inventive. Maybe you rent a studio for your projects or set aside a "do not disturb" zone at home.

Thinking of sprucing up your lair? Cosmetic tweaks to your space are fine now, but hold off on major renovations or splurges until Venus is direct mid-November. That Beaux-Arts chandelier might be perfect for your dining room—or it could feel a little too Gilded Age. Measure, create AI mockups, look at everything you can before making your final purchase.

On October 25, Venus begins the second leg of the retrograde in charming, social Libra and your outgoing third house, until November 13. You know how to make an entrance, Leo, but what if, instead, you focused on reading the room? That could make you even MORE of a beloved star. The third house is the platonic partnership zone of the zodiac wheel so concentrate your energy on friends and collaborators who have always brought sparkle to your social life. There will be no shortage of topics to discuss!

One note of caution: The people closest to you may not fully "get" your latest genius idea—and you will have plenty of those now that unbridled Jupiter is touring Leo and your trailblazing first house. Should they react with skepticism or a side-eye, don't take it personally. Sometimes loved ones project their own fears onto your ambitions. Protect your motivation by being selective about who gets a sneak peek at your plans and save the venting for a trusted confidant who can hold space without judgment.

2026
LEO

12 MONTH OVERVIEW

January MONTHLY HOROSCOPE

Fine-tune your flow, Leo! With the Sun in Capricorn until the 19th, your "healthy, wealthy and wise" sixth house is in the spotlight. Perfect timing for getting your 2026 routines into gear. Start with a clean-up mission: declutter, update apps, create workflows that make life hum like a well-tuned machine. By the time the Capricorn new moon rolls in on the 18th, you'll be ready to kick off a fitness and eating regimen that is both enjoyable and energizing. Make sure you add enough soul to those goals! On the 3rd, the year's first full moon arrives in Cancer and your spiritual twelfth house. Notice where you're being a perfectionist and let go a little. Surrender leads to serenity. Lovebirds Venus and Mars huddle close in Capricorn until the 17th, helping you tend to the administrative parts of relationships: syncing schedules, coordinating budgets. Both planets shift into Aquarius after the 23rd, energizing your seventh house of partnerships for the rest of the month. Your closest connections get a surge of passion and purpose now! Nurture the ones that support your long-term vision for your life. When the Sun strides into Aquarius on the 19th, you're keen to collaborate. Who's worthy of a starring role beside you? That adjacent throne may soon be occupied. Already found your royal plus-one? Pour more time and energy into making your bond solid. And while the month sets a brisk pace, your inner life also beckons. On the 2nd, wounded healer Chiron turns direct in Aries, giving you courage to say yes to an adventure you've been hesitant to take. On the 26th, dreamweaver Neptune drifts back into Aries for a 13-year stay, inviting you to expand your horizons in soulful ways—through study, spirituality and journeys that change how you see the world.

February MONTHLY HOROSCOPE

Who's gonna keep you warm this February, Leo? The heatgiving Sun blazes through Aquarius and your seventh house of partnerships until the 18th, spotlighting connection, chemistry, and collaboration. Where do you crave more balance—or a heaping dose of passion? Relationships are a dance, so let yourself lead sometimes and follow other times. The year's only Leo full moon puts you center stage on the 1st, boosting your confidence and ushering in a milestone moment. Then, on February 17, the Aquarius new moon arrives as a catalytic solar eclipse—the first here since 2018—just as the Year of the Fire Horse begins. A relationship could accelerate suddenly, or a surprising new alliance might reroute your path in thrilling ways. Until February 10, Venus sizzles in Aquarius, smoothing bonds and bringing extra magnetism to your partnerships. Afterward, she plunges into sultry Pisces and your eighth house, cranking up the intensity in love and

joint ventures. Need more structure around your goals? Disciplined Saturn re-enters Aries on February 13, beginning a two-year cycle of steady growth in your ninth house. Big dreams in media, education, or long-distance travel will demand effort but could expand your world dramatically. Valentine's Day follows with the steady Capricorn moon, favoring thoughtful, grounded gestures over flashy ones. Pisces season begins on the 18th, heating up your eighth house of intimacy and joint investments. Themes of trust, desire, and shared resources take center stage. With Mercury retrograde here from February 26 to March 20, contracts and commitments need extra care—but this cycle also invites you to have the conversations you've been avoiding. Whether about money, intimacy, or emotional truths, honesty now paves the way for deeper bonds and wiser investments.

March MONTHLY HOROSCOPE

Ready, set, introspect! Your inner world is rich this March as the radiant Sun, Mercury retrograde, courageous Mars and a Pisces new moon (on the 18th) move through your eighth house of intimacy, shared resources and transformation. Where do you need to let go in order to grow? Release what no longer fuels you so there's space for bonds and ventures that truly do. The total lunar (full moon) eclipse in Virgo on the 3rd strikes your second house of money and values, pushing a financial matter to resolution. Are you spending wisely, or is it time to adjust your approach? A reality check now can save you from stress later. On March 2, Mars enters Pisces for a six-week stay, intensifying desire and stirring passion in both business and romance. Joint ventures, loans or collaborations may require quick action. Love gets adventurous after March 6, when Venus buzzes into Aries and your ninth house of travel and expansion. A relationship could be reinvigorated by a trip, or you may feel drawn to someone with a very different worldview. Philosophical Jupiter ends a four-month retrograde on the 10th, moving ahead in Cancer and your twelfth house of closure and healing. Old baggage can finally be released, making space for renewal. On the 20th—the spring equinox—the Sun enters Aries, igniting your ninth house of exploration. Mercury stations direct the same day, ending three weeks of miscommunication. Time to plan your next big journey or dive into a project that stretches your horizons!

April MONTHLY HOROSCOPE

Adventure is calling, Leo! The radiant Sun charges through Aries and your ninth house of expansion until the 19th, daring you to take bold risks. Where do you feel called to stretch? Say yes to the bucket list trip, enroll in the masterclass, share your vision with the world. The Libra full moon on April 1 lights up your third house of communication, bringing a contract, writing project or conversation to culmination. Speak with courage—your words carry extra weight now. After April 9, fiery Mars storms through Aries for six weeks, urging you to act on your big ideas. Just be mindful not to scatter your energy in too many directions at once. On the 17th, the new moon in Aries opens fresh horizons in your ninth house, fueling wanderlust and giving cosmic clearance to launch an entrepreneurial project, write a book or spend a month (or year!) abroad. The steady Taurus Sun shifts into your ambitious tenth house on the 19th, turning the spotlight onto career breakthroughs and public recognition. Until April 24, Venus also graces Taurus, making professional partnerships especially rewarding. The plot twist arrives on the 25th, when radical Uranus leaves Taurus after seven years and rockets into Gemini until 2033. With your eleventh house now electrified, friendships, collaborations and community ties will be transformed. Expect sudden alliances, paradigm-shifting connections and group endeavors that catapult you into the future.

May MONTHLY HOROSCOPE

Career momentum builds this month, Leo, as the vibrant Sun powers through Taurus and your tenth house of achievement and recognition until May 20. Step into leadership roles and showcase your talents. The full moon in Scorpio beams into your fourth house of home and family on the 1st. Repair a rift with a relative and make any important decisions about your living situation that you've been putting off. Alchemical Pluto pivots into its annual retrograde on the 6th, backing up through Aquarius and your seventh house of partnerships. Between now and October 15, address brewing power dynamics in your closest bonds. The Aquarius quarter moon on May 10 also highlights this area. Mother's Day could be best celebrated with glamorous pampering and cultural activities. Think: mani-pedis and brunch at a museum. Supermoon season begins on the 16th with the Taurus new moon planting the seeds for professional growth in your tenth house. Set six-month career goals and get into action! Then, on the 20th, the Sun shifts into Gemini and your collaborative eleventh house kicking off a month of energizing teamwork and social expansion. Magnetic Venus hovers in Gemini and your eleventh house until the 18th, boosting your popularity in group settings. Then, Venus slips into Cancer and your twelfth house, deepening private emotions, while fiery Mars charges into Taurus and your tenth house, fueling ambition and drive. Relationships may feel like a dance between vulnerability and visibility. Balance your cozy time with the power couple vibes. The Sagittarius full moon on the 31st is a blue moon. Landing in your fifth house of romance, fame and creativity, this rare lunation brings another burst of recognition right at the end of May. Take a bow, Leo!

June MONTHLY HOROSCOPE

Welcome to the collaboration station! The Sun beams through Gemini and your eleventh house of community and technology until June 21. Rally allies and share your vision widely. Tap the apps and AI helpers to make life easier. The June 14 Gemini new moon—the second supermoon in a rare three-part series—sparks fresh beginnings with friendships, networks or group projects. Sync with people who are playful and innovative. Meanwhile, go-getter Mars powers through Taurus and your tenth house of career until June 28, giving you momentum to push a professional project to the next level. A key shift comes June 19 when "wounded healer" Chiron moves into Taurus for a three-month preview of its 2027-2034 stay. Since 2018, Chiron has pushed you to become more independent and authentic. This summer's focus turns to your ambitions, helping you redefine what success means on your own terms. On June 21, the Sun slips into Cancer and your twelfth house just in time for the solstice and Father's Day. Reflection, release and rest help you integrate the past year before your season begins. In love, Venus lingers in Cancer until the 13th, making private connections especially sweet. Then she strides into Leo, your first house, turning up your magnetism and drawing admirers like moths to a flame. Now for the biggest news of the month—make that the YEAR! A major growth cycle begins June 30 as abundant Jupiter strides into Leo for the first time in over a decade, lighting up your first house until July 26, 2027. This is your green light to go big—invest in yourself, launch bold ventures and lead with heart. June closes with a Capricorn full moon on the 29th in your sixth house of work and wellness. A project could land in your lap and you may be pumped about a fitness goal. Just note that Mercury turns retrograde in Cancer (for three weeks) the same day, so pace yourself and don't overcommit.

July MONTHLY HOROSCOPE

Countdown to birthday season! But first, you've got some behind-the-scenes business to handle. Until the 22nd, the Sun travels through Cancer and your twelfth house of rest and release, joined by Mercury retrograde here until the 23rd. Close out chapters, clear clutter (emotional and otherwise) and guard your energy like the precious resource it is. The Cancer new moon (a supermoon) on the 14th brings a turning point in your healing journey. Therapy breakthroughs, endings you didn't know you needed or even a spiritual awakening could surface. Trust that clearing makes way for renewal. On July 7, mystical Neptune pivots retrograde in Aries, beginning five months of reflection in your ninth house of truth and wisdom. Then, on the 26th, Saturn follows suit, pushing you to question your beliefs and long-term trajectory. Are you building your future on foundations that feel authentic—or just habitual? Get honest with yourself. Popularity soars as go-getter Mars energizes Gemini and your collaborative eleventh house all month. Expect nonstop invites, but be discerning about what you say "yes" to! The curtain rises on the 22nd when the Sun enters Leo for a month, amplifying your confidence, magnetism and creative fire. Venus adds sparkle to your money zone from the 9th, helping you earn, save or invest with style. After Mercury stations direct on the 23rd, you'll be ready to make key decisions about your next chapter. The biggest headline arrives on the 26th, when the karmic South Node enters Leo for the first time in nearly two decades. Simultaneously the North Node revs up your partnership destiny in Aquarius. Until March 2028, fated relationships will shape your path—ones that allow you to fully shine. The 29th is also major! For the first time in over a decade, the Sun and Jupiter unite in Leo for the annual "Day of Miracles," amplifying your charisma and visibility. On the same day, the Aquarius full moon crowns your relationship sector, spotlighting a defining moment for love, partnership or collaboration. Solo or partnered (or both!), you're claiming center stage!

August MONTHLY HOROSCOPE

Happy birthday season, Leo! With the Sun blazing through your sign until the 22nd, the stage is yours—so lean in and own it. On August 3, Chiron pivots retrograde in Taurus and your tenth house of career and public image, resurfacing old wounds around recognition and success. This five-month cycle isn't about grinding harder; it's about rewriting your definition of achievement and stepping into authority on your own terms. A mentor or past opportunity could reappear, reminding you of how far you've come. By the 11th, Mars shifts into Cancer and your twelfth house of intuition and closure. Channel that drive inward: Rest, restore and lean into therapy, journaling or other healing outlets. Eclipse season bursts open on the 12th with a total solar eclipse in Leo—the first in your sign since 2019—bringing a dramatic personal plot twist. You could debut a bold new direction, shed an identity that no longer fits, or launch a project that feels like your truest self. Venus enters Libra on the 6th, boosting your charisma and sparking ideas that deserve to be captured. Think: podcasts, manuscripts, creative collabs with viral potential. When the Sun enters Virgo on the 22nd, it's time to ground your birthday buzz in practical plans and smart financial choices. The Pisces lunar eclipse on the 28th shakes up your eighth house of intimacy and shared resources. A relationship or joint venture could reach a turning point—are you all in or all out? Choose or lose. August ends on a brilliant note on the 31st as Jupiter in Leo forms a rare trine with Saturn in Aries, blending expansion with structure. Channel this momentum into a milestone victory that feels both thrilling and sustainable.

September MONTHLY HOROSCOPE

Money's on your mind this September and you need to get serious about your resources. The Virgo Sun illuminates your second house of money and security until the 22nd. Treat your budget like a VIP guest list: Only the essentials get in. Audit subscriptions, reorganizing your closet to see what you actually wear, then splurge on one quality piece instead of three fast-fashion finds. Meanwhile, Mars is powering through Cancer and your private twelfth house until the 27th, rousing buried emotions. Process through journaling, therapy, art, even some cathartic playlist-making. Better out than bottled up, Leo! On the 10th, the year's only Virgo new moon lands in your money zone, priming you for a financial fresh start. A new gig, client or income stream could appear. Keep your eyes open for practical opportunities. That same day, Uranus pivots retrograde in Gemini and your eleventh house of friendships. Over the next five months, you'll be reevaluating your circles and looking for intentional meetups with people who inspire you. Ardent Venus hovers in Libra and your third house until the 10th, making casual hangs and short trips extra sweet. Then it dives into Scorpio and your fourth house of home, shifting your attention to family, nesting and private, romantic connections. Heads-up: From October 3 to November 13, Venus will be retrograde. Strengthen trust and communication NOW to avoid meltdowns starting next month. The fall equinox on the 22nd kicks off Libra season and your social life will be buzzing with activity. With your locally zoned third house lit for a month, you won't need to travel far to find your people. On the 17th, Chiron (the wounded healer asteroid) backs into Aries and your expansive ninth house, urging you to heal limiting beliefs. And the Aries full moon on the 26th could bring a travel opportunity, perhaps one with an educational component. Freedom and authenticity are non-negotiables as the month winds down. Speak your truth, but use tact.

October MONTHLY HOROSCOPE

What's happening in your lion's den? On October 3, harmonizer Venus spins retrograde in Scorpio and your domestic fourth house, where it lingers until the 25th before sliding into Libra and your communication sector until November 13. Renovations could stall, family tensions might bubble or your living situation could feel uncertain. Ask yourself: Is this frustration pointing to where you need stability—or where it's time for change? The Sun moves through Libra until the 23rd, energizing your third house of ideas and connections. While you're buzzing with inspiration, the Libra new moon on the 10th could bring kindred spirits who want to team up on your projects. Meanwhile, Mars is on fire in Leo all month, supercharging your motivation. Channel this momentum toward personal projects. You can get stalled missions in motion, but make sure you don't steamroll people in the process. Alchemical Pluto turns direct on the 15th, reigniting progress in partnerships that stalled over the summer. Then on the 23rd, the Sun dips into Scorpio and your home zone—the same day Venus retrograde aligns with the Sun in a rare Cazimi. A breakthrough around family or your living situation could shift the ground beneath your feet. Mercury joins the retrograde brigade on the 24th and this time, the messenger planet is backing up through Scorpio. Brace for crossed signals on the home front. A pinnacle career moment arrives with the Taurus full moon on the 26th. Grab the brass ring or pivot to pursue a role that fits your evolving vision.

November MONTHLY HOROSCOPE

Home is where the heat is this November, Leo. With the Scorpio Sun anchoring your domestic fourth house until the 22nd, family, roots and emotional foundations demand attention. But don't rush ahead with any initiatives. Until the 13th, messenger Mercury is retrograde in Scorpio and design-star Venus is backing up through Libra. This twin mayhem could leave you feeling torn between private obligations and public ambitions. Slow down and tend to your base in the first half of the month. On the 9th, the Scorpio new moon brings some positive momentum for Château Leo. Host a family gathering (chosen fam counts!) or start pinning decor ideas for a post-retrograde update. Make sure you get out and circulate, too! Red-hot Mars is blazing through Leo until the 25th, dialing up your charisma and drive. During this large-and-in-charge cycle, your leadership can move mountains. But take care not to bulldoze people with single-minded ambition. You're in playful spirits after the 22nd, once the Sun bounds into Sagittarius and your passionate fifth house (AKA "the Leo house"). Play Head Elf and get the holiday merriment underway. This four-week cycle is prime time to showcase your talents and make a daring romantic gesture. A group project hits a milestone with the Gemini full supermoon on the 24th. Next question: Is there further to go together or is it time to move on elsewhere? Mars leaves your sign on the 25th and settles into pragmatic Virgo for the rest of 2026. Financial focus sharpens and your hustle could pay off with year-end wins. Streamline spending, negotiate confidently and invest in what stabilizes you.

December MONTHLY HOROSCOPE

You don't have to RSVP "yes" to every invitation to feel adored, Leo—but this December, the spotlight follows you regardless. The Sagittarius Sun glows in your fifth house of creativity, romance and play until the 21st, coaxing you onto the middle of every dance floor. A glamorous reboot arrives with the new moon in Sag on the 8th, inspiring you to debut a passion project, accept a dazzling date or simply revel in festive sparkle. Two outer planets—sensible Saturn and dreamy Neptune—conclude five-month retrogrades in Aries on the 10th and 12th, respectively, sharpening your perspective on travel, education or a big-picture pursuit. Suddenly, the horizon looks both clearer and closer. With motivator Mars driving through Virgo and your second house of income all month, your instincts around earning and spending are strong. Invest in statement pieces or meaningful experiences, but resist frittering away your reserves. Desire intensifies after the 4th, when Venus returns to Scorpio and your domestic fourth house. A cozy dinner at home or heartfelt reconnection with family could prove far more rewarding than a crowded soirée. On the 12th, expansive Jupiter pivots retrograde in Leo for four months, urging you to refine your focus rather than scatter your brilliance. Capricorn season arrives with the solstice on the 21st putting you into "elf mode." Give the world service-with-a-smile but honor your boundaries and need for rest. You'll be the first one to hit the gym when it opens on the 26th and you're keen to close the year on a healthy note. Need to forgive (even if you don't forget)? The full Cancer supermoon on the 23rd helps you release a longstanding grudge. Wrap the year on a soulful, salubrious note. With a radiant Sun-Mars trine this NYE, you may prefer a candlelit ceremony, sound bath or meditation to a noisy soiree. There's so much to reflect on and gratitude is the vibe.

Read your extended monthly forecast for life, love, money and career! astrostyle.com

VIRGO IN 2026

| ALL THE PLANETS IN VIRGO IN 2026 | YOUR 2026 HOROSCOPE | TOP 5 THEMES FOR VIRGO IN 2026 | LOVE HOROSCOPE + LUCKY DATES | MONEY HOROSCOPE + LUCKY DATES |

Virgo in 2026

Your year of:
INNER GROWTH, SUPPORT,
PROFESSIONAL BREAKTHROUGHS

**STOP PERFECTING THE PAST
AND START INVESTING IN THE FUTURE.**

In 2026, your inner world calls for reflection, asking you to release habits and roles that no longer serve you. At the same time, a current of excitement ripples through your career—goals feel alive and opportunities arrive that push you to think bigger. Can you hold both the quiet work of letting go and the thrill of stepping up? Relationships and partnerships become the bridge, reminding you that true success is built on trust, patience and shared vision. By December, you'll feel clearer, lighter and more aligned with the ambitions that matter most.

THE PLANETS IN Virgo

THE SUN
AUG 22–SEP 22

Happy birthday season! With the Sun in your sign, you're clear to take chances, chase fresh adventures, and command the spotlight.

NEW MOON
SEP 10
11:27PM, 18°26'

Happy bonus New Year! Set your intentions for the next six months, then take a brave step forward. Your fans await!

FULL MOON, TOTAL LUNAR ECLIPSE
MAR 3
6:38AM, 12°54'

Manifestation moment! Your work of the past six months bears fruit. Celebrate your progress and harvest the rewards—which might come with a surprising twist under this lunar eclipse.

MERCURY
AUG 25–SEP 10

Hold court! When charismatic Mercury zips through your sign, your social status soars. Work the room, make connections—but keep your commitments realistic to avoid overpromising.

VENUS
JUL 9–AUG 6

Love is in the air! When the galactic glamazon struts through your sign, your powers of seduction skyrocket. Irresistible charm, luxe tastes and flirtatious vibes abound—just keep an eye on your budget.

MARS
NOV 25–DEC 31

Motivation is off the charts when energetic Mars blazes through your sign every couple of years. You're bold, driven, and unstoppable—but watch that combative streak and ease up on the intensity.

SOUTH NODE
JAN 1–JUL 26

Life feels both surreal and karmic when the lunar South Node backs up through your sign (for 18 months) every 18.5 years. Surrender to the vision quest and prepare to let go of unworkable habits. This will all make sense when the cycle ends.

Virgo in 2026
HIGHLIGHTS

KARMIC RELIEF: SOUTH NODE FINISHES ITS STAY IN VIRGO

You've been on a cosmic refinement tour since January 2025, Virgo, and 2026 delivers the final edits. With the karmic South Node in your sign until July 26, you're shedding habits, identities and perfectionist patterns that no longer fit. This cycle asks you to stop tweaking and start living. Delegate tasks instead of micromanaging. Assemble a signature look that doesn't require multiple edits throughout the day. Share about a passion even if it's not fully formed. Across the sky, the North Node in Pisces is pushing you to embrace empathy, partnership and connection. Meant-to-be people show up in your world, as if fate brought you together. Follow your curiosity and see where it leads.

EMOTIONAL AND FINANCIAL ALCHEMY: SATURN AND NEPTUNE IN ARIES

Saturn and Neptune resume their slow dance through Aries and your eighth house, spotlighting intimacy, money and transformation. Saturn pushes you to manage debt and set boundaries in your closest partnerships starting February 13. Shared (or inherited) resources could be the stepping stone to wealth if you invest wisely. Neptune, which streams back into Aries from January 26, 2026 until 2039, calls for forgiveness, compassion and deep healing. This is the year to update your financial systems and to get real about your closest bonds. Couples may move toward deeper commitment while solo Virgos could use therapy, journaling or energy work to crystallize what intimacy and security look like for you.

LUNAR WAKE-UP CALL: ECLIPSE IN VIRGO ON MARCH 3

On March 3, a total lunar eclipse lights up your sign, bringing a lightning-bolt awakening. This supercharged full moon serves epiphanies that can't (and shouldn't) be ignored about the role you play in the world. If it's time for a personal pivot, don't fight the change. Circumstances may shift suddenly, forcing you to adapt. Disconcerting as this can be, it's in your best interest. Whether it's quitting a draining job, ending a one-sided friendship or finally breaking a cycle of self-criticism, this eclipse clears the slate so you can step into your evolving power. Treat it like your personal New Year—rituals, journaling even a solo getaway can help anchor the shift. By the time the Virgo new moon arrives on September 10, you'll be ready to set some groundbreaking intentions.

CAREER REINVENTION: URANUS ENTERS GEMINI APRIL 25
After seven years of shaking up your belief systems, changemaker Uranus beams into Gemini and your tenth house of career until 2033. You're not just climbing the ladder—you're rocketing into a new space. Expect sudden pivots in your profession, leadership or public reputation. Over the coming seven years, success requires you to think outside the box. New tech, new titles, even a totally new industry, could be calling. Learn AI tools or sign up for a course in a field you never considered before. The world is your innovation station—don't be afraid to disrupt yourself.

MERCURY RETROGRADES: REVIEW THE TIES THAT BIND
Mercury turns retrograde three times in 2026, putting relationships and communication at the forefront. From February 26 to March 20, the backspin is in your seventh house of partnerships. A past connection could resurface or you may need to renegotiate terms with a current collaborator or mate. From June 29 to July 23, Mercury reverses in your eleventh house of friendships and group ventures. Old friends may reappear, or you could rejoin a team or community you once left behind. The final cycle, October 24 to November 13, moves through your third house of communication and short trips. With Venus also retrograde in Libra, expect crossed wires and tech snags along with heartwarming reconnections with friends. Use this time to clarify agreements and restore harmony to your closest circles.

RECHARGE AND REIMAGINE: JUPITER SHIFTS INTO LEO JUNE 30
After thirteen months of energizing Cancer in your eleventh house of community and long-range goals, Jupiter packs up and heads into Leo on June 30. Translation: sabbatical vibes incoming. For the next year, your twelfth house of rest, imagination and healing takes the spotlight. This is a cycle for stepping back, refueling your spirit and letting your creativity unfurl without pressure. Think artist retreats, solo travel, meditation marathons or simply leaving space to dream. Sometimes the biggest breakthroughs arrive when you're not "trying" but wandering, resting or daydreaming into possibility.

DESTINY SHIFTS: NODES ENTER AQUARIUS AND LEO JULY 26
On July 26, the Lunar Nodes change signs, opening up a fate-fueling 20-month cycle. Lather, rinse, repeat? That's how you'll grow now. With the North Node in Aquarius, your evolution comes from daily routines, health and systems. Across the board, the South Node in Leo encourages you to release outdated patterns of overwork or behind-the-scenes burnout. Build wellness habits you can actually stick to: meal prep, group fitness, sleep sanctity and a morning ritual that doesn't involve doomscrolling.

COMMUNITY, CREATIVITY AND CONNECTION CHECK: VENUS RETROGRADE THIS FALL
From October 3 to November 13, Venus retrogrades through your zones of friendships, creativity and communication, asking you to pause and reassess. Old alliances may resurface, a collaborative project could be revived, or you might realize certain groups no longer feel aligned. Love also gets a review: Conversations with a partner may circle

back to unfinished business, or an old flame could slide into your DMs. Venus retraces this patch of sky every 8 years (minus 2°), flashing you back to fall 2018. What stories were unfolding then in your social life, creative passions or love life? This time, you're wiser and more discerning. Use this cycle to reconnect with people and projects that still light you up, and release the ones that don't.

MARS BLAZES INTO VIRGO AT THE YEAR'S END

Finish the year strong! Motivator Mars moves into Virgo on November 25 and sticks around unusually long thanks to a retrograde from January 10 to February 21, 2027. As the 2026 holiday season buzzes, you'll feel driven to optimize everything. Resist nitpicking people and focus on setting up sustainable systems that can support your goals. To avoid overwhelming yourself (and everyone around you who's just trying to catch some holiday cheer) pick one mission that matters and build repeatable sprints around it. When the red planet turns retrograde next year, you can revisit stalled projects, refine workflows and renegotiate roles. Pace yourself, Virgo—consistency turns this extended stay into serious leverage.

Love
VIRGO 2026 FORECAST

The year kicks off with a decadent surprise: Venus and Mars are together in Capricorn until January 17, igniting your fifth house of passion. Even you, Virgo, the zodiac's meticulous planner, might be swept into a situation that refuses to fit into neat little boxes. (We know you like spreadsheets, but you can't chart chemistry.) Or your relationship could move in a frisky direction. Indulge the playfulness. Early this year, love looks more like champagne and midnight confessions than bullet points and pros-and-cons lists.

Then, on February 10, Venus glides into Pisces and your seventh house of partnerships, setting up Valentine's Day for serious soul connections. The destiny-dusted lunar North Node is already in this sign—and has been since January 11, 2025—where it's bringing major revelations about what a healthy commitment looks like for you.

Across the aisle, the karmic South Node hovers in Virgo, reminding you that it takes two to tango. While this nodal cycle wages on until July 26, you'll continue to have wakeup calls about the role you play in both healthy and unhealthy dynamics. Highlight March 3 in neon! The full moon in Virgo is also an eye-opening total lunar eclipse. Expect sudden pivots, cosmic curveballs and maybe even a "How did I not see this before?" epiphany.

Relationships are the ultimate mirrors. What you see reflected back to yourself will be illuminating. You'll get more such reminders from another pair of planets. Starting February 13—and lasting for two years, stabilizing Saturn and hypnotic Neptune will dance together through Aries and your playing-for-keeps eighth house. Part of you wants guarantees. What does the future hold and where is this heading? Another half of you will prefer to keep things nebulous. But come on, Virgo: If you reserve the right for an out-clause it's only fair to extend that to your partner, right? True intimacy isn't about having every answer etched in stone. It's about staying present when things feel uncertain.

Communication is one of your sign's strengths so talk, talk, talk and talk some more. Sexually, the Saturn-Neptune merger, which is most intense in the first quarter of the year, could bring some fascinating exploration. Saturn sets boundaries, Neptune dissolves them. Sounds like the opener to some spicy erotic fiction, outfitted with leather and maybe a mistress' dungeon. This duo could also bring reality checks around money, sex and shared resources. If you've been dodging tough conversations, Saturn insists you define terms. But Neptune reminds you not to choke out the magic with rigidity.

On June 30, limitless Jupiter drifts into Leo and your dreamy twelfth house for a 13-month stay. Love may feel like a hazy reverie—healing, intoxicating, or a mix of both. If you've been carrying the weight of an old chapter, this transit can help you release it. Or you could tumble headlong into a connection that feels fated but hard to define. Keep one foot on the ground while the rest of you sways in the clouds.

The Pisces lunar eclipse on August 28 is a defining moment for partnerships, landing in your seventh house of commitment. A relationship could take a turn in a surprising direction—which could shock you in a good way. Or an episode could occur that makes it impossible to ignore that your paths are diverging. This is the final Pisces lunar eclipse in a series that has been rocking your relationship realm since Fall 2024.

Even if one door closes, another opportunity could come knocking within a short time. A past figure could be involved, thanks to Venus retrograde from October 3 to November 13. Tread lightly if you're stoking those embers. Situations that start (or restart) while the love planet is in reverse are often unreliable. That's not to say they're doomed, but recalibration may be required once the love goggles come off mid-November. Coupled Virgos may revisit an issue that you THOUGHT was resolved. A flirtation with a friend could surface, or a misunderstanding could take on more weight than it should. Pausing before you react keeps everything in perspective.

Lucky for you, the year ends on a steamy note! Passionate Mars storms into Virgo on November 25, extending its stay until early 2027. Lust levels rise, but so can nitpicking squabbles. Direct that heat into physical activities, in and out of the bedroom, before it sparks unnecessary drama.

By year's end, you'll have danced through destiny pivots, healing reveries and fiery tests. Your 2026 love lesson? Let go of the myth of perfect romance and embrace the messy, magical truth. This year, intimacy means leaving a few boxes unchecked.

Money & Career

VIRGO 2026 FORECAST

In 2026, you're invited to play a longer game, Virgo—one built on purpose, precision and presence. Since January 11, 2025, the karmic South Node has been slowly gliding through your sign, guiding you toward a deeper understanding of who you are and what truly matters. You've outgrown busywork for its own sake. Your focus is on aligning effort with meaning. Early in 2026, you'll start to see results from any shifts you've made in the past year. On March 3, a total lunar eclipse arrives with the annual Virgo full moon, bringing a breakthrough opportunity and increased visibility. Make sure you're ready for your close-up!

Starting February 13, Saturn and Neptune circle back together in Aries and your eighth house of shared resources, long-term investments and wealth strategy. This potent pairing launches a two-year cycle of financial maturity and imaginative thinking. Serious Saturn calls for structure—budgeting, paying down debt or managing money with greater confidence. Meanwhile Neptune encourages you to invest in what feeds the soul as well as the bank account. Art, spiritual education or conscious enterprise could become part of your portfolio. Whether you're exploring partnerships, retirement planning or a creative investment, aim for both security and significance.

Professional horizons broaden dramatically starting April 25, as innovative Uranus buzzes into Gemini and your tenth house of career and leadership until 2033. You got a taste of this experimental energy mid-2025, and now the full revolution begins. Technology, media or AI-driven tools could reshape how you work, and new industries may pull your curiosity in unexpected directions. If your role at work has felt too narrow, think bigger—and maybe broadcast those ideas to a wider audience. The biggest challenge might be releasing perfectionism (a Virgo pitfall) and allowing yourself to experiment.

Networking will be a growth engine while expansive Jupiter sails through Cancer until June 30, lighting up your eleventh house of teams and collaboration. Influential allies and mentors are within reach. Attend conferences, join mastermind groups or simply reconnect with peers who inspire your next chapter. On June 30, Jupiter slips into Leo and your introspective twelfth house for 13 months, shifting the focus inward. You may work with a coach or spiritual teacher, or step into a creative sabbatical that helps you refine your vision. Behind-the-scenes projects could become surprisingly lucrative.

The next big career theme kicks off on July 26, when the fateful North Node moves into Aquarius and your practical sixth house until March 2028. Time to systematize your success so you can work smarter, not harder. This 20-month cycle rewards organization, consistency and disciplined effort. But don't try to do it all yourself! This is the "service sector" of the zodiac, so tap into your community. Whether you're bartering or hiring, helping hands are all around you. If your offerings have grown too complex, here's a chance to streamline your services. Volunteer or mentorship work can also open professional doors now. Watch how the pros do it, then adapt what fits.

As the year wraps, Mars charges into Virgo on November 25, revving up your motivation. Finish the year strong by making sure yours is the name on the VIPs' lips. Start conversations on social media and share what you've learned. You don't have to be the expert of everything, Virgo, just the curator of things that everyone needs to know!

TOP 5 THEMES FOR *Virgo* in 2026

1	2	3	4	5
TRANSFORM FROM THE INSIDE OUT	BUILD WITH YOUR PEOPLE	REDEFINE SUCCESS	UPGRADE YOUR SYSTEMS	SPEAK WITH HEART

1 TRANSFORM FROM THE INSIDE OUT

NEPTUNE IN ARIES
JANUARY 26, 2026–MARCH 23, 2039

SATURN IN ARIES
FEBRUARY 13, 2026–APRIL 12, 2028

Deep, powerful shifts are stirring in the most private corners of your chart, Virgo—and they won't be ignored. Two of the slowest, most fate-shaping planets in astrology, Neptune and Saturn, are settling into Aries this year, activating your eighth house of sex, shared resources and profound psychological transformation. What began as a simmer during their sneak previews in 2025 becomes a full-on slow boil in 2026, as both commit to these subterranean depths for the long haul.

This isn't light work—far from it. Saturn, the planet of structure and accountability, wants receipts, commitments and real results. Neptune, the cosmic dream-weaver, dissolves boundaries, stirs your soul and asks you to surrender to the unknown. Together, they make an odd yet potent pair—especially when swimming through this emotionally complex terrain. For perspective: The last time Saturn and Neptune joined forces in Aries was in 1702. Yes, you're working with magic that hasn't visited Earth in over 300 years. This rare alignment is here to transform you at the root.

You got a taste of this shift in 2025: Neptune drifted into Aries from March 30 to October 22, softening your defenses and awakening spiritual yearnings around trust, intimacy and merging. Saturn joined in from May 24 to September 1, giving you an early look at the deeper commitments that lie ahead—to people, to healing, to your own evolution. Now, Neptune anchors in for a mystical 13-year journey starting January 26, while Saturn launches a two-year boot camp from February 13.

Circle February 20 in bold red ink: Saturn and Neptune form an exact conjunction at 0° Aries on that date—their only precise meeting during this cycle. This potent moment fuses Neptune's longing for soulful union with Saturn's demand for tangible structure. Translation? You're not just idealizing what true connection "might" be. You're manifesting it, with all its messy, vulnerable, transformative glory.

The eighth house rules intimacy—but not the casual, swipe-right kind. This is psychological nakedness, financial entwinement, deep merging partnerships that push you to examine where you hold power…and where you give it away.

You may be drawn into situations that reveal your hidden fears around trust and surrender. Think of it as a two-year initiation. While unhurried Saturn slogs through Aries until April 12, 2028, rushing is not allowed. Slow down to discover what an authentic union actually requires—from you and from anyone you invite into your inner sanctum.

If you already have plenty of experience here, buckle up. You might discover hidden layers of yourself or your partner. Secrets may emerge, ones neither of you meant to bury—or maybe you did. One or both of you could go through a life cycle change that impacts your attraction or the way you relate to each other. Even the most die-hard soulmates aren't guaranteed to evolve through life in tandem. You may be challenged to hold space for someone through an experience that feels more like a test than a triumph—at least until you get to the other side. Once you do, you'll know each other MORE than you ever dreamed possible.

On the most personal level, this cycle could completely transform your relationship with sex, Virgo. The eighth house doesn't do casual—it craves depth, trust, and the kind of soul-baring connection that rewires you from the inside out. Neptune here can stir powerful desires for spiritual union and erotic exploration, dissolving old fears about vulnerability in the bedroom. Meanwhile, Saturn demands honesty about your needs, boundaries, and where you might hold back out of shame or control. How exciting! In 2026, you may shed old baggage around pleasure and heal from past betrayals. Through the new experiences—and maybe a great somatic therapist—you can learn how to share your body and heart with a new level of trust.

Money matters come up, too. The eighth house governs shared finances, investments, inheritances, taxes and long-term wealth planning. Saturn demands a clear-eyed audit: Where are you overextended? Where are you undervaluing your worth? Neptune's presence can cloud judgment or stir financial idealism. Balance gut feelings with grounded strategy. When in doubt, seek expert advice rather than trying to figure out complex fiscal decisions with a Google search.

Virgos who own property or have children, this would be a great year to write your will. Not because it's "your time," we're not saying that. The peace of mind for caring for your loved ones is worth its weight in platinum. If you have aging parents, talk to them about setting up a family trust or making sure any debt they have is settled. Do they have a life insurance policy or other assets you need to know about? These types of conversations aren't always easy to have, but the eighth house rules all life and death matters. Virgo, you always feel better when prepared, even if you're years away from having to deal with any losses.

This cycle will test your boundaries, your ability to let go, and your beliefs about what it means to be truly intimate—with yourself, with a partner, with the bigger mysteries of life. That's the point. You're not meant to stay the same. You're meant to transform—through love, loss, trust, healing, and ultimately, empowerment.

The eighth house is where alchemy happens. It's where you rise from the ashes of an old version of yourself, purified and renewed. Let these planetary heavyweights guide you through the fire. By the time Saturn exits Aries in 2028—and especially when Neptune moves on in 2039—you'll be sharper, softer and more certain of what (and who) you truly want in your life.

2 BUILD WITH YOUR PEOPLE

JUPITER IN CANCER
JUNE 9, 2026–JUNE 30, 2026

CEO of Everything? No, no, Virgo, that is NOT the role you want to apply for this year. Permission to be a team player is roundly granted in 2026. Such a relief for your helpful, industrious sign!

You're halfway through "more is more" Jupiter's thirteen-month spring through Cancer, which began on June 9, 2025. As the red-spotted planet barrels through your collaborative eleventh house until this June 30, no one has to rip the controls from your clutch. Hopefully, you've already begun to embrace the art of delegating.

If not, well, make that your first resolution of the year. Perhaps that means getting a few ducks in a row while Jupiter finishes out its four-month retrograde until March 10. Organize your systems, create SOPs, Asana boards and private GPTs. Then turn them into your version of an operations manual. It's okay to share a few of your go-to systems, as long as you're not giving away trade secrets.

If you don't have a supersquad assembled yet, begin the casting process in earnest. While it's not always easy for a perfectionist Virgo to loosen the reins, this cycle is proof that you don't have to do it alone to do it right. Scout people whose work ethic matches yours, but who bring their own genius to the table.

Quick question: Can you automate that? Jupiter's journey through your tech-savvy eleventh house helps you maximize time. Bring in an AI helper to handle the tedium. Why burn out on busywork when you could focus on high-impact ideas? "Let's ask ChatGPT" could become your new favorite phrase.

If your online presence needs a glow up, you're in luck. Media-savvy Jupiter in the communal eleventh house loves to amplify your voice. There's no better time than the first half of 2026 to grow a loyal following. It doesn't have to be a public, all-access thing, either. Maybe you're ready to build a tight-knit community on a turnkey—or on an app that you create, develop and sell subscriptions to all on your own. If you're looking to shine as a creator, be careful not to spread yourself too thin. Pick one or two platforms where your message can really make an impact.

Not that you should spend every moment of your spare time recording YouTube Shorts. As you open up whitespace in your calendar, your social life keeps on thriving. As one of the Mercury-ruled signs (along with Gemini), you thrive on daily doses of conversation, laughter and connection. Hey, it's science! Joyful interactions boost your levels of the feel-good hormone oxytocin. Posse up with your people regularly—for Friday night dinners, book clubs, karaoke, crafting, anything that lets you relax and enjoy their company.

Then again, you may feel like flexing your Virgo event-planning muscles in the first part of the year. Gather your besties for a winter trip. How about a food tour through Positano or a weekend at a hot springs spa in the Southwest? A voluntourism trip would also be meaningful as worldly Jupiter rolls through your humanitarian eleventh house. If none of your BFFs are free to join, consider going anyway. A curated tour experience could be magical, and with your popularity soaring, you could wind up making friends for life with others on the journey.

Speaking of humanitarianism, Jupiter can amplify your messaging should you want to use your voice for good. Add a social impact twist to your work. Lucky Jupiter in Cancer brings momentum to apply for a grant, fundraise for a cause or become the ultimate community cheerleader.

This year, you can be the glue that brings people together for something bigger than themselves. Just make sure the responsibilities don't wind up sticking to you alone. Remember, Virgo, delegating is your new superpower in 2026, even when you're on a do-good mission!

JUPITER IN LEO
JUNE 30, 2026 – JULY 26, 2027

Ready for a celestial sabbatical? A sweet escape could lure you off the grid mid-year, when Jupiter heads into Leo and your twelfth house of dreams, surrender and spirituality for thirteen months. You haven't experienced this cycle in over a decade, since July 2014 to August 2015. Chances are, you're in a very different place in your life now. Nevertheless, the assignment is the same: Let go so that you can grow.

That's a tall order for the zodiac's not-so-secret control freak. While you're fine going with the flow here and there, you're much more comfortable with a clear-cut itinerary. Yet, from June 30, 2026 to July 26, 2027, your mantra might as well be, "Virgo plans, the universe laughs."

Or how about this upgrade? Virgo plans, the universe delivers a better option. This is lucky Jupiter we're talking about here, the planet of "more." Its focus is always on broadening your horizons, which sometimes means pushing you out of your comfort zone so you can actually SEE what else is out there.

That MIGHT involve traveling to a different part of the world, but in your twelfth house, Jupiter's journeys are as much of an internal voyage as an actual trip. Because the red-spotted planet will be in creative Leo, whatever you learn about your inner workings could become the springboard for an artistic project. The métier doesn't matter. You could write fiction, choreograph a dance piece, put together your one-Virgo show. The point is that you're moving the energy instead of feeling bogged down by trauma and limiting beliefs.

It's okay if you're not ready to pick up a paintbrush or guitar right away. When Jupiter first steps into Leo this June 30, you might be flooded with a host of feelings that you've been avoiding for years. Give yourself ample space to process them. Like we said, the journey is largely inward now. And it's one worth taking! Between now and July 2027, expect accelerated emotional healing and spiritual growth. Quiet breakthroughs arrive when you finally release the reins and allow yourself to be supported.

Some Virgos could check out of the grind altogether for a bit. Maybe you'll post up in a sleepy surf town or take that cross-country road trip in an Airstream trailer. Even if you stay put, the busy social life you enjoyed in early 2026 could slow to a near halt. The energy you devoted to the outside world now needs to come home to you and your innermost circle.

And surprise! Jupiter can move the needle in places you swore you would never change. You may be amazed by how naturally outmoded situations fade away. Stale jobs, toxic connections, old stories—blargh! In joyful Leo, Jupiter helps you release the ties that bind without the usual angst. But don't wait for the universe to rip unhealthy situations from your cold and clutching hands. Practice loosening your grip, Virgo, and allowing emotions to arise. Repression is what causes depression. While, those tears? They are your gift.

Healing could be your number one priority for the second half of the year. For your wellness-oriented sign, this will feel quite inspiring. Maybe this is the excuse you needed to book the weeklong detox at a desert spa or join an online mastermind oriented around health. Stress, inflammation, microplastics—these seem to be at the root of so many issues right now—and you may need to confront their deleterious influence on your life.

One of the biggest gifts this cycle can bring? Forgiveness, both for yourself and others. Even if you never say your quiet thoughts out loud, you can be a harsh critic. The kinder you are to yourself, the easier it becomes to cut other people some slack.

Your body, mind and spirit want to feel free, so give them what they deserve. Get recommendations for therapists, bodyworkers and spiritual healers. Start a mindfulness practice. (And you thought you were a die-hard journaler before?!) This "soul work" is all preparation for a powerful, new 12-year cycle that begins on July 26, 2027, when Jupiter circles back to Virgo for the first time since mid-2016. Do the inner excavation now and you'll be more than ready to rise—lighter, freer and crystal clear about what you want to create next!

3 REDEFINE SUCCESS

URANUS IN GEMINI
APRIL 25, 2026 – MAY 22, 2033

Time to remix your professional playlist, Virgo! First step? Delete the elevator music and yacht rock. Then, start exploring more experimental genres. Work may be anything BUT business as usual for you starting April 25, 2026. The reason? Wild child Uranus buzzes back into Gemini, setting off a seven-year surge through your goal-getting tenth house of ambition and success. Like Virgo Beyoncé's turn as a country music superstar, you are poised for your own era of groundbreaking reinvention.

You got a sneak preview of this electrifying energy from July to November 2025. If your brain lit up with wild new ideas, or you found yourself questioning what it REALLY means to "succeed," consider that your pregame show. It's officially Go time after April 25, as the side-spinning planet circles back to Gemini until May 22, 2033.

This isn't your typical climb-the-ladder phase. In fact, you might toss the whole ladder and build a spiral staircase instead—one that doubles as an art installation and maybe a trapeze. Either way, forget about coloring inside the lines. With Uranus in your status-driven tenth house, innovation IS the structure. You're being called to redefine what success looks like on your own visionary terms.

That's easier said than done for many a Virgo. Even the edgiest among you find comfort in systems, results and a clear, linear path from point A to point B. Disruptive Uranus would rather take a detour, looping around point Q then back to G before inventing a brand-new alphabet. This roller coaster ride will feel disorienting at times, but that's the point. Over the next seven years, experimentation is the way forward. Instead of attempting to have all the answers BEFORE you begin, rewards come as you prototype, test, tweak and try again. Adopt a startup mindset and apply it to your familiar path. You'll discover hidden gems and "money left on the table" sitting right under your own nose.

Gemini rules communication, ideas, media and technology. With inventive Uranus charging up this sign, your messaging matters. If you've got something to say—and of course you do—play around with different platforms. While it's important to keep your audience in mind when crafting your ideas, know this: People want to hear YOUR unique perspective. Public speaking, digital content creation, social media, app design: Whatever your métier, your voice is an important part of this next phase of evolution. Bring on the clever hot takes Virgos are famous for.

Since Uranus is the futuristic planet, many Virgos will be drawn to emerging industries this year. Heck, you could help shape one from scratch. Is there an AI helper for that? Ethical technology, digital health, remote work infrastructure, new education models—these are all Uranus-in-Gemini frontiers. Over the next seven years you could be swept along in the wave of progress, both in your professional and personal life.

Even if you're happily engaged in an analog career or possibly eyeing retirement, don't be surprised if Uranus in Gemini makes itself known in the social corners of your life.

Virgos may find themselves involved in politics or humanitarian work, especially on the Gemini-ruled local level.

Already making your zip code a better place to live? Neighbors (and neighborhood officials!) in high places could take notice of you. Get out and circulate. Synergies will spark anywhere from a town hall meeting to an ice cream social. Still, quality control is key. Unpredictable Uranus might send some flaky collaborators your way, so vet thoroughly. If the energy's off, don't force an alliance.

And get ready to challenge a few of your sign's famous control issues. No one loves a plan more than a Virgo, yet micromanaging every step limits your potential. You may have to iterate more than you're comfortable with. Run the reports, but don't ignore your gut when it tells you that defying the early data is the right move.

Your work-life balance takes on a new rhythm, too. The tenth house rules structure, but Gemini craves movement and variety. Maybe you go hybrid, freelance or shift into project-based work. Traditional career paths may not be extinct, but they're definitely not the only way forward now. Virgos who have garnered considerable expertise may be ready to break out as the boss of your own consultancy or agency.

By the time this cycle wraps in 2033, you may have a few professional pivots under your belt. Maybe you'll become the version of yourself you always knew was possible, but never quite had the room to become. Get ready to taste the sweetness of success in a whole new variety of flavors.

Let go of the need to have everything done "just the way I like it." When the planet of surprises shows up in Gemini, you're poised for growth, but it comes from curiosity rather than any known quantities.

4 UPGRADE YOUR SYSTEMS

LUNAR NODES IN LEO AND AQUARIUS
NORTH NODE IN AQUARIUS, SOUTH NODE IN LEO JULY 26, 2026–MARCH 26, 2028

Exhale, Virgo. On July 26, the karmic South Node finally leaves your sign, not to return for another 18 years. Since January 11, 2025, you've carried this heavy cosmic weight, navigating a period of soul-searching that may have felt like an endless "dark night of the soul." But the gift is clarity—you've been stripped of illusions and recalibrated to your truest self.

Much of the past 18 months, with the North Node in Pisces and your seventh house of partnerships, taught you crucial lessons about collaboration. Relationships of every kind—romantic, professional, platonic—served as mirrors, showing you both your strengths and your blind spots. You've learned where true reciprocity exists, and where imbalance leaves you drained. Now, as that cycle winds down, you step into the next chapter with clearer boundaries and a stronger sense of who you want beside you.

Midyear, with the North Node moving into Aquarius and your sixth house of routines on July 26, you're ready for a radical life overhaul. Think of it as cosmic spring cleaning, where efficiency meets innovation. Streamline your schedule, refine your diet and adopt sustainable wellness rituals. This is about creating rhythms that nourish rather than deplete you. Meanwhile, the Leo South Node simmers in your twelfth house, revealing subconscious patterns that trip you up. People-pleasing, self-sacrifice, numbing out—watch for the old defaults creeping in. This fresh, 20-month cycle calls for courage: Observe, release and replace those outworn methods with practices that strengthen rather than drain.

Trigger alert: Buried grief or hidden wounds may resurface. Let them. Journaling, therapy, creative rituals—even a good cry—will unblock what's been weighing you down. As emotions flow, your vitality rises. Aquarius rules the nervous system, so explore neuroplasticity: Rewire your brain through new skills, daily movement or meditative breathing. Small, consistent actions now create lasting transformation.

Professionally, the North Node in your work sector points you toward growth. Don't be afraid to restructure your role, explore new projects, or propose innovative systems within your company. This isn't about overextending yourself, however, so watch out for that tendency. The tech-savvy Aquarius North Node can help you to work smarter. Batch tasks, automate where you can, and work with AI as your helper to speed certain tasks. Burnout is the shadow of this cycle, but it's avoidable if you treat your time as sacred.

The last time the nodes activated this axis was June 2006 to December 2007. Echoes from that period could return, perhaps through old habits, work patterns or even colleagues. Take the wisdom from that chapter but don't repeat the mistakes. This time, you're crafting a life that's sustainable, nourishing and aligned with who you've become.

5 SPEAK WITH HEART

VENUS RETROGRADE IN SCORPIO AND LIBRA
VENUS RETROGRADE IN SCORPIO: OCTOBER 3–25
VENUS RETROGRADE IN LIBRA: OCTOBER 25–NOVEMBER 13

Pause, Virgo—don't hit send on that impulsive text! Loose lips (and fingertips) might not just sink ships this fall, they could run your love life straight into choppy waters. From October 3 to November 13, ardent Venus, the romantic planet of beauty, harmony and desire, slips into a rare six-week retrograde, an event that only happens every 18 months. This time, her backspin takes place in two zodiac signs. From October 3 to 25, Venus steals back through emotionally intense Scorpio and your third house of communication and peers. Then, from October 25 to November 13, she rocks the boat in Libra and your sensual, security-minded second house.

For most of October, your challenge will be to refine your delivery, especially with those closest to your heart. Are you being a straight-shooter, Virgo? Or are you couching truth in dry wit or sarcastic jabs? Even your compliments may sound more like the delivery of a Critic's Choice Award—and people may be offended by your hot takes. Dial up your sensitivity radar. Aim for clarity and kindness, letting your trademark thoughtfulness guide every conversation.

The investigative third house also rules platonic love, sibling bonds and community ties. If a friendship has grown distant or overly transactional, you won't be able to stay mum. But who should you talk about this with first? Venus' trademark diplomacy may be AWOL during the retrograde, so it might be best to run your feelings by a savvy sounding board before you attempt any repair work.

If this feels like an easy fix, Venus' reverse commute offers a heartfelt opportunity to restore warmth and mutual respect. Rebuild bridges through shared activities—cooking meals together, coworking sessions or even signing up for a skill-building class together. Venus is the planet of love and, yes, you can expect both friction and some unexpected sparks to fly this fall. Feelings may develop for someone in your friend circle or a casual acquaintance. Advance with care, especially if this exploration could jeopardize your bond or create awkwardness within your social circle. Chemistry can flare up in a flash and fade just as quickly during this phase. Make sure anyone you pursue is genuinely available and that you're ready for something more than a fleeting thrill.

Touch is important and you could find yourself craving a different level of affection once Venus glides back into Libra and your tactile second house from October 25 to November 13. If you've been keeping someone at a polite distance, you may suddenly feel like pulling them close. In other cases, you might actually prefer a little LESS canoodling. Deliver this information with sensitivity since your partner could take your change of pace personally. Make sure they know, "It's not you, it's me." Single Virgos: Hugs from friends, massages and cuddling pets all do wonders to fill your oxytocin tanks.

Budget check! Venus also governs money and Libra rules your second house of possessions and valuables. Have you been indulging in guilty pleasures without tallying the long-term costs? The retrograde inspires a gentle financial recalibration. You don't have to strip away pleasure, but you DO need to consider sustainability. Trim back excess spending and, more importantly, look at where your generosity may be draining your resources. That friend who's been staying in your guest room while she gets back on her feet might be ready to pay you a little rent. And you don't have to pick up the tab for every brunch, even if you're earning a higher wage.

Create a few buckets for personal investments. That fifty dollars you dropped on someone's steak and eggs (again!) could be earning you compounding interest in an index fund. Same for an extra few hundred bucks that a "roomie" contributes to the pot. We're not suggesting that you stop treating. Just include yourself on that roster!

Looking for new revenue streams? A former collaborator could resurface with a project worth considering. Run those LinkedIn searches while you're at it. A colleague from your past may be working in a field you'd love to enter. If you're at a job you love, use the gracious Venus energy to strengthen your connection to the key people in your office—and industry! Show up at those conferences, evening mixers and virtual seminars. Someone you've casually vibed with in the past could soon play an important role in your professional future.

2026 VIRGO

12 MONTH OVERVIEW

January MONTHLY HOROSCOPE

Joy and creativity fuel your January. Um, you're so NOT ready to stop celebrating yet! With the Sun beaming into Capricorn until the 19th, your festive, flamboyant fifth house is activated. Stave off the winter blues with dinner parties, clubbing, concerts and shows. Embrace your role as hygge season entertainment director—especially when the Cancer full moon lights up your communal eleventh house on the 3rd. Here's your cue to organize ongoing winter activities for your network or get involved in a meaningful group project. On the 18th, the Capricorn new moon puts fame and creativity in the spotlight. What do you want to be known for in 2026? Actions you begin now will blossom over the coming six months. Lovebirds Venus and Mars travel in Capricorn until the 17th, then in Aquarius after the 23rd, reminding you that romance thrives when paired with practical support. You know how to be of service, Virgo, but how about receiving it in return? Practice makes perfection. Wellness goals take the spotlight as the Sun enters Aquarius on the 19th. Time to commit to that eating plan and start using the gym membership you paid for. And while outer progress is key, your inner landscape matters just as much. On the 2nd, wounded healer Chiron turns direct in Aries, helping you work through financial or intimacy-related stress. Then on the 26th, dreamweaver Neptune re-enters Aries for a 13-year cycle, transforming the way you trust, merge and build deeper bonds.

February MONTHLY HOROSCOPE

Get your systems in order, Virgo. February spotlights wellness, work, and the art of efficiency as the pragmatic Sun moves through Aquarius and your sixth house until the 18th. Where could life run more smoothly? Streamline your days, refine your rituals, and set yourself up for success. The courageous Leo full moon on the 1st illuminates your twelfth house of release, nudging you to shed draining habits or close a lingering chapter. Then, on February 17, the Aquarius new moon arrives as a game-changing solar eclipse—the first here since 2018—just as the Year of the Fire Horse begins. A fresh work project, a lifestyle upgrade or even a new daily routine could ignite quickly. Until February 10, Venus in Aquarius brings sweetness to collaborations and teamwork. After that, she drifts into Pisces and your seventh house, putting relationships and romance front and center. Partnerships feel more affectionate and cooperative now, both personal and professional. Saturn re-enters Aries on February 13, launching a two-year cycle of accountability in your eighth house of intimacy and shared resources. Money and commitments will demand long-term planning. Valentine's Day follows with the Capricorn moon, perfect for a cozy, creative date that feels thoughtful yet simple. Pisces season begins on the 18th, activating your seventh house of partnerships and one-on-one bonds. Step into Pisces season on the 18th by prioritizing your closest partnerships. Lean into collaboration, but also be clear about boundaries. When Mercury retrograde begins here from February 26 to March 20, revisit old agreements or clarify expectations that feel fuzzy. Don't shy away from hard conversations—they'll help you transform fragile bonds into resilient ones.

March MONTHLY HOROSCOPE

Two is your magic number this March as the Sun, Mercury retrograde, lusty Mars and a Pisces new moon (on the 18th) energize your seventh house of partnerships. What do you want from your closest connections, and what needs to change? Be honest about what you're giving and what you're receiving—true balance will only come when both sides match. The total lunar (full moon) eclipse in Virgo on the 3rd lands in your sign and your first house of identity. A personal goal or project could reach culmination, or you may decide it's time to show up differently in the world. This eclipse puts you on notice: Are you living authentically? Some massive shifts may be in store if you need to "true up" to your soul's calling. On March 2, can-do Mars enters Pisces for a six-week stay, heating up your relationship sector and demanding action. Be direct about your needs, and don't shy away from tough conversations. Romance grows more intense after March 6, when Venus enters Aries and your eighth house of intimacy. Expect sparks, but also deeper questions about trust and commitment. On the 10th, expansive Jupiter ends a four-month retrograde in Cancer and your eleventh house of community and friendships. Social plans begin flowing again and group projects gather steam. Aries season kicks off on March 20—the spring equinox—shifting focus to your eighth house of transformation and shared resources. Mercury stations direct the same day, clearing three weeks of crossed signals. With communication finally back on track, you can strengthen your bonds and move partnerships to the next level.

April MONTHLY HOROSCOPE

Seismic shifts are stirring this April, Virgo. The Sun powers through Aries and your eighth house of intimacy and transformation until the 19th, urging you to look at what needs to change so you can feel truly secure. What's weighing on you—financially, emotionally, spiritually? Take it seriously and start strategizing. This sultry cycle heightens erotic energy, too. What happens behind closed doors should stay there! On the 1st, the Libra full moon beams into your second house of money and values, bringing clarity around income or a financial agreement. Make decisions that reflect your worth. Then, fiery Mars storms into Aries on the 9th, stirring passion and intensifying close bonds, but also heightening power struggles if you're not careful. Channel this high-intensity six-week cycle into shared ventures that benefit everyone. The new moon in Aries on the 17th opens the door to new financial arrangements, joint ventures or deeper intimacy. By the 19th, the steady Taurus Sun shifts into your expansive ninth house, bringing inspiration through travel, study or publishing. Until April 24, Venus also glides through Taurus, making connections feel adventurous and enriching. Then comes the tectonic shift: On the 25th, side-spinning Uranus wraps up its seven-year stay in Taurus and blasts into Gemini until 2033. With your tenth house of career now electrified, you're entering an era of reinvention and bold professional breakthroughs. Expect surprises, pivots and opportunities to be recognized in new ways.

May MONTHLY HOROSCOPE

Distant horizons beckon! The Taurus Sun streams into your ninth house of travel, study and big-picture growth until the 20th, urging you to stretch beyond known terrain. Travel, study and mingle multiculturally. When the Scorpio full moon lights up your third house of communication on the 1st, action will be buzzy on the local scene, too. Kindred spirits pop up and you could seal the deal on a collaboration. Deep-diving Pluto turns retrograde in Aquarius and your sixth house of wellness and routines from May 6 to October 15. Slow down and refine daily systems so they support your long-term vitality. The Aquarius quarter moon on May 10 also spotlights this area—Mother's Day could be the perfect time for a mindful family ritual, like a walk in nature or cooking a nourishing meal together. Supermoon season begins on the 16th as the year's only Taurus new moon energizes your adventurous ninth house. Spread your wings, Virgo! This is the start of a six-month window of worldly exploration. Then, on May 20, the Sun enters Gemini and your tenth house of career, putting professional goals front and center. Step into visibility and show the world what you're capable of. Until May 18, magnetic Venus glides through Gemini and your tenth house, boosting your professional charm and helping you gain recognition and visibility. Then, on the 18th, Venus shifts into Cancer and your eleventh house of community, while fiery Mars charges into Taurus and your ninth house. Romance could blossom through shared ideals, travel or group activities. That's a good reason to get out and circulate! The month ends on May 31 with the expansive Sagittarius full blue moon in your fourth house of home and family, bringing a domestic decision or milestone to light. Trust the process. You're laying foundations that will stand the test of time.

June MONTHLY HOROSCOPE

Ambition is your fuel this month, Virgo, as the Sun treks through Gemini and your tenth house of career and public image until June 21. Recognition is within reach if you step up and show off your skills. The June 14 Gemini new moon—the second supermoon in a rare three-part series—lands here, too, sparking opportunities in leadership or long-term goals. Meanwhile, Mars powers through Taurus and your ninth house of expansion until June 28, urging you to pursue study, travel or projects that stretch your horizons. A turning point comes June 19 when "wounded healer" Chiron dips into Taurus for a three-month preview of its 2027-2034 stay. Since 2018, Chiron has pressed on your intimacy zone, demanding deeper honesty in relationships and shared resources. This summer, its focus shifts to your beliefs, nudging you to heal old doubts and reclaim faith in your own path. On June 21, the Sun slides into Cancer and your eleventh house, just in time for the solstice and Father's Day. Celebrate with friends or a group gathering—community is where your energy thrives during Cancer season! In love, Venus lingers in the sign of the Crab until the 13th, highlighting romance through shared activities and group connections. Then she struts into Leo and your twelfth house, pulling desire behind the scenes and adding a dreamy, fantasy-fueled element to love. On June 30, Jupiter shifts into Leo and your twelfth house, starting a thirteen-month chapter of healing, reflection and release. Stepping back will set the stage for a powerful reinvention when lucky Jupiter heads into Virgo on July 26, 2027. Your inner work now paves the way for outer breakthroughs then. The month wraps with the Capricorn full moon on June 29 in your fifth house of passion and self-expression. A romance or creative project could peak, but with Mercury retrograde in Cancer beginning the same day, choose carefully what you reveal over the coming three weeks.

July MONTHLY HOROSCOPE

Rally your crew, Virgo! July puts teamwork front and center. With the Sun powering through Cancer and your eleventh house of community until the 22nd, it's all about shared visions and collective wins. Mercury retrograde here until the 23rd brings old allies back into your orbit or revives a group project worth reworking. The Cancer new moon (a supermoon) on the 14th charges up your eleventh house, too, sparking a milestone moment in your friendships or reminding you which bonds are truly ride-or-die. On July 7, mystical Neptune turns retrograde in Aries and your eighth house, peeling back the layers of intimacy, trust and shared resources. Then, on the 26th, Saturn follows suit, demanding you reinforce boundaries and take responsibility for what (and who) you merge with. Meanwhile, driven Mars dominates Gemini and your ambitious tenth house all month, pushing you to take bolder steps in your career. Pitch, present, apply—just pace yourself so you don't burn out. Once Leo season kicks off on the 22nd, the vibe shifts: Slip behind the scenes to rest and recharge your creative batteries. But peek out a bit, too! Venus enters Virgo on the 9th, boosting your magnetism and making you impossible to overlook. Once your ruler Mercury stations direct on the 23rd, collaborations flow smoother and long-stalled plans pick up steam. The big turning point arrives July 26, when the karmic North Node lands in Aquarius and your sixth house for the first time in nearly 20 years. Until March 2028, your destiny revolves around building habits, systems and wellness routines that keep you sharp and sustainable. July ends with fireworks on the 29th as the Sun and Jupiter unite in Leo for the "Day of Miracles," delivering a powerful spiritual download. At the same time, the Aquarius full moon lights up your sixth house, pushing you to implement new rituals that fuse vision with structure. Team up, Virgo—you'll go further, faster.

August MONTHLY HOROSCOPE

Birthday season is on the horizon, Virgo, but first comes a behind-the-scenes recalibration while the Sun simmers in Leo and your transitional twelfth house until the 22nd. Tie up loose ends and replenish with some unapologetic poolside lounging. On August 3, Chiron turns retrograde in Taurus and your ninth house of expansion, nudging you to revisit an old dream tied to travel, learning or publishing. Something once shelved could be worth dusting off—this time with wiser eyes and a clearer plan. On the 11th, Mars charges into Cancer, revving up your social life and group projects. Collaboration fuels momentum now, but choose your crew carefully. The right allies can multiply your impact, while the wrong ones scatter your energy. Eclipse season ignites on the 12th with a total solar eclipse in Leo—the first here since 2019—activating your twelfth house of closure and renewal. A chapter could end abruptly, clearing space for the fresh start that arrives with your birthday season. Venus enters Libra on the 6th, highlighting your second house of money and values. Go ahead and treat yourself, but lean into investments that are both beautiful and useful. The Sun sails into Virgo on the 22nd, energizing your first house of identity and kicking off your personal new year. Reset your priorities and carve out space to explore passions that are purely your own. On the 28th, the Pisces lunar eclipse lights up your seventh house of partnerships, bringing a relationship to a turning point. Whether you're defining the bond, renegotiating the terms or parting ways, hovering in limbo won't be an option. August wraps with rare cosmic convergence on the 31st, as Jupiter in Leo trines Saturn in Aries. Expansion meets structure: Commit to a plan with staying power and roll up your sleeves!

September MONTHLY HOROSCOPE

It's birthday season, Virgo, and the limelight is all yours! With the Sun blazing through your first house of identity until the 22nd, you've got cosmic permission to celebrate yourself. Book that photoshoot, launch the project you've been quietly perfecting or plan a party where the guest list reflects who you've become. Meanwhile, Mars is energizing Cancer and your eleventh house of community until the 27th, firing up collabs, group projects and social events. Say yes to the not-so-random invite, even if it feels a little intimidating. The year's only Virgo new moon lands on the 10th, pressing the reset button. Set "me-first" intentions for your next spin around the Sun—whether it's a health goal, a brand refresh or a life-changing experience that's been on your bucket list for years. That same day, Uranus pivots retrograde in Gemini and your ambitious tenth house, putting your career strategy under review for the next five months. Are you climbing a ladder you still want to be on? Value-driven Venus lingers in Libra until the 10th, highlighting your money zone, then dips into Scorpio and your third house of communication. Pitch, write or workshop your ideas. You'll have magnetic charm and persuasive power. Advance notice: From October 3 to November 13, Venus retrograde could slow negotiations, so tee up important convos before then. Libra season begins with the fall equinox on the 22nd, refocusing your energy on finances and stability. On the 17th, Chiron backs into Aries and your eighth house of intimacy and shared resources, helping you heal old wounds around trust and vulnerability. And the Aries full moon on the 26th shines a light on your most sacred bonds. Whether you're signing a lease, deepening a commitment or cutting ties, it's a turning point in how you invest—your time, your energy and your heart.

October MONTHLY HOROSCOPE

Use your words wisely, Virgo. On October 3, diplomatic Venus turns retrograde, first sliding back through Scorpio and your communication sector until the 25th, then into Libra and your money zone until November 13. Misunderstandings could drag conversations in circles, and financial issues may resurface. But what if these detours are your chance to renegotiate? Where have you been underselling yourself—or overexplaining? Dig deeper to figure out what a "win-win" looks like. The Sun continues its tour of Libra until the 23rd, spotlighting your second house of income and security. The Libra new moon on the 10th could mark a new chapter for your finances—whether it's updating your rates, applying for a higher-paying role or creating a budget that finally sticks. Mars blazes through Leo and your twelfth house all month, demanding downtime. Ignore rest at your peril; exhaustion could sneak up fast. Pluto ends its retrograde on

October 15 in Aquarius and your sixth house of work and wellness, finally pushing forward any stalled projects or health goals. Then on the 23rd, the Sun shifts into Scorpio and your communication zone, the same day Venus aligns with the Sun in a rare Cazimi. Expect a moment of clarity with a sibling, colleague or collaborator—and the confidence to share something you've kept under wraps. Mercury retrograde begins on the 24th in Scorpio, garbling texts and tangling travel plans. Double-check details before you hit "send" or "book trip." By the Taurus full moon on the 26th, your ninth house of travel and expansion is illuminated. This is the wider lens you've been craving, so peer beyond your comfort zone for answers and opportunities.

November MONTHLY HOROSCOPE

Your words carry weight this November, Virgo, so wield them with care. With the Scorpio Sun spotlighting your third house of communication until the 22nd, conversations, writing and ideas are your currency. But don't rush to make any big announcements just yet. Until the 13th, Mercury is retrograde in Scorpio while Venus backspins through Libra. Misunderstandings and crossed wires are likely, especially around money and everyday interactions. Edit, refine, rehearse—then release after midmonth. On the 9th, the Scorpio new moon brings kindred spirits out of the woodwork. One of these "soul friends" could be the perfect partner for an initiative that you roll out over the coming half year. Test the waters with a short-term project first. Behind the scenes, make-it-happen Mars is recharging its batteries until the 25th, resting in Leo and your healing, restorative twelfth house. Old stresses or secret frustrations could flare, but this is also your chance to clear them. Schedule downtime for therapeutic activities and wrap projects that drain your energy. When the Sun shifts into Sagittarius on the 22nd, home and family take center stage. Host cozy dinners, craft nights and holiday gatherings at Château Virgo. In the market for a move? Relocation plans could get underway. The full supermoon in Gemini on the 24th puts your career in the spotlight. A project could reach a stunning milestone bringing long-due recognition. Ready to pivot? This lunar lift reveals where to steer your ambitions. The most exhilarating news comes on the 25th when, for the first time in two years, heatseeking Mars bursts into Virgo. With the red planet in your trailblazing first house for the rest of the year, you can overcome personal blocks and kick a personal initiative into high gear. Use this momentum to lead the charge—but pace yourself so you don't burn out before 2026 is through!

Read your extended monthly forecast for life, love, money and career! astrostyle.com

December MONTHLY HOROSCOPE

The fun is happening under your roof—and wherever you cozy up—this month! As the Sagittarius Sun warms your fourth house of family and foundations until the 21st, you're craving up-close-and-personal moments with your people. The new moon in Sagittarius on the 8th brings a chance to reset the hearth: Refresh your décor, initiate a heart-to-heart or plan a holiday gathering that feels soul-nourishing. Two outer planets—goal-getting Saturn and idealistic Neptune—end five-month retrogrades in Aries on the 10th and 12th, respectively, clarifying where you stand in key partnerships. The path to deeper commitment—or a cleaner break—finally comes into view. With motivator Mars powering through Virgo all month, you're brimming with drive and charisma. Push ahead on personal projects but be mindful of coming on too strong before you've warmed up your "audience." Venus returns to Scorpio and your third house of communication after the 4th, sweetening conversations and drawing kindred spirits your way. On the 12th, expansive Jupiter pivots retrograde in Leo and your reflective twelfth house. Before exhaustion creeps in, open some whitespace in your calendar to recharge, dream and commune with the muse. Those disco naps will come in handy after the 21st: Capricorn season begins with the solstice, firing up your festive, romantic fifth house. Indulge your playful side and make space for joy. The Cancer full supermoon on the 23rd could bring a group effort to a grand finale, just in time to raise a toast before the holidays. Forget about tucking in early on NYE. An adventurous Sun-Mars trine pushes the envelope with your plans. Drape yourself in sequins and dance in 2027, ideally on a new part of the globe.

LIBRA IN 2026

| ALL THE PLANETS IN LIBRA IN 2026 | YOUR 2026 HOROSCOPE | TOP 5 THEMES FOR LIBRA IN 2026 | LOVE HOROSCOPE + LUCKY DATES | MONEY HOROSCOPE + LUCKY DATES |

Libra in 2026

Your year of:
ASCENSION, ADVENTURE, UNBRIDLED JOY

AIM THE SPOTLIGHT AT YOUR AMBITIONS, LIBRA.

This is a breakout year for career and community. Projects scale, your name circulates in bigger rooms, your platform finds its people. Build a team that matches your pace. There is strength in numbers now, Libra, whether two, twenty or ten thousand! Let yourself take up space, in the stylish way your sign prefers. 2026 offers a chance to refresh your digital footprint: portfolio tight, bio sharp, content consistent. But be discerning about who enters your fold. This is your year for doing excellent work with excellent people. By December you'll be backed by a network that opens doors, ones you're ready to strut through like an MVP.

THE PLANETS IN Libra

THE SUN
SEP 22–OCT 23

Happy birthday season! With the Sun in your sign, you're clear to take chances, chase fresh adventures, and command the spotlight.

NEW MOON
OCT 10
11:50AM, 17°22'

Happy bonus New Year! Set your intentions for the next six months, then take a brave step forward. Your fans await!

FULL MOON
APR 1
10:12PM, 12°21'

Manifestation moment! Your work of the past six months bears fruit. Celebrate your progress and harvest the rewards.

MERCURY
SEP 10–30

Hold court! When charismatic Mercury zips through your sign, your social status soars. Work the room, make connections—but keep your commitments realistic to avoid overpromising.

VENUS
AUG 6–SEP 10
OCT 25–DEC 4
RETROGRADE IN LIBRA:
OCT 25–NOV 13

Hello, gorgeous! When the galactic glamazon struts through your sign, your powers of seduction skyrocket. Irresistible charm, luxe tastes, and flirtatious vibes abound—just keep an eye on your budget. During the retrograde, old flames could make a dramatic return.

Libra in 2026
HIGHLIGHTS

JUPITER CROWNS YOUR CAREER UNTIL JUNE 30

Power, purpose and visibility are on tap, Libra. With Jupiter perched at the top of your chart until June 30, this is your once-in-12-years chance to rise into your most ambitious self. Go after the promotion, launch the dream project. With some gentle-but-consistent nudging you'll finally get recognized for your gifts. Update your portfolio, hire a brand photographer or say yes to that panel invite. Your work doesn't just land this year, it reverberates.

LOVE LESSONS: SATURN AND NEPTUNE IN ARIES

As of February 13, Saturn and Neptune spend two full years together in Aries, activating your relationship house. Stable Saturn demands boundaries, standards and accountability in love. Fantasy-agent Neptune brings compassion and romance—but also fog if you're not clear about what you want. The combo means it's time to refine your partnerships. If single, don't settle; if attached, get real about where you're headed. Think couples therapy, relationship coaching or even a new creative collab with your partner. Durable, dreamy connections are your theme.

NETWORK EXPANSION: JUPITER SHIFTS INTO LEO JUNE 30

Send out a casting call—and cast a wider net! As global Jupiter moves into Leo on June 30, your eleventh house of friendships and future goals lights up for 13 months. Your mission expands and so does your circle. Collaborations could lead to breakthrough opportunities. Your social media presence may explode. Don't leave this up to chance. Start crafting the right branding and messaging so that you go viral for something you're proud of. Networking is your superpower now. Join the mastermind, sign up for conferences, get involved in political and community organizing. It's all about who you know and who you network with.

PHILOSOPHY RESET: URANUS ENTERS GEMINI APRIL 25

After a seven-year deep dive into intimacy and transformation, experimental Uranus sails into Gemini and your ninth house of beliefs, travel and wisdom until 2033. Your worldview is about to get radically realigned. Expect steep (but fascinating!) learning curves and mind-expanding adventures. Book the far-flung trip, start the degree program or dive into a spiritual practice you've only skimmed. This cycle wants you to explore widely and think bigger than your current bubble.

MERCURY RETROGRADES: RETHINK YOUR RHYTHM

Mercury turns retrograde three times in 2026, urging you to slow down and refine the way you work, earn and lead. From February 26 to March 20, the messenger planet rewinds through your systematic sixth house. A wellness goal or office project may need a second look, or you might revive a workflow that once kept life on track. From June 29 to July 23, Mercury reverses in your tenth house of career. Old professional contacts could resurface or you may need to revise a long-term goal before moving forward. The final cycle, October 24 to November 13, spins backward in your second house of money and security. With Venus also retrograde in your sign, this period could highlight spending patterns or a past income stream returning to the mix. Use these pauses to reset your pace and bring your ambitions into balance.

MIRROR MOMENTS: LIBRA FULL AND NEW MOONS

Mark April 1 for the Libra full moon—a clarifying reveal around identity, relationships and self-image. Notice where you've over-given or under-asked. Is it time for an adjustment? Edit commitments, refresh your look and express the boundary out loud. On October 10, the Libra new moon offers a clean slate for your brand, voice and partnerships. Since it lands mid–Venus-retrograde season, consider this your cue to do some deeper research. Shuffle through your archives. An old, half-finished initiative could be the inspiration you're looking for!

RECONFIGURE ROMANCE: VENUS RETROGRADE OCTOBER 3 TO NOVEMBER 13

From October 3 to November 13, your ruling planet Venus is retrograde. The first part of the transit rewinds through Scorpio (October 3-25), spotlighting money, values and daily rhythms. When the love planet retrogrades in your sign (October 25 to November 13), it's deeply personal: Your identity and relationships come under review. But this isn't a cosmic takedown—it's a glow-up in disguise. You're being asked to realign with what feels authentic, not what pleases everyone else. Venus retrogrades repeat every 8 years (minus 2°), so this one links directly to fall 2018. Think about who you were becoming then and the choices you made about love, style or self-worth. Now, you're wiser and more self-possessed. Use this cycle to reconnect to rich relationships that reflect the real you.

DESTINY SHIFTS: NODES MOVE INTO AQUARIUS AND LEO

Until July 26, the South Node in Virgo helps you heal from self-sabotage while the North Node in Pisces rebuilds you through healthy routines. Clear ghost tasks from your calendar, swap doomscrolling for a wind-down routine. If you get easily overwhelmed, stack micro-habits—like a 10-minute stretch and a glass of water. Automate the boring money stuff and let "good enough" beat perfection. After July 26, the North Node lands in Aquarius and the South Node slides into Leo, turning the lights up on joy, creativity and community. This is your cue to trade performative hustle for genuine play. Block weekly hours for creative pursuits. Fun is back on the menu as a high-priority item!

Love

LIBRA 2026 FORECAST

The year begins on a cozy note with Venus and Mars cuddled up in Capricorn and your domestic fourth house until January 17. You might be tempted to hibernate, play house or swap keys. Just monitor your moods. (Yes, Libra, "love nest" sounds cute until you're negotiating who does the laundry.) Fortunately, by January 23, the vibe shifts in a far more romantic direction! Both Venus and Mars strut into Aquarius and your fifth house of passion. Suddenly it's not about Netflix and nesting—it's glamorous dinner dates, rose-petals on the bed and tickets to the opera. The February 17 solar eclipse Aquarius new moon launches the Year of the Fire Horse, fanning flames. Passion projects and passion partners, full steam ahead.

But here's where things take a serious turn. Beginning February 13, Saturn and Neptune join forces in Aries and your seventh house of relationships, where they'll stay paired for two years. Saturn wants to DTR, Neptune wants to keep things fluid. This odd-couple mash-up is a masterclass in balance (your specialty). The challenge? To identify your relationship ideals without trapping yourself in rigid titles or escaping into dreamy what-ifs.

Have you been stringing someone along? (Um, whoops!) Saturn's march through Aries until April 2028 forces you to stop playing both sides of the scale and decide what you really want. Craving a partner who's all in, or are you more enchanted by the fantasy? Maybe what you want IS a casual relationship, one with lots of room for personal autonomy. Whatever the case, Saturn will test bonds for durability, while fantasy-agent Neptune helps you find clever ways to keep the magic alive.

By summer, destiny comes knocking. On July 26, the North Node heads into Aquarius and your fifth house of romance for the first time in nearly three decades! With transformational Pluto already here, get ready for a 20-month cycle of milestones. Engagements, weddings, pregnancies or other defining moments could lie ahead. Whether you're coupled or single, you could experience legacy-level love.

But it's not going to be all buttercream-frosted cake and tea roses. From June 19 to September 14, wounded healer Chiron makes a brief visit to Taurus and your eighth house. Old pain around rejection, betrayal or vulnerability may surface. Alas, you won't be able to push these aside, Libra, not if you want to move to the next level of Cupid's gameboard. Healing those wounds creates space for intimacy that's truly nourishing. With a safe partner, role-playing power dynamics could be fascinating fodder for this evolution. Chiron here can help Libras heal from sexual shame and trauma, but it's not an overnight journey. The asteroid returns to Taurus for a longer journey in April 2027. Be gentle with yourself and communicative with the one(s) you love.

Now for some excellent news! Your ruling planet, ardent Venus, spends a huge chunk of the summer and fall in Libra! Her first pass through your sign is from August 6 to September 10, which could mitigate some of Chiron's influence and give you the courage to pursue the kind of love you want. Venus returns to Libra again from October 25 to December 4, but this time with a twist: a retrograde phase that lasts until November 13 (which begins in Scorpio and your second house of self-worth from October 3 to 25). The assignment for Venus' second lap? Learning to lovingly assert self-sovereignty instead of bending to keep the peace. Yes, Libra, everyone loves your diplomacy, but sometimes saying "no" is the most loving act you can offer yourself—and your relationships.

By year's end, you'll have redefined what partnership means on your terms. The nudge? Stop auditioning for the role of "perfect partner" and step into your own power. As you claim greater autonomy you can still leave room for soul-level connection. When you show up as your full, unfiltered self—without pushing anyone away—love finds its natural balance.

Money & Career

LIBRA 2026 FORECAST

Talk about genius, Libra: In 2026, you're blending artistry with enterprise—and doing it on your own terms. Live-out-loud Jupiter is touring Cancer and your ambitious tenth house until June 30, a cycle that began June 9, 2025, and now hits full stride. You kick off the year feeling enterprising, ready to grow your influence and expand your reach. Whether you're stepping into a leadership role, pitching a creative project or building a business, your vision is scaling up. The challenge? Staying free enough to follow inspiration while managing the real-world demands that come with success.

Since January 11, 2025, the destiny-fueling North Node has been moving through Pisces and your methodical sixth house, highlighting HOW you handle your tasks, not just what you produce. You're learning to design systems that support creativity instead of stifling it. Use the first part of the year to streamline workflows, integrate AI tools and delegate tasks that drain your focus. Efficiency equals freedom now. Across the zodiac, the South Node continues through Virgo and your guided twelfth house until July 26. Make space for imagination and mentorship. Quiet time and trusted advisors will be key ingredients in your next-level success.

On February 13, Saturn and Neptune join forces in Aries and your partnership zone, kicking off a two-year chapter of structured collaboration. The right alliances could open doors that solo efforts never could. Pro-level Saturn helps you define the business terms of a partnership or contract, while soulful Neptune invites you to choose collaborators who share your ideals and creative spark.

A major shift arrives when Uranus finally departs Taurus and your eighth house of shared resources, debt and investments on April 25, wrapping a seven-year roller coaster ride that began in 2018. You've likely faced fluctuations in income and trust. But you've also learned resilience. Now that rocky road of feast and famine (and maybe a bit of debt, to boot) comes to an end. As Uranus zips into Gemini and your ninth house of expansion and education until 2033, your focus widens. Freedom becomes your currency as new opportunities emerge through international projects, travel, publishing or teaching. Libras who are gainfully employed could work more independently after April 25.

Midyear, momentum accelerates. When Jupiter enters Leo on June 30, your fifth house of self-expression lights up, pushing you to step into the spotlight. Polish up your personal branding and get ready to self-promote. This 13-month cycle could bring media work, performance or a pursuit that lets your creative voice shine. That trend deepens on July 26, when the karmic South Node moves into Leo and this same expressive zone for a 20-month stay. You have something meaningful to share with the world, so put your message out there!

Financial reflection arrives this fall, when Venus—your ruling planet—turns retrograde from October 3 to November 13. Rethink your spending and make sure your resources are flowing toward projects that truly inspire you. By year's end, your creative power is undeniable—and so is your strategic edge!

TOP 5 THEMES FOR *Libra* in 2026

1	2	3	4	5
PARTNER POWERFULLY	GO PRO	EXPAND YOUR WORLDVIEW	STEP ON STAGE	KNOW YOUR WORTH

1 PARTNER POWERFULLY

NEPTUNE IN ARIES
JANUARY 26, 2026–MARCH 23, 2039

SATURN IN ARIES
FEBRUARY 13, 2026–APRIL 12, 2028

Dreamy duets are ahead for you in 2026, Libra! That should be music to your ears, which are forever perked for partnership opportunities. Romantic, business and soulfully creative pairings take center stage as two outer planets—disciplined Saturn and dreamy Neptune—weave through Aries and your seventh house of one-on-ones.

These two planets couldn't be more different: Neptune is the poet of the zodiac, ushering in spiritual love, unconditional trust and an unfettered desire to merge. Saturn is the builder, insisting on clear roles, contracts and real-world accountability.

You got an early preview of this oddball energy in 2025 when Neptune wandered into Aries from March 30 to October 22, softening your romantic walls and inviting you to share your feelings with radical honesty. Saturn followed suit from May 24 to September 1, offering a taste of what true partnership requires. Now Neptune submerges in Aries for a numinous 13 years, until 2039. Saturn hunkers down for two focused years, inviting a deeper excavation of your most important social connections between now and April 12, 2028.

February 20 is a major day! That's when Saturn and Neptune form an exact conjunction at 0º Aries, their only one during this shared journey. These two planets only unite in the sky every 35 to 40 years, but they haven't bonded in the Ram's realm since 1702! Yes, this is an ultra-rare moment when mystical meanderings meet sober reality checks.

Fortunately, it doesn't have to harsh your quixotic buzz. If you've been thinking about co-leading an initiative, starting a business with a trusted partner or launching something collaborative, this period is primed for turning a handshake deal into something structured and legally sound. You'll feel magnetically drawn to connections that go beyond infatuation—ones where emotional ease pairs with logistical synergy. For example, you lean into a romantic relationship, and it thrives because you're willing to have the tough conversations and uphold your shared agreements. Or you form a business partnership where creative magic meets clear contracts, ensuring equal effort and mutual trust.

Nevertheless, Neptune's foggy energy CAN blur the lines. Stay aware, Libra. You could begin idealizing your partner, ignoring red flags or slipping into codependency disguised as devotion. Catch yourself before Saturn steps in with the REALLY tough love. No vague promises, no "we'll see." Real partnership demands clear expectations, honest conversations and healthy boundaries.

If you're ready to formalize your 'ship, 2026 could bring engagements, co-signed leases and shared purchases. Time to build something lasting, Libra? Don't be coy. Saturn wants you to send a clear message to your other half.

Warning: Neptune might sabotage this initiative with half-baked plans. Spell out your desires clearly. People will appreciate the no-nonsense directives, as long as you deliver them sweetly.

Has an important connection soured in recent years? There's big healing potential in 2026, Libra. Neptune softens old resentments and opens the door to forgiveness. Simultaneously, Saturn gives you the courage to say what needs to be expressed.

Together, they'll also guide you to release outdated relationship patterns and let go of connections that drain your energy. If you've been holding onto an old tether, cut it with compassion and grace.

Drama isn't off the table—Saturn and Neptune ARE in fiery Aries, after all. But their blend of romance and rigor can serve up partnerships that are emotionally charged and fundamentally stable. Saturn's time in your seventh house until 2028 gives you the runway for real endurance. By then, a few VIP bonds could feel like fortresses built on trust, devotion and mutual respect.

When Neptune moves on to Taurus in 2039, you may look back and see that this cosmic duet taught you not just how to love deeply, but how to love intelligently. This isn't just a season of synergy, Libra. It's a turning point in how you love, collaborate and co-create.

2 GO PRO

JUPITER IN CANCER
JUNE 9, 2026–JUNE 30, 2026

Those gold-plated ambitions? Upgrade them to platinum level, Libra. As 2026 begins, you're halfway through lucky Jupiter's climb through Cancer and your tenth house of success and achievements. The abundant planet has been revving its turbine engines on behalf of your career since June 9, 2025—and it's only halfway through its journey! You have until June 30 to maximize this cycle, which only comes around every 12-13 years.

Keep polishing your crown, Libra, but don't get too comfortable leaning back on your throne. Responsibilities continue stacking up this year. If you want to reap the rewards, you need to put in a steady effort. While the first leg of this cycle may have felt like a soft launch, 2026 is the year to show up like a pro. And yes, that means trading a bit of carefree spontaneity for real-world structure. But the prestige, recognition and security you gain will be worth every spreadsheet and strategy session. Professionally, this cycle could be one of the most profitable (and liberating!) eras you've experienced in over a decade. Even better?

You have an opportunity to truly stabilize your income. If you've been working as an independent contractor, you could land a long-term "whale" client who covers the majority of your earnings. What relief it will be to NOT hop from gig to gig. Are you running your own venture? Tighten up your offerings so you can position yourself as a premium player. Think: fewer one-off services, more full-fledged packages and monthly retainers.

Jupiter in this powerhouse position wants you to aim for the top. Doors are opening, Libra! Meet the universe halfway by tapping one of your convivial sign's top skills: networking. Surround yourself with people who have already arrived at the destination you're angling for. Apply for membership at an exclusive social club, get nominated for a board seat, or if you're just getting started, volunteer at an organization that draws like-minded, successful people. You never know who you'll meet while stuffing gift bags for a charity gala—an activity that comes with a bonus of giving back, which your justice-loving sign is all about.

With worldly, freedom-loving Jupiter involved, the digital nomad life may tempt you. But don't race off to a remote villa too quickly. Until June 30, you may need to log more hours at HQ—in a centralized hub that allows you to see people IRL. Even if your work is remote, YOU will benefit from grounding yourself in a main location. That's not to say you won't travel for work in the first half of 2026. You could attend industry expos and conferences, possibly scouting locations for your next big expansion.

And if your work keeps you on the move, come up with easy systems, like keeping a bag packed with essentials like a go-to travel outfit, mini versions of your favorite products, chargers and other must-haves.

Got wisdom to share? Since Jupiter rules higher education, it's time to unleash "Professor Libra" on the world. Get yourself booked to speak at conferences, host a summit, lead a masterclass. Even if these activities aren't immediately profitable, the exposure puts you in the orbit of the power players and helps to position you as a subject matter authority.

The tenth house is the realm of the archetypal masculine, so don't be surprised if philosophical Jupiter gets you ruminating on your relationships with the guys in your life. And because the red-spotted planet is rolling through sentimental Cancer, you could heal and strengthen your emotional bonds with these dudes that you adore. Daddy issues or straight-up rage at the patriarchy could also flare up. Jupiter is all about authenticity. If you plan on talking this out, show up with your truth—and hold space for theirs, too. But don't force yourself if you're still processing. What you DON'T want to do this year is glaze over your pain to try to make peace.

For some Libras, this may also bring a necessary reckoning. Jupiter's freedom-loving vibe could push you to put healthy distance between yourself and a male figure who no longer aligns with your path. If you feel that tug, be thoughtful. These decisions can echo for years. Before cutting ties, try creating clearer boundaries first. A little space might be exactly what both hearts need to heal and reset.

Bottom line? Jupiter wants you to grow your influence—and enjoy every VIP experience you can! You're not just looking for a seat at the table in 2026, you're building your own damn dining hall. And if you play your cards right, you'll be feeding yourself and the people you love for years to come.

JUPITER IN LEO
JUNE 30, 2026 – JULY 26, 2027

Make way for the Libra dream team! This June 30, horizon-expanding Jupiter swings into Leo, firing up your collaborative eleventh house until July 26, 2027. After hustling through the first half of 2026, you may be feeling lonely at the top—or a bit limited in what you can achieve on your own. Loosen up the reins. If you want to expand (and have fun doing so!), allow your solo missions to evolve into joint ventures.

With jetsetting Jupiter leading the charge, dream collaborators could hail from every corner of the globe. Long-distance partnerships, international clients or projects that cross time zones will stretch you into uncharted territory. Sure, you may need to share the profits. But think of it this way: You'll have a much bigger pie to slice when you combine your magic with other MVPs.

The eleventh house rules technology, too, making this thirteen-month transit prime time for turning your genius into an online empire. Got an idea for an app, TikTok Shop, podcast or a digital course? Global Jupiter amplifies your reach through the digital realm. If you own an existing business, you could increase your earnings through special offerings such as a paid subscription or downloads.

If you need to raise capital for a venture, this community-driven vibe says: Don't go it alone. Crowdfunding, angel investors or pooling resources with other visionaries could get your ideas off the ground. Don't sit on your brilliance. Gather your supporters, film your pitch and get your GoFundMe or Patreon page up and running.

Whether you're working or playing, get ready for a popularity surge. People want to be near you—and maybe even BE you, which is quite flattering. And well deserved! You'll vibe easily with friends from all walks of life. Ambassador Jupiter in your avant garde eleventh house can draw you to artists, activists, thought leaders and visionaries. People who essentially march to the beat of their own drums. Be the bridge, Libra. During this Jupiter-in-Leo cycle, it's almost your duty to bring people together.

As the zodiac's sign of justice, you'll quickly resonate with this: The eleventh house is the humanitarian zone. Big-hearted Jupiter in Leo could guide you toward a meaningful mission in the second half of the year—politics, advocacy or, yes, justice work. Your level of involvement in a cause may deepen, too. Step up as a community organizer, run for office, or volunteer with a movement that needs your diplomatic skills. Your voice has the power to bring people together, Libra.

At its core, Jupiter in your eleventh house reminds you that your community is your greatest currency. Let that be the excuse you didn't need to go full-on social butterfly. When you expand your network, you expand your world. Keep your ideas flowing, your devices charged and your wingspan wide. Your people are waiting, and your future is, too.

3 EXPAND YOUR WORLDVIEW

URANUS IN GEMINI
APRIL 25, 2026 – MAY 22, 2033

Pack your bags, Libra. This April 25, experimental Uranus hands you a one-way ticket to a destination that lies well past the edge of your known universe. For the second time since 2025, the planet of upheaval and innovation zips into Gemini and your ninth house of travel, higher learning and limitless expansion. And oh, the places you will go between now and May 22, 2033!

You got a brief taste of this journey in 2025. From July 7 to November 7, detours beckoned while Uranus took its first spin through Gemini since 1941-49. But did it reset your entire compass? Probably not. Your sign is famous for carefully weighing every decision. Spontaneous Uranus might not have got you to leap without a net, but it probably got your stalled engines turning.

The Uranus-in-Gemini odyssey begins in earnest starting this April 25 as you officially enter a seven-year era of expansion—mentally, spiritually, maybe even geographically. So, Libra, what's next? Discovering that is where the magic lies. Rather than observing, reading or scrolling, get ready to find meaning through lived experience. There's no telling where one conversation or seminal trip could lead you now. If you lean into the spirit of exploration, Uranus in variety-loving Gemini could broker one of the most adventurous chapters you've had in your entire life.

Has your world felt small or restricted? That could change on a dime after April 25. Everywhere you look, there's something new to absorb and learn. While the ninth house rules education, unconventional Uranus could guide you away from the ivory tower. Your personal growth experiences may emerge from a self-paced course, a coding bootcamp, or a weeklong retreat in the Andes. Not to say a PhD program is off the table, but you may enroll in one that has customizable scheduling or even pays you to earn your degree. (Yes, that is a thing!)

No need to rush the application process. High-minded Uranus in this philosophical zone could find you questioning everything, including some long-held beliefs. Your mindset is evolving, Libra, and by the time 2033 rolls around, you might even change religions, political allegiances or embark on a new spiritual journey. Radical reboots are possible with Uranus in the ninth house. Give yourself time to explore a variety of perspectives before you declare yourself a party member. (Not that we have to twist your arm here, Libra.)

Even if you're NOT in school, you could become obsessed with decoding the "big picture"—and not in a navel-gazing, coffeeshop philosopher kind of way. Uranus in Gemini helps you build bridges between ideas and action. Got a theory? Test it. A hunch? Follow it. This transit rewards those who walk their talk—and teach what they've learned along the way.

Libra writers and mediamakers could hit an exciting renaissance moment since both Gemini and the ninth house rule publishing. As techie Uranus plugs in, you could move away from those old-school, analog tools. AI developments that have others clutching their pearls could help you string together some genius content. Uranus is the futurist, making you perfectly suited to adopt all the latest apps or blow up on social media, Substack, YouTube, or a platform that hasn't even been invented yet. Let your voice and ideas become part of the zeitgeist!

And here's a bonus: The ninth house is also the domain of entrepreneurship. Uranus here might not just change your perspective—it could change your career path entirely. You could invent something that disrupts an entire industry or launch a business that's years ahead of the curve. If an idea lights you up and solves a real-world problem, it's worth developing now.

You may also start to feel restless in relationships, particularly the ones that feel too small for the person you're becoming. That doesn't mean cutting off people cold turkey (unless, of course, you know in your heart that you need to). But you'll crave connections that are rooted in growth, exploration and shared ideals. Stagnation is a deal-breaker with Uranus in the sign of the Twins.

And a word about limits. If you've been downplaying your abilities, waiting until you're "ready" or thinking you need a gold-plated résumé to pursue your vision—Uranus is here to blast that myth to bits. Stop stressing about a 10-year plan. Instead, see what you can do with a mix of nerve, a strong Wi-Fi connection and the willingness to learn from your mistakes.

Uranus in Gemini won't send you on a straight line to enlightenment, no. You're embarking on a seven-year hike up the switchbacks of self-realization. There may be moments where you lose sight of the trail or your GPS glitches out. That's part of the experience. Until May 22, 2033 your mission is this: To follow the ideas, people and opportunities that make your inner compass spin with excitement. They're leading you SOMEWHERE, Libra, but you won't find the destination unless you take the first step, then the next one after that.

STEP ON STAGE

LUNAR NODES IN LEO AND AQUARIUS
NORTH NODE IN AQUARIUS, SOUTH NODE IN LEO JULY 26, 2026–MARCH 26, 2028

Lights, camera, Libra! On July 26, 2026, the fateful North Node leaps into Aquarius and your fifth house of passion, fame and creative expression, inviting you to step into a starring role until March 26, 2028. Across the wheel, the karmic South Node lands in Leo and your eleventh house of groups and collaborations, asking you to stop hiding behind the crowd and to fully own your artistry.

Since January 11, 2025, the North Node in Pisces has spotlighted your sixth house of work, wellness and service, while the South Node in Virgo tugged at your twelfth house of endings and release. That cycle was about discipline and healing—getting your routines in order, addressing burnout and learning to let go. Now, the narrative shifts dramatically. This nodal cycle dares you to put your heart and soul into play and to find joy in being seen.

During this 20-month cycle, the Aquarius North Node hands you a cosmic permission slip to court recognition. What are you most proud of, Libra? Whether through your artistry, performance or a creative project that bears your unique signature, it's time to share your gifts with the world. No more downplaying your brilliance! Lean into platforms that showcase your talents, from digital stages to live spotlights. You don't need to wait for a gatekeeper to validate you. Share your work, and the right eyes will find it.

Romance may feel fated under these skies. Single Libras could tumble into whirlwind affairs that light up every corner of your world. Established couples might rediscover the thrill of romance via shared adventures and creative projects. (Time to have your musician S.O. create a score for your memoir?) You'll still crave those heart fluttering moments—Libra always does—but the deeper lesson is about learning to bask in affection without losing balance. Fertility is also heightened, so if parenthood is on your mind, this cycle could bring that dream closer.

With the karmic South Node in Leo, your friendships and networks come up for review. While you'll still thrive in community, this cycle helps you distinguish between people who amplify your light and those who siphon it away. Certain alliances may fade as you gravitate toward collaborators who celebrate, not compete with, your shine.

If you've overextended yourself to keep the peace in groups, this cycle gives you the clarity to step back. It's not about ghosting everyone! That's going to bring regrets. But you WILL feel best once aligned with the teams and circles that truly support your vision. Your karmic homework? Trade approval-seeking for authenticity and let your star rise without apology.

By the end of this 20-month chapter, Libra, you'll understand that sharing your gifts isn't self-indulgent—it's your dharma. The more you allow yourself to create, to love and to dazzle, the more your world (and the people in it) will thrive.

5
KNOW YOUR WORTH

VENUS RETROGRADE IN SCORPIO AND LIBRA
VENUS RETROGRADE IN SCORPIO: OCTOBER 3–25
VENUS RETROGRADE IN LIBRA: OCTOBER 25–NOVEMBER 13

Cuffing season isn't canceled this fall, Libra, but it IS under formal review. This October 3, your cosmic custodian Venus spins into her biennial retrograde. This unavoidable event happens every 18 months, and when it does, all things Venus-ruled—romance, fashion, justice, values—can take an unexpected turn for the chaotic.

While this may cause temporary turbulence, there's always a silver lining to be found. Pull the focus away from other people—and seize the opportunity for self-work and moreover, self-LOVE. That alone could wind up getting lopsided relationships back on an even keel once the love planet resumes direct motion on November 13.

We're not saying this Venus retrograde will be a walk in the park. For the first time since 2018, the beatific planet is backing up through YOUR sign for part of the journey. From October 3 to 25, the retrograde begins in Scorpio and your second house of self-worth and personal finances. Then, from October 25 to November 13, Venus steals back into Libra and your first house of identity and self-expression.

Look back eight years in your calendar. What was happening between October 5 and November 16, 2018? You may see some patterns repeating with love or money—or coming up for further excavation. You've evolved since then, of course, Libra, and you may have some progress that's worth celebrating!

During the Scorpio leg of the retrograde, from October 3 to 25, the focus is on fortifying your security. That goes for both your bank account AND the value you put on yourself. As Venus reverses through this fixed water sign, you may need to tighten your belt, especially when it comes to some of your retail therapy indulgences. Please, Libra, don't attempt to go on a full austerity plan or slip too far into punishing practices like, "No going out to dinner and shows for three weeks!" Cinching off your connection to pleasure is a recipe for a rebellious binge.

Instead, embrace the creative challenge. Meet for happy hour or snacks instead of a full-course meal. Attend (or host!) a clothing and home goods swap. Organize game and movie nights with people who adore you through all your ups and downs. What will really buoy your spirit during Venus retrograde is surrounding yourself with people who see you, love you and cherish you.

During this time, you may have a few panicked moments, wondering whether a relationship or financial arrangement is truly mutual. In the process, you will also recognize where you've been underselling your own worth. If scarcity fears start creeping in, take a breath before acting on impulse. Clutching tighter—whether to a lover, a paycheck or an outdated self-image—won't fix the root issue. Instead, channel these feelings into safe, supportive spaces: a heartfelt conversation with a trusted confidante, a deep dive in therapy or through your own artistic expression. Graceful Libra, you have a rare gift for transforming raw emotions into beauty, and this retrograde could serve as your creative spark.

From October 25 to November 13, Venus backspins through your airy, refined sign, and things get personal. Your appearance, your closest relationships and even your sense of identity could be ripe for reinvention. Not that you should make any drastic changes before November 13! Tattoos, major haircuts, injections and cosmetic procedures should be avoided as much as possible during Venus retrograde, unless you're just doing "maintenance." Even then, deliver clear instructions! Question the stylist who casually muses, "I think we need to cut a few inches off the ends" before they start shearing away.

Don't be surprised if you suddenly feel a new, romantic side of yourself emerging. With vixen Venus whipping things up, you could tap into sultry powers that have lain dormant for too long—or possibly ones you haven't explored before.

Give some genuine thought to this question: What makes me feel sexy, magnetic and receptive to love? Keep drilling down with your exploration. Beauty and style are your sign's calling cards, but there's much more going on below the surface. Have you allowed these parts of yourself to have free rein before? By the time November 13 rolls around, you can start trotting out some new looks and attitudes in public. Before then, get to know them in your own private way.

Be extra aware of your people-pleasing reflexes, especially if they keep you from voicing your needs. If you've been twisting yourself into knots to keep the peace, this is your cosmic cue to practice the art of a guilt-free "no." This six-week cycle can help you reclaim your independence without sacrificing your natural grace. That might mean renegotiating boundaries in love, redefining a professional role or stepping away from connections that require you to play small.

Venus retrograde can stir up emotional waves, so lean into grounding self-care: nourishing meals, restorative sleep, consistent movement and plenty of hydration. While you can't control the actions of others, you can guard your energy and stand firm in your truth. By the time Venus stations direct on November 13, you'll emerge with a stronger sense of self-worth and the clarity to attract relationships, opportunities and beauty that reflect the very best of you.

2026 LIBRA

12 MONTH OVERVIEW

January MONTHLY HOROSCOPE

Home is where the magic (and the mayhem) is this January, Libra. With the Sun in Capricorn until the 19th, your fourth house of domesticity and emotional roots takes the spotlight. Time to cozy things up: redecorate, host friends or simply give yourself permission to hibernate with style. But don't think you can hide out for long—the Cancer full moon on the 3rd beams into your ambitious tenth house, pulling you onto center stage. A project could earn applause, or you may realize it's time for a career pivot. On the 18th, the Capricorn new moon pulls your focus back indoors. What foundations—at home and in your personal relationships—do you want to strengthen over the next six months? Venus and Mars, the celestial lovebirds, nestle together in Capricorn until the 17th, infusing your private life with warmth and even a little passion. After the 23rd, they sashay into Aquarius and your fifth house of romance and creativity. Translation? Fun is back on the agenda. Start booking concert tickets, pick up your paintbrush/guitar/poetry journal. Flirt shamelessly and see who nibbles. The Sun joins the Aquarius party on the 19th, supercharging your flamboyant side. Who cares what people think? You're ready to take up space without apology. And while life heats up socially, your inner world gets a tune-up, too. On the 2nd, wounded healer Chiron turns direct in Aries, smoothing over relationship bumps and reminding you that balance takes practice. Then on the 26th, dreamweaver Neptune floats back into Aries for a 13-year stay, elevating love into a spiritual journey. Get ready for partnerships that are less about pretty appearances and more about profound connection.

February MONTHLY HOROSCOPE

What lights you up, Libra? February is your invitation to create, play and love boldly as the radiant Sun powers through Aquarius and your expressive fifth house until the 18th. Where do you want to take a risk—with your art, your heart, or both? Now's the time! The playful Leo full moon on the 1st beams into your eleventh house of community, bringing a group project to completion or spotlighting shifts in your social circle. Then, on February 17, the Aquarius new moon arrives as a dramatic solar eclipse—the first here since 2018—just as the Year of the Fire Horse begins. A romance could heat up, or a passion project might surge forward faster than expected. Until February 10, Venus shimmers in Aquarius, boosting your charm and magnetism. Afterward, she glides into Pisces and your sixth house, turning daily routines into rituals of beauty and care. Saturn re-enters Aries on February 13, starting a two-year cycle in your partnership zone. Relationships may feel weightier, but the bonds you forge now can be built to last. Valentine's Day follows with the Capricorn moon, encouraging gestures that are heartfelt and grounded, even if understated. Use Pisces season starting on the 18th to refine your daily routines. Streamline, simplify, and bring beauty into your small habits. Mercury retrograde from February 26 to March 20 could scramble schedules, so protect your peace by double-checking details. Reintroduce past practices that kept you grounded—like a fitness class, meal prep, or journaling ritual—and watch them work wonders now.

March MONTHLY HOROSCOPE

Streamline your routines—or create a new workflow if life has slipped into chaos. Your spring training begins early as the Sun, Mercury retrograde, driven Mars and a Pisces new moon (on the 18th) activate your sixth house of health, habits and daily work. What systems need fine-tuning so your life runs more smoothly? Start with the basics: clear boundaries, neat schedules and realistic goals. The total lunar (full moon) eclipse in Virgo on the 3rd beams into your twelfth house of closure and healing. You may feel called to release a lingering situation, end a draining cycle or finally take a break from pushing yourself so hard. Whew! Energizer Mars sails into Pisces for a six-week stay on March 2, energizing your wellness sector. Channel this drive into exercise, healthier habits and productive routines—but don't push yourself so hard you burn out. Love gets a booster shot after March 6, when Venus enters Aries and your seventh house of partnerships. Relationships heat up quickly, and new commitments may form. On the 10th, no-limits Jupiter wraps a four-month retrograde in Cancer and your tenth house of career. Professional momentum picks up and long-delayed opportunities come back around. Are you ready to step into a bigger role? The Sun enters Aries at the spring equinox on March 20, spotlighting your relationship zone. Mercury stations direct the same day, clearing three foggy weeks of miscommunication. Partnerships of all kinds move forward, and you'll feel ready to collaborate with clarity and confidence. Make it a double, Libra!

April MONTHLY HOROSCOPE

Partnerships take the spotlight, Libra! The glowing Sun sails through Aries and your seventh house until the 19th, highlighting relationships of all stripes. Where do you need more balance, clarity or compromise? Be proactive and reset the scales with nakedly honest conversations. On April 1, the Libra full moon beams into your sign, spotlighting your individuality and putting you front and center. A personal project could peak or you may decide to make a defining move. Fiery Mars storms into Aries on the 9th, ramping up both passion and conflict in partnerships. Use this intensity to address issues head-on instead of letting resentment build. The new moon in Aries on the 17th brings fresh opportunities in your relationship sector, whether through untapped alliances or deeper commitments. When the Sun moves into Taurus on the 19th, your eighth house of intimacy and shared resources takes focus, inviting concrete connections and transformative bonds. Venus joins the steady Taurus Sun until April 24, adding heat and harmony to romance. Then comes the cosmic shake-up: On the 25th, disruptive Uranus leaves Taurus after seven years and rockets into Gemini until 2033. With your ninth house of travel, learning and perspective now activated, expect paradigm shifts in how you grow, explore and share your wisdom with the world. Relocation plans may take shape quickly for some Libras out there!

May MONTHLY HOROSCOPE

Nothing superficial for you this May, Libra! Until the 20th, the Taurus Sun works its magic in your eighth house of intimacy, shared resources and transformation, spicing up the vibe. Your vulnerability is a sexy superpower. On the 1st, the Scorpio full moon beams into your money sector, forcing a reality check about how you're earning, spending or investing your energy. Ditch the pricey subscriptions and low-energy situationships. On the 6th, Pluto turns retrograde in Aquarius and your creativity corner until October 15, pushing you to review how you express passion, joy and artistry. The quarter moon on the 10th highlights this, too: Mother's Day could mean karaoke in the living room, painting with your kids or another playful ritual that brings art into family time. On the 16th, the Taurus new supermoon opens doors in your intimacy zone, offering a fresh slate in joint ventures or personal bonds. Gemini season begins on the 20th, blasting open your ninth house of adventure. Book a trip, enroll in that workshop—the further from home, the better. Until the 18th, Venus tours Gemini and your ninth house, spicing up romance with someone from a different culture or sparking chemistry with a long-distance love interest. Then, Venus moves into Cancer and your career zone while Mars powers into Taurus and your passion sector. Power couple pursuits heat up and single Libras could meet their match through work. The month wraps with the Sagittarius blue full moon on the 31st, spotlighting your communication zone. Drop that podcast episode, hit publish on the essay, or finally say the thing you've been rehearsing in your head.

June MONTHLY HOROSCOPE

Adventure beckons this month, Libra, as the Sun blazes through Gemini and your ninth house of exploration, learning and expansion until the 21st. Feed your wanderlust and say yes to experiences that broaden your worldview. The June 14 Gemini new moon—the second supermoon in a rare three-part series—lands in this zone, inviting you to launch travel plans, enroll in a course or publish your ideas. Meanwhile, Mars powers through Taurus and your eighth house until June 28, intensifying intimacy, finances and personal transformation. On June 19, "wounded healer" Chiron enters Taurus for a three-month preview of its 2027-2034 stay. Since 2018, Chiron has tested your closest partnerships, pushing you to balance independence with commitment. This summer's focus shifts to shared resources and vulnerability, urging you to heal old wounds around trust. On June 21, the Sun slides into Cancer and your tenth house, just in time for the solstice and Father's Day. Recognition could arrive from authority figures or family members—an affirmation of your hard work. In love, Venus lingers in Cancer until the 13th, boosting your professional magnetism and making career connections sparkle. Then she struts into Leo and your eleventh house, igniting romance through friendships and group activities. Get ready for liftoff! Jupiter rockets into Leo and your eleventh house of community and future visions on June 30, a cycle that lasts until July 2027. Collaborations, networking and friendships could catapult you into new opportunities. Surround yourself with people who expand your worldview. The month ends with the Capricorn full moon on June 29 in your fourth house of home and family. A domestic project or emotional matter could reach resolution, but with Mercury retrograde in Cancer beginning the same day, be cautious about major decisions over the next three weeks.

July MONTHLY HOROSCOPE

Keep rising up the ladder, slowly and deliberately, Libra. With the Sun traveling through Cancer and your ambitious tenth house until the 22nd—and Mercury retrograde here until the 23rd—your professional path is under revision. Old projects, mentors or opportunities may circle back, giving you a chance to refine your goals with greater clarity. The Cancer new moon (a supermoon) on the 14th could mark a major milestone for your work or public image. Step forward thoughtfully: Visibility is valuable, but only when you're aligned with what you want to be known for. On July 7, mystical Neptune pivots retrograde in Aries, beginning five months of introspection in your partnership zone. Then, on the 26th, taskmaster Saturn also turns retrograde here, doubling down on the call to re-examine your closest bonds. Not everything needs to be locked in—this is about assessing what strengthens you and what drains you. Meanwhile, motivator Mars energizes Gemini and your ninth house all month, inspiring travel, study and cross-cultural connections. Feed your curiosity and pursue adventures that expand your worldview. When Leo season kicks off on the 22nd, your focus pivots to friendships and group projects. Venus in Virgo from the 9th highlights behind-the-scenes healing and closure work, while Mercury's direct turn on the 23rd smooths professional communication. The real shift comes on July 26, when the lunar North Node enters Aquarius and your fifth house for the first time in nearly two decades. Through March 2028, your destiny is tied to love, creativity and living with more joy. July wraps with fireworks on the 29th as the Sun and Jupiter unite in Leo for their annual "Day of Miracles," fueling community-driven wins. Simultaneously, the Aquarius full moon lights up your fifth house, delivering a creative or romantic breakthrough just in time for August!

August MONTHLY HOROSCOPE

Who gets true VIP status in your world, Libra? The Leo Sun is shining in your community zone until the 22nd, revealing true friends. On August 3, soothsayer Chiron pivots retrograde in Taurus and your eighth house of intimacy and shared resources, surfacing old trust issues or financial entanglements that need another look. This is your chance to renegotiate terms—emotional or monetary—so they feel equitable. Mars blasts into Cancer and your tenth house of ambition on the 11th, making you hungry for visibility. Polish that LinkedIn profile, pitch the project or take the floor at the team meeting. Just don't sprint so hard that you flame out before the finish line. Eclipse season kicks off on August 12 with a total solar eclipse in Leo—the first here since 2019—sparking revelations in your eleventh house of teamwork and tech. A groundbreaking project involving social justice or a disruptive industry could pull focus. With Venus, your ruler, gliding into Libra on the 6th, you've got no shortage of main-character energy. Expect to turn heads in business and love, but save your final rose for generous partners only. On the 22nd, Virgo season shifts the vibe into your twelfth house of reflection. Go analog more often, close some tabs. You need to recharge before your birthday spotlight next month. On the 28th, the Pisces lunar eclipse lands in your sixth house of wellness, catalyzing big changes in your daily rhythms. A new supplement, biohack or wellness routine could actually stick this time. August wraps with cosmic fireworks on the 31st as Jupiter in Leo harmonizes with Saturn in Aries, blending risk and structure. A partnership—romantic, creative or professional—could crystallize into something both exciting and built to last.

September MONTHLY HOROSCOPE

Ready for a reset, Libra? September begins with the Virgo Sun tucked into your twelfth house of rest and reflection, nudging you to slow down before your birthday season kicks off. Think: yoga retreats, writing poetry in cafés, reclaiming your mornings with a slower ritual. Not that you'll come to a standstill. With ambitious Mars powering through Cancer and your tenth house of career until the 27th, professional opportunities heat up. Don't burn yourself out chasing every shiny lead. On the 10th, the Virgo new moon spotlights your twelfth house, encouraging you to release what's no longer serving you: a draining obligation, a digital time-suck or even an outdated belief. The same day, Uranus pivots retrograde in Gemini and your expansive ninth house, sparking a five-month review of your big-picture plans. Revisit a stalled venture or a pilgrimage you've been postponing. Seductive Venus (your ruling planet) lingers in your sign until the 10th, giving you charm to spare. Use it for everything from first dates to negotiating deals. Then the enchanting planet moves into Scorpio and your second house, whetting your appetite for luxury while softening your willpower. Put solid budgets in place, including an entertainment budget. You don't want to leave spending up to chance, especially since Venus turns retrograde from October 3 to November 13. (You're on notice!) The fall equinox on the 22nd is your cosmic new year as the Sun moves into Libra. You're back in your element and ready to pursue novel experiences, especially ones that double as growth opportunities. On the 17th, Chiron slips into Aries and your relationship zone, helping you heal old wounds around commitment and partnerships. And by the Aries full moon on the 26th, you could reach a turning point in love or business. Negotiations, proposals or a fresh chapter in your personal life are on the horizon.

October MONTHLY HOROSCOPE

Press reset, Libra. On October 3, Venus—your galactic guardian—spins retrograde, backing through Scorpio and your money house until the 25th, then moonwalking into Libra and your first house of identity until November 13. Cash flow could get tight and your confidence may need a tune-up. But this isn't a setback—it's a makeover in progress. Where are you ready to stop overspending or overgiving? What parts of your look, brand or vibe deserve a bold refresh? Use this six-week cycle to make necessary adjustments. There's lots to celebrate, too, like birthday season! The Sun beams through

Libra until the 23rd, spotlighting your personal goals and giving you cosmic clearance to put yourself first. The Libra new moon on the 10th is a pivotal day for setting your Q4 intentions. What personal goals do you want to achieve before 2026 wraps? Moreover, who can help you bring them to life? Make-it-happen Mars blazes through Leo and your teamwork zone, making it easy to draw support. Easy does it, though. Overcommitting to every invite could leave you drained, so pick the circles that feed your spirit. October 15 ends Pluto's retrograde in Aquarius and your creativity zone, reviving momentum around romance, art or even parenting matters. Then on the 23rd, the Sun slides into Scorpio and your money sector, the same day Venus aligns with the Sun in a rare Cazimi. You'll see clearly what (and who) is worth your investment. An old source of money could wake up again. Heads-up: Mercury retrograde begins on the 24th in Scorpio, so transactions and budgeting could get messy. Keep receipts, and pause before any big splurge. A relationship or financial bond could hit a turning point near the Taurus full moon on the 26th. Commit or quit? You won't be keen to straddle any fences as October draws to a close.

November MONTHLY HOROSCOPE

Know your value, Libra! With the Scorpio Sun energizing your second house of income and values until the 22nd, money matters and self-worth are front and center. But tread carefully in the first half of the month. Until the 13th, messenger Mercury is retrograde in Scorpio AND, more consequentially, your ruler Venus is backing up through Libra. This could bring budgeting blunders or second-guessing about your personal path forward. Use this time to reassess: Are you respecting your limits at work and in relationships? You may need to reset boundaries—or reorient people to the new, self-loving you. On the 9th, the Scorpio new moon refreshes your financial picture. A raise, new revenue stream or smarter plan could be on the table. Go-getter Mars powers through Leo until the 25th, energizing collaborations. Your calendar could fill with events, group projects and opportunities to network. Inspiring new allies are everywhere! Protect your bandwidth and pick your teams wisely. The social buzz continues to surge once Sagittarius season begins on the 22nd. With your third house of communication and local activities alight, you won't have to travel far from home to find your entertainment fix—not to mention your fans. Write, podcast, step up as an influencer on the socials. People want to hear what you have to say! Opportunity rolls in from afar with the Gemini full moon—a potent supermoon—on the 24th. With your global ninth house in its beams, you could book some pre-holiday travel or connect to an audience far from home base. Make time for rest and reflection after the 25th. Hotheaded Mars cools out in Virgo and your restorative twelfth house for the remainder of the year. Clearing the decks (in between all those parties and international engagements), will set you up for a powerful start to 2027.

December MONTHLY HOROSCOPE

Call it a holiday whirlwind, Libra—you're busier than most this December, but it's exactly the kind of buzz you thrive on. The Sagittarius Sun lights up your hyper-mobile third house until the 21st, keeping you in constant motion. On the 8th, the new moon in Sagittarius illuminates the perfect adventure buddies. Race off on a quick getaway and livestream along the way. Two outer planets—strategic Saturn and visionary Neptune— wrap up five-month retrogrades in Aries on the 10th and 12th, respectively, bringing clarity to your closest partnerships. Whether in love or business, you'll know which bonds can truly go the distance. With motivator Mars recharging its batteries Virgo and your twelfth house all month, you may have some energy dips to contend with. But your subconscious is alive with insights. Carve out quiet space for reflective journaling and dates with the muse. Venus re-enters Scorpio on the 4th, adding a touch of luxe and romance to your holiday season. Just watch your spending! Jupiter turns retrograde in Leo on the 12th. Scale back to meaningful gatherings with people who inspire you. You'll be ready for some hardcore nesting once Capricorn season and the solstice arrive on the 21st. Cozy traditions and bonding with your inner circle win out over chasing every invitation. Take a bow on the 23rd when the Cancer full supermoon manifests a professional milestone or an achievement worth celebrating. NYE networking could set you up with opportunities for early 2027. A soulful NYE is in store as the Capricorn Sun syncs with Mars in Virgo. Ring in the New Year at a candlelight meditation, concert or anywhere that elevates your spirit.

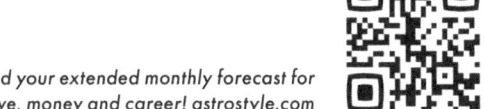

Read your extended monthly forecast for life, love, money and career! astrostyle.com

SCORPIO IN 2026

| ALL THE PLANETS IN SCORPIO IN 2026 | YOUR 2026 HOROSCOPE | TOP 5 THEMES FOR SCORPIO IN 2026 | LOVE HOROSCOPE + LUCKY DATES | MONEY HOROSCOPE + LUCKY DATES |

Scorpio in 2026

Your year of:
TRAVEL, SUPPORTIVE ROUTINES, ANCESTRAL HEALING

GIVE YOURSELF ROOM TO ROAM, SCORPIO!

In 2026, the wider world beckons. Say yes to adventures that push you past your comfort zone. Each leap feeds into your bigger goals, and before long, doors you never imagined stepping through start swinging open. For your change-resistant sign, this can be unmooring. Anchor yourself through daily rituals, repeatable routines and steady habits. These become the scaffolding that holds everything (including you!) together. Creative momentum that you build upon this year can provide exciting shifts around home and career. By December, you'll be standing taller on a foundation you actually trust—success that feels expansive AND sustainable.

THE PLANETS IN Scorpio

THE SUN
OCT 23–NOV 22

Happy birthday season! With the Sun in your sign, you're clear to take chances, chase fresh adventures, and command the spotlight.

NEW MOON
NOV 9
2:02AM; 16°53'

Happy bonus New Year! Set your intentions for the next six months, then take a brave step forward. Your fans await!

FULL MOON
MAY 1
1:23PM; 11°21'

Manifestation moment! Your work of the past six months bears fruit. Celebrate your progress and harvest the rewards.

MERCURY
SEP 30–DEC 6
RETROGRADE IN SCORPIO:
OCT 24–NOV 13

Hold court! When charismatic Mercury zips through your sign, your social status soars. Work the room, make connections. Keep your commitments realistic to avoid overpromising—especially during the retrograde, which could scramble signals or resurface old drama.

VENUS
SEP 10–OCT 25
DEC 4–31
RETROGRADE IN SCORPIO:
OCT 3–25

Love is in the air! When the galactic glamazon struts through your sign, your powers of seduction skyrocket. Irresistible charm, luxe tastes, and flirtatious vibes abound—just keep an eye on your budget. During the retrograde, old flames could make a dramatic return.

Scorpio in 2026
HIGHLIGHTS

ADVENTURE CALLS: JUPITER IN CANCER UNTIL JUNE 30
Pack your bags, Scorpio! Peripatetic Jupiter is soaring through Cancer and your ninth house of travel, study, mediamaking and general life expansion until June 30. This is your permission slip to think (and move) big. Jet off on that bucket-list trip, apply for the fellowship, pitch your story to a broader audience. Personal growth will be seismic this year, whether through traditional education or experiential learning. The key is saying yes to opportunities that stretch you—even if they feel a little intimidating at first.

DAILY ROUTINES GET A SOULFUL UPGRADE: SATURN AND NEPTUNE IN ARIES
Disciplined Saturn and devotional Neptune team up in Aries for two years starting February 13. With your systematic sixth house in their crosshairs, the little things count mightily. Saturn wants structure—consistent workouts, clean eating, healthy boundaries around stress management. Fluid Neptune calls for creativity and compassion. How can you weave healing and purpose into your day-to-day? Upgrade your tech tools, commit to regular exercise or swap the endless scroll for a morning meditation app. While effort is required, it's less about grinding and more about finding rhythms that nourish you long-term.

PARTNERSHIP SHAKE-UP: URANUS ENTERS GEMINI APRIL 25
On April 25, Uranus exits Taurus after seven years of rocking your relationship zone. You've had your fair share of romantic wildcards, surprise endings and unconventional partnerships since 2018. Now Uranus dives into Gemini for a seven-year tour of your eighth house of intimacy, shared resources and transformation. Expect breakthroughs around finances (investments, loans, inheritances) and a deeper excavation into what it means to truly be vulnerable. Joint ventures may take off unexpectedly, while old fears around trust could finally dissolve.

MERCURY RETROGRADES: PAUSE BEFORE YOU LEAP
Mercury turns retrograde in water signs three times in 2026, giving you time to revisit passions, big plans and personal goals. From February 26 to March 20, the rewind moves through Pisces and your fifth house of love, creativity and self-expression. An old flame could reappear or you might dust off a project that once lit you up. From June 29 to July 23, Mercury backtracks in Cancer and your ninth house of travel, education and

publishing. Trips may stall or you could return to a course of study or idea you'd shelved. The final retrograde, October 24 to November 13, lands in Scorpio and your first house of self. With Venus also retrograde in Libra, you'll be rethinking how you come across to others. Are people misreading your messaging, style and signals? This is an opportunity to refine your front-facing presentation, but wait until after November 13 for any major updates.

MILESTONE MOONS: SCORPIO LUNATIONS IN MAY AND NOVEMBER
Circle May 1 for the Scorpio full moon, your annual mirror moment. Something you've outgrown could finally fade out, making space for the next chapter. Let go with ritual—journal, burn a list, write a letter that you never send. Then on November 9, the Scorpio new moon arrives during Venus and Mercury retrogrades. A clean slate, yes, but one best approached with curiosity, not contracts. Soft-launch your ideas, plant seeds in private and let your intentions marinate. By the time the retrograde fog lifts after November 13, you'll know exactly which dreams are worth watering.

VENUS RETROGRADE: ROMANCE AND IDENTITY REVIEW
Venus, planet of love, beauty and values will be retrograde for six weeks this fall, which is an especially poignant cycle for you. From October 3 to October 25, Venus cycles back through Scorpio, bringing some disruptive waves in your closest relationships. Is there enough room for you to be yourself with the people you love? Are you feeling seen, cherished and appreciated? Before you start hurling accusations, it might be up to YOU to set better boundaries—or show up more consistently so that others know that you care. Then from October 25 to November 13, Venus slips into Libra, guiding you into reflection mode and encouraging rest, creativity and healing. Consider this a chance to reclaim your magnetism and update your standards. Venus repeats her retrograde pattern every 8 years (minus 2°), so this one flashes you back to fall 2018. Who were you loving then? How did you express yourself? What did you believe you deserved? Use this retrograde to honor your evolution and call in relationships that meet you at your new level of power.

DESTINY SHIFTS: NODES ENTER AQUARIUS AND LEO JULY 26
Until July 26, the South Node in Virgo and North Node in Pisces spotlight your community and creativity, asking you to balance group involvement with personal expression. Midsummer, the Nodes pivot into Aquarius and Leo, pulling focus toward

your home and career. The next 20 months may ask: How do you balance private life with public ambition? This is the cycle where you could transform your role in both spaces.

TRUTHS HIT HOME: PLUTO RETROGRADE IN AQUARIUS

Your ruling planet Pluto turns retrograde in Aquarius and your domestic sector from May 6 to October 15, spotlighting family dynamics, home base and ancestral healing. With the karmic Lunar North Node flowing through Aquarius after July 26, you'll be inspired to shift whatever feels misaligned. This may be the year you uncover stories from your lineage, renovate your space or confront patterns you've inherited. Therapy, genealogy research and a major declutter could feel downright cathartic. The more you clear, the stronger your foundation becomes.

Love

SCORPIO 2026 FORECAST

As hard as it can be for you to NOT control the narrative of your love story, try, Scorpio, try. This year the stars want you to swap a bit of strategy for spontaneity. 2026 opens on a playful note with Venus and Mars mingling in Capricorn until January 17, lighting up your third house of communication. Flirty banter, witty DMs and local adventures keep things humming. Adding to the fun? No-limits Jupiter is on a pleasure cruise through Cancer and your adventurous ninth house until June 30. Love thrives when you break routines! Say yes to new experiences that expand your horizons like overseas baecations, long-distance relationships or cross-cultural dating.

Romance heats up just in time for Valentine's Day. Venus slips into Pisces and your fifth house of passion on February 10, followed by lusty Mars from March 2 to April 9. You could meet a "person of interest" through creative pursuits, parties or playful encounters. Good reason to sign up for that life-drawing class or indoor pickleball league! In relationships, this cycle revives fun and attraction. Here's where your planning powers (and charm!) can be utilized. Score those VIP concert tickets or a two-top reservation at the restaurant with the three-month waitlist.

With the fateful North Node in Pisces and your fifth house until July 26, destined developments are on tap. This cycle, which began on January 11, 2025, could usher in milestone moments that feel scripted by fate. The fertile fifth house rules children, romance and creative expression, so some Scorpios may be talking baby names or planning engagements. Others might find themselves swept up in a whirlwind romance that inspires art, music or a future memoir. Across the aisle, the karmic South Node in Virgo pushes you to stop polling friends or family for approval. Maybe your new flame isn't "type-approved" by your crew—or maybe you're realizing you've been editing yourself to fit in. What you DON'T need for your love life this year is a focus group.

A game-changing moment arrives near April 25, when wild-card Uranus exits Taurus and your relationship house after seven bumpy years. Expect the dust to finally settle around old partnerships—breakups, reconciliations, or even just the stop-start drama that's kept you guessing. But this isn't your cue to release the reins. Now, Uranus darts into Gemini and side-spins through your erotic eighth house until 2033. Sex could become more exploratory; intimacy, less about control and more about raw honesty. New ways to share financial resources (or separate them for the sake of peace) emerge. Let yourself experiment!

Venus makes her annual visit to Scorpio starting on September 10—and this year she's blessing you with her presence twice (re-entering on December 4)! Excitement crackles, along with red-hot chemistry when the love planet cruises through your sign. You're in the driver's seat so make your desires clear.

And don't stall, because from October 3 to 25 the love planet will flip retrograde in your sign. This could bring a round of romantic déjà vu. Exes creep out of the social media woodwork or your S.O. pushes every one of your buttons. Instead of deploying your famous sting, take a step back. The full retrograde lasts until November 13, with the second half taking place in Libra and your boundary-blurring twelfth house. During that time, Mercury will also be retrograde in Scorpio (October 24 to November 13), muddling communications. Suffice it to say, it's best NOT to make any binding romantic decisions between October 3 and November 13!

Retrograde season might stir the ghosts of lovers past, but come December 4, Venus returns to Scorpio in full power until January 7, 2027. Whatever detours your love life takes this fall, you'll get a clean slate and a clear-eyed view about how to wrap 2026. You won't just be ending the year on a sultry note, you'll be ending it on your own terms, wiser, sexier and ready to write the next chapter of your love story without apology!

Money & Career

SCORPIO 2026 FORECAST

Strategist? Storyteller? Quiet empire-builder? However you label it, Scorpio, 2026 pulls you out of hiding and onto influential terrain. Lucky Jupiter is soaring through Cancer and your ninth house of growth and global ventures until June 30, expanding your appetite for freedom—and for meaningful work. Media or education projects could take off under this enterprising influence. You may travel for business, court international clients or blend your expertise into a new offering that reaches far beyond your current circle. Even if you're working within a larger company, this is an intrapreneurial moment. Innovate from the inside out.

Starting February 13, Saturn and Neptune team up in Aries and your practical sixth house, ushering in a two-year cycle of structure-meets-imagination. Reevaluate how you work—your systems, routines and the habits that shape your results. Are you holding yourself to impossible standards in some areas while letting others slide? Saturn helps you streamline and professionalize, while Neptune keeps your approach inspired. "Imagineering" is your keyword: Use creativity to design processes that make your day-to-day both productive and fulfilling.

Meanwhile, financial experimentation is in the stars. On April 25, innovative Uranus rockets into Gemini and your eighth house of shared resources, investments and long-term wealth. You may find yourself drawn to new forms of capital—tech stocks, crypto, startups or AI-related ventures. This is a brilliant period for innovation around money, but it comes with a caveat: volatility. Not every "next big thing" will pan out. Hedge your bets and diversify before taking major leaps. This same transit can awaken fresh perspectives around intimacy and trust, both emotional and financial.

Midyear, your professional life gets a major boost. Abundant Jupiter enters Leo on June 30 for a 13-month tour of your tenth house of career and reputation. Don't be surprised if you suddenly feel ready to chase a "BHAG" (big, hairy, audacious goal). This cycle brings opportunities for promotion, leadership or launching a venture under your own name. The world's watching, but you're not freaking out, Scorpio. Nope—you're ready to deliver.

Integrity must anchor your ambition. On July 26, the karmic South Node also enters Leo for a 20-month stay, reminding you that HOW you achieve success matters as much as the victory itself. Some Scorpios could part ways with an organization that no longer aligns with their values, or build something better from the ground up.

Financial reality takes center stage this fall, when money-minded Venus turns retrograde in Scorpio from October 3 to 25. Tighten your belt, review your budget and resist impulse spending. A short pause in luxury purchases or speculative risks could free up funds for what truly counts.

TOP 5 THEMES FOR Scorpio in 2026

1	2	3	4	5
ALIGN BODY AND SOUL	BROADEN YOUR HORIZONS	REDEFINE POWER AND TRUST	CREATE SANCTUARY	RECLAIM YOUR MAGIC

1 ALIGN BODY AND SOUL

NEPTUNE IN ARIES
JANUARY 26, 2026–MARCH 23, 2039

SATURN IN ARIES
FEBRUARY 13, 2026–APRIL 12, 2028

What happens when the cosmic dreamer meets the planetary taskmaster in your sixth house of health, habits and hustle? You're about to find out, Scorpio. (Spoiler alert: Drop and give us twenty…down dogs.) A rare convergence of structured Saturn and spiritual Neptune is coming to Aries and your systematic sixth house for a multi-year stay. Starting in early 2026, your whole approach to wellness, productivity and purpose is set to evolve.

While Saturn and Neptune have radically different agendas, they each bring an essential lesson to this new chapter of your life. Neptune serves up mindfulness, meditation and a strong urge to dial back the stress. Meanwhile, Saturn charges you up with discipline, strapping on the weighted vest and getting you out for walks, strength training and plant-based meals.

In 2025, you got a taste of this clean, green agenda. Idealistic Neptune waded into Aries from March 30 to October 22, while Saturn took a brief spin there from May 24 to September 1. But the real work (and magic) begins in 2026, as both planets return to the Ram's realm for their longer treks: Neptune for thirteen years (until 2039), Saturn for two more years (until April 12, 2028). This is a rare opportunity to tune into the subtle cues of both your body and soul—and start designing a lifestyle that honors them.

February 20 marks a major milestone! For the first time since 1702 (seriously), Saturn and Neptune form an exact conjunction at 0° Aries. This is the only time they'll make a direct hit during their parallel tour through the realm of the Ram. And it might be one of 2026's most defining moments for how you care for your body, build your schedule and pursue meaningful work. While Neptune inspires a soulful vision for your daily routines, Saturn asks, "So what's the plan?" Together, they challenge you to turn lofty ideals into actual habits, and to streamline systems so you're not always running on fumes. Get ready for an early wave of spring cleaning and spring training.

This might feel like a seismic shift, especially coming off Neptune's foggy, fifteen-year float through Pisces and your passionate, glamorous fifth house. As the focus downshifts to a more pragmatic energy, you might feel a temporary sense of sadness, the way one does when a wildly indulgent vacation is coming to an end. While it's true that a hedonistic era is winding down, you will quickly grow to enjoy this new phase. Imagine waking up every day with energy, purpose and the sense that your time is being spent on what truly matters.

Sure, this will require discipline—that's Saturn's stock in trade. There will be days when Neptune's influence makes you want to drift, dream and float through your hours. That's fine! Just don't get lost in the mist. Saturn is here to help you build a container for all of Neptune's mindfulness quests. Whether it's a new morning ritual, biohacking for optimized health or a more inspiring way to work, every part of you is craving alignment. While your intuition is always strong, pay equal attention to physical signs. Your body will send messages if you're veering off course. Listen—and respond—with self-compassion, not cruelty or punishment.

Some Scorpios will develop a truly powerful relationship with health care practitioners this year. Saturn wants everything backed by blood tests and X-rays while Neptune taps into the spiritual side of healing. You might do well to look for a functional MD who has a traditional med school background but focuses on natural and preventative techniques before immediately writing you a pharmaceutical prescription. And hey, Scorpio, there's nothing wrong with needing a Western medicine solution! Regardless, you can tune your body by reducing stress, exercising more, eating clean—and supplementing with things like massage and acupuncture.

If burnout's been creeping in, Neptune's long tour through your sixth house urges you to create a more fluid and restorative rhythm. Beware the temptation to sacrifice too much in the name of service. Boundaries are essential when it comes to giving, and that goes for every area of life. Just because you can do it all doesn't mean you should. (Office martyr or family doormat? NOT a good look!) Saturn will help you radar in on where your time is best spent, and which responsibilities can be handed off, restructured or released altogether.

This year is also powerful for reevaluating your workflow. If your job (or an aspect of it) isn't lighting you up, Neptune may start flashing you signs toward a more fulfilling path. You might feel called to healing, teaching or creative service work. But Neptune doesn't always show the full picture. Before you leap, consult Saturn. Is this idea sustainable once the initial buzz wears off? Do you have the support, the skills, the financial plan to make it viable? Saturn's presence reminds you: There's no rush. Let the vision ripen. Do your research. Lay the groundwork.

You may feel a tug-of-war between dreaming big and dealing with the daily grind. But this tension is precisely where your power lies. Structure doesn't have to stifle your imagination, Scorpio. In fact, it can liberate it. The more efficiently you manage your time and energy, the more space you'll have for the pursuits that nourish your spirit. That's the sweet spot! A life that feels both purposeful and pleasurable.

If you've struggled to stick with routines, Saturn can help you lock into habits that actually last. And with Neptune in the mix, those habits might include journaling, breathwork or meditation, along with your fitness and nutrition goals. Keep your system flexible enough to adapt to changing moods and needs. You're a water sign, after all. Rigidity isn't your thing.

By the time Saturn exits Aries in 2028, your lifestyle could be optimized in some truly impressive way. You'll have a clearer sense of how to protect your energy, pace your efforts and pour your gifts into work that truly serves a higher purpose. That's what this rare planetary pairing is here to teach you, Scorpio. Don't rush the process. Let it unfold, one intentional step at a time.

2 ALIGN BODY AND SOUL

JUPITER IN CANCER
JUNE 9, 2026–JUNE 30, 2026

That hermit life? Forget about slipping into any such vibe, Scorpio. Jupiter is only halfway complete with its thirteen-month journey through Cancer and your ninth house of travel, expansion, and bold new frontiers. Since June 9, 2025, the red-spotted titan has been luring you to parts unknown. If you start 2026 with an incurable case of wanderlust, you're right on cosmic schedule.

While Jupiter soars through Cancer until June 30, you can gain altitude in every corner of your life. The ninth house is Jupiter's happiest place in the zodiac AND it's "exalted" in

Cancer, which essentially means this is the most powerful place it can be. There's really only one direction to look in now and that is up.

As a water sign, you can appreciate Jupiter in Cancer for even more reasons. This transit's nurturing waves can help you feel (and stay) in your intuitive element—all while you push past your edges and take a few gambles. No one loves a privacy policy more than you, Scorpio, but has your personal firewall become impenetrable? With live-out-loud Jupiter in this candid zone, you could soften some of those barriers and welcome a few new "strangers" into your fold.

Already know more people than you can keep up with? Radar in on a handful of MVPs and see them a bit more regularly. Bonus if they live in a foreign country (or have a vacation home there) or share your travel style.

You'll always need your alone time, of course—and we'd never deny you that. Hang on to a few social survival tactics. Limit marathon meetups, build in downtime between events, and call in a trusty plus-one when you need backup. Chances are you'll be having too much fun to stay steeped in awkwardness for long.

Not sure what to focus on? Follow your curiosity! Or keep following it. As 2026 begins, there's a good chance you've already dipped your toes in international waters or expanded your mind with new philosophies. Both Jupiter and the ninth house are associated with broadening your horizons—with travel, education, experiences and entrepreneurial projects.

Apply for that Real ID, passport or visa and get ready to roll. Work could take you to far-flung destinations. Think: global summits, creative conferences or off-sites in cities you've never set foot in before. The ideas you bring home could evolve into your next big thing, especially if you draw from your cultural roots or ancient wisdom traditions.

Learning and teaching are also top of the syllabus now. Maybe you're halfway through a degree program, or you've got a podcast brewing on a topic close to your heart. If you've got a story to tell, share it. This is prime time to pitch a book, film or project that crosses borders—

literally or metaphorically. Don't underestimate the power of your hard-won expertise. People want to learn from you.

Of course, every Jupiter cycle has its lessons. Truth bombs detonate easily when Jupiter's in the no-holds-barred ninth house, and your signature sting can do harm. Fortunately, in sensitive Cancer, Jupiter adds a softening filter. Save some of those scorching hot takes for "internal debriefings" with the BFFs you trust won't spill any tea. One of your greatest lessons in the first half of the year could be refining your delivery.

If you're a secretive Scorpio, the opposite may occur. Jupiter in Cancer can spur a round of refreshing realness. Unlock a few hidden parts of yourself and make an effort to share more personal details with trusted friends and family. Vulnerability hangovers may happen, but they'll pass. Drop the mask and invite people in who see and love all of you, not just the polished version.

JUPITER IN LEO
JUNE 30, 2026 – JULY 26, 2027

Warmup time is over, Scorpio! You're headed for a much bigger league starting this June 30, when "more is more" Jupiter ascends to the top of your chart. With the abundant planet in Leo and your tenth house of career ambition and prestige until July 26, 2027, you could hit a new professional peak.

If you're ready to strike out on your own, Jupiter's entrepreneurial energy can help you launch a venture that puts your name on the map. As the planet of publishing and international relations, that might involve producing some sort of media or working with an overseas supplier to produce goods. Not quite ready to exit the company life? Think "intrapreneurially" and pitch ideas to the C-suite. Jupiter supplies a powerful nudge to climb the ranks into a more prestigious role—one that provides the authority and independence you crave.

Not every opportunity will land in your lap once Jupiter leaves Cancer. While it hustles through Leo and your industrious tenth house, you'll need to show up and stake your claim. Polish that pitch deck, update your portfolio and tap your network for influential introductions.

Some Scorpios could take on a leadership role, becoming "the face of" a major project or public campaign. Even if you're more comfortable pulling strings behind the scenes, you can't stay hidden forever. Jupiter wants the world to see what you're truly capable of!

Warning: Life may feel a touch "Game of Thrones" during this thirteen-month cycle. Jupiter is a high-roller and in Leo, it wants you to be the King/Queen/Royal of (fill in the blank). Good thing the Scorpio spirit is a competitive one. (Just make sure you don't veer into cutthroat terrain.) While Jupiter pours Miracle-Gro on your goals, you may become so focused on achieving a result that you forget to pay attention to anything else. That's a recipe for burnout, o' obsessive one, so take breaks between all those breakthroughs. Travel could tie into your success story, too. You may take meetings in far-flung cities, lead international teams, or build a global client base. Craving an industry switch or next-level title? Consider working with a coach or mentor who's already climbed the mountain you want to scale. This is a once-in-12-years window to turn your ambitions into real power moves. Don't squander it! If you recently left corporate or took a break from the grind, you may find yourself lured back to an executive role in the second half of 2026.

No matter what you're up to, keep your game face on, Scorpio. You'll be spending more time than usual in the public eye. That may feel a bit unnerving for a sign who loves to keep certain cards close. But Jupiter's "full exposure" approach will push you to own your story. Got a skeleton or two rattling in the closet? Don't wait for someone else to expose it. Tell your truth on your own terms. Your confessions could turn you into an unlikely hero, earning you respect as a role model for authenticity.

This cycle is also a big one for your relationships with masculine energies—fathers, mentors, bosses, brothers or male colleagues. The tenth house rules this realm, and Jupiter's candid influence could bring long-overdue evolutions to how you relate. A no-holds-barred conversation may clear the air—and possibly reestablish boundaries with a man in your orbit. Trust that honesty now will set the stage for healthier, more supportive bonds down the road.

3 REDEFINE POWER AND TRUST

URANUS IN GEMINI
APRIL 25, 2026 – MAY 22, 2033

A chemistry experiment is bubbling, Scorpio, so put on your lab coat—maybe over some sexy lingerie. Starting April 25, iconoclast Uranus returns to Gemini for a seven-year run through your eighth house, the zone of money, power and sex. This arena happens to be your home turf, so even as every corner of your life feels ripe for transformation, you'll embrace this disruptive energy wholeheartedly.

You got a sneak peek of Uranus in Gemini last year, from July 7 to November 7, 2025, when the side-spinning planet did a quick preview tour through your eighth house. A few strange desires may have bubbled up then, ones you couldn't help but pursue. You longed for depth and intimacy, but also liberation from obligation. Does that sound like a paradox? It definitely is, and one that you have seven more years to learn how to navigate.

Buckle up for one of the most personally transformative cycles of your life. The eighth house is among the most soul-searching places in the zodiac. This zone governs sex, death, rebirth, power dynamics and the mysteries we usually tuck under the rug. It also rules spiritual bonding and joint ventures, emotional and financial alike. With boundary-busting Uranus zapping through this territory from April 25, 2026 until May 22, 2033, you'll be deconstructing a lot. Whew! Goodbye outdated relationship patterns. It's time to transform your approach to trust and merging.

Not that this will be a linear process. One moment, you might crave an all-consuming connection. The next? Space, autonomy and five devices on Do Not Disturb. That's the incongruity you'll be dancing with for most of the next decade: Gemini's thirst for freedom versus the eighth house's hunger for depth. This isn't cosmic purgatory. It's your invitation to create a new intimacy blueprint that honors both deep loyalty and your mental independence.

Forget the old scripts about control, silent expectations or trying to read someone's vibe like a classified file. Uranus in Gemini says: Speak your truth. And not just in relationships. This is your moment to bring forth the projects, passions and visions you've been quietly shaping. Enough behind-the-scenes strategizing. Uranus wants your work out in the

zeitgeist. Pitch that concept, post the article, publish the 'zine. Tell your story in the searing way that only a Scorpio can.

Vulnerability hangovers may be a regular thing—we know, we know. But here's the gift of Uranus in witty, curious Gemini: It helps you move through discomfort with humor and perspective. That intense moment you keep replaying? Turn it into a comedy sketch or an ironic song that is also hardcore relatable. When you lift the mask, Scorpio, you let people into your most endearing parts.

Financially, this transit could overhaul your relationship with wealth, especially any shared assets. Collaborative ventures with the right people could bring untold bounty. Meanwhile, financial entanglements that handcuff you to unreliable collaborators should get the snip. As a Scorpio, you're known for making smart investments and demanding clear agreements. This is no time to compromise on that! Make sure your money moves align with your values. Just resist the urge to rush. Uranus can make you impulsive and you need to read (and re-read) the fine print before committing to anything.

On a soul level, your inner world could go full sci-fi. The eighth house rules energetic exchanges, and with Uranus here, you may be drawn to tantra, somatic healing or deep shadow work. Psychic downloads and epiphanies could arrive regularly—but not necessarily when you're meditating. With Uranus in verbose, interactive Gemini, you could talk your way into the best possible strategies. Bring on the savvy sounding boards!

As secretive as the eighth house can be, Uranus in Gemini urges you to experiment with selective visibility. Let people see the parts you usually guard with barbed wire and a sly smirk. Ditch the all-or-nothing mindset. To foster deeper connection, you must let yourself be messy and in motion. One of the greatest gifts of this transit? The courage to show up in full color and evolve in plain sight. By 2033, you could emerge with a radically new understanding of love, trust and your own psychic power. But take it one breakthrough at a time. Start with a single stuck dynamic you're ready to shift—and if you can laugh at it along the way, you've already unlocked the next level.

4 CREATE SANCTUARY

LUNAR NODES IN LEO AND AQUARIUS
NORTH NODE IN AQUARIUS, SOUTH NODE IN LEO JULY 26, 2026–MARCH 26, 2028

Ready for a karmic deep dive, Scorpio? On July 26, 2026, the destiny-shaping North Node settles into Aquarius and your fourth house of home, family and roots until March 26, 2028. For the next 20 months, your growth edge will come from nurturing your foundations, even as your ambitions continue to call. Simultaneously, the South Node shifts into Leo, activating your tenth house of career and public image. The cosmic lesson? Like a towering oak, you can't rise to soaring heights without strong roots.

Since January 11, 2025, the North Node has been in Pisces and your fifth house of romance, creativity and self-expression, while the South Node moved through Virgo and your eleventh house of groups and community. The karmic call has been luring you into the spotlight to share your talents. Life has felt more romantic—by design—as you've opened up to things that bring you joy. You've also realized the need to pull back from draining collectives.

Now, the spiritual compass points you back home to tend to your sanctuary. After July 26, this becomes a fundamental key to thriving everywhere else. The North Node's path through Aquarius pushes you to invest in your inner world. During this 20-month cycle, questions about where you live, who you live with and how secure you feel at your core will rise to the surface. A move, renovation or family milestone could be part of this journey. More importantly, though, you're being called to create a base of operations that feels nourishing, supportive and authentically you.

While your design-savvy sign requires a well-appointed home, does your environment feed your soul? Aquarius is a metaphysical, community-oriented sign. You may reset your space to include a meditation area and gathering spaces for the people you love. Living communally may appeal to some Scorpios out there, which is fine as long as you have at least one decent-sized room of your own, ideally with a trustworthy lock on the door.

This cycle may bring karmic shifts in your family relationships. Ancestral healing work could be especially potent now, whether you're unpacking generational patterns or consciously rewriting them. If old wounds resurface, don't sweep them under the rug or bury them in the secret catacombs of your subconscious. Address them with compassion and, if needed, the guidance of mentors or healers. On a lighter note, you might be drawn to create new traditions or build chosen family bonds that feel just as strong as blood ties.

Across the wheel, the Leo South Node highlights your tenth house of success and public standing. You've been steadily building your reputation, but this transit reminds you that accolades alone won't sustain you. Beware of clinging too tightly to external validation or chasing visibility at the expense of your well-being. Yes, your ambition is admirable, but is it aligned with the life you actually want to come home to? The South Node's lesson is clear: Don't lose yourself in the performance of success.

Career-wise, the Leo South Node doesn't spell the end of your professional drive—it simply asks you to be intentional about what you're building and why. Some Scorpios may release a role that no longer resonates, while others could shift their focus from chasing titles to pursuing meaningful impact. If you've been living for applause, it's time to ground your goals in authenticity. You have so much wisdom to share, Scorpio! Don't hide your light. Just direct the cameras toward the narrative YOU want to share with the world.

Romantically, the Aquarius North Node in your domestic fourth house can bring turning points around cohabitation, marriage or starting a family. Even if you're single, you'll crave deeper emotional safety in your connections. This cycle prioritizes bonds that feel like home, whether that's a partner, close friends or your actual household.

By the time this cycle wraps in March 2028, Scorpio, you'll have built foundations that support both your private life and your public presence. True transformation isn't just about power plays in the outside world—it's about creating a sanctuary where your soul can rest, recharge and rise again, stronger than ever.

5
RECLAIM YOUR MAGIC

VENUS RETROGRADE IN SCORPIO AND LIBRA
VENUS RETROGRADE IN SCORPIO: OCTOBER 3–25
VENUS RETROGRADE IN LIBRA: OCTOBER 25–NOVEMBER 13

Your love life could slip into a lower gear this fall, but don't panic, Scorpio. This isn't a stallout! Rather, it's a rare opportunity to recalibrate all things romantic in your universe.

On October 3, ardent Venus, the planet of romance, beauty and pleasure, embarks on a six-week retrograde, an unavoidable cycle that comes around every 18 months.

In 2026, you will feel the Venus retrograde more intensely than most other signs. The reason? For the first time since Fall 2018, the celestial love goddess will retreat through Scorpio (until October 25) stirring up turbulence in your first house of identity and self-sovereignty. After that, Venus slips back into Libra for the second half of the retrograde, until November 13. With your self-focused first house and your dreamy, mysterious twelfth in Venus' crosshairs, this six-week cycle is certain to bring waves of unrest followed by profound epiphanies.

No, your love life is NOT doomed, Scorpio! (No need to spiral!) Yet, the first three weeks of Venus retrograde will feel especially personal. With the rewind taking place in Scorpio from October 3 to 25, you will crave meditative time alone and space to go within. Don't miss this opportunity to pull back and check in with yourself. Give yourself a pass to step back from the crush of romantic and social demands. While it might not please the people who have grown used to you being at their beck and call, it's necessary if you want to bring your best self to the table.

Take an honest assessment: Are your relationships meeting you where you are now? Or are they stuck in an unfulfilling time warp? Before stagnant energy pulls you into a doom loop, get back in touch with what brings YOU joy. Perhaps you've been so focused on what everybody else needs that you've lost touch with your own. Until you create some unstructured "me time" to putter, make art and music, dance, dream or just be, you won't be able to articulate your desires.

If only people had your psychic skills! Have you been waiting for someone to read between the lines and figure out what you need? You might THINK you've been dropping obvious hints, but with Venus retrograde, you don't want to leave anything up to chance. Spell it out, Scorpio—heck, hand them an instruction manual. (We're only half kidding.)

Think back to October 5 to November 16, 2018, the last time Venus retrograded through Scorpio and Libra. Did that period spark similar feelings, events or relationship questions? Patterns that arise now could feel like déjà vu—not because you haven't grown, but because Venus is giving you a second shot at handling them with your current wisdom and self-awareness.

Single Scorpios might want to hide dating app profiles for a few weeks. A little hibernation can help you reconnect with what you truly want, rather than chasing sparks with someone who isn't actually aligned with your deeper values. By the time Venus turns direct mid-November, you'll have a clearer sense of the qualities—and the kind of energy—you want to invite in.

If you're in a relationship, get ready for a planetary PSA: Autonomy is a crucial ingredient in long-term chemistry. You need to feel like your own person, not half of a two-headed unit. Give each other room to breathe while also checking in consistently. Absence can make the heart grow fonder—but with Venus in reverse, silence can just as easily trigger old insecurities. Make a point to send thoughtful messages or plan simple, low-stress meetups to keep the connection warm.

Venus is also the cosmic muse, and her slowdown can help you focus on a creative or personal project that's been on your back burner for too long. Just be mindful of the retrograde trap: getting swept into intense but questionable connections. When Venus slips into Libra and your secretive twelfth house on October 25, the temptation of a mysterious soul will be hard to resist. Your logical brain might be sending up red flags (Avoidant! Narcissist!) but the chase will feel scintillating. Emotional affairs can be just as seductive. You'll know you've crossed the line if you find yourself obsessively replaying conversations or rearranging your schedule for "chance" encounters.

But this is cause for reflection, Scorpio! Is there something missing from your current connection that needs to be repaired? Or are you bored and in need of a reconnection to one of YOUR personal passions? Maybe the person you're really missing in your life is…you. So before you project any existential angst onto your love life, dive back into activities that make your soul sing.

On a more superficial note, hold off on drastic aesthetic changes while Venus, the celestial style queen, is in reverse. That edgy haircut or full-sleeve tattoo might feel like a thrilling idea in the moment but could bring regrets. Same goes for big-ticket purchases—especially anything driven by strong emotions. If you're feeling the itch to splurge, channel it into mood boards, creative brainstorming or research. With a little fine-tuning, you could set yourself up for an exciting post-retrograde comeback. By November 13, you'll have sharper instincts, stronger boundaries and a renewed sense of what—and who—is worth your time, energy and heart.

2026
SCORPIO

12 MONTH OVERVIEW

January MONTHLY HOROSCOPE

Your words land like arrows this month, Scorpio, so aim wisely. With the Sun in Capricorn until the 19th, your third house of communication is buzzing. Pitch the project, start the podcast or finally have the conversation you've been circling around. Your message has extra impact now. On the 3rd, the Cancer full moon lights up your adventurous ninth house, pushing you to think expansively. Here's your cue to travel or immerse yourself in studies that broaden your worldview. Too many options to choose from? By the Capricorn new moon on the 18th, you'll be ready to commit to an adventurous mission. Venus and Mars, the cosmic lovers, cozy up in Capricorn until the 17th, infusing your interactions with charm and a few cat-and-mouse games. After the 23rd, both shift into Aquarius and your fourth house of home, drawing your attention to behind-the-scenes encounters. Coupled Scorpios could bring their sexy cohabitation goals to life. After the Sun settles into Aquarius on the 19th, nesting instincts are seriously activated. Refresh your decor and entertain regularly. Your health deserves a tune-up, too. On the 2nd, wounded healer Chiron pivots direct in Aries, reminding you to reset daily habits that support your wellbeing. Then on the 26th, dreamweaver Neptune floats back into Aries for a 13-year stay, inviting you to turn everyday routines into soulful rituals.

February MONTHLY HOROSCOPE

Settle down at base camp, Scorpio. February brings your focus to home, family and emotional roots as the grounding Sun moves through Aquarius and your fourth house until the 18th. Where do you need more stability—or simply a softer place to land? Prioritize spaces and people that nurture you. The regal full moon in Leo beams into your tenth house of career on the 1st, pushing a professional project to culmination and bringing recognition for your hard work. Bravo, Scorpio! Then, on February 17, the Aquarius new moon arrives as a potent solar eclipse—the first here since 2018—just as the Year of the Fire Horse begins. If you're ready to change something in your personal life, this will be the catalyst! Until February 10, Venus in Aquarius smooths domestic matters and may inspire you to beautify your space. Afterward, she drifts into Pisces and your fifth house, reigniting creativity and turning romance into something playful and magnetic. On February 13, Saturn re-enters Aries, beginning a two-year cycle in your health and routine zone. Structure becomes essential to success. Habits and work rhythms require discipline, but they'll also bring lasting strength. Valentine's Day follows with the Capricorn moon, favoring heartfelt conversations and grounded gestures over anything grandiose. Pisces season begins on the 18th, sending a wave of fresh inspiration through your fifth house of romance and creativity. Love takes an imaginative turn while artistic pursuits gain soulful glow. Mercury retrograde here from February 26 to March 20 could slow new projects, but it's ideal for revisiting half-finished ideas or reigniting a passion you set aside. Old flames may resurface too, giving you closure—or maybe one more chapter.

March MONTHLY HOROSCOPE

Passions fire on all cylinders this March as the Sun, Mercury retrograde, lusty Mars and a Pisces new moon (on the 18th) activate your fifth house of love, creativity and self-expression. What do you want to pour your heart into, Scorpio? Prioritize the projects, people and passions that light you up from the inside. The total lunar (full moon) eclipse in Virgo on the 3rd activates your eleventh house of community and collaboration. A group project may reach a turning point, or you could redefine your role within a friendship or organization. On March 2, unbridled Mars shifts into Pisces for a six-week stay, fueling romance and artistic inspiration. Don't hold back—this is your time to play, perform and create with childlike wonder. Love gets even more magnetic after March 6, when Venus enters Aries and your sixth house of health and routines. A relationship may flourish through shared daily activities, or sparks could fly with someone you meet at work. On the 10th, adventurous Jupiter ends a four-month retrograde in Cancer and your ninth house of expansion. Travel, education and horizon-broadening plans that stalled since last year suddenly will gain traction. Media projects take off at a gallop. Aries season kicks off with the spring equinox on the 20th, spotlighting your sixth house of wellness and service. Mercury stations direct the same day, ending three weeks of mix-ups. From this point forward, routines feel easier to manage, and you'll have the clarity to refine both work and love.

April MONTHLY HOROSCOPE

Daily rhythms get a shake-up this April, Scorpio, but don't resist the call to change. The Sun charges through novelty-seeking Aries and your sixth house of habits and health until the 19th, urging you to redefine your systems. Where could life run more smoothly, perhaps with the help of support staff and AI? Make practical tweaks that reduce stress. This will open up more time for you to get out and roam. On the 1st, the Libra full moon lights up your twelfth house of rest and release, encouraging closure and self-care. Tie up loose ends or let go of what's been draining you. Fiery Mars storms into Aries for six weeks on the 9th, supercharging your productivity but also testing your stamina. Focus on efficiency so you don't burn out. The new moon in Aries on the 17th brings a fresh slate for wellness, work projects or daily rituals. By the 19th, the grounding Taurus Sun moves into your seventh house of partnerships, shifting the focus to collaboration and connection. Until April 24, Venus also travels through Taurus, bringing harmony and attraction to relationships. Then, the big reveal: On the 25th, Uranus ends its seven-year stay in Taurus and rockets into Gemini until 2033. With your eighth house of intimacy and transformation lit up, brace for breakthroughs in relationships, finances and your emotional depth. This era will push you to embrace change instead of resisting it.

May MONTHLY HOROSCOPE

Partnerships headline your month, Scorpio, as the Taurus Sun charges through your seventh house until the 20th. Whether it's romance, business or a creative duo, you're being asked to define the terms. On the 1st, the full moon lands in your sign, spotlighting your personal needs and a milestone you've been working toward. Think: soft launch of a new personal brand, hard launch of a reputation-boosting project. On the 6th, Pluto turns retrograde in Aquarius and your home zone through October 15, stirring deep reflection on roots and family patterns. The Aquarius quarter moon on the 10th could make Mother's Day nostalgic. Cook a meal of family recipes and anchor into cozy traditions. On the 16th, the Taurus new supermoon activates your partnership house, prompting defining moments in love or alliances. Then, Gemini season kicks off on the 20th. With the Sun streaming through your eighth  house of intimacy, sexy times, financial merges, or maybe all three, are ahead. Until the 18th, Venus in Gemini fuels intensity in your eighth house, upping the stakes on desire and drawing resources your way. Then, Venus shifts into Cancer and your adventure zone while Mars storms into Taurus and your relationship sector. Romance heats up with someone who challenges you to grow. Coupled? Reignite passion by planning a daring escapade with your S.O. The month ends with the Sagittarius blue full moon on the 31st in your money house. News about a job or work situation could arrive. Be ready to act quickly should opportunity strike!

June MONTHLY HOROSCOPE

Your urge to merge heats up this June as the Sun powers through Gemini and your deep-diving eighth house until the 21st. Intimate bonds, joint finances or shared resources could demand your attention. This is sexy season, too, but make sure there's enough trust to accompany the lust. The June 14 Gemini new moon—the second supermoon in a rare three-part series—lands here, too, offering breakthroughs in investments, partnerships and erotic explorations. Meanwhile, Mars charges through Taurus and your seventh house of relationships until June 28, stirring both passion and conflict. Pro tip: Channel this heat into building stronger bonds rather than battles of will. On June 19, "wounded healer" Chiron moves into Taurus for a three-month preview of its 2027-2034 stay. Since 2018, Chiron has highlighted health and work struggles, pushing you to refine your systems. This summer, the healing shifts to partnerships, encouraging you to confront patterns of imbalance and cultivate healthier dynamics. On June 21, the Sun soars into Cancer and your worldly ninth house, just in time for the solstice and Father's Day. Travel, study or sharing wisdom could inspire meaningful family traditions. In love, Venus lingers in Cancer until the 13th, drawing romance through travel, learning or cross-cultural connections. Then she struts into Leo and your tenth house, turning professional settings into fertile ground for inspiration. Your career climbs to new heights beginning June 30, when expansive Jupiter rises into Leo and your tenth house for the next thirteen months. Recognition and leadership opportunities are within reach! If you're ready to claim your place in the spotlight, the universe is backing you. The month wraps with the Capricorn full moon on June 29 in your third house of communication. A writing project, conversation or contract could come full circle, but with Mercury retrograde in Cancer starting the same day, avoid rushing commitments over the next three weeks.

July MONTHLY HOROSCOPE

Spin the globe, but mindfully, this July. With the Sun in Cancer and your adventurous ninth house until the 22nd—and Mercury retrograde here until the 23rd—you could be on the move this month, revisiting favorite locations for a nostalgic voyage. The Cancer new moon (a supermoon) on the 14th may greenlight a big trip, perhaps with a learning component. Plan with care (because, Mercury retro) but don't miss out on a growth opportunity. On July 7, Neptune turns retrograde in Aries, beginning five months of review in your wellness zone. If you've been fueled by iced lattes and adrenaline, your body might force a reset. Saturn follows on the 26th, demanding structure: meal-preps, sleep goals or even a digital detox. All month long, firecracker

Mars in Gemini crackles through your eighth house, intensifying relationships and accelerating money moves. This lusty cycle could bring spicy developments to your love life, too—privacy, please! Leo season arrives on the 22nd and your career kicks into high gear. Time to claim authority and get to work on developing one of your big 2026 goals. With Venus in Virgo from the 9th, get out and circulate! A well-placed introduction could connect you to collaborators worth their weight in gold. Mercury direct on the 23rd helps you seal deals with confidence. The biggest shift comes on the 26th, when the North Node moves into Aquarius and your home zone for the first time in 20 years. From now through March 2028, roots and family become your growing edge—whether you're nesting, buying property or healing generational dynamics. On the 29th, the Sun and Jupiter align in Leo for the annual "Day of Miracles," amplifying career momentum. The Aquarius full moon brightens your home sector the same day, bringing a milestone on the domestic front. Casa Scorpio could become the hub for some exciting ventures as the month wraps.

August MONTHLY HOROSCOPE

Dress to impress, Scorpio! Your career zone is lit by the Leo Sun until the 22nd, so even your beach days could yield some promising professional connections. On the 3rd, soothsayer Chiron pivots retrograde in Taurus and your seventh house of partnerships, surfacing old patterns in your closest bonds. If dynamics feel lopsided, it's time for some radical honesty. Therapy sessions, couples' check-in, even a podcast binge on attachment styles—healing comes when you name what's really at play. On the 11th, Mars blazes into Cancer and your adventurous ninth house, stoking wanderlust. Over the next two months, expand your horizons through travel, study or cultural exploration. Eclipse season begins on the 12th with a total solar eclipse in Leo—the first here since 2019—igniting your tenth house of career and public image. A professional breakthrough or leadership opportunity could arrive suddenly, catapulting you into a more visible role. Ardent Venus enters Libra on the 6th, slipping into your twelfth house and adding a touch of nostalgia to love. Old flames or unfinished emotional stories may resurface, inviting closure—or possibly a second chance. Let your fantasies be your guide when the lights go down. Virgo season kicks off on the 22nd. Networking and group endeavors are especially fruitful as the Sun activates your eleventh house of community and collaboration. On the 28th, the Pisces lunar eclipse pushes you further into the public. From fame to romance, people want to see more of you, Scorpio! But it's up to you to decide how much you REALLY want to share. Vulnerability, in the right dose, can foster trust. The key? All parties must be invested if you want this to be worth the effort. Career goals get a solid boost on the 31st when enterprising Jupiter in Leo trines stabilizing Saturn in Aries. Stop forcing stalled agendas and follow the string of green lights that are flashing in a different direction.

September MONTHLY HOROSCOPE

Life is a team sport this September, Scorpio. With the Virgo Sun lighting up your eleventh house of groups and collaboration, your best opportunities flow in via friends, colleagues and networks. Sign up for networking brunches and volunteer projects. Join that creative collective you've been eyeing. Motivator Mars blazes through Cancer and your adventurous ninth house until the 27th, bringing out your spontaneous side. Book a last-minute getaway or dive into a class. Whatever expands your horizons is solid gold. On the 10th, the Virgo new moon energizes your eleventh house, sparking new alliances and future-focused goals. Someone you meet now could be a game-changer for a project or your social world. But can you trust them? That same day, Uranus pivots retrograde in Gemini and your eighth house of intimacy and shared resources. Over the next five months, review financial entanglements and take your sweet time developing emotional bonds. Venus lingers in Libra until the 10th, fueling fantasies and softening your boundaries in love. Then, come out from your boudoir. The planet of amour heads into Scorpio, amplifying your magnetism and putting love (and fashion!) front and center. But be fair warned: Venus retrograde is looming from October 3 to November 13. Make any style changes and romantic pivots now while your sensibilities are solid. The fall equinox on the 22nd turns your focus back to rest and restoration as the Sun slips into Libra for a month. On the 17th, Chiron backs into Aries and your sixth house of health and work, reminding you to prioritize routines that actually support your energy. And the Aries full moon on the 26th could bring a breakthrough around wellness or work-life balance. Whether it's a new fitness habit, a schedule revamp or simply saying no more often, align your daily rhythm with your long-term vitality.

October MONTHLY HOROSCOPE

Flip to the selfie camera, Scorpio, and take a look at your reflection. On October 3, Venus retrogrades in your sign until the 25th, then rewinds into Libra and your twelfth house of closure until November 13. Aspects of your personal brand may feel out of sync with the Scorpio you're becoming. The call to shed what no longer fits is too loud to ignore. Simultaneously, which new layers of yourself are you ready to discover? This introspective cycle will be illuminating. The Sun travels through Libra until the 23rd, activating your twelfth house of rest and reflection. The Libra new moon on the

10th invites you to clear space. Wrap up a draining project, declutter your physical and digital environments. There's plenty of progress on deck, too. Go-getter Mars blazes through Leo and your tenth house of career all month, keeping the spotlight on professional ambitions. Focus on elite opportunities and try to bypass the middleman. Good news! Your ruler, alchemical Pluto, ends its annual, five-month retrograde on October 15. As Pluto powers forward in Aquarius and your fourth house of home and family, issues that stalled since spring may finally shift.

Then on the 23rd, the Sun moves into Scorpio, recharging your vitality for a month of birthday celebrations. The same day, Venus retrograde aligns with the Sun in a rare Cazimi. This could bring a powerful identity reset, one that may shift relationships in the process. But, sigh...Mercury retrograde begins the next day, October 24, also in Scorpio. Until November 13, your best bet is to enjoy nostalgia and keep yourself occupied with old friends—expecting delays with plans and plenty of crossed signals as you go. Don't take every pause personally. A powerful partnership could solidify near the Taurus full moon on the 26th. Make the most of this defining moment and speak up for what you need!

November MONTHLY HOROSCOPE

Keep on celebrating, Scorpio! With the Sun in your sign until the 22nd and the year's only Scorpio new moon arriving on the 9th, the stage is set for birthday season reinvention. Fresh starts around identity, style and personal goals are on your mind. But—here's the rub: Until the 13th, publicist Mercury is retrograde in Scorpio AND style-queen Venus is retrograde in Libra, slowing your rollout. You may wrestle with self-doubt, tech hiccups or the sense that your plans aren't quite ready for prime time. Don't force a debut (and wait on that drastic haircut). Instead, edit, rehearse and refine your mood boards. By midmonth, your clarity and charisma return and you'll be ready to unveil the "new you" with impact. Meanwhile, go-getter Mars powers through Leo until the 25th, supercharging your tenth house of career and leadership. Big opportunities are brewing, but so are power struggles if you charge ahead without buy-in. Choose influence over intimidation and you won't lose allies on your climb to the top. Sagittarius season begins on the 22nd. As the Sun highlights your second house of income and values, financial focus sharpens. Negotiate for better pay, upgrade your skills or invest in something lasting. Speaking of investments, a backer could put resources behind your vision near the Gemini full supermoon on the 24th. This "all or nothing" energy demands clarity, however, and situationships could crumble if they can't be defined. After the 25th, Mars shifts into Virgo and your eleventh house of community for the rest of the year. Collaborations and group efforts take off, but guard your energy. Your magnetism is strong. Save it for projects that amplify your vision.

December MONTHLY HOROSCOPE

Call it a money makeover, Scorpio—this December is all about your bottom line and sense of security. The Sagittarius Sun energizes your second house of income and values until the 21st, urging you to tighten your grip on finances and invest (time, energy, resources) in what truly sustains you. On the 8th, the new moon in Sagittarius sparks fresh momentum for earnings: a raise, a side hustle or a smart investment could be in the works. Disciplined Saturn and imaginative Neptune wrap up five-month retrogrades in Aries on the 10th and 12th, respectively, helping you streamline routines and sharpen your daily flow. With motivator Mars firing through Virgo and your collaborative eleventh house all month, say yes to group projects, community events and holiday mixers. (And avoid getting sucked into organizational politics!) Venus re-enters Scorpio on the 4th, wrapping you in a little extra shimmer for the season. Spotlight moments are yours; take the initiative in love! On the 12th, abundant Jupiter turns retrograde in Leo and your tenth house of career. If professional demands are spiraling, scale back to essentials and protect your energy. Capricorn season and the solstice arrive on the 21st, lighting your third house of communication. Local happenings, short trips and lively exchanges keep you busy through year's end. The Cancer full supermoon on the 23rd spotlights your ninth house of travel and expansion. A year-end getaway materializes, or you could get word of a long-distance opportunity that's worth pursuing in early 2027. NYE networking could set you up with even more opportunities, thanks to a galvanizing Sun-Mars trine. Head to an event filled with people you need to meet!

Read your extended monthly forecast for life, love, money and career! astrostyle.com

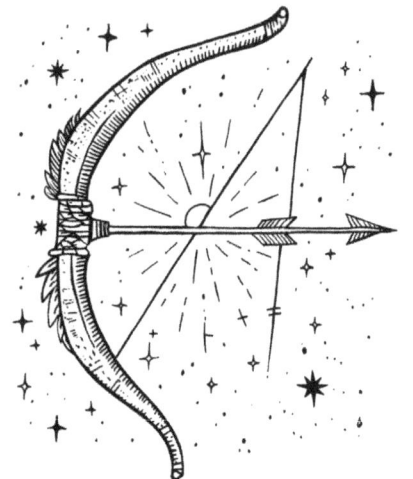

SAGITTARIUS IN 2026

| ALL THE PLANETS IN SAGITTARIUS IN 2026 | YOUR 2026 HOROSCOPE | TOP 5 THEMES FOR SAGITTARIUS IN 2026 | LOVE HOROSCOPE + LUCKY DATES | MONEY HOROSCOPE + LUCKY DATES |

Sagittarius in 2026

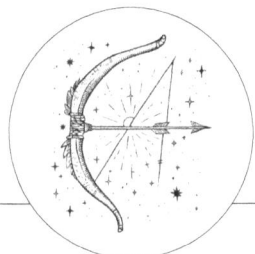

Your year of:
WEALTH BUILDING, GLOBAL EXPANSION, RECLAMATION

AIM WITH PRECISION, ARCHER.

Adventure calls—it always does—but this year requires intentional strategy. Novelty is great. A mission that matters? That's worth pouring yourself into. Avoid getting pulled onto FOMO-induced detours and take time to map out a blueprint for your "build." Say yes to experiences that expand your skills and your reach. Then, most importantly, finish what you start. Achieving one impactful milestone (with style and fanfare, naturally) beats chasing ten half-formed ideas. The new vibe for 2026? Enjoying the sweet taste of success on your own terms without draining your resources in the process.

THE PLANETS IN Sagittarius

THE SUN NOV 22–DEC 21	Happy birthday season! With the Sun in your sign, you're clear to take chances, chase fresh adventures, and command the spotlight.
NEW MOON DEC 8 7:52PM, 16°57'	Happy bonus New Year! Set your intentions for the next six months, then take a brave step forward. Your fans await!
FULL MOON MAY 31 4:45AM, 09°56'	Manifestation moment! Your work of the past six months bears fruit. Celebrate your progress and harvest the rewards.
MERCURY DEC 6–25	Hold court! When charismatic Mercury zips through your sign, your social status soars. Work the room, make connections—but keep your commitments realistic to avoid overpromising.
LILITH JAN 1–SEP 14	Black moon Lilith is associated with the female journey through scorn, rage, empowerment and sexual liberation. When it visits your sign, you may work through issues around shame and belonging.

Sagittarius in 2026
HIGHLIGHTS

START DEEP, THEN GO WIDE: JUPITER IN CANCER UNTIL JUNE 30

No skimming the surface in the first half of the year! Your ruler, peripatetic Jupiter, is on a dive mission in Cancer, plumbing the depths of your intimate, erotic and transformational eighth house. Who you allow into your inner circle matters greatly. Make sure their trust is earned before you spill state secrets. Focus on strengthening the ties that bind. You could merge resources with a partner (romantic or business-wise) or commit to a long-term relationship structure. Since the eighth house rules investments, someone may bankroll one of your dreams. (Time to write that business proposal!) Money could flow in through an inheritance, settlement, property sale or tax return, setting you up for future wealth.

SPIN THE GLOBE: JUPITER BLAZES INTO LEO JUNE 30

After all that soul-mining, it's time to stretch your legs. On June 30, you are back in your exploratory element! Worldly Jupiter bounds into Leo and your ninth house (AKA "the Sagittarius house") and activates the part of your chart that rules travel, publishing and bold leaps of faith for 13 months. Suddenly the world feels like your oyster again—and you're ready to chase any "pearl" that glimmers with possibility. Reminder, Sagittarius, to take a beat and figure out if there's actually a "there" there—before you book the trip or circulate the company-wide memo. Still, this cycle is a time of extreme growth, one you haven't experienced since mid-2014 to mid-2015. Independent projects, education (teaching and studying), media and public speaking call you out to shape the culture at large!

CREATIVE ALCHEMY: SATURN AND NEPTUNE IN ARIES

Stoic Saturn and numinous Neptune unite again beginning this February 13—in Aries, firing up your fifth house of romance, creativity and fame. For the next two years, you'll have to balance their "odd couple" vibes. Saturn calls for discipline while Neptune adds inspiration. Purposeful play is the name of the game, whether you're making love or art. The magic happens when you give your passions structure—set deadlines for your projects, carve out sacred time for love and treat joy like the serious business it is.

RELATIONSHIPS REVOLUTIONIZED: URANUS ENTERS GEMINI APRIL 25

Enough grinding, Archer! On April 25, Uranus blasts out of your sixth house of work and daily rhythms and rockets into Gemini, sparking a seven-year remix of your relationship story. Partnerships come from the most unexpected places, opening up freedom in your schedule and allowing you to bloom in the areas where you feel most excited to plant seeds. Stale relationship dynamics may dissolve quickly—with some connections withering on the vine as you move into this new era. If you've been craving freedom, this cycle delivers. Swipe with curiosity, draft agreements with care, and stay open to allies who stretch your perspective in the best way.

FIERCE INDEPENDENCE: BLACK MOON LILITH IN SAGITTARIUS UNTIL SEPTEMBER 14

From January through mid-September, Black Moon Lilith stirs up your sign, awakening radical independence and untamed self-expression. During this 9-month cycle (which happens every nine years), you are uninterested in fitting into boxes—or in being polite about it. Use this energy to explore alternative paths. Launch a culture-shifting project, revamp your image, advocate for yourself without apology. Just beware of burning bridges! Can you claim your truth without torching your networks? Try that first.

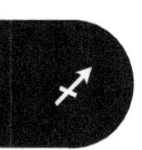

MERCURY RETROGRADES: REWORK YOUR ROOTS

Mercury turns retrograde three times in 2026, slowing you down to reassess home, intimacy and spirituality. From February 26 to March 20, the messenger planet rewinds through your domestic fourth house, which could bring friction with relatives or under your roof. From June 29 to July 23, Mercury backtracks in your eighth house of intimacy, shared resources and long-term commitments. You may renegotiate financial agreements, revisit trust issues or reconnect with a sexy someone from your past. The final retrograde, October 24 to November 13, lands in your twelfth house of closure and healing. With Venus also retrograde in Libra, expect old emotions or unfinished business with friends to resurface. Use this time to rest, reflect and release before turning the page on a new chapter.

MILESTONE MOONS: SAGITTARIUS LUNATIONS IN MAY AND DECEMBER

On May 31, the Sagittarius full moon illuminates your progress since late 2025, helping you celebrate wins and clear what's holding you back. Then, on December 8, the Sagittarius new moon gives you a powerful fresh start. These lunations are cosmic checkpoints—treat them like strategy sessions. Set goals, book the ticket or take the leap that scares you (in the best way).

DESTINY AT THE CROSSROADS: LUNAR NODES SHIFT

Until July 26, the South Node in Virgo and North Node in Pisces tug you between career and home. You're being asked to loosen perfectionism around professional ambition while nurturing deeper roots in your personal life. Then mid-summer, the Nodes pivot into Aquarius (North) and Leo (South), opening a 20-month cycle around communication, learning and truth-telling. Your destiny lies in what you say and how you express it. What message are you ready to broadcast, and who needs to hear it most?

LOVE AND FRIENDSHIPS ON PAUSE: VENUS RETROGRADE THIS FALL

Every so often, the universe hits pause on matters of the heart, and fall 2026 is one of those times. From October 3 to November 13, Venus rewinds through Scorpio and Libra, slowing the pace in your friendships, networks and hidden desires. Old collaborators could circle back, or you may question whether certain groups still feel like your people. Venus retraces this territory every 8 years (minus 2°), flashing you back to fall 2018. Think of it less as déjà vu, more as proof of how much you've evolved. This time, you get to choose from a place of clarity, not compromise.

Love

SAGITTARIUS 2026 FORECAST

What's the rush, Archer? 2026 starts with a sensual slowdown as cosmic canoodlers Venus and Mars cozy up in Capricorn until January 17. As they warm your second house of security and values, you may be craving stability more than your usual whirlwind romances. (Yes, Sag, even you sometimes like a little Netflix-and-savings-account.) Focus on building confidence and intimacy that actually lasts, not just the thrill of the chase.

Finding that elusive balance of stability and excitement is a major theme of your 2026, in fact. Beginning February 13, traditional Saturn and fantasy-agent Neptune unite in Aries and your fifth house of romance for a rare two-year run. Passion is as much about follow-through as it is about fireworks now. Your sign thrives on excitement, yet this is your chance to pair that thrill with staying power, weaving both magic and structure into love. This cycle could bring milestones like engagements, pregnancies or the intoxicating rush of new courtship—moments that ask you to honor both the spark AND the lasting bond they're meant to create.

Spring jolts you awake! Ardent Venus heats it up in Aries from March 6 to 30, and lusty Mars follows suit from April 9 to May 18. In your glamorous, demonstrative fifth house, you'll be more effusive as the temperatures rise.

Still, you won't be your usual, unfettered self in the first half of the year, so don't force the PDA. Until June 30, your ruler, liberated Jupiter, flies under the radar in Cancer. In your erotic and mysterious eighth house, the red-spotted planet can intensify intimacy. This first half of the year might feel heavier, with cravings for deep bonding, solitude or healing old wounds.

The tide turns dramatically after June 30, as Jupiter gallops into Leo for a 13-month joyride through your adventurous ninth house. You're back in your wildly free-spirited element—traveling, expanding and loving out loud. (Here's hoping you didn't saddle yourself to an introvert with an "us against the world" mentality earlier this year!) But heads up: The South Node also enters Leo on July 26, warning against any "exploration" that skews destructive. Avoid burning bridges in a panicked moment of restlessness. The August 12 Leo solar eclipse could reveal a passionate epiphany, reminding you that romance can be both wild and wise.

Another reason love could take an unpredictable turn this year? Innovative Uranus circles back into Gemini on April 25, hard-launching its seven-year stay in your partnership province. You could radically shift the way you "do" relationships. Ample autonomy becomes non-negotiable as you embrace unconventional dynamics. Self-styled romance has always been the Sagittarius way, but between now and 2033, you could take that to new levels: Non-monogamy, LAT, long-distance, creative arrangements. Find whatever fits YOU and don't bother plugging into someone else's template.

But that's not all the spice that 2026 is serving. Black Moon Lilith—the point in the sky associated with erotic empowerment—is in Sagittarius until September 14. Lilith only comes to your sign every nine years (last time was 2014-15) so you might reconnect to some buried desires that you tucked away back then. This cosmic wild child wants you to own every part of yourself—especially the messy, rebellious sides you usually tame for love. Still, this comes with the PSA: Don't trample a partner's feelings or let lust consume you to destructive levels. The shadowy aspect of Lilith can bring obsession or arouse shame. Fantasize freely. Act consciously.

This fall, Venus retrogrades October 3 to November 13 through Scorpio and Libra, rattling your twelfth and eleventh houses. Old patterns, secret attractions or friends-turned-flings may resurface. And with Mercury retrograde overlapping from October 24 to November 13, communication could get messy. This might be a forced timeout for Archers whose love lives have spun a little out of control. Nothing wrong with taking a breather to recenter and figure out what (and who) belongs on your 2027 romantic bingo card.

By year's end, you'll have learned that true love isn't just a spark, it's a flame you consciously feed. Keep your adventurous heart open, but add a little discipline to the passion. Freedom feels even sweeter (and hotter) when you have a home base to fly back to.

Money & Career

SAGITTARIUS 2026 FORECAST

Is it worth it? That's your guiding question in 2026, Sagittarius. The answer depends on what exactly you're building. Your ruling planet, Jupiter, spends the first half of the year in Cancer and your eighth house of wealth, investments and shared resources. This year is less about hustle, more about leverage. Suddenly your appetite for risk is lower, but your earning potential rises as you make smarter plays. Learn about compounding interest, real estate deals or joint ventures that can grow your long-term security. Strategic partnerships and financial education pay dividends now, so raise your money IQ and start thinking about legacy, not just income.

Meanwhile, the South Node continues its stay in Virgo and your tenth house of career until July 26, reminding you that success without meaning simply won't satisfy you. The March 3 total lunar eclipse in Virgo could bring sudden shifts in your professional life, perhaps an unexpected offer or an opening at the top. Read the fine print before you leap; this opportunity could be major, but it will require discernment and balance.

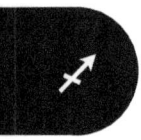

On February 13, Saturn and Neptune make contact in Aries and your expressive fifth house, kicking off a two-year cycle that brings structure and imagination to your creative life. This is your moment to cultivate both visibility and credibility. Saturn helps you polish your craft, develop discipline and project authority, while Neptune restores artistry and authenticity. Whether you're leading a team, performing or building a personal brand, you're front-facing now. The world is taking note.

Wave goodbye to the grind—or at least, the most exhausting parts of it. On April 25, Uranus concludes its seven-year shake-up through Taurus and your sixth house of work and wellbeing, a cycle that began in 2018. You've paid your dues and learned what truly supports your productivity. When Chiron passes through Taurus from June 29 to September 17, you'll get a chance to heal old scarcity narratives or burnout patterns that have limited your potential. Then, as Uranus enters Gemini and your seventh house through 2033, you'll attract dynamic collaborations. Contractual or partnership changes could be disruptive at first but lead to breakthroughs—and possibly a better deal than the one you had before.

Your entrepreneurial spirit roars back to life midyear! On June 30, Jupiter strides into Leo and your ninth house of expansion, publishing and global ventures. This 13-month cycle pushes your ambition on a bigger stage. Get ready to captivate new audiences and explore international opportunities. It's the perfect time to blend wisdom with wanderlust! Some Archers will dive into teaching, writing or advanced study. On July 26, the karmic South Node joins Jupiter in Leo. Keep your ethics spotless as you grow or it's going to be lonely at the end of the day.

Simultaneously, the fateful North Node shifts into Aquarius and your communicative third house, sparking opportunities for collaboration, local partnerships and short-term projects until March 2028. You may juggle multiple gigs or develop a versatile skill set that keeps your schedule—and your mind—buzzing.

After years of recalibration, 2026 restores your natural optimism and drive. Build what's worth keeping, share what you know, and remember: The bigger your vision, the stronger your foundation needs to be.

TOP 5 THEMES FOR Sagittarius in 2026

1	2	3	4	5
CREATE A MASTERPIECE	INVEST WITH INTENTION	REDEFINE RELATIONSHIPS	SPREAD YOUR MESSAGE	HEAL YOUR HEART

1 CREATE A MASTERPIECE

NEPTUNE IN ARIES
JANUARY 26, 2026–MARCH 23, 2039

SATURN IN ARIES
FEBRUARY 13, 2026–APRIL 12, 2028

Get ready to step onto your biggest stage yet, Sagittarius. Early this year, two cosmic heavyweights—Neptune and Saturn—settle into Aries for long runs through your fifth house of creativity, romance and fame. You may be the producer, director AND the star of this production. That's what being an independent multihyphenate is all about, right? You got a teaser of these transits in 2025, when mystical Neptune dipped into Aries from March 30 to October 22, rousing your inner artiste. Structured Saturn joined in from May 24 to September 1, hinting at the dedication this next chapter demands.

Now, in 2026, the real show begins. On January 26, numinous Neptune returns to Aries, launching a 13-year odyssey through your realm of artistry, romance and joyful risk-taking. Saturn follows close behind on February 13, starting a two-year boot camp designed to help you shape those sweeping dreams into a tangible (and profitable!) structure. For a sign as vision-driven as you, this cosmic combo could be exactly what you need to finally bring your grandest ideas to life.

But this journey won't be quick or linear. Neptune dissolves boundaries and fuels fantasy; Saturn demands structure, discipline and precision. That duality will be most apparent on February 20, when Saturn and Neptune join forces in Aries for an ultra-rare exact conjunction. This is their only direct meeting during their parallel paths in Aries—and the first time they've teamed up in the Ram's realm since (drumroll, please) 1702! You're standing at the starting line of a new era. And it's equal parts intoxicating and intense. Romance? For many Archers, it may become both magnetic and revealing. Neptune stirs an irresistible craving for cinematic love, where every kiss feels fated and every glance sets your soul ablaze. But Saturn may toss a bucket of ice water on that dream, insisting you pause long enough to vet the person behind the pulsing desire. Do they have what it takes to go the distance with a fireball like you? Can you build something sustainable together? Those dreamy eyes better come with a five-year plan if you want to avoid rude awakenings later.

This same tension may pop up in your creative life. One minute you're swept away in an artistic reverie; the next, you're staring down a deadline or revising a pitch deck. For best results, let sensible Saturn provide a container for Neptune's fluid nature. Otherwise, you'll get scattered, shape-shifting so often that nothing actually gets produced.

While Saturn demands excellence, Neptune softens that harsh edge. In 2026, you have the green light to stop waiting for the "perfect" moment to share your gifts. Put your creations into the world, even if they are still somewhat in beta. Each performance, post or prototype is a stepping stone toward mastery. There will be moments this year when getting your work in front of a test audience is the only way you'll be able to massage it. You need to see how people respond!

Bring a sense of wonder to the process. The fifth house rules children, joy and your unfiltered self-expression. Tend to both your inner child and the ones you may be raising—kids, fur babies, nieces and nephews. As you tap into a more playful, free-flowing rhythm, expect deeper bonding and spontaneous discoveries—whether with your kids, your creative works or your own exuberant soul.

With Saturn in the mix, expect to hit a few speedbumps. This isn't the planet of overnight fame or effortless love. As Saturn moves through your fifth house from 2026 to 2028, there will be creative blocks to work through, along with moments of doubt. But Saturn rewards those who persist. If you show up, commit and practice, you'll find your rhythm—and your audience.

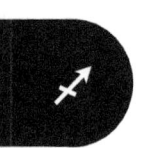

As much as Neptune can make one feel like Peter Pan, Saturn is the planet of adulting. Playtime without proper rest, self-care and resources is a recipe for a dumpster fire. Stop showing up at work with dark circles under your eyes because you were up late scrolling, partying or finishing an assignment that you blew off for too long. Not cute, Archer, not if it's becoming your new normal.

Your image and reputation may be more important to you in 2026 than they've been in a while. People are watching you this year, Sagittarius, and, yes, they want you to be authentic. While it's fine to be quirky, saucy and edgy, go easy on the salaciousness. Image matters when planets pulse through the fifth house. Your sign can rock a collegiate or ironic teen look well into your AARP years, but still. Saturn is requesting a little more polish—at least when you're on duty. Refine your wardrobe and elevate your visuals. You don't have to turn into some stuffy, soulless cardboard cutout. (As if!) Just lift to the next evolution with a sophisticated spin on your signature style.

One last reminder: Pace yourself. Neptune in Aries will dial up your excitement to a fever pitch. There's so much to see, do and accomplish—and everyone wants a piece of your magic! Treat this like a marathon, not a sprint. After all, Neptune is in Aries until 2039. Build in rest days, creative retreats and screen-free weekends. Keep your body grounded and your heart wide open. You only get this stardust-and-steel combo once in a lifetime, Sagittarius, and you want to be feeling your best when your standing ovation arrives!

2 INVEST WITH INTENTION

JUPITER IN CANCER
JUNE 9, 2026–JUNE 30, 2026

You're far from "the shallow" now, Sagittarius! In fact, you might just set a new depth record in 2026. As the year begins, your galactic guardian Jupiter is submerged in watery Cancer and your mysterious, alchemical eighth house. You're halfway through this thirteen-month cycle, which began on June 9, 2025. Odds are, you've already experienced some of the "money, power, respect" vibes that it promises to deliver.

Take a New Year's audit: What (and who!) are you investing your time, energy and resources into? Choose wisely and you could turn a tiny drop of possibility into an ocean of opportunity. But it goes both ways. NOT knowing when to throw in the towel—or pivot to a smarter strategy—can leave you drowning in debt.

We know which money moves you prefer, Sagittarius! (Yes, the ones that leave you in the black, not in the red.) With Jupiter in Cancer until June 30, you may have to let go of a dream that's not materializing, or at least, put it on the back burner until Jupiter soars into Leo this coming June 30.

Instead, focus on investments that compound over time. This doesn't just apply to your 401(k) or IRA account. People are among your richest resources while Jupiter makes waves in nurturing Cancer. Instead of chasing shiny things, go for smart bets. The work may be a little tedious and NOT as exciting as you'd prefer. But the stability you'll create for yourself? That will be worth every moment spent poring over financial projections, Gantt Charts and quarterly reports.

Jupiter is "exalted" in Cancer, meaning that the Crab's castle is its most powerful placement in the zodiac. With this security-loving vibe afoot, you have a prime opportunity to level up your wealth. Real estate, crypto, stocks—they're all on the (trading) table. Be smart and diversify your portfolio. A profitable home sale or purchase of an investment property (or both) could figure in.

WHO you merge with matters more than ever now. This is a potent window to attract backers for a venture, but couple your optimism with due diligence! The eighth house can be a murky place and people may not show their true faces immediately. The last thing you need is to be sitting in court (with a warehouse full of merch) because you named your product after a heavily lawyered, trademarked brand. Everything needs extra research and speculation during this cycle, Sagittarius. Temper your impatience and do the digging!

That goes for your love life, too. As Jupiter in Cancer stirs the waters of your erotic eighth house, you long for deeper intimacy and soulful connections. Although your sexual appetite can expand in new directions, loyalty and emotional safety will be your real turn-ons now. For many Archers, this cycle could bring a powerful alliance that has "happily ever after" written all over it. Engagements, business partnerships and other twosomes can blossom before June 30.

Still, you may feel oddly guarded in the first half of the year—the opposite of your usual raw, unfiltered self. Careful not to keep too much mystery going. What you DON'T need is to sell someone on an image that you cannot maintain. Ice Queen? Unbothered? That's so NOT you. Authenticity is your sign's superpower, even if you drip out the information instead of broadcasting it on the first date.

You could be drawn to someone who has "a past" or a shadowy chapter that isn't quite closed. Don't kid yourself, Sag. Getting tangled up in situations like this WILL affect you. Tough decisions may lie ahead, including breaking away from a person who you love, but has A LOT of soul work left to do.

Stay far away from "intermittent feeders," too: People who dangle the carrot of a relationship or attention, then snatch it away periodically. This is a recipe for obsession! Your brain literally can't help it. If the one you adore says, "I'm not ready," don't make it your private mission to change their mind. Pull back and put the focus on YOU. Your inner life will be rich during this Jupiter cycle. Once you detach from the cat-and-mouse games, you'll enjoy your own company in ways you haven't for years.

Wherever you are on Cupid's timeline, a relationship that's been percolating could reach a defining moment before June 30. You might combine assets, sign a lease together, or even make things official with paperwork, whether that's a marriage license, a will, or a prenup. On the flipside, if a bond has run its course, Jupiter here can also bring the courage (and resources) to make a clean break. Either way, clarity comes when you face the facts head-on.

Feeling ready for a total life overhaul? The eighth house is the realm of radical reinvention, from a career pivot to a full-blown identity metamorphosis. Just remember: Jupiter loves a shortcut, but transformation that sticks requires patience. Do the deep work behind the scenes instead of racing ahead on a gut feeling. Therapy, coaching or energy work might help you break through old blocks and unearth hidden fears. It's amazing what can shift when you're willing to look at your shadows instead of outrunning them.

This isn't your usual "see what sticks" year, Sagittarius. The foundation you build now can set you up for major abundance and soul-deep connection when Jupiter bursts into Leo this summer. Invest your energy—and your heart—wisely.

JUPITER IN LEO
JUNE 30, 2026 – JULY 26, 2027

Bigger, stronger, faster! That's your mantra in the second half of 2026, Sagittarius. On June 30, your ruling planet Jupiter blazes into fellow fire sign Leo, igniting your ninth house of travel, expansion and mind-opening experiences until July 26, 2027. Get ready to rocket into a whole new stratosphere of growth and adventure! Because the ninth house is your natural domain (you're the zodiac's ninth sign), it's like a double shot of good fortune. You're back in your globetrotting element, with the wide world calling your name.

And no more censoring yourself or hiding your shine! After thirteen tight-lipped months of Jupiter in Cancer, the abundant planet's ascent into spotlight-stealing Leo lifts the veil. Unfiltered Sagittarius energy is exactly what the world wants now. Reclaim your role as the zodiac's Most Outspoken. Your raw honesty, unbridled optimism and novel ideas are the trifecta that people are craving. No space is off limits. You can share your truth on stage, at a university, in a documentary or a bestselling book. Cast a wide net. Jetsetting Jupiter could find you an eager audience halfway across the globe.

Need to brush up your skills? Both Jupiter and the ninth house rule higher education, which could inspire you to apply for a degree program or special training. Athletic Archers could spend vacation time doing teacher training. If you're already a master of your métier, share that knowledge. Develop your own workshops, seminars or retreats. Your wisdom is in wider demand than you may realize.

Entrepreneurial Archers will love this Jupiter-in-Leo cycle to help structure your business for ultimate freedom. More independence, less micromanagement? Yes, please. Sure, big "whale" clients who pay hefty retainers are great, but don't underestimate the power of the masses. A million minnows can add up to the same payout when you reach them with a course, a subscription, or an idea that goes global.

The door could open for a major move. If you've been dreaming of living abroad (and what self-respecting Sagittarius hasn't?), a dream opportunity could land in your lap. You don't have to sell your house and put everything in storage—unless you're legit ready for that. Maybe you spend a semester in Tokyo, do a six-month house swap in Spain, or hit the road as a digital nomad touring through beach and mountain towns. Even a short sabbatical or spiritual pilgrimage could change your life in ways you can't predict. You might just fall in love with one of these home-away-from-home locations. With Jupiter, you need to release control and let the adventure be your guide.

3 REDEFINE RELATIONSHIPS

URANUS IN GEMINI
APRIL 25, 2026 – MAY 22, 2033

Long-term partnership or a personal reinvention tour? Starting this April 25, you may no longer see the two as separate experiences. Disruptor Uranus takes up residence in Gemini and your seventh house of committed relationships, ushering in a seven-year revolution in how you connect, love and collaborate—until May 22, 2033. If you've been longing for a different kind of intimacy, something wilder, more electric, more tailored to YOU, this is your era, Sagittarius.

You got the first glimmer of this energy last year, when Uranus dipped briefly into Gemini from July 7 to November 7, 2025. Perhaps a fascinating stranger crossed your path and you made it your business to stay in touch. Or a current relationship began to unravel in ways you didn't expect, bringing both grief and a new opening for freedom.

As the side-spinning planet returns to Gemini for seven years on April 25, your entire approach to relationships is set for a radical metamorphosis. The seventh house is the domain of "we," but Uranus demands that every "we" begin with an honest "me." What do you need in order to feel seen? Supported? Free? These aren't rhetorical questions anymore, Sagittarius—they're your new relationship non-negotiables.

Coupled? The traditional trajectory may suddenly feel stifling—if it doesn't already for your liberated sign. That doesn't mean storybook love is off the table, but who says you can't have a happily-ever-after that's authored according to what your heart wants? Maybe it's separate homes or a long-distance love. Wild, spiritual intimacy that unfolds between solo retreats and creative sabbaticals. A version of partnership that suits your forward-thinking nature is evolving now, Sagittarius, and guess what? Commitment and independence CAN co-exist.

Single? This cycle could introduce lovers who don't fit any archetype you've previously desired—or even recognized. An age gap, a cultural gulf, a soul connection forged through a 2AM message board conversation: Uranus doesn't care what it LOOKS like. It cares what energy it sparks in you. Uranus is the planet of electricity, and you need partners who wake up your kundalini/life-force energy!

But here's where that gets a little complicated. Renegade Uranus can spin up your sign's attraction to the troubled types. You could weather a few false starts or find yourself hung up on the exactly WRONG kind of person simply because they get your adrenaline pumping. Expect déjà vu, cosmic chemistry and karmic patterns to finally break. The rush of the chase is something your sign hungers for. The upgrade? Keep a high bar when it comes to your targets. Pursuing someone simply to get their attention or validation? Such a waste of time. How about racing together, side-by-side after shared adventures, with someone who is eager to be your plus-one? We promise you: this kind of chase will be far more fulfilling.

Uranus in Gemini doesn't stop at romance. As the planetary ruler of technology and innovation, Uranus can completely revamp how you connect in your professional partnerships, creative duos and long-term collaborations. Think: virtual studios, AI-assisted projects, working with teams scattered across time zones. You're not looking for passive followers or feel-good agreements—you want co-creators who bring heat to the table, who challenge your thinking and sharpen your vision. With Uranus in the mix, alliances may form in lightning-strike fashion, and just as quickly catapult you into some of your most groundbreaking work yet.

Discernment, however, will be your saving grace. Uranus moves fast, and Gemini energy can be slippery. That exciting new venture? Define the terms and have a lawyer draft them into a contract. Put your agreements somewhere other than the group chat. Keep communication clear and frequent, even if the connection feels fated. Magic still needs maintenance if it's going to last.

And here's where Uranus takes it deeper: The seventh house can also reveal projections, those pieces of yourself you've unconsciously outsourced to others—your fears, your longings, even your resistance to truly being seen. Under this transit, you may notice those patterns more vividly than ever. That's your cue to own them. The only way to stop the loop is to speak your truth out loud, even if it rattles the status quo.

Uranus in your partnership house isn't here for "settling down," Sagittarius. But it IS about showing up for your truth and your desires. For the relationships that don't just accept your growth but evolve alongside it. The most transformative union of your life might just begin with the boldest act of all—being unapologetically, unmistakably yourself.

4 SPREAD YOUR MESSAGE

LUNAR NODES IN LEO AND AQUARIUS
NORTH NODE IN AQUARIUS, SOUTH NODE IN LEO JULY 26, 2026–MARCH 26, 2028

Local vibes, limitless possibilities! That's your new mantra starting July 26, as the destiny-driven North Node sails into Aquarius and your communicative third house, where it will remain until March 26, 2028. This 20-month cycle spotlights your messaging (global!) while bringing a bounty of allies close to home. Instead of scanning the horizon, pay attention to where your feet are planted, Archer; there are rich opportunities to be mined and shared. Whether you're pitching an "experience" type event, launching a podcast or leading a neighborhood initiative, your message will resonate far and wide. The key? Keep it clear, specific and accessible—your talent now lies in making the complex simple.

From January 11, 2025, until July 26, 2026, the North Node in Pisces fired up your domestic fourth house while the South Node moved through Virgo and your tenth. That cycle pushed you to balance home life with career ambition, reminding you that your foundation has to support your big leaps. In the first half of 2026, you may feel a bit more anchored, possibly dealing with upgrades to your living situation. Midyear, with the nodes shifting into Aquarius and Leo, you're ready to use your voice, share your ideas and build networks that move your worldly visions forward.

This cycle could connect you with kindred spirits who match your pace and vision. Surprise twist? Someone you once pegged as a rival may actually turn out to be a crucial collaborator. Since the third house rules siblings, colleagues and neighbors, karmic ties could emerge in your closest circles. Scribble down agreements and clarify commitments—Sag loves to wing it, but this time, written contracts keep everyone honest.

Got a message to broadcast? The mic is yours! And your voice could quickly gain traction. The North Node in Aquarius favors fresh, future-forward platforms, so think about tapping into virtual communities or tech-savvy projects that let your ideas travel fast. From Spotify to Substack, people want to hear your hot takes. Want to position yourself as an expert? Start publishing, teaching or keynoting on your area of genius. By the time this cycle is done, you could be known as the Archer who cracked the code everyone else was overcomplicating.

Meanwhile, across the wheel, the karmic South Node shifts into Leo and your ninth house of global expansion, higher education and big-picture dreams. This is familiar territory for you, since the ninth house shares many qualities with Sagittarius, the ninth sign. And here's an interesting twist: Lucky Jupiter, your ruling planet, travels alongside the South Node for the first 13 months. That means your "behind-the-scenes" work could carry just as much weight as what you broadcast. One moment you're center stage, the next you're studying, researching or quietly expanding your worldview. The dance between spotlight and sabbatical will keep you growing in dynamic ways.

For some Sagittarians, this could bring international opportunities—multi-city living, digital nomad life or clients based halfway across the world. Others may go back to school or explore new certifications that sharpen your skills. Spiritually, the ninth house is your wheelhouse, so don't be surprised if you're drawn to revisit old philosophies or dive into a fresh practice that expands your sense of meaning.

The trick is balance: The North Node in Aquarius keeps your arrows trained on clear, local targets, while Jupiter and the South Node help you refine the wisdom behind them.

By March 2028, Sagittarius, you'll emerge as both a trusted voice in your community and a global visionary whose words carry serious weight.

5 HEAL YOUR HEART

VENUS RETROGRADE IN SCORPIO AND LIBRA
VENUS RETROGRADE IN SCORPIO: OCTOBER 3–25
VENUS RETROGRADE IN LIBRA: OCTOBER 25–NOVEMBER 13

Your romantic optimism is legendary, Sagittarius—but even your free-spirited heart can't gallop past every feeling. From October 3 to November 13, emotional bypassing could catch up with you. And all you can do is stop and process.

The reason for this? Ardent Venus, the magnetic planet of love, beauty and harmony, shifts into a six-week retrograde, an uncancellable event that only happens every 18 months. The love planet begins the reflective backspin in intense, shadowy Scorpio and your mystical twelfth house of closure, healing and illusions from October 3 to 25. Then, she drifts back into charming, diplomatic Libra and your visionary, team-spirited eleventh house until November 13. The result could be a season of emotional truth-telling that starts behind the scenes, then ripples into your social circles.

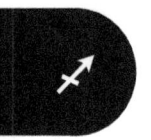

The Scorpio leg of the backspin (October 3 to 25) is your cue to turn inward. Have you been carrying the weight of an unresolved loss, breakup or personal disappointment? No more sidestepping your emotions, Sagittarius. It's time to face them with courage and support. (No, you don't have to grieve alone!)

You might realize it's time to close the chapter on someone who simply can't meet you halfway—whether that's a romantic partner, a once-close friend, or even a group whose values no longer match your own. Letting go doesn't erase the beautiful moments you shared. It simply frees you from replaying the painful parts on an endless doom loop.

Think back to October 5 to November 16, 2018, the last time Venus retrograded through Scorpio and Libra. Did you experience similar closures, or a shift in who you allowed into your inner circle? Those themes could echo now, offering a second chance to respond with more wisdom, boundaries and self-respect.

If you feel stuck ruminating on "the one that got away," Venus retrograde is NOT necessarily the time to reach out for a reunion. That said, don't be surprised if a former flame slides into your DMs. There's no hard-and-fast rule against reconnecting with a healthy person from your past during Venus retrograde. Should you sense that timing may finally be right for the two of you, gentle investigation might actually bring a beautiful reunion.

Yet, if you know this person is officially toxic and unable to meet you where you are today, keep that door slammed shut. What you might do, Archer, is create a personal closure ritual. Build a small altar with mementos to honor what you're releasing. Write letters you'll never send—but might burn as part of the ritual. By late October, when Venus slips into Libra, you may feel ready to give away a box of those keepsakes and clear the emotional space. If seeing the reminders is too raw, allot yourself "grief time" each day to journal, meditate or read something nourishing. As much as you may THINK you're ready for your next big adventure, some inner journeys can't be rushed.

Coupled Archers may uncover old, buried wounds that need another round of dressing. Although Venus retrograde can feel destabilizing, it also offers an opening for deep healing—IF you and your partner face challenges honestly. A few sessions with a skilled counselor could help you reconnect, rebuild trust and strengthen your bond.

Single? Your normally sharp instincts may be a little foggy this fall. The Scorpio portion of the backspin could pull you toward complicated types in October. Yes, including those enigmatic "mystery magnets" from your past. Tempting as it is to saddle up for a familiar ride, keep a trusted friend on speed dial to help you avoid déjà vu heartbreak.

Once Venus moves into Libra from October 25 to November 13, the spotlight shifts to your friendships, networks and collaborative dreams. An old pal could reappear, or a past group project might get a second wind. Before you leap back in, ask yourself: Am I doing this because it feels right for who I am now—or because I'm afraid to miss out? FOMO can be a great motivator for you, Archer, but it can also get you in over your head and cause friction when you pull out mid-project. Better to think things through for a few weeks before signing on.

In the meantime, fill your calendar with cultural events and classes that feed your soul. Creative outlets—photography, dance, that cooking class—can help you reconnect to your playful, expressive self. By November 13, you'll have a much clearer sense of which relationships and communities genuinely elevate your life, and you'll be ready to step forward with your signature optimism, tempered by hard-earned discernment.

2026 SAGITTARIUS

12 MONTH OVERVIEW

January MONTHLY HOROSCOPE

Look who's starting 2026 like a boss! Savvy money moves top your January agenda, Sagittarius. With the Sun in Capricorn until the 19th, your second house of income and security takes center stage. Pore over those spreadsheets and make good use of that budgeting app. You want to start this year on stable footing. On the 3rd, the Cancer full moon beams into your intimate eighth house, bringing a financial turning point and deepening an important bond. Prepare to feel like your most sexy and magnetic self. A moneymaking opportunity could arrive with the Capricorn new moon on the 18th. This one could pay off handsomely by midsummer. Venus and Mars snuggle in Capricorn until the 17th, charging up your earning power—and your sensual side. After the 23rd, they buzz into Aquarius and your third house of communication. Flirt alert! Stave off winter blahs with witty banter, electric connections and fun indoor activities—from pickleball to trivia nights. When the Sun joins the Aquarius crew on the 19th, your social life surges. Time to get your voice into the zeitgeist, too: Substack, YouTube, even local political gatherings. But while you're charging forward, love and creativity beg for some attention, too. On the 2nd, Chiron corrects course in Aries, helping you reopen your heart and shake off old romantic blocks. Then on the 26th, Neptune re-enters Aries for a 13-year stay, turning joy into a spiritual practice. Make playtime non-negotiable—it's where the magic happens now!

February MONTHLY HOROSCOPE

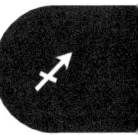

The floor is yours, Sagittarius! February supercharges your voice as the radiant Sun travels through Aquarius and your third house of communication until the 18th. What message do you need to put out into the world? Don't hold back. Your words can inspire and mobilize others now. On the 1st, the theatrical full moon in Leo lights up your expansive ninth house, spotlighting travel, media projects and education. Time to develop that curriculum, maybe while nibbling on a baguette in a Paris cafe. Then, on February 17, the Aquarius new moon arrives as a catalytic solar eclipse—the first here since 2018—just as the Year of the Fire Horse begins. A contract, conversation or opportunity could spark radical change and open new doors fast. Until February 10, Venus in Aquarius makes your words magnetic, smoothing collaborations and turning everyday interactions into chances for connection. Afterward, she drifts into Pisces and your cozy fourth house, bringing warmth to your home life and intimacy to your relationships. On February 13, Saturn re-enters Aries, beginning a two-year cycle in your creative and romantic zone. Passion projects and love will demand focus, but the rewards could be long-lasting. Valentine's Day follows with the Capricorn moon, reminding you that the most meaningful gestures are simple and sincere. Pisces season kicks off on the 18th, pulling focus to your fourth house of home and emotional foundations. Nesting becomes a form of magic now: rearrange furniture, add a ritual corner, reconnect with family traditions. With Mercury retrograde here from February 26 to March 20, family talks or real estate matters may stall, but you'll also get the chance to process old feelings and heal past dynamics. Think of this as emotional spring cleaning, creating space for the life you want to grow into.

March MONTHLY HOROSCOPE

Back to base camp you go, Sagittarius! This March, the Sun, Mercury retrograde, driven Mars and a Pisces new moon (on the 18th) charge up your fourth house of roots and domestic life. Do you feel grounded where you are, or is it time to make a change? Trust your instincts. Your gut will tell you whether to stay put or branch out. On the 3rd, a total lunar (full moon) eclipse in Virgo ignites your tenth house of career and public image. A professional milestone could arrive suddenly, or you may realize you've outgrown a role and need to pivot. On the 2nd, go-getter Mars charges into Pisces for a six-week stay, fueling action on the home front. Renovations or even a move may demand your attention. Careful not to get sucked into family drama under this aggravating cycle. Romance and creativity heat up after March 6, when Venus enters Aries and your fifth house of passion and play. Single Archers could meet someone who matches your zeal, while couples rediscover their spark through wildly adventurous dates. Your cosmic ruler, abundant Jupiter, wraps up its four-month retrograde on the 10th and powers ahead in Cancer and your eighth house of intimacy and shared resources. Financial support, loans or joint ventures may finally move forward.

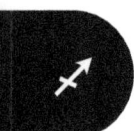

An investment could pay off handsomely and people may want to put dollars behind your dreams. Emotional connections deepen as old trust issues begin to heal. The Sun beams into Aries on March 20—the spring equinox—igniting your fifth house and inspiring you to create, flirt and take risks. Mercury stations direct the same day, lifting three foggy weeks of confusion. With your natural enthusiasm restored, you are back in your element! Launch novel projects and follow your heart—it's the Sagittarius way!

April MONTHLY HOROSCOPE

Romance and creativity heat up this April, Archer! The dazzling Sun blazes through Aries and your playful fifth house until the 19th, urging you to pour energy into love, passion projects and self-expression. Where do you want to take a risk? Follow your joy—it's your truest compass. The Libra full moon on April 1 lights up your friendship sector, bringing a team project to completion or clarifying your role in a group. On the 9th, fiery Mars storms into Aries for six weeks, giving you the courage to chase love, show off your talents or embrace playful adventures. The new moon in Aries on the 17th opens doors in your creative and romantic life, offering fertile ground for fresh beginnings. By the 19th, the steady Taurus Sun grounds you in your sixth house of wellness and routines, asking you to balance passion with practicality. After a hedonistic month, you're ready to get back into those workouts and clean up your eating habits. You'll feel like your active, energized self in no time. Venus in Taurus until April 24 sprinkles that same healthy energy into your love life and social plans. Meet for bike rides instead of brunches and make sure your dates have more green flags than red ones. Then comes a rare shift: On the 25th, Uranus leaves Taurus after seven years and rockets into Gemini until 2033. With your partnership zone electrified, relationships will evolve in radical, unexpected ways. Look forward to unconventional alliances, surprising unions and dynamic collaborations that keep you on your toes.

May MONTHLY HOROSCOPE

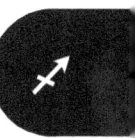

Clean, green living is the vibe this May, Sagittarius, as the Taurus Sun supercharges your sixth house of health and routines until the 20th. Where can you simplify? Think: healthy eating, better sleep hygiene and upgrading your workflow with smarter systems. On the 1st, the Scorpio full moon lights your twelfth house, urging you to drop the bad habits—or toxic ties—that drain your vitality. Pluto spins retrograde in Aquarius on the 6th, backing up through your communication zone through October 15. Are people not quite "getting" you? Rethink how you're showing up in conversations, social media and in your community. The quarter moon on the 10th makes Mother's Day a great excuse for a road trip with a few fun detours along the way. On the 16th, the Taurus new supermoon in your sixth house resets your habits. How can you move more and stress less? This may involve adopting a pet! Gemini season kicks in on the 20th, electrifying your partnership house. Suddenly, "me" becomes "we" again. Until the 18th, Venus in Gemini makes love and work collaborations feel effortless. Then, Venus glides into Cancer and your intimacy zone while Mars enters Taurus and your wellness house. Passion gets practical and suddenly, supporting each other's growth becomes the sexiest thing you can do. On the 31st, the Sagittarius blue full moon shines in your first house of identity, giving you a dramatic curtain call. Reveal your next chapter and watch the world swoon!

June MONTHLY HOROSCOPE

Two is your magic number this June! As the Sun blazes through Gemini and your seventh house of partnerships until the 21st, relationships take center stage, from business alliances to romantic bonds. The June 14 Gemini new moon—the second supermoon in a rare three-part series—lands here as well. Get ready for a bounty of contracts, partnership opportunities and powerful new connections. Meanwhile, Mars powers through Taurus and your sixth house until June 28, firing up your energy for work, wellness and routines. Stay disciplined, but also take breaks, so you don't burn out. A turning point arrives June 19 when "wounded healer" Chiron enters Taurus for a three-month preview of its 2027-2034 stay. Since 2018, Chiron has spotlighted your creative and romantic zone, which has radically shifted your outlook on love. This summer, the healing work shifts to health and habits, nudging you to mend old patterns and build supportive systems. On June 21, the Sun enters Cancer and your eighth house, just in time for the solstice and Father's Day, putting intimacy and shared resources in the spotlight. In love, Venus lingers in Cancer until the 13th, drawing you deeper into passion and emotional honesty. When she struts into Leo and your ninth house, adventure fuels romance, and couples may bond through travel or big-picture dreams. Passport, please! The global scene calls louder than ever as your ruling planet Jupiter soars into Leo on June 30, energizing your ninth house until July 2027. Publishing, travel and higher learning are blessed—follow your curiosity and watch it open doors you never imagined. The month closes with the Capricorn full moon on June 29 in your second house of money and values. A financial decision or self-worth breakthrough could arrive, but with Mercury retrograde in Cancer launching the same day, think long-term before locking things in.

July MONTHLY HOROSCOPE

July calls for depth over dazzle, especially when it comes to relationships. With the Sun in Cancer and your intimate eighth house until the 22nd—plus Mercury retrograde here until the 23rd—partnerships demand reconfiguration. From joint finances to erotic attractions, don't move further until trust is cemented. Tough but illuminating conversations are ahead. The Cancer new moon (a supermoon) on the 14th could bring resolution to a romance or business deal. Don't minimize what gets revealed. Imaginative Neptune turns retrograde in Aries on July 7 which could inspire you to rethink your personal brand. Take it slowly as Saturn's retrograde on the 26th adds gravitas: Make sure you're presenting yourself like the pro you are. Lusty Mars in Gemini ignites your relationship zone all month, heating up duos of every kind. Sparks could fly—but so could tempers. Stay present, and turn conflict into connection. Once Leo season begins on the 22nd, excitement returns for your independent ventures. Mediamaking, study and travel, yes, please! Venus in Virgo from the 9th sprinkles star power over your career, too. Don't be shy about sharing wins on LinkedIn or Instagram. When Mercury stations direct on the 23rd, delayed contracts and negotiations start moving forward. July 26 brings a huge headline: The North Node enters Aquarius and your communication house until March 2028. Your destiny lies in your messaging, whether through writing, podcasting or leading conversations that shape global thinking. On the 29th, the Sun and Jupiter unite in Leo for the "Day of Miracles," energizing travel and big-picture dreams. The very same day, the Aquarius full moon lights up your communication sector. Make way for a viral moment, breakthrough conversation or announcement that sets you on a thrilling new path.

August MONTHLY HOROSCOPE

Time to get organized and set yourself up for success! On the 3rd, Chiron turns retrograde in Taurus and your sixth house of work and wellness, nudging you to revisit habits, routines or projects that have been draining instead of sustaining. Refine your systems so they actually support you. Travel and entrepreneurship also top the list of must-do's while the Sun shimmers in Leo until the 22nd. Yes, Archer, you need to feel free…but also connections. Lusty Mars dives into Cancer and your eighth house on the 11th heating up your urge to merge. Invest in people and projects that give back in kind. Eclipse season kicks off on the 12th with a total solar eclipse in Leo—the first to hit your globally expansive ninth house since 2019! A sudden opportunity to teach, publish or hop a flight could reroute your trajectory. Let your insatiable wanderlust be your guide. Convivial Venus glides into Libra on the 6th, lighting up your eleventh house of community. Muses and allies are everywhere you turn, so say yes to cultural activities, networking events and motivating group chats. Your career kicks into high gear on the 22nd, when the Sun blazes into Virgo for a month. Update your bio, prep your fall launch or line up speaking gigs—you're in demand as summer winds down. On the 28th, the Pisces lunar eclipse sends frissons through your domestic fourth house, expediting matters at Sagittarius Central. A move, renovation or shift in family dynamics may finally crystallize. August wraps on a golden note: Your bountiful ruler Jupiter (currently in Leo)

forms a rare fire trine with Saturn in Aries on the 31st. As expansion meets discipline, a risk you've been taking could finally anchor into a lasting payoff!

September MONTHLY HOROSCOPE

September puts your ambitions front and center, Archer. With the Virgo Sun at the top of your chart in your tenth house of career and achievement, you're in boss mode until the 22nd. Bring on the promotions and pitches. Post regularly on LinkedIn and apply to be part of an elite group. Hotshot Mars is firing up Cancer and your eighth house of shared resources until the 27th, which could bring momentum around investments. Read the fine print though! It's easy to rush into binding agreements when you're this fired up. Mars could create a sexy stir, too, so look up from those screens and see who's scoping you out, Sagittarius! On the 10th, the Virgo new moon lights up your professional zone. A leadership role or high-visibility project could arrive. That same day, game-changing Uranus pivots retrograde in Gemini and your relationship house, beginning a five-month review of partnerships. Romantic or business connections may need fine-tuning to keep pace with your evolving goals. Until the 10th, Venus hangs out in Libra and your eleventh house of community, then it dips into Scorpio and your twelfth house of rest, encouraging you to recharge behind the scenes. Heads-up: Venus retrograde (October 3 to November 13) could rustle toxic relationship patterns—another reason to set clear boundaries now. Libra season begins with the fall equinox on the 22nd. Prioritize friendships and community again. You need to do more than work, work, work. On the 17th, Chiron backs into Aries and your passionate fifth house, bringing healing opportunities around romance, creativity or even parenting. By the Aries full moon on the 26th, a love story or playful pursuit could reach a turning point. Reconnect to your killer sense of humor. Laughter is medicine for the soul.

October MONTHLY HOROSCOPE

Take stock, Sagittarius. This October 3, harmonizing Venus retrogrades through Scorpio and your twelfth house of closure until the 25th, then slips into Libra and your community zone until November 13. While old connections could resurface, a collaboration might stall. Unfinished creative work could circle back around. Discombobulating as this might be, the universe asking you to consider everything carefully. Which relationships deserve a second chance, and which need to stay in the permanent archives? The Sun sails through Libra until the 23rd, spotlighting your eleventh house of teamwork. Helping hands are everywhere, especially near the Libra new moon on the 10th. Jump into a group event that widens your network. Simultaneously, heatseeking Mars blazes through Leo and your ninth house all month, fueling wanderlust and energizing visionary ideas. Watch out for FOMO: Overbooking your calendar with travel, classes and adventures could spread you too thin. October 15 ends Pluto's retrograde in Aquarius and your communication zone. A stalled contract, pitch or writing project could finally gain traction. Then on the 23rd, the Sun dives into Scorpio and your twelfth house, the same day Venus retrograde meets the Sun in a rare Cazimi. Closure is imminent: Make peace with the past and clear space for what's next. If you need to grieve any goodbyes, Mercury turns retrograde in Scorpio on the 24th, giving you three weeks to slip behind the scenes and process. Keep sensitive conversations offline and vet people carefully. It's a little too easy to fall in love with people's potential. The Taurus full moon on the 26th could bring a wellness breakthrough. Overhaul your routines so they support your vitality during the cold months.

November

MONTHLY HOROSCOPE

Clear the decks, Sagittarius. With the Sun in Scorpio lighting your twelfth house of closure and healing until the 22nd—and the year's only Scorpio new moon arriving on the 9th—you're invited to rest, release and reset. But here's the plot twist: Until the 13th, analytical Mercury is retrograde in Scorpio while convivial Venus retrogrades in Libra, dredging up unfinished business with groups or making you question certain alliances. Don't rush to cut ties or sign on for new commitments. Observe and see what happens if you make clear requests for support. By midmonth, you'll know what (and who) belongs in your life and what's better left behind. Your adventurous spirit soars nonetheless! Go-getter Mars charges through Leo until the 25th, bringing spirited visions for travel, study and entrepreneurial ventures. Your worldview is stretching this month, along with a desire to do, see and have it all. But…you're a human, not an octopus, remember? Prioritize what brings an ROI and don't get your tentacles wrapped up in too many places. Birthday season begins on the 22nd as the Sagittarius Sun brings four weeks of fresh-start energy just as the year is winding down. Leverage holiday gatherings to unveil your next big move and forge alliances with people who motivate and empower you. One or two of the people you encounter could have "power couple" potential, which becomes clear near the Gemini full supermoon on the 24th. A duo could reach a turning point that day, too: whether that's inking an official deal or deciding to go separate ways. On the 25th, Mars moves into Virgo and your tenth house of career for the rest of the year. Professional momentum surges, putting you in the running for leadership. Finish with a crown of feathers in your cap! You're writing the prologue to an ambitious 2027.

December MONTHLY HOROSCOPE

You're the main event this December! The Sun blazes through your sign until the 21st, illuminating your first house of identity and reinvention. On the 8th, the Sagittarius new moon serves a fresh start: Unveil a bold look (sequins for brunch?), pitch an idea over gingerbread lattes, set intentions that stretch well into 2027. Two outer planets—strategic Saturn and visionary Neptune—end five-month retrogrades in Aries on the 10th and 12th, respectively, pumping you up with inspiration. A half-written screenplay, an unfinished podcast or a stalled love story could suddenly surge forward. With motivator Mars powering through Virgo and your tenth house of ambition all month, career momentum builds. But easy, trailblazer! Pace yourself so you don't turn into the office Grinch. Venus re-enters Scorpio on the 4th, gliding into your twelfth house of reflection. Counter the holiday buzz with soulful rituals: sound baths, quiet cuddling (people or pets!), meditative crafts. On the 12th, your ruler Jupiter pivots retrograde in Leo which could tamp down some of your wanderlust for four months. The upside? You'll have to focus on opportunities that you overlooked close to home. Tighten your belt—and your schedule—after the 21st when Capricorn season and the solstice deliver a reality check. Budget smartly, invest in lasting pieces (a tailored coat, well-crafted décor), and close the year with a sense of stability. A partnership could crystallize with the Cancer full supermoon on the 23rd, bringing a deep sense of security. Simultaneously, you may exit something you've outgrown. The Capricorn Sun syncs with Mars in Virgo this NYE, directing you to a celebration that's stylish and intentional: rooftop fireworks, a vision-board party or a room full of fascinating people who'll shape your 2027.

Read your extended monthly forecast for life, love, money and career! astrostyle.com

CAPRICORN
IN 2026

| ALL THE PLANETS IN CAPRICORN IN 2026 | YOUR 2026 HOROSCOPE | TOP 5 THEMES FOR CAPRICORN IN 2026 | LOVE HOROSCOPE + LUCKY DATES | MONEY HOROSCOPE + LUCKY DATES |

Capricorn in 2026

Your year of:
LEGACY BUILDING, PARTNERSHIP, INTIMACY

WHO DESERVES A SEAT AT YOUR TABLE, CAPRICORN?

This year is all about alliances that amplify your reach—in love, creativity and career. You're a powerhouse on your own, but the right counterpart multiplies your impact. Think clear roles, shared vision and genuine give-and-take. Early in the year, you're exploring new commitments and collaborations. Midyear, you're ready to thin the herd. Who do you trust? You're ready to go "all in" with loyal people who energize you on a cellular level. Home remains your anchor all year, so make sure your base is solid. By December, your circle feels defined and you're growing from a place of sexy certainty!

THE PLANETS IN Capricorn

THE SUN
JAN 1–19
DEC 21–31

Happy birthday season! With the Sun in your sign, you're clear to take chances, chase fresh adventures, and command the spotlight.

NEW MOON
JAN 18
2:52PM, 28°44′

Happy bonus New Year! Set your intentions for the next six months, then take a brave step forward. Your fans await!

FULL MOON
JUN 29
7:57PM, 8°15′

Manifestation moment! Your work of the past six months bears fruit. Celebrate your progress and harvest the rewards.

MERCURY
JAN 1–20
DEC 25–31

Hold court! When charismatic Mercury zips through your sign—twice in 2026—your social status soars. Work the room, make connections—but keep your commitments realistic to avoid overpromising.

VENUS
JAN 1-17

Love is in the air! When the galactic glamazon struts through your sign, your powers of seduction skyrocket. Irresistible charm, luxe tastes, and flirtatious vibes abound—just keep an eye on your budget.

MARS
JAN 1-23

Motivation is off the charts when energetic Mars blazes through your sign every couple of years. You're bold, driven and unstoppable—but watch that combative streak and ease up on the intensity.

LILITH
SEP 14–DEC 31

Black moon Lilith is associated with the female journey through scorn, rage, empowerment and sexual liberation. When it visits your sign, you may work through issues around shame and belonging.

Capricorn in 2026
HIGHLIGHTS

LAY YOUR FOUNDATION: SATURN MOVES INTO ARIES ON FEBRUARY 13

Big shifts are underfoot, Capricorn. On February 13, your ruling planet Saturn settles into Aries and your domestic zone until April 2028. This is about building your base—literally and metaphorically. Renovate your space, redefine family roles, focus on emotional security. Dreamy Neptune also heads into Aries (on January 26), spending much of 2026 in close contact with Saturn. Engage your imaginative side for these pursuits. Casa Capricorn is a soulful and well-appointed hub for fun and productivity this year!

RELATIONSHIPS EXPAND: JUPITER IN CANCER UNTIL JUNE 30

Until June 30, Jupiter blesses your seventh house of partnerships, expanding one-on-one connections in love, business or creative collabs. Single Sea Goats could meet someone with long-term potential, while couples may deepen commitment. Professionally, this is a stellar time to team up with a coach, agent or partner who helps elevate your work. Say yes to contracts that align with your vision, but don't be afraid to negotiate terms that reflect your worth.

DEEP TRANSFORMATION: JUPITER SHIFTS INTO LEO JUNE 30

On June 30, abundant Jupiter does a costume change, slinking into Leo and your eighth house of seduction, shared resources and transformation. This 13-month cycle could put your trust to the test. You need to go "all in" to reap the rewards, but people must also pass your loyalty test. Soul-mingling sexiness and asset-merging wealth are on Jupiter's table in the second half of the year. Syncing up with powerful people can help you soar. The catch? With unfiltered Jupiter in dramatic Leo, you need to drop the mask and bring your naked vulnerability to the table. Passion isn't just expected, it's demanded. Face your fears and reap the rewards!

INNOVATION AT WORK: URANUS ENTERS GEMINI APRIL 25

After shaking up your fifth house of romance and play since 2018, Uranus moves into Gemini on April 25, launching a seven-year remix of your work, health and daily systems. The routines you've leaned on may suddenly feel stale, making space for fresh approaches. Remote-first schedules, AI tools or wellness practices that once seemed "fringe" could become your new normal. This cycle is about experimentation. If a habit, gadget or workflow boosts your energy and output, it might be worth adopting.

CAPRICORN NEW AND FULL MOONS: INITIATE AND MANIFEST

Your sign hosts two potent lunations this year: the Capricorn new moon on January 18 and the full moon on June 29. Think of January's new moon as a bonus New Year—a cosmic reset for intentions and reinvention. Who do you want to be six months from now? Set goals that stretch you, not just ones you can tick off quickly. By June 29, the Capricorn full moon spotlights your progress and holds up a mirror to your growth. Mark both dates as checkpoints: Journal your vision, create a ritual or gather your closest people for a milestone dinner.

MERCURY RETROGRADES: REVISIT THE CONVERSATION

Mercury turns retrograde three times in 2026, spotlighting communication, partnerships and your wider network. From February 26 to March 20, the backspin lands in your third house of communication and short trips. Double-check travel plans and contracts. Reconnect with siblings, old friends and people you collaborated with in the past. From June 29 to July 23, Mercury reverses in your seventh house of partnerships. Past relationships may resurface, or a current union could require renegotiation. The final retrograde, October 24 to November 13, runs through your eleventh house of teamwork. With Venus also retrograde in Libra, you may reevaluate your role in a group, or consider whether certain alliances still fit. Each cycle is a chance to refine your connections so they support you, not drain you.

AMBITION UNLEASHED: BLACK MOON LILITH IN CAPRICORN SEPTEMBER 14 TO JUNE 2027

Starting September 14, Black Moon Lilith stirs your sign for a nine-month tour, awakening untamed ambition and fierce independence. During this cycle (which comes every nine years), you may feel less patient with authority figures or structures that box you in. Channel this energy into leadership roles, activism and projects that let you call the shots. Just be mindful of power struggles—your anger is potent, but it needs direction.

DESTINY SHIFTS: NODES ENTER AQUARIUS AND LEO JULY 26

Until July 26, the South Node in Virgo and North Node in Pisces highlight a tension between belief systems and practical skills. Let go of outdated doctrines or rigid philosophies and lean into everyday tools that sharpen your voice. By mid-summer, the Nodes shift into Aquarius (North) and Leo (South), launching a 20-month chapter focused on values, money and intimacy. Your destiny lies in clarifying what's yours to build and what you share. Where are you ready to claim your power—and where do you need to trust more deeply?

PUBLIC IMAGE RESET: VENUS RETROGRADE THIS FALL

From October 3 to November 13, Venus retrogrades through your career and social sectors, pausing progress and inviting review. Public image, reputation and professional alliances may feel in flux. A past collaborator or mentor could return with unfinished business. Venus cycles back to the same retrograde territory every 8 years (minus 2°), linking this to fall 2018. Think about the career moves, branding decisions or leadership roles you were navigating then. This time, you can refine them with a wiser perspective.

Love
CAPRICORN 2026 FORECAST

Cupid's got you in his crosshairs at the start of 2026 with love planets Venus and Mars entwined in Capricorn until January 17. Love is in the air, but you might not be eager to pin yourself down into something serious. No matter your status, bask in the attention from admirers and flirt like it was your second job. (Yes, we know how to motivate a Sea Goat!)

This could very well be a major year for relationships, Capricorn. Philosophical, free-spirited Jupiter is flowing through both Cancer and Leo all year, the rulers of your seventh house of commitment and your intimate, erotic eighth. No matter how you try to dodge the DTR talk, the "Where are we heading?" conversation keeps circling back. Once the red-spotted planet heads into Leo on June 30, this may feel less like a ball and chain and more like an anchor—steadying rather than restricting. Jupiter's 13-month stay in the lion's den confirms what your sign innately knows: Building something lasting with a partner can be one of the most rewarding journeys. Your mid-year focus turns to shared resources, permanent bonds, even merging households. As long as they agree to furnish in Room & Board, you might give up a little of your famous control.

The March 3 total lunar eclipse in Virgo activates your ninth house of expansion and adventure. Don't be surprised if you catch feelings for someone with a different passport or a completely unique worldview. Long-distance love could ignite. Or you could encounter someone who you can't shake the feeling that you've met in a past life. Explore with both eyes open.

Seeking stability? Highlight April 25 on the calendar and set up a reminder alarm. Disruptive Uranus exits Taurus and your passionate fifth house after seven unpredictable years. The roller coaster of romantic ups and downs could finally end. Now, the side-spinning planet heads into Gemini, electrifying your sixth house of routines until 2033. This could reshape the way you "do" relationships, from the healthy habits you share with a partner to the quirks you will and won't put up with in a mate. Uranus is the planet of surprises and you may be shocked to discover that something you were laidback about in the past (a partner's occasional smoking habit, laundry on the floor) becomes a hard no. Put more structures in place to keep the relationship flowing smoothly. Scheduled date nights might seem cliché but they can guarantee that you won't put off your partner for other obligations seven nights a week.

Romance blooms along with the spring tulips! Ardent Venus tours Cancer from May 18 to June 13, showering your relationship zone with magic. Lusty Mars picks up the baton late summer, keeping passion high from August 11 to September 27. You might not have to do much more than step into a room full of attractive people to get the party started.

But no dodging the shadow work! On September 14, Black Moon Lilith enters Capricorn for nine months. Lilith is associated with erotic empowerment as well as any shame or rage around sexuality. When this karmic point arrives in your sign every nine years, you may grapple with a few of your own inner restrictions and conflicts. If you've been playing the role of "perfect partner," Lilith demands authenticity. The right person won't be rattled by your intensity—they'll be drawn to it. That said, finding an outside source of support (read: not your partner) would be a wise move. Some processing is best done with an objective third party, especially when it comes to the shadowy pain points that Lilith can churn up.

Fall tests your ability to balance love with other aspects of your busy life. Venus spins retrograde from October 3 to November 13, first in Scorpio and your rebellious eleventh house (until October 25), then in Libra and your goal-getting tenth house. Old crushes could reappear, or blurred lines at work may spark questions. With Mercury retrograde overlapping, tread carefully because mixing business and pleasure could complicate both.

By December, you'll have weathered sudden attraction, deep explorations about "the future of us" and a few cosmic curveballs. What you're here to learn in 2026 is that commitment doesn't have to limit you. When you put the right structures in place, it can also amplify the best parts of yourself.

Money & Career

CAPRICORN 2026 FORECAST

Big picture, bigger purpose. With lucky Jupiter touring Cancer and your seventh house of partnerships until June 30, collaboration is your growth path. This 13-month cycle, underway since June 9, 2025, encourages you to experiment with alliances that stretch your reach. Negotiate new contracts, test potential partnerships or explore co-branded ventures that highlight complementary skills. The right teammate or client could help you scale faster than you imagined.

Meanwhile, the North Node continues its journey through Pisces and your communicative third house until July 26, nudging you to diversify your interests and connect locally. Short-term projects, writing and teaching all thrive in the first half of the year. Follow your curiosity and keep your message adaptable. It's okay if you don't see instant results: You're gathering data for what comes next. Across the sky, the karmic South Node slips through Virgo and your expansive ninth house. This reflective phase is perfect for distilling big-picture lessons into tangible formats. Material you gather could evolve into a course, book or digital offering. Pay special attention around the March 3 total lunar eclipse in Virgo, when inspiration may strike in full color.

On February 13, Saturn and Neptune join forces in Aries and your domestic fourth house, beginning a two-year cycle that merges discipline with devotion. You may put down deeper roots—literally or figuratively—committing to something that anchors you. Wealth may grow through a home-based business, a family venture or work that integrates personal values with professional purpose. Saturn stabilizes your foundation while Neptune reminds you to lead with heart. If you have extra space or an ADU, you might monetize it as a rental property.

Time to overhaul your workflow? On April 25, Uranus rockets into Gemini and your analytical sixth house, where it will stay until 2033. If you've been operating on outdated systems, innovative Uranus will prompt an upgrade. You could adopt new technology, master AI tools or streamline your day-to-day with smarter processes. Flexibility is key: less grind, more flow.

Momentum accelerates midyear. On June 30, Jupiter shifts into Leo and your eighth house of investments, joint resources and long-term wealth. You're ready to deepen your financial strategy—perhaps by pooling assets, restructuring debt or exploring passive-income streams. Trusted advisors, collaborators and mentors can play pivotal roles here.

Shortly thereafter, on July 26, the destiny-fueling lunar nodes change signs, heading into your money zones for a 20-month chapter of financial evolution. The North Node will be in high-minded Aquarius and your second house of earnings and self-worth. Meaningful ways of making and spending money could evolve between now and March 2028. Across the zodiac, the South Node in Leo and your shared-resources sector reminds you that generosity and collaboration can still be profitable. Sharing is caring, and it could save you a bundle.

By year's end, you'll have tested, built and refined the frameworks that can sustain your next decade of growth. 2026 rewards you when you combine curiosity with strategy. Stay open, stay grounded and keep building something that lasts.

TOP 5 THEMES FOR Capricorn in 2026

1	2	3	4	5
FORTIFY HOME BASE	STRENGTHEN YOUR BONDS	INNOVATE ROUTINES	CREATE LASTING WEALTH	RENEGOTIATE RELATIONSHIPS

1 FORTIFY HOME BASE

NEPTUNE IN ARIES
JANUARY 26, 2026–MARCH 23, 2039

SATURN IN ARIES
FEBRUARY 13, 2026–APRIL 12, 2028

What does it mean to feel "at home," Capricorn? In 2026, you can ponder that both literally and spiritually. Your foundation is set for a soulful renovation as two powerful outer planets, Neptune and Saturn, settle into Aries and your fourth house of roots, family and emotional intelligence.

The energy of the zodiac's Ram is fiery, independent and pioneering. That's quite the contrast for the zone that rules your sense of security! Some Sea Goats may be pondering a change of address. Others will be upgrading your entire approach to nourishment and nurturing—both of yourself and the ones you adore.

You got a sneak peek of both transits in 2025, so this shift may already be underway for you, Cap. Numinous Neptune drifted into the Ram's realm from March 30 to October 22, making you feel a lot less rooted. Then, your ruler, stabilizing Saturn, joined in briefly from May 24 to September 1. Dreamy ideas started shaping into actual lifestyle adaptations or the early plans for such renovations.

In 2026, these longer cycles really take root. Neptune anchors in Aries for a mystical 13-year stay beginning January 26. Saturn returns for a two-year boot camp starting February 13.

Circle February 20 as a major moment! That's when Saturn and Neptune form an exact conjunction at 0° Aries, their only precise alignment in their shared journey through the Ram's realm. And here's some fascinating data: These two heavenly heavy hitters only unite every 35 to 40 years in the sky. Even more rare? The last Saturn-Neptune conjunction in Aries was way back in 1702! So yeah, this is a really big deal.

Epiphanies flow in as soulful Neptune's longing for a sacred space fuses with Saturn's steady insistence on bricks, budgets and boundaries. Your vision for home and family is evolving in 2026. So is your willingness to do the adult-level work to make it a reality.

All the while, you'll have to take into account the decidedly awkward energy of this planetary pairing!

Neptune in your cozy fourth house casts a gentle, spiritual glow over your living space. You may crave more softness in your design, along with a new level of artistry. We wouldn't be surprised to see you turning nooks and open shelves into altars. Expect to become more aware than ever of the energy in each room, adjusting with feng shui and space clearings. Your tastes could shift from the practical to the mystical. This isn't about rearranging furniture. In 2026, you're literally curating the vibe.

Caution flag: No-limits Neptune can dissipate common sense. It's easy to bite off more than you can chew or develop a serious case of scope (and budget!) creep when designing your ideal home. It's fine to have daydreams about opening a retreat center or buying a villa in Puglia. Please don't ignore your galactic guardian Saturn who advises you to run the numbers and draft the plan. Oh, and have the stone-hewed 19th-century Masseria with 28 hectares of land planted with olive trees inspected—even if it looks like every Fellini film you've ever drooled over. Honor your intuition, but don't ignore your spreadsheets. That fixer-upper fantasy might be a dream come true, but only if it aligns with your real needs, budget and long-term security.

On the flip side, you may feel like downsizing so you can travel more freely. Escapist Neptune in this part of your chart for the next 13 years will need regular time AWAY from base. Saturn favors minimalism, too. Selling a too-big empty nest could be the ticket to freedom, allowing you to live in a vibrant, culturally rich neighborhood—or rent a pied-a-terre there.

Family dynamics will take on a more soulful tone this year. Compassionate Neptune can help you soften old resentments or finally forgive a relative from which you've felt estranged. Saturn, meanwhile, pushes you to have the hard talks, clarify expectations and establish healthy boundaries. With both planets focusing on elderhood, some Capricorns will have to put more time into supporting an aging relative. If you're caregiving, stay mindful of burnout. Neptune can lure you into sacrificial behaviors but Saturn will remind you that draining yourself helps no one.

Ready to break some generational patterns? This is an ideal year for ancestral healing—both in the literal and woo sense. As the fourth house connects to your roots, subconscious Neptune can unearth buried memories and toxic family patterns. Saturn invites you to name them, then find tangible ways to update your neural pathways. Therapy, somatic work or simply telling the truth can loosen old knots that have kept you bound for years.

By the time Saturn exits Aries in 2028, your concept of "family" and "sanctuary" could look very different. Our bet? It will feel more authentic, peaceful and true to who you've become. And when Neptune finally moves on in 2039? You'll know how to create a home you can carry within you, no matter where in the world you roam.

2 STRENGTHEN YOUR BONDS

JUPITER IN CANCER
JUNE 9, 2026–JUNE 30, 2026

Double down on those duos, Capricorn! You're halfway through a rare Jupiter cycle that's lighting up your seventh house of partnerships. While the abundant planet buzzes in Cancer until June 30, think in pairs: business partners, romantic bonds, creative collaborators—you name it. If you've been used to climbing mountains solo, this is the year to welcome some solid company on the trail.

But not just anybody. There's a paradox to contend with. Hedonistic Jupiter is the planet of independence, so it's not exactly at home in this "just the two of us" zone. Ever since it camped out in Cancer on June 9, 2025, you may have felt your moods swinging wildly. One minute, you're craving closeness, the next, you need to get away from your favorite humans and take a gulp of air. The ideal partner for you is someone who respects your autonomy and has a full life of their own—but isn't SO busy that they never have time to meet up for concerts, fancy dinners and all the prestigious events you're invited to (often to collect an award). A tall order? Sure, but not an impossible one to fill.

Look back to 2013-14 for clues, which was the last time Jupiter was in Cancer. You may have planted seeds for a relationship pattern that's now evolving or completing. If you've been together with someone since then, this doesn't have to spell a breakup—sometimes it's about breakthrough. The sign of the Sea Goat ages in reverse, after all, and you may find yourself longing for more fun with each passing year. Take the initiative and make it happen.

Could you afford to release some obligations, even a sense of unspoken duty that you really don't need to be carrying anymore? Jupiter loves to fly free! Look for ways to lighten your load—not by quitting, but by inviting greater cooperation. The people you love will show up for you, Capricorn, but you have to let them know how.

And yeah, you might have to give up a measure of control. So the towels are folded instead of rolled and the toothpaste is squeezed from the middle of the tube. Pick your battles! It's better than saddling yourself with all the work then simmering with resentment. Allow Jupiter in Cancer's co-creative vibe to work its magic. The more you plan adventures or build projects side by side, the stronger your bond becomes.

Once Jupiter ends its four-month retrograde this March 10, you could find an optimal window to mix business with pleasure. Team up on a shared venture or just stash away cash for an epic baecation. A big, soul-expanding trip could be just what you need to reconnect. Think beyond the five-star resort with golf course and swim-up bar. Take a dip in Iceland's Blue Lagoon (and stay in an igloo) or go on a culinary trip through the French countryside where you stay, sip and make decadent meals at a centuries-old château. Since Cancer rules all things domestic, a more local trip could also be lovely.

If you're single—and loving or hating it—expect the unexpected. In your opposite sign of Cancer, Jupiter may expand your tastes to lean toward people who are way outside what you've gone for in the past. Challenge yourself to stay put and explore. As long as there's a physical attraction, you could be delightfully surprised. As the galactic ambassador, Jupiter could spark your interest in a cross-cultural connection, long-distance relationship or even a vacation romance.

Bear in mind that Jupiter IS the truth-teller of the cosmos. If there's tension bubbling beneath the surface of a close partnership, you may already feel that mask slipping off. Bottled-up frustrations could come pouring out—and your words could sound a lot harsher than you intend. Don't shy away from necessary dialogues. Just keep your eye on the real goal: growth. If attempting these convos alone gets too charged, seek outside perspective from a therapist, spiritual guide or coach.

Jupiter does have a liberating streak. If you've outgrown a bond—and you've made attempts to repair it—this cycle could make the case for moving on. Not an easy choice for loyal Capricorns, but staying stuck just delays the healing.

Business and creative alliances are equally blessed under this transit. Cancer sits opposite you on the zodiac wheel, so the magic happens when you find your complement—that yin to your yang. Scout out partners who pick up where you leave off, and vice versa. Jupiter is "exalted" in Cancer, so this could be one of the most potent times in over a decade to step into your power-couple era. We don't have to remind a Capricorn to keep your standards high. Just don't elevate them SO much that no one gets through the door.

JUPITER IN LEO
JUNE 30, 2026 – JULY 26, 2027

If the first half of the year doesn't sort the wheat from the chaff, just wait. On June 30, Jupiter settles onto Leo's throne, spending thirteen months in your all-or-nothing eighth house. While you may have experimented wildly (or even modestly) in the first half of the year, the results are in. Unless you're utterly captivated with a clear-cut vision of a shared future, you won't be in the mood to stick around and "see how it goes."

Does that seem a little harsh? Yeah, it is. But it's also pretty kind. Why drag on an affiliation when you know it's only going to end up falling apart? The good news is, you won't have to hustle to find the right people. Instead, you can now easily magnetize them to you. Jupiter in Leo elevates your sex appeal, more than you may realize! The ultra-potent eighth house is the domain of intimacy, erotic energy, wealth and shared resources. Your "money, power, respect" era is officially underway while Jupiter's here until July 26, 2027.

To avoid breaking hearts, beam your charms selectively. The power of your purr is so alluring that it's easy to lead people down a dead-end path. You know how to keep your circle tight, Capricorn, so stick to your standards. That's how you'll draw in the powerful, creative and undeniably sexy souls who match your vibe and inspire you to keep on elevating.

Jupiter is the cosmic explorer, and in the second half of 2026, it could lead you into some seriously steamy terrain. You might know how to keep your nose to the grindstone, but a Sea Goat off duty? That's where the "play hard" part of the equation comes in. And after June 30, your idea of a good time may involve indulging your erotic appetite, experimenting with a buffet of kink that wasn't previously on the menu. The stage is set with all sorts of theatrical props, thanks to Jupiter in Leo. Play out a fantasy or dive deep into the world of sacred sexuality practices. You're poised to discover what real intimacy feels like—and here, the only masks allowed are the silk blindfolds you invite your "play partner" to tie on.

And it's not just physical! A growing relationship could go full-tilt now, moving from casual to committed in a heartbeat. You're a loyal sign, but this cycle asks you to go beyond duty and toward real, soul-baring connection. If you've been skimming the surface in love, Jupiter's truth serum will push you to get raw and honest.

On the flipside, if embers are fading, Jupiter in Leo can help you make a gracious exit—or a dramatic one, the choice is yours. The eighth house is where bonds get broken and sealed. When truth-teller Jupiter lands here, there's not much grey area about what is right for you. That goes for both personal and professional relationships.

We don't recommend cutting ties rashly—or because you developed a crush on your sexy coworker with the bulging pecs and sleeve tattoos. New relationship energy doesn't last forever. Still, there may be richer terrain to explore after the "I can't wait to rip your clothes off" period. Relationships are the ultimate mirrors, reflecting back to us the good, bad and the brilliant. It's up to you to decide whether or not you want to keep forging ahead. Many long-term couples swear that their breakdowns led to the most important healing and intimacy they experienced together.

Single Capricorns: You don't have to wait until you "have it all together" (a day that never comes) before you start dating. Fears, anxiety and attachment issues are always going to arise once you make yourself vulnerable—and nothing can stir 'em up quite like the search for romance. But the above advice applies. Those early "will they or won't they?" bumps can make the whole getting-to-know-you-process a fascinating experience. If nothing else, think of all that you'll learn about yourself.

If this feels cringey, relax. This Jupiter cycle isn't only about sex. Leo rules the "mad money" part of your chart, pointing to lump sums of cash, passive income and investments that compound over time. If you'd rather obsess over spreadsheets than slipping between the sheets, we'll applaud you either way.

While ownership is your default mode, you may have people lining up to back your vision during this phase. Get your investor deck ready. There's money to be made when you share the risk and the reward. Capricorns in the C-suite could expand their vision for how to make bank. Instead of (or in addition to) collecting a paycheck, you might build wealth from royalties, commissions or affiliate sales. Jupiter in the eighth house can bring a lump sum of cash from an inheritance, legal settlement or tax return.

It takes money to make money, so keep putting it into assets that grow over time. They might be ones you create yourself, especially with enterprising Jupiter at the helm. Either way, there's no time like the present to raise your financial IQ.

With Jupiter magnifying your eighth house until July 2027, you're not just stacking cash—you're planting money trees that keep bearing fruit for years to come. Look for smart ways to invest in assets that appreciate: property, stocks, a share in a lucrative venture. If you've been wanting to learn the fine art of passive income, now's the time to master it.

Remember, the eighth house favors collaboration, too. You don't have to bankroll your empire alone! Invite in the right partners, investors or patrons who believe in your vision as much as you do. Keep your standards high, your paperwork airtight and your trust well-placed. Build slowly, but think big. You've earned the right to create wealth on your terms and Jupiter in regal Leo wants you to claim it.

3 INNOVATE ROUTINES

URANUS IN GEMINI
APRIL 25, 2026 – MAY 22, 2033

Life-as-usual? Not for long, Capricorn. Starting April 25, iconoclast Uranus dives into Gemini and your sixth house of health, habits and daily operations, where it will stir your routines until May 22, 2033. Think of it as a seven-year lifestyle lab, with you as both the scientist AND the experiment.

You got a taste of this energy from July 7 to November 7, 2025, when Uranus took a quick four-month spin through this productivity zone. Even in that short window, you may have felt the urge to scrap your old systems in favor of something sleeker, simpler—or just more your general vibe. Maybe you reorganized your workspace, discovered a new training app, or realized your daily routine was more grind than gain.

There's no doubt about it: A change is due. Uranus hasn't been in Gemini since 1941-49, so this is fresh cosmic territory. For you, it's all about optimizing how you move through your days—how you work, fuel your body and recharge your energy. It's time to design rhythms that keep you sharp and inspired instead of stuck on autopilot.

For the past seven years, Uranus was in Taurus, shaking up your fifth house of fun and personal expression. While this cycle loosened your grip on "the way things have always been done" you're ready for something more concrete. In Gemini, Uranus' energy shifts the focus from "Why am I doing this?" to "How can I make this work beautifully and efficiently?" That's not something you have to answer on the spot! Between now and 2033, experimentation becomes your new normal.

The influence of Uranus in Gemini doesn't stop at your workday routine. As the planet of technology and innovation, you'll tap into tools that rewire how you work, collaborate and take care of yourself. When it comes to your professional life, you could go full remote or join forces with a virtual team scattered across time zones. Maybe your "office" becomes a mix of coworking hubs, walking meetings and pop-up work sessions in places that spark your creativity.

While the gym membership is a must for destressing, wearable health tech tracks your stress and nudges you toward better habits. Sci-fi, metaphysical Uranus could lead you to approaches you once considered too "woo." Biohacking—think infrared saunas, cold plunges, nootropics and sleep-optimizing tech—could go from fringe curiosity to part of your everyday routine. Longevity science might capture your interest, leading you to experiment with nutrition protocols, intermittent fasting or data-driven fitness regimens. This isn't about chasing trends for the sake of novelty, Capricorn. It's about collecting insights on what genuinely enhances your energy, mood and focus.

Your sixth house also rules daily maintenance, and with Uranus here, the old "no pain, no gain" mentality won't fly. You might swap punishing workouts for joyful movement you actually look forward to. Or use AI-assisted training programs that adapt to your goals and recovery needs. Tracking apps could become your accountability partner, showing you how even small changes ripple into bigger gains. Over time, you may become your own health scientist, fine-tuning everything from hydration to circadian rhythms.

That said, not every shiny new tool will be worth your time. Uranus moves fast, and Gemini can scatter your focus. Vet ideas before you commit and test-drive systems before you integrate them fully. Get agreements in writing if you're partnering with others on business or health ventures—especially the exciting, fast-moving ones.

The sixth house also rules service and self-improvement, so this transit could push you to confront the habits, beliefs or relationships that quietly drain your energy. Maybe you've been overextending yourself, micromanaging everyone around you, or holding yourself to an impossible standard. Uranus will push you—sometimes abruptly—to drop what's not working so you can free up bandwidth for what does.

By the time Uranus leaves Gemini in 2033, you could be living in a radically different rhythm—one that prizes clarity, vitality and purpose over busyness. Let yourself try new things in the name of progress! You're building a daily life that feels as sharp and intentional as your best power suit, yet as comfortable as your favorite worn-in joggers. In short: systems that serve YOU, not the other way around. That's what we call a win-win.

4 CREATE LASTING WEALTH

LUNAR NODES IN LEO AND AQUARIUS
NORTH NODE IN AQUARIUS, SOUTH NODE IN LEO JULY 26, 2026–MARCH 26, 2028

Back to mogul mode you go, Capricorn! If the first half of 2026 lures you out into the world of "everyday people," the second half reminds you of your gifts as a steady, strategic leader—no matter what the goal. On July 26, the destiny-dusted lunar North Node moves into Aquarius and your second house of income and values, where it will stay until March 26, 2028. Slow and steady financial growth can bring newfound stability during this 20-month cycle. That could mean tightening up a few expenses or making smarter choices about where your money goes. Think of it less as cutting back and more as redirecting resources into savings, investments and opportunities that will pay off in the long run.

This cycle isn't just about covering your costs; it's about building wealth. With the South Node crossing into Leo and your eighth house of shared resources, collaboration is key. Consider ways to pool assets or bring in outside funding. Maybe you apply for a mortgage, look into small business loans or court investors who can help scale your ideas. Strategic alliances could unlock the kind of financial freedom you've been craving.

If the last 18 months of the Pisces-Virgo nodal cycle (January 11, 2025 to July 26, 2026) helped you expand your network, now's the time to cash in those connections. The relationships you've nurtured are ripe with potential. Don't wait for offers to land in your lap. Speak up and make specific requests. Closed mouths don't get fed, Capricorn. Your brave ask could lead to a breakthrough opportunity that changes your life.

The Leo South Node also pushes you to approach money with analysis, not impulse. Real estate, index funds, or even dipping a cautious toe into digital assets could be worth exploring. Diversification is your friend. The more you learn about financial systems, the more leverage you'll have to create security.

If you've let retirement planning slip, this is your cosmic nudge to get serious. Even small, consistent contributions can snowball into significant savings thanks to compounding growth. A broad, balanced portfolio—think mutual funds or index funds—offers a safer bet than trying to pick the next hot biotech stock. Corporate Capricorns should look into employer matching programs, while entrepreneurs can benefit from setting up a SEP IRA or similar vehicle. The key is automation: Set up regular transfers so you don't even have to think about it. Money that bypasses your checking account can't tempt you into spending it.

Career-wise, your hard work is ready to pay off. If you've been loyal to one company for years, it's time to leverage that experience into a promotion or higher salary. Don't be afraid to explore opportunities elsewhere if you're undervalued. Self-employed Caps can raise rates, repackage services or experiment with subscription models that bring in steady cash. This isn't about chasing quick wins; it's about building the kind of stability that gives you room to grow.

Your mindset is just as important as your strategy during this nodal cycle. Treat money as a tool—something to put to work for your goals, not a source of obsession or avoidance. Align your spending and saving with what truly matters. Reminder: In addition to things like "building my dream home" or "putting my kid through college," you need to reward yourself. Include the kind of experiences that make life feel rich, full and joyous—that bucket-list trip to your ancestral homeland or to see one of your favorite artists perform at an overseas music festival.

Here's the liberating twist: Stability doesn't limit you—it sets you free. The more secure your financial base, the more energy you'll have to invest in your vision of "a life well lived." When you're not bogged down by stress about bills, you can devote yourself fully to the creative, big-picture projects that only you can bring to life. That's something your ambitious sign can get behind!

5. RENEGOTIATE RELATIONSHIPS

VENUS RETROGRADE IN SCORPIO AND LIBRA
VENUS RETROGRADE IN SCORPIO: OCTOBER 3–25
VENUS RETROGRADE IN LIBRA: OCTOBER 25–NOVEMBER 13

Knowing the "right" people is one of your not-so-secret weapons for success, Capricorn. But starting this October 3, you may need to pause from your expansion efforts to fortify a few key alliances. Diplomatic, harmonious Venus shifts into her biennial, six-week retrograde, putting the focus on people who are already part of your world.

This unavoidable backspin takes place every 18 months, but every 8 years will repeat through the same zodiac signs. (Flashback to a cycle that hasn't happened since Fall 2018!) From October 3 to 25, Venus slips back through Scorpio and your eleventh house of teamwork, community and technology. Then, from October 25 to November 13, she moonwalks into diplomatic Libra and finishes the retrograde in your tenth house of ambition, public image and long-term success. It's not simply "all about who you know" this fall—it's all about the effort you put into those VIP bonds.

The first leg of Venus retrograde, in Scorpio and your people-loving eleventh house, could pull you back into the orbit of an old crew. Scroll through the deep archives of your social media timelines and contact lists. A forgotten group interest could pique your attention again. (Remember THAT?) Whether it's a book club, a creative collective or a political action network, nostalgia calls you back to explore it again.

One word of caution: When diplomatic Venus is in snooze mode, you could develop a case of selective amnesia. Why DID you step back from that group in the first place? Along with fond memories, this cycle could dredge up difficult dynamics which splintered you the last time around. If you're reviving a team effort, make sure expectations, commitments and boundaries are crystal-clear from the start. Doing so can create the right foundation for a successful second act.

This phase also prompts an honest audit of your inner circle. Have certain friendships faded due to busy schedules—or is it because your values have evolved in different directions? A reconnection could be healing, but it could also confirm that some bonds were meant to stay in the past. If you do rally the old squad, keep travel and ticket purchases flexible. Venus retrograde has a way of tossing logistical curveballs, especially when friends are spread across time zones.

When Venus slides back into Libra on October 25, the spotlight shifts to your professional sphere. Old contacts could resurface with intriguing offers, or you might revisit a stalled project with renewed clarity. If you've fallen out of touch with a career contact, reach out in a graceful manner. In other words, don't rush to pitch any ideas. Just start with a gentle check-in to the tune of, "We haven't connected for a while, and you were on my mind. What have you been up to lately?"

Have you lost your enthusiasm for work you once loved? Lean into the artsy and justice-oriented sides of Venus. Creative solutions can breathe new life into your work; so can connecting what you're doing to an important cause. Put your competitive streak in the timeout chair until Venus turns direct on November 13. Rather than rushing into a public launch, use these weeks for strategic refinement and behind-the-scenes relationship building. The connections you strengthen now could lead to significant breakthroughs in the months ahead.

Romantically, Venus retrograde is a clear sign to ease off the accelerator. If you're getting to know someone, let the story unfold instead of rushing to define it. Retrogrades peel back the layers slowly, revealing truths you might miss if you push too hard. Still hung up on someone whose behavior is inconsistent (at best)? This is your cue to stop waiting for crumbs—you deserve so much better than that! Step back, reclaim your energy and leave room for a partner who's all in.

Couples could find themselves deep in talks about shared goals and timelines. Maybe one of you is chasing a career milestone while the other dreams of more downtime—or your visions for a shared lifestyle need some finessing. Use this retrograde window for exploratory conversations rather than firm commitments. Swap ideas for how to balance ambition with rest, or test out small changes like adjusting your weekly routines, planning a mini escape, or carving out dedicated time for each other that isn't overshadowed by work or chores. The aim is to fine-tune the way you move through life together so it feels sustainable for both of you.

2026 CAPRICORN

12 MONTH OVERVIEW

January MONTHLY HOROSCOPE

It's your season, Capricorn—charge into the New Year like you mean it! With the Sun beaming in your sign until the 19th, your trailblazing first house is lit up. You have momentum for whatever you desire, from refreshing your look to tackling a daring fitness goal to launching a vanity project that will take the world by storm. Don't let anyone dissuade you from "doing you," but stay open to partnership possibilities near the 3rd, when the first full moon of 2026 lands in Cancer and your dynamic duo zone. A relationship could also reach a turning point near this day, especially if one (or both) of you is craving more togetherness—or more independence. Save a few resolutions for the 18th when the Capricorn new moon hits the cosmic reset button. What do you want to be known for in 2026? Actions you take now will ripple forward for months. Venus and Mars travel in tandem through your sign until the 17th, boosting your magnetism (and yes, your sex appeal). After the 23rd, they move into Aquarius and your money sector, reminding you that self-worth and net worth are deeply connected. When the Sun shifts into Aquarius on the 19th, there's even more emphasis on your earnings. Time to stabilize income and value your time properly. But beneath the ambition, your foundations need tending, too. On the 2nd, Chiron turns direct in Aries, easing family dynamics and helping you find peace at home. And on the 26th, dreamweaver Neptune re-enters Aries for a 13-year cycle, inspiring you to root yourself in places—and relationships—that feel soulful.

February MONTHLY HOROSCOPE

Secure the bag, Capricorn! February puts money and values front and center as the determined Sun powers through Aquarius and your second house until the 18th. Where do you need to strengthen your fiscal foundation? Start with small, consistent habits that grow into lasting security. The full moon in Leo beams into your eighth house on the 1st, pushing a contractual matter to resolution. Can you finally put a power struggle or debt behind you? Facing it head-on will bring the freedom you crave. On February 17, the Aquarius new moon arrives as a decisive solar eclipse—the first here since 2018—just as the Year of the Fire Horse begins. A new income stream or investment could appear suddenly. Until February 10, Venus in Aquarius enhances your financial magnetism. Afterward, she slides into Pisces and your third house, sharpening your words and making your communication particularly persuasive. Just don't dangle any promises you have no intention of keeping. On February 13, structured Saturn re-enters Aries, beginning a two-year cycle in your domestic sector. It's time to create stronger foundations at home and within family dynamics. Valentine's Day follows with the Capricorn moon, making YOU Cupid's favorite this year. On the 18th, Pisces season turns the spotlight to your communicative third house. Your inbox may overflow, but so will your idea bank. Mercury's retrograde here from February 26 to March 20 could scramble details, but it's also a gift for revisiting pitches, editing drafts, or reconnecting with neighbors and siblings. Conversations you thought were over may loop back around, this time with a chance to say what you really mean. Clarity comes from reflection first, then action.

March MONTHLY HOROSCOPE

Step up to the mic, Capricorn! You're a veritable fount of ideas this March as the Sun, Mercury retrograde, go-getter Mars and a Pisces new moon (on the 18th) energize your third house of communication. This is your month to write, teach and get your message out—but also to listen carefully. Dive into those think tanks and brainstorm freely. On the 3rd, a total lunar (full moon) eclipse in Virgo strikes your ninth house of expansion and big-picture plans. A media project, educational pursuit or travel opportunity could reach a pivotal point. Are you ready to commit to a path that stretches you beyond the familiar? Take the leap—you're more prepared than you think. Mars moves into Pisces on the 2nd for a six-week stay, revving up conversations, negotiations and networking. Use this influence to pitch ideas, reconnect with siblings or revitalize community ties. Love takes a tender turn after March 6, when Venus enters Aries and your fourth house of home. Cozy, heartfelt connections matter more than grand gestures now, and couples may focus on creating a sanctuary together. On March 10, abundant Jupiter ends a four-month retrograde in Cancer and your seventh house of partnerships. Relationships that stalled or felt unclear since last year can finally gain traction, and supportive allies may step in. Aries season begins with the spring equinox on the 20th, illuminating your domestic zone. Mercury stations direct the same day, ending three foggy weeks. Home and family plans move forward again. Roll out the welcome mat and let the nesting commence!

April MONTHLY HOROSCOPE

Home becomes your anchor this April, Capricorn. The grounding Sun moves through Aries and your domestic fourth house until the 19th, pulling focus to your family, roots and emotional foundations. Do your surroundings support the life you're trying to build? If not, begin shaping them to match your vision. On the 1st, the Libra full moon lights up your tenth house of career, bringing a professional milestone to culmination. Radical Mars storms into Aries for six weeks on the 9th, energizing household matters but also testing patience in difficult interpersonal dynamics. Pour this energy into constructive change—a new kitchen, maybe—rather than clashes with the toxic branches of your family tree. The new moon in Aries on the 17th invites you to plant fresh roots or start a new domestic chapter. Rearrange furniture, relocate or just set better boundaries with the people who darken your doorstep. On the 19th, the steady Taurus Sun brightens your fifth house of creativity and romance, shifting your mood to playful and passionate pursuits. Until the 24th, Venus also travels through Taurus, adding sweetness and harmony to love and artistic projects. Then, a seismic change: On the 25th, revolutionary Uranus ends its seven-year stay in Taurus and rockets into Gemini until 2033. With your sixth house now activated, daily routines, health and work will undergo a radical transformation. Expect breakthroughs in how you manage time, wellness and productivity.

May MONTHLY HOROSCOPE

Passion takes the wheel this May, Capricorn, as the Taurus Sun lights up your fifth house of romance and creativity until the 20th. Make time for art, pleasure and romantic experiences—with or without a partner. On the 1st, the Scorpio full moon illuminates your eleventh house of groups and friendships: A collab could wrap, or you may realize you've outgrown a certain crew. Exit gracefully and move on to greener pastures. On the 6th, Pluto turns retrograde in Aquarius and your money sector until October 15, asking you to rethink spending, investments and worth. The quarter moon in Aquarius on the 10th could make Mother's Day both elegant and traditional. Spare no expense. On the 16th, the Taurus new supermoon charges up your fifth house, a green light for new love affairs and creative breakthroughs. Then Gemini season begins on the 20th, shifting your attention to wellness and systems. Set up the practical scaffolding that supports your life goals—and your art! Until the 18th, Venus in Gemini adds harmony to your work and daily rhythms. Then, the love planet slips into Cancer and your partnership house while Mars charges into Taurus and your fifth. Open yourself up to people who you might normally be a little overwhelmed by. Big love energy is on deck and you're ready to greet it with passion. The month ends with the Sagittarius blue full moon on the 31st, shining into your twelfth house. Release a long-standing burden—closure is the ultimate power move.

June MONTHLY HOROSCOPE

Bring on the practical magic! As the Sun treks through Gemini and your sixth house of work and wellness until the 21st, streamline your routines, tighten systems and put healthy habits in place. The June 14 Gemini new moon—the second supermoon in a rare three-part series—lands here as well, calling for stress-busting lifestyle upgrades. Meanwhile, Mars charges through Taurus and your fifth house until June 28, fueling creativity, romance and playful self-expression. Channel this energy into passion projects—or passion itself. On June 19, "wounded healer" Chiron enters Taurus for a three-month preview of its 2027-2034 stay. Since 2018, Chiron has pressed on family and home matters, surfacing insecurities about belonging. This summer, the focus shifts to your self-expression and love life, helping you heal through joy and vulnerability. On June 21, the Sun shifts into Cancer and your seventh house of partnerships, just in time for the solstice and Father's Day. Relationships, romantic or professional, could feel especially meaningful now. In love, Venus lingers in Cancer until the 13th, adding sweetness and harmony to your closest bonds. Then she struts into Leo and your eighth house, intensifying passion and turning up the heat in intimacy. The big news of the month arrives on June 30! Limitless Jupiter powers into Leo and your eighth house of intimacy, shared resources and transformation, where it will remain until July 2027. Get ready to deepen bonds, attract investments and feel more tapped into your spiritual side than you have in years. The month peaks with the Capricorn full moon on June 29 in your first house of identity and self-expression. You may reach a personal milestone or step into the spotlight, but with Mercury retrograde in Cancer starting the same day, proceed thoughtfully in partnerships over the next few weeks.

July MONTHLY HOROSCOPE

Relationships move to the top of your priority list this month, Capricorn. With the Sun in Cancer and your partnership zone until July 22—and Mercury retrograde here until the 23rd—you may be renegotiating an agreement, reviving an old connection or redefining what commitment looks like now. The Cancer new moon (a supermoon) on the 14th brings clarity: Whether it's making things official or deciding it's time to part ways, you'll know where you stand. After the 7th, you'll reevaluate home and family dynamics as therapeutic Neptune begins a five-month retrograde in Aries. Are you escaping into work to avoid personal issues? Your wise ruler Saturn follows suit on the 26th, pressing you to create firmer boundaries before the end of 2026. Put healthy habits in place as you go! Energizer Mars charges through Gemini, activating your sixth house of health and routines all month. While this transit supercharges productivity, it also raises stress levels. Streamline your calendar instead of saying yes to everything. When Leo season kicks in on the 22nd, your attention shifts to intimacy and shared resources. This sultry cycle could bring you closer to one (or two) special souls. Money's in focus, too: From mortgages to investments, your funds deserve careful review. There's fun to be had once Venus swings into Virgo on the 9th, boosting your appetite for travel and learning. This could be the summer to enroll in a certification program or book that long-haul trip. Once Mercury turns direct on the 23rd, partnership conversations flow without static. Fiscal developments accelerate after July 26, when the fateful lunar North Node enters Aquarius and your money sector for the first time in nearly 20 years. Until March 2028, your destiny revolves around financial independence and building lasting security. Start exploring revenue streams that match your values instead of chasing quick wins. Closing out the month, the Sun and Jupiter unite in Leo for the "Day of Miracles" on the 29th, amplifying shared financial opportunities. Simultaneously, the Aquarius full moon lights up your income zone. You could wrap July with a raise, a side hustle taking off or a money mindset shift that changes everything!

August MONTHLY HOROSCOPE

Your heart takes the lead this August, as the Leo Sun bursts through your intimate, soulful eighth house until the 22nd. On the 3rd, healer-feeler Chiron pivots retrograde in Taurus and your passionate fifth house, resurfacing old stories about love or confidence that are ready for an upgrade. Get real. Sharing your vulnerability could be the very thing that deepens a connection or unlocks your artistry. Make-it-happen Mars charges into Cancer and your partnership zone on the 11th, serving dynamic duo energy left and right. Whether it's a business alliance, a romance or teaming up with a project partner, passion and synergy run high. Eclipse season kicks off August 12 with a total solar eclipse in Leo—the first here since 2019—igniting your eighth house of intimacy and shared resources. A financial merger, joint investment or transformative relationship could accelerate suddenly, demanding trust and full presence. Venus enters Libra on the 6th, polishing your tenth house of career and reputation. Use the last days of summer to sharpen your brand, update your digital footprint and step onto a more influential stage. You've got natural authority, Capricorn, and people are watching. Virgo season fuels your ninth house of wisdom and exploration starting on the 22nd. How will you expand next? Here's your cue to book a retreat, sign up for a fall masterclass series or share your expertise more widely. The Pisces lunar eclipse on the 28th could bring a turning point in a platonic partnership. Don't hang on out of habit! August wraps with a rare gift: On the 31st, Jupiter in Leo forms a harmonious trine with Saturn in Aries, giving you the courage to take a calculated risk around home, financial investments and long-term relationships. If all the players are stable and "all in" you have the makings of a victory on your hands.

September MONTHLY HOROSCOPE

Adventure is calling, Capricorn! With the Virgo Sun blazing through your ninth house of travel, learning and expansion until the 22nd, September invites you to broaden your horizons. This could look like booking a fall getaway, signing up for a workshop or diving into a spiritual practice that gels with your philosophy on life. Meanwhile, Mars is powering through Cancer and your partnership zone until the 27th, adding passion—and maybe some friction—to your closest bonds. Use this dynamic energy to collaborate, but watch for clashes if egos

get in the way. On the 10th, the Virgo new moon energizes your ninth house, sparking opportunities around travel, entrepreneurship or higher education. A project with a global reach could get a green light. That same day, Uranus pivots retrograde in Gemini and your sixth house of work and wellness, nudging you to refine your routines and experiment with new systems over the next five months. Until the 10th, Venus lingers in Libra and your tenth house of career, boosting your charm with higher-ups and giving you extra magnetism in professional settings. Then Venus dips into Scorpio and your eleventh house of community, making networking and team projects especially rewarding. Heads-up: Venus retrograde from October 3 to November 13 could slow collabs, so invest now in the alliances that matter most. The fall equinox on the 22nd doubles down on career as the Sun moves into Libra and your public tenth house. Roll up your sleeves and get working on a project that inspires you. On the 17th, Chiron backs into Aries and your domestic fourth house, highlighting healing around family and home. And by the Aries full moon on the 26th, you may feel a powerful urge to reset your foundations—whether that's moving, renovating or finally mastering the work-life balance thing.

October MONTHLY HOROSCOPE

Steady your aim, Capricorn. On October 3, Venus retrogrades through Scorpio and your eleventh house of groups until the 25th, then slides into Libra and your career zone until November 13. Team efforts may stall, alliances could wobble or you might feel unsure about your role in a community. But maybe this pause is helping you refine your vision. Who belongs in your circle—and who doesn't? The Sun beams through Libra until the 23rd, spotlighting your tenth house of career and status. The Libra new moon on the 10th could deliver a new role, a leadership opportunity or a chance to showcase your expertise. Simultaneously, motivator Mars blazes through Leo and your eighth house all month, heating up shared finances and intimacy. You're an attractive force, Capricorn, but look out! Jealousy or power struggles could creep in if boundaries aren't crystal clear. On October 15, Pluto ends its retrograde in Aquarius, reigniting momentum around your finances. Then on the 23rd, the Sun enters Scorpio and your eleventh house of friends and networks, the same day Venus retrograde fuses with the Sun in a rare Cazimi. Get ready for intense revelations about who's truly aligned with your long-term goals—and who isn't worth the energy. Mercury slips into retrograde (in Scorpio) on the 24th, crossing wires in group chats and team projects. Expect delays, so pad your deadlines. Romance is in the spotlight with the Taurus full moon on the 26th, Venus retrograde be damned! Keep your heart open, especially with people who feel safe and familiar.

November MONTHLY HOROSCOPE

Rally your people, Capricorn. With the Sun in Scorpio activating your eleventh house of community and collaboration until the 22nd—and the year's only Scorpio new moon landing on the 9th—you're in team-building mode. But the first half of the month may test your patience. Until the 13th, social Mercury is retrograde in Scorpio while convivial Venus retrogrades in Libra, stalling progress on group projects or causing friction in your professional circles. Use this time to fine-tune roles, boundaries and expectations. By midmonth, the right allies rise to the surface and momentum returns. Meanwhile, make-it-happen Mars powers through Leo until the 25th, charging your eighth house of intimacy and shared resources. Joint ventures heat up, whether in business, finances or love—but so do power struggles if transparency is lacking. Direct that intensity toward strategic moves, not battles of will. Once Sagittarius season begins on the 22nd, the Sun slips into your twelfth house of rest and reflection. You'll crave quiet, healing and space to recharge before your birthday season begins on December 21. The Gemini full supermoon on the 24th lights up your sixth house of wellness and work. A project could reach completion or you may get a reality check about your schedule. Are you balancing productivity with sustainability? Adjust accordingly. Then on the 25th, Mars sails into Virgo and your global ninth house for the rest of the year. Wanderlust spikes, and opportunities for studying, teaching or long-distance travel surge. Expand your world, Capricorn! Opportunity awaits in unexplored terrain.

December MONTHLY HOROSCOPE

Until the solstice, the Sagittarius Sun shimmers in your twelfth house of reflection, healing and behind-the-scenes magic. What can you release before your birthday season? Swap doomscrolling for meditation; mix up mocktails instead of uncorking another bottle of wine. Trade one late-night party for a candlelit bath, especially with the new moon on the 8th. Your ruler, dependable Saturn, along with compassionate Neptune, wrap up five-month retrogrades in Aries on the 10th and 12th, respectively, bringing clarity to home and family matters. Renovations, relocation or a boundary with difficult relatives suddenly makes sense. Wanderlust washes over you in waves all month, while motivator Mars powers through Virgo and your adventurous ninth house. Sign up for a post-holiday retreat, hit the ski slopes and mingle multiculturally. Venus re-enters Scorpio on the 4th, bringing an experimental vibe to your love life. Someone who's "not usually my type" could melt your resistance. With Jupiter turning retrograde in Leo on the 12th, you'll need to watch finances carefully for the coming four months. Don't Scrooge out, just invest wisely. Birthday season begins with the solstice on the 21st and you're ready for your annual reboot! Debut a new look or tee up a launch for early January. A partnership could come to fruition under the Cancer full supermoon on the 23rd. Seek support from people whose skills complement yours. And NYE? The Capricorn Sun syncs with Mars in Virgo, setting you ablaze with visionary fire. Host or attend a party with fellow movers and shakers whose 2027 goals are a match for your own!

Read your extended monthly forecast for life, love, money and career! astrostyle.com

AQUARIUS IN 2026

| ALL THE PLANETS IN AQUARIUS IN 2026 | YOUR 2026 HOROSCOPE | TOP 5 THEMES FOR AQUARIUS IN 2026 | LOVE HOROSCOPE + LUCKY DATES | MONEY HOROSCOPE + LUCKY DATES |

Aquarius in 2026

Your year of:
DESTINY FULFILLMENT, CREATIVITY, PRACTICAL MAGIC

THAT'S GENIUS, AQUARIUS!

In 2026, inspiration doesn't just visit—it takes up permanent residence in your daily life. Your assignment? Channeling your flashes of brilliance into projects that shift the culture around you. This is the year to stop trimming your edges to fit what's popular and start letting your quirks be the headline. When you show up with full presence instead of keeping one foot out the door, relationships flourish and collaborators line up to support you. By year's end, playful experiments could crystallize into real influence, positioning you as the innovator who not only dreams it up but delivers results!

THE PLANETS IN Aquarius

THE SUN
JAN 19–FEB 18

Happy birthday season! With the Sun in your sign, you're clear to take chances, chase fresh adventures, and command the spotlight.

NEW MOON, ANNULAR SOLAR ECLIPSE
FEB 17
7:01AM, 28°50'

Happy bonus New Year! The first eclipse in your sign since 2018 rockets you into a new league. Set intentions with care, considering every possible angle.

FULL MOON
JUL 29
10:36AM, 06°30'

Manifestation moment! Your work of the past six months bears fruit. Celebrate your progress and harvest the rewards.

MERCURY
JAN 20–FEB 6

Hold court! When charismatic Mercury zips through your sign, your social status soars. Work the room, make connections—but keep your commitments realistic to avoid overpromising.

VENUS
JAN 17–FEB 10

Hello, smokeshow! When the galactic glamazon struts through your sign, your powers of seduction skyrocket. Irresistible charm, luxe tastes and flirtatious vibes abound—just keep an eye on your budget.

MARS
JAN 23–MAR 2

Motivation is off the charts when energetic Mars blazes through your sign every couple of years. You're bold, driven and unstoppable—but watch that combative streak and ease up on the intensity.

PLUTO
JAN 1-DEC 31
RETROGRADE IN AQUARIUS:
MAY 6–OCT 15

Your soul undergoes a profound metamorphosis as intense, alchemical Pluto spends its second full year (of nineteen) in your sign. Outmoded parts of your identity may burn away as you rise like a phoenix from the ashes. Connect to your raw power by doing shadow work.

NORTH NODE
JUL 26–DEC 31

The destiny-fueling North Node begins an 18-month tour through your sign, connecting you to your passion and purpose. This cycle, which only happens every 18.5 years, may put you through your paces but helps to true you up with your authentic self.

Aquarius in 2026
HIGHLIGHTS

REINVENTION STATION: URANUS ENTERS GEMINI APRIL 25

Mark the date, Aquarius—your ruling planet Uranus changes signs and, for you, that's headline news. On April 25 it strides into Gemini for a seven-year stay, firing up your fifth house of creativity, romance and self-expression. Translation? Your passions get a radical reboot. Love stories arrive out of left field, artistic projects take wild new forms and your personal style could surprise even you. Launch the podcast, try on a new aesthetic or shake up your dating life—what starts as play could evolve into your next defining chapter.

USE YOUR VOICE: SATURN AND NEPTUNE IN ARIES

Saturn and Neptune spend most of 2026 in Aries, energizing your third house of communication, ideas and local connections. Saturn says: Structure your message. Neptune digs deeper: Make it inspiring. Whether you're teaching, writing, podcasting or building community through local platforms, this combo makes your words magnetic. Start the newsletter, polish the pitch deck or carve out regular writing hours. With the right blend of discipline and vision, your ideas can truly move people.

YOUR GALACTIC RESET: AQUARIUS SOLAR ECLIPSE FEBRUARY 17

Mark February 17 for a shake-up, Aquarius—your annual new moon arrives as a solar eclipse, the first in your sign since 2018. Eclipses act like cosmic plot twists, jolting you onto a new path before you've had time to overthink it. Surprises may surface quickly, calling for nimble decisions or an instant pivot. You could debut a new look, launch a passion project or experience a personal turning point that shifts how others see you. Treat it like a birthday reset: Set intentions, gather your allies and claim the reinvention. Watch for the story to crest at the Aquarius full moon on July 29, when the changes begun in February reveal their full shape.

HEALTH IS WEALTH: JUPITER IN CANCER UNTIL JUNE 30

Until June 30, abundant Jupiter blesses your sixth house of work and wellness. This isn't just about hitting the gym—it's about aligning body, mind and daily rhythms. You could land a new job, join a team that fits your values or overhaul your routines with tools that actually stick. From habit-tracking apps to coworking memberships, invest in systems that make life flow easier.

MERCURY RETROGRADES: REDEFINING YOUR VALUE

Mercury turns retrograde three times in 2026, pushing you to rethink money, work rhythms and career goals. From February 26 to March 20, the rewind moves through your second house of income and self-worth. Review spending, renegotiate pay or reconnect with a past income stream. From June 29 to July 23, Mercury steals back through your sixth house of health, habits and daily routines. Schedules may go sideways, projects get delayed or wellness plans require a reset. The final backspin, October 24 to November 13, lights up your tenth house of career. With Venus also retrograde in Libra, this period highlights your public image—an old professional contact may reappear, or you might rethink your long-term goals. Each retrograde reminds you: Progress sticks when you take time to refine the details.

LOVE AND RELATIONSHIPS EXPAND: JUPITER ENTERS LEO JUNE 30

Relationships—romantic, professional and creative—become major growth zones in the second half of the year. On June 30, Jupiter shifts into Leo and your partnership house for 13 months. Single Water Bearers could meet someone game-changing, while couples may take big steps (moving in, rings, joint ventures). Professionally, partnerships could expand your reach in massive ways. The secret sauce? Choose collaborators who amplify your vision instead of competing with it.

DESTINY CALLING: NORTH NODE LANDS IN AQUARIUS JULY 26

Who do you think you are, Aquarius? That's a profound question to explore in the second half of the year. On July 26, the lunar North Node enters Aquarius for the first time in nearly two decades, kicking off a 20-month soul directive. This is your call to live your truth, step into leadership and align with your purpose. Across the sky, the South Node in Leo urges you to release toxic partnerships or people-pleasing tendencies. Show up fully, without apology. Eclipses across the Aquarius-Leo axis will supercharge this theme until March 2028, stirring up karmic corrections around identity and relationships. Enjoy your independence without isolation.

PRESS PAUSE: VENUS RETROGRADE THIS FALL

From October 3 to November 13, Venus retrogrades through your career and expansion zones, stirring questions about your ambitions and how they meld with your vision of love. You may rethink a project, revisit a long-term goal or pause to reassess whether the direction you're pursuing is aligned with your relationship values. Venus repeats her retrograde path every 8 years (minus 2°), so fall 2026 mirrors fall 2018. What was shifting in your love life back then—and how did your life plans figure in? This round offers a chance to integrate those lessons and choose something that supports YOU.

Love
AQUARIUS 2026 FORECAST

If you're up in the clouds at the start of 2026, don't rush back down to earth. Lovebirds Venus and Mars linger together in Capricorn until January 17, swirling through your fantasy-fueled twelfth house. You may prefer to avoid some inconvenient realities—like returning to work post-holidays or leaving your vacation romance on another continent—but c'est la vie. Or, you could be nursing a bit of heartache and simply want to stay in your healing bubble.

This could all shift quite rapidly on January 23, as both Venus and Mars will have moved into Aquarius. Hibernation, schmibernation. The love planets push you out of your cave to flirt and organize romantic winter activities. While Venus moves on by February 10, lusty Mars hangs out in your sign until March 2, practically guaranteeing that the groundhog won't be the only one, er, popping up to say hello.

The Year of the Fire Horse brings another fresh start on February 17, arriving with the new moon in Aquarius—which happens to be a game-changing solar eclipse. Hidden desires jolt awake! This gets further amplified with the second eclipse in this pairing, the March 3 lunar (full moon) eclipse in Virgo and your erotic eighth house. Sudden developments—anything from accelerated passion to a hard truth—could push a relationship to its next stage. A spicy attraction could consume you. This could fall far outside the range of your "usual type." And for you, Aquarius, that's saying something!

The electrifying updates don't stop there. On April 25, your galactic guardian Uranus logs into Gemini for a seven-year stay in your fifth house of love, passion and creativity. Welcome to the liberation station, Aquarius. (Even if you thought you were already there.) With your rebellious ruler in this whimsical zone until 2033, love becomes (even more) unconventional, experimental and dynamic AF. Since the fifth house rules celebrations and fertility, there could be weddings, children and co-created projects on deck. All mapped out with an Aquarian twist!

Summer raises the volume. From June 13 to July 9, Venus struts through Leo and your relationship house, turning everyday interactions into high-voltage encounters. Then on June 30, indie-spirited Jupiter beams into Leo for the first time since 2014, super-sizing your partnership zone for the next 13 months. Your love life becomes a main stage act, not a side project. This is expansive, electric energy that can draw in a soulmate-caliber match or inspire a long-term upgrade to an existing bond. Think bigger, Aquarius:

The person you join forces with now should multiply your freedom, not fence you in. With worldly Jupiter at the helm, they might not even live in the same city as you. Travel could figure in, even if that means jetting around like a global power couple.

A destiny checkpoint arrives July 26, when the lunar nodes head into Aquarius (North Node) and Leo (South Node). How do you balance your drive for individuality with your desire for togetherness? This 20-month transit spawns a fascinating inquiry, one that is sure to bring some evolution. The August 12 Leo solar eclipse could bring sudden developments like a whirlwind commitment or, in some cases, a breakup that frees you for truer love.

But that's not all! Lusty Mars storms through Leo from September 27 to November 25, igniting passion—and maybe power struggles if egos collide. With so much action hitting your relationship zone, you might actually be relieved to slip into the forced timeout of Venus retrograde from October 3 to November 13.

This slowed-down cycle gives you a chance to catch your breath, review the events of the year and maybe reconnect to someone who you glossed over accidentally. Coupled Aquarians have a chance to evaluate and recalibrate: Are you climbing in the same direction or marching to different drummers? Some new ways of supporting each other could emerge, just in time for 2027. The cosmic memo is undeniable as the year winds down: The right partner won't try to polish away your quirks but will be a cheerleader for your undeniably original ways!

Money & Career

AQUARIUS 2026 FORECAST

An inside-out transformation is underway, Aquarius, and your money is no exception. With wealth-agent Pluto powering through Aquarius for its second full year (of twenty), this is a reinvention era for your professional identity and earning power. You're not here for flash-in-the-pan wins. Nope, you're building an empire, one innovative idea at a time. Focus on legacy investments, long-range strategies and business models that reflect your values. The next chapter of your success story involves depth over speed.

Work—and the way you do it—is also transforming. With prosperous Jupiter in Cancer and your sixth house of service and efficiency until June 30, you're rewriting the rules of the modern workplace. Think: More flexibility, less burnout. Some Aquarians may pioneer "intrapreneurial" projects within established companies, while others design hybrid careers that blend multiple income streams. Apps, robotics, AI tools—whatever helps you automate and optimize—will boost both your productivity AND your profits. Surround yourself with capable people who can help your ideas scale. This is your chance to build a workflow that works FOR you, not against you.

On February 13, Saturn and Neptune conclude their respective tours of Pisces and your second house of income, launching a new chapter that rewards everything you've built since 2023. The seeds you planted could now bear tangible fruit—especially ventures tied to creativity, spirituality or community service. You might partner with local businesses, host classes, or develop new offerings for friends and neighbors. Don't be afraid to monetize some of your magic. That blend of artistry and practicality could evolve into a steady stream of income.

Your path could become public after April 25, as your ruling planet Uranus rockets into Gemini and your fifth house of fame, entrepreneurship and creative leadership for a seven-year stay. Time for a brand reboot! Your professional image—and possibly your entire business model—could shift in dramatic and exciting ways. You may step into a leadership role, launch a content channel or claim your place as an industry influencer.

Whatever your medium, your goddess-given originality is your market advantage. Keep your visuals sharp and your messaging fearless. Aquarius, you ARE the brand.
A midyear money wave could arrive via a contractual partnership starting June 30, when Jupiter strides into Leo and your seventh house of partnerships for thirteen months. Align with pros who complement your skill set, whether through a joint venture, shared investment or co-founded business.

Destiny doubles down starting July 26, as the lunar North Node moves into Aquarius for the first time in nearly three decades. You'll feel an undeniable pull toward purpose-driven success. The next 20 months push you to align your career with your calling, even if that means launching something on the side while you build your safety net. The more courageous authenticity you bring to your vision, the more unstoppable you become.

TOP 5 THEMES FOR Aquarius in 2026

1	2	3	4	5
BROADCAST YOUR TRUTH	MASTER YOUR CRAFT	LIVE AS ART	REVOLUTIONIZE EVERYTHING	REDEFINE YOUR DESIRES

1 BROADCAST YOUR TRUTH

NEPTUNE IN ARIES
JANUARY 26, 2026–MARCH 23, 2039

SATURN IN ARIES
FEBRUARY 13, 2026–APRIL 12, 2028

Break time's over, Aquarius, it's time to log back into life—and life as you've never known it. A whole new era of connection is calling in 2026, as intuitive Neptune and ambitious Saturn kick off long treks through Aries. As they fire up your third house of communication, cooperation and innovation, you'll be in your genius element. That's far too rich a gift to keep to yourself! Better still, you won't have to travel far from home to make an impact. The third house is the locally zoned segment of the zodiac wheel. Wherever your mail is being delivered, you're changing the game.

You got a teaser of this energy already in 2025. Neptune drifted into Aries from March 30 to October 22, arousing meaningful conversations and the kind of mind-bending ideas Aquarians are famous for. Your co-ruler Saturn dropped into Aries from May 24 to September 1, providing an early nudge to beta test those wild visions in real life. In 2026, it's official: Neptune anchors in the Ram's realm for 13 years starting January 26, and Saturn returns for two focused years from February 13.

Even more impactful? These two heavenly heavyweights make an exact conjunction at 0° Aries on February 20, fusing dreams and discipline. Saturn and Neptune only unite like this every 35 to 40 years, but they haven't met up in Aries since 1702! Under this influence, your social world is up for a remix, but not in a random "work the room" way. Use your intuition and charm to foster the types of connections that feed your soul. Whether you click under the stars at a plant medicine ceremony or via a LinkedIn search (or both!), all that matters is that you care about a common cause.

From there, how can you turn a vision into a tangible mission? While hazy Neptune dreams, hardcore Saturn demands a plan. Want to teach, write or spread your message? This cycle helps you craft it with precision and purpose. Fiery Aries rules your third house of writing, media and community initiatives. What will you do with this rare energy, Aquarius? Everything's on the table, from publishing a company-wide newsletter, cultivating a hyper-local start-up, or finding a building with friends that you turn into a communal living space. Whatever you go after, Saturn says: "Stick with it. Make it real." Meanwhile, Neptune softens your rational edges and stirs curiosity about mystical or artistic forms of communication. Write poetry, record a podcast, or learn to read Tarot for your neighborhood squad. Aquarius is the sign that rules astrology, so 2026 could be your year to finally study all those planets, signs, houses and aspects.

Ties with siblings or neighbors may also transform, not necessarily in an easy way. If they've been fraying for a while, you could snip them off for good—or step back in a serious way. As Neptune incites a craving for meaningful exchanges and Saturn calls for purposeful connection—the kind that supports both your independence and your wild ideas—people you can count on become the new gold standard.

Since the third house rules short trips and micro-adventures, expect more "get in the car and go" moments. Yoga retreats in nearby towns, creative staycations at Airbnbs, or simply rediscovering the hidden gems in your own backyard—this is your new idea of an affordable good time.

By the time Saturn exits Aries in 2028, you'll know exactly which conversations, collabs and communities are worth your energy. And you'll have built the real-life connections to keep your brilliant mind inspired for years to come. When Neptune finally floats on in 2039, you may look back and realize that building an intentional community was your greatest masterpiece.

2 MASTER YOUR CRAFT

JUPITER IN CANCER
JUNE 9, 2026–JUNE 30, 2026

Healthy, wealthy and wise? That's not just a goal for you as 2026 kicks off—hopefully, it's already becoming your official lifestyle. Vitality-boosting Jupiter is halfway along its 13-month tour through Cancer, bringing a mindful touch to your sixth house of work and wellness until June 30, 2026.

No matter where you are on the "spud to stud" ratio, couch-potato-ing your way through the winter months should not be an option. Even if you're not the first person to unroll their yoga mat on January 2, don't wait too long to rev up the kinetic energy. Make loving your body a top resolution for the year ahead. Your mood and productivity levels will soar!

And that's a good thing for another reason than simply your physical well-being. The sixth house rules daily work. With nourishing Cancer in charge of this zone, bake self-care into every part of your life. Instead of thinking, I'll get to the gym (or start my clean eating regimen) when I hit this deadline, consider these things an essential part of the success process.

It isn't breaking news that good nutrition is linked to attention span and exercise is brain food. The hurdle to overcome may lie in setting up a routine that you can realistically stick to. Fortunately, as one of the four fixed signs, you thrive with a repetitive schedule. Maybe it's waking up an hour earlier to do sunrise yoga—or stopping at the gym on four set days each week before you go home or meet friends for dinner.

Since Jupiter is the global nomad, how about kicking it all off with a wellness retreat, Aquarius? If you have the funds stacked, take your winter break at a resort that boasts organic fare, mindfulness activities (sound baths, meditation gardens) and detoxing with saunas and daily workout classes. Got a miniscule budget with a Miraval appetite? Organize friends for an Airbnb weekend (or week). You can take turns preparing fresh, vegan meals, stream workouts and do guided meditations together.

This is also your chance to get more personal with your wellness. A little biohacking can go a long way in 2026. Enough wondering about hidden sensitivities or nagging health questions. Approaches that blend Eastern and Western care are always Aquarius-approved. In addition to your regular MD checkups, meet with a specialist who can test your hormone levels or design a microbiome-balancing menu that optimizes gut health. Staying active should feel like a gift, not a grind. Water-sign Cancer wants movement to be as restorative as it is invigorating, so paddleboarding, swimming laps, or even beachside yoga could become your new go-to's. At home, carve out a cozy corner for stretching or streaming quick workouts. Consistency is more important than perfection.

Apply the same systematic approach at the office, too. What tasks can be bundled or even divided up differently among Team Aqua? Completing busy work has a certain fulfillment to it, but you could find yourself drowning in administrative activities early this year. Investing in support could open up your schedule for more high-earning activities. You just have to get off the hamster wheel. Hiring a house cleaning service or bookkeeper is a "gamble" worth taking with Jupiter in Cancer.

Don't be surprised if new professional opportunities come with a wider reach. Some Aquarians could pivot toward freelance work or global collaborations that keep things fresh and exciting. And hey, if you enjoy the aforementioned busywork, go get certified. Project management is one of your sign's specialties—well, at least the more Saturnian Aquarians out there (Uranian Aquarians might be too busy blowing up the lab). From Agile to PMP, earning your credentials can help you command more cash.

Streamlining your expenses may also be necessary. Jupiter's hedonistic impulses are curbed by cautious Cancer and the savvy sixth house. How can you do more with less, Aquarius? Your lifehacking could wind up spawning some new algorithms that open up time and energy for you and everyone in your orbit. That's a win-win worth aiming for!

JUPITER IN LEO
JUNE 30, 2026 – JULY 26, 2027

Love is in the air, Aquarius—the kind that could make even the most hardened cynic among you believe in "happily ever after." On June 30, daring Jupiter leaps into Leo and your seventh house of commitment. As the lucky planet infuses your closest bonds with expansion, truth and adventure until July 26, 2027, you may become Cupid's biggest cheerleader.

And no, you don't have to define "relationships" the same way your muggle neighbors do. A twosome (or two twosomes) just needs a clear set of agreements. That's all. With Jupiter in Leo's liberating influence boosting your courage, you could draft your ideal "state of the union" and see who is willing to get on board. While there is always going to be SOME compromising, there's no denying that we each have a unique set of circumstances that lead to fulfillment. With Jupiter in passionate Leo, lukewarm attractions just won't cut it.

Even the zodiac's liberated Water Bearer (yes, you!) could find yourself happily ensconced in a twosome—or leveling up a partnership that's ready to go the distance. But this may also be where the rubber meets an irreparable pothole in the road. If it's time to part ways from a significant other, the breakup may be faster and easier than either of you anticipated. And as long as Leo-ruled egos stay in check, you stand a chance of remaining dear friends. It's the Aquarius way!

Have you been getting closer to a special someone? Timelines speed up under Jupiter's eager influence. Screw the destination wedding, Aquarius. You might be getting hitched at City Hall after June 30. But don't skip the lavish celebration, even if a ceremony isn't involved. Hedonistic Jupiter in Leo wants to celebrate any milestone with Dionysian flair. Elopement post-party, divorce party, "I'm marrying myself" party—all valid causes for revelry.

Whatever sort of partnership ambitions you have, know this: Between now and next summer, you're in a major growth cycle that can turn "me" into a rock-solid "we." Rule No. 1: Jupiter wants you to broaden your horizons. Cast a wider net and embrace the idea that opposites really do attract. Whether you have designs on marriage, a creative collab or a joint business venture, look for someone whose strengths balance yours—the yin to your yang, the calm anchor to your rebellious streak.

Since Jupiter is the globalist, cross-cultural romances could be wildly fulfilling. And don't dismiss a long-distance spark! For a sign that treasures personal space, a little geographical breathing room might be the secret ingredient that keeps things sizzling.

Happily attached? Use this lucky thirteen-month stretch for true co-creation. If you've felt like two ships passing in the night, make a conscious effort to drop anchor in the same port. And hey, that doesn't have to be home base! Book a couples' retreat, schedule a bi-monthly weekend getaway, plan a bucket-list trip to a spiritual vortex or overseas music festival.

Jupiter's entrepreneurial vibe could also inspire you to mix business with pleasure. If you've ever thought of co-owning a company with your S.O., now's the time to test the waters. This sort of thing can go spectacularly wrong, however, so it's not something to gamble with. But if you CAN play to both of your strengths—and not resort to control tactics or spend every off-duty moment talking about launch strategies—this Jupiter cycle could help you bank some long-lasting financial security together.

Awkward as it might seem, consider writing up a formal agreement with an attorney. This can set expectations and actually be an insurance policy against future blowups. When you're working with friends, family or a love interest, the relationship is even more essential to protect. Hitting resistance to the idea? That might be a red flag. Our Aquarius friend Suzie taught us this spot-on mantra: Ambiguity breeds contempt.

But if you get it all in writing? You're golden. Maybe you'll launch a side hustle with your sweetie, buy some acreage with a bestie or co-create a product with your sibling that combines your talents. Think like a power couple. Two brains are better than one when you have a shared vision.

When you choose your plus-ones wisely, you unlock a whole new level of joy, stability and success. Jupiter in Leo reminds you that you don't have to do it all by yourself, Aquarius—nor do you have to organize an army of ten or twelve. With Jupiter in your seventh house, the real magic is found in the space between you and that one other person who you trust implicitly.

3 LIVE AS ART

URANUS IN GEMINI
APRIL 25, 2026 – MAY 22, 2033

Life may imitate an installation art exhibit starting this April 25, Aquarius—and you are the "work" that draws rave reviews from the critics. Your celestial ruler Uranus hurls itself in a brand-new direction, moving into Gemini and your fifth house of celebrity, romance and creative expression until May 22, 2033. Currently flying under the radar? That could change at a considerable clip as the side-spinning planet buzzes through Gemini. Prepare to field admiring stares, droves of fans and even cult-hero status over the next seven years.

It's about damn time! After seven years spent under the soft mood lighting of Uranus in Taurus, you've had enough time to tweak your foundations and redefine what "home" even means. Now you're ready to bask in something a little more glamorous. Or a lot more! This isn't just a casual glow-up, Aquarius, it's a full on renaissance.

You got a sneak peek of Uranus in Gemini from July 7 to November 7 2025, when your cosmic custodian took a four-month tour through this expressive zone. If your heart started beating louder—or your camera roll filled up with concept boards and OOTD selfies—you're already tuning in to this frequency. Now comes the real invitation: to live as art. How can you design your days, and your relationships, with the flair of someone who knows exactly who they are becoming? That's a challenge worth accepting.

The fifth house is where joy resides. With renegade Uranus here, pleasure becomes political, daring and unapologetically personal. Yes, Aquarius, it's time for you to take up (more) space. You might do it by hanging your art in a gallery or directing a short film. Maybe you'll dress like every sidewalk is your runway. Whatever the case, start broadcasting a message: I'm no longer asking for space. I'm taking it.

Romantically, this transit tilts the axis. For some Water Bearers, it's time to disrupt the domestic default. Maybe you break free from a stagnant routine or surprise yourself by falling—hard—for someone outside your usual orbit. Long-distance affairs, electrifying flings, love that plays by its own rules: all possible, and likely. Even in committed partnerships, you'll crave a fresh script. Think less "matching mugs" and more "separate studios, shared vision board."

And yes, there could be spotlight moments. The fifth house rules fame—and with Uranus, the rise is rarely linear. One TikTok could ignite a book deal. An offhand comment might spiral into a viral quote. But before you chase virality, ask yourself: "What's the legacy I'm building?" Fame fades but resonance endures.

Uranus in Gemini also demands discernment. Your ideas may flow faster than you can articulate them at times, which can send you into a spiral. Develop a curation practice. Not every sketch needs to become a capsule collection. Not every lover needs a drawer at your place. Protect the intimacy of your process, and remember: Mystery can be magnetic.

Above all, this is your time to take yourself—and your joy—seriously. Not in the heavy, obligatory way, but with the same care a couturier takes when crafting a gown. With Uranus in Gemini, your life becomes a canvas, a stage, a manifesto. You don't need to explain yourself to everyone. Just find the ones who are fluent in your language—and create something unforgettable together.

4 REVOLUTIONIZE EVERYTHING

LUNAR NODES IN LEO AND AQUARIUS
NORTH NODE IN AQUARIUS, SOUTH NODE IN LEO JULY 26, 2026–MARCH 26, 2028

At last! The world is ready for your groundbreaking brand of leadership, Aquarius. And starting July 26, it's time to claim your destiny. For the first time in nearly two decades, the fateful North Node soars into your sign, putting you at the helm of worldwide evolution. Buckle up (and strap on your space helmet). This 20-month cycle, which lasts until March 26, 2028, will launch you into a period of profound reinvention. Your image, your leadership, your very sense of identity are evolving at warp speed. While there will be applause, you're not here to put on a show. You're here to change the whole damn system.

In the first half of 2026 (and since January 11, 2025), the North Node has been trekking through Pisces and your grounded second house, while the South Node lingered in Virgo and your eighth house of intimacy and shared resources. Your focus has been on balancing material security while parsing through deeper intimacy issues. Now, as the nodes shift onto your axis, the story pivots to your individuality, your self-expression, your ability to lead in ways that only an Aquarian disruptor can.

This is no time to downplay your presence. The North Node in Aquarius dares you to crank the volume on your quirks, blast your message through the cosmic bullhorn, and stop auditioning for approval. Think back to June 23, 2006 to December 18, 2007, the last time this nodal cycle unfolded. What risks did you take then that helped you grow? Themes from that period could resurface, but this time you're playing with more wisdom and gravitas. A coach, mentor—or even a full-on "rebrand" moment—could give you the confidence to strut onto this next stage like it's your own Met Gala.

Partnerships won't vanish, but they'll shift shape. With the South Node—and super-expansive Jupiter until summer 2027—anchored in Leo and your seventh house, you'll crave more independence within relationships. Think: less handholding, more parallel play. Some karmic bonds could boomerang back for a remix, while others dissolve if they can't flex with your authenticity. The cosmic test? Can you be fully you and still be in this partnership? If not, rewrite the script. Jupiter's megaphone may even inflate certain dynamics, spotlighting where you've been over-giving or dimming your glow.

Working together, the lunar nodes call for authenticity in action. Want to broadcast your brilliance? Start that podcast, lead the workshop, get yourself on a panel at a thought leader conference like SXSW. If you're still in the "discovery" phase about what's next for your life, invest in your self-development. Book a retreat, join a mastermind or stage-dive into a workshop (or playshop) that pushes you further. Even seemingly small shifts—like revamping your online presence or doing a photo shoot that captures your "main character energy"—can ripple out into career-making opportunities.

Circle November 2027 in neon highlighter: The North Node will conjoin transformational Pluto at the same degree of Aquarius, a once-in-a-lifetime cosmic collab that could supercharge your influence. A reinvention you've been slow cooking behind the scenes could break wide open, turning you into an industry icon. Let that be your motivation to get your theories rock solid and your work pressed into a portfolio that people can access.

By the time this nodal cycle wraps in March 2028, you'll be living louder, walking taller and leading with radical authenticity. Your assignment? Invest in your growth, polish your platforms and practice sovereignty in every connection. Aquarius, you weren't born to blend into the chorus line—you were born to headline the whole tour.

5 REDEFINE YOUR DESIRES

VENUS RETROGRADE IN SCORPIO AND LIBRA
VENUS RETROGRADE IN SCORPIO: OCTOBER 3–25
VENUS RETROGRADE IN LIBRA:
OCTOBER 25–NOVEMBER 13

Your plans for love and adventure may ease into a slower rhythm this fall—and honestly, it could feel like a blessing. Ardent Venus will be retrograde from October 3 to November 13, a six-week cycle that helps you refine and realign your desires. This is a golden opportunity to reconnect to your own heart instead of worrying about what everyone else wants. In the process, a few of your forgotten "love goals" could come back into sharp clarity.

Disclaimer: This cycle, which only happens every 18 months, CAN feel like an unanticipated rerouting from your GPS. If you suddenly get confused about what direction to take next, DON'T just forge ahead with a questionable option and hope that you'll figure it out as you go. Making rash or uninformed decisions about your romantic, creative or social future is not advised during Venus retrograde.

This time around, the planet of romance, beauty and harmony is backspinning through a pair of signs. From October 3 to 25, the retrograde is in seductive Scorpio and your tenth house of career, public image and long-term goals. Then, from October 25 to November 13, Venus moonwalks into gracious Libra and your ninth house of travel, higher learning and big-picture dreams.

The first phase, in penetrating Scorpio, could spark a reckoning about how your relationships and professional goals intersect. Have you been so laser-focused on your personal ambitions that romance has slipped to the sidelines? Or, conversely, has love distracted you from an important life mission? Either way, Venus retrograde here challenges you to define what true balance looks like.

Coupled Water Bearers, the structure of your relationship may require some refining. Use October to each talk through your individual priorities in love, life and work. What support does each of you really need? Beyond that, is it fair and reasonable to expect the other one to provide that? Taking the pressure off a few areas of your shared life can be a game-changer. Maybe you bring a friend along on a work trip when your S.O. is too busy to take time off, or you drop off laundry instead of fighting over who is going to wash the towels and dark load this week.

Keep these conversations bite-sized and manageable. Schedule regular check-ins with your significant other—or anyone who shares responsibilities with you. Create a shared calendar to sync your worlds, and make space for quality connection outside of business talk. You may discover that some long-term visions don't quite align—and that's okay. Creative compromises might take a little digging, but retrogrades are ideal times for going beyond the surface or what's obvious.

When Venus slips back into Libra from October 25 to November 13, your ninth house takes the wheel, stirring a craving for space, freedom and fresh horizons. This is where absence really can make the heart grow fonder. You or your partner might have travel, study or work plans that pull you apart for a while—but that doesn't have to be a bad thing. Distance can add spark. Just keep communication consistent while you're apart.

Single? Venus retrograde can turn your thoughts toward "the one that got away." Before you romanticize the past, be brutally honest about why things ended. If the only

obstacle was timing, this backspin could offer a do-over—but take it slow and wait until after November 13 for clarity. And if an ex keeps drifting into your orbit, interfering with your dating goals, you may need a period of no-contact so you can heal and fully move forward.

Professionally, Venus retrograde in Scorpio (October 3–25) asks you to tread carefully in workplace relationships. Temper your maverick streak and show that you can be a team player—even when you disagree with higher-ups. If someone hurls a curveball your way, you don't have to open up your catcher's mitt and race after it. De-escalate as much as possible and focus on getting yourself centered before you put up a much-needed boundary.

Business owners may need to dig deeper for client leads or fresh creative inspiration this fall. The silver lining? That's a challenge that could lead you in all sorts of fascinating directions! Step into networking spaces that align with your bigger vision. Be open to serendipitous introductions. A casual conversation now could evolve into a powerful collaboration in the months ahead!

2026
AQUARIUS

12
MONTH OVERVIEW

January MONTHLY HOROSCOPE

Clear the decks, Aquarius. The Sun simmers in Capricorn until the 19th, resting in your twelfth house of closure and healing. Wrap up lingering projects, prioritize rest and let go of what doesn't belong in your 2026 story. What is standing in the way of you feeling healthy, wealthy and wise? You'll get a clear view of this on the 3rd as the Cancer full moon shines into your sixth house of health and routines. Make any necessary shifts. You can start rebooting your energy with exercise, rest and healthy eating again. By the time the Capricorn new moon arrives on the 18th, you'll be ready to shed a draining obligation and create space for new beginnings. Lovebirds Venus and Mars roll together in Capricorn until the 17th, directing romance and passion behind the scenes. While fantasies will be rich, you might not have the most energy for "the hunt." But don't worry. By the 23rd, both Venus and Mars will have moved into Aquarius, cranking up your magnetism and charm. When the Sun also enters Aquarius on the 19th, your birthday season officially begins. Step boldly into the spotlight and declare what you want for the year ahead. Just don't forget the inner work that makes your shine sustainable. On the 2nd, Chiron pivots direct in Aries, helping you smooth out communication glitches and reconnect with powerful allies. Then on the 26th, Neptune drifts back into Aries for a 13-year stay, giving your words spiritual resonance. Speak with compassion, Aquarius—your voice is your superpower.

February MONTHLY HOROSCOPE

It's your cosmic reset, Aquarius—what new version of you is ready to emerge? The radiant Sun blazes through your sign until the 18th, putting you in the driver's seat of that exploration. This is your chance to reinvent stale aspects of your life and show the world who you've become. On the 1st, the passionate Leo full moon beams into your partnership zone, clarifying a key relationship. A commitment could deepen—or you may realize it's time to reset the balance. Then, on February 17, the Aquarius new moon arrives as a rare solar eclipse—the first in your sign since 2018—just as the Year of the Fire Horse begins. Sudden opportunities could arise that thrust you onto the main stage. Your independent nature cannot be contained, so goodbye to anyone who tries to restrict you! Venus in Aquarius amplifies your magnetism through the 10th; use it to promote your ideas or strengthen your personal brand. Afterward, the love planet drifts into Pisces and your second house, grounding romance in reality (sigh). On February 13, sound Saturn re-enters Aries, beginning a two-year cycle in your communication sector. Prepare to get serious about your messaging, your studies and the way you share your ideas.

Valentine's Day follows with the Capricorn moon, encouraging depth over display. Pisces season begins on the 18th, illuminating your second house of money and values. Your financial picture may shift, but this is also your chance to align spending with what truly matters. Mercury retrograde here from February 26 to March 20 might delay payments or scramble budgets, but it's also perfect for reworking a financial plan, renegotiating terms, or resurrecting an idea for income.

March MONTHLY HOROSCOPE

How secure do you feel in the world, Aquarius? With the Sun, Mercury retrograde, Mars and a Pisces new moon (on the 18th) flowing through Pisces and your second house of money and values, your eye is on the bottom line. Where do you need to stabilize, and where can you invest with confidence? Build your safety net first, then branch into bigger opportunities. On the 3rd, a total lunar (full moon) eclipse in Virgo activates your eighth house of shared resources and intimacy. A financial partnership, loan or joint venture could reach a decisive turning point, or you may need to release an arrangement that no longer works. This sexy eclipse could also help you seal the deal on a scintillating relationship. Life slips into a more manageable pace on March 2, as go-getter Mars leaves Aquarius and enters Pisces for a six-week stay. You're determined to earn more and pursue lucrative opportunities. Just watch impulsive spending under this influence. Love gets lively after March 6, when Venus enters Aries and your third house of communication. Expect flirty banter, late-night talks and sparks flying in your daily exchanges. Lucky Jupiter ends a four-month retrograde on the 10th and pushes forward in Cancer and your sixth house of health and work. Routines that stalled since last year pick up again, and opportunities appear for new jobs or wellness breakthroughs. The Sun sails into Aries at the spring equinox (March 20), energizing your third house of ideas and connections. Mercury stations direct the same day, untangling three weeks of crossed wires. Conversations, contracts and plans finally smooth out, giving you the clarity to move forward. Partner up with peers and triple your productivity!

April MONTHLY HOROSCOPE

Ideas fly fast and furious this April, Aquarius—try to capture as many of those gems as you can! The illuminating Sun lights up Aries and your third house of communication and intellect until the 19th, sparking conversations, passion projects and connections. What message do you need to share? Don't hold back. Your words could inspire the masses and draw kindred spirits into your orbit. On April 1, the Libra full moon shines

in your ninth house, bringing a media project, travel plan or academic goal to fruition. The call to broaden your horizons will be too loud to ignore, so go ahead and make that daring leap towards an exciting experience. Firecracker Mars storms into Aries for six weeks on the 9th, bringing momentum to collaborations but sharpening your tongue. Use the heat to persuade, not provoke. You may not realize how harsh you sound! The new moon in Aries on the 17th offers a fresh start in contracts, conversations and networking. Circulate! Life settles down a bit on the 19th as the Taurus Sun settles into your domestic fourth house, bringing grounding energy to home and family matters for a month. Venus also lingers here until April 24, adding a cozy vibe in affairs of the heart. Then, the turning point: On the 25th, your ruler, shock-jock Uranus, ends its seven-year stay in Taurus and rockets into Gemini until 2033. With your fifth house of love, creativity and passion now electrified, expect exciting new romances, bold artistic ventures and unscripted ways of expressing yourself. Life may feel like an improv show some days, but roll with it. You'll navigate the spontaneous experiments like a Nobel-Prize-winning scientist!

May MONTHLY HOROSCOPE

Home base calls this May, Aquarius, as the Taurus Sun illuminates your fourth house until the 20th. Nurture your nest, reconnect with family and create space that feels like a true sanctuary. The Scorpio full moon on the 1st beams into your career house, spotlighting recognition or a project milestone. Don't be afraid to brag! People will be inspired by what you've created. On the 6th, Pluto turns retrograde in Aquarius until October 15, inviting an inner review of your identity and public persona. The Aquarius quarter moon on the 10th reinforces this—Mother's Day might be the perfect moment to honor your roots while acknowledging how much you've contributed to the family tree. On the 16th, the Taurus new supermoon energizes your domestic sector: Start fresh with a move, a reno project or a new ritual that makes home your happy place. Gemini season begins on the 20th, shifting focus to your fifth house of love and creativity. Let yourself play! Until the 18th, Venus in Gemini ignites flirtations and artistic collaborations. Then, Venus flows into Cancer and your wellness zone while Mars powers into Taurus and your domestic fourth house. Love grows through simple, everyday rituals. Couples may bond through cooking together or weekend nesting. The Sagittarius blue full moon on the 31st lands in your eleventh house, spotlighting friendships or a game-changing collab. Future alliances are waiting. Say yes to the invite!

June MONTHLY HOROSCOPE

June lights a fire under your passions as the Sun blazes through Gemini and your fifth house of romance, creativity and play until the 21st. Follow your heart and dare to put your art—or your affections—on display. The June 14 Gemini new moon, the second supermoon in a rare trilogy, lands here as well, setting the stage for a summer love story or igniting inspiration for a project that could captivate an audience. Meanwhile, driven Mars charges through Taurus and your domestic fourth house until June 28, making home life anything but quiet. Redecorate, rearrange or host gatherings that turn your space into a hub of connection. A notable cosmic shift arrives on June 19, when "wounded healer" Chiron enters Taurus for a three-month preview of its 2027–2034 stay. Since 2018, Chiron has prodded at your communication style, forcing you to find your voice—even in difficult moments. Now the emphasis shifts to healing family dynamics and rewriting generational scripts. Think therapy breakthroughs, heartfelt kitchen-table talks or even creating new rituals that anchor you. On June 21, the Sun glides into tender Cancer for the solstice and Father's Day, highlighting your wellness-oriented sixth house. This is your cue to refine your routines and invest in the rituals that keep your body and spirit in sync. Venus lingers in Cancer until the 13th, helping you find love in simple acts of care. But when she struts into flamboyant Leo and your seventh house, sparks fly—expect grand gestures, power-couple vibes or sizzling chemistry with someone new. By June 30, Jupiter also leaps into Leo for a thirteen-month tour, blessing your partnerships with growth and opportunity. Whether romantic, business or creative, choose connections that expand your world. The month ends with the Capricorn full moon on June 29 in your twelfth house of release and renewal. A behind-the-scenes project or a long-awaited healing process could culminate. But with Mercury retrograde in Cancer starting the same day, give yourself permission to move slowly, guard your energy and savor the closure over the coming three weeks.

July MONTHLY HOROSCOPE

Time to get your systems in order, Aquarius. With the Sun in Cancer and your sixth house of health and routines until July 22—and Mercury retrograde here until the 23rd—you'll be fine-tuning everything from schedules to workflows. Don't slack on self-care! The Cancer new moon (a supermoon) on the 14th spotlights wellness. Blast through stress by doing less busywork and enjoying more meaningful engagements. On July 7, Neptune pivots retrograde in Aries, beginning five months of review in your communication zone. Watch for burnout from endless group chats and digital overload. Saturn's retrograde here on the 26th doubles down on the need for boundaries—muting notifications may be your best productivity hack. There's fun and glamour to be had, too! Firecracker Mars charges through Gemini and your fifth house of passion and creativity all month, stoking romance and giving your summer projects serious heat. Once Leo season lights up your partnership zone on the 22nd, relationships could get more serious and defined. With Venus in Virgo after the 9th, money and intimacy talks turn constructive. This is a great month for hashing out details of shared resources or long-term plans. By the time Mercury stations direct on the 23rd, you may be ready to put those deal points in writing. The game-changer arrives July 26, when the North Node moves into Aquarius and your first house for the first time in nearly two decades. Step into your destiny, Water Bearer! Until March 26, 2028, you are in an accelerated era of personal growth—and your transformation could turn you into a global role model. On the 29th, the Sun and Jupiter meet in Leo for the annual "Day of Miracles," energizing your relationship house with serendipitous connections. The very same day, the year's only Aquarius full moon puts you firmly in the spotlight. A personal goal you've been working toward could finally crystallize—and the world is ready to see the new you!

August MONTHLY HOROSCOPE

People are your priority this August—and an attractive "opposite" could wow you before Leo season wraps on the 22nd. On the 3rd, Chiron pivots retrograde in Taurus and your fourth house of home and family, surfacing old wounds around belonging and stability. This is your cue to unpack family patterns, maybe through therapy, guided journaling or finally addressing the "unspoken stuff." On the 11th, Mars charges into Cancer and your sixth house of work and wellness, boosting your stamina and helping you power through projects. Go full force with your healthy living goals, but don't forget to build in recovery time. Watch out for stress at work. Manage expectations and don't slip into "office martyr" mode. Eclipse season kicks off on the 12th with a total solar eclipse in Leo—the first in this sign since 2019—shaking up your seventh house of partnerships. A relationship could turn a sharp corner, whether through sudden commitment, a surprising new connection or a revelation about what balance really looks like to YOU. Venus in Libra from the 6th blesses your ninth house of wisdom and wanderlust. Oh, the places you could go, both in and out of the bedroom. After the 22nd, Virgo season spotlights your eighth house of intimacy and shared resources. Money talks and heart-to-hearts take center stage, giving you clarity around what (and who) deserves your full trust. This is also "sexy season" for you, Aquarius, so don't overbook your social calendar with random events. On the 28th, the Pisces lunar eclipse beams into your second house of money and values, catalyzing a financial shift that could require some pivots. August wraps with cosmic synergy on the 31st as Jupiter in Leo trines Saturn in Aries, solidifying contracts and collaborations. Define your partnerships, Aquarius! That's how you'll anchor them into something real and enduring.

September MONTHLY HOROSCOPE

Shake things up, Aquarius! September is anything but boring. With the Virgo Sun cruising through your seductive and intimate eighth house, surface-level just won't cut it. You're craving soul-baring honesty, sexy innuendoes and maybe even a little financial strategy talk over cocktails. Meanwhile, Mars is powering through Cancer and your sixth house of wellness and routines until the 27th, motivating you to tweak your habits. Try a new workout app, test a meal prep hack, schedule those checkups you've been putting off. On the 10th, the Virgo new moon activates your eighth house, helping you reset around money, sex or emotional bonds. This could be the start of a joint venture that's worthy of your fullhearted investment. That same day, Uranus (your ruler) turns retrograde in Gemini and your fifth house of love and creativity. Over the next five months, you may rethink how you express yourself in romance or art. Sometimes a remix is better than a reinvention. Venus lingers in Libra and your expansive ninth house until the 10th, fueling wanderlust, independent ventures and your "eternal student" mindset. Then Venus slides into Scorpio and your career zone, spotlighting your ambitions and making you extra magnetic with decision-makers. Just note: Venus retrograde (October 3 to November 13) could slow the pace, so get in any key pitches and proposals early. The fall equinox on the 22nd turns the spotlight back to big-picture growth as Libra season kicks in. Off-season travel could be rewarding and affordable. Pack your bags and go! On the 17th, Chiron backs into Aries and your communication house, bringing healing around your voice and how you connect. And the Aries full moon on the 26th lights up that same zone. Share your message. Make that big reveal. Your ideas could literally go viral, Aquarius.

October MONTHLY HOROSCOPE

You may need to shift gears this month, Aquarius, so stay nimble. On October 3, convivial Venus retrogrades through Scorpio and your tenth house of career until the 25th, then rewinds into Libra and your ninth house of expansion until November 13. Romantically, you may discover that your goals are out of alignment or that you're drawn to a different vision of love. This doesn't have to be a dealbreaker, but don't suppress the needs that are stirring inside you. The people in your life may be more flexible than you realize. The Sun streams in Libra until the 23rd, spotlighting your worldly, expansive ninth house. The Libra new moon on the 10th nudges you toward fresh horizons. Book an overseas trip, sign up for a workshop or challenge yourself with an indoor sports team this fall. Lusty Mars blazes through Leo and your partnership zone all month, making cuffing season spicy. Warning: That same fiery energy could heat up conflicts. Choose your battles. October 15 ends Pluto's retrograde in Aquarius, unlocking the next level of a personal reinvention you've been shaping since the alchemical planet entered your sign in November 2024. Then on the 23rd, the Sun shifts into Scorpio and your ambitious tenth house—the same day Venus retrograde aligns with the Sun in a rare Cazimi. Your love goals come into sharp focus now, which may require some adjustments to the way you "do" relationships. Don't take your eye off the ball at work. Mercury slips into a retrograde on the 24th, backing up through Scorpio and your career zone until November 13. Keep receipts, copious notes and backups handy. Domestic matters are spotlighted with the Taurus full moon on the 26th. Stabilize your base as the first line of defense against curveballs from the outside world.

November MONTHLY HOROSCOPE

Keep career goals in your crosshairs this November, but move ahead strategically. With the Scorpio Sun shining at the top of your chart, your tenth house of ambition and public image is lit until the 22nd. Add in the year's only Scorpio new moon landing on the 9th and you're poised for a professional reboot. But patience first. Until the 13th, personal planets Mercury and Venus are retrograde, making negotiations, contracts or travel plans messy. Instead of forcing outcomes, refine your goals and polish your pitch. By midmonth, opportunities align, and you'll be ready to make your move. In the meanwhile, get out and network! Excitable Mars powers through Leo until the 25th, energizing your seventh house of partnerships. Dynamic duos—romantic, business or creative—keep you busy! The red planet can stir impatience though. Careful not to push your agenda or make unilateral decisions. Even if you see a dreamy future ahead, you need to advance at a pace that works for BOTH of you. Group efforts pick up steam after the 22nd, as the Sun surges into Sagittarius and your eleventh house of teamwork and tech (AKA "the Aquarius house"). Your influence stretches far when you plug into the right circles. Be ready for your closeup on the 24th, when the Gemini full supermoon beams into your fifth house of fame, creativity and romance. Get ready for a milestone moment with your artistry, or a dramatic arc to a love story. Either way, you'll be happy to have everything out in the open. There's plenty bubbling backstage, too, especially once Mars moves into Virgo and your seductive, mysterious eighth house from the 25th.

You're ready to hit the accelerator on a private initiative. With the red planet revving your engines here for the rest of the year, you're ready to go "all in," but make sure you know exactly what's involved. Once you commit, it will be hard to quit!

December MONTHLY HOROSCOPE

You're not exactly the type to stay in one lane, Aquarius—and this December, why would you? The Sagittarius Sun fires up your eleventh house of community and future visions until the 21st, turning gatherings into launchpads. On the 8th, the new moon in Scorpio ignites fresh connections: Apply for club memberships, pitch a collab. RSVP "yes" to a holiday mixer where "right place, right time" magic can happen. Two outer planets—your strategic co-ruler Saturn and fantasy-agent Neptune—end five-month retrogrades in Aries on the 10th and 12th, respectively. Confusion clears and you'll be able to articulate your ideas as a strong message. While you can see both sides of an argument, you may have to pick a team. With motivator Mars charging through Virgo and your eighth house all month, people will demand your loyalty. Sexy sparks could heat into exothermic chemistry fast. There's a thin line between love and hate, however, so don't let passions overtake common sense. Your reputation gleams as Venus floats back into Scorpio on the 4th. Dress for the role you want to play (at work and in love) and don't be shy about a little strategic self-promotion. On the 12th, Jupiter spins retrograde in Leo and your partnership house. Pace yourself in relationships and allow people a chance to reciprocate. Settle down for a long-ish winter's nap on the 21st (winter solstice) when the Sun retreats to Capricorn and your transitional twelfth house. Rest up before Aquarius season begins in a month! The Cancer full supermoon spotlights self-care on the 23rd, getting you pumped about your post-holiday glow-up. (What are the holiday hours at your gym?) The Sun in Capricorn syncs with Mars in Virgo this NYE, which could electrify and exhaust you. Make your cameo near (or in!) the DJ booth, then slip off to make a vision board.

Read your extended monthly forecast for life, love, money and career! astrostyle.com

PISCES IN 2026

| ALL THE PLANETS IN PISCES IN 2026 | YOUR 2026 HOROSCOPE | TOP 5 THEMES FOR PISCES IN 2026 | LOVE HOROSCOPE + LUCKY DATES | MONEY HOROSCOPE + LUCKY DATES |

Pisces in 2026

Your year of:
SOUL PURPOSE, STABILITY, SELF-WORTH

DESTINY KEEPS CALLING, PISCES!

And this year, the volume grows louder. The upgrade in 2026? Instead of feeling like a distant dream, your vision takes a shape you can actually hold. Creative sparks are abundant, but so is the discipline to anchor them into projects, practices or offerings that bring stability—and even revenue. Romance and artistic expression both rise to the surface, reminding you that love fuels your best work. But no slipping down any slopes! Mid-year, healthy routines become the fuel that keeps your magic in motion. By year's end, what once felt nebulous pours into form, the perfect blend of spiritual inspiration and material-world results.

THE PLANETS IN Pisces

THE SUN FEB 18–MAR 20	Happy birthday season! With the Sun in your sign, you're clear to take chances, chase fresh adventures, and command the spotlight.
NEW MOON MAR 18 9:23PM, 28°27'	Happy bonus New Year! Set your intentions for the next six months, then take a brave step forward. Your fans await!
FULL MOON, PARTIAL LUNAR ECLIPSE AUG 28 12:18AM, 04°54'	Manifestation moment! Your work of the past six months bears fruit. Celebrate your progress and harvest the rewards—which might come with a surprising twist under this lunar eclipse.
MERCURY FEB 6–APR 14 RETROGRADE IN PISCES: FEB 26–MAR 20	Hold court! When charismatic Mercury zips through your sign, your social status soars. Work the room, make connections. Keep your commitments realistic to avoid overpromising—especially during the retrograde, which could scramble signals or resurface old drama.
VENUS FEB 10–MAR 6	Hello, smokeshow! When the galactic glamazon struts through your sign, your powers of seduction skyrocket. Irresistible charm, luxe tastes, and flirtatious vibes abound—just keep an eye on your budget.
MARS MAR 2–APR 9	Motivation is off the charts when energetic Mars blazes through your sign every couple of years. You're bold, driven, and unstoppable—but watch that combative streak and ease up on the intensity.
SATURN JAN 1–FEB 13	Saturn visits your sign every 29.5 years for a 3-year visit, and its tour through Pisces finally wraps up on February 13. It hasn't been easy with the planet of discipline and focus in your sign since March 7, 2023. But the progress you've made? Epic!
NORTH NODE JAN 1–JUL 26	The destiny-fueling North Node begins an 18-month tour through your sign, connecting you to your passion and purpose. This cycle, which only happens every 18.5 years, may put you through your paces but helps to true you up with your authentic self.

Pisces in 2026
HIGHLIGHTS

A COSMIC SEND-OFF: NEPTUNE LEAVES PISCES JANUARY 26

Take a bow, Pisces. On January 26, your ruling planet Neptune exits your sign after a 15-year odyssey that began in 2011. You've shapeshifted, dreamed, healed and surrendered in ways few others will ever experience. This departure marks the end of a deeply personal era and sets the stage for a new chapter. Honor how far you've come—through rituals, reflection or even a simple night under the stars. The identity you forged during this cycle will anchor you for decades to come.

NEW FOUNDATIONS: SATURN AND NEPTUNE IN ARIES

Shortly after Neptune moves on to Aries, it teams up with Saturn in the Ram's realm (starting February 13) for a transformational tour through your second house of self-worth, money and values. Saturn wants you to build structure—budgets, boundaries, systems. Neptune adds imagination and meaning, encouraging you to align resources with purpose. This two-year duet is your chance to get financially fluent while creating abundance in line with your core values. Download the money app, revisit your rates, invest in projects that feed both your wallet and your spirit.

FATE FINDS YOU: NORTH NODE IN PISCES UNTIL JULY 26

Until July 26, the North Node travels through Pisces, spotlighting your identity and purpose. This is your karmic "main character" moment, urging you to claim your voice and trust your instincts. Across the sky, the South Node in Virgo asks you to release codependency and perfectionism in relationships. Prioritize authenticity over approval. Before the North Node heads into Aquarius and your numinous twelfth house on July 26, it delivers a powerful send-off. Expect revelations, endings and epiphanies about your purpose for being in this world.

CREATIVE FUEL: JUPITER IN CANCER UNTIL JUNE 30

Bountiful Jupiter spends the first half of the year in Cancer, energizing your fifth house of romance, creativity and joy. Love feels lighter, artistic projects leap off the page, canvas or dressmaker's form. This 13-month cycle, which began on June 9, 2025, is pushing you into the limelight. Let yourself be seen and admired, even if you're simply turning heads with your runway-worthy style. Fun is non-negotiable so prioritize play once again. Joy is your compass—follow what makes you feel alive!

MILESTONE MOONS: PISCES NEW AND FULL MOONS

Circle March 18, Pisces! Your annual new moon is a cosmic clean slate for personal goals and self-expression. Think of it as your bonus New Year's Day, perfect for setting intentions that reflect who you're becoming. Then, on August 28, the Pisces full moon arrives as a partial lunar eclipse, amplifying the energy tenfold. This eclipse spotlights your growth, revealing which dreams are ready to manifest and which chapters you're ready to close. Use these dates as checkpoints to honor your evolution.

WORK AND WELLNESS GLOW-UP: JUPITER ENTERS LEO JUNE 30

Health is wealth, Pisces, especially starting this June 30! Revitalizing Jupiter grapevines into Leo for 13 months, spotlighting your sixth house of wellness and work. Think: less hustle, more flow. Upgrade your systems with tools that streamline your day, from habit-tracking apps to AI project managers. Wellness could become a lifestyle: meal-prepping, joining a fitness community or finally sticking to that sleep schedule. When your daily rhythms align, everything else falls into place.

HOMECOMING ENERGY: URANUS ENTERS GEMINI APRIL 25

Since 2018, Uranus has stirred your third house, shaking up communication, learning and local ties. On April 25, it moves into Gemini and your fourth house of home and family, where it will stay until 2033. Big shifts could follow—relocation, renovation or a complete reinvention of your household dynamics. This transit is also a chance to rewrite family narratives and heal ancestral patterns. Surprises may crop up—an unexpected roommate, a sudden desire to put down roots or a living situation that changes overnight. Flexibility is your best tool as home becomes the most exciting—and unpredictable—part of your world.

MERCURY RETROGRADES: REWRITE YOUR STORY

Mercury turns retrograde three times in 2026, pressing pause on personal goals, love and big-picture plans. From February 26 to March 20, the backspin is in Pisces and your first house of self. Expect delays around personal initiatives or image changes, and take extra time to clarify how you're showing up. From June 29 to July 23, Mercury rewinds in your fifth house of romance, creativity and passion projects. An old flame may resurface or you could revisit an artistic pursuit that once inspired you. The final cycle, October 24 to November 13, lands in your ninth house of travel, learning and expansion. With Venus also retrograde in Libra, you may reconnect with an old mentor, revisit plans for school or retrace the steps of a past adventure. Each retrograde asks you to slow down, revise and realign so your vision grows stronger.

THE PATH PROGRESSES: LUNAR NODES SWITCH SIGNS JULY 26

Until July 26, the South Node in Virgo and North Node in Pisces highlight a dance between relationships and selfhood. Old patterns of over-giving are ready to go, while the North Node urges you to step into your own authority. Mid-summer, the Nodes pivot into Aquarius (North) and Leo (South), igniting a 20-month cycle of healing, creativity and daily rhythm. Your destiny lies in weaving soulful practices into your routine. What will you release to make room for rituals that truly restore you?

RELATIONSHIPS UNDER REVIEW: VENUS RETROGRADE THIS FALL

Relationships, power dynamics or financial entanglements may come up for review this fall. From October 3 to November 13, Venus retrogrades through your intimacy and wisdom zones. You might reconnect with a partner, revisit unresolved money matters, or rethink what intimacy really means to you now. Venus retraces this retrograde territory every 8 years (minus 2°), linking fall 2026 to fall 2018. What was happening with love, trust and shared resources back then? This is your chance to close the loop and move forward with clarity.

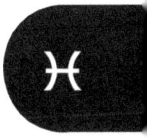

Love

PISCES 2026 FORECAST

Love is always on the menu for you, Pisces, the zodiac's Most Romantic. But this year brings lessons in balance: How can you prioritize partnership without losing the most essential parts of yourself? The lunar nodes are carrying out the final third of their mission, which began back on January 11, 2025. With the evolutionary North Node sailing through Pisces until this July 26, you're finally learning what it means to "put myself first." Who knew this could be the LEAST selfish act of all? When you're in flow state, everyone's in flow state.

Meanwhile, the karmic South Node has been rolling through Virgo and your seventh house of partnerships, revealing all the ways you have sacrificed your own identity to be part of a "we." That's just not going to cut it in 2026, Fish. But rebalancing drives up all sorts of excruciating feelings, many that fall in the "anxious attachment" camp. Expect "aha" moments that change how you view relationships. The March 3 total lunar eclipse in Virgo could spotlight truths you've avoided, including pressure you've unwittingly put on a partner.

Stay open to love from new categories! Indie-spirited Jupiter sails through fellow water sign Cancer and charges up your adventurous ninth house until June 30. Single Fish could date someone who lives long distance or hails from a different culture or provenance than your own. Travel and romance make a perfect pairing in the first half of 2026. Even if you don't board a plane with a partner, you may leave the trip with one. (Or said "new partner" could be a relaxed and refreshed version of your S.O. who desperately needed a baecation!)

You'll host the love planets, Venus and Mars, early in the year, too. Seductress Venus glides into Pisces on February 10, making you V-Day royalty, and keeping you in minx mode all the way until March 6. Lusty Mars follows suit on March 2, cranking up the spring fever vibes through April 9. Love could feel more like a game of catch-and-release during this time, with you slipping away from anyone who wants to snare you in their net. A major shift begins February 13, one that's been years in the making. Restrictive Saturn leaves your sign after clamping down on your joy since March 2023. That's not all! On January 26, your ruler, dreamy Neptune, also wraps a 15-year tour through your sign that began back in 2011. Between Saturn's mojo-dulling influence and Neptune's fog of illusions, it hasn't been easy to get your romantic footing in recent years. But starting mid-February, things change. For the next two years, both planets nest in Aries and your sensual-but-sensible second house. Settling down is still on the menu, Pisces, even (and especially) if you take your sweet time. (Slow-moving Saturn approves!) While the ringed planet moves on after two years, Neptune will be in Aries until 2039, keeping your runaway fantasies anchored in reality.

The summer brings togetherness: Venus tours Virgo and Libra from July 9 to September 10, activating your relationship houses. Connection feels lighter, easier and more fun. On August 28, the final eclipse in Pisces—a partial lunar (full moon) eclipse wraps up a 2.5-year series. Suppressed needs bubble to the surface. No more hiding who you are or what you want in love!

While you could race into some exciting new romantic terrain early fall, get ready to pump the brakes on October 3. Ardent Venus spins retrograde until November 13, backspinning through Scorpio and Libra. Negotiating freedom versus togetherness could get complex now. How much space do you need? How about your love interest? The two of you could be out-of-sync during this six-week cycle, but don't despair. This is an opportunity to plumb some new depths as you figure out the right rhythm. When Venus backs through Libra from October 25 to November 13, you may feel like exploring a kink. Do so with care, because you could open up a portal to shadowy feelings, even past trauma.

Lusty Mars moves into Virgo and your seventh house of partnerships on November 25, setting up an extended stay until February 21, 2027. Relationships could feel intense, passionate, maybe a bit complicated—and you're here for it all! If you began 2026 feeling like an escape artist, you'll end it clear, and ready to pursue the one that makes your heart skip a beat.

Money & Career

PISCES 2026 FORECAST

Destiny keeps calling—so how can you monetize that? With the North Node sailing through Pisces until July 26, you're still under a 19-month spotlight that began January 11, 2025. The universe is practically auditioning you for the role you were meant to play. And here's the best part: A few constraints lift in Q1.

Since March 2023, taskmaster Saturn has been swimming in your sign, making you feel like it's been two steps forward, one step back. On February 13, the ringed realist leaves Pisces (see you in 29 years!) and hunkers down in Aries, activating your second house of income and self-worth for two years. Saturn's practical influence helps you price your talent properly, build sustainable systems and turn creative capital into actual currency.

That's not all! On January 26, your dreamy ruler Neptune follows the same path, officially leaving Pisces (for 150 years!) for a 13-year residency in your financial sector. Dreams that have been languishing in the "someday" zone start to crystallize into a tangible format. No need to go big, Pisces, just start taking the first few steps and let things evolve organically.

Are you ready for your close-up? Abundant Jupiter beams through Cancer and your expressive fifth house until June 30, luring out the artist and performer in you. Whether you're stepping onstage or composing in a private studio, you can't stop the faucet of divine inspiration. Repeat after us: Visibility equals viability. (At least in the first half of the year!) Drum up the courage to pitch, post, audition and promote. Polish up your front-facing materials: photo shoot, web presence, socials.

Work-from-home life could take a futuristic turn, too. On April 25, innovative Uranus rockets into Gemini and your domestic fourth house, where it will camp until 2033.

Family—or chosen family—may play an unexpected role in your professional evolution. You might build a studio in your living room, launch a family business or create digital products that serve households or women and children.

Midyear, the mood shifts from freestyle to focused. When Jupiter moves into Leo and your systematic sixth house on June 30 (its first visit here in over a decade), it's time to get organized. This 13-month transit helps you transform raw inspiration into repeatable results. Measure twice, cut once. Helpful assistants who share your work ethic will be key to your success.

On July 26, the lunar nodes change signs, adding both a stabilizing and charitable element to your work for 20 months. The karmic South Node joins Jupiter in Leo, while across the sky, the North Node flows out of Pisces and into Aquarius and your compassionate twelfth house. The more you give, the more the universe gives back, whether you're donating a portion of proceeds, mentoring or creating a product that helps people in need at a fair cost.

Financially, pay close attention this fall. Venus turns retrograde from October 3 to November 13, and an investment could reveal hidden strings—or unexpected rewards. Steer clear of anything promising "instant riches." If it sounds too good to be true, it is. Audit your portfolio for ethical alignment, but don't dismiss the possibility that a dormant asset could start paying again.

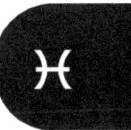

TOP 5 THEMES FOR Pisces in 2026

1	2	3	4	5
TURN VISION INTO VALUE	CLAIM THE SPOTLIGHT	INNOVATE AT HOME	ADD SOUL TO YOUR GOALS	RESTRUCTURE ROMANCE

1 TURN VISION INTO VALUE

NEPTUNE IN ARIES
JANUARY 26, 2026–MARCH 23, 2039

SATURN IN ARIES
FEBRUARY 13, 2026–APRIL 12, 2028

Get ready for a turning point that will only come once in your lifetime, Pisces. In 2026, your ruling planet Neptune paddles out of Pisces after 15 years of flowing through your first house of identity and initiative. Since 2011, you've been swimming in your own waters—dissolving boundaries, reinventing your personal brand (multiple times, even), and exploring the most radical edges of your imagination. On January 26, Neptune rides a wave into Aries and your sensible second house. As this new phase wages on until 2039, your focus shifts from "Who am I?" to "How do I bring my gifts into the world?"

If we haven't emphasized it enough, this is a huge deal, Pisces! Neptune only visits your sign every 165 years. Your galactic guardian's move out of your sign may feel like you're waking from a long, mystical dream.

And that's not all! On February 13, stalwart Saturn wraps up a tough, three-year journey through Pisces and joins Neptune in Aries until April 12, 2018. After hosting taskmaster Saturn since March 7, 2023, you'll feel like a huge weight has been lifted. You're free to go create and explore—now with a newfound confidence about who you are and what you need to feel happy and fulfilled.

You already got a brief taste of this transition in 2025. From March 30 to October 22, Neptune darted into Aries. Saturn joined last year, too, from May 24 to September 1. Over the coming two years, these two planetary powerhouses will help you translate your visions into something tangible, and possibly monetizable. (Never say never!)

Let's hover on February 20, a very important date! For the first time since 1702, Neptune and Saturn unite at the same degree of Aries. It's the only time they'll meet this closely during this entire cycle, and for you, it's a moment of powerful re-grounding. Start blending your biggest dreams with real-world discipline.

2026 HOROSCOPE GUIDE

The second house is your foundation for all things practical: your income, possessions, daily security, and most importantly, your relationship with value. That includes both what you have and what you believe you deserve. With confident, courageous Aries governing this part of your chart, it's a bit of a tightrope act. Sometimes, you may feel completely shut out, a victim of the world's unfair practices. Then, you can swing wildly into the opposite direction, risking a bit of entitlement or diva-ish behavior.

There's a middle ground to aim for, Pisces, and 2026 is the year to find it. While Neptune has no "off" switch, Saturn is nothing if not disciplined. You don't have to settle for less than you desire, but you might find yourself wanting to trim back excess this year. Where is your "just right" sweet spot?

This cycle could nudge you toward work that feels more aligned with your spirit AND your sense of security. With intuitive Neptune guiding you, you may feel called to earn through creative or compassionate pursuits—art, music, film, spiritual teaching, healing, or designing beautiful things people love and value. You might monetize gifts that once felt too personal to share.

At the same time, Saturn's practical push keeps your feet on the ground. Get real about what it takes to make your soulful ideas sustainable. Bone up on your traditional business skills, even if it feels dry at first. They will serve as the sturdy container for your magic.

Together, these planets invite you to balance giving and receiving. You're here to do meaningful work that feeds your spirit—but not at the cost of draining your bank account or sacrificing your own stability. As Saturn and Neptune settle in for this long haul, you'll discover that the more you honor your worth, the easier it is for the world to do the same.

For the past decade and a half, Neptune in Pisces has made you a master at flowing with life's currents. But it may also have left you drifting, unsure where you stand—especially when it comes to money, confidence and what you truly deem valuable. Now, as both planets advance into your second house of finances, possessions and self-worth, you're ready to build something solid.

Are you ready to let go of an old scarcity mindset? Or the guilt that can creep in when you start to thrive? Neptune wants you to see that abundance doesn't make you less spiritual. It helps you share your gifts freely, without fear of running dry.

But don't forget Saturn's lesson: Your big ideas need a framework. Dream all you want— but draft the plan, stick to the budget, and ask for what you're worth. You might finally price your art or start charging for your healing gifts. This is an excellent year to turn one of your creative talents into a practical revenue stream. The key? Keep your visions rooted in reality. Neptune can lure you into magical thinking; Saturn helps you separate hope from hype.

You're at the starting block of a major manifestation cycle, Pisces, one that grows out of your most authentic self-expression. But that evolution won't happen overnight. Saturn is slow and steady, but in impulsive Aries, you might feel the tug-of-war between wanting it now and trusting the process. By the time Saturn exits Aries in 2028, you'll stand on firmer financial and emotional ground than you've known in years. And when Neptune finally leaves Aries in 2039? You'll look back and see just how profoundly you transformed your self-worth, and how your gifts turned into something the world can see, touch and value.

2 CLAIM THE SPOTLIGHT

JUPITER IN CANCER
JUNE 9, 2026–JUNE 30, 2026

Your imagination continues to be one of your greatest assets in 2026, Pisces. (Block anyone who tells you otherwise!) Abundant Jupiter is halfway through its 13-month stint in Cancer and your playful, spotlight-stealing fifth house. Your creative world is brimming with potential until June 30. Heck, it might already be in full bloom! Wherever you are on the journey, don't stop now. You have the cosmic green light to take up space— romantically, artistically, stylistically and all of it!

No need to rush off to rehearsal. To magnetize attention, you just have to be your radiant, unfiltered self. The fifth house governs fame, and Jupiter's generous touch can push you onto stages or make it impossible for anyone to ignore your efforts. Even if you aren't TRYING to make a spectacle of yourself, don't be surprised if you find yourself painting, performing or sharing your gifts with a wider audience.

When life feels THIS theatrical, you might as well dress for the part you want to play. (Read: scene-stealing, bossed up and glamorous!) While comfort-loving Cancer may skew "granny chic," this is not the year to hide your killer style behind a crocheted afghan throw. (Of course, if you turn said throw into an ironic shawl, you might kick off a viral trend.) Curate some flowing, photo-ready pieces, colors that light you up, and details that make you feel ready for your close-up at a moment's notice.

Opportunities for public acclaim will come in waves, but so might a few nerves about stepping into the spotlight. Sensitive Pisces, you cherish the serenity of your private world. It's easy to feel exposed when your work—or heart—is on display. But it's not your fate to be a starving artist in perpetual throes of unrequited love. This is your time to stand behind your gifts with pride—but we get it if you balk when it's time to toot your own bugle. If you need help stating your worth, consider adding a savvy agent or rep to your dream team. Let friends be your marketing team by posting about your offerings and leaving glowing reviews.

And not that we have to tell a Pisces this, but don't give up on Cupid! Lucky Jupiter's tour through your fifth house can spark new flames or dial up the passion in an existing relationship. Playfulness is the glue for love now. Whether it's planning a decadent baecation, getting lost in a foreign metropolis together, or dressing to the nines for a cultural night out, shared experiences will keep your hearts wide open.

Geographically undesirable? That doesn't have to be a dealbreaker, even with the red-spotted planet getting cozy in homebody Cancer. Long-distance bonds are blessed under this globe-trotting influence. As long as your time together feels intimate, don't rule out a lover from another zip code or time zone. A move for love could even be in the cards, or you might find yourself cheering on your partner's next big leap, trusting you'll grow together through every new adventure.

Do you know in your heart that your relationship could use a tune-up? Sweeping the tough stuff under the rug won't fly when truth-seeker Jupiter is around. This philosophical cycle could direct you to a couples' workshop in an off-grid retreat center, where you shut down your devices for sessions in co-regulating breathwork, mirroring and partner massage. (Bring your sense of humor and your raw, beating heart!) And even if you're just parked in your own living room, honest conversations and brave vulnerability are on deck.

Pisces on the fertility track have cosmic blessings working overtime, too. Jupiter's amplifying effect could support your family goals, whether that means planning for a pregnancy, exploring IVF, or taking practical steps like freezing eggs for the future. Not ready for a school of mini-Fish just yet? Take extra precautions. Jupiter loves to multiply whatever you're already working with!

Whatever your heart's biggest wish is—love, art, joy—Jupiter's presence n your fertile fifth house reminds you that life is meant to be lived out loud. Say yes to experiences that make you feel radiant and even a tiny bit out of your depth. Reveal your talents, pour your passion into what you love, and don't rush offstage until you've soaked up the well-deserved applause.

JUPITER IN LEO
JUNE 30, 2026 – JULY 26, 2027

That's a wrap, Pisces! After a high-key stretch in the spotlight, you'll be ready to head back to your metaphoric trailer and revel in a much-needed round of self-care. On June 30, Jupiter unrolls its bamboo yoga mat in Leo and your sixth house of wellness, daily routines and work. As it does, it blesses you with thirteen months of pure revitalization until July 26, 2027. Time to yell, "Cut!" on some of those hedonistic indulgences of early 2026, and embrace clean, green living again. Let visions of adaptogenic mushrooms, cooling sleep masks and flowy barre classes dance through your head.

Not that you'll be supine, watching the clouds, for the entire thirteen months. The sixth house is the administrative zone of your chart. All of your daily routines, including your professional ones, are getting a healthy makeover. In regal Leo, Jupiter wants you to feel like the Queen or King of Pentacles in the Tarot: entitled to the best while also dutiful, responsible and wise. Set up systems that help make your repeating tasks flow like a well-tuned machine. As much fearmongering as there is about humans being replaced by technology, see what happens if you make an AI helper your partner in crime. That will leave more time for activities no machine has yet been able to nail: ones that require your deep level of empathy and psychic attunement.

Mixing Eastern and Western wisdom can help you find the perfect wellness cocktail for your unique body chemistry. Curious? Preventative care like acupuncture, Chinese herbs and colon hydrotherapy (worth looking into as Pisces rules the elimination system) can go far to keep your body balanced when you get your annual physical. A food allergy test could even unlock hidden sensitivities that have been slowing you down. Who knows? Maybe dairy isn't the villain you thought it was, or maybe it absolutely is!

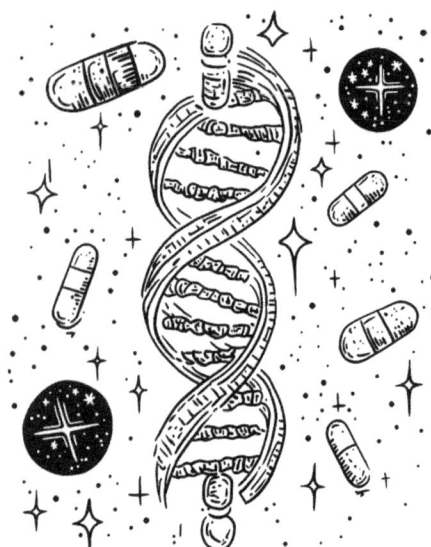

If you're already fascinated by nutrition, as many forward-thinking Fish are, this cycle could inspire you to go pro. Maybe you'll get certified in a holistic healing modality, train as a nutrition coach, or work with a doctor to try superfood supplements, hormone replacement therapy (HRT) or a personalized vitamin stack.

Exercise will feel incredibly inviting, too—even celebratory—with Jupiter in passionate, festive Leo. The second half of the year could find you shouting mantras in a Soul Cycle class or becoming a regular at sober, daytime dance parties. If it's been a while since you prioritized fitness, Jupiter's boost will get you moving again. Start slow with gentle stretches, long walks or pool workouts, and watch your stamina grow. Before you know it, you might be participating in a charity 5K.

Feeling burnt out by work? Before you quiet-quit, this freedom-loving cycle can get you on the road to independent work. It may be worth discussing "other arrangements" with your current employer or clients. Rather than lose a gem like you, they might be willing to figure out a remote work sitch or rehire you as a contractor instead of a full-time employee. If you have some PTO dates banked, take them as soon as you can after June 30. A couple weeks of restorative time away might do more than you realize.

Even while in decadent Leo, Jupiter in the sixth house favors simplicity. Where could you scale back expenses or make your funds go farther? With some careful planning, you may be able to work less and still enjoy a soul-nourishing lifestyle, albeit one that doesn't involve quite so much impulse spending.

With entrepreneurial media maven Jupiter at the helm, you could feel a strong pull to launch your own business or take your current hustle global. Writing, teaching, podcasting or filming a documentary could be powerful ways to share what you know. Don't hold back just because you're "not an expert yet." You've got wisdom that people need now.

Jetsetting Jupiter could open new doors for travel, too. Maybe you'll land a contract that sends you abroad for a while or take an extended work-from-anywhere adventure. A year in the London office? A wellness retreat in Costa Rica? Why not? Your routines CAN be flexible and life-enhancing now, not soul-draining.

One note: Jupiter in your sixth house can pile your calendar with busy work if you don't stay mindful. Guard your energy by streamlining your systems, delegating where you can and carving out real downtime. Balance is your true superpower between June 30, 2026 and July 26, 2027—the sweet spot where vitality, productivity and joy all meet.

3 INNOVATE AT HOME

URANUS IN GEMINI
APRIL 25, 2026 – MAY 22, 2033

Home isn't just where you rest your head, Pisces, it's where you recharge your magic. And beginning April 25, 2026, radical Uranus drops anchor in Gemini and your domestic fourth house, reshaping your concept of sanctuary until May 22, 2033. You got a whisper of what's to come last year, when the side-spinning planet did a teaser tour through Gemini from July 7 to November 7, 2025. Maybe your space suddenly felt too small. Or the emotional climate in your inner circle shifted from cozy to chaotic. That was your cosmic clue: Something deeper is calling for reinvention.

This isn't just about Frette sheets or Farrow & Ball paint—though, by all means, indulge. With Uranus in your home zone, you're designing from the soul outward. Think less "Pinterest board," more "emotional feng shui." What kinds of spaces allow your creativity to have free rein? Who in your life exudes the warmth of a comforting hearth—and who drains the energy from the room before they've even taken off their shoes?

Pisces, your nature is fluid and porous. You absorb the mood of a space before you even realize it's happening. While that empathy is your gift, it's also your Achilles' heel—especially when boundaries blur. Now you have a new mission: To master the art of erecting a psychic border. Not to shut people out, but to preserve your own peace and keep relationships in the proper balance. (Read: No one feeling guilty, obligated or codependently drained.) From shared walls to shared DNA, the relationships closest to you may go through seismic shifts. Some bonds will deepen, others will dissolve. Through it all, you'll be asked to define (or redefine) what your comfort zone looks and feels like.

This will be a process, so keep an open mind. Uranus is the "mad scientist," renegade and disruptor of the skies. What you REALLY want might be something you've never even thought of having before. Living arrangements could become more experimental. You might split your time between cities, retreat to a tiny house in the woods, or try a co-living space that nourishes both your mind and heart.

The fourth house rules family, but with Uranus here, "chosen family" could become just as essential as the one you were born into. Curate your circle with intention. You need people who honor your emotional intelligence and communicate with curiosity. With Uranus in interactive Gemini, you aren't looking to isolate into a solitary cave. Your home could become the hub for a parade of interesting characters from your romantasy book club to your political action nonprofit and even a few psychedelic ceremonies. Host with intention, Pisces!

Since Uranus is the techie planet, this cycle could spark innovations in how you create and maintain your sanctuary. Think smart-home devices that adjust lighting to match your mood, air-purifying systems that help you breathe easier, or energy-efficient upgrades that align with your eco-values. Wellness at home could take center stage, too—maybe you carve out a meditation room, install a red-light therapy corner, or use tracking apps to monitor your sleep, hydration and stress. The goal isn't a showroom-perfect house; it's a living, breathing space that evolves with you.

This is also a potent time for emotional and ancestral healing. Family roles, inherited stories, even childhood conditioning may come up for review. You might start (or resume) therapy, explore epigenetics or simply have that overdue heart-to-heart with someone who played a key role in your origin story. Remember, healing doesn't always require a dramatic confrontation. Sometimes it starts with rearranging the furniture, lighting a candle and choosing softness over silence.

That said, your emotions may short-circuit here and there under this erratic transit. Gemini governs communication and Uranus is famously impulsive, so be mindful about when—and how—you speak your truth. A poorly timed outburst at the dinner table could reverberate far beyond the moment. Practice emotional intelligence as a spiritual discipline. When you do speak up, aim for clarity over crisis.

Over the next seven years, your mission is to create a space—both physical and emotional—that reflects who you're becoming, not just where you've been. A sanctuary that protects your tenderness, amplifies your artistry and supports the rhythms of your soul. Think private sanctum meets creative atelier. Mood board meets moon ritual. Create a home by YOUR design, Pisces.

4 ADD SOUL TO YOUR GOALS

LUNAR NODES IN LEO AND AQUARIUS
NORTH NODE IN AQUARIUS, SOUTH NODE IN LEO JULY 26, 2026–MARCH 26, 2028

Less hustle, more flow? That's a recipe your dreamy sign can get down with. And after a busy first half of 2026, you'll be so ready to sink into that groove this summer. Good news! Starting July 26, 2026, the lunar nodes shift into Leo and Aquarius until March 26, 2028, pulling you into a cycle that values soul over speed. The karmic South Node settles into Leo and your sixth house of work, health and routines, while the destiny-driven North Node plants its flag in Aquarius and your twelfth house of spirituality, release and healing. Step off the hamster wheel and rediscover the restorative rhythm that makes you feel whole.

Since January 2025, you've hosted the North Node in Pisces—a rare era of bold reinvention that only comes around every 18 years. During this time, you redefined your independence and pushed toward personal milestones. But this hasn't been a walk in the park! For a good deal of this nodal cycle, you've also carried the weight of Saturn in your sign, demanding structure and discipline. Neptune, your ruling planet, was simultaneously wrapping up its 14-year stay in Pisces, dissolving old illusions and asking you to dream with purpose. Growth didn't come easy. It came through grit, reality checks and deep inner work. But…you did it!

As the North Node slides into Aquarius this July 26, your soul work takes center stage. The training wheels are off, Pisces, and the focus turns inward: healing, releasing and finding peace. This is your wheelhouse! The twelfth house shares similar qualities to Pisces, the twelfth sign, so you are bound to embrace this dream spell.

Old fears or unfinished emotional business may rise up, but only so you can finally set them down. This is shadow work, therapy, meditation, breathwork—the practices that clear away the static. Honestly, Pisces, you have always been here for that kind of internal deep dive. Now, the universe gives you permission to focus, guilt-free, on exploring the fascinating discovery of your psyche. Creativity doubles as medicine during this cycle. Write, paint, dance, make music. Serendipitous encounters are everywhere you turn, so pay attention to the people who come across your path. Mentors, healers or "earth angels" appear right on cue to guide you through the fog. Across the zodiac, the Leo South Node tugs on your sixth house of wellness and daily routines. Reminder, Pisces: Your body is your soul's address here on Earth. If you want to soar across the astral plane, you need to take "stellar" care of your physicality. Get yourself back into powerful practices. Cook nourishing meals, turn your morning rituals into ceremony, reclaim your evenings as sacred resets. Watch out for the sixth house shadow, though—perfectionism, micromanaging, busywork disguised as progress. Ask yourself often: Is this routine helping me thrive, or am I just running on autopilot?

Your health and workflow may issue wake-up calls, too. It may be necessary to simplify your systems and streamline tasks. Outsource what drains you instead of being a martyr. You might actually SAVE money in the long run by hiring assistance. Think of it as clearing the energetic clutter so your spirit has room to breathe. Your body is your vessel, and this cycle wants you to treat it with reverence: rest, move, eat clean, manage stress. The better you care for the container, the more freely inspiration can pour through you.

Service will also be a theme. The twelfth house asks you to offer your compassion in tangible ways like volunteering with a charitable organization. If you're in a leadership role, create space for underrepresented voices or launch initiatives that support collective healing. Even the smallest acts ripple out in ways you can't always see.

Remember, Pisces: Enlightenment isn't found in a grand gesture—it's woven into the rhythms of everyday life. The difference is in the awareness you bring to even the smallest actions. By March 2028, you'll emerge lighter, wiser and more spiritually attuned. The reinvention of the past few years will crystallize into a quiet confidence. You won't need to prove your growth anymore—you'll simply embody it, naturally, like water flowing back to the sea.

5 RESTRUCTURE ROMANCE

VENUS RETROGRADE IN SCORPIO AND LIBRA
VENUS RETROGRADE IN SCORPIO: OCTOBER 3–25
VENUS RETROGRADE IN LIBRA: OCTOBER 25–NOVEMBER 13

Like Pisces Rihanna, you've got a talent for finding love in a hopeless place—and yes, a hopeful one, too. But starting October 3, it's time to turn that siren song inward. Amorous Venus begins a six-week retrograde, backing up through Scorpio and your truth-seeking ninth house until October 25, then drifting back into Libra and your eighth house of eroticism and unbreakable bonds until November 13.

Your inner world is a deep, cinematic ocean, Pisces, and when Venus shifts into reverse every 18 months, you get a golden opportunity to dive down to the hidden reefs—those beliefs, desires and patterns that quietly shape your love life.

While this can churn up a flood of feelings, take heart. This retrograde won't have the same raw intensity as the last one that directly impacted your sign when Venus reversed through Pisces from March 27 to April 12, 2025. Consider this more of a choppy current than a hurricane.

The first leg of the retrograde is in Scorpio, which could make you feel like an intimacy investigator on the hunt for buried feelings. Not that you'll have to dig deep to find them. Raw emotion could bubble to the surface demanding to be dealt with. Nevermind whether or not the timing of this is "inconvenient," Fish. You may have to stop in your tracks and get honest with yourself about something that needs to evolve or change in your love life.

Check in with yourself: Have you been glossing over a simmering issue with rose-colored reassurances, hoping it will resolve on its own? While the love planet slips back through Scorpio and your no-BS ninth house, it's impossible to delude yourself. (And yes, this IS a good thing.) Positive thinking has its charms, but it can't replace an honest conversation. Stop painting watercolor rainbows over something that needs a sharper outline. Diplomatic Venus can help you address problem areas without wounding anyone's pride. The gift of this cycle is the chance to revisit the past and make it better—or at least, to walk away knowing you've spoken your truth. Yes, some moments will be uncomfortable, but once you open the floodgates, you'll feel lighter, freer and more in control of your own story.

In your closest bonds, put long-range visions on the table and see where they align and where they diverge. Differences don't have to spell doom. This discovery could open doors to creative solutions. Could you live in different places part of the year? Restructure finances temporarily so one of you can apply for a PhD program? While you might not land on a solution until Venus turns direct on November 13, the gift of the retrograde is that it can help you look in new directions and drum up richly creative solutions.

Need a romantic reboot? Before October 25, you might find your mojo by revisiting a place that makes you feel luminous. No one loves a seaside escape like a Pisces, and should you find yourself wandering around the Greek Isles or the California coast, there's no telling who might be drawn in by your windswept allure. Can't get away? Day trips to artsy towns can also rev your engines. Flirt with the gallery owners and the literary hottie working at the used bookstore. Shameless? Absolutely—and there's nothing wrong with that. The trick is to NOT mentally turn every moment into a happily-ever-after scenario in your imagination.

When Venus retreats into Libra from October 25 to November 13, the focus shifts to more private affairs. With your erotic eighth house getting seduced by Venus retrograde, attractions could be both highly magnetic and intensely messy if you let go of the wheel. (So don't.) Past lovers could resurface, particularly those with a knack for disappearing just when things start to warm up. Before you get pulled back into a toxic riptide, remind yourself why you jumped ship in the first place.

That said, if you're feeling wistful over "the one that got away," Venus's pivot could bring them back into your orbit. If the connection seems like it has life left in it, cautiously explore, making sure to lay all your truths on the table. The conditions don't have to be flawless, but they should be ones you can honestly live with. You may be the one who has some explaining to do. Avoid getting defensive and focus on showing all the ways you HAVE evolved and grown. That could set the stage for reparations.

Chemistry brewing with someone new? Slow the pace, no matter how much the "cuffing season" vibes are infecting you with the urge to merge. It's a little too easy to be blinded by people's charisma and potential, projecting qualities onto them that may (or may not) ever emerge. Alas, not everyone who sweeps you off your feet will stick around to create a soft landing.

While in Libra and your eighth house, Venus retrograde may trigger an inquiry about your sexuality, turn-ons and what you need to feel trusting and secure. You don't have to throw yourself into the arms of a player to figure this out! An intellectual inquiry might be the best place to start. Read books, attend workshops, watch TED Talks on the subject. If you have a trusted "play partner" this could be a spicy journey that ignites new dimensions of pleasure.

By November 13, you'll have a sharper sense of who can meet you at your depths and how you want to be loved. Whether you choose to recommit, release or keep exploring, you'll move forward with stronger boundaries, richer self-knowledge and a more deliciously self-assured sense of your own worth.

2026
PISCES

12 MONTH OVERVIEW

January MONTHLY HOROSCOPE

The future is looking bright—and you can't stop thinking about what's ahead this month. With the Sun in Capricorn until the 19th, your communal eleventh house (AKA the innovation station) is alive and buzzing. Network, join forces or launch a group project. Your influence is amplified through collaboration. But don't get lost in the crowd! On the 3rd, the first full moon of 2026 arrives in Cancer swinging a spotlight into your fifth house of fame. Romance could heat up, or a creative project might finally reach the finish line. Take time to properly celebrate and let the universe know, "I want more!" Missing a few puzzle pieces on Team Fish? The new moon in Capricorn on the 18th could shine a light on fresh alliances who make your mission sing. Venus and Mars pair up in Capricorn until the 17th, which brings warmth and conviviality to your social interactions. Get out and circulate while you can! After the 23rd, both Venus and Mars will have slipped into Aquarius and your restful twelfth house, pulling you behind the scenes for more private connections (and yes, a little fantasy-fueled romance). Energy flags after the 19th as the Sun also moves into Aquarius. Rest and recharge during this four-week cycle so you'll be in fighting shape once your birthday season begins late February. Practical details demand attention this month, too: On the 2nd, soothsayer Chiron pivots direct in Aries, helping you reset finances and strengthen your sense of self-worth. The 26th is a major day! Your ruling planet Neptune officially wraps its 14-year tour of Pisces, not to return again for over 150 years! As the numinous planet drifts through Aries for a 13-year tour, your relationship with abundance is up for reinvention. Build prosperity in ways that nourish your bank account AND your spirit.

February MONTHLY HOROSCOPE

Clear the decks, Pisces—February calls for rest, reflection and release before your season begins. The Sun quietly streams through Aquarius and your twelfth house until the 18th, asking: What needs clearing so you can start fresh? Tie up loose ends and let go of old baggage to make room for what's next. On the 1st, the full moon in Leo shines into your systematic sixth house, urging you to revamp routines or complete a lingering project. Are your daily systems supporting you or draining you? A few tweaks now can restore your energy. On February 17, the Aquarius new moon arrives as a karmic solar eclipse—the first here since 2018—just as the Year of the Fire Horse begins. A chapter may close, opening the door for renewal in every way. Expect epiphanies! Until February 10, Venus in Aquarius enhances intuition and draws in private connections. Then the love planet parades through Pisces, boosting charisma and making you an irresistible force through

March 6. And here's your victory lap: On February 13, Saturn finally departs your sign, ending a grueling cycle that began on March 7, 2023. For nearly three years, Saturn tested you, toughened you and pushed you through your paces. Now, it won't return for almost three decades. Feel the weight lift! As Saturn moves into Aries, a new two-year cycle in your financial zone begins, asking you to build lasting stability. Valentine's Day follows with the Capricorn moon, spotlighting friendships and reminding you to cherish your circle. Happy birthday season, Pisces! When the Sun returns to your sign on the 18th, it's time for a personal reboot. Mercury retrograde in Pisces from February 26 to March 20 may feel like a slow start, but use it to shed an old skin and sketch the blueprint for your next chapter. Honor your own rhythms as you go!

March

MONTHLY HOROSCOPE

What do you want to initiate, Pisces? March is your month to shoot your shot, as the Sun, Mercury retrograde, unstoppable Mars and a new moon on the 18th light up Pisces and your first house of identity and fresh starts. Do your research (because, Mercury's retrograde in your sign until the 20th), then take the daring leap. The total lunar (full moon) eclipse in Virgo on the 3rd beams into your seventh house of partnerships, bringing a relationship to a crossroads. Will you deepen the commitment or decide it's time to part ways? Either choice brings clarity, as long as you get off the fence. Lusty Mars moves into Pisces for a six-week stay this March 2, charging you with vitality and drive. Use this burst of energy to pursue your personal goals and projects—but pace yourself so you don't burn out. Love and pleasure get a softer glow after March 6, when Venus leaves your sign and slips into Aries and your second house of values. You'll crave stability and security in relationships, and you may also attract partners who appreciate your worth. On March 10, no-limits Jupiter ends a four-month retrograde in Cancer and your fifth house of passion and creativity. A romantic connection or creative pursuit that stalled now gathers momentum. Results could fly in fast, so buckle up! Birthday season wraps on the 20th as you pass the torch to Aries for the spring equinox. With your second house of security and self-worth alight for four weeks, you're ready to monetize those big ideas you've been kicking around. Mercury stations direct in Pisces the same day, untangling three weeks of mixed signals. Finances and personal goals start moving forward again. You're so ready for this relaunch!

April MONTHLY HOROSCOPE

Money is top of mind this April, Pisces, and at the root of so many changes you're ready to make. The radiant Sun powers through Aries and your second house of income and values until the 19th, reminding you to take your resources seriously. Where do you need more security? Start by building budgets and prioritizing sustainable earning strategies. On April 1, the Libra full moon illuminates your eighth house of intimacy and shared resources, pushing you to resolve a financial arrangement. An investment could pay off handsomely, but you may need to cut ties with one partner and strengthen them elsewhere. This scintillating lunation could shine a light on a sexy keeper, too. Coupled Fish could make another aspect of your relationship rock solid. After April 9, fiery Mars storms into Aries for six weeks, fueling your drive to earn—but also tempting you to overspend. Channel the energy into building stability rather than draining resources trying to compete with the so-called "in crowd." On the 17th, the new moon in Aries brings a fresh wave of income streams or a chance to rebuild financial foundations. But no need to go it alone! Kindred spirits arrive with Taurus season on the 19th. As the Sun streams into your third house of cooperation and communication, your words have persuasive power. Don't bother talking people into anything, though. Look for win-wins and your connections will go the distance. Venus joins the Sun until April 24, helping your ideas land with charm and magnetism. The month ends with a dramatic shift on the 25th, when radical Uranus leaves Taurus after seven years and rockets into Gemini until 2033. With your domestic sector activated, family life and your home environment will undergo surprising, liberating transformations. Put down roots or pull them up—you're ready to create a sacred space by your own design.

May MONTHLY HOROSCOPE

Words carry weight this May, Pisces, as the Taurus Sun radiates through your communicative third house until the 20th. Pitch ideas, propose deals and let your voice be heard—maybe through a podcast or style blog? More mediamaking incentive comes on the 1st when the Scorpio full moon beams into your ninth house, spotlighting a publishing project or academic milestone. Opportunity could knock from halfway around the globe! On the 6th, Pluto turns retrograde in Aquarius and your twelfth house of healing until October 15, calling for inner reflection and a bit more solitude. The Aquarius quarter moon on the 10th could make Mother's Day more introspective—journal, meditate or create a ritual that honors your lineage. On the 16th, the Taurus new supermoon lands in your third house, giving green lights to contracts, writing projects

or important convos. Then Gemini season begins on the 20th, putting the focus on your fourth house of home. Roll out the welcome mat for houseguests, redecorate and make your space feel like a sacred oasis. Until the 18th, Venus in Gemini sweetens family ties and makes nesting fun. Then, on the 18th, Venus moves into Cancer and your fifth house while Mars powers into Taurus and your buzzy third. Flirty banter and late-night convos could turn up the heat. Someone from your friend circle could show more "benefits" than simply platonic vibes. Explore. On the 31st, the Sagittarius blue full moon illuminates your career house. Recognition could arrive suddenly. Your work is ready for its big reveal!

June MONTHLY HOROSCOPE

Give me sanctuary! June draws you inward as the Sun simmers through Gemini and your domestic fourth house until the 21st. Nurture your roots, feather your nest and spend meaningful time with the people who love you unconditionally. The June 14 Gemini new moon—the second supermoon in a rare three-part series—lands here, too, bringing a fresh chapter for home and family. A move, renovation or milestone could unfold faster than you expect, so get ready to pivot. Meanwhile, energetic Mars charges through Taurus and your third house until June 28, filling your calendar with short trips, bold ideas and lively conversations. Don't just talk about it—act on what excites you. A turning point arrives on the 19th when "wounded healer" Chiron dips into Taurus for a three-month preview of its 2027–2034 stay. Since 2018, Chiron has pressed on your self-worth and money story. This summer, the healing shifts to your voice—literally. Share your story and reclaim your power through words. On the 21st, the Sun strides into Cancer and your playful fifth house, right on cue with the solstice and Father's Day. Creativity, romance and joy take the spotlight. In love, Venus lingers in Cancer until the 13th, adding warmth and tenderness. Then she struts into Leo and your sixth house, where passion merges with daily rituals. Show love through acts of service. Dates might even look like meal prep or working out together. Your health and habits get a major boost on June 30 when expansive Jupiter settles into Leo and your sixth house for a thirteen-month stay. Streamline routines, refine systems and prioritize wellness. Small wins add up to big results. The month ends with the Capricorn full moon on the 29th, illuminating your eleventh house of friendships and community. A group project or social effort could wrap up successfully. But heads up: Mercury turns retrograde in Cancer (for three weeks) the same day, so triple-check plans to avoid crossed wires in your circle.

July MONTHLY HOROSCOPE

A joyful July is in store for you, Pisces. Soak it up! With the Sun in Cancer and your playful fifth house until July 22—plus Mercury retrograde here until the 23rd—you'll be revisiting creative projects, old flings or even abandoned hobbies. The Cancer new moon (a supermoon) on the 14th brings a huge heart-opening moment with someone who can meet you on your passionate level. Numinous Neptune, your ruling planet, shifts retrograde in Aries on July 7, beginning five months of reflection about what you consider valuable. This is your cue to tighten budgets, reassess expenses and pull back from stressful obligations. Your manifestation powers are mighty, so get clear on your needs and wants. Saturn's retrograde here on the 26th reinforces the message: Stability comes from data and discipline, too. Meanwhile, go-getter Mars charges through Gemini and your domestic fourth house all month, firing up home projects—and also (glug) family debates. Channel the energy into productive domestic plans and get support for navigating stress with your inner circle. Don't burn bridges by trying to hash things out while tempers are flaring. Once Leo season begins on the 22nd, the spotlight shifts to healthy daily routines. You might reset your hours, hire a trainer or change your eating habits to restore energy. Venus in Virgo from the 9th brings a happy buzz for relationships. Partnership conversations may surface alongside your self-improvement kick. (Turn your bedroom buddy into your gym buddy!) When Mercury stations direct on the 23rd, romance and creative talks smooth out, making it easier to commit to a shared vision. July 26 brings a destiny shift: The North Node enters Aquarius and your twelfth house for the first time in nearly 20 years. Until March 2028, your growth lies in rest, healing and spiritual exploration. This is also the end of the North Node's tour of Pisces that began on January 11, 2025. Time to integrate all the lessons of that identity-shifting cycle. The Sun and Jupiter unite in Leo for the annual "Day of Miracles" on the 29th, serving important news around work and health. Simultaneously, the Aquarius full moon beams into your twelfth house helping you release what no longer serves you. Let go—and watch how much lighter your path becomes.

August MONTHLY HOROSCOPE

Precision is a must, Pisces! With the Sun in Leo and your analytical sixth house until the 22nd, every detail matters. On the 3rd, Chiron pivots retrograde in Taurus and your third house of communication, spotlighting old narratives and peer dynamics that need fine-tuning. Surprise! Conversations you avoided now hold the key to healing. On the 11th, hyperkinetic Mars storms into Cancer and your passionate fifth house, firing up romance, play and artistic expression. Follow what excites your heart! Eclipse season begins dramatically on the 12th with a total solar eclipse in Leo—the first here since 2019—poking that same sixth house of wellness and daily routines. Are your habits lifting you up or quietly draining you? This lunar lift could deliver a sudden job, project or lifestyle shift that makes the answer clear. Venus in Libra from the 6th illuminates your eighth house of intimacy and shared resources, inviting deeper trust in relationships and sharper instincts with money. Where do you need to merge, Pisces? And where should you keep boundaries firm? Use this four-week cycle to figure out those things. More illumination arrives when the Sun beams into Virgo and energizes your partnership zone on the 22nd. You're ready to define alliances that support your growth and say goodbye to the ones that weigh you down. On the 28th, the annual Pisces full moon arrives as a game-changing lunar eclipse! As it lifts the curtain in your first house of identity, it marks a milestone moment. What role no longer fits? Shed an old skin and step into visibility with renewed confidence. August closes with rare cosmic alignment on the 31st as Jupiter in Leo harmonizes with Saturn in Aries, blending expansion with discipline in your work and money sectors. A creative project, side hustle or wellness practice could finally gain traction, proof that consistency pays off.

September MONTHLY HOROSCOPE

Power to your partnerships, Pisces! With the Virgo Sun lighting up your seventh house of relationships until the 22nd, collaboration is the name of the game. You'll thrive in duos—whether that's a romantic date night, co-working session or teaming up on a passion project. Until the 27th, red-hot Mars is firing up Cancer and your fifth house of romance and creativity, adding sparks to your love life and fueling playful self-expression. Bring on the five-part date nights, DJ sets and outfits that make the style bloggers chase you down on the streets. On the 10th, the Virgo new moon brings a fresh start in your closest ties. A relationship could turn official, or you may attract a promising new collaborator. That same day, Uranus pivots retrograde in Gemini and your domestic fourth house, beginning a five-month review of your home life. Is it time for a move, a reno or just better boundaries with relatives or roommates? Think it through strategically. Seductive Venus lounges in Libra and your eighth house until the 10th, stirring intimacy and deep emotional bonds. Then it slides into Scorpio and your ninth house, amplifying wanderlust, learning and spiritual exploration. Heads-up: Venus retrograde from October 3 to November 13 could stall travel or expansion plans, so lock in logistics now. The fall equinox on the 22nd keeps the focus on shared resources and deeper connections as Libra season begins. You may be ready to make a relationship "officially official" in some area of your life. On the 17th, Chiron backs into Aries and your second house of money and self-worth, offering healing around finances and confidence. The Aries full moon on

the 26th could bring a huge money breakthrough. Know your worth, Pisces, and price accordingly!

October

MONTHLY HOROSCOPE

Your scope is broadening, Pisces, but you can't escape your past. On October 3, Venus retrogrades through Scorpio and your ninth house of growth until the 25th, then slides into Libra and your eighth house of intimacy until November 13. Certain relationships could feel perilously close to a "make it or break it" moment. Before you go to extremes, use this six-week cycle to see what creative solutions you can devise together. Magic may be reviveable! You'll get some support in the intimacy department from the Libra Sun until the 23rd, plus the new moon in Libra on the 10th, both of which are in your sexy, soul-baring eighth house. Work is busy while Mars powers through Leo and your sixth house all month. Pack your schedule too tightly and stress could take the wheel. Instead, tap the energizing planet to get your fall fitness plan going and set up savvy systems at work. Transformer Pluto turns direct in Aquarius on the 15th, helping you integrate a few parts of your personality that you've been hiding out of fear or shame. You'll feel back in your emotionally astute element when Scorpio season begins on the 23rd. The very same day, Venus retrograde meets the Sun in a rare Cazimi. With your philosophical ninth house activated, expect a profound revelation that shapes your worldview. Sign up for a class, rev up your spiritual practice. A conversation that opens your eyes could help move the needle on a stagnant relationship. But alas, Mercury turns retrograde in Scorpio on the 24th, making it harder to trust that people are being upfront with you. Take time to get to know them and reveal personal information bit by bit. One friendship could prove to be true blue during the Taurus full moon on the 26th—a day that your words will hit home with the zeitgeist. Share your message!

November MONTHLY HOROSCOPE

You're ready to leap, Pisces, but first, secure your net. With the Scorpio Sun stretching across your ninth house of expansion until the 22nd, wide-open vistas are calling. The year's only Scorpio new moon lands on the 9th, dangling enticing opportunities before you: adventure travel, international conferences, self-development workshops.

Tempting, yes—but wait a beat. Until the 13th, personal planets Mercury and Venus are retrograde, and your grand plans may hit turbulence with timing, money or logistics. Rather than force the launch, refine your ideas. Update your portfolio, revisit an unfinished manuscript or start scouting destinations you'll actually book once the skies clear. By midmonth, the path is open, and you'll achieve lift-off. In the meantime, Mars fires through Leo until the 25th, energizing your sixth house of self-care and efficiency. Upgrade your systems with color-coded tabs, sleek studio workouts, meal-delivery kits that save you time. Your discipline delivers results quickly, but be careful not to push yourself so hard that you get discouraged. Progress, not perfectionism, Pisces. Career goals come into sharp relief after the 22nd, when the Sun rises to the top of your chart in Sagittarius and your tenth house of ambition. Lean into the seasonal soiree circuit as an opportunity to rub shoulders with VIPs and bend the ear of an exec. Matters close to home demand your attention during the Gemini full supermoon on the 24th. Tap in with family to figure out holiday plans. If you're ready to change something about your living situation, this lunar lift could bring the push you need. Whatever's on deck, don't go it alone! On the 25th, excitable Mars struts into Virgo and your seventh house of partnerships for the rest of the year. Expect fireworks in your closest bonds—some a bit too thrilling for your taste. Maybe it's a business deal speeding ahead, a whirlwind romance heating up or a relationship suddenly due for renegotiation. You're all in, Pisces. Just make sure the commitment you choose is one you actually want to keep.

December MONTHLY HOROSCOPE

On Dasher! On Dancer! The Sagittarius Sun powers through your tenth house of ambition until the 21st, spotlighting your goals and achievements. Holiday soirées double as networking events. No apologies for gracefully talking shop! On the 8th, the new moon in Sag hands you a professional reset: Post something meaningful on LinkedIn, take a VIP colleague out for a holiday lunch to set the stage for 2027. Masterful Saturn and your ruler, visionary Neptune, end five-month retrogrades in Pisces on the 10th and 12th, respectively, clearing away doubt about the contribution that you make to the world. Upgrade your boundaries so the energy vampires can't drain your reserves. With motivator Mars charging through Virgo and your partnership house all month, duos become extra dynamic. Lean into relationships that feel like equal parts support system and spark. Just make sure you aren't falling in love with mere potential. Once Venus re-enters Scorpio on the 4th, your romantic truths come spilling out. Let them! If your calendar feels like a marathon of commitments, scale back on the 12th, as Jupiter pivots retrograde in Leo and your wellness zone. Prioritize workouts that recharge you (think: reformer Pilates or a long walk with a podcast) and swap one boozy night on the town for a skincare-and-sage night in. Popularity surges as the solstice arrives on the

21st, ushering in Capricorn season. The more is the mightier! A love story could reach a sentimental turning point during the Cancer full supermoon on the 23rd, and a passion project earns its applause. The Sun clinks glasses with Mars in your partnership zone this NYE. Whether you're dreaming up resolutions with your partner or chatting up an intriguing reveler by the open bar, you're ready to set off fireworks with someone who can match your imagination and zeal!

Read your extended monthly forecast for life, love, money and career! astrostyle.com

JANUARY

JANUARY
Moon Phase Calendar

SUN	MON	TUE	WED	THU	FRI	SAT
				CLARIFY **1** ○ ♊	REVIVE **2** ○ ♊ ☾ 8:09 AM	ILLUMINATE **3** ○ ♋ Full Moon 5:03AM
INTEGRATE **4** ○ ♋ ♌ 8:44AM	RADIATE **5** ○ ♌	ATTRACT **6** ○ ♌ ♍ 11:57AM	UNIFY **7** ○ ♍	HARMONIZE **8** ◐ ♍ ♎ 7:06PM	EXPAND **9** ◐ ♎	CONFRONT **10** ◐ ♎ Last Quarter
TRANSITION **11** ◑ ♎ ♏ 5:55AM	REFLECT **12** ◑ ♏	BROADEN **13** ◑ ♏ ♐ 6:34PM	RETHINK **14** ◑ ♐	LIBERATE **15** ● ♐	COMMIT **16** ● ♐ ♑ 6:47AM	INNOVATE **17** ● ♑
INITIATE **18** ● ♑ New Moon 2:52PM ♑→♒ 5:18PM	ALIGN **19** ● ♒	ENERGIZE **20** ● ♒	COMMUNICATE **21** ◐ ♒ ♓ 1:50AM	TRANSFORM **22** ◐ ♓	EMPOWER **23** ◐ ♓ ♈ 8:26AM	PROPEL **24** ◐ ♈
STABILIZE **25** ◐ ♈ First Quarter ♉ 1:05PM	BUILD **26** ◑ ♉	INTENSIFY **27** ◑ ♉ ♊ 3:55PM	CONVERSE **28** ○ ♊	CONNECT **29** ○ ♊ ♋ 5:32PM	NURTURE **30** ○ ♋	CREATE **31** ○ ♋ ♌ 7:09PM

Times listed are Eastern US Time Zone

KEY

♈ ARIES	♌ LEO	♐ SAGITTARIUS	**FM** FULL MOON
♉ TAURUS	♍ VIRGO	♑ CAPRICORN	**NM** NEW MOON
♊ GEMINI	♎ LIBRA	♒ AQUARIUS	**LE** LUNAR ECLIPSE
♋ CANCER	♏ SCORPIO	♓ PISCES	**SE** SOLAR ECLIPSE

JANUARY 3, 5:03 AM
full moon in Cancer #1 (13°02')

CANCER FULL MOON CRYSTAL

SELENITE

This calm and soothing gemstone forms in long bands and has a high, clear and pure vibration. Named after Selene, the goddess of the Cancer-ruled moon, this crystal is believed to help the flow of bodily fluids and support fertility. Since selenite does not hold negative charges, it is fantastic to use to neutralize your own energy. Like a "crystal crab shell," selenite is often used to make a protective energetic "grid" around your house or workspace.

CANCER FULL MOON = CELEBRATE!

Your divine emotional intelligence

The importance of creating safe spaces

The power of family—blood-related or chosen

Intuitive hits that guide you toward your dreams

The healing power of water

Mother figures and your own maternal instincts

1

JANUARY 18, 2:52PM

new moon in Capricorn (28°44')

CAPRICORN NEW MOON CRYSTAL

GARNET

This grounding, blood-red stone helps with focus and keeps you disciplined while you tick off your Capricorn season goals. Garnet enhances life-force energy and vitality during the winter months.

CAPRICORN NEW MOON = FOCUS

Set goals that challenge and inspire you

Elevate your image to be more professional

Connect to authority figures and mentors

Make a long-term plan

JANUARY
MONTHLY HOTSPOTS

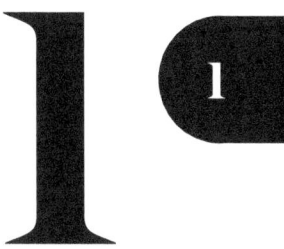

JAN 1

MERCURY-NEPTUNE SQUARE
Welcome to 2026! The year opens with a chatty Gemini moon in its Waxing Gibbous phase, which will ripen to a full moon on the 3rd. Whether it's the bubbles wearing off or the cosmic weather, you might need a few moments away from the crowds. As expressive Mercury in visionary Sagittarius butts up against nebulous Neptune in escapist Pisces, mere words won't capture those 2026 resolutions. Lean into Neptune's artistry and make a vision board with images that captivate your intuition. Then, tap into Mercury's wordsmithing powers by journaling your intentions for the year ahead. Later in the day, Mercury moves into a new sign. Get started on this with a strong cup of coffee, even with a few people over brunch.

MERCURY IN CAPRICORN (JAN 1-JAN 20)
Talk about timing! After a meditative morning, mental Mercury marches into goal-getter Capricorn at 4:11pm ET, revving up your resolutions. Nestled in this stoic sign, Mercury helps you plan, strategize and negotiate with a larger game in sight. This doesn't mean you should abandon your lofty 2026 visions. With clear-headed Capricorn's precision, you can set those dreams to a realistic timeline. Got an "impossible" goal for the year? Break it into phases with defined milestones and watch it start to feel totally feasible! Reach out to mentors and invest in an expert training (all the domain of Capricorn) to fill in the blanks. Not ready to get quite so linear on the first day of the year? There's no rush—Mercury is in Capricorn for nearly three weeks.

JAN 2 CHIRON RETROGRADE ENDS IN ARIES
Speak up! Healing comet Chiron, which has been retrograde since July 30, 2025, moves forward in firebrand Aries. While Chiron helps you identify your needs and advocate for them, there may have been a few messy attempts. Reminder: What reads as assertive to one person could come off as aggressive to another. Starting today, seek healthy ways to access the conviction that lies underneath your anger and outrage. Is there a core value, a belief that you feel has been violated? Take

the time to identify it before you confront anyone. In the best-case scenario, you can have a productive conversation instead of a fight. Learning longtime techniques like Non-Violent Communication or the three-step Imago Dialogue (mirror, validate, empathize) could transform a relationship that's veering into toxic waters. That said, if you're dealing with narcissism (a shadow trait of Aries) or an abusive dynamic, the best form of healing might come through rebuilding your own self-esteem outside of this particular relationship. In mythology, Chiron revived himself in order to heal others. What you learn could end up being a golden lesson that you share with others down the line.

JAN 3 CANCER FULL MOON (5:03AM; 13°02')

Feel those feelings! The year's first full moon arrives in caring Cancer, spotlighting the holiday afterglow...or aftermath. Cancer is the sign of home and family, and the "festive season" can stir up quite a lot around these topics. Whether you're basking in nostalgia or stewing in resentment, the emotions roused by this lunar light will be anything but mild. With the moon opposing peacemaker Venus and combative Mars (both in Capricorn), your unprocessed feelings could manifest as an angry outburst, a torrent of tears or even as extreme fatigue. Since it's the weekend, sleep in if you can, or do something cathartic and self-soothing. Ask a nurturing friend or relative for advice, or pour a mug of tea and fill up a few journal pages. Does your personal space look like a disaster zone of gift wrap and half-unpacked suitcases? Use this domestic full moon to get things back in order.

JAN 6 SUN-VENUS MEETUP

Today's meetup of the confident Sun and magnetic Venus in Capricorn could help you start the year feeling like a boss. Where would you like to express your leadership or be recognized in 2026? Stride boldly into the first workweek of the year and radiate charisma! A compelling person could sweep you up in their aura. Dazzled though you may be, remember that they're still a mere mortal. Admiration is one thing, but hoisting them onto a pedestal can lead to disappointments for both of you.

JAN 7 VENUS-MARS MEETUP

How far will you go to prove your loyalty? Cosmic lovers Venus and Mars unite in devoted Capricorn today. Romantic gestures are nice, but consistent action is the love language that speaks volumes. Capricorn is a long-term planner, and you may be questioning whether a relationship or friendship can go the distance. Do the mature thing and talk about it. Better to lay your cards on the table and know where you stand than to be left fantasizing about a future that only one of you wants! Is everyone on board? Turn talks to what you can build together as a duo this year.

JAN 9

VENUS-JUPITER OPPOSITION
Craving comfort or itching for a challenge? Today, the "benefics" Venus and Jupiter break from their simpatico stance and lock into a power struggle. With Jupiter in nurturing Cancer and Venus in status-seeking Capricorn, your heart and head may be pulling you in dueling directions, making satisfaction a fleeting prospect. Sentimental feelings clash with practical considerations, and the tension between emotional security and worldly ambition could leave couples second-guessing their bond. Attached? One partner may be craving deeper intimacy while the other's laser-focused on long-term goals. Don't confuse distraction with disinterest, though! Talk it out before you let assumptions build walls. Single? Chemistry could spark in unexpected places, but don't rush to lock anything down. Let connections unfold slowly and see who shows up for the real you. A case of "grass is greener" could make it hard for you to give anyone a fair chance.

SUN-MARS MEETUP
Who's an unstoppable force today? You are! As the confident Sun and fearless Mars unite in ambitious Capricorn, they send you on a mission—and nothing can stand in your way. Just check in with yourself throughout the day to make sure you're not coming across as too competitive or aggressive, as this combustible mashup can make people a little ruthless. More aura, less ego. When you exude leadership, people will naturally gravitate to you.

JAN 10

SUN + MARS OPPOSE JUPITER
Don't believe the hype—or feed it! With both the Sun and combative Mars facing off against outspoken Jupiter, emotions can spin stories faster than the facts can keep up. Someone may talk a big game, tugging on your heartstrings, or trigger knee-jerk reactions that spiral into heated debates. Before you know it, tall tales and strong opinions are flying, leaving everyone unsure what (or who) to believe. Enjoy the colorful narratives, but check the receipts before you sign on—or start promising more than you can deliver. If words get too sharp, take responsibility quickly. A real apology ("I'm sorry for hurting you") goes a lot further than a defensive justification. And if you're the one on the receiving end, don't stew—set a clear boundary and see who's mature enough to respect it.

THIRD QUARTER MOON IN LIBRA
Avoiding a touchy topic? Not today. With the waning quarter moon in Libra lending its diplomatic touch, it's time to initiate the conversation you've

been dodging. Approach it with grace, not grit. A calm, composed tone will take you further than defensiveness or finger-pointing. If you've been hurt, speak from your experience instead of trying to score points. And if you discover that you misread the situation? Own it. A heartfelt apology can clear the air and lay the groundwork for real understanding.

JAN 14 MERCURY-JUPITER OPPOSITION

Know-it-all alert! As mouthy Mercury and candid Jupiter face off, people could try to one-up each other—and get a dig in for good measure. Tap out of this toxic trap and be careful not to push anyone's buttons today. Trying to concentrate? Good luck! The Mercury-Jupiter opposition could be a minefield of distractions. Between family members texting you and the temptation of a dishy group chat, staying focused could be a Herculean effort. Under pressure of a deadline? Don your headphones, turn on some binaural beats and drown out the drama. Is someone trying to pitch you a big idea? If it sounds too good to be true, this exaggeration-prone transit makes it likely that it is.

JAN 15 VENUS-URANUS TRINE

Feeling stuck in a romantic rut? Venus in Capricorn syncs up with unconventional Uranus in Taurus, shaking up stale dynamics with a well-timed twist. Both planets are grounded in earth signs, so while change is welcome, it needs to come with structure. Single? A spark could fly with someone who challenges your usual type or introduces you to a new way of loving. Attached? Disrupt the routine before it disrupts you. Instead of seeking thrills elsewhere, co-create an experience that breaks from your norm. Try role-swapping for a day or plan a date with no script. Novelty doesn't have to mean chaos—just a little reinvention.

JAN 17

VENUS IN AQUARIUS (JAN 17–FEB 10)

Romance gets a remix as Venus sails through Aquarius until right before Valentine's Day, dialing down the drama and shifting the tone from wild to mild. Cupid might be off the clock, but connection is still in the air—just on less traditional terms. Think friendship-first vibes, creative chemistry and conversations that veer into the unexpected. Single? You could meet someone intriguing through your social circle or a shared cause, and sparks may fly online more than in person. Partnered? This is the moment to talk about the kind of relationship that truly fits your lifestyle, not just the one you inherited from tradition. From unconventional living arrangements to bold family planning, nothing's off-limits. You don't have to act on every idea, but naming your truth makes space for authenticity—and gives love room to grow without constraint.

SUN-URANUS TRINE

Seeking a professional change in 2026 or an additional source of income? Think outside the box! The ambitious Capricorn Sun fist-bumps unconventional Uranus in Taurus, lending a creative twist to how you think about work and money. Spend time contemplating what would make you feel fulfilled professionally. If you draw a blank, think about the way you'd like to FEEL when you start your workday. Let that emotion guide you. With innovative Uranus in the mix, you could get additional insights by pulling a Tarot card, free-writing or breaking out of your weekend routine. Do something different today and a lightning-bolt insight could hit you!

JAN 18

MERCURY-MARS MEETUP

Need a little time to think about it? Today, contemplative Mercury and action planet Mars connect in discerning Capricorn. It's a good day to ask all your questions and do research before making a big decision. But don't deliberate for too long or you could miss an opportunity. Try to get those answers in the next 48 hours so you can give a clear "yes" or "no." Is someone giving you a hard sell, or are you the one applying pressure? A gentle reminder or a mutually agreed upon deadline is cool. Being pushy? Not so much.

CAPRICORN NEW MOON (2:52PM; 28°44')

The first new moon of 2026 arrives in Capricorn and delivers a jolt of ambition and focus. This is your cue to set the bar higher—not just for what you do, but for how you want to grow this year. What would it look like to stretch beyond your current limits? With the moon conjunct clever Mercury and go-getter Mars, and also in a favorable trine to innovative Uranus, think way outside the box. There's almost nothing that can't be achieved with courage, curiosity and conviction now! Aim high, but also get specific. Rather than spread yourself thin trying to accomplish a zillion things, double-click on a couple of meaningful goals and build out a master plan. A coach, mentor or strategic partner could help you chart the course. Lay the foundation now and by the June 29 Capricorn full moon, you could be standing on a whole new summit.

JAN 19

MERCURY-URANUS TRINE

When you've got a lot on your plate, it can be easy to overthink things. Don't second-guess yourself today! As cerebral Mercury and inventive Uranus team up in stabilizing earth signs, it's time to make a decision and stick to it. Got a big idea but hesitant to take the plunge? Frame it as an experiment and dive in with conviction. Even if you eventually pivot, there's so much to learn from engaging in the process. As the saying goes, you miss 100 percent of the shots you don't take.

SUN IN AQUARIUS (8:45PM) (JAN 19-FEB 18)

As the Sun shifts into Aquarius, collective energy takes the wheel. Over the next four weeks, it's not just about what you accomplish, but who you build it with. This is a time for collaboration and community, not solo missions. Whether you're teaming up on a project, swapping ideas or rallying around a cause, seek out synergy and shared purpose. Shifts may unfold in your social sphere, nudging you toward groups that reflect your evolving ideals. Need more structure? Digital tools, from AI assistants to project management apps, can help your crew run like clockwork. Aquarius also rules progress and humanitarianism, so ask yourself: How can your work contribute to the greater good, even outside the bounds of business as usual?

VENUS-PLUTO MEETUP

Don't form impressions based solely on appearances. As attractive Venus and enigmatic Pluto connect, the pages of the book could be far more interesting than its cover! The key? You'll have to forge in deeper to find out. When it comes to sharing your own story, be more of a whodunit than a tell-all novel. With both planets in collaborative Aquarius, people may flock to you, wanting to join forces. Set the bar high if you're going to team up; you shouldn't jump right in and hope for the best. Be discerning! Come up with a clear set of qualifications and then conduct your due diligence on the candidates. Your research might reveal that a low-key person is actually an unexpected VIP!

JAN 20

MARS-URANUS TRINE

Whoa there! Today, rabble-rouser Uranus in Taurus syncs up with excitable Mars in Capricorn, which could send you off to the races, especially with a work or business project. Just be mindful not to give anyone a case of whiplash! Accelerate gradually before you break the speed limit. With both planets in structured earth signs, create processes and workflow systems before you start throwing around cash. Mars is a trailblazer by nature—but in traditional Capricorn (where it's "exalted"), you'll thrive when you back your bold ideas with a solid plan. Innovative Uranus rules technology, and in Taurus, it rewards simplicity. Find an app that makes your life easier so you can build your empire while still having time for family dinners, an evening workout and some good old-fashioned unwinding.

MERCURY IN AQUARIUS (11:41AM) (JAN 20-FEB 6)

Superconnector Mercury shifts into group-centric Aquarius today, giving your social life (both online and IRL) an energetic infusion. Instead of going it alone, tap into the power of the collective. Group projects pick up steam between now and February 6. Aquarius rules humanitarian efforts: How can you use your social contacts, communication skills or media savvy to make the world a better place? Let other people's grand visions educate and enliven you, and team up in the name of change. This is an excellent time for networking and online ventures, so use every available channel to spread your message.

JAN 21 SUN-MERCURY MEETUP

Synergistic sparks will fly as the confident Sun aligns with outspoken Mercury in Aquarius. Ideas zing around like live wires, and group chats or brainstorms could lead to a flash of collective genius. That said, not every voice will harmonize. This revealing meetup could spotlight who's in sync and who's throwing off the rhythm. If someone's not pulling their weight or is constantly shifting the vibe, don't beat around the bush. The Sun-Mercury conjunction gives you the guts to confront them directly. No need to be in-your-face or to shame anyone. Just ask them point-blank if they're in—or if they want to make a graceful exit and find something that's a better fit, no hard feelings. This is an excellent day to sharpen your compassionate leadership skills.

JAN 22 MERCURY-PLUTO MEETUP

Words cut deep as Mercury meets power player Pluto, cranking up the intensity in conversations and negotiations. This is not a day for small talk. Keep your message sharp and speak only when you've chosen your words with care. Whether you're pitching an idea, probing for answers or making your case, precision is everything. High-level minds are drawn to substance, so aim to impress the players—not the sideline spectators. If you sense something lurking beneath the surface, start asking smarter questions.

JAN 23

MARS IN AQUARIUS (JAN 23- MAR 2)

Rally the troops! Mars charges into visionary Aquarius, firing up your drive to connect, collaborate and create systemic change. Over the coming weeks, you'll thrive in group settings where ideas fly and everyone brings something unique to the table. The goal? Building something bigger than yourself. This Mars cycle pushes you to think beyond personal wins and toward collective progress. Idealism runs high, but so does innovation. Channel that electric energy into brainstorming sessions, humanitarian efforts or cutting-edge tech projects. Feeling overstimulated? Slow the pace, find your breath and remember—you don't have to lead the whole revolution in one day.

SUN-PLUTO MEETUP

Power dynamics come into sharp focus as the Sun aligns with shadowy Pluto today for their yearly Cazimi, a meetup that dials up the intensity. Since the Sun illuminates what Pluto conceals, you may shift your entire strategy based on what's uncovered! From 2025 until 2043, they'll team up in communal Aquarius each year. During this time, group settings become the arena for unleashing bold moves and savvy agendas. Alliances could shift quickly, and competition gets fierce. If your social circle feels shaky, reassess who really has your back. And even with trusted teammates, stay alert. A seemingly selfless offer could carry hidden motives. Play smart, observe everything and don't be too quick to reveal your hand.

JAN 25 FIRST QUARTER MOON IN TAURUS

Quiet luxury, anyone? Today's waxing quarter moon in sensible, sensual Taurus marries decadence with the appropriate amount of restraint. How can you indulge your senses without breaking the bank or falling asleep in a comfort food coma? Check your budget and see what you can allot. Maybe it's a few hours at a Korean spa or shopping for a cashmere scarf instead of a total wardrobe overhaul. Simple pleasures could also fill your tanks, like movies and warm conversation over hot cocoa with a friend who lifts your spirits. If something's worn out or uninspiring, replace it with a more elevated piece. Function matters, but so does form. Treat yourself to upgrades that feel as good as they look.

JAN 26–MAR 23, 2039 NEPTUNE IN ARIES

Instant karma, let's go! After a short preview from March 30 to October 22, 2025, spiritual Neptune blasts into flash-fire Aries for the long haul, staying in this impulsive, trailblazing sign for 13 full years! As a slow-moving outer planet, Neptune takes more than a decade to transit through every sign, shaping generational trends. After 14 years in watery Pisces, which Neptune has journeyed through since 2011, this signals a dramatic turn. The last Neptune-in-Aries cycle spanned from 1862 to 1875, a period marked by rapid industrial growth and deep societal upheaval—from abolition to women's suffrage to the U.S. Civil War. This round could once again be laced with urgency. While Neptune blurs lines and leans toward passivity, Aries thrives on action and confrontation. Mixed together, these two disparate forces demand a new kind of courage—one that blends empathy with brave initiative. Whether it's tech-driven transformation that creates opportunities to disenfranchised people, new healing frontiers in wellness or social movements born from raw instinct, we'll need resilience while Neptune traverses Aries until 2039. Get ready for a long crash course in spiritual firepower.

JAN 27 MARS-PLUTO MEETUP

How far are you willing to push for change? As driven Mars unites with power broker Pluto in iconoclastic Aquarius, you'll get a surge of determination that can be revolutionary at best and bring destructive group-think at worst. This high-voltage meetup, which happens every couple of years, ignites fierce ambition and bold strategy. As hotheaded Mars and transformer Pluto meet in Aquarius for the first time since 2024, their cosmic conjunction could incite everything from political protests to power struggles to dramatic shifts in alliances. Channel your outrage with caution, because it can tip into domination or tunnel vision. Stay focused on the common agenda. No matter how urgent a matter feels, you need to be careful that your attempts to solve problems don't turn destructive.

JAN 29 MERCURY-VENUS MEETUP

With chatty Mercury pinging affectionate Venus, your mind and heart are in sync. Bring those big ideas out of the clouds and figure out how to make your romantic or creative dreams a reality. Need to get something off your chest? Today's stars set the stage for a loving and compassionate conversation. With both planets in objective Aquarius, you'll be able to keep a cool head if you need to work through a conflict. Pro tip: Focus on common goals and finding a solution that best serves all.

FEBRUARY

FEBRUARY
Moon Phase Calendar

SUN	MON	TUE	WED	THU	FRI	SAT
SHINE **1** ♌ Full Moon 5:09PM	GROUND **2** ♍ 10:21PM	AWAKEN **3** ♍	ORGANIZE **4** ♍	RETHINK **5** ♎ 4:33AM	ADAPT **6** ♎	BALANCE **7** ♏ 2:13PM
CHALLENGE **8** ♏	RELEASE **9** ♏ Last Quarter	SOFTEN **10** ♐ 2:22AM	EXPLORE **11** ♐	ADVANCE **12** ♑ 2:44PM	STRUCTURE **13** ♑	REFLECT **14** ♑
TRANSITION **15** ♒ 1:17AM	LIBERATE **16** ♒	RESET **17** ♒ New Moon & Solar Eclipse 7:01AM ♒→♓ 9:09AM	ENVISION **18** ♓	INITIATE **19** ♓ ♈ 2:39PM	UNITE **20** ♈	FORTIFY **21** ♈ ♉ 6:31PM
EXPAND **22** ♉	INTEGRATE **23** ♉ ♊ 9:29PM	DECIDE **24** ♊ First Quarter	REFINE **25** ♊	REVIEW **26** ♊ ♋ 12:11AM	DISRUPT **27** ♋	EXPRESS **28** ♋ ♌ 3:17AM

Times listed are Eastern US Time Zone

KEY

♈ ARIES	♌ LEO	♐ SAGITTARIUS	**FM**	FULL MOON
♉ TAURUS	♍ VIRGO	♑ CAPRICORN	**NM**	NEW MOON
♊ GEMINI	♎ LIBRA	♒ AQUARIUS	**LE**	LUNAR ECLIPSE
♋ CANCER	♏ SCORPIO	♓ PISCES	**SE**	SOLAR ECLIPSE

FEBRUARY 1, 5:09PM
full moon in LEO (13°04')

LEO FULL MOON CRYSTAL

TIGER'S EYE

This confidence-boosting stone contains the power of the mid-day Sun, the ruler of Leo. Use Tiger's Eye to enhance creativity and connect to personal agency. With its swirling hues of amber and brown, this talisman directs your attention to what's truly important in your life.

LEO FULL MOON = CELEBRATE

The unique way that you shine

The people who make your heart sing

Your romantic nature

Your fashion sense

Your childlike wonder

The places where you feel like a natural leader

Your fiercely competitive streak that won't let you quit on yourself

FEBRUARY 17, 7:01AM

new moon in Aquarius (28°50')

AQUARIUS NEW MOON CRYSTAL

APOPHYLLITE

High vibes: incoming! This spirit-elevating stone enhances Aquarian-ruled hope for the future. As a clear-hued cluster, the light apophyllite emits encourages self-reflection and gratitude while energizing the soul.

AQUARIUS NEW MOON = FOCUS

Experiment with new technology and techniques

Break out of the box with style and social expression

Connect to community, activism and humanitarian work

FEBRUARY
MONTHLY HOTSPOTS

FEB 1 FULL MOON IN LEO (5:09PM; 13°04')

St. Valentine is swinging by early this year, so might as well make the celebration a doubleheader. As the year's only full moon in Leo brings peak passion to this Sunday, there could be rapid developments in your romantic life. If you've been stuck in a nebulous situationship, this lunation can push things in a more definitive direction over the coming two weeks (peak manifesting time). Already attached? Time to quit sweeping THAT topic under the rug and search for creative solutions instead. If you're in a good place, bring more fun and play into your bond. There's more to life than paying the bills. This fame-fueling full moon can make you a head-turner AND a headliner. If you've been hustling to achieve, you could soon be taking a strut down life's long red carpet. If you want this newfound level of fame to last more than 15 minutes, challenge yourself to be even MORE of a leader than you already are.

FEB 3 URANUS RETROGRADE ENDS

Fasten your seatbelt and watch out for whiplash. Side-spinning Uranus pivots out of retrograde and charges forward in steady Taurus for its final stretch through this stubborn earth sign—an era we won't experience again for another 84 years. This rebellious backspin, which began last September 6, may have stirred up surprises in your finances, home life or sense of security. As Uranus corrects course, expect a few days of extra erratic energy, so steer clear of chaos and avoid getting pulled into anyone's drama. Since May 2018, Uranus has been shaking up your ideas of stability and what it means to feel grounded. By April 25, you'll close the books on this once-in-a-lifetime chapter as the cosmic disruptor begins a seven-year journey through Gemini. Embracing uncertainty has become part of the lesson, but any exciting changes on the horizon deserve a thoughtful plan. For the rest of the week, unplug when you can: reduce screen time, craft, cook, do a gentle fitness class to keep yourself rooted.

FEB 5 MERCURY-URANUS SQUARE

Need to plump up your earnings? Don't wait for a future client to slide into your DMs. Under today's galvanizing square between Mercury in Aquarius and spontaneous Uranus in Taurus, you could hit on a brilliant idea for how to use your talents to earn some bank. For example, can you use your writing, design or social media skills to launch a sideline freelance business? With a little hustle and muscle, you could open up a fresh income stream. If it's time to upskill for the AI era, this could be your cue to sign up for some training or practice using tools that could raise your salary in the near future.

FEB 6–APR 14 MERCURY IN PISCES

Hygge season just got sweeter as social Mercury flutters into poetic Pisces for ten weeks. Under the influence of the flowy Fish, attractions take on a life of their own. But don't let communication get too vague. This extended cycle, which lasts until April 14, includes a retrograde (February 26 to March 20). Assumptions could cause you to crash if you attempt to ride on them. That said, the fluid nature of Pisces supports softer boundaries, which can help you break through the ice. Deep healing awaits those willing to plunge into the stormy surface of the psyche. Keep the creative supplies on hand and turn your discoveries into cathartic works of art.

FEB 8 VENUS-URANUS SQUARE

Before you prep your morning pour-over, a genius idea may already be percolating. Capture it as a napkin sketch as you get caffeinated, then share it with the "big idea" trusted people in your friend circle. The lively discussion that ensues could evolve into an actual game plan in a matter of hours! Since Venus is in money-minded Taurus, make sure you're clear about what you're willing to share—both in terms of the glory AND the profits. With curveball-throwing Uranus in the mix, failing to talk about this now could devastate a friendship or turn into a legal arbitration. Who needs that?!

FEB 9 THIRD QUARTER MOON IN SCORPIO

What just happened there? Under last week's feverish full moon in Leo, situations may have galloped ahead at a breakneck pace. Big ideas were tossed around, deals discussed, and some overly optimistic promises might have slipped out. But what do you actually have to show for all that? Today's waning quarter moon in intense Scorpio helps you dig deeper to separate fact from fiction. If you're serious about a plan, put a real offer on the table or start sourcing the tools you need. Scorpio's probing energy wants you to cut through the fluff and find out what's real. No more half-baked commitments or empty hype. Romantically, this

moon can shine a light on any sparks that flew last week. Is there true potential here, or was it just heat without substance? Shine your bright light of truth on the situation and trust what you uncover.

FEB 10–MAR 6 VENUS IN PISCES

Just in time for Valentine's Day, Venus heads into Pisces—one of its most potent ("exalted") placements on the zodiac wheel. There's poetry in everything during this enchanted transit, which may spur a romantic and artistic renaissance. Make time to meditate, daydream and court the muse. Relaxing will put you in a receptive state that's ideal for heart-opening moments. The downside of Venus in Pisces is that it can make people a bit gullible. Pisces is the master of illusions (and delusions). And while this might work well for, say, composing sonnets, it can be dodgy when it comes to screening amorous candidates. Run the background searches to avoid falling head over kitten heels for someone who isn't 100 percent available or reliable.

FEB 12 MERCURY-NORTH NODE MEETUP

What message is your intuition trying to deliver? Today's alignment of Mercury and the destiny-driven North Node in Pisces helps you tune in to ideas that can guide your next brave step forward. Conversations may feel fated, and the right word at the right time could shift your entire perspective. Don't get stuck trying to rationalize every detail. Esoteric Pisces energy asks you to simply open up your channels and allow inspiration to flow—even if you can't see the final destination yet. A line in a book, an unusual sighting or an animal that appears in your path could hold an important clue. Stay open to signs and synchronicities.

FEB 13–APR 12, 2028 SATURN IN ARIES

Atten-hut! Taskmaster Saturn plants itself firmly in Aries today, kicking off its first full tour through the Ram's realm since 1999. You got a sneak peek of this energy during Saturn's brief visit from May 24 to September 1, 2025—and now it's here for a solid two years, until April 12, 2028. This cycle brings a powerful blend of discipline and drive, encouraging you to take bold action while staying focused on your long-term goals. Just know: Progress won't always feel smooth. Saturn is in "fall" in Aries, one of its least comfortable positions, since the planet's measured approach doesn't always mesh with Aries' impulsive spirit. As you learn how to direct your passion into productive channels, you may wrestle with restlessness. While it may take a few tries to hit your stride, original ideas you initiate during this once-every-three-decades cycle can change the game!

FEB 14 VALENTINE'S DAY, MOON-JUPITER OPPOSITION

This Valentine's Day calls for a balance between classic romance and genuine connection. The Capricorn moon tugs you toward traditional gestures—candlelit dinners, overflowing bouquets, a Michelin-star dinner. You may feel the urge to do it "properly" and make it look picture-perfect. But across the sky, expansive Jupiter in Cancer reminds you that what really matters is how loved and cared for you feel. An intimate setting, a cozy meal at home, or heartfelt words might mean more than any over-the-top spectacle. Find the sweet spot. If your partner would light up at a grand gesture, go ahead and splurge. Just make sure it comes from the heart, not the need to impress. This day isn't about impressing on the 'gram. It's about creating a moment that feels warm, real and memorable for you both.

FEB 15 SUN-URANUS SQUARE

They don't call them "human resources" for nothing. Some people can be an incredible asset, while others end up being more expensive than they're worth. Today, as the outgoing Aquarius Sun locks horns with hardheaded Uranus in Taurus, it's worth taking a closer look at the company you keep. Are certain friends nudging you toward splurges that are beyond your budget? While there's nothing wrong with treating yourself, there's no joy to be found in racking up debt. When your values don't align with the people around you, it can cost you more than money—it can quietly drain your spirit. Vocalize your limits. Chances are, others may be feeling the same social pressures.

FEB 16 MERCURY-JUPITER TRINE #1 OF 3

Words have the power to open hearts today—but they can also hit raw nerves if you're not mindful. As expressive Mercury in Pisces forms a sensitive angle to candid Jupiter in Cancer, it's easy to spill your guts, revealing things you'd normally keep tucked away. This "say anything" vibe can be incredibly freeing, especially with people who are deserving of your trust. Feel like extending an olive branch? Being the first to apologize can build a bridge that heals an old rift. Creative collaborations can thrive under this open-hearted energy, too. Team up with someone who shares your vision and see what magic you can make together.

FEB 17

NEW MOON IN AQUARIUS (7:01AM; 28°50'; ANNULAR SOLAR ECLIPSE)

Today's supercharged new moon in Aquarius is also an annular solar eclipse. And it marks the first eclipse on the Leo-Aquarius axis since 2019, reigniting themes of individuality, community and bold self-expression. This cosmic reset also lines up with Lunar New Year's Eve, as we say goodbye to the sensual Wood Snake and gallop into the Year of the Fire Horse. The Fire Horse is all about freedom, courage and unstoppable momentum. Paired with Aquarius's trailblazing spirit, you're encouraged to break from the herd and let your unconventional ideas run wild between now and February 6, 2027. Make space for different opinions. You don't have to agree on everything to move forward together. Plant seeds for what you want to innovate, experiment with, or completely reimagine. The ideas you hatch now could carry you into galaxies unknown!

VENUS-NORTH NODE MEETUP
Haven't we met before? Love feels as fated as a Bridgerton episode today as ardent Venus aligns with the destiny-driven North Node in Pisces. This rare and dreamy meeting opens the door to connections that feel meant to be. Existing relationships may flow into soul-stirring new territory. You could feel a strong pull toward a "stranger" who feels eerily familiar. Share a secret hope, plan an artistic escape, or simply soften old patterns that may be blocking your ability to truly get close.

FEB 18–MAR 20 SUN IN PISCES (10:52AM)
Life is but a dream as the Sun shines into Pisces' watery realm for the next four weeks. After Aquarius season's social flurry, micro-analysis and YOLO adventures, you're ready to recharge your batteries. Mind, body, soul: How can you bring the three back into divine communion? Compassionate Pisces stirs your deepest wells of empathy, all while stoking your creativity and intuition. Tune in to your subconscious and turn that inner dialogue into music, art or healing words that help others. But watch those porous boundaries. While your compassion runs deep, be mindful of pulling people onto your lifeboat who don't want to be saved. Escapism will be tempting (and sweet!), but know your own limits to avoid falling down a slippery slope.

FEB 20 SATURN-NEPTUNE MEETUP
Talk about a cosmic paradox. Today, boundary-setting Saturn meets boundary-dissolving Neptune at 0° Aries—a super-rare alignment that hasn't happened at the same zodiac degree since 1989, and not in Aries since 1702! Saturn wants structure, discipline and clear lines in the sand. Neptune prefers to blur them into limitless possibilities. And fiery Aries is a bold, impulsive sign that isn't exactly comfortable for either planet. This unusual mashup invites you to get real about a vision you've only been daydreaming. Don't expect instant clarity. This is the beginning of a brand-new cycle, and it may feel murky or frustrating at first. Since Aries energy is all about new beginnings, take the first step, even if it's imperfect. This could be the starting block of a dynamic new era if you're willing to balance faith with a practical roadmap.

FEB 22 VENUS-JUPITER TRINE
Are you a safe space? With Venus in compassionate Pisces forming a flowing trine to big-hearted Jupiter in caring Cancer, this is the perfect moment to show people you've got room for their whole messy, beautiful selves, no judgment. While

small gestures count, don't be afraid to pump up the volume if it feels right. Jupiter loves a grand, genuine show of goodwill. Treat someone to dinner or grab a pair of tickets to a show. Organize a gathering that makes everyone feel seen and appreciated. In love, the connection of these two "benefics" can set the stage for genuine proclamations. Trust grows when people know you're in their corner for the long haul.

FEB 24 FIRST QUARTER MOON IN GEMINI

Feeling stuck in your own head? The waxing quarter moon in Gemini today nudges you to branch out and gather fresh input. This moon might shine in the sign of the Twins, but that doesn't mean you have to duplicate yourself! Instead of teaming up with someone who's just like you, look for a partner whose strengths complement—not mirror—yours. Don't be surprised if this connection pops up close to home. With locally minded Gemini leading the way, the synergy you're seeking might be right in your own neighborhood.

FEB 26 MERCURY RETROGRADE IN PISCES

Back up all your important data, switch to stronger passwords, and submit any lingering paperwork now! Mercury turns retrograde for the first time this year, backtracking through Pisces until March 20. In the Fish's kaleidoscopic waters, few things are as they appear. Brace for crossed wires, false starts and missing details. Take nothing at face value, not even people's enthusiastic promises or cheerful nods of approval. If you really want to know what someone's thinking, you'll probably have to ask them outright. Even then, expect a little vagueness or mixed signals. When in doubt, slow down, clarify, and keep your sense of humor handy. It'll help you navigate these murky waters with minimal stress.

FEB 27

MARS-URANUS SQUARE

Good luck keeping the peace with anyone who pushes your buttons today. Combative Mars crashes into a complicated square with combustible Uranus and all hell could break loose. With both planets in stubborn, fixed signs—Mars in Aquarius and Uranus in Taurus—tempers flare as egos and ideologies clash. If you've been a little too agreeable, this dustup can push you to your breaking point. Most people won't be willing to bend on their principles or "take one for the team." If you're feeling too heated to hash things out diplomatically, steer clear of situations that are potential powder kegs. This might be a better moment for privately clarifying your anger rather than attempting to hold a summit between warring factions.

SUN-NORTH NODE MEETUP

Your destiny comes alive in 5D today as the Sun aligns with the fateful North Node in boundless Pisces. You may catch a glimpse of yourself as bigger, braver or more capable than you've dared to imagine. The truth? That can feel both thrilling and intimidating. Watch for imposter syndrome creeping in. There's no honor in hiding your light or shrinking your dreams to make others comfortable. Pisces energy reminds you that your vision matters, even if it's still taking shape. Take a step toward that bigger version of you. Share an idea, say yes to an opportunity, or simply allow yourself to believe that you're ready for this next chapter.

FEB 28 MERCURY-VENUS MEETUP

When Mercury cozies up to Venus in dreamy Pisces, those sweet nothings could turn into sweet somethings if you let them. Poetic texts, heartfelt confessions and quiet time together. It all flows easily under this wistful vibe. But don't just toss your words into the ether. How can you anchor your daydreams in reality? Follow that tender talk with a thoughtful gesture. Plan an actual date or spell out your desires instead of hinting. Pisces loves fantasy, but a little follow-through turns wishful thinking into true connection.

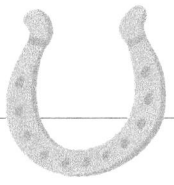

MARCH

MARCH
Moon Phase Calendar

SUN	MON	TUE	WED	THU	FRI	SAT
RADIATE **1** ♌	FLOW **2** ♌ ♍ 7:34AM	REVEAL **3** ♍ Full Moon & Lunar Eclipse 6:38AM	SYNTHESIZE **4** ♍ ♎ 1:56PM	EXPAND **5** ♎	INITIATE **6** ♎ ♏ 11:01PM	FUSE **7** ♏
STABILIZE **8** ♏	HARMONIZE **9** ♏ ♐ 11:37AM	ADVANCE **10** ♐	ADJUST **11** ♐ Last Quarter	PLAN **12** ♐ ♑ 12:07AM	GROUND **13** ♑	REORGANIZE **14** ♑ ♒ 11:13AM
ASSERT **15** ♒	IMAGINE **16** ♒ ♓ 7:16PM	HEAL **17** ♓	BEGIN **18** ♓ New Moon 9:23PM	TRANSITION **19** ♓ ♈ 12:03AM	IGNITE **20** ♈	ACTIVATE **21** ♈ ♉ 2:35AM
MERGE **22** ♉	ADAPT **23** ♉ ♊ 4:19AM	CONVERSE **24** ♊	ENDURE **25** ♊ ♋ 6:33AM First Quarter	MEND **26** ♋	STABILIZE **27** ♋ ♌ 10:10AM	LEAD **28** ♌
EXAMINE **29** ♌ ♍ 3:33PM	CULTIVATE **30** ♍	EQUALIZE **31** ♍ ♎ 10:51PM				

Times listed are Eastern US Time Zone

KEY

♈ ARIES	♌ LEO	♐ SAGITTARIUS
♉ TAURUS	♍ VIRGO	♑ CAPRICORN
♊ GEMINI	♎ LIBRA	♒ AQUARIUS
♋ CANCER	♏ SCORPIO	♓ PISCES

FM FULL MOON
NM NEW MOON
LE LUNAR ECLIPSE
SE SOLAR ECLIPSE

MARCH 3, 6:38AM
full moon in Virgo (12°54')

VIRGO FULL MOON CRYSTAL

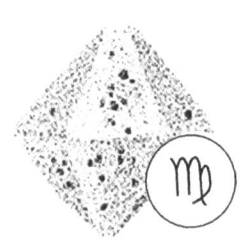

MOSS AGATE
With its swirls of green, this stone connects you to the healing powers of nature. Moss Agate is known to ease anxiety and reduce people-pleasing and judgment that can creep in under Virgo's watch.

VIRGO FULL MOON = CELEBRATE!

The serenity of a freshly cleaned space

Streamlined systems

Your helpful spirit

Being of service to those in need

Taking great care of your body by eating clean and exercising

The magic of nature and organic beauty

MARCH 18, 9:23PM

new moon in Pisces (28°27')

3

PISCES NEW MOON CRYSTAL

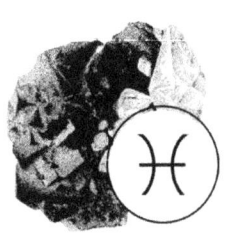

AMETHYST

This relaxing purple crystal increases inner peace and tunes you in to your Pisces-ruled intuition. Keep amethyst by your bedside to sanctify sleep and invite powerful messages from your dreams.

PISCES NEW MOON = FOCUS

Connect to your dreams, spiritual exploration

Find creative outlets

Give back

Inspire others

Form supportive alliances

Express empathy so people feel seen and understood

MARCH
MONTHLY HOTSPOTS

MAR 2–APR 9 MARS IN PISCES

Surrendering to the flow could be your most productive move over the next six weeks, as make-it-happen Mars drifts through dreamy Pisces. Just when you sit down to tackle your to-do list, your imagination pulls you in a different direction. That's not always a bad thing—just carve out dedicated windows for daydreaming and keep one eye on the clock. Add soul to your goals: How can your work uplift others, helping them feel seen, valued and inspired? Maybe it's time to bravely face an old wound or get to the root of an emotional pattern that's been holding you back. Warning: Guilt or anger might bubble up as you let go, but trust that each feeling carries a lesson. Tap into the courage of warrior Mars and the empathy of gentle Pisces—together, they'll guide you toward healing and growth.

MAR 3 FULL MOON IN VIRGO (6:38AM; 12°54'; TOTAL LUNAR ECLIPSE)

Get ready for an unflinching life edit. Today's full moon in Virgo—a total lunar eclipse—radars in on anything you've been avoiding, especially when it comes to your daily routines. If you've let healthy habits slide over the winter or you've fallen behind at work, this jarring lunation delivers a much-needed wake-up call. Eclipses reveal what's been hiding in the shadows. Since this one falls close to the karmic South Node, don't be shocked if you are forced to deal with one of your longstanding "bad habits." Have you been overexerting yourself lately? Pump up the self-care. Virgo's meticulous energy wants you to streamline your life without overcomplicating it. Simple and manageable steps will stick best. Need extra help staying on track? Let technology handle the parts that feel messy or unclear. Is there an app or tool that can do the heavy lifting for you? An AI companion or smart scheduler could be exactly what you need to stay focused, especially with Virgo's love of progress-tracking and tidy systems.

MARCH 5 SUN-JUPITER TRINE

Emotions run high today, but so does your optimism. As the intuitive Sun in Pisces forms a supportive trine to generous Jupiter in Cancer, feelings you'd normally suppress could flow out. Ah, what a relief! The scene is set for heartfelt conversations, acts of compassion and colorful dreams about your future. Plan a cozy after-work hang with a beloved relative or a friend who feels like home. Keep the tissues handy.

With these two irrepressible planets joining forces, one (or both!) of you could shed some much-needed tears. Share your hopes, fears and even a few secrets. Just keep one foot on the ground. Today's bright alignment can make everything look possible—which is wonderful, but practical details matter, too. Keep the vision alive, but take it one inspired step at a time.

MAR 6–MAR 30 VENUS IN ARIES

Follow your bliss! Cupid's pink-hued spotlight cranks up to its highest setting as amorous Venus charges into Aries until March 30. Love comes in many forms during this charmed annual phase—uplifting friendships, erotic experimentation and a magnetic pull toward your own passions. Single? This indie-spirited cycle is a time to savor your freedom. Let yourself dabble in different dating pools, if you feel like dating at all! Attached? Fall back in love with an old hobby or interest, even if no one else shares it. You might wind up setting a new trend. With beauty-maven Venus helming the operation, this is prime time to start pulling new looks. (Just wait until Mercury turns direct on March 20 before unleashing any major style renovations.) Confidence is your most alluring accessory now!

MAR 7

SUN-MERCURY MEETUP

Buried feelings rise to the surface under today's union of the Sun and Mercury retrograde in Pisces. Use this rare sync-up to parse through information that's been lingering in the shadows. Feeling upset? While you may feel an urge to send a text or call an "offending party," pump the brakes. Until Mercury turns direct on March 20, it's best to process it all with caring-yet-objective outsiders. Soothe frazzled nerves with soulful self-care. A long walk, yin yoga and a hot bath can be balm for your soul. Closure is around the corner, but today, it begins with internal reflection.

VENUS-NEPTUNE MEETUP

Rose-colored glasses are firmly in place under today's enchanting union of romantic Venus and mystical Neptune in bold Aries. This cosmic haze can make everything—and everyone—look fetching, but their allure may be masking some troubling traits. With the line between fantasy and reality so blurry, take time to discover the full spectrum of who people are before you get swept away by their "potential." Your own magnetism could be dialed way up, especially if you stay present and actually make eye contact with people in the room instead of staring at your screens. Hey there, hey! Let your "fans" bask in your glow, but be mindful not to make promises you can't keep.

MAR 8 VENUS-SATURN MEETUP

Sexy AND stable? That combo might sound like a non-existent chupacabra, but surprise! As sensual Venus aligns with responsible Saturn in Aries, you could discover someone who delivers the ideal total package. Chemistry warms up steadily under this red-hot alignment, so pay attention to any instinctual hits you get about a fascinating character who SEEMS to have lasting potential. There's a paradox to contend with here: Venus can be a hopeless romantic while Saturn demands clear boundaries and a responsible approach to amour. You don't have to sacrifice one for the other—in love, friendship or any sort of collaboration. Not every flicker of attraction will survive Saturn's endurance tests, of course. But if you sense something brewing, it's definitely worth a deeper look!

MAR 9 MERCURY-JUPITER TRINE #2 OF 3

Undeniable truths bubble to the surface today, demanding examination. Warning: Don't broadcast every epiphany to a general audience! Reflective Mercury is retrograde in boundary-blurring Pisces—and for the second time this year, it forms a tender trine to expansive Jupiter, who is also retrograde (in Cancer). With these watery energies swirling about, it's tough to make sense of the amplified emotions that arise. You are prone to saying things you'll regret—and even blurting them out at the worst possible moment. Do you desperately need to get something off your chest? Choose safe (and private!) spaces to share what's on your mind—and only unleash around people who can be trusted to keep this info confidential. Pro tip: Do this BEFORE your big meeting or any event where you have to put on a brave face. Forget about having any tough talks with people who irk you. Under these skies, you won't have an off switch, plus you may feel too raw to hold down a rational conversation.

MAR 10 JUPITER RETROGRADE ENDS

Emotional limbo, begone! After drifting in reverse since November 11, expansive Jupiter pivots direct in Cancer, helping you take action on all those feelings you've been processing over the past four months. You might need a primal scream, ugly cry or an extra therapy session. Go for it! The energetic release will be a huge psychic relief. Starting today, matters close to your heart begin to flow in a forward direction again. Decisions about your home and family life that have been muddled since the fall become clear again. With risk-taker Jupiter at the helm, you may feel ready to explore some daring possibilities around where to live—and who to live with. Honest conversations with your inner circle are forthcoming. Before truth-teller Jupiter moves on to Leo on June 30, you could lift the mask and reveal parts of your identity that you've been shielding. No pressure though! Building up new support networks might be the best first step.

MAR 11 THIRD QUARTER MOON IN SAGITTARIUS

You want to change the world, but how about starting with one corner of it? The waning quarter moon in big-thinking Sagittarius reminds you that Rome wasn't built, retrofitted or toured in a day. Check in: Are you overcommitting or spreading yourself too thin? Use this balancing lunar checkpoint to adjust your plans, especially if you're trying to map out adventurous travel or budget for the next steps of an ambitious, entrepreneurial project. Opinions flow freely under these candid skies, which can make for lively discussions. Just try not to drag any of your allies while you're sharing your hot takes. Respectful disagreement, please!

MAR 13 MARS-NORTH NODE MEETUP

Heed the call! Your intuition is revving in high gear today, as driven Mars aligns with the fateful North Node in Pisces. This ultra-rare conjunction pushes you toward your dreams, some that may defy logic. This is not the moment for step-by-step strategies. Instead, get into a quiet, meditative space where you can tune in to your inner compass. Your subconscious contains clues about "next steps," even if you can't see the full map yet. Throughout the day, you might feel a sudden burst of courage or find yourself pulled in a direction that totally was NOT on your BINGO card. If discomfort bubbles up, don't back down. It's a sign you're breaking through your own limits.

MAR 15 MERCURY-MARS MEETUP

Tempers and truths collide under today's fiery union of Mercury retrograde and combative Mars. With both planets in sensitive Pisces, conversations easily get tangled in old misunderstandings. Resentment might bubble up, especially if one person's been shouldering too much adult responsibility while the other's been coasting like a pre-teen on holiday break. If you're feeling aggressive—or aggressively defensive—take a time out and go cool down. With Mercury still retrograde until March 20, your attempts to clear the air might stir up more confusion. You might need to smash a few plates or scream into a pillow for the time being, since these skies are not conducive to resolution.

MAR 17 MERCURY-NORTH NODE MEETUP

Old narratives resurface under today's fated union of the destiny-driven North Node and Mercury retrograde in esoteric Pisces. A conversation from the past, an unresolved question, or a buried dream could be playing on repeat in your head—or living there rent-free against your wishes. As much as you want it to go away, get curious. There's wisdom to unpack in whatever circles back. Don't rush to formulate answers or draw empirical conclusions. Instead, slow down and ask yourself, "Where am I feeling this in my body?" Is it a racing heart, a pounding in your temples? Place your hands there for comfort; stretch. This swell of emotion may be best healed somatically instead of attempting to logic it out. Make art, dance, play music or book a healing bodywork session to move the current of energy through you.

MAR 18 NEW MOON IN PISCES (9:23PM; 28°27')

The spiritual veil is thin today as the year's only new moon in Pisces blurs the line between fantasy and reality. Open up the floodgates to your imagination. This is one of the best times all year to receive divine downloads and you'll want to capture each sparkling gem from your psyche. Find a quiet spot to unplug and meditate. You'll be surprised by what surfaces when you give yourself space to listen. If you've been clinging to something that's outlived its purpose—an old story, a draining obligation, a lingering attachment—consider today the beginning of a gentle "letting go" process. You don't have to rip the Band-Aid off all at once. Just start tying up the loose ends and mapping out a better replacement for whatever you're leaving behind.

MAR 20

SUN IN ARIES (10:46AM), (MAR 20 - APR 19), SPRING EQUINOX

Triple-down on the celebration! Today marks the spring equinox AND the astrological New Year as the solar calendar flips over and begins anew with Aries Season. Ready for a fresh start? Game on! And don't spend another second dwelling on winter's seasonal "sins." We won't argue that a loaded, garlic-crust pizza goes perfectly with a six-hour streamish sesh, but it's time to "un-Hygge" yourself. Replace craft supplies with garden tools and couch potato-ing with breezy walks around your neighborhood. Live-out-loud Aries season is a time to grab life by the horns and push the envelope on maximalism. Since Aries is #1 in the zodiac, the competitive vibes will be fierce for the next four weeks. Are you living on your edge? Go for the gold! And if you happen to out-run a few narcissists with your hard-won victory, revel in it with your full chest. It's a personal growth experience for them AND you!

MERCURY RETROGRADE ENDS IN PISCES (3:33PM)

Lift the gag orders! A few hours after Aries season begins, messenger Mercury wakes up from its choppy, three-week retrograde. While the messenger planet backstroked through the murky waters of Pisces since February 26, the emotional currents felt more like a riptide—and regularly overtook everyone's better senses. If you found yourself crying "inexplicably" or for a solid reason, you'll have to admit that the tears were healing. But enough of this three-hanky drama, it's time to hug it out. With Mercury back on track, the chronic misunderstandings give way to healing reconciliations. Contracts that were held up in red tape could finally move into the negotiation (and signing!) phase. But don't lose the important message Mercury retrograde taught about the pitfalls of skimming the surface instead of finding out what lies beneath. Move ahead with new resolve to slow down, get every question answered and read the fine print.

MAR 21 MARS-JUPITER TRINE

Courage and compassion work hand in hand under an uplifting trine between motivated Mars in Pisces and expansive Jupiter in Cancer. Normally, these no-holds barred planets are too busy forging ahead on their independent missions to pause and process emotions. But with both planets in sensitive water signs, it's essential to read the room. First and foremost, make sure you're not bulldozing anyone's feelings on your climb to the top. Check in with your crew and let everyone air their current mood. As long as you steer the conversation in a proactive direction, this will strengthen the team's bond. If you've been waiting for a sign to chase a soulful goal, it could show up serendipitously under this alignment. As you ascend, set yourself up to win by rallying a solid support network. Have you hit a wall? Don't stubbornly forge ahead against all odds. Today, you might need to lean on your squad for expert advice, brainstorming and important referrals. And it goes both ways. Sharing YOUR wisdom has a ripple effect on your community.

MAR 22 SUN-NEPTUNE MEETUP

Inspiration strikes like a lightning bolt as the radiant Sun merges with fantasy-agent Neptune. This cosmic connection is a historic one! After meeting up in Pisces since 2012, the Sun and Neptune begin a new 14-year duet in Aries. This means that for the next decade and a half, the annual "Neptune Cazimi" will take place in the Ram's realm, catalyzing inspired action instead of dreamy drifts. Today's flashes of insight can launch you toward a powerful initiative. Quiet your mind so you can pick up that signal. While you're at it, take a break from rigid to-do lists and create space for your ideas to flow freely. Try mind mapping, vision-boarding or go on a walk and talk into your voice notes app as if you're having a conversation with the muse. While you might not end the day with a ten-part project-plan in Asana, that's not the point! Let yourself dream as if there are no limits.

MAR 25

SUN-SATURN MEETUP

Your strength gets tested—and fortified—under today's annual Sun–Saturn meetup. For the first time in three decades, they're teaming up in unstoppable Aries, ensuring that you won't back down without a fight. This annual "Day of Challenges" can feel weighty, but don't resist the growth opportunities. Any breakdowns that occur could be blessings in disguise, revealing where your plans require more structure to succeed. If obstacles reveal cracks in the foundation, don't quit. But do pause to find smart solutions instead of powering through against all odds. Seek out people whose stories and wisdom inspire you to be more courageous. You might even hire one of them as your personal adviser.

FIRST QUARTER MOON IN GEMINI

Ideas take shape one conversation at a time under today's waxing quarter moon in Gemini. This lunar checkpoint is a better day for evaluation than productivity. While you may be eager to get a mission to the finish line, take a moment to tighten all the screws and seek expert feedback on your progress thus far. If your mind feels scattered, pick one idea with real potential and give it your full focus. A promising partnership could reveal itself under this lunar light, especially if you can't stop talking to someone who just "gets" you. Since this is a balancing quarter moon, proceed with care. Test the waters with a short-term project to see how your styles actually mesh in real time.

MAR 26 VENUS-CHIRON MEETUP

Old hurts around love, trust or self-worth could resurface today as Venus aligns with wounded healer Chiron in courageous Aries. But so can a new perspective on how to heal them. This isn't a day to beat yourself up for past mistakes. It IS about meeting your pain head-on so you can finally move past it. Start by extending compassion to yourself and honoring all your feelings. Unstoppable Aries reminds you that loving yourself fiercely is an act of true courage. Then, take account of your growth. Make a list of all the things you've learned since this painful event—better still, read that list to a caring friend. As you acknowledge how far you've come, you might see ways that you still want to evolve. Take a brave step in that direction, whether it's signing up for a workshop, applying for a new job or nurturing a healthy new friendship that is emerging.

MAR 30–APR 24 VENUS IN TAURUS

Sweet sensuality fills the air as affectionate Venus returns to her cozy home in tactile Taurus, awakening your senses and whetting your appetite for life's simple, earthy pleasures. Indulge in what delights you: nourishing meals, fresh flowers, luxe linens, and long, lingering moments with your familiars. Under Taurus's steady influence, "too much of a good thing" might feel just right. Relationships can deepen and stabilize over the coming four weeks, but the Bull likes to take its time. Savor the slow and sultry build-up and choose connections that feel grounded and true. Couples: Turn daily routines into rituals. Brewing a perfect cup of morning coffee and sitting down to pay bills together CAN be bonding experiences.

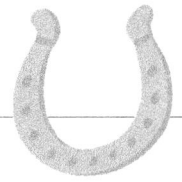

APRIL

4

APRIL
Moon Phase Calendar

SUN	MON	TUE	WED	THU	FRI	SAT
			RECONCILE **1** ○ ♎ Full Moon 10:12PM	MEDITATE **2** ○ ♎	NAVIGATE **3** ○ ♏ 8:11AM	PENETRATE **4** ◐ ♏
CONFRONT **5** ◐ ♏ ♐ 7:32PM	ROAM **6** ◐ ♐	EXAGGERATE **7** ◐ ♐	ENVISION **8** ◐ ♐ ♑ 8:04AM	CONSTRUCT **9** ◑ ♑	DISCERN **10** ◑ ♑ Last Quarter ♑→♒ 7:55PM	DETACH **11** ◑ ♒
BRAINSTORM **12** ◑ ♒	DISSOLVE **13** ● ♒ ♓ 4:55AM	CHANNEL **14** ● ♓	MOBILIZE **15** ● ♓ ♈ 10:04AM	SYNTHESIZE **16** ● ♈	EMBARK **17** ● ♈ New Moon 7:52AM ♈→♉ 11:58AM	ROOT **18** ● ♉
GROUNDBREAK **19** ◐ ♉ ♊ 12:18PM	DECLARE **20** ◐ ♊	TRANSLATE **21** ◐ ♊ ♋ 1:00PM	TEND **22** ◐ ♋	ELECTRIFY **23** ◐ ♋ ♌ 3:41PM First Quarter	ROAR **24** ◐ ♌	TINKER **25** ◐ ♌ ♍ 9:04PM
DEBATE **26** ◐ ♍	OPTIMIZE **27** ◐ ♍	WEAVE **28** ○ ♍ ♎ 5:03AM	MEDIATE **29** ○ ♎	PROBE **30** ○ ♎ ♏ 3:02PM		

Times listed are Eastern US Time Zone

KEY

- ♈ ARIES
- ♉ TAURUS
- ♊ GEMINI
- ♋ CANCER
- ♌ LEO
- ♍ VIRGO
- ♎ LIBRA
- ♏ SCORPIO
- ♐ SAGITTARIUS
- ♑ CAPRICORN
- ♒ AQUARIUS
- ♓ PISCES
- **FM** FULL MOON
- **NM** NEW MOON
- **LE** LUNAR ECLIPSE
- **SE** SOLAR ECLIPSE

APRIL 1, 10:12PM
full moon in Libra (12°21')

LIBRA FULL MOON CRYSTAL

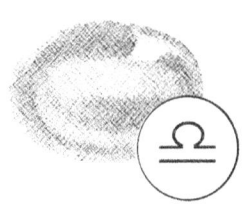

ROSE QUARTZ
This pale pink crystal is the stone of pure love, radiating the compassion and romance of Libra. Said to be beneficial for heart healing and fertility, Rose Quartz carries goddess energy and can be used for inspiration and protection.

LIBRA FULL MOON = CELEBRATE!

The power of partnerships and synergistic connections

Dressing up and socializing

Transcendent music and the arts

Peaceful moments of serenity

The parts of your life that are in beautiful balance

APRIL 17, 7:52AM
new moon in Aries (27°29')

ARIES NEW MOON CRYSTAL

CARNELIAN

This vibrant orange stone wakes up the sacral chakra to connect you to your instinctual truth. Use carnelian to enhance confidence and creativity as you step into your Aries-inspired power. This crystal also supports with new beginnings.

ARIES NEW MOON = FOCUS

Sharpen your competitive edge

Blaze your own trail

Take the initiative with people and activities that matter to you

Try new things

APRIL
MONTHLY HOTSPOTS

APR 1 FULL MOON IN LIBRA (10:12PM; 12°21')

Peak relationship moments ahead! As the year's only Libra full moon lights up the skies, connections that have been percolating since last fall could arrive at a defining moment. Couples may decide to make their status public and Instagram official. For others, the question may be: Are you in or are you out? Enjoying someone's company is only half the equation. How secure and connected do you feel when apart? If you're perpetually anxious or suspicious, it might not be your "attachment issues." Transparency is a must in order to build trust and you both need to lay your cards on the table. If differing life goals are creating a rift, this full moon can help you hash out a creative compromise. Remember: Things don't have to be split 50/50 in order to feel fair. Trying to force that might be part of the breakdown. Could you divide up responsibilities to play to each person's strengths? Let the negotiating commence!

APR 3

MERCURY-JUPITER TRINE #3 OF 3

Clear the air to move things forward! Today, messenger Mercury in Pisces forms its third and final trine to outspoken Jupiter in Cancer. If you've been stuck in endless loops—half-finished conversations, messages left on Read or signals that are harder to read than hieroglyphics—you may be ready to throw in the towel. Is there a ray of hope left? Try one final time to get everyone on the same page. With both planets in emotional water signs, tempers can run hot. Have those heart-to-hearts in private, far from anyone who might misread the situation and start damaging rumors.

VENUS-PLUTO SQUARE

First impressions may be deceiving today, so don't make assumptions based on someone's jaw-dropping style or savvy intellect. Convivial Venus in Taurus wants to take everything at face value, but there's more to the story than meets the eye. A tense beam from sneaky Pluto in Aquarius could be concealing important data. Find out people's history—and motives—before casting them in any sort of role in your life. Red flags won't be obvious, so you'll need to do some digging. Probe without going overboard. Ask a few personal questions and see how they respond. Healthy skepticism will be your saving grace.

APRIL 5 SUN-JUPITER SQUARE

Even the healthiest bonds need breathing room—in fact, it's practically a requirement. Take the space you need today, before you explode with frustration. With the fiery Aries Sun squaring Jupiter in moody Cancer, you're not doing anyone a favor by sidelining your own agenda or being a people pleaser. Reassure friends and family that you're not disappearing. You can always check in with them throughout the day. But claim enough autonomy to follow your own inspiration, otherwise, resentment could bubble up fast. A little independence now will make your reunions that much sweeter. Meet up for Sunday dinner or share pics from your day of discoveries so your loved ones feel included.

APR 9–MAY 18 MARS IN ARIES

Spring fever kicks into overdrive as red-hot Mars charges into its home sign of Aries for six spicy weeks. This raw, revitalizing energy wants action—the kind that might require a helmet and stunt double. Tap into this unstoppable momentum: Kick off an ambitious project, train for a race, pursue your romantic interest with sexy fervor. Mars in Aries amps up your competitive spirit and makes you fearless about advocating for yourself. The only catch? It can be hard to gauge whether (or not) you're coming on too strong. If you register shock on anyone's face, dial down the intensity—and offer a genuine apology if you stepped on their toes.

APRIL 10 THIRD QUARTER MOON IN CAPRICORN

Time for a Q2 goal review! Today's waning quarter moon in success-driven Capricorn helps you fine-tune a mission that you started (and maybe drifted from) in the beginning of the year. Even if you've had your eyes steadily on the prize, that vision alone may not have manifested your desired results. Don't be discouraged! This is your opportunity to pull yourself back on track. Get the facts and figures straight. Crunch the numbers, review milestones, and determine what support you need to get past the next hump. Did you bite off more than you can chew? Your grand plan might need to be broken into phases, and that's okay. Scaling back doesn't mean giving up. It's an opportunity to lay a solid foundation for success.

APR 13 MARS-NEPTUNE MEETUP

Courage and compassion? You'll have bottomless supplies of both today as Mars and Neptune unite in can-do Aries. Action planet Mars fires up your drive, while mystical Neptune rustles your idealistic spirit. Together, they push you to chase something that feels meaningful on a soul level. The only catch? It will be hard to think practically with this hasty (and hazy!) energy afoot. While a wild idea could come together magically, it could also turn into an expensive dumpster fire if you act in haste. Best to keep it on the whiteboard for a few days, then revisit it when saner heads prevail.

APR 14–MAY 2 MERCURY IN ARIES

Goodbye, mental fog, hello cerebral tsunami! Insanely original ideas pop up like daffodils as Mercury dashes into Aries until May 2. After the messenger planet's prolonged passage in nebulous Pisces (including a retrograde from February 26 to March 20), your mind snaps back into action—quick, sharp and brimming with possibilities. With so much mental firepower, you'll be an idea machine for the next few weeks. Capture your best brainstorms on a whiteboard, audio memo or anywhere you care to record them. But wait a beat before leaping into action. Rushing ahead impulsively is a surefire way to make costly mistakes. Give yourself a little time to gestate. Run the numbers, think through the long-term effects. You want diamond-level possibilities, not distractions.

APR 16

SUN-CHIRON MEETUP

Compassion starts with YOU today, as the Sun makes its annual connection with wounded healer Chiron in self-sovereign Aries. Old anger or self-sabotaging patterns could bubble up, revealing where it's time for an upgrade. Forget powering through with tough love. Where can you be kinder to yourself—and then, by extension, offer that to everyone around you? A little self-forgiveness goes a long way now, turning what once felt like a weakness into a source of strength. Treat yourself like the work in progress you are, and you'll inspire others to do the same.

MERCURY-NEPTUNE MEETUP

Answers may feel just out of reach today as savvy Mercury gets lost in nebulous Neptune's fog. Words might tumble out before you've sorted through what you actually want to communicate. As a general rule, pause before blurting unprocessed thoughts. If conversations start to go sideways, excuse yourself quickly before they blow up into a five-alarm drama. This isn't the best day for major declarations, but it's

a beautiful one for connecting to your inner child, if you step away from the noise. A quiet walk, a solo journaling session, or time to daydream could help you tune into a message from the most powerful part of your subconscious.

APR 17 NEW MOON IN ARIES (7:52AM; 27°29')

If you're ready to turn to a fresh page in your personal history, lean into the the annual new moon in Aries which arrives this morning! These moonbeams reset the lunar "clock," bringing a refreshing perspective on, basically, everything. If leaving the past in the past means moving away from people and situations that aren't in your best interest, so be it. Or maybe you just put them on ice for a while as you fearlessly explore the new. Aries is the first sign of the zodiac—daring and impulsive. This is one of the best days of the year for starting a new solo project or striking out on an independent (and spontaneous!) path. Circle September 26—the date of the corresponding FULL moon in Aries—to achieve any personal milestones that you begin reaching for now. And starting today, think: limitless possibilities!

APR 19

MARS-SATURN MEETUP

Green flags, green lights—if you're getting the go-ahead today, don't stall! Make-it-happen Mars teams up with legacy-building Saturn in fearless Aries. This dynamic duo delivers the perfect mix of courage and discipline, giving you the juice to tackle a big mission that's been stalled on the tarmac. Green light! But don't just charge ahead blindly—map out your game plan before you hit the gas. If you've been spinning in circles, take a pit stop to troubleshoot the roadblocks and adjust your route. Any obstacles you hit now are really course corrections in disguise. Stick with it: Patience, persistence and fearless follow-through will carry you straight across the finish line.

SUN IN TAURUS (9:39PM) (APR 19–MAY 20)

Taurus season begins with anything but a sluggish start! After four weeks of Aries' feisty ambition, it's time to buckle down with the Bull. The Ram lit your creative fire and shot you out of your comfort zone like a cannon. No doubt, you're buzzing with a zillion grandiose ideas. Now practical Taurus steps in to help you polish any rough-cut visions into sparkling gems. Let the assembly lines roll to get your plans in motion—but don't overlook this sign's love of life's simple luxuries. Beauty isn't optional now; it's an essential part of every equation. FYI, those aesthetic upgrades don't have to cost a fortune. Since Taurus is both sensible and sensual, the next four weeks are as much about savoring the process as they are about delivering results. Every detail matters so take your time to do it right.

APR 20 MERCURY MEETS SATURN + MARS

Contracts, commitments, and bold conversations are all on deck as Mercury aligns with both Saturn and Mars in Aries. Words carry serious weight under this double meetup, so choose them wisely. With Saturn in the mix, talks could get heavy fast, and pushing too hard for your way might make people feel cornered. Back up your vision with a concrete plan that proves you can actually deliver. At the same time, Mars cranks up your confidence—and your volume—making it easy to pitch daring ideas or tackle topics you've been avoiding. Just beware: What feels "brutally honest" to you could land as plain brutal to someone else. Advocate for yourself, absolutely, but finesse your delivery so you win allies instead of shutting doors.

APR 23 VENUS-URANUS MEETUP

Itching to break free from a romantic rut? As Venus links arms with wildcard Uranus in sensual Taurus, sparks could fly in the most unexpected ways. Couples caught in a loop may feel the frisson of excitement return—or the urge to carve out some breathing room. Flying solo? You could find yourself magnetized to someone refreshingly different from your "type." Just keep impulsive moves in check. What feels thrilling at night might look dicey by morning. Luckily, a dash of novelty—whether that's a playful date idea, a bold bedroom move, or simply switching up your routine—might be all you need to reignite the passion. Just be careful not to rock the boat so hard that it capsizes a commitment.

APR 24

VENUS IN GEMINI (APR 24-MAY 18)

Wordplay is foreplay—and a full-on aphrodisiac—as Venus flits into witty Gemini for a few weeks. Don't hold back those clever quips, late-night texts, or cheeky fruit emojis. Couples can reignite sparks with pillow talk that goes deeper (or dirtier) than usual, while singles may find themselves juggling multiple crushes or drawn to someone totally outside their usual lane. Just be mindful: With Gemini's mercurial vibes, it's easy to mix signals or lose track of your own story. Keep things light, playful, and experimental. Join a trivia team, try out a quirky hobby together, or start a podcast with your S.O. Venus in Gemini reminds you: Love thrives on curiosity and fun.

FIRST QUARTER MOON IN LEO

Let your inner child call the shots as the waxing quarter moon beams through vibrant Leo. If the daily grind has snuffed out your sense of wonder, hit pause and plug back into play. Book tickets to a show, dance it out at a live set. Rally a ride-or-die friend (or flirty plus-one) for an impromptu overnight adventure. Not in the mood to mingle? Pour this creative surge into a passion project that lights you up. The lesson of today's lunar lift-off: When you follow joy, you're on the right path.

APR 25

SUN-PLUTO SQUARE

Interactions could get a little prickly today as the unwavering Taurus Sun squares off with shadowy Pluto in Aquarius. Power struggles and buried resentments may pop up where (and when) you least expect them. Instead of sidestepping the tension, face it head-on. This clash can be the catalyst for a genuine breakthrough if you don't run away from it. Let secrets rise to the surface. Sure, it will sting to discover that one (or both) of you has been less than transparent. Once the truth is in the open, you'll see how to resolve this brewing dilemma. What emerges can clear the air and rebalance power dynamics, setting the stage for a more honest connection going forward.

URANUS IN GEMINI (APR 25, 2026–MAY 22, 2033)

Welcome to the innovation station—this time for the long haul! After last year's four-month teaser, revolutionary Uranus is now fully plugged into Gemini's grid until 2033. Get ready for a thrilling mix of excitement, disruption and game-changing ideas to permeate the world. Everything's up for reinvention: how you communicate, connect, learn, and share your truth with the world. Daily routines could flip overnight. Friendships might evolve in surprising ways. Your fascination with cutting-edge tech could hit warp speed. Uranus's mission? To shake you free from stale patterns and push you to think in bold, flexible ways. Stay curious, adaptable and ready to pivot. The more you embrace change, the freer—and more inspired—you'll feel.

APR 26 MERCURY-JUPITER SQUARE

Time for a reality check! With fast-talking Mercury in fiery Aries clashing with aggrandizing Jupiter in Cancer, your grand visions could hit a few practical speed bumps—especially if family or close friends are involved. Instead of going full steam ahead, run your ideas past a trusted sounding board. Their grounded advice could be exactly what you need to turn an ambitious scheme into a workable plan. And don't make any unilateral decisions today, unless you want to deal with mutiny on your team tomorrow. Enthusiasm is great fuel. Just make sure you've got a solid roadmap—and people's genuine buy-in—before you burn rubber.

APR 28 VENUS-PLUTO TRINE

Chemistry is off the charts today as flirty Venus in Gemini harmonizes with intensifier Pluto in Aquarius. A lusty attraction can ignite out of nowhere, heating up faster than you can (almost) control. A friend could suddenly reveal potential to be "more" and you might start rethinking what commitment even means. Just know that this spicy sync-up can hijack your willpower. Blurred lines can get messy if you're not honest about your motives. Enjoy the magnetic pull, but keep one foot on the ground so passion doesn't morph into a hot mess or obsession. Leave the party early if you're worried about things spiraling into something you'll regret.

5

MAY

MAY
Moon Phase Calendar

SUN	MON	TUE	WED	THU	FRI	SAT
					REVEAL **1** ○ ♏ Full Moon 1:23PM	SOLIDIFY **2** ○ ♏
TRAVERSE **3** ○ ♏ ♐ 2:33AM	SURGE **4** ◔ ♐	CHALLENGE **5** ◔ ♐ ♑ 3:06PM	RECONSIDER **6** ◑ ♑	FORTIFY **7** ◑ ♑	EVOLVE **8** ◑ ♑ ♒ 3:27AM	DISRUPT **9** ◗ ♒ Last Quarter
REDIRECT **10** ◗ ♓ 1:39PM	IMAGINE **11** ◗ ♓	INITIATE **12** ◗ ♓ ♈ 8:04PM	ASSERT **13** ● ♈	CONVERSE **14** ● ♈ ♉ 10:31PM	SUSTAIN **15** ● ♉	MANIFEST **16** ● ♉ New Supermoon 4:01PM ♉→♊ 10:23PM
SPARK **17** ● ♊	BLEND **18** ● ♊ ♋ 9:46PM	DEEPEN **19** ◐ ♋	TRANSITION **20** ◐ ♋ ♌ 10:48PM	EMBOLDEN **21** ◐ ♌	DISTILL **22** ◐ ♌	SORT **23** ◐ ♌ ♍ 2:57AM First Quarter
OPTIMIZE **24** ◓ ♍	COORDINATE **25** ◓ ♍ ♎ 10:34AM	COMPEL **26** ◯ ♎	REFRAME **27** ◯ ♎ ♏ 8:53PM	RESIST **28** ◯ ♏	TRANSFORM **29** ◯ ♏	EMBARK **30** ◯ ♏ ♐ 8:45AM
EXPAND **31** ◯ ♐ Full Moon 4:45AM						

Times listed are Eastern US Time Zone

KEY

- ♈ ARIES
- ♉ TAURUS
- ♊ GEMINI
- ♋ CANCER
- ♌ LEO
- ♍ VIRGO
- ♎ LIBRA
- ♏ SCORPIO
- ♐ SAGITTARIUS
- ♑ CAPRICORN
- ♒ AQUARIUS
- ♓ PISCES

- **FM** FULL MOON
- **NM** NEW MOON
- **LE** LUNAR ECLIPSE
- **SE** SOLAR ECLIPSE

MAY 1, 1:23PM
full moon in Scorpio (22°13')

SCORPIO FULL MOON CRYSTAL

HEMATITE

This silvery stone is a great protection while under the spell of empathic, intuitive Scorpio. Hematite reflects and deflects any negative energy so you don't absorb it. With its high iron content, it also helps circulate Scorpio-ruled blood and wake you up for springtime.

SCORPIO FULL MOON = CELEBRATE!

Your loyal and caring spirit

Intense exchanges

The sexiest parts of yourself

The ways you've transformed your struggles into gold

True friendship

Resourcefulness and raw creative expression

Supermoon

MAY 16, 4:01PM

new moon in Taurus (25°58')

TAURUS NEW MOON CRYSTAL

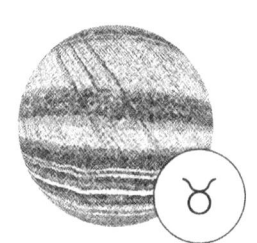

BLUE LACE AGATE

This soothing, soft blue stone helps you relax and tap into a deep inner calm. Blue Lace Agate unblocks the Taurus-ruled throat chakra so you can speak your truth and share what's valuable to you.

TAURUS NEW MOON = FOCUS

Define your values

Set up healthy and rewarding routines

Enjoy arts and culture

Simplify complexities

Budget

Get out in nature

MAY 31, 4:45AM
full moon in Sagittarius (9°56')

SAGITTARIUS FULL MOON CRYSTAL

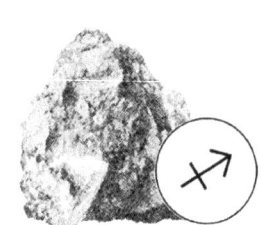

BLUE APATITE
This turquoise-hued crystal represents Sagittarian optimism and restores a positive, proactive approach to life. Blue Apatite activates the throat chakra and can help you speak your truth under this live-out-loud full moon.

SAGITTARIUS FULL MOON = CELEBRATE!

The spirit of wanderlust

Your unvarnished truths

Loved ones who live far away

The passport stamps you've collected or hope to one day

Visionary ideas that you're bringing to life

Diversity, inclusivity and cross-cultural connections

MAY
MONTHLY HOTSPOTS

MAY 1

FULL MOON IN SCORPIO (1:23PM; 11°21')
Passion, power, and partnerships are at a fever pitch under today's full moon in Scorpio. Brace yourself: Smoldering attractions could boil over into bodice-ripping encounters—or reveal confessions best kept under wraps. (Privacy, please!) But this lunation isn't just about seduction. Since Scorpio also rules joint ventures and shared resources, money-making opportunities could pop up on your radar. Over the next two weeks, what happens in the boardroom could be just as sizzling as what unfolds in the bedroom. With investments, inheritances, loans, and taxes under Scorpio's domain, a lucrative deal could be on the table. Choose your collaborators wisely, then lawyer up and make those bonds "officially official."

MERCURY-CHIRON MEETUP
Words can be medicine today as messenger Mercury joins forces with Chiron in courageous Aries. A truth you've struggled to articulate may finally come tumbling out—and along with this admission, a wave of relief. Don't worry about nailing the perfect script. What matters is the courage to speak up, even if your voice shakes as you do. Sit down with a trusted sounding board and turn your inner monologue into a confessional dialogue. As you give language to your feelings, you could talk your way into epiphanies, creative solutions and above all, self-forgiveness.

MAY 2–MAY 17 MERCURY IN TAURUS
Practical magic! As thoughtful Mercury roots into Taurus, your attention turns to money, security, and the tangible resources that keep life running like a well-oiled machine. Over the next couple of weeks, you could lay the groundwork for a lucrative project or discover smart new ways to stretch your earning power. Budgeting, managing resources, scheduling and any sort of project management get the cosmic green light now. Good news! Mercury Taurus insists that the process doesn't have to be dry as unbuttered toast. Light a candle, cue up your favorite playlist, and make the numbers-crunching process into a soulful ritual. Mercury in Taurus rewards patience and persistence. Keep your eyes on the long game in all that you do. Step by step, slow and steady progress adds up to something lasting.

MAY 4 MARS-JUPITER SQUARE

Daredevil alert! As go-getter Mars in Aries locks horns with boundless Jupiter in Cancer, you might wake up fully ready to charge into action. The square between these thrillseeking planets can crank up both passion and impulsivity. Tempted to make a hasty move? A promise that you're not even 50 percent sure you can deliver on? Just…don't. With both planets in emotionally charged water signs, it's most important that you keep relationships intact—and that requires honesty and integrity. Before you act unilaterally, loop in the people who'll be affected. What feels like "obvious leadership" to you might land as steamrolling to them. Get buy-in first, then you can move ahead without bruising feelings or damaging trust.

MAY 5 MERCURY-PLUTO SQUARE

Power struggles could flare today as messenger Mercury in stubborn Taurus locks horns with manipulative Pluto in Aquarius. Mixed signals, unspoken tension, and domination games—what's going on here, anyway? Nefarious behavior could creep into your interactions, especially around money and resources. If you sense someone's playing games, resist the urge to clap back. Instead, keep your cool and let them underestimate you. A calm poker face buys you time to gather facts—and may even prompt people to reveal their hand. Bottom line: The less reactive you are, the stronger your position becomes.

MAY 6–OCT 15 PLUTO RETROGRADE IN AQUARIUS

Power to the people? As alchemical Pluto pivots retrograde in Aquarius for the next five months, group dynamics may need a serious recalibration. If you're collaborating with a team, community, or institution, this is a golden window to review what's working—and what's not. Untangle loose ends, streamline workflows, and divvy up duties so everyone plays to their strengths. If a key role needs to be filled, consider circling back to a former colleague or ally who could be the missing puzzle piece. Since Pluto is rewinding through digital Aquarius, keep an eye on your online presence. Old posts could resurface, or you may realize you've been giving the opinions of your TikTok followers more energy than they deserve.

Set healthy boundaries with your screen time and redirect some of that energy into IRL community. Real transformation happens when you're face-to-face, not just screen-to-screen.

MAY 9 THIRD QUARTER MOON IN AQUARIUS

Restless much? Today's quarter moon in innovative Aquarius urges you to break free from stale routines and test-drive new approaches. Float an edgy idea and you could attract the very collaborators who can help you develop it and bring it to life. Let tech be your sidekick: Streamline with AI, apps and smart systems. Don't sleep on people-powered progress either. Check your group dynamics: Are you fostering true community or letting too many cooks spoil the broth? Yes, it's important to make sure everyone has a voice, but you also need to align around roles and accountability. Innovation requires follow-through to make it stick.

MAY 14 SUN-MERCURY MEETUP

Laser focus can move mountains today as the Sun syncs up with interactive Mercury in Taurus. This pragmatic pairing helps you plow through lingering tasks and tie up loose ends hanging overhead. Every box you tick brings a wave of relief—and a well-deserved sense of pride. Reward yourself with small treats as you reach each milestone. Got some "practical magic" to share? Recruit a brainstorming buddy or bounce ideas with someone who complements your strengths. Slow and steady may win the race, but with the right collaborator, you'll get there faster and actually enjoy the ride.

MAY 16

MARS-CHIRON MEETUP

Fuse getting short? Anger doesn't have to spiral into destructive outcomes. Today, it can point the way to healing as fiery Mars connects with wounded healer Chiron in Aries. If you've been snapping at people (or silently stewing), ask yourself: Is this about unspoken boundaries, skipped self-care, or just plain exhaustion? Naming the source is the first step toward shifting it. Start with small changes like taking a real lunch break, saying no when you're maxed out, or swiftly correcting people when they make false assumptions about you. (Those microaggressions DO add up.) Honor your limits instead of pushing past them.

NEW MOON IN TAURUS (4:01PM; 25°58'; SUPERMOON)

Practical magic is in the air as the year's only Taurus new moon—a powerful supermoon—plants fresh seeds for abundance, security, and everyday comfort. This lunar reset asks: What do you truly value? How can you spend and save in ways that honor both your pleasure and your priorities? Even small upgrades—like replacing worn-out basics with quality investment pieces—can be a game-changer now. Align your dollars with your values by supporting businesses that reflect your ethics. Craving more stability or a new income stream? Polish your pitch deck, refresh that LinkedIn, or set intentions around work that sustains you. With this supermoon's extra voltage, a smart move today (and over the next two weeks) could attract an offer worthy of a "hell yes"!

MAY 17–JUN 1 MERCURY IN GEMINI

Novel ideas are flying at warp speed as quicksilver Mercury zips through its home sign of Gemini until June 1. This chatty, curious cycle revs up your social life and makes it easy to strike up connections close to home. Short-term collabs are especially blessed now—think pop-up projects or trial runs that could pave the way for longer partnerships later this year. With attention spans running short, focus on tasks that keep your brain engaged without bogging you down. Move your body to keep thoughts flowing: Take walks, hop on your bike, or explore your neighborhood. And start right away! Mercury meets up with wildcard Uranus (in Gemini) today, bringing lightning bolts of genius and conversations that flip your perspective in the best way. Stay loose and follow the spontaneous threads. One surprising spark could open a whole new channel of thought.

MAY 18

MARS IN TAURUS (MAY 18-JUN 28)

Put together a playlist heavy on the slow jams. As driven Mars settles into earthy Taurus for the next six weeks, your motivation kicks in—but at a pace that's deliberate, not frantic. This is prime time to tackle your to-do list with a clear head and get your finances on solid footing. A bill may come due or money matters could demand extra attention. While Mars can pile on the pressure, Taurus reminds you to balance hustle with pleasure: Savor music, art, nature, or a well-earned splurge that's both luxe AND practical. In love, Taurus leans toward traditional courtship, but impatient Mars might speed things up, pushing bonds into serious territory sooner than expected. Watch out for stubborn standoffs. With combative Mars in headstrong Taurus, neither side will be eager to bend. Then again, the making up could be well worth the showdown.

VENUS IN CANCER (MAY 18-JUN 13)

Sweet sanctuary! As Venus gets cozy in nurturing Cancer, you're invited to turn your space into a heartwarming hub. Spruce it up with eye-catching art, lush greenery, and pillow piles that make the couch impossible to leave. Once your pad is properly zhuzhed, invite your inner circle to enjoy it with you. 'Tis the Venus season for Sunday dinners, movie nights, pre-game drinks. Couples may be ready for big next steps in the domestic department (gulp). Whether you're swapping keys, meeting families, or picking out baby names, you'll feel the call to bring your lives closer together. Single? Venus in Cancer can make you equal parts guarded and eager to settle into something secure. But be mindful not to let "interested" read as "clingy." This transit thrives on warmth, tenderness, and emotional safety—but definitely not speed. Lean into those vibes and let relationships unfold at their natural pace.

MAY 19 MERCURY TRINE PLUTO + SQUARE THE NODES
Conversations could pack a punch today as Mercury in Gemini trines probing Pluto in Aquarius while squaring the lunar nodes. Words carry extra weight, and even a casual chat could veer into unexpectedly personal—or revealing—territory. If the TMI starts making you nervous, change the subject before you learn more than you bargained for. On the flip side, your own words may scatter in a dozen directions, making it tricky to land your point. The cosmic push-pull between relaxing into the moment and overanalyzing every detail could leave you second-guessing what you REALLY want to say. Strategy is your saving grace: Keep a little mystery in your back pocket, read body language as much as words, and if the fog won't lift, hit pause until your gut (or a little extra research) guides the way forward.

MAY 20–JUN 21 SUN IN GEMINI (8:37PM)
Calling all social butterflies! The Sun flits into lively Gemini, ushering in four weeks of connection, conversation, and community. With Gemini ruling all things local, start exploring right outside your front door. Sip an iced latte from a new café, browse a neighborhood gallery, or try that Pilates studio you always walk past. Since Gemini also governs transportation and "twos," you might be inspired to split your time between zip codes, take a quick road trip, or even test-drive a weekend in a nearby town. Craving more human contact on the job? Trade your solo grind for a coworking space and see how much more energized you feel. Off-duty, media-savvy Gemini might nudge you to start a Substack, host a book swap, or even pitch your story to the press. One note: Gemini energy moves at warp speed. Capture every brainstorm in your Notes app before it vanishes as quickly as it arrived.

MAY 22

VENUS-NEPTUNE SQUARE
Mixed signals can muddy the waters as nurturing Venus in Cancer clashes with smoke-machine Neptune in Aries. What feels warm and genuine one moment could come across as pushy or confusing the next. Be honest about your preferences instead of trying to charm your way into (or out of) something. Today, even the best intentions may be agonizingly misconstrued. If you're

seeking advice, source it from people with legit experience instead of that TikTok talking head. The wrong hot take could whip up your fervor and turn YOU into the spreader of fake news. Get the full story before you share anything.

SUN-URANUS MEETUP

Surprise! As the Sun syncs up with unpredictable Uranus in quick-witted Gemini, this Friday takes a left turn you couldn't have scripted. This rare cosmic mashup delivers lightning flashes of genius and shake-ups that spark major upgrades. Don't cling too tightly to your plans—last-minute news or detours could reroute your evening in the best way. What first feels disruptive might actually be a breakthrough in disguise. Stay experimental: Try a different approach, test a fresh system, or ask for input from someone you'd never normally consult. Under these skies, the magic happens when you stay curious and pivot on a dime.

MAY 23 FIRST QUARTER MOON IN LEO

Pops of color and poetic proclamations? Yes, please! Crank up the volume a few extra notches under today's waxing quarter moon in Leo. While you don't want to overreach, you also don't want to underwhelm. Sprinkling in some flamboyant touches can bring just the right amount of "theatah" into everything you do. Dare to stand out—whether you're pitching an idea, dressing up for a night out, or putting your talents on display. Just keep your audience in mind. How can you engage and inspire them instead of simply seeking their applause? When everyone gets to be part of the magic, it's a win-win.

MAY 26 MARS SQUARE PLUTO + SUN TRINE PLUTO

Who's the boss? Power dynamics come to the forefront today as pugnacious Mars in Taurus locks horns with Pluto in Aquarius while the Gemini Sun forms a tantalizing trine to the same planet. One side of this cosmic mix can spark control struggles, money clashes, or tempers that combust when compromise runs dry. If shady vibes are swirling around shared resources or trust, don't kid yourself. The wisest move may be to bow out before someone else's lack of integrity drags you down. Yet with the Sun also harmonizing with Pluto, you've got a powerful edge: intrigue. Instead of baring all, play it cool and share just enough to spark curiosity—whether that's a flirty DM or a teaser of a big idea. Strategic mystery keeps you magnetic while protecting your energy and your reputation.

MAY 28 VENUS-SATURN SQUARE

Assumptions can muddy the waters today as sensitive Venus in Cancer clashes with boundary-hound Saturn in Aries. If you're doing more than your share at home, work or in a relationship, hit pause. Not only does an unequal effort kill the vibe, it can make everyone want to abandon ship. Before you write people off as "users" or "slackers," have you clearly established limits? Don't expect people to read your mind. What seems obvious to you might never have crossed theirs. Instead of stewing in resentment, spell out what you need. Then, invite others to vocalize their requirements. Getting on the same page might take a little negotiating, so don't rush to consensus. A bigger exploration may be required before you figure out how to fairly balance the load.

MAY 31 FULL MOON IN SAGITTARIUS (4:45AM; 09°56)

Say yes to the quest! Today's full moon in visionary Sagittarius dares you to stretch beyond the safe and familiar. Under the Archer's globetrotting spell, opportunities roll in from afar. Over the coming two weeks (peak manifesting time for this full moon) you could be packing your bags for an epic journey. Can't get away? Broaden your horizons through experiential learning like a personal growth workshop or hands-on course in anything from Shibori fabric dyeing to Portuguese cooking. Sagittarius is the zodiac's gambler, and normally this full moon is prime time for rolling the dice on your dreams. But with cautious Saturn in Aries trining the moon, aim for "calculated risks" that come with a safety net. What's important is that you aim in the direction of something that feels meaningful today. Whether you hit the bull's-eye or miss the mark, you'll gain wisdom—and stories—that only come from trying.

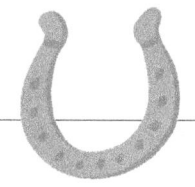

JUNE

JUNE
Moon Phase Calendar

SUN	MON	TUE	WED	THU	FRI	SAT
	ORIENT **1** ♐ ♑ 9:19PM	STRATEGIZE **2** ♑	QUESTION **3** ♑	EVALUATE **4** ♑ ♒ 9:46AM	CONNECT **5** ♒	ENCHANT **6** ♒ ♓ 8:43PM
INTUIT **7** ♓	SURRENDER **8** ♓ Last Quarter	ATTRACT **9** ♓ ♈ 4:33AM	ENDURE **10** ♈	FOCUS **11** ♈ ♉ 8:28AM	PRESERVE **12** ♉	REIGNITE **13** ♉ ♊ 9:06AM
INITIATE **14** ♊ New Supermoon 10:54PM	SYNTHESIZE **15** ♊ ♋ 8:14AM	IMAGINE **16** ♋	POLARIZE **17** ♋ ♌ 8:05AM	CELEBRATE **18** ♌	CULTIVATE **19** ♌ ♍ 10:36AM	ASSESS **20** ♍
INVITE **21** ♍ ♎ 4:55PM First Quarter	DECIDE **22** ♎	INFLUENCE **23** ♎	SHIFT **24** ♎ ♏ 2:43AM	STABILIZE **25** ♏	AIM **26** ♏ ♐ 2:41PM	BROADCAST **27** ♐
ACCELERATE **28** ♐	ILLUMINATE **29** ♐→♑ 3:19AM Full Moon 7:57PM	EXPAND **30** ♑				

Times listed are Eastern US Time Zone

KEY

- ♈ ARIES
- ♉ TAURUS
- ♊ GEMINI
- ♋ CANCER
- ♌ LEO
- ♍ VIRGO
- ♎ LIBRA
- ♏ SCORPIO
- ♐ SAGITTARIUS
- ♑ CAPRICORN
- ♒ AQUARIUS
- ♓ PISCES
- **FM** FULL MOON
- **NM** NEW MOON
- **LE** LUNAR ECLIPSE
- **SE** SOLAR ECLIPSE

Supermoon

JUNE 14, 10:54PM
new moon in Gemini (24°03')

6

GEMINI NEW MOON CRYSTAL

PHANTOM QUARTZ
Shift your Gemini-ruled mindset with this protective, empowering stone. Phantom Quartz facilitates unexpected breakthroughs and promotes personal growth.

GEMINI NEW MOON = FOCUS

Sharpen your communication style

Write and make media

Become active in your local community

Socialize with new people

Flirt and joke!

Pair up on short-term collaborations

JUNE 29, 7:57PM
full moon in Capricorn (8°15')

CAPRICORN FULL MOON CRYSTAL

ARAGONITE
Release anger and frustration and get unstuck. Whatever obstacle is standing in your way, this stone is here to help you break through, just like the can't-stop-won't-stop persistence of Capricorn.

CAPRICORN FULL MOON = CELEBRATE!

People you admire—heroes and mentors

Family legacies

Customs that you want to carry on

Enduring friendships and business relationships

Your most ambitious ideas

Institutions or organizations that you believe in and support

JUNE
MONTHLY HOTSPOTS

JUN 1–AUG 9 MERCURY IN CANCER
Shhh...privacy, please! As messenger Mercury slips into sensitive Cancer for an extended ten-week stay (retrograde alert: June 29–July 23), discretion becomes your superpower. Keep confidences close to the vest—both IRL and online—because oversharing could come back to haunt you. That said, heartfelt exchanges also flourish under this transit. With Mercury in Cancer's nurturing waters, conversations grow deeper, warmer, and more compassionate. Listen with care, speak with kindness, and give people extra space to air their feelings. This cycle is also perfect for tending to your nest. Spruce up your home or work zone so your environment feels as comforting as your favorite childhood "blankie." And when it's time to venture out? Say yes to bonding time with your closest crew. Bring on the beach days, barbecues, and summer bonding that creates lifelong memories.

JUN 3 MERCURY-NEPTUNE SQUARE
Head versus heart? Rational Mercury in sensitive Cancer locks into a tense square with dreamy Neptune in impulsive Aries, and your decision-making could get cloudy fast. One part of you wants to stick to the plan, while the other is ready to toss the rulebook and follow a wild hunch. With both planets in bossy cardinal signs, pride makes it harder to see straight. If you're feeling foggy, pause before you leap. Try the "10-10-10" test: How will this choice impact you in ten minutes, ten months, or ten years? That quick check-in can help you separate a valid signal from static noise.

JUN 8 THIRD QUARTER MOON IN PISCES
Languishing at a plateau? Today's quarter moon in dreamy Pisces helps you leap off it and get back in the flow. Inspiration starts with immersion. Wander through an art exhibit, browse a used bookstore, or simply soak in other people's brilliance until your own wheels start turning. Instead of asking ChatGPT to solve every dilemma, step away from screens. Tune into what you see, hear, and feel IRL. Staying mindful could reveal a surprising, actionable solution hiding in plain sight. Pisces energy also supercharges your manifesting powers. A supportive person might be a text (or a passing thought) away. Don't be shocked if someone pops into your mind and then

shows up out of nowhere. If burnout's creeping in, give yourself permission to slow down. Book a massage, take a long bath, or just unplug for a few hours of calm.

JUN 9 VENUS-JUPITER MEETUP

Love is in full bloom! As affectionate Venus cozies up to generous Jupiter in tender Cancer, relationships of all kinds get a heart-expanding glow-up. If you've been watering your bonds with steady care, today could bring a bumper crop of sweetness and connection. And if you've been a little distracted? This cosmic combo offers the perfect chance to pivot. See what a difference you can make with a sweet and caring gesture. Drop off a card, treat for coffee, send a supportive voice note. What matters most is that you let your inner circle know that they are cherished. A little reassurance doesn't just go a long way—it multiplies. In romance, chemistry bubbles in the coziest of ways. Couples may feel inspired to nest, cook together, or talk about growing the family (fur babies count, too). Single? Keep your heart open. Jupiter's expansive touch could draw in someone with long-term potential who feels like "home."

JUN 10 MERCURY-SATURN SQUARE

Thick skin required. Mercury in sensitive Cancer locks horns with Saturn in blunt Aries today, stirring defensive vibes and prickly pushback. Don't jump to conclusions about other people's motives. What looks rude or inconsiderate may have more layers than you realize. Knee-jerk reactions could backfire fast. If you're resisting something "on principle," ask yourself what's really underneath that. Is it a fear of losing control? Not having all the answers? Keep imposter syndrome in check, but make sure you've done your homework so you can stand your ground for the right reasons.

JUN 13–JUL 9 VENUS IN LEO

Love goddess Venus struts onto Leo's catwalk, bringing out the spotlight-stealing siren in us all. Get ready! Over the next few weeks, summer love could quickly accelerate from mild to wild. Don't snooze on invites that promise a bevy of beautiful, fascinating people to flirt with. Whether you're on the hunt for romance or a creative collaborator, everyone's talents are on eye-popping display. That includes yours, so don't miss the chance to strategically self-promote. You could set yourself up for long-term gains by boldly sharing your gifts. Be vocal with your praise and gracious when you're in the spotlight receiving accolades. Flattery might not get you everywhere, but it can certainly move the needle now. Flamboyant style updates are on deck, so think: maximalist. But hurry and book that salon appointment before Mercury turns retrograde on June 29!

JUN 14 NEW MOON IN GEMINI (10:54PM; 24°03'; SUPERMOON)

Call in the besties! The year's only Gemini new moon—a potent supermoon to boot—ignites fresh starts through your friendships, networks, and peer-to-peer connections. This is prime time to strengthen your circle or welcome new allies who share your wavelength. Look up from your phone and make eye contact. Your perfect partner-in-crime could be hiding in plain sight. Since Gemini also rules siblings, neighbors, and coworkers, this lunation may open a brand-new chapter with someone who's been part of your daily orbit all along. Information is gold under these curious skies. Feed your mind with books, podcasts, or even a mastermind group that keeps you learning. Just a note: Gemini's charm runs high, but don't rush to hand over the keys to your queendom. Take the time to see who can actually walk their talk.

JUN 16 VENUS-NEPTUNE TRINE

Oh, the places you COULD go. With romantic Venus trining fantasy-agent Neptune—both in passionate fire signs—there's no telling what sultry scenario you might dream up. Lift the guardrails and let your mind roam off-leash. While you don't have to act upon every urge (and probably shouldn't), getting in touch with your desires can be instructive. What do you long to experience more of in love—or maybe a whole lot less? This energizing fire trine melts barriers and fosters soulful connections. However, that blast of heat could leave you vulnerable to a charming raconteur. Keep the discernment filters on. If you're typically reserved or tend to keep a stiff upper lip, drop the armor just enough to share what you really feel. It could pave the way for a spicy adventure!

JUN 17 VENUS-PLUTO OPPOSITION

Are you sensing a betrayal or is there a chance you might be reading things completely wrong? As Venus in passionate Leo opposes furtive Pluto in Aquarius, trust issues spiral. Don't ignore suspicious behavior (leaving the room to answer a phone call or a late-night text on bae's home screen). But rather than violating anyone's privacy, start with a conversation. You might be able to resolve this with a few pointed questions. Even if the truth isn't what you WANT to hear, it's better to know the real deal. Pay attention to red flags and don't think twice about leaving any situation where you feel uncomfortable or unsafe. Better safe than sorry!

JUN 19–SEP 17 CHIRON IN TAURUS

Karmic shift ahead! For the first time since 1983, wounded healer Chiron dips into earthy Taurus, offering a sneak preview of a longer transit that begins in earnest next spring. During this short passage, old wounds around money, security, and self-worth may rise to the surface—especially those tied to family conditioning or ancestral patterns. Do the values you live by today truly match the ones you were raised with? Or is it time to update, modernize, and make them your own? As you tap in to these tender spots, you'll discover a gift: the ability to turn your scars into wisdom and share it with others walking similar paths. Your healing becomes their healing. Use this window to notice what still needs attention, so you'll be ready to dive into the deeper work when Chiron returns to Taurus from April 14, 2027, until May 5, 2034.

JUN 21-JUL 22 SUN IN CANCER (4:24AM), SUMMER SOLSTICE

Welcome home, in every sense of the word. The Sun slips into tender Cancer and reaches its peak in the sky at the summer solstice. The next four weeks turn the spotlight on family, connection, and emotional nourishment. Think nesting and guesting: Pack up for a camping trip, invite beloved relatives for a long weekend, meet your college roomies at the beach. Nostalgia may tug you back to a favorite childhood haunt—perfect since Mercury will be retrograde for a good part of Cancer season this year. (You've been notified.) Close to home, you might feel inspired to start new traditions that loved ones will treasure for years to come. Raw emotions can bubble up now and you may find yourself "in a mood" more often than usual. Consider this a cue to pile on the self-care. You may feel less social during this sensitive and solitary spell, so treasure your time alone when you can get it. Don't isolate for too long. Letting people witness your feelings can be deeply healing. Creativity is cathartic, too, whether you're writing song lyrics in a hammock or watercolor painting with your kids. The muse is in the house, literally!

JUN 22 FIRST QUARTER MOON IN LIBRA

Want to increase the peace? Here's a novel idea: Stop sidestepping conflict. Today's quarter moon in diplomatic Libra reminds you that facing friction head-on is the fastest path to resolution. This lunar lift helps you navigate rough patches with balance, strategy, and a touch of grace. Stand up for yourself, but let facts—not just feelings—guide the conversation. Stay open to other viewpoints, and if you realize you missed the mark, own it. A moment of humility can heal more than a perfectly timed clapback. Since it's Father's Day, timing is everything. If there's something you need to work out with a dad-figure in your life, best to NOT stage the conversation in the midst of the celebration. Literally keep things harmonious with a playlist heavy on old-school tracks from his "coming of age" era.

JUN 25

VENUS-SATURN TRINE

When was the last time you mapped out your love goals? As ardent Venus in Leo locks arms with serious Saturn in Aries, your romantic ideals collide with reality—in the best possible way. Sparks are exciting, but keeping love alive over time takes devotion and a shared sense of purpose. What systems can you put in place to nurture your bonds? Maybe it's contributing to a joint vacation fund every month or carving out weekly "sacred time" together for dates, no excuses. Single? Give Cupid some structure. Set a challenge for yourself, like hitting one new social event per week where you're bound to meet kindred spirits. Stuck in a situationship? If you're craving more than they can offer, bless and release. And if you're the one who doesn't see a future, be grown-up enough to set them free instead of ghosting or "Banksying."

SUN-NEPTUNE SQUARE

Martyr alert! As the Sun in nurturing Cancer clashes with sacrificial Neptune, you could slide into "doing-the-most" mode—a surefire recipe for feeling drained, resentful, or underappreciated. If you're acting more like a caretaker than a collaborator, pause and ask: What's really driving this? Fear that others won't come through? Worry they'll blow up if you don't anticipate their every need? Neither extreme is sustainable—or fair. Time to hang up the superhero cape (maybe for good). When you move at a balanced pace, you create space for others to rise, contribute, and show they're capable, too. But if you keep overfunctioning, don't be surprised if they lean back and let you carry the load. Step aside and let teamwork actually mean teamwork.

JUN 28–AUG 11 MARS IN GEMINI

The pace picks up as passionate Mars charges into persuasive, quick-witted Gemini, turning everyday life into an open marketplace. Whatever you're pitching, people may line up to buy in—whether or not actual money changes hands. But here's the catch: If you want to foster trust, make sure you can actually deliver. This buzzy transit can also stir up fast-talking charlatans or devil's advocates who argue just to keep the debate alive. Don't rush into a dynamic duo without first vetting the facts or testing your chemistry on a small project. Keep an eye on your screen time, too. Mars in this gadget-loving sign can pull you into a constant

scroll of texts and alerts that eat up precious hours. Log off when you can. There are far more fascinating conversations waiting for you in the real world.

JUN 29

MERCURY RETROGRADE IN CANCER (JUN 29-JUL 23)
Mercury spins into its second retrograde of 2026, this time backing up through sensitive, nostalgic Cancer. For the next three weeks, take extra care with anything involving family, home projects or heartfelt conversations. Double-check messages before you hit send. Emotions can run high and misunderstandings may crop up if you're not crystal clear. This is an ideal time to revisit old memories, sort through family keepsakes, or reconnect with relatives you haven't heard from in a while. But don't let sentimentality cloud your judgment. If you need to set clearer boundaries, practice saying what you mean with kindness AND firmness. And if you're feeling overwhelmed, resist the urge to isolate into your shell. Reach out for support from the people who know you best.

FULL MOON IN CAPRICORN (7:57PM; 08°15')
Time for a midyear check-in! The annual full moon in goal-getter Capricorn spotlights your ambitions, helping you measure what's on track—and what needs a serious upgrade. Remember those resolutions you set at the late-December Capricorn new moon? Revisit them now: Which ones still light a fire, and which deserve to be released? Capricorn energy loves a practical plan, so retool your blueprint for success with clear milestones you can actually hit. But don't forget to celebrate along the way. Pause to acknowledge how far you've already come in 2026, and give thanks to the people who've supported your climb. Got a promising idea brewing? Run it past a trusted sounding board before you scale the mountain. A little reality check now can help you turn a lofty dream into an achievement worth toasting.

JUN 30–JUL 26, 2027 JUPITER IN LEO
All the world's a pride parade! For the first time since 2015, larger-than-life Jupiter struts into flamboyant Leo, where it will hold court for the next thirteen months. If you've been keeping a low profile, step out of the wings and claim center stage in the arena that's right for YOU. Since June 9, 2025, Jupiter's tour of Cancer encouraged you to nurture family ties, tend to your emotional foundation, and create a sense of lasting security. That groundwork now becomes the launchpad for your next big act. Fashion, romance, creativity—Leo demands it all in red-carpet-worthy 8K. Share your gifts widely and adopt a warm, generous approach (Leo rules the

heart, after all). Bloviating Jupiter doesn't have an off switch, however, so this cycle comes with an ego alert. While it's fine to be a little performative, real confidence radiates from within—and doesn't require a crowd's applause. For the next thirteen months, leadership shines when you inspire and empower others. (Think "director lifting up the entire cast.") Play your role with courage and heart, but leave space for others to bask in the spotlight, too. Done right, Jupiter in Leo helps you strut proudly AND magnify the brilliance of everyone around you. That's how you create a legacy worth remembering.

JULY

JULY
Moon Phase Calendar

SUN	MON	TUE	WED	THU	FRI	SAT
			EXPOSE **1** ♑ ♒ 3:33PM	LIBERATE **2** ♒	AWAKEN **3** ♒	SPARK **4** ♒ ♓ 2:30AM
EMPOWER **5** ♓	RESTRICT **6** ♓ ♈ 11:07AM	REFLECT **7** ♈ Last Quarter	RECENTER **8** ♈ ♉ 4:31PM	REPAIR **9** ♉	SUPPORT **10** ♉ ♊ 6:42PM	CONVERSE **11** ♊
ILLUMINATE **12** ♊ ♋ 6:46PM	INTERRUPT **13** ♋	BEGIN **14** ♋ New Supermoon 5:44AM ♋→♌ 6:35PM	ENTHRALL **15** ♌	FINE-TUNE **16** ♌ ♍ 8:07PM	REFINE **17** ♍	ADVANCE **18** ♍
REBALANCE **19** ♍ ♎ 12:57AM	EXPAND **20** ♎	ASSERT **21** ♎ First Quarter ♏ 9:35AM	TRANSFORM **22** ♏	REALIGN **23** ♏ ♐ 9:07PM	PURSUE **24** ♐	ELEVATE **25** ♐
REDIRECT **26** ♐ ♑ 9:44AM	REVEAL **27** ♑	DISTILL **28** ♑ ♒ 9:46PM	CELEBRATE **29** ♒ Full Moon 10:36AM	RECHARGE **30** ♒	DRIFT **31** ♒ ♓ 8:14AM	

Times listed are Eastern US Time Zone

KEY

- ♈ ARIES
- ♉ TAURUS
- ♊ GEMINI
- ♋ CANCER
- ♌ LEO
- ♍ VIRGO
- ♎ LIBRA
- ♏ SCORPIO
- ♐ SAGITTARIUS
- ♑ CAPRICORN
- ♒ AQUARIUS
- ♓ PISCES

- **FM** FULL MOON
- **NM** NEW MOON
- **LE** LUNAR ECLIPSE
- **SE** SOLAR ECLIPSE

JULY 14, 5:44AM
new moon in Cancer (21°59')

CANCER NEW MOON CRYSTAL

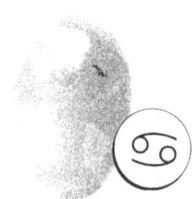

MOONSTONE
Like the moon-ruled sign of Cancer, this iridescent bluish-white stone is associated with the divine feminine and fertility. Moonstone supports with birthing new ideas and tuning in to your destiny.

CANCER NEW MOON = FOCUS

Spend time near water

Connect to family

Get in touch with your emotions

Nourish yourself with good food and close friends

Spruce up your spaces so you feel at home everywhere

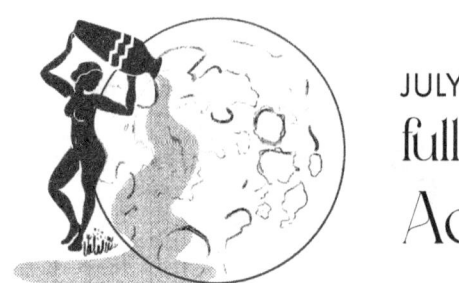

JULY 29, 10:36AM
full moon in Aquarius (6°30')

AQUARIUS FULL MOON CRYSTAL

LABRADORITE

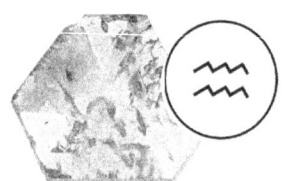 

Rainbow-hued labradorite looks different from every angle, reflecting the diversity and originality that Aquarius celebrates. An "illusion-buster," this stone protects us from over-serving others. Labradorite enables big-picture thinking and is powerful for meditation and insight.

AQUARIUS FULL MOON = CELEBRATE!

Your weirdest ideas

Teams and communities where you feel seen and embraced

Your sharing and accepting spirit

Technology that keeps you connected

Hopes and dreams for the future

Your idealistic nature that refuses to give up on humanity

JULY
MONTHLY HOTSPOTS

JUL 4 MARS-URANUS MEETUP
Talk about fireworks! Feisty Mars connects the dots with disruptive Uranus in quick-thinking Gemini—their first exact conjunction since the 1940s. Words can become your sharpest weapon or your most useful tool. Wield them wisely today. With these mischievous planets here, a little mental sparring CAN be fun. Just avoid getting sucked into petty mind games. This clever combo can stir up sharp-tongued debates, half-baked ideas, or arguments where people twist the facts to win. If you can keep conversations grounded, you might crack open genius solutions and radical new ways of thinking. Intellectual chemistry could get spicy fast. Spend time getting to know the person whose mind fascinates you!

JUL 5 MARS-PLUTO TRINE
Your brilliance can't be contained today! As driven Mars in quick-witted Gemini harmonizes with powerhouse Pluto in visionary Aquarius, both in cerebral air signs, your mental firepower is off the charts. What do you really want? Mars gives you the guts to go for it, while Pluto reveals the pressure points and pathways to success. Be bold but strategic: Woo the decision-makers with sharp ideas, clever hooks, and just enough intrigue to keep them leaning in. With this cosmic combo, think like a chess master. Stay a few moves ahead and position yourself where no one can miss your genius.

JUL 6 SUN-SATURN SQUARE
Got a knot in your stomach? It may not just be the rushed breakfast you shoveled down before your 8AM meeting. As the sensitive Cancer Sun locks horns with structured Saturn, buried emotions could bubble up, demanding attention. Have you been biting your tongue or bottling resentment to keep the peace? That pressure needs a release valve. Tune in to your inner dialogue like a wise parent calming a restless child. Acknowledge what's really bothering

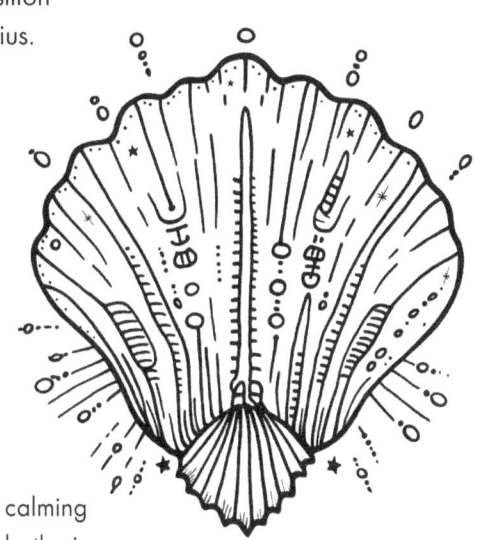

you—without guilt or judgment. Once you name it honestly, you can start reshaping the situation. Today's growth comes from addressing issues with patience and maturity, not sweeping them under the rug.

JUL 7

THIRD QUARTER MOON IN ARIES

Actions speak a thousand times louder than words under today's waning quarter moon in go-getter Aries. If you view something, DO something. It's not enough to point out the problem. You'll win support by showing you're ready to roll up your sleeves. Skip the helpless act! Aries energy celebrates courage, not complaints. Even if you're tackling something tricky, deliver your message with fire-in-the-belly conviction. Propose a solution, outline your next step, and watch people rally behind you. Confidence is contagious, and when you lead with action, you turn potential skeptics into willing teammates.

NEPTUNE RETROGRADE IN ARIES (JUL 7-DEC 12)

Your psyche gets a much-needed sabbatical as Neptune begins its annual five-month retrograde—this time in fiery Aries for the first full backspin since the 1870s! If life has felt like a nonstop swirl of emotions and impulses, this slowdown may come as a relief. At last! A chance to catch up on all the internal messages you've been leaving on "read." Have knee-jerk reactions or bursts of impulsivity been tripping you up? Trace those flare-ups back to their roots. These might be surface-level smoke signals for deeper wounds that want healing. Look back to your early childhood, the time of life that Aries, the zodiac's baby, rules. Ask your mom or older relatives about your birth story—or even what was happening in your mother's life while you were in utero. Those experiences may still be shaping your neural pathways today. Neptune's retrograde is your chance to bring those subconscious patterns into the light. Journaling, therapy, dream work, or energy healing could be powerful tools now. The more awareness you cultivate, the more you can channel Aries' fiery energy into conscious choices rather than reflexive reactions. By December, you could feel more sovereign in your own skin—and less ruled by echoes of the past.

JUL 9-AUG 6 VENUS IN VIRGO

Practical magic is the ultimate love potion for the next few weeks as Venus shifts into mindful Virgo. As romance gets a healthy "makeunder," trade drama for grounded gestures and fuss-free devotion. With wellness in the spotlight, reboot daily rituals that restore your glow. You don't have to give up the champagne and cheese boards—just enjoy them as the occasional treat instead of daily rituals. For the next few weeks, don't underestimate the power of sushi and mocktails after a high-vibe yoga class. Virgo's love language is thoughtful acts of service. Show up for your partner in small, meaningful ways and find hacks that make BOTH of your lives easier. Single? You could meet someone intriguing on a self-improvement path. That's added incentive to train for a 5K, book a wellness retreat, or sign up for a skill-building seminar.

JUL 10 VENUS TRINE CHIRON + CONJUNCT THE SOUTH NODE

Talk is cheap, but actions tell the real story. With Venus in Virgo harmonizing with wounded healer Chiron in Taurus, you may meet (or recognize) someone whose integrity feels like a breath of fresh air. If you've been lowering your standards to keep the peace, this is your cosmic cue to raise the bar. Healthy love and trust are built through consistency, responsibility, and mutual respect. At the same time, Venus meets the karmic South Node, dredging up old flames or patterns for review. An ex or unresolved dynamic could resurface, offering a chance to heal, forgive, or finally release what no longer serves. Don't confuse history with destiny. By binding up those loose ends and demanding meaningful follow-through, you set the stage for future connections that are solid, safe, and built to last.

JUL 12 SUN-MERCURY RETROGRADE MEETUP

A nostalgic day is in store as the Cancer Sun beams into a heart-to-heart with Mercury retrograde. Flip through old photo albums, dig up family keepsakes, or call a relative to hear those stories that never made it into the group chat. You might uncover something that deepens your sense of belonging—or helps you connect the dots on who you are now. On the home front, don't brush aside squeaks, leaks or odd rattles. Mercury retrograde loves a "gotcha," so do a quick check to keep small fixes from turning into big headaches. Inspect to protect!

JUL 13 VENUS-URANUS SQUARE

Stop hovering! Too much togetherness or micromanaging energy could have you itching to break free under today's Venus-Uranus square. While one (or both) of you may feel like ghosting, that will only worsen the situation. Underneath the anxious vibes may be some attachment wounds. How can you offer—or ask for—reassurance? Clear statements are mitigating: "I'm in a meeting until 3" or "Let's have dinner at 7" (followed by an Open Table invite). But careful not to pander to anyone's neediness or make other people responsible for your abandonment fears. Can't be with the one you love? Seize the golden opportunity to hang out with a new friend!

JUL 14 NEW MOON IN CANCER (5:44AM; 21°59'; SUPERMOON)

Circle the wagons! Today's Cancer new moon—also a potent supermoon—spotlights your closest bonds and pumps up the cozy, nostalgic feels. If you've let your MVPs slip to the back burner, it's time to bring them front and center. Sing their praises, set plates for them at your table, or carve out one-on-one time that shows how much you value them. This supermoon could also spark inspiration around home and hearth. From a hot real estate lead to a vision for your dream décor, fresh ideas are in the air. (Antiquing road trip? Approved.) Recharging near water is especially therapeutic now. Slip off for a swim, a soak, or a shoreline stroll. One caveat: With Mercury retrograde swirling, caretaking can quickly turn into over-functioning. Take on what you can manage and let the rest roll in with the next tide.

JUL 18 URANUS-PLUTO TRINE #1 OF 2

Power meets progress! For the first time since 1921-22, alchemical Pluto and radical Uranus form a rare, flowing trine—this time in visionary Aquarius and curious Gemini. This generational alignment launches a two-year wave of transformation that could redefine society as we know it. Breakthroughs in technology, communication, science, and collective movements for freedom are just the beginning. On a personal level, you're invited to crack apart stale systems and innovate boldly for your future self. What old structures or patterns are begging to crumble so your wildest ideas can finally take root? Uranus brings the shocks, Pluto delivers the power, and together they're here to reinvent the playing field. The first tremors arrive now, but watch for an even more dramatic turning point around the second trine on November 29. This is history in the making. Lean into it with courage, curiosity, and vision.

JUL 20

JUPITER-NEPTUNE TRINE

Get ready for liftoff! For the first time in more than a century, starry-eyed Jupiter in Leo flows into a rare trine with mystical Neptune in Aries. With both planets in fiery, future-forward signs, your imagination is set to warp speed. Visionary ideas, artistic downloads, and spiritual awakenings could arrive in a divine deluge today. Just pace yourself when it comes to acting on these ideas. Jupiter and Neptune both love to dream big, but they're not famous for reading the fine print. Before you leap, scan the landing. Today's energy is best for wild, unfiltered brainstorming: "Wouldn't it be amazing if...?" Let the possibilities spill out onto paper, into your Notes app, or in a mind-map session with your most creative friend. You'll have plenty of time later to edit and refine. For now, give yourself permission to dream beyond boundaries.

JUPITER-PLUTO OPPOSITION

Imagineers wanted! Today's high-powered opposition between expansive Jupiter and alchemical Pluto floods the zone with bold ideas and grand visions. But before you chase the shiny object, pop the hood and check the wiring. Not every glittering concept is worth the long-term cost—especially if it complicates community dynamics or stirs up drama in your love life. Balance front-end glamour with back-end reality checks. Do the logistics, tech specs, and social ripple effects actually support your dream? When in doubt, slow your roll, refine, and research. The best ideas will hold up under scrutiny—and those are the ones worth betting on.

JUL 21 FIRST QUARTER MOON IN LIBRA

No more sweeping tension under the Turkish kilim! It's time to face the music and find a sweeter tune. Today's quarter moon in fair-minded Libra, the zodiac's master of compromise, helps you navigate tricky dynamics with poise. Think of this as a cosmic checkpoint: a chance to smooth over rough edges and restore balance where things have gotten wobbly. Yes, thorny truths may need to be aired before harmony returns, but don't let stormy feelings eclipse the facts. Stay curious, own your part, and hold others accountable—without blame or shame. Keep your focus on win-wins. The most ingenious solutions often appear when everyone is willing to meet halfway.

JUL 22–AUG 22 SUN IN LEO (3:13PM)

Curtains up! The Sun struts into flamboyant Leo for its annual four-week reign, turning life into a cosmic talent show. Passion, playtime, and PDA take center stage, so let your hair down and amplify your creative self-expression. With Mercury wrapping up its retrograde tomorrow (July 23), you've got a green light for your grand debut—no more excuses. Leo rules the spine and the heart, reminding you to bring more backbone and warmth into your interactions. Where could you stand taller? Where could you love louder, with your full chest? This regal solar cycle is the perfect moment to raise the bar on your self-worth and courageously own your gifts. Just watch the shadow side: entitlement. Royal energy is meant to uplift the whole kingdom, not just your throne. Lead with generosity, and everyone wins.

JUL 23 MERCURY RETROGRADE ENDS (6:58PM)

Exhale—Mercury retrograde is officially over! Since June 29, the messenger planet's backspin through tender Cancer may have stirred up old family drama, reopened childhood wounds, or left you tangled in emotional misunderstandings. Maybe you butted heads with a relative, sparred with a longtime friend, or found yourself looping on anxious "what-ifs." Now, as Mercury corrects course and powers forward in Cancer for a few more weeks, you've got a golden window to smooth things over. Reach out to your inner circle, clear the air, and mend fences where needed. And if someone from your past popped back into the picture during retrograde? The fog will lift soon, revealing whether this connection deserves a role in your future—or should be filed permanently in your archives.

JUL 26–MAR 26, 2028
LUNAR NODES IN AQUARIUS (NORTH) AND LEO (SOUTH)

Destiny takes a high-fidelity turn as the karmic lunar nodes shift into Aquarius (North Node) and Leo (South Node) for the first time in nearly two decades. For the next 20 months, the fateful North Node in futuristic, community-minded Aquarius urges us to innovate, collaborate, and design smarter ways to live, work, and care for one another. Expect major updates to social systems. Bring an open mind plus a willingness to beta-test better models. Meanwhile, the South Node in Leo calls time-out on grandstanding and ego-driven "I alone can fix it" theatrics. If power has been misused, karmic invoices may come due. The sweet spot? Tap Leo's warmth, generosity, and play to bring people together—then channel that mojo into Aquarian ingenuity that lifts the collective.

JUL 27 SUN OPPOSITE PLUTO + TRINE NEPTUNE

Plot twist! The proud Leo Sun faces off with shrewd Pluto in Aquarius while also syncing harmoniously with visionary Neptune in Aries. Power plays could bubble up like a binge-worthy drama, so watch for charm offensives that feel a little too smooth. Vet people's motives before granting VIP access, and check yourself, too—are you projecting old fears onto those who've actually earned your trust? Not every intensity spike is a red flag. Meanwhile, Neptune sprinkles some magic, opening your third eye to sudden flashes of genius, serendipitous invites, or adventures that stretch your comfort zone. Say yes to detours—a rooftop happy hour, a spontaneous road trip, or a midday vision board session could spark unexpected breakthroughs. The cosmic reminder? Real power is knowing when to step back and when to lean in. Let inspiration guide you along the way.

JUL 29

VENUS-MARS SQUARE

Where is the love? Win-wins will be hard to negotiate thanks to a challenging dust-up between Venus and Mars. With Venus in critical, detail-oriented Virgo, do your best to focus on solutions rather than zeroing in on other people's faults. Yet Mars is tossing up a word salad in Gemini, turning even the most basic-level conversations into mind-boggling debates. You may need an outside party to help you find a compromise. If you've hit a romantic plateau, this Mars-Venus square is your cue to shake things up. With both planets in mutable signs, bring in some movement by literally changing locations, going for a walk or meeting up for a sporty date.

SUN-JUPITER MEETUP, "DAY OF MIRACLES"
Nobility and generosity reign supreme as the radiant Sun and bountiful Jupiter align for their once-a-year meetup—known as a Cazimi. For the first time since 2014, these power players hold their couer-a-couer in big-hearted Leo, amplifying your courage, creativity and a flair for the dramatic. Been craving more attention and recognition? During this "Day of Miracles," the Sun and Jupiter cast their golden glow on your self-expression, passion projects and personal leadership. Embrace this surge of positive momentum! Share your gifts generously and let the world see you in all your luminous glory.

FULL MOON IN AQUARIUS (10:36AM; 06°30')
Rally the crew! The full moon in visionary Aquarius invites you to gather your people and celebrate how far you've come—together. This isn't just a fleeting flash of inspiration; it's the payoff for six months of wild ideas, experiments and radical collaboration. Conjunct transformative Pluto, trine rebellious Uranus and opposite boundary-pushing Jupiter, this lunar high point pulls you in the opposite direction of anything stale or small-minded. The next two weeks are prime time to push unconventional plans across the finish line. Maybe you're launching a disruptive podcast, rolling out a local mutual aid hub, or testing AI in a way that solves a real problem. Don't hold back your innovative notions. Aquarius energy loves a rebel with a good cause. Celebrate wins, give credit where it's due, and keep asking: "How can we do this even better TOGETHER?"

AUGUST

AUGUST
Moon Phase Calendar

SUN	MON	TUE	WED	THU	FRI	SAT
						TRANSCEND **1** ♓
	KEY ♈ ARIES ♌ LEO ♐ SAGITTARIUS **FM** FULL MOON ♉ TAURUS ♍ VIRGO ♑ CAPRICORN **NM** NEW MOON ♊ GEMINI ♎ LIBRA ♒ AQUARIUS **LE** LUNAR ECLIPSE ♋ CANCER ♏ SCORPIO ♓ PISCES **SE** SOLAR ECLIPSE					
FLOW **2** ♈ 4:37PM	REVISIT **3** ♈	ANCHOR **4** ♈ ♉ 10:35PM	STABILIZE **5** ♉ Last Quarter	MATURE **6** ♉	SHIFT **7** ♉ ♊ 2:08AM	COMMUNICATE **8** ♊
TRANSITION **9** ♊	UNVEIL **10** ♋ 3:46AM	SYNCHRONIZE **11** ♋	AWAKEN **12** ♌ 4:38AM New Moon Solar Eclipse 1:37PM	ACTIVATE **13** ♌ ♍ 6:18AM	PURIFY **14** ♍	EXPAND **15** ♍ ♎ 10:20AM
HARMONIZE **16** ♎	NAVIGATE **17** ♎ ♏ 5:46PM	DEEPEN **18** ♏	INTENSIFY **19** ♏ First Quarter	PROPEL **20** ♏ ♐ 4:30AM	CONSTRAIN **21** ♐	CLARIFY **22** ♐ ♑ 4:59PM
HEAL **23** ♑	FORTIFY **24** ♑	EVALUATE **25** ♑ ♒ 5:02AM	EVOLVE **26** ♒	INTEGRATE **27** ♒ ♓ 3:04PM	CULMINATE **28** ♓ Full Moon Lunar Eclipse 12:18AM	SOOTHE **29** ♓ ♈ 10:38PM
CHARGE **30** ♈	STABILIZE **31** ♈					

Times listed are Eastern US Time Zone

Total Solar Eclipse

AUGUST 12, 1:37PM

new moon in Leo (20°02')

LEO NEW MOON CRYSTAL

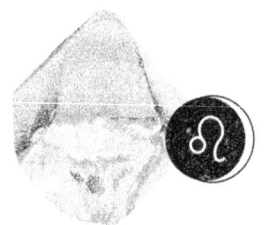

CITRINE

Golden Citrine glows with the regal, joy-inducing hue of Leo! This stone boosts ambition and self-esteem while helping you attract abundance during one of the most creative seasons of the year.

LEO NEW MOON = FOCUS

Find your place to shine

Spend time with kids

Take a leadership role

Host and attend glamorous parties

Enjoy romance and playtime

AUGUST 28, 12:18AM
full moon in Pisces (4°54')

PISCES NEW MOON CRYSTAL

ANGELITE
This pale blue stone activates the Pisces-ruled upper chakras (throat, third-eye and crown), allowing your mind to download messages from your angels, guides and your higher self. Angelite can dissolve emotional or energetic boundaries that may be holding you back from progress.

PISCES FULL MOON = CELEBRATE!

Your secret fantasies

Your creative spirit

Messages from your dreams

People who inspire you to think beyond current limitations

Compassion and empathy

Blurry lines that don't need to be sharpened

The beauty in "ugly" things

AUGUST
MONTHLY HOTSPOTS

AUG 3-SEP 17 CHIRON RETROGRADE IN TAURUS

Wounded healer Chiron begins its annual retrograde today, backing up through security-seeking Taurus until September 17, then continuing its reverse journey through Aries until January 6, 2027. This is the first Chiron retrograde in Taurus since 1983, a cycle that could stir ancient pain around money, stability, and your sense of belonging on Earth itself. Chiron's glyph is shaped like a key, a reminder that healing opens doors. Between now and mid-September, you unlock transformation not by hoarding resources, but by extending support. Whether you donate money or goods, share hard-earned wisdom, or simply stand in solidarity with people who need allies, your generosity becomes medicine. On a global level, Chiron asks us to face collective wounds tied to Taurus-ruled realms: financial inequality, exploitation of the planet, and the ways comfort has been unevenly distributed. Healing begins when we learn to re-root together.

AUG 6

THIRD QUARTER MOON IN TAURUS

Time to get grounded! Today's quarter moon in sensible, steady Taurus brings you back to your core priorities and principles, reminding you that not every "urgent matter" deserves your precious energy. Bottom-line the basics, clear out the clutter and trim any unnecessary expenses. If your no-frills approach starts to feel too stark, reintroduce a few sexy luxuries—mindfully and within your means. Taurus loves life's sensual pleasures, ideally when they have a practical application. This resource-savvy moon might inspire you to organize a clothing swap, rediscover treasures in your own closet, or give old goods a stylish, upcycled twist.

VENUS IN LIBRA (AUG 6-SEP 10)

Cue the cosmic love song! Venus, the planet of beauty, pleasure and romance, waltzes home to her native sign of Libra for the next five weeks. Translation? Harmony, style and sweet connections are back on the menu. From your wardrobe to your living room, sprinkle in luxe touches that make everything feel like an upgrade. In relationships, Venus in Libra restores fairness and flow, helping you smooth over jagged edges and rekindle the art of compromise. Couples can rediscover their groove, while singles may spark with someone who's more "opposites attract" than carbon copy. (Think yin meeting yang and realizing it's actually the perfect duet.) With Venus in this convivial air sign, get ready for a social whirlwind, packed with sophisticated meet and greets, glamorous date nights and elegant soirées. Fancy!

SUN-SATURN TRINE

Passion fuses with purpose as the courageous Leo Sun teams up with can-do Saturn in Aries. If you've been uninspired, raise the stakes. With both of these heavy-hitters in fearless fire signs, it will take a worthy challenge to keep you engaged. Visualize your "BHAG"—that big, hairy, audacious goal that makes your heart race with excitement. Picture yourself nailing it, then break it down into the very first step. Tiny, consistent actions now can snowball into something legendary. Leaders and trailblazers, remember: With great power comes great responsibility. Saturn wants you to build a legacy, so roll up your sleeves and commit to the work.

AUG 9-25 MERCURY IN LEO

Grab the mic and reclaim your roar! With expressive Mercury sashaying into spotlight-stealing Leo for three sizzling weeks, the whole world becomes your stage. Got a pitch, proposal or proclamation to make? Don't just say it—serve it. Think storytelling, bold visuals and a dash of theatrical flair. Under this fire sign's influence, conversations go from casual chitchat to full-on declarations. Expect grand gestures, unapologetic PDA and relationships that debut like a Broadway opening night. Make your entrance impossible to ignore—whether that's in a leopard-print bikini, sequined jumpsuit or vintage couture dripping with drama. Mercury in Leo reminds us that charisma is currency, and right now, you've got an unlimited credit line. Spend it like a star.

AUG 10 VENUS-PLUTO TRINE + VENUS-NEPTUNE OPPOSITION

Romance is dialed up to cinematic levels today, but…is this legendary love or just smoke and mirrors? With enchanting Venus syncing to sultry Pluto, sparks fly through soulful conversation, shared secrets and magnetic chemistry. That witty polymath or passionate activist could leave you spellbound, and for couples, vulnerability is the ultimate aphrodisiac. Peel back a hidden layer and you might find yourself connecting on a soul-deep level. But! Venus also faces off with misty-eyed Neptune, blurring lines between fantasy and reality. Someone's aura may be irresistible, but before you dive headlong into their dreamscape, ask: Are they truly present, or just playing muse for the moment? Under this haze, even minor slights can sting, and it's easy to fall for potential rather than what's real. The sweet spot? Enjoy the chemistry, but keep your eyes open. Let yourself revel in the magic of the moment, remembering that real love embraces the unfiltered version, flaws and all.

AUG 11

MARS IN CANCER (AUG 11-SEP 27)

Home sweet haven? As fiery Mars sets up camp in Cancer, the action shifts squarely to your nest for the next six weeks. That might be a mixed bag with the aggro planet here—especially since Mars is "in fall" in Cancer, its toughest position in the zodiac. As a result, household energy could swing from cozy bonding to cabin-fever clashes in seconds flat. Minimize flare-ups as best you can. Set clear ground rules and carve out private nooks where everyone has breathing room. On the plus side, this go-getter cycle can spark inspired reno projects or a home-based side hustle. When tensions spike, don't stick around waiting for things to explode. Staying OUT more often might be your best plan for mitigating conflict during this transit. Scout out your "satellite" locations: a favorite coffee shop, a gym with great classes, even your BFF's spare bedroom. As long as you feel at home there, you'll be golden.

MERCURY-PLUTO OPPOSITION + MERCURY-NEPTUNE TRINE

Mixed messages much? With quicksilver Mercury in Leo caught between probing Pluto in Aquarius and dreamy Neptune in Aries, conversations could swing from cryptic to spiritually inspired. On the one hand, a tense Mercury-Pluto opposition might stir up mind games, half-truths or sly digs. Instead of overanalyzing, ask directly: "What did you mean by that?" A straight answer can save you hours of spiraling. But don't tune out completely because a soulful Mercury-Neptune trine is also in play, flooding the airwaves with compassion and creative downloads. You may feel like you're reading minds or channeling pure inspiration. Just remember to stay grounded in your own needs (hydrate, stretch, eat something real) so you don't disappear into someone else's agenda. The cosmic combo could hand you both a piercing insight and a poetic breakthrough—all in the same breath.

VENUS-URANUS TRINE

Feeling boxed in by your usual romantic flow? Today's liberating trine between convivial Venus in Libra and wild-card Uranus in Gemini helps you break out of stale routines that are dragging down your mojo. Keep an open mind and see where a little experimentation takes you. With both planets in sociable air signs, you don't have to blow up your whole playbook. But a little detour could do wonders for your love life. Single? Experiment with softening your filter instead of scanning for flaws. You might find yourself swooning for someone refreshingly outside your "type." Long-term couples can revive the spark by mixing up your extracurricular time. What bands are coming to town this week? Is there a new cultural hotspot you want to try? Get out and play!

AUG 12 NEW MOON IN LEO (1:37PM; 20°02'; TOTAL SOLAR ECLIPSE)

Lights, camera, eclipse! Today's Leo new moon is no ordinary lunation. It's a total solar eclipse, the first in this sign since 2019, and it's handing you a megawatt passion reboot. If you've been downplaying your talents or censoring your voice, here's your cue to take the stage. That "little idea" you've been toying with? Under this lunation, it could swell into a full-blown production worthy of a standing ovation. The catch? Leo loves the spotlight, but this eclipse won't tolerate smoke and mirrors. If you embellish too much or cut corners, the cracks will show. Instead, showcase what you're genuinely proud of and let your natural brilliance do the heavy lifting.

AUG 15 MERCURY-JUPITER MEETUP

Say it loud and proud! Messenger Mercury and jubilant Jupiter sync up in Leo, giving your words extra oomph. Don't be shy about hitting "share" if you've earned your bragging rights. This cosmic mashup practically begs you to be your own hype machine. Rally your crew to repost, recommend and help you create a bigger buzz. You could cross paths with someone whose conviction lights a fire under you. Just watch that you don't get swept up in a cult of personality. Allow them to inspire you, but keep your own mic turned up.

AUG 17 MARS-NEPTUNE SQUARE

Passive, meet aggressive. Indirect signals fly as Neptune in Aries clashes with Mars in Cancer. If you're not careful, you could get pulled into other people's conflicts and end up taking sides before you know the full story. Stay alert. This galactic grudge match can obscure facts so deeply that you're left in an emotional tailspin. Someone might give you the old razzle-dazzle, talking a big game with zero follow-through. And if you're the song-and-dance act? Don't make promises you can't keep. Save those jazz hands for when you're truly equipped to deliver.

AUG 17 MERCURY-SATURN TRINE
Big dreams need blueprints! As messenger Mercury in spotlight-stealing Leo syncs with taskmaster Saturn in Aries, shore up your vision with structure and scaffolding. Whether you're polishing a project or making a pivotal call in your personal life, it's not enough to simply follow "a feeling." Saturn wants proof, plans and practical next steps. Map out your moves, set clear deadlines and, if needed, call in an experienced mentor to stress-test your strategy.

AUG 19 FIRST QUARTER MOON IN SCORPIO
And...cut! After basking in the exotic limelight of last week's total solar eclipse in Leo, today's first quarter moon in Scorpio pulls you backstage for a reality check. Beneath the glow of recent wins, what's really motivating you? Are you driven by authentic passion or the need to prove something? Scorpio rules power, privacy and transformation, and this lunar checkpoint calls for a deeper audit of your intentions. Are you steering from intuition or ego? Nothing wrong with basking in the life of a showgirl (or uh, something like that). But this moon favors shadow work over spotlight moments. By addressing what's hidden, you'll clear emotional clutter and step into next week's closing lunar eclipse with sharp instincts and a stronger sense of purpose.

AUG 21 VENUS-SATURN OPPOSITION
Have you let your guard down a little too much lately? With gracious Venus in Libra clashing with stern Saturn in Aries, today's skies remind you that strong boundaries are sexy, too. If you've overridden your instincts just to keep the peace, step back and realign with your non-negotiables. Unsure of someone's true role in your life? Resist snap judgments under this befuddling opposition. Red flags do deserve attention, but your radar may be fuzzy, blurring the line between a workable flaw and a true deal-breaker. Watch a little longer before deciding which is which.

AUG 22-SEP 22 SUN IN VIRGO (10:19PM)
After an indulgent month, it's time to simplify. The Sun shifts into devotional Virgo, bringing you back to earthy, easy pleasures. This industrious solar season can fill your calendar with administrative duties, but how can you turn those routines into rituals? Spruce up your workspace with plants and mood-lifting accessories like crystals and art prints. Slip on stylish basics in comfy cottons, linens and breathable fabrics—yes, even when you're dashing to the gym or picking up the kids. While you're on a roll, systematize your life for ease. Make extra portions at dinner so tomorrow's lunch is ready to grab. Start a Pinterest board of clever storage ideas and efficiency hacks. And remember: Some of the best things in life are still free. Bring on the sunrise walks, waning beach days and yoga in the park. Earthy Virgo wants you to enjoy the very last drops of summer!

AUG 25 - SEP 10 MERCURY IN VIRGO

Just in time for back-to-school season, mindful Mercury returns to one of its home signs, detail-loving Virgo. Bring order to the late-summer sprawl. Stress-busting routines and healthy habits can stick now—if you actually commit to them. Tempted by every rooftop invite? Fine, but balance it with early nights, clean eats, and a screen curfew that lets your nervous system actually recharge. With the communication planet in this meticulous earth sign, planning ahead and tracking progress will set you up for success. Editing, refining and polishing projects is favored, but watch the perfectionism trap. Virgo loves precision, but don't let endless tweaks stall your forward motion.

AUG 27 SUN-MERCURY MEETUP

Don't underestimate the difference you make! As the Sun teams up with Mercury in service-driven Virgo, small acts of kindness pack a powerful punch. Surprise a coworker with an almond croissant from their favorite bakery, help a neighbor wrestle the recycling bins, or offer to water a friend's plants. At work, slip out of autopilot mode and embrace the Virgo mantra: work smarter, not harder. Download that project-management app, clear the clutter from your desk, or finally conquer that nagging file backlog. Feeling maxed out? Ask for support before you hit a wall. Got wisdom to share? Skip the fluff and deliver the practical nuggets people can actually use.

AUG 28

FULL MOON IN PISCES (12:18AM; 04°54'; PARTIAL LUNAR ECLIPSE)

Logic won't cut it under today's lunar eclipse in esoteric Pisces. With the veil between worlds thinner than gossamer, you may glimpse the "source code" behind life itself. Get ready for a day of uncanny synchronicities and miracles big and small. Meditate, pull a tarot card, or jot down your dreams; messages may arrive in symbols rather than straight lines. But brace for curveballs. This eclipse squares off with unpredictable Uranus in Gemini, stirring up revelations that could flip old assumptions on their head. An "enemy" may suddenly look more like someone to pity, sparking an unexpected wave of compassion. That doesn't mean excusing bad behavior, but it could open a door to forgiveness—or to finally saying, "Enough." Sometimes the most sacred act of love is drawing the boundary that protects your peace.

MERCURY SQUARE URANUS + SUN SQUARE URANUS

Expect the unexpected! With both the Sun and Mercury in meticulous Virgo clashing with disruptive Uranus in quick-thinking Gemini, your best-laid plans could take some wild detours. Control freakery won't help here—it'll only make you spin faster. Mercury's square warns against overpromising or skipping steps. If your ideas sound great in theory but the details don't add up, Uranus will expose the cracks. Break big visions into doable, bite-sized milestones so they don't crumble under their own weight. Meanwhile, the Sun's square stirs up power struggles and contrarian energy. Someone may push back just for the sake of rebellion—or you may be the one itching to break free. Before you get caught in endless debates, ask yourself: Does this need fixing right now? Probably not. Keep your cool, pick your battles, and stay grounded in facts. Flexibility is your superpower today!

AUG 31 JUPITER-SATURN TRINE #1 OF 2

Passion and purpose sync up today, helping you find your cruising altitude around an important mission. With buoyant Jupiter in showstopping Leo, the urge to stage life like a Tony Award production is real. But retrograde Saturn in Aries isn't here for the theatrics. What it does reward is focus, structure and patience. Maybe you don't need so many moving parts? A streamlined vision can be just as satisfying, especially if it frees you to try new tactics and forge heartfelt connections. Whatever the case, move ahead with integrity. Skip the shortcuts, refine your process, and let yourself play the long game. This is the first of two supportive Jupiter-Saturn trines (round two lands April 3, 2027). Build now, dazzle later and your vision will stand the test of time.

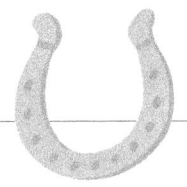

SEPTEMBER

SEPTEMBER
Moon Phase Calendar

SUN	MON	TUE	WED	THU	FRI	SAT
		PERSEVERE **1** ♓ ♉ 4:01AM	GROUND **2** ♉	PROCESS **3** ♉ ♊ 7:47AM	DECIDE **4** ♊ Last Quarter	EXCHANGE **5** ♊ ♋ 10:30AM
CARE **6** ♋	REKINDLE **7** ♋ ♌ 12:49PM	CENTER **8** ♌	EDIT **9** ♌ ♍ 3:35PM	SEED **10** ♍ New Moon 11:27PM	REFOCUS **11** ♍ ♎ 7:52PM	REVEAL **12** ♎
INVENT **13** ♎	TUNE **14** ♎ ♏ 2:44AM	EXPOSE **15** ♏	JOURNEY **16** ♏ ♐ 12:41PM	REDISCOVER **17** ♐	CONSTRAIN **18** ♐ First Quarter	STRENGTHEN **19** ♐ ♑ 12:55AM
COMMIT **20** ♑	BUILD **21** ♑ ♒ 1:14PM	RELATE **22** ♒	IMAGINE **23** ♒ ♓ 11:24PM	SURRENDER **24** ♓	DISSOLVE **25** ♓	CULMINATE **26** ♓→♈ 6:23AM ♈ Full Moon 12:49PM
HEAL **27** ♈	REVOLUTIONIZE **28** ♈ ♉ 10:40AM	RECONCILE **29** ♉	PENETRATE **30** ♉ ♊ 1:26PM			

Times listed are Eastern US Time Zone

KEY

- ♈ ARIES
- ♉ TAURUS
- ♊ GEMINI
- ♋ CANCER
- ♌ LEO
- ♍ VIRGO
- ♎ LIBRA
- ♏ SCORPIO
- ♐ SAGITTARIUS
- ♑ CAPRICORN
- ♒ AQUARIUS
- ♓ PISCES
- **FM** FULL MOON
- **NM** NEW MOON
- **LE** LUNAR ECLIPSE
- **SE** SOLAR ECLIPSE

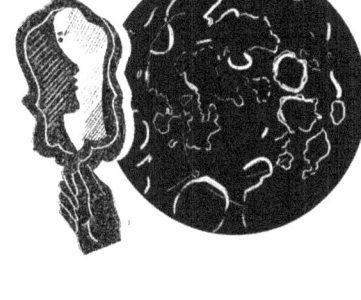

SEPTEMBER 10, 11:27PM

new moon in
Virgo (18°26')

VIRGO NEW MOON CRYSTAL

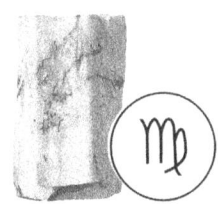

LEPIDOLITE
This soothing stone is also called the "grandmother stone" or "peace stone." Use it to calm your nerves and ease the worrying tendency that Virgo can stir up. Lepidolite encourages us to quiet inner criticism and embrace self-love and compassion.

VIRGO NEW MOON = FOCUS

Adopt (or cuddle) a pet

Work out and eat clean

Hire service providers and assistants

Practice random acts of kindness

Embrace healthy routines

Implement efficient systems

Break projects into actionable steps

SEPTEMBER 26, 12:49PM
full moon in Aries (3°37')

ARIES FULL MOON CRYSTAL

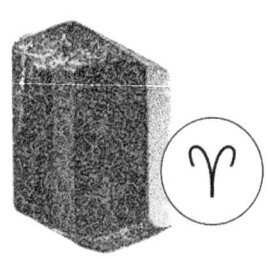

BLOODSTONE
A dramatic dark-green with flecks of red, this stone is historically given to brave warriors. Use bloodstone to build resilience and pump up self-confidence as you step out as an individual. This circulation-boosting crystal enhances vitality and makes you feel alive.

ARIES FULL MOON = CELEBRATE!

Your inner (and outer) baddie

New experiences you're brave enough to try

Your competitive nature

Every unique feature that makes you a rare individual

Your fighting spirit that won't give up

SEPTEMBER
MONTHLY HOTSPOTS

SEP 1 MARS-SATURN SQUARE
Go fast to go slow? As Mars in emo Cancer locks into a tense square with cautious Saturn in Aries, it can feel like you're flooring the gas while the universe yanks the emergency brake. Tempted to skip the messy parts and fast-forward to the fun? Bad idea. This aspect demands due diligence—red flags ignored now will only wave with greater intensity later. On the flip side, if your walls are sky-high, you could be the one stalling progress. Real intimacy requires risk. Lower the drawbridge, show your cards, and let people in.

SEP 4 THIRD QUARTER MOON IN GEMINI
Where's the gray area? That's exactly where your focus belongs under today's waning quarter moon in Gemini. Nothing is strictly black or white now, so zoom in on the nuances. A sharper observation could reveal the missing piece—or show you that what (or who) you've been seeking has been right under your nose all along. If you made a snap call, this prismatic moon nudges you to widen your lens and consider fresh perspectives. Need to change your tune? Swallow your pride and say so.

SEP 10

VENUS IN SCORPIO (SEP 10-OCT 25)
Secrets, soul merging and smoldering sparks ahead! Venus slinks into seductive Scorpio until October 25, lingering here longer than usual thanks to a six-week retrograde that begins October 3. Forget about "keeping it casual" this fall. Cuffing season comes with a high-security lock in 2026. Savor your chemistry in private and enjoy steamy secrets without pressure to tell a single soul. Dating? A few cat and mouse games can be sexy during this alluring cycle. But don't be TOO mysterious! Interested parties may get frustrated and give up unless you drop enough breadcrumbs to keep them following your trail. Couples can grow much closer with Venus in Scorpio. The big requirement: Trust has to run as deep as lust, especially when retrograde revelations surface after October 3. Rein in jealousy and possessiveness, which can run rampant now—not a good look!

URANUS RETROGRADE IN GEMINI (SEP 10–FEB 8, 2027)

Rethink, rewrite, rebel! Radical Uranus kicks off its annual five-month retrograde, moonwalking through curious, quick-talking Gemini. Your inner mad scientist is getting a hush-hush reboot, so between now and early next year, rethink how you communicate, connect, and share ideas with the world. Question stale beliefs, explore impact-driven perspectives, and play in Gemini's playgrounds of media, learning, and tech. Behind the scenes, dive into that secret screenplay, lay tracks for your future EP, or tinker with your next big app. This is gold-star energy for reskilling—especially hands-on, digital, or mobile-friendly. Stay open to unconventional inspo: What looks radical today could be tomorrow's genius breakthrough.

NEW MOON IN VIRGO (11:27PM; 18°26')

Bless this mess? Nope, not under today's neat-freak new moon in Virgo. It's time to get organized. With la luna squaring unpredictable Uranus, surprise disruptions could expose exactly where your systems need an overhaul. Before you lose critical data or can't find your keys (again!) while you rush out the door, open your Notes app and draft a plan. Build a shelving unit, upload digital files on a secure cloud server, donate clothes to a shelter. Could your meals be cleaner, your sleep more sacred? Stock up on fresh produce, stash wholesome snacks like raw almonds and turn your bedroom into a sanctuary. Uranus's jolt to this new moon might feel disruptive at first, but it's clearing space for routines that truly keep you humming along.

SEP 12 MERCURY TRINE PLUTO + MERCURY OPPOSITE NEPTUNE

Say it like you mean it—but check yourself before you overpromise. Today's persuasive Mercury–Pluto trine supercharges your words with passion and intensity, giving you the charm and strategy to win people over fast. But with Mercury also facing off against slippery Neptune, clarity could be in short supply. Decision-making may feel murky, so double-check that everyone's actually on the same page. Use Pluto's laser focus to pitch ideas that are truly mutually beneficial, but guard against Neptune's haze by leaning on structure—a spreadsheet, clear notes, or a reality check from a trusted ally. Bottom line: Your words carry weight today, so make sure they inspire trust, not confusion.

SEP 13 MERCURY-URANUS TRINE

The zodiac's two brainiest planets sync up today as Mercury in Libra forms a flowing trine with unconventional Uranus in Gemini. This Mensa-level air-sign combo can spark ingenious ideas, breakthrough solutions and a meeting of the minds that flips your usual approach on its head. Entire industries could get a jolt—or maybe you'll finally break free from a frustrating thought pattern that's kept you stuck. Pitching an idea? Prep what you can, but skip the hard sell. Stay present, flexible and responsive to people's questions. This is quick-thinking magic at its best—trust it!

SEP 14–JUN 10, 2027 LILITH IN CAPRICORN

Reclaim your throne—or build your own from scratch. As Black Moon Lilith strides into Capricorn, the zodiac's CEO, the parts of yourself that you once dismissed or exiled demand a seat at the boardroom table. This isn't about squeezing into someone else's version of success. It's about defining it on your own terms. Capricorn's disciplined, legacy-minded energy helps you turn raw truth into strategy, transforming old rejections into a source of power. You may even become an authority in an area that was once a private pain. Any story that said you weren't "enough" in the eyes of the system? Time to rewrite it. Larger life goals may shift as Lilith reveals the hidden impacts of following society's archaic rules. Rage against the Capricorn-ruled patriarchy may reach a fever pitch under Lilith's empowered hand.

SEP 15 VENUS-PLUTO SQUARE (#1 OF 3)

Can you handle the heat? Today marks the first of three sizzling Venus-Pluto squares in 2026, with Venus prowling through seductive Scorpio and squaring off with intense Pluto in Aquarius. Passions run deep, but so do the power plays. Raw desires and buried fears about trust and control can bubble to the surface, making relationships feel both magnetic and volatile. Secrets may come to light or you might find yourself craving soul-baring intimacy that leaves zero room for deception. The chemistry is electric, but don't let manipulation sneak in. Get radically honest about what you want—and what you're no longer willing to tolerate.

SEP 17 – APR 14, 2027 CHIRON RETROGRADE IN ARIES

Stand up—don't blow up! Wounded healer Chiron charges ahead in fiery Aries, wrapping up a cycle that began in 2018. This final lap delivers closing lessons on the power of healthy anger. Suppressing upset feelings only makes them boil into rage. The world has certainly reflected that during Chiron's eight-year tour of the Ram's realm. Starting now, you're invited to drop the martyr act and advocate for yourself with courage and clarity. Just remember: There's a fine line between assertiveness and scorched-earth aggression. Chiron's medicine is about turning old wounds into wisdom and pain into purpose (its symbol is literally a key). Use this passage to unlock your strength, rewrite your story, and stand your ground—without torching the very bridges you still need to cross.

SEP 18

MERCURY-SATURN OPPOSITION

Analysis paralysis alert! With Mercury in diplomatic Libra facing off against Saturn in headstrong Aries, part of you wants to weigh every option while another part just wants to race ahead. If you've been winging it, consider this a cosmic checkpoint. Do you need more structure? Is outdated tech slowing you down? Take time to tighten your plan and cover the essentials—even if it stalls production a little. Lay solid groundwork today and you'll move much faster tomorrow.

FIRST QUARTER MOON IN SAGITTARIUS

Does "work-life balance" feel more like a riddle than an attainable reality? Today's balancing quarter moon helps you recalibrate fast. Hitting your targets is great—but at what cost? Scan your to-do list: are you spreading yourself too thin instead of delegating? Trying to do it all could jam up your bigger mission. If life pressures have your shoulders up by your ears, dial it back. Logging off for yoga or a long walk might boost productivity more than pushing through one more task. Stuck in a rut? These steady moonbeams could highlight a way forward. Sign up for a course or go wander in search of inspiration. Anything from a bookstore run to a trip out of town counts!

SEP 22– OCT 23 SUN IN LIBRA (8:05PM), FALL EQUINOX

Ditch the lone-wolf act and go find your pack! Libra season begins with the fall equinox, launching a solar-powered month for partnerships and dynamic duos, in both business and love. Keep an open mind: Your best connections may come from people who don't fit your usual type. Need to strike a deal? This diplomatic cycle gives you extra edge at the bargaining table. Look for win-wins that leave everyone smiling. Existing bonds could deepen fast, too. Ready to make it official? Add an exclusivity clause, put a ring on it, or decide what "next level" looks like for you. And since Libra is the zodiac's aesthete, this season is also perfect for beautification. Update your wardrobe with one statement piece, refresh your décor with flowers, candles and art. Whenever possible, bring more grace into your daily interactions.

SEP 25 SUN-NEPTUNE OPPOSITION

Stuck in a swirl of indecision? As the wavering Libra Sun locks horns with foggy Neptune in Aries, good luck finding clarity. Just when you think you've landed on the "right" answer, another option pops up that seems just as compelling—or completely confusing. Even your go-to advisors may be spinning under these hazy skies. Don't waste energy forcing hidden truths into the light. Some details just won't surface today. Instead, focus on what you can control. Lean into Libra's gift for grace and diplomacy in tricky conversations—or table those talks until tomorrow!

SEP 26

SUN-PLUTO TRINE

Your allure is off the charts as the Libra Sun syncs up with magnetic Pluto in Aquarius. Use this captivating energy wisely! A witty remark can hook people's interest, but too much dry humor could land as an unintended dig. Dial back the sarcasm and aim for clarity, especially if you're presenting a complex idea that may need extra explanation. While a touch of intrigue keeps people leaning in, don't be so mysterious that you lose your audience. Give others room to respond before unleashing your next thought.

FULL MOON IN ARIES (12:49PM; 03°37')

Today's fiery full moon in Aries—sitting shoulder-to-shoulder with dreamy Neptune—floods you with confidence and a swirl of emotions. You want to show up unfiltered, fully authentic, and deep in your baddie era, but read the room! There's a line between empowered and entitled. Advocate for yourself without veering into self-absorption. Aries loves to be Number One, so competitive vibes are strong. Toss your name in the ring for a leadership role, but use your influence to uplift other rising stars, too. With Neptune sitting close to the full moon, compassion flows—but so can old frustrations. Channel that intensity into healthy outlets. Hit the punching bag, vent to a trusted friend or belt it out at karaoke. The feels are potent today, and they need to be released!

SEP 27–NOV 25 MARS IN LEO

Let your inner big cat roar! Mars charges into Leo for the first time in nearly two years, and the competition for the spotlight is on. Your job? Find an authentic way to stand out. Hint: Be more of yourself, not less. With Mars in Leo, there's no such thing as "too much"—though sometimes the quietest presence in the room makes the biggest impact. A warm personality and contagious enthusiasm will outshine even the fiercest OOTD, but why not treat life like a costume party? In love, this transit sparks fiery clashes as easily as passion. Skip the text fights and redirect that feisty Mars energy to the bedroom—where lust-out-loud, sheet-tangling chemistry awaits. (Did someone say make-up sex?) With Mars in Leo, the spoils go to the boldest hearts.

SEP 28 SUN-URANUS TRINE

Feeling restless? If you've hit a plateau, today's Sun-Uranus trine could jolt you with the urge to shake things up. Just don't toss common sense to the wind. With the Libra Sun syncing to renegade Uranus in Gemini, sudden flashes of inspiration could tempt you to leap into uncharted territory without a plan. If your gut says "go for it," listen— but read all the safety instructions before you start "experimenting."

SEP 30–DEC 6 MERCURY IN SCORPIO

Say less. As messenger Mercury dives into secretive Scorpio, your words pack extra power, but so does your silence. Don't feel pressured to spill every detail—or any at all. Let people earn your trust as you turn the getting-to-know-you phase into a delicious unfolding. Advance warning: Mercury spins retrograde (alongside Venus) from October 24 to November 13. Plan ahead with extra security measures. Update your passwords, change your privacy settings on the socials, assign new codes for all your locks. A sultry ex or intriguing frenemy could slip back into your DMs at some point during this cycle. If you'd rather not open that door again, you might want to block 'em for your own self-protection.

OCTOBER

OCTOBER
Moon Phase Calendar

SUN	MON	TUE	WED	THU	FRI	SAT
				CONNECT **1** ♊	CHALLENGE **2** ♊ ♋ 3:54PM	RECKON **3** ♋ Last Quarter
REASSESS **4** ♋ ♌ 6:54PM	INSPIRE **5** ♌	RECONCILE **6** ♌ ♍ 10:53PM	CLARIFY **7** ♍	POLISH **8** ♍	BALANCE **9** ♍ ♎ 4:11AM	INITIATE **10** ♎ New Moon 11:50AM
MAGNETIZE **11** ♎ ♏ 11:21AM	INVESTIGATE **12** ♏	ROAM **13** ♏ ♐ 8:59PM	EXPAND **14** ♐	SHIFT **15** ♐	REINFORCE **16** ♐ ♑ 8:57AM	ESTABLISH **17** ♑
STRATEGIZE **18** ♑ First Quarter ♒ 9:40PM	REVOLUTIONIZE **19** ♒	INTENSIFY **20** ♒	CONFRONT **21** ♒ ♓ 8:35AM	IMAGINE **22** ♓	MERGE **23** ♓ ♈ 3:53PM	RECLAIM **24** ♈
BEAUTIFY **25** ♈ ♉ 7:35PM	EMBODY **26** ♉ Full Moon 12:12AM	STABILIZE **27** ♉ ♊ 9:02PM	SYNTHESIZE **28** ♊	REFLECT **29** ♊ ♋ 10:06PM	CLASH **30** ♋	PROTECT **31** ♋ ♌ 9:18PM

Times listed are Eastern US Time Zone

KEY

- ♈ ARIES
- ♉ TAURUS
- ♊ GEMINI
- ♋ CANCER
- ♌ LEO
- ♍ VIRGO
- ♎ LIBRA
- ♏ SCORPIO
- ♐ SAGITTARIUS
- ♑ CAPRICORN
- ♒ AQUARIUS
- ♓ PISCES

- **FM** FULL MOON
- **NM** NEW MOON
- **LE** LUNAR ECLIPSE
- **SE** SOLAR ECLIPSE

OCTOBER 10, 11:50AM
new moon in Libra (17°22')

LIBRA NEW MOON CRYSTAL

MALACHITE
Green like the heart chakra, this stone supports the profound emotional transformations we can make during Libra season. Malachite also invites wealth and prosperity into your home, perfect for this time of beauty and abundance.

LIBRA NEW MOON = FOCUS

Find synergies

Nurture romantic relationships

Enjoy art, music and fashion

Beautify everything

Network to build your contact list

OCTOBER 26, 12:12AM
full moon in Taurus (2°46')

TAURUS FULL MOON CRYSTAL

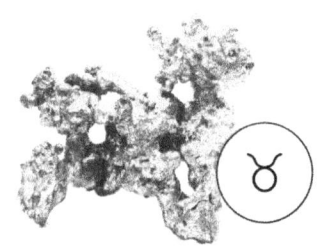

COPPER
One of the Earth's most healing materials, copper brings the signature stability of earth-sign Taurus. This gem balances the chakras and shifts stagnant energy, charging you up to connect with loved ones during holiday celebrations. The weight of copper grounds you as you to tap into the quantum field—the place of limitless ideas and possibilities.

TAURUS FULL MOON = CELEBRATE!

The simple things that bring you joy

The beauty of nature

Your favorite music and artists

Finding holiday gifts that are sustainable and earth-friendly

Creating a comfortable home environment

Food that you love

OCTOBER
MONTHLY HOTSPOTS

OCT 2

MERCURY SQUARE MARS + PLUTO

Should you ease in slowly or let it all hang out? With Mercury in secretive Scorpio clashing against flamboyant Mars in Leo and power-player Pluto in Aquarius, intense conversations could ignite in seconds. One moment you're whispering confidences, the next it's ego flare-ups, ideological tug-of-wars or hidden agendas on parade. Guard your personal data—especially from people who overshare freely. What feels like harmless tea-spilling could hand someone the very ammo they'll later use against you. Honesty is powerful, but today's stars advise: edit, edit, edit. Say just enough to advance the dialogue, keep a few cards tucked away, and bow out before you're dragged into a complex scenario.

MARS-NEPTUNE TRINE

As flamboyant Mars in Leo high-fives dreamweaver Neptune in Aries, the whole world feels like improv night. "To thine own self be true" could echo as today's unofficial anthem, with these boundary-busting planets egging on bold moves and headline-grabbing displays. Expect no shortage of spectacles—some dazzlingly inspired, others so off-key they're chilling. Guard your associations carefully! If you amplify the wrong voice, their missteps could boomerang back on you. And before you hit "post" on your own spicy rant, pause for a gut check. One impulsive share could ignite a firestorm that takes forever to extinguish.

OCT 3

THIRD QUARTER MOON IN CANCER

The errands can wait! Soothe your senses under today's quarter moon in nurturing Cancer. Add creature comforts to your weekend lineup. Brew a favorite tea, putter around in slippers and sweats. Under these balancing moonbeams, you might get the urge to spruce up a messy corner of your home. Tackle projects in bite sizes today so you don't get overwhelmed. When (and if!) you're feeling social, keep it chill. Linger over brunch with a loved one or invite a couple friends over to watch a show you all love. Searching for a new

place to call home? Don't snooze on those Redfin alerts. Your dream listing could pop up just as you're rearranging a bookshelf or clearing out a closet.

VENUS RETROGRADE (OCT 3-NOV 13)

Scorching hot, icy cold, lukewarm again! Relationships could cycle through every temperature over the next six weeks as ardent Venus spins retrograde. The love planet reverses course every 18 months, but this is the first time in eight years she's moonwalked through Scorpio and Libra. During the retrograde, Venus switches her status from evening star (visible in the night sky) to morning star (visible just before dawn). Metaphorically, seize the opportunity to put old love stories to bed and write a fresh chapter for amour. From October 3 to 25, Venus begins her reverse commute in sultry Scorpio, unearthing buried feelings about trust, loyalty, and erotic chemistry. Then from October 25 to November 13, she rewinds into Libra, shaking up otherwise peaceful dynamics. Old conflicts may resurface and jealousy could flare. There's no slapping a Band-Aid on it this time—Venus retrograde demands you drill down to the root of the issue. And surprise: It's not about pointing fingers. While it takes two to tango, this backspin helps you recognize your role in any relationship that's on shaky ground. Self-compassion is equally vital, especially as you parse through old hurts and attachment wounds that trace back to childhood. Double down on self-care and supportive practices—journaling, meditation, couples' therapy. Exes may resurface, but proceed with caution. Toxic patterns love to repeat themselves during Venus retrograde. Unless you've both done the work, keep that chapter closed.

MARS-PLUTO OPPOSITION

Pride, power plays, and hidden agendas—brace yourself for some added intensity today! With fiery Mars in Leo facing off against controlling Pluto in Aquarius, an already-tense atmosphere teeters on the brink of explosive drama. It's all too easy to get pulled into a psychological tug-of-war where one wrong word ignites a full-blown feud. Your greatest strength (and biggest challenge) will be staying calm. Refuse to be drawn into anyone's mind games. No matter how tempting it is to clap back, shut it down instead. If you want to keep the upper hand, walk away before things escalate.

OCT 4 SUN-SATURN OPPOSITION

Libra season tempts you to keep the fête going—another VIP party, a splurge-worthy purchase, one more round for the table. Nothing wrong with a little luxury! But when indulgence tips into approval-seeking or avoidance, balance goes out the window. Cue Saturn in Aries, opposing the Sun and serving a much-needed reality check. Where are you overextending yourself to keep the peace or gain status? Today's skies call for recalibration: Reassess your commitments, reset your boundaries, and remember that joy doesn't have to break the bank or destroy your hard-won healthy habits.

OCT 6 MERCURY-VENUS RETROGRADE MEETUP

Like it or not, buried feelings bubble up today as Mercury collides with Venus retrograde. Old hurts, grudges, or unspoken desires could demand airtime, and you may feel like you'll explode if you don't get them off your chest. With verbal Mercury in the mix, putting thoughts and feelings into words can spark powerful insights. Just choose your sounding board wisely. Venting to a pot-stirrer could leave you feeling exposed—or worse, even more upset. If you want real perspective (and you do), confide in someone you trust who can help you process without fanning the flames. Revelations may arrive mid-conversation, but hold off on the dramatic "we need to talk" speech. With both planets in deep-diving Scorpio, more epiphanies are still on their way.

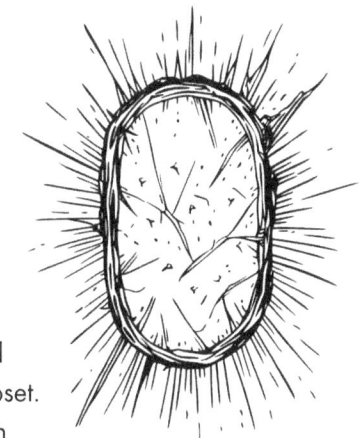

OCT 10

NEW MOON IN LIBRA (11:50AM; 17°22')

Where's the missing link in your life? Today's Libra new moon kicks off a six-month cycle that energizes partnerships of every kind—romantic, professional, creative, you name it. New moons are cosmic starting blocks, so take time to clarify what you truly need before you send out any casting calls. Which skills, perspectives, or qualities would genuinely strengthen your vision? Jot them down and get specific. Reflect on past experiences, too. What have you learned? Note what you absolutely do—and don't—need in a plus-one. If you're already in a relationship, realign goals and make sure the roles you've each taken on still feel supportive. And while you may adore someone, don't shoehorn them into the wrong part. That could create more strain than synergy.

VENUS-MARS SQUARE #2 OF 2

The cosmic lovebirds clash again—and this round has teeth. Unlike July's skirmish in flexible mutable signs, today's square between retrograde Venus in Scorpio and Mars in Leo lands in stubborn fixed signs. Values may collide, so ask yourself: Are you blowing up a minor difference or staring down a genuine dealbreaker? Today could serve a smorgasbord of righteousness, pride, and a flat-out refusal to budge. Don't ignore legitimate red flags, but think twice before torching a bridge you might later regret. Not sure? Let Venus' retrograde (through November 13) buy you time. Space and patience could reveal whether this tension is a growth edge or a line in the sand.

OCT 15 PLUTO RETROGRADE ENDS

The winds of change pick up speed! After five months of deep recalibration, transformative Pluto pivots direct in progressive Aquarius. Since May 6, Pluto's backspin has pushed you to examine the systems, networks, and alliances most in need of a radical overhaul. Now, with the metamorphic planet moving forward, you can start putting your world-bettering ideas into motion—slowly but surely. No rush: Pluto is only at the dawn of its two-decade journey through Aquarius (lasting until January 19, 2044). Sweeping shifts in technology, social equity, and collective connection will shape what you're building. Strengthen community ties and remember—real power multiplies when you stand with allies.

OCT 16 MARS-SATURN TRINE

The right balance of "hit the gas" and "ride the brakes" could arrive today when speed racer Mars harmonizes in a dynamic duet with steady Saturn. Although these two planets operate at very different paces, they're both blazing through bold fire signs—and during this flowing trine, they'll have each other's back. This is not the day to charge ahead without a solid plan in place. Saturn, the ruler of time, has no problem being the tortoise to Mars in Leo's hare. Use this planetary pairing to pop the hood and give those big ideas a tune-up so everything runs like a well-oiled machine. After that, it will be easy to move the needle on stalled projects or passion pursuits without "scratching the vinyl" in haste. Just make sure every move has a smart strategy behind it, while leaving room for some inspired spontaneity.

OCT 18 FIRST QUARTER MOON IN CAPRICORN

Is "work-life balance" starting to feel more like a riddle than reality? Today's first quarter moon in Capricorn offers a clarifying pause to see what needs adjusting. Ambition is admirable, but if your weekend is swallowed by catch-up mode, that's a red flag. Instead of powering through another round of chores or emails, delegate—or just drop—a few tasks so you can actually enjoy your downtime. This lunar lift favors quality over quantity. Feeling restless about the week ahead? Use today to sketch out a smarter system or explore a new skill that excites you. Even a short workshop, podcast, or training module could leave you inspired and reset for Monday.

OCT 20 VENUS-PLUTO SQUARE #2 OF 3

Temptation with a twist! The second of 2026's three Venus-Pluto squares dials up the intensity. With Venus retrograde in Scorpio, old flames, unresolved desires, or shadowy trust issues could surface from the depths. Secretive Pluto in Aquarius adds an edgy, unpredictable layer, stirring up obsessions, jealousy, or power plays. An ex may resurface, but before you crack open Pandora's box, ask yourself: Is this true closure—or just a replay of old patterns? While magnetism is undeniable, manipulation lurks in the shadows. Use this raw, revealing energy to face deep fears around intimacy. Be honest, be brave, but don't get dragged back into games you've already outgrown.

OCT 23

SUN IN SCORPIO (5:38AM), (OCT 23-NOV 22)

Money, power, sex! The zodiac's most magnetic season begins as the Sun slips into Scorpio until November 22. Where could you merge "yours" and "theirs" for a true win-win? This resourceful cycle favors trusted twosomes, whether you're teaming up on a business venture, pooling funds for an investment, or simply splitting a subscription. You may also spot a few leaks in your budget. Time to trim the excess and let your profit margins grow. Because Scorpio rules transformation, be intentional with your focus. Energy flows where attention goes, and your manifesting powers are supercharged now. Don't be surprised if someone you were "just thinking about" suddenly texts. And if it's a late-night flirtation? Sultry Scorpio season knows exactly how to dial up the heat.

SUN-VENUS MEETUP

Today marks a major moment for love and desire! The Sun and retrograde Venus unite at the same degree of Scorpio, forming an "inferior conjunction"—a rare cosmic alignment that only happens every 584 days, right in the heart of Venus's backspin. As Venus ends her "evening star" phase, she disappears from the sky for a few days. Think of this as a new moon for your love life: a blank canvas for mapping your next romantic chapter. You might even want to ritualize the magic of this "Venus Cazimi." Create a love altar with photos, symbols of your dream relationship, or sweet mementos with your S.O. Add a few favorite crystals, pull a tarot card, and let it bask in the sunniest window you can find. Done with a toxic tie? Channel that energy into writing a goodbye letter—then burn it instead of sending it. (Don't worry, you can write a more effective draft after Venus turns direct November 13.) In a few days, Venus will reappear as a "morning star," appearing in the sky at dawn. Ask yourself: What am I ready to put to rest—and what (or who) am I ready to welcome in?

OCT 24-NOV 13 MERCURY RETROGRADE IN SCORPIO

Expressive Mercury turns retrograde in Scorpio, kicking off a cosmic masquerade ball that lasts until November 13. With this backspin unfolding in the zodiac's most secretive sign—and alongside Venus's retrograde in Scorpio and Libra—take nothing at face value. Both planets remain retrograde until November 13, making matters of love, money, and communication especially tricky. Old secrets and unfinished emotional business could resurface, demanding resolution. The challenge? People may not present true to form, and key details could be concealed. If something feels off, channel your inner private investigator and dig quietly behind the scenes—but first, ask if it's even worth your energy. Resist the pull to chase taboos, plot revenge, or let your shadow side run the show. Scorpio energy can stir up obsessions best left alone. Guard your own confidences like a hawk; even a casual tea spill could snowball into a serious breach of trust.

OCT 25 VENUS RETROGRADE ENTERS LIBRA

Venus, planet of romance, beauty, and life's finer things, is still spinning backward. Today she slips from intense, smoldering Scorpio into her home sign of harmony-seeking Libra, where she'll remain retrograde until November 13. If the past few weeks felt like a plunge into karmic entanglements and unresolved passions, this next phase shifts the focus to the delicate art of partnership. Passion or drama? The scales could swing either way as Venus retraces her steps through Libra. Everyone will crave more TLC, but don't expect it to flow perfectly in both directions. Keeping the give-and-take balanced will require extra effort. Exes may resurface, swearing they've changed, but stay clear-eyed about what's real and what's just déjà vu. Wedding on the calendar? No need to cancel the caterers or run off to Vegas. Still, a little premarital counseling couldn't hurt—and for good measure, plan a vow renewal on your first anniversary. (Happily, Venus will NOT be retrograde next fall!)

OCT 26

FULL MOON IN TAURUS (12:12AM; 02°46')

Say yes to abundance! Today's full moon in financially savvy Taurus shines a revealing light on your money mindset. How are you navigating the material world? Sensible yet sensual Taurus is ruled by pleasure goddess Venus. This sign adores its luxuries, but make sure your essentials are covered before you splurge. As ruler of the five senses, this lunar energy reminds you that the simplest comforts can be the sweetest: curling up with a hot mug of tea, cooking a beloved family recipe, soaking in a long bath. Over the next few days, take an unflinching look at your budget. A tense square to intense

Pluto in Aquarius could expose an overlooked expense that needs your attention. Use this lunar moment to anchor a sustainable, soul-nourishing routine—one that lets you savor life's pleasures without tipping into excess.

SUN-PLUTO SQUARE

Tension simmers beneath the surface as the penetrating Scorpio Sun locks into a challenging square with shadowy Pluto in Aquarius. This clash can stir up old resentments or hidden agendas that no one's eager to air out. Yet burying them deeper may only make the pressure mount. Sometimes the dread of confrontation is more draining than facing it head-on. Scorpio's unflinching energy wants to get to the bottom of things, while Pluto in Aquarius pushes for radical reinvention and freedom. You may feel torn between clinging to what's familiar and stepping boldly into new terrain. Use this friction to dismantle stale patterns, but don't strong-arm your way through or people will just rebel against you.

OCT 30 MERCURY-MARS SQUARE #2 OF 3

Round two! Mercury, now retrograde in secretive Scorpio, clashes again with outspoken Mars in Leo, reviving a tense dynamic from earlier this month. Conversations that were left dangling could reignite—only this time, the stakes (and tempers) run even hotter. With Mercury in reverse, misunderstandings are likely and confidential info could spill out at exactly the wrong moment. Resist the urge to flex or fire back if someone tries to provoke you; aggression will only fan the flames. If old resentments bubble up, you don't have to air your grievances on the spot. Not every thought needs to be publicized today. Handle delicate truths with care and remember: Some battles are better defused than fought twice.

OCT 31 HALLOWEEN

This Halloween is basically two parties in one. By day, the moon lingers in cozy Cancer—perfect for carving pumpkins, baking spiced treats, and binging spooky classics under a blanket. But don't even think about ghosting the celebrations, because just after midnight, the moon struts into flamboyant Leo, cranking the volume all the way up on the costumed revelry. After passing out candy, you'll be ready to take your sequins, feathers, and light-up features out on the town. Before you go, ask yourself: How can I raise the bar on my look? A mask or face paint is cute, but the Leo moon wants nothing less than a full-on character transformation.

NOVEMBER

NOVEMBER
Moon Phase Calendar

SUN	MON	TUE	WED	THU	FRI	SAT
PRIORITIZE **1** ♋ ♌ 12:18AM Last Quarter	CONVEY **2** ♌	DIRECT **3** ♌ ♍ 3:28AM	ILLUMINATE **4** ♍	SITUATE **5** ♍ ♎ 9:38AM	SOFTEN **6** ♎	PREPARE **7** ♎ ♏ 5:40PM
TRANSFORM **8** ♏	COMMIT **9** ♏ New Moon 2:02AM	SPARK **10** ♐ 3:36AM	EXPLORE **11** ♐	ELEVATE **12** ♐ ♑ 3:27PM	CLARIFY **13** ♑	REFINE **14** ♑
INNOVATE **15** ♑ ♒ 4:24AM	EXPAND **16** ♒	CONSTRUCT **17** ♒ First Quarter ♓ 4:19PM	STRETCH **18** ♓	REALIGN **19** ♓	IGNITE **20** ♓ ♈ 12:52AM	COMPETE **21** ♈
EMBARK **22** ♈ ♉ 5:10AM	ENVISION **23** ♉	CULMINATE **24** ♉→♊6:10AM Gemini Full Supermoon 9:53AM	REBEL **25** ♊	RETHINK **26** ♊ ♋ 5:51AM	NEST **27** ♋	RESOLVE **28** ♋ ♌ 6:21AM
ADVANCE **29** ♌	SOLIDIFY **30** ♌ ♍ 9:13AM					

Times listed are Eastern US Time Zone

♈	ARIES	♌	LEO	♐	SAGITTARIUS	
♉	TAURUS	♍	VIRGO	♑	CAPRICORN	
♊	GEMINI	♎	LIBRA	♒	AQUARIUS	
♋	CANCER	♏	SCORPIO	♓	PISCES	

FM FULL MOON
NM NEW MOON
LE LUNAR ECLIPSE
SE SOLAR ECLIPSE

NOVEMBER 9, 2:02AM

new moon in Scorpio (16°53')

SCORPIO NEW MOON CRYSTAL

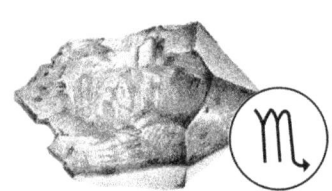

SERPENTINE
With its dramatic swirls of pale yellow and ash grey, this crystal activates the Scorpio kundalini energy, helping you transcend your ego and detoxify your body. Serpentine creates a bridge between the physical and spiritual realms so you can access ancient wisdom and messages from your guides.

SCORPIO NEW MOON = FOCUS

Build trusted bonds

Share secrets

Form strategic partnerships

Explore your erotic nature

Join forces (and finances)

Give everything you do more sizzle and spice

NOVEMBER 24, 9:53AM
full moon in Gemini (2°20')

GEMINI FULL MOON CRYSTAL

DALMATIAN JASPER

This black-and-white-flecked stone helps balance the yin and yang of dualistic Gemini. Dalmatian Jasper can evoke a sense of childlike wonder along with bursts of hope and joy—all while supporting the release of anger and resentment.

GEMINI FULL MOON = CELEBRATE!

Friends who are always up for a hangout

The silly things that make you laugh

Your favorite local haunts

People who are easy to flirt with (no strings attached)

Inside jokes

Books, movies and experiences that stimulate your mind

NOVEMBER
MONTHLY HOTSPOTS

NOV 1 THIRD QUARTER MOON IN LEO

Don't let anyone dim your shine! Today's quarter moon in Leo smooths out the rough edges and polishes them to a gleam. Forget "mid" or "basic"—under these skies, a sprinkle of sparkle is just right. Revive yourself with a burst of glamour, but keep it calibrated. Take a cue from Leo style icon Coco Chanel: "Before you leave the house, look in the mirror and take one thing off." The same principle applies to your calendar, too. Feeling weighed down by obligations? Lighten your load. Since Leo rules the heart and spine, a cardio class, dance session, or even a chiropractic tune-up could help you get back in balance.

NOV 4 SUN-MERCURY RETROGRADE MEETUP

What do you reveal—and what stays behind the curtain? As the Sun shadow-dances with Mercury retrograde in Scorpio, hidden parts of your personality may surface. Expect a layer-cake of feelings to emerge, too, from magnetic attraction to simmering anger to pangs of empathy. Since the Sun illuminates but retrograde Mercury obscures, it's tricky to know how much to share socially. While you don't want to come off as overly mysterious, this is not the day to be an open book. Trust issues could flare, even in the most rock-solid relationships. Do your best not to react impulsively. Under these sensitive skies, egos are more fragile than usual.

NOV 9 NEW MOON IN SCORPIO (2:02AM; 16°53')

Is it gonna last forever? The year's only Scorpio new moon ushers in a powerful new chapter for your deepest investments—emotional, spiritual, financial, and yes, erotic. A connection that begins today could grow into a profound soul bond over the next six months. If a relationship is giving "happily ever after," explore it with courage. This resourceful lunation spotlights shared finances, passive income, and property matters. Over the next couple weeks, you may get the green light to move ahead on a deal involving merged resources. (We recommend waiting until Mercury and Venus both direct on November 13 before making the final call!) Don't overlook your most important asset: your own vitality. If your energy's been low, get a blood-panel done to check all your levels and tend to hormone health. Pleasure is fuel under Scorpio's watch. Nourish it like a sacred investment with sensual practices that awaken your whole system.

NOV 13

MERCURY RETROGRADE ENDS

At last! Fall's dodgy, befuddling interactions begin to clear as Mercury pivots out of a three-week retrograde in Scorpio. With the silver-tongued messenger reversing since October 24, little has been as it seemed. Starting today, wires slowly but surely begin to uncross. Cutthroat dynamics ease into healthy competition—or even (gasp!) cooperation—since Mercury's U-turn reminds us that sharing resources beats hoarding them. That said, don't drop all your defenses. This retrograde may have unmasked a few shady characters. If someone's integrity doesn't hold up, retract the benefit of the doubt and move on. Otherwise, keep vetting your agreements carefully and read the fine print with a magnifying glass.

VENUS RETROGRADE ENDS

Mercury's not the only planet correcting course! Venus is back on the scene, ready to redeem herself for the transgressions of the past six weeks. Since October 3, the love planet has been slogging through a retrograde cycle, challenging hearts and libidos everywhere. This backspin was extra intense since it took place in two of the most relationship-oriented signs: first seductive Scorpio, then marriage-minded Libra, since October 25. Venus turns retrograde every 18 months, and while these phases might afford people a chance to dive deeper into relationship bonding and exploration, they can still rile tension. Starting this evening, the tide turns in a positive direction. Venus spends the rest of 2026 in direct motion retracing her steps through committed Libra then, after December 4, in intimate, ultra-sexy Scorpio. Situations that seemed like lost causes could be blessed with a do-over—and someone you wrote off might actually earn the right to a second chance.

NOV 16 MARS-JUPITER MEETUP

Deck the halls with glitz and glamour. Today's rare Mars-Jupiter conjunction in showstopping Leo sets your spirit ablaze with confidence, charisma and a craving for celebration. Mid-November might usually feel low-key, but not with this cosmic combo: Leo energy wants a full-on festive vibe. Think sparkling outfits, big-hearted gestures and a little extra razzle-dazzle in every plan. Still plotting those end-of-year goals? This star-powered mashup says: Dream bigger and dress

louder. Be more generous with your talents and your holiday spirit. Whether you're planning an over-the-top Friendsgiving or crushing an end-of-year project at work, do NOT (we repeat, do not) shrink to fit in. Mars the warrior and Jupiter the gambler want you to roll the dice on your authentic self-expression. When you shine your light, you give others permission to do the same.

NOV 17 FIRST QUARTER MOON IN AQUARIUS

"Password123" isn't gonna cut it anymore. Today's waxing quarter moon in tech-savvy, community-minded Aquarius urges you to tighten things up—online and off. Digitally, do a quick data audit: Beef up your logins, disable unnecessary location sharing, and tweak those privacy settings so you're not giving away more than you intend. In real life, scan your inner circle. Does trust run deep, or are certain chat threads just breeding gossip and low vibes? If you've been bonding with coworkers over a shared nemesis, shift the conversation. Suggest a morale-boosting brainstorm or a fun offsite event to revive team spirit. And if it's been too long since you saw your besties, organize a cozy fall hang—pumpkin spice optional!

NOV 18 SUN-JUPITER SQUARE

Subtlety is your secret weapon today as the penetrating Scorpio Sun clashes with show-stealing Jupiter in Leo. You may feel tempted to put it all out there, but resist! There's power in restraint. Jupiter in Leo wants a nationally televised debut, while the Scorpio Sun prefers to drip out details for maximum intrigue. If you're flirting with overexposure, keep a few cards tucked close. Not every story needs the spotlight, and quiet confidence speaks louder than a flashy announcement today. Let people lean in, wonder, and crave your next move. Call it seduction 101: Mystery will keep them coming back for more.

NOV 19 SUN-MARS SQUARE

Next stop: King's Landing? As the stormy Scorpio Sun locks horns with fiery Mars in Leo, tempers could flare and power struggles erupt on a dime. Hotheaded reactions, vengeful jabs, and "I must win at all costs" energy may make it feel like everyone's battling for the throne. Keep your stinger sheathed! Flexing your clout just to intimidate will only cast YOU as the villain. Instead, channel the heat into something physical—a sweaty workout can burn off the angst. Creatively, this cosmic clash has benefits too. With focused effort, you can smash through a block. Just don't expect perfection on the first try. Draft, revise, and polish until your vision gleams.

NOV 22–DEC 21 SUN IN SAGITTARIUS (2:23AM)

Go beyond the familiar! The Sun blazes into expansive, open-hearted Sagittarius for the next month, inspiring you to stretch past your usual circles and connect with people from all walks of life. Stay curious and inclusive. A fresh perspective could lead you to new friends, mentors, collaborators—or even a business partner. Sagittarius is the zodiac's entrepreneur and truth-teller. Even as the year winds down, you may feel inspired to launch a media project or broadcast your message to a wider audience. This is a "come one, come all" cycle. Play connector for your crew, or seek out a fresh talent pool to support your next big idea. Straight talk is another Sag specialty, so if there's air to clear, seize the moment before holiday busyness takes over. Should wanderlust strike, answer the call. A quick pre-holiday escape could reset your spirit. If that's not possible, start plotting your next grand adventure—from a cross-country road trip to a once-in-a-lifetime retreat. Widen your horizons and keep your optimism burning bright.

NOV 23 SUN-NEPTUNE TRINE

Ask, believe, receive! The universe drops signs straight into your lap today as the adventurous Sagittarius Sun fist-bumps mystical Neptune in Aries. What—or who—catches your eye? Follow that spark. It may not be the ultimate answer, but it could be the breadcrumb that leads you closer to what you truly want. With this rare fire trine ablaze, passion and possibility align in perfect balance. Watch for people who radiate magnetism and carry a wild, open-hearted spirit that fuels growth. Pay attention to any intuitive hits you get. They'll guide you toward opportunities that make you feel vividly, unmistakably alive.

NOV 24 FULL MOON IN GEMINI (9:53AM; 02°20'; SUPERMOON)

Get that wish list ready! Today's full supermoon in curious Gemini urges you to speak your desires into existence. Want something? Dare to say it out loud. This lunation forms a trine to magnetic Pluto and a conjunction to humanitarian Uranus, giving your words the power to move people. Share boldly—a post about the holiday charity you're backing could draw the kindred spirits you've been looking for. Collaboration is also in the air. DM someone whose work inspires you and see what doors open. That missing puzzle piece could come from a peer—a sibling, coworker, or neighbor who surprises you with exactly what you need. If you don't ask, you don't get.

NOV 25

SUN-URANUS OPPOSITION

For the first time since the 1940s, the adventurous Sagittarius Sun faces off against unpredictable Uranus in curious Gemini. Everyone's nerves might feel extra jumpy under this cosmic tug-of-war. Steer clear of button-pushers and resist the urge to stir the pot yourself. Plans could flip in a heartbeat, so keep your schedule loose and your sense of humor intact. Trying to force a firm answer or a big decision? Not today. Instead, lean into Sagittarius' free-spirited vibe and Gemini's knack for flexibility. A last-minute twist could reveal an option you'd never have considered otherwise. Stay nimble, keep your mind open and remember: Sometimes the detour leads to the best story of all.

MARS IN VIRGO (NOV 25-FEB 21)
Take your inner elf OFF the shelf and start spreading the holiday spirit! Action planet Mars settles into service-oriented Virgo for the rest of 2026. Roll up your sleeves and pitch in to support your loved ones with holiday planning and end-of-year prep. Bitten off more than you can chew? This fix-it-up cycle helps turn lofty plans into something more manageable—and healthier. Streamline gift lists and budgets. Try lighter takes on festive favorites (simpler side dishes, gingerbread cookies sweetened with maple syrup and dates). Virgo's mindful touch also inspires a tidy-up. Clear cluttered spaces and prep your body for the indulgent season with a few extra workouts each week—if only to balance out your love of a cookie tray. Just keep an eye on the nitpicking. Mars in Virgo can crank up criticism, and if you want to reach New Year's without a family feud, some opinions are better left unsaid.

NOV 29 URANUS-PLUTO TRINE #2 OF 2
Power meets progress—again! The second Pluto–Uranus trine of 2026 doubles down on radical reinvention, as visionary Pluto in Aquarius syncs with experimental Uranus in Gemini. This rare, generational aspect fuels breakthroughs that reshape how we connect, communicate, and build community—an ongoing storyline through 2028. Because Uranus is retrograde, this round asks you to dig deeper. What outdated structures or stale beliefs are ready to be scrapped for good? Shocking revelations might open the door to an unconventional path, one that sets you free from what's always been done. On a personal level, the magic lies in experimenting with new ways of thinking. Which part of your future is ready for an upgrade? And how far into the quantum field are you willing to go to make it happen? You're quickly discovering that old limits are no longer standing in the way!

NOV 30 SUN-SATURN TRINE
Take the lead with warmth and wisdom! As the vibrant Sagittarius Sun teams up with scrappy Saturn in Aries, you can push year-end goals forward without steamrolling anyone. This cosmic combo favors creative leadership. Empower your crew with encouragement and genuine interest in their ideas. People thrive when they know you believe in them—and soar when they feel seen in their highest light. Whether you're managing a holiday project, hosting family, or coordinating a last-minute getaway, show that you value every contribution. And don't forget your sense of humor!

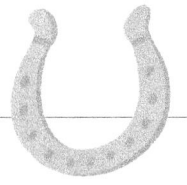

DECEMBER

DECEMBER
Moon Phase Calendar

SUN	MON	TUE	WED	THU	FRI	SAT
		DISCERN **1** ♍ Last Quarter	REALIGN **2** ♍ ♎ 3:04PM	MEDIATE **3** ♎	DISTURB **4** ♎ ♏ 11:35PM	INVESTIGATE **5** ♏
EXPAND **6** ♏	VISUALIZE **7** ♏ ♐ 10:07AM	LAUNCH **8** ♐ New Moon 7:52PM	STIR **9** ♐ ♑ 10:09PM	GROUND **10** ♑	STABILIZE **11** ♑	TRANSITION **12** ♑ ♒ 11:06AM
AWAKEN **13** ♒	BRIDGE **14** ♒ ♓ 11:36PM	ENCHANT **15** ♓	SOFTEN **16** ♓	INITIATE **17** ♓ First Quarter ♈ 9:34AM	AFFIRM **18** ♈	ESTABLISH **19** ♈ ♉ 3:30PM
FORTIFY **20** ♉	REFOCUS **21** ♉ ♊ 5:27PM	EXPRESS **22** ♊	CULMINATE **23** ♊→♋ 4:58PM Full Supermoon 8:28PM	COMFORT **24** ♋	REFLECT **25** ♋ ♌ 4:12PM	CONFUSE **26** ♌
OBSERVE **27** ♌ ♍ 5:13PM	REFINE **28** ♍	CONFRONT **29** ♍ ♎ 9:27PM	CONSERVE **30** ♎ Last Quarter	MOTIVATE **31** ♎		

Times listed are Eastern US Time Zone

KEY

- ♈ ARIES
- ♉ TAURUS
- ♊ GEMINI
- ♋ CANCER
- ♌ LEO
- ♍ VIRGO
- ♎ LIBRA
- ♏ SCORPIO
- ♐ SAGITTARIUS
- ♑ CAPRICORN
- ♒ AQUARIUS
- ♓ PISCES
- **FM** FULL MOON
- **NM** NEW MOON
- **LE** LUNAR ECLIPSE
- **SE** SOLAR ECLIPSE

DECEMBER 8, 7:52PM

new moon in Sagittarius (16°57')

SAGITTARIUS NEW MOON CRYSTAL

LAPIS LAZULI
This bright blue, high-vibrational stone helps you tap into your inner wisdom and gain confidence with self-expression. Lapis Lazuli connects you to the Sagittarian values of integrity, clarity and intuition.

SAGITTARIUS NEW MOON = FOCUS

Turn each day into an adventure

Travel to new places—locally and globally

Broaden your social horizons

Speak your truth while hearing new perspectives

Study and invest in self-development

Make media and share your message

DECEMBER 23, 8:28PM
full moon in Cancer #2 (2°14')

CANCER FULL MOON CRYSTAL

SELENITE

This calm and soothing gemstone forms in long bands and has a high, clear and pure vibration. Named after Selene, the goddess of the Cancer-ruled moon, this crystal is believed to help the flow of bodily fluids and support fertility. Since selenite does not hold negative charges, it is fantastic to use to neutralize your own energy. Like a "crystal crab shell," selenite is often used to make a protective energetic "grid" around your house or workspace.

CANCER FULL MOON = CELEBRATE!

Your divine emotional intelligence

The importance of creating safe spaces

The power of family—blood-related or chosen

Intuitive hits that guide you toward your dreams

The healing power of water

Mother figures and your own maternal instincts

DECEMBER
MONTHLY HOTSPOTS

DEC 1 THIRD QUARTER MOON IN VIRGO

Don't sweat the small stuff—but don't sweep it aside either. Today's quarter moon in meticulous Virgo spotlights the tiny details that keep life humming like a well-tuned engine. Give your plans a loving polish. Is everything clear, organized, and typo-free? Before hitting send on an important message, run it by a sharp-eyed friend who can catch what you might miss. If perfectionism creeps in, pause for a reality check. Are your expectations higher than people can realistically deliver right now? This lunar checkpoint can help you find capable helpers—or inspire you to simplify your plans so you're not juggling more than necessary. A few thoughtful tweaks today could save you a mountain of stress later.

DEC 2 JUPITER-CHIRON TRINE

Big-hearted Jupiter in radiant Leo forms a rare connection to wounded healer Chiron in brave Aries, helping you shed lingering feelings of insufficiency. If you've been hiding behind a cloak of invisibility, this expansive aspect can reveal where you're ready to step into the spotlight and be truly seen—flaws, gifts and all. Old wounds around recognition and validation soften now, replaced by genuine self-belief. Your voice, talents and presence matter!

DEC 4

MERCURY-JUPITER SQUARE

It's easy to take things personally today as Mercury in probing Scorpio locks into a tense square with larger-than-life Jupiter in Leo. Competitive vibes could flare, especially if someone seems to be hogging all the attention or overshadowing your efforts. But before you let jealousy get the best of you, pause and check in: Could envy be pointing you toward something you truly want? Use it as a compass instead of a trap. This cosmic clash can help you uncover where you're craving more recognition or room to shine—then find a stage that's meant to be yours.

VENUS IN SCORPIO (DEC 4-JAN 7, 2027)

If you thought your love life couldn't get more intriguing, guess again. Venus returns to magnetic Scorpio for the second time this year, adding one last swirl of passion and depth to 2026. From September 10 to October

25—much of it during her retrograde—hidden feelings and old attractions resurfaced. Now you get a second chance to cultivate genuine intimacy. Secrets may emerge, but if handled with care, they can strengthen your bond. If trust wobbled, the next four weeks offer solid ground to rebuild it. Venus in Scorpio favors loyalty that runs soul-deep, so be sure you're ready to give (and receive!) that level of devotion before reopening any doors.

MARS-URANUS SQUARE

Avoid making impulsive moves today—especially in relationships—as hotheaded Mars in practical-but-picky Virgo locks into a tense square with unpredictable Uranus in Gemini. An urge to shake things up could feel strong, but the fallout could be devastating. Resist! And keep those sharp-tongued clapbacks in check. The line between "productive change" and "total chaos" is razor-thin now. Make sure you are fully briefed before charging ahead on any missions. Or, wait a beat. This buzzy energy is best used for researching, brainstorming and tasks that require mental agility.

DEC 6–25 MERCURY IN SAGITTARIUS

Authenticity is back on trend as messenger planet Mercury fires arrows into Sagittarius' domain. But if you let the cat out of the bag, be ready to defend your principles with tiger-level fierceness. Instead of getting tangled in endless debates, use the next few weeks to explore perspectives beyond your echo chamber. Your worldview could expand in surprising ways. In Sagittarius, Mercury is blunt—sometimes brilliantly sharp, sometimes cutting. Once words are spoken, there's no walking them back. That gamble could even get you canceled, so lean into open-mindedness rather than playing the know-it-all. Build bridges with humor when it's appropriate. As Sagittarian Mark Twain reminded us, the human race "has one really effective weapon, and that is laughter."

DEC 7 MERCURY-NEPTUNE TRINE

Warm connections flow with ease today as outspoken Mercury in Sagittarius harmonizes with dreamy Neptune in Aries. This gentle trine blends candor with compassion, helping you speak your truth without trampling anyone's feelings. If you've been waiting for the right moment to clear the air, share your heart, or offer forgiveness, the cosmic mic is on. Inspiration also runs high! Capture any intuitive flashes and creative downloads, which could be gems worth polishing in the days ahead.

DEC 8

MERCURY-URANUS OPPOSITION

An ambitious vision may need a reality check today, as Mercury in Sagittarius faces off with unpredictable Uranus in Gemini. If you've been charging ahead without testing the details, a sudden twist could reveal where things aren't as solid as they seemed. Stay flexible—what looks like an annoying detour might save you from a bigger mess down the line. Beware the contrarian. A rabble-rouser could throw a last-minute wrench into travel or communication plans. Keep your cool, think on your feet and have a backup plan ready.

NEW MOON IN SAGITTARIUS (7:52PM; 16°57')
Shots of truth serum on the house! The final new moon of 2026 lands in tell-it-like-it-is Sagittarius. At last, the freedom to speak your mind—while entertaining your audience with raucous tales. New moons are starting blocks, and this one is a rocket launcher into galaxies far and wide. Would a change of scenery refresh your feed and revive your spirits? Let these nomadic moonbeams inspire a spontaneous getaway. Or set up those fare savers and start socking away funds for the 2027 retreat you bookmarked months ago. Close to home, this lunar lift doubles as diversity training. When was the last time you went beyond surface-level exchanges with someone from a vastly different background than your own? This philosophical new moon creates space for curiosity and some refreshing real talk.

DEC 9

MERCURY-MARS SQUARE #3 OF 3
For the third and final time this season, Mercury squares off with Mars—this round featuring Mercury in big-picture Sagittarius and Mars in detail-driven Virgo. The earlier clashes in October stirred secrets and egos. Now, the risk is overanalysis that derails progress. You may feel torn between seeing the whole forest (Mercury in Sag) and obsessing over every single tree (Mars in Virgo). Heated debates over details could flare, so choose your battles wisely. Stay flexible, resist the urge to dismantle something just to prove a point, and don't let perfectionism stall your momentum. Avoid the weeds, and you could turn this into one of the most productive days of the week.

VENUS-PLUTO SQUARE #3 OF 3
Round three! Venus clashes with Pluto for the third and final time this season, stirring up another emotional storm system. This time, however, Venus has finished her retrograde and is charging full steam ahead in smoldering Scorpio. If power struggles or buried feelings erupted earlier this fall, they could resurface now—this time with a chance to resolve or transform them. Deep attractions and hidden agendas may bubble back up, igniting potent waves of desire, jealousy or control. Secrets could surface and trust issues may feel especially raw. Woosh! Passion is undeniable, but it's easy to slip

into obsession or manipulation if you start to feel insecure. Channel this energy into honest dialogue about what you truly crave—without the games.

DEC 10 SATURN RETROGRADE ENDS
Taskmaster Saturn straightens out after a five-month retrograde in fierce, independent Aries. Since July 26, Saturn's backspin has challenged you to look at how you assert yourself, set boundaries and take charge of your goals. It may not have been easy—growing up rarely is—but you've likely gained priceless lessons about self-leadership, courage and personal responsibility. Now, with Saturn moving forward, put that wisdom into action. Where do you need to show up with more discipline or resilience? Saturn rules mentorship. In the days ahead, you may be tapped to guide others through something you've mastered yourself.

DEC 11 MERCURY-SATURN TRINE
Santa's not the only one making lists today! With Mercury in adventurous Sagittarius aligning with Saturn in steady Aries, your holiday visions could creep from "modest" to "all-star extravaganza." Before you overstuff the sleigh, ground those grand ideas in a realistic plan. What can you actually wrap up today without turning it into a stress-fest? Trim back anything that feels too much like a major production, and find that balance between dashing through the snow and pacing yourself like a pro.

DEC 12

NEPTUNE RETROGRADE ENDS
What's next? For the past five months, that question may have lingered without resolution as Neptune's retrograde in Aries stirred deep reflection about your identity and purpose. You may have felt foggy or uninspired, but as the numinous planet corrects its course today, clarity begins to filter back in. Clear signals come from your own psyche—perhaps along with messages from ancestors and guides. Begin dreamweaving again, now with decisive action. Pull out half-finished creative projects and return to a spiritual practice that may have languished since the retrograde began on July 7. As Neptune turns direct, generosity and compassion flow more freely, too, nudging you to embody the season's giving spirit. Bye-bye, Scrooge—the rest of 2026 is all about open hearts and soul-sized gifts.

JUPITER RETROGRADE (DEC 12-APR 12, 2027)
Lights, camera…reflection! With starry-eyed Jupiter backpedaling through flamboyant Leo, the "greatest show on Earth" takes an intermission. Use this pause to rehearse, refine and rebuild—whether that means polishing your creative work, training as a leader or refreshing your brand. Why not enroll in a

little "star school" while you're at it? Painting, music, acting, public speaking—anything that helps you shine with ease belongs on the roster. Leo also rules fertility, play and the pure joy of self-expression, so surround yourself with the children in your life—or let your own inner child run the show. Laugh, create, play without judgment. That simple joy heals old fears of being seen and builds real confidence. By the time Jupiter powers forward in April, you'll be ready to step into the spotlight again—this time radiating a joy that can't be ignored.

DEC 17 FIRST QUARTER MOON IN PISCES

What's NOT being said? Slow down and listen under today's quarter moon in intuitive Pisces. Subtle cues—body language, tone, a sudden gut feeling—speak louder than words. If Sagittarius season has tempted you to overshare, balance that openness with a touch of mystery. Hold back, observe, say less. Has life been buzzing with plans and parties? Recentering is essential: slip into quiet moments for rest and spiritual check-ins. Go easy on stimulants like sugar or caffeine, and let your system reset. This midpoint moon can spark bursts of divinely inspired imagination. Your inner voice grows strongest when you give it the quiet to be heard.

DEC 18 SUN-JUPITER TRINE

Mic drops incoming! The radiant Sun in Sagittarius links up with retrograde Jupiter in Leo, handing you the cosmic megaphone. Your words, your moves, your mere presence—everything comes with extra sparkle today. But with Jupiter retrograde, don't get swept up in "opening night" vibes. Think of it as a dress rehearsal where you can test out material, refine your lines and figure out what really lands with your audience. Start with your inner circle—the folks who hype you up without judgment—then take your truth to a wider stage. Holiday party? Instagram post? Spontaneous karaoke mic grab? All fair game. Share your story with joy, and let the applause teach you where to shine brighter next time.

DEC 21–JAN 20 SUN IN CAPRICORN (3:50PM)

It's beginning to look a lot like solstice! The shortest day of the year in the northern hemisphere ushers in steadfast Capricorn season, guided by the tireless Sea Goat who climbs any mountain, no matter how steep. Enjoy the holiday revelry, but in between family gatherings, channel this earth sign's gift of discipline, patience and practicality. Over the next four weeks, ambitious Capricorn inspires you to set clear goals and make steady, step-by-step progress. Cast your gaze forward—where do you want to be by 2027? Start sketching a realistic roadmap now. This grounded sign also calls for generosity with boundaries. Pass along your hard-won wisdom, mentor someone just starting out, or extend a hand to a friend in need. Whatever you invest—in people or in projects—will circle back in time, stronger and sweeter than before.

DEC 23

SUN-NEPTUNE SQUARE

Feeling scattered? The sensible Capricorn Sun locks horns with dreamy Neptune in impulsive Aries today, making it all too easy to drift off course. Bring yourself back to Earth by focusing on a single goal instead of chasing a dozen half-baked ones. Sort your unfinished tasks into two piles: "Save it for 2027" and "Get on it ASAP." This cosmic combo is perfect for mapping out the final details of your holiday plans. Who's bringing dessert? Are you stocked on wine? Take a moment to rally your people and share the plan—a little structure today means more time to actually enjoy the festivities tomorrow.

MERCURY-JUPITER TRINE

Holly jolly vibes incoming! With festive Mercury in Sagittarius teaming up with generous Jupiter in warmhearted Leo, spread good cheer far and wide. Big ideas and sweet gestures flow easily—think last-minute gift-wrapping parties with friends or teaming up on errands. Is someone making a Costco run? Maybe they could pick up some items on your list while you slip an extra pie in the oven for them to serve at their dinner tomorrow. You may be feeling especially magnanimous, but careful you don't make promises that you can't realistically keep. Before you offer to pick anyone up from the airport, check what you've already committed to. Keep the spirit big but your tasks doable, so you actually have energy left to ENJOY the holiday spirit!

FULL MOON IN CANCER (8:28PM; 02°14'; SUPERMOON)

Just in time for the holidays, the final full moon of 2026 slides down Cancer's garland-strewn chimney. With emotions running high under this potent supermoon, even a small caring gesture can warm someone's heart. Home and family take center stage, inspiring you to nest, whip up comfort food or open your doors to someone needing extra TLC. Missing a loved one? Reach out with a sweet call or message. Wrap your words with compassion. Sometimes the coziest gift is simply making someone feel safe and understood. Thinking about a change at home? From fresh decor to a new address, this full moon can spark the shift. Too busy with the holidays to make a big change? Pull together a mood board so you don't lose your momentum!

DEC 25–JAN 13, 2027 MERCURY IN CAPRICORN

Master strategist Mercury slides into ambitious Capricorn on Christmas Day, adding a grounded, elegant note to the festivities. This is a natural moment to honor traditions and raise a toast to the steady providers and wise elders who helped shape your story. Over the next few weeks, as Mercury moves through this industrious earth sign, your thoughts may drift toward the year ahead—and even further. Sketch out your 2027 goals, keeping budgets, timelines and practical steps in mind. The Sea Goat favors plans with staying power. Polish your proposals, refine your pitch or simply share your ideas with clarity. The more intentional your words, the wider the doors will swing open.

DEC 26 MERCURY-NEPTUNE SQUARE

It might be Boxing Day, but your mind is busy unwrapping a dozen half-formed ideas. With analytical Mercury in practical Capricorn squaring off with hazy Neptune in impulsive Aries, your logical side wrestles with your desire to drift off like a fluffy cloud on the horizon. One minute you're mapping goals for the new year; the next, you're tempted to toss plans aside for an exciting detour. Keep your feet on the ground as you sort through options. Take a quiet moment to reflect before making any big promises. And if you're feeling foggy, tackle small tasks you can check off with confidence—one box at a time!

DEC 29 SUN-SATURN SQUARE

Your 2027 resolutions start to crystallize as the steady Capricorn Sun squares tough-love Saturn in Aries today. This combination shines a light on what's working—and what really isn't. Maybe you've promised more than you can deliver, or you're bumping up against limits you can't ignore. Don't see this as defeat. Instead, get honest about the results you want and the habits you'll need to shift to get there. Go back to the drawing board, adjust your plan and brainstorm supportive daily actions like checking in with an accountability buddy. A few thoughtful tweaks now will set you up for resolutions that actually stick in the new year.

DEC 30

MERCURY-SATURN SQUARE

Unless you're actually trying to squeeze blood from a stone, today's planetary face-off might be your cue to stop wasting energy when it's not going anywhere. With rational Mercury in Capricorn squaring off with headstrong Saturn in Aries, some people may dig in their heels just to prove a point. If you're hitting constant resistance, take it as your sign to walk away—or at least put this on ice until 2027. Use your resources wisely by shifting your focus to something that CAN move forward. When the universe closes one door, it's often giving you space to find a better one that actually opens.

THIRD QUARTER MOON IN LIBRA

Have you been putting off an important discussion or avoiding a conflict that's been brewing amid December's holiday stress? Today's waning quarter moon in Libra urges you to stand up for what's fair and just. This diplomatic energy supplies a level head as you wade into tricky waters. Even if you're feeling wounded or defensive, resist the urge to strike back—that will only inflame the situation. If the facts are on your side, you'll be fine. But a little digging could also reveal that you're partly in the wrong. If so, own it and say the words that heal: "I'm sorry."

DEC 31

SUN-MARS TRINE

It's the final morning of 2026—and the Sun in organized Capricorn forms a supportive trine to productive Mars in detail-driven Virgo. Translation? You've got fuel to confirm every last piece of your New Year's Eve, so the night goes off without a hitch. Use this can-do energy to run last-minute errands, prep your outfit and double-check who's bringing what to the party. Check the weather and make sure reservations are all set. If you're hosting, this earthy trine rewards practical steps and thoughtful touches—think playlists, extra snacks or a cozy wind-down plan for later. A little effort early in the day will free you up to be in full celebration mode once the clock strikes midnight.

MERCURY-MARS TRINE

Raise a glass and ring in 2027 with words as sharp as your outfit! Tonight's Mercury-Mars trine gifts you with clear, confident conversation—and a little extra swagger to back it up. With strategic Mercury in no-nonsense Capricorn syncing to action-hungry Mars in Virgo, your plans can run like clockwork without feeling stiff. Meanwhile, the waning crescent moon in Libra sprinkles on charm, lightening the mood even if you're slipping in some truth bombs at midnight. Stay grounded so you can savor it all: the champagne fizz, the whispered confessions, and that electric surge of hope as the clock strikes twelve. The next chapter begins in 3, 2, 1...

THE SUN IN 2026

PLANNING WITH THE SUN
The Zodiac Seasons

Planning with The Sun: The Zodiac Seasons
Break out the cake and candles! On the third week of every month, the Sun changes signs and initiates a brand-new zodiac "season." These four-week cycles show where opportunities are brightest and where your efforts will yield the sparkliest results. Think of each solar season like a costume party. What is it like to live like a Gemini or a Pisces for a month? Try it on for size!

season	focus
CAPRICORN DEC 21, 2025 10:03AM Winter Solstice	Earthy Capricorn's drive makes this the month to aim higher; then apply steady, disciplined effort to hit your goal. Network with VIPs during Capricorn season. Mentor someone younger or new to the game.
AQUARIUS JAN 19 8:45PM	Weird is wonderful during airy, eccentric Aquarius season. Allow yourself to stand out in the crowd while also embracing the spirit of community. You can be different AND belong when this air sign rules the skies.
PISCES FEB 18 10:52AM	Compassionate, creative Pisces season invites you to feel deeply and heal wholly. Dive into your emotions and alchemize them into art—your empathy becomes your magic during this watery spell.
ARIES MAR 20 10:46AM Spring Equinox	Fiery Aries is the first sign in the zodiac, making this season all about blazing trails and starting fresh. Get to know what makes you tick by daring to do more things independently.
TAURUS APR 19 3:56PM	Rooted earth sign Taurus reminds us of the importance of comfort and security. Review your finances, update your accounts, create a budget—both for practical necessities and life-enhancing luxuries. Inspect your personal goods—clothing, furniture, dwelling, accessories—and ensure everything is in good working order.

season	focus
GEMINI MAY 20 8:37PM	How well do you collaborate? Gemini season highlights communication and connection. Skip assumptions and start asking curious questions—that's the key to crafting true win-wins under this air sign's reign.
CANCER JUN 21 4:24AM Summer Solstice	Home sweet sanctuary! Nurturing Cancer, a cardinal water sign, rules family and emotional roots. Reconnect with loved ones and make your space a cozy, supportive haven that flows with your current life.
LEO JUL 22 3:13PM	We all have a special light to shine, as fire sign Leo reminds us. Lift the curtain during this zodiac season and show the world what you're made of. Let your wilder romantic nature come out to play and wear your heart on your sleeve!
VIRGO AUG 22 10:19PM	Earthy Virgo is the sign of service. Where would a random act of generosity make a difference for someone else? Be humble and helpful. The simplest approach is the best during this season.
LIBRA SEP 22 8:05PM Fall Equinox	Peace, love and harmony! These are lofty ideals, but Libra season invites us to live them. Practice the kindness, collaboration and balance this air sign encourages—and let opposites attract by staying open to different energies.
SCORPIO OCT 23 5:38AM	Sultry, transformative Scorpio dives fearlessly into life's mysteries and primal urges. This intuitive water sign season dares you to explore your deepest desires and bring your raw passion to the surface.
SAGITTARIUS NOV 22 2:23AM	What's happening on the other side of the globe, fence or aisle? Fire sign Sagittarius is the zodiac's ambassador. Reach across so-called boundaries to learn what makes others tick during this season. Travel or plan your next amazing journey.
CAPRICORN DEC 21 3:50PM Winter Solstice	The Sun swings back around into Capricorn at the end of every year putting the focus on the traditional side of this sign. Get to know a family custom and look for special ways you can provide support and happiness to your inner circle.

THE MOON IN 2025

MOTIVATE & MANIFEST WITH THE
New & Full Moons

MOTIVATE AND MANIFEST WITH THE MONTHLY MOON PHASES

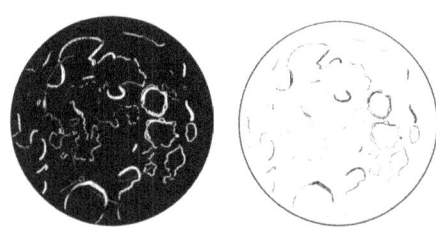

Following moon cycles is a great way to set goals and reap their benefits. Astrologers believe that our energy awakens at the new moon, then peaks two weeks later at the full moon. By tracking the moon, we can tap into our intuition and set goals that match our energy levels best throughout the month.

NEW MOONS mark beginnings and are the optimal time to kick off any new projects or plans. Lay the groundwork for what you want to manifest in the coming six months. Set intentions or initiate action while you have this lunar lift creating momentum.

FULL MOONS emonies where you get to show off and celebrate your hard work of the past six months. Full moons dial up feelings and can provoke emotional outpourings. It's time to cash in—or cash out, if you're ready for something new.

SUPERMOONS a new or full moon that arrives at a closer-than-usual distance to Earth. Supermoons occur about three or four times a year, some years more often. There are five supermoons in 2026, indicated in the table below.

PLAN YOUR LONG-TERM GOALS BY THE MOON (SIX-MONTH WINDOW):

Each new moon falls in a specific zodiac sign. Six months later, a full moon occurs in the very same sign, completing the cycle. Tracking the moon's journey by zodiac sign is a great way to set longer-term goals every year.

PLAN YOUR SHORT-TERM GOALS BY THE MOON (TWO-WEEK WINDOW):

Every month, the skies deliver a new moon and full moon, spaced two weeks apart. Set intentions and begin projects at the new moon, then check in at the full moon—is this idea a keeper? In the weeks between the new and full moon we have a quarter moon, a great time to balance. The quarter moon phase is either waxing (growing from new to full) or waning (dwindling from full to new).

phase	date	focus/celebrate
FULL MOON **CANCER #1** (13°02')	JAN 3 5:03AM	**Celebrate:** Bonds with your family and inner circle of friends, the places where you feel at home, nostalgic memories, creative alone time.
NEW MOON **CAPRICORN** (28°44')	JAN 18 2:52PM	**Focus:** Set goals that challenge and inspire you, elevate your image to be more professional, connect to authority figures and mentors, make a long-term plan.
FULL MOON **LEO** (13°04')	FEB 1 5:09PM	**Celebrate:** The unique way that you shine, the people who make your heart sing, your romantic nature, fashion sense, childlike wonder, the places where you feel like a natural leader and your fiercely competitive streak that won't let you quit on yourself.
NEW MOON **AQUARIUS** (28°50')	FEB 17 7:01AM	**ANNULAR SOLAR ECLIPSE** **Focus:** Experiment with new technology and techniques, break out of the box with style and social expression, connect to community, activism and humanitarian work.
FULL MOON **VIRGO** (12°54')	MAR 3 6:38AM	**TOTAL LUNAR ECLIPSE** **Celebrate:** The serenity of a freshly cleaned space, streamlined systems, your helpful spirit, being of service to those in need, taking great care of your body by eating clean and exercising, the magic of nature and natural beauty.
NEW MOON **PISCES** (28°27')	MAR 18 9:23PM	**Focus:** Connect to your dreams, spiritual exploration, find creative outlets, give back, inspire others, form supportive alliances, express empathy so people feel seen and understood.

phase	date	focus/celebrate
FULL MOON LIBRA (12°21′)	APR 1 10:12PM	**Celebrate:** The power of partnerships and synergistic connections, dressing up and socializing, transcendent music and the arts, peaceful moments of serenity, the parts of your life that are in beautiful balance.
NEW MOON ARIES (27°29′)	APR 17 7:52AM	**Focus:** Sharpen your competitive edge, blaze your own trail, take the initiative with people and activities that matter to you, try new things.
FULL MOON SCORPIO (11°21′)	MAY 1 1:23PM	**Celebrate:** Your loyal and caring spirit, intense exchanges, the sexiest parts of yourself, the ways you've transformed your struggles into gold, true friendship, resourcefulness and raw creative expression.
NEW MOON TAURUS (25°58′)	MAY 16 4:01PM	**SUPERMOON** **Focus:** Define your values, set up healthy and rewarding routines, enjoy arts and culture, simplify complexities, budget, get out in nature.
FULL MOON SAGITTARIUS (9°56′)	MAY 31 4:45AM	**Celebrate:** The spirit of wanderlust, your unvarnished truths, people you love who live far away, the passport stamps you've collected or hope to one day, visionary ideas that you're bringing to life, diversity and cross-cultural connections.
NEW MOON GEMINI (24°03′)	JUN 14 10:54PM	**SUPERMOON** **Focus:** Sharpen your communication style, write and make media, pair up on short-term collaborations, socialize with new people, become active in your local community, flirt and joke!

phase	date	focus/celebrate
FULL MOON **CAPRICORN** (8°15')	JUN 29 7:57PM	**Celebrate:** People you admire—heroes and mentors, family legacies, customs that you want to carry on, enduring friendships and business relationships, your most ambitious ideas, institutions or organizations that you believe in and support.
NEW MOON **CANCER** (21°59')	JUL 14 5:44AM	**SUPERMOON** **Focus:** Nourish yourself with good food and close friends, spruce up your spaces so you feel at home everywhere, connect to family, spend time near water, get in touch with your emotions.
FULL MOON **AQUARIUS** (6°30')	JUL 29 10:36AM	**Celebrate:** Your weirdest ideas, teams and communities where you feel seen and embraced, your sharing and accepting spirit, technology that keeps you connected, hopes and dreams for the future, your idealistic nature that refuses to give up on humanity.
NEW MOON **LEO** (20°02')	AUG 12 1:37PM	**TOTAL SOLAR ECLIPSE** **Focus:** Express yourself through art and style, enjoy romance and playtime, spend time with kids, take a leadership role, host and attend glamorous parties, find your place to shine.
FULL MOON **PISCES** (4°54')	AUG 28 12:18AM	**PARTIAL LUNAR ECLIPSE** **Celebrate:** Your secret fantasies, your creative spirit, messages from your dreams, people who inspire you to think beyond current limitations, compassion and empathy, blurry lines that don't need to be sharpened, the beauty in "ugly" things.
NEW MOON **VIRGO** (18°26')	SEP 10 11:27PM	**Focus:** Embrace healthy routines, work out and eat clean, implement efficient systems, hire service providers and assistants, break projects into actionable steps, be of service, adopt a pet.

phase	date	focus/celebrate
FULL MOON ARIES (3°37')	SEP 26 12:49PM	**Celebrate:** Your inner (and outer) bad bitch, new experiences you're brave enough to try, your competitive nature, every unique feature that makes you a rare individual, your fighting spirit that won't give up.
NEW MOON LIBRA (17°22')	OCT 10 11:50AM	**Focus:** Find synergies, network to build your contact list, nurture romantic relationships, enjoy art, music and fashion, and beautify everything.
FULL MOON TAURUS (2°46')	OCT 26 12:12AM	**Celebrate:** The simple things that bring you joy, the beauty of nature, your favorite music and artists, finding holiday gifts that are sustainable and earth-friendly, creating a comfortable home environment and food that you love.
NEW MOON SCORPIO (16°53')	NOV 9 2:02AM	**Focus:** Build trusted bonds, share secrets, join forces (and finances), form strategic partnerships, explore your erotic nature, give everything you do more sizzle and spice.
FULL MOON GEMINI (2°20)	NOV 24 9:53AM	**SUPERMOON** **Celebrate:** Friends who are always up for a hangout, the silly things that make you laugh, your favorite local haunts, people who are easy to flirt with (no strings attached), inside jokes, books, movies and experiences that stimulate your mind.
NEW MOON SAGITTARIUS (16°57')	DEC 8 7:52PM	**Focus:** Turn each day into an adventure, broaden your social horizons, travel, study and self-development goals, make media, speak your truth.
FULL MOON CANCER #2 (2°14')	DEC 23 8:28PM	**SUPERMOON** **Celebrate:** Bonds with your family and inner circle of friends, the places where you feel at home, nostalgic memories, creative alone time.

ECLIPSES IN 2026

Eclipses

THESE YEARLY MOON MOMENTS SHAKE UP LIFE AS WE KNOW IT

Eclipses arrive four to six times each year, igniting unexpected changes and turning points. If you've been mired in confusion, an eclipse may force you to act, whether you're ready or not. Unanticipated events arise and demand a radical change of direction. Since eclipses reveal shadows, get ready for buried truths and secrets to explode into the open. Situations that are no longer "meant to be" are swept away without notice. Shocking though their delivery may be, eclipses help open up space for progress.

SOLAR VERSUS LUNAR ECLIPSES

A **solar eclipse** takes place when the new moon passes between the Sun and the Earth, temporarily blocking out the light of the Sun. The effect is like a spiritual power outage—you either feel wildly off center or your mind becomes crystal clear in the darkness.

Lunar eclipses arrive at full moons. The Earth passes directly between the Sun and the moon, cutting off their "communication" and casting a blood red shadow on the full moon. Situations could pivot abruptly or come to a sudden, unceremonious halt. There's no way around it. During a lunar eclipse, you have to deal with the stormy feelings that arise.

FEB 17	MAR 3	AUG 12	AUG 28
Eclipse #1	*Eclipse #2*	*Eclipse #3*	*Eclipse #4*
7:01AM	6:38AM	1:37PM	12:18AM
Annular Solar Eclipse in Aquarius (28°50')	Total Lunar Eclipse in Virgo (12°54')	Total Solar Eclipse in Leo (20°02')	Partial Lunar Eclipse in Pisces (04°54')

All dates and times in Eastern Time Zone

Eclipse #1

FEB 17 (7:01 AM) ANNULAR SOLAR ECLIPSE IN AQUARIUS (28°50')

Ready to spark a revolution? The 2026 new moon in Aquarius is also the first eclipse to land in the sign of the Water Bearer since 2016. That's not all! This lunation initiates a new eclipse series on the Aquarius-Leo axis that runs until January 2028. If you've been stuck in a rut, that ends today. As an annular "ring of fire" solar eclipse, this lunation incites breakthrough innovations and collective progress. Release outdated thinking and envision a future that aligns with your highest ideals. The Lunar Year of the Fire Horse begins today, too, doubling down on the call to blaze new trails and ignite world-changing momentum. Technology, community and social impact are part of the narrative.

Eclipse #2

MAR 3 (6:38AM) TOTAL LUNAR ECLIPSE IN VIRGO (12°54')

Spring cleaning is an inside job under the 2026 full moon in Virgo, a total lunar eclipse. As the Earth's shadow turns the moon blood red, draw your gaze inward for some all-important shadow work. This analytic and emotional lunation helps you identify patterns running beneath the surface, especially around wellness and the ways you show up in service to others. Ditch the harsh self-criticism and embrace the opportunity for honest illumination. Which habits sustain you and which slowly drain your energy? Use this eclipse to clear space—not just in your calendar or cupboards, but in the corners of your psyche—so the next chapter can take root.

Eclipse #3

AUG 12 (1:37PM) TOTAL SOLAR ECLIPSE IN LEO (20°02')

A dramatic reset roars in with the 2026 new moon in Leo, a breathtaking total solar eclipse. As the Sun is completely veiled, you're called to rediscover the true source of your light—your spiritual self. This eclipse echoes the seismic August 21, 2017 "Great American Eclipse" and marks the first Leo eclipse since January 2019. Get ready for a powerful continuation of themes around courage, creativity and self-expression. Where are you ready to reclaim the spotlight—or step into it for the first time? Use this lunation to plant seeds for joy and passion, ones that come from the pure thrill of expressing yourself freely.

Eclipse # 4

AUG 28 (12:18AM) PARTIAL LUNAR ECLIPSE IN PISCES (04°54')

What are you holding on to—and are you finally ready to release it? The partial lunar eclipse in Pisces can accelerate your "letting go" process. As the Earth's shadow partially crosses the Moon, you may see clearly where you've been holding on too tightly or avoiding deeper feelings that have been uncomfortable to process. Epiphanies await as this eclipse turns your focus to intuition, healing and emotional well-being. Old dreams or creative callings might resurface, reminding you of what truly feeds your soul. Let this be your catalyst to clear emotional baggage and realign with what feels meaningful on a soul level.

INNER PLANETS IN 2026

Mercury

Messenger Mercury is the ruler of information, communication and our intellectual processes. The closest planet to the Sun, Mercury orbits through each zodiac sign for approximately three weeks. These cycles shape our cultural interests. From the topics we're buzzing about to the ways we communicate, whatever sign Mercury is occupying plays a role.

date	sign	what's going on
JAN 1	CAPRICORN	Conversations are serious, goal-oriented, and focused on results. Practicality prevails, but communication can feel rigid or overly formal.
JAN 20	AQUARIUS	Communication takes a visionary, innovative turn. Discussions are future-focused and idealistic, but emotions may be overlooked in favor of logic.
FEB 6	PISCES	Words become dreamy, poetic, and intuitive. Interactions are compassionate and imaginative, but clarity can drift and misunderstandings may occur.
FEB 26	RETROGRADE IN PISCES	Communication gets foggy, and compulsions override logic. Daydreaming takes over, leading to confusion or missed details. Revisit plans with extra care.
MAR 20	DIRECT IN PISCES	Clarity returns after a muddled period. Intuition and creativity flow smoothly again, making it easier to express emotions and connect with others on a deeper level.
APR 14	ARIES	Communication is fast and direct. Attention spans are short, so speak in bullet points. Watch for impulsive words and fiery reactivity.
MAY 2	TAURUS	Conversations slow down and become more thoughtful. People are practical and grounded. Stubbornness may creep in, but decisions are steady and deliberate.
MAY 17	GEMINI	The mind races with curiosity and multitasking rules. Ideas flow quickly and conversations are lively, but focus can be scattered.

date	sign	what's going on
JUN 1	CANCER	Words are infused with emotion. Communication becomes nurturing and intuitive, but mood swings can cloud clarity. Speak from the heart.
JUN 29	RETROGRADE IN CANCER	Family friction can get gnarly during this three-week cycle. Everyone's extra-sensitive. Keep a firm privacy policy in place and respect people's space.
JUL 23	DIRECT IN CANCER	Find compassionate people who can witness you without judgment. We need our feelings to be validated in a healthy way. Allow them to be heard by people who "get" you.
AUG 9	LEO	Speak with flair and confidence! Conversations take on a dramatic tone, but watch out for self-centeredness. Creative expression thrives.
AUG 25	VIRGO	Communication is detailed, analytical and efficient. It's time to plan, organize and solve problems, but don't get lost in perfectionism.
SEP 10	LIBRA	Diplomacy and balance rule conversations. It's all about finding harmony and weighing both sides, but decision-making won't be easy.
SEP 30	SCORPIO	Conversations go deep and reveal hidden truths. Words can be intense, investigative and transformative—just avoid obsessiveness or secrecy.
OCT 24	RETROGRADE IN SCORPIO	Secrets come to light and intense conversations resurface. Emotions run deep, so be cautious with power struggles and avoid obsessive thinking. Reflect before you react.
NOV 13	DIRECT IN SCORPIO	Conversations regain intensity but with more focus and control. Secrets and hidden truths that surfaced during the retrograde can now be addressed with clarity and depth.
DEC 6	SAGITTARIUS	Communication becomes bold, optimistic and blunt. It's time to talk big ideas and philosophy, but be mindful of exaggeration or tactlessness.

date	sign	what's going on
DEC 25	CAPRICORN	Conversations are serious, goal-oriented and focused on results. Practicality prevails, but communication can feel rigid or overly formal.

Venus

Venus is the planet of love, beauty and luxury, lending its decadent energy to every zodiac sign for three to five weeks each year. Who will we fall for…and how? Venus sets the love language of the moment, determining the right romantic moves for pleasure and passion.

date	sign	what's going on
JAN 1	CAPRICORN Since DEC 24, 2025	No apologies for being attracted to ambition, or tradition! This power-couple cycle sets the stage for impressive co-creation—the kind that you can take to the bank and the altar!
JAN 17	AQUARIUS	Ready, set, experiment! Push the envelope and explore a kink. Don't be surprised if you find yourself attracted to a friend you never thought of "like that" before.
FEB 10	PISCES	Love becomes dreamy, compassionate and romantic. Emotions are deep and poetic, but boundaries may blur. Idealism rules relationships and creativity.
MAR 6	ARIES	Passion ignites as love becomes bold, adventurous and spontaneous. You're ready to take charge in romance, but impatience and impulsiveness can stir drama.
MAR 30	TAURUS	Love is sensual, stable and grounded. Relationships focus on pleasure, loyalty and comfort, but possessiveness or stubbornness may also creep in.

date	sign	what's going on
APR 24	GEMINI	Flirtation and curiosity dominate as love turns lighthearted, intellectual and social. Keep conversations lively and fun, but beware of scattered or superficial interactions.
MAY 18	CANCER	Love becomes nurturing, emotional and protective. You crave deeper connections and security, but watch out for moodiness or clinginess in relationships.
JUN 13	LEO	Romance is grand and dramatic. Self-expression and affection flow boldly, but be mindful of attention-seeking behavior or letting ego drive your love life.
JUL 9	VIRGO	Love takes a practical, devoted turn. You show affection through helpful acts and attention to detail, but watch for perfectionism or over-criticism.
AUG 6	LIBRA	Romance thrives on balance, harmony and beauty. Relationships are diplomatic and fair, but indecision and people-pleasing could hinder deeper connections.
SEP 10	SCORPIO	Love is intense, passionate and transformative. Deep bonds are formed, but emotional power struggles or jealousy can lead to turbulence.
OCT 3	RETROGRADE IN SCORPIO	What felt sexy and mysterious in the past could suddenly spin up serious trust issues. Don't rush to accuse—but watch for red flags. Who's on top? Power struggles disrupt harmony.
OCT 25	RETROGRADE IN LIBRA	Old relationship patterns resurface, especially around fairness, codependency or unspoken resentment. The urge to keep the peace may mask deeper disconnects.
NOV 13	DIRECT IN LIBRA	Clarity returns to your closest bonds along with the ability to compromise. Sweet gestures and luxe gifts are the salve.
DEC 4	SCORPIO	Seduction is an art form, but who—and what—is truly worth your devotion? If it's not a "Hell, yes!" it's a "Hell, no!" now.

Mars

Mars is the planet of action, drive and ambition, pushing you to take bold steps toward your goals. Mars brings a burst of energy when it transits through a sign for six to eight weeks on average and supports with tackling big projects or asserting yourself in key areas of life.
Knowing when to harness Mars' dynamic influence helps you plan for periods of high motivation, but be mindful—Mars can also stir up conflict if not channeled wisely.

date	sign	what's going on
JAN 1	**CAPRICORN** Since DEC 15, 2025	Time to do, be and have the best. Zero in on success and hustle for the victory. Align with VIPs and influencers. Prestigious endorsements can open doors, so network strategically and join key industry circles.
JAN 23	**AQUARIUS**	Be an agent of change and get your community aligned on the same page. Focus on commonalities and shared goals while creating an inclusive space for everyone's voice to be heard.
MAR 2	**PISCES**	Plumb the depths, exploring life's mysteries and bringing more empathy into daily interactions. Work to uplift others, making them feel seen, valued and inspired. Carve out time for creativity.
APR 9	**ARIES**	Use this double dose of warrior energy to advocate for yourself. If egos and tempers rage, channel that ferocity into a physical outlet. Take initiative on personal projects. Don't overthink it—just get into action on the first step.
MAY 18	**TAURUS**	Tackle your to-do list, but do so gently. Savor simple pleasures like art, music and nature. If extra funds land in your wallet, treat yourself to a luxurious but practical splurge. Slow and steady wins the race.
JUN 28	**GEMINI**	It won't take much convincing to get people on board with your wild schemes! But to maintain trust, be sure you can deliver the goods. Don't rush into a duo without a chemistry test. Monitor screen time and opt for seeing people IRL.

date	sign	what's going on
AUG 11	CANCER	You'll feel protective and motivated to take care of home and family. Be mindful of passive-aggressive tendencies or emotional outbursts.
SEP 27	LEO	Bold, confident and dramatic, you're ready to take center stage and fight for what you want. Your energy is high, but watch out for pride or over-the-top reactions.
NOV 25	VIRGO	Energy becomes focused and efficient. You'll want to tackle tasks with precision and productivity, but perfectionism or nitpicking could cause frustration.

All dates and times in Eastern Time Zone

OUTER PLANETS IN 2026

Jupiter

Jupiter, the planet of expansion and abundance, blesses you with growth opportunities during its year-long tour through each zodiac sign. Whether it's luck in finances, learning or personal growth, Jupiter helps you plan for periods of optimism and possibility. This is your time to dream big and pursue goals that push your boundaries!

date	sign	what's going on
JAN 1	**RETROGRADE IN CANCER** Since NOV 11, 2025	Reflect on how you seek emotional and domestic security. Reassess your connection to family, home and inner growth, as this retrograde calls for revisiting and realigning emotional priorities.
MAR 10	**DIRECT IN CANCER**	Emotional expansion and nurturing energy reign. Focus on deepening relationships and building a sense of security. This is a time for growth through family, home and emotional fulfillment.
JUN 30	**LEO** Until JUL 26, 2027	Confidence, creativity and self-expression get a massive boost. Steal the spotlight—but don't let anyone rob you of your joy while you're out "doing you." Opportunities flow when you lead with heart and let your authentic light shine.
DEC 12	**RETROGRADE IN LEO**	Lower the curtain for some behind-the-scenes productions. Rehearse your lines, quietly restore your confidence and figure out where you need a stricter privacy policy. If you're in charge of too much, find ways to delegate or cooperate.

Saturn

Saturn brings structure, discipline and long-term success. The ringed taskmaster lends its sobering energy to a single zodiac sign for two to three years, helping you plan for serious commitments, hard work and personal growth. Saturn asks you to build a strong foundation before reaching for success. Persistence pays off under its watchful eye.

date	sign	what's going on
JAN 1	PISCES	Discipline meets dreams as Saturn helps you structure your spiritual growth and creative pursuits. It's a time to turn fantasies into reality, but stay mindful of escapism or avoiding responsibilities.
FEB 13	ARIES	Time to take bold, decisive action toward your goals. Saturn's presence in Aries encourages leadership and initiative, but be cautious of impatience or a "my way or the highway" attitude.
JUL 26	RETROGRADE IN ARIES	Reflect on how you've been asserting yourself and pursuing your goals. This retrograde invites you to slow down, reassess your leadership style and correct impulsive actions. It's a time to refine your strategies for long-term success.
NOV 27	DIRECT IN ARIES	The pause ends—and now it's go time, but with precision. Lessons from the retrograde sharpen your instincts, turning impulsive urges into strategic action. With clearer focus and a steadier pace, daring moves can finally gain lasting traction.

Uranus

Uranus is the planet of innovation, surprise and rebellion, shaking things up during its seven-year cycles through each sign. Plan for unexpected changes, breakthroughs and moments of liberation when Uranus transits. Embrace the opportunity to break free from old patterns and think outside the box.

date	sign	what's going on
JAN 1	RETROGRADE IN TAURUS Since NOV 7, 2025	As Uranus takes its final retrograde spin through Taurus for another 84 years, financial curveballs and shifting values could rattle your foundations. This isn't just disruption—it's a last call to break free from outdated habits and redefine security on your own terms. Get inventive with resources and explore unconventional paths that can sustain you for the long haul.
FEB 3	DIRECT IN TAURUS	As Uranus makes its final direct turn in Taurus after eight retrogrades in this sign, clarity around money and personal values clicks into place. Breakthroughs may shift how you build stability while embracing change, especially with finances and possessions. This is your green light to lock in lasting security on new, more liberated terms.
APR 25	GEMINI	Innovation takes flight in communication, learning and adaptability. This is a time for experimental ideas and unconventional thinking—expect major shifts in how you connect with others and process information.
SEP 10	RETROGRADE IN GEMINI	Reassess how you communicate and adapt to changing circumstances. This period is about reflecting on new ideas or exciting collabs that require further refinement before moving forward.

Neptune

Neptune, the planet of dreams and spirituality, brings each sign periods of heightened imagination, creativity and intuition. Its lengthy 14-year stay in each sign allows you to plan for spiritual growth and artistic endeavors, and to draw from the deep well of your psyche. Be careful. Neptune's foggy influence can blur reality, so check those facts.

date	sign	what's going on
JAN 1	**PISCES** Since OCT 22, 2025	As Neptune wraps its final chapter in Pisces in our lives, imagination, intuition and empathy reach their peak. This closing act opens portals for healing, creativity and deep spiritual connection, helping you integrate the lessons of the past fourteen years. Let your inner world spill into outer beauty through art, music and soulful rituals as you prepare to carry this wisdom into the next era.
JAN 26	**ARIES**	Bold dreams and visionary action take the stage. Neptune in Aries pushes you to pursue your ideals with courage and creativity—just watch out for impulsive decisions or chasing unrealistic goals.
JUL 7	**RETROGRADE IN ARIES**	Revisit your dreams and ideals with a critical eye. This retrograde invites you to reflect on bold actions and fine-tune your approach to turning visions into reality.
DEC 12	**DIRECT IN ARIES**	Clarity returns to your vision, igniting purposeful momentum. After months of soul-searching, you're ready to chase your dreams with focus (and fire!). Intuition and courage work in tandem now—trust the call, but keep your feet on the ground.

Pluto

Pluto is the planet of transformation and power, driving deep inner change over its long transits. Each sign experiences Pluto's influence for over a decade, making it a time to plan for profound personal growth, shedding of old identities and doing important shadow work that allows for emotional and spiritual evolution.

date	sign	what's going on
JAN 1	AQUARIUS	Deep transformation arrives through technology, innovation and social structures. You're called to embrace personal and collective change—expect radical shifts in how you relate to community and power.
MAY 6	RETROGRADE IN AQUARIUS	Time to revisit and reassess the transformations happening in your social life. This retrograde slows down the revolutionary changes, giving you space to reflect on personal growth and societal shifts.
OCT 15	DIRECT IN AQUARIUS	The pace of transformation accelerates once again. You'll feel empowered to embrace change, take control of your future and contribute to the collective evolution with renewed determination.

The Lunar Nodes

The lunar nodes, with their 18-month cycles, show where destiny calls and where you must release outmoded ways. The North Node points to your growth path, while the South Node guides you in letting go of outdated habits. Plan for karmic shifts, major life changes and alignment with your higher purpose.

date	sign	what's going on
JAN 1	**NORTH NODE IN PISCES SOUTH NODE IN VIRGO** Since JAN 11, 2025	Put some steam behind your dreams. The North Node in Pisces encourages you to tap into your compassion and divine inspiration, while the South Node in Virgo helps you release the need to micromanage and over-analyze, opening space for creativity and emotional connection.
JUL 26	**NORTH NODE IN AQUARIUS SOUTH NODE IN LEO** Until MAR 26, 2028	Aim your energy toward the future. The North Node in Aquarius urges you to align with innovation, community and visionary goals, while the South Node in Leo helps you release the need for constant validation and personal spotlight. Shift from ego-driven pursuits to collective progress. You'll create space for true collaboration and world-changing ideas.

Chiron

Chiron, the "wounded healer," helps you address deep emotional wounds and past traumas. Chiron is a comet that orbits between Saturn and Uranus; it takes about 50 years to move through all 12 zodiac signs. As it moves through a sign, Chiron offers a time for reflection, healing and personal growth. Plan for moments of vulnerability and the courage to transform pain into wisdom.

date	sign	what's going on
JAN 1	**RETROGRADE IN ARIES** Since JUL 30, 2025	Reflect on past wounds related to self-worth and personal power. This retrograde encourages deep introspection, helping you uncover and heal old insecurities about asserting yourself.
JAN 2	**DIRECT IN ARIES**	Heal through courage and self-empowerment. You're confronting wounds around identity and independence. Embrace vulnerability to build inner strength.
JUN 19	**TAURUS**	Attention turns to security, self-worth and personal values as Chiron visits Taurus for the first time since 1983. Old money wounds or scarcity patterns may surface, inviting introspection. This brief visit plants the seeds for a new relationship with abundance.
AUG 3	**RETROGRADE IN TAURUS**	Revisit old fears around money and worthiness—not to undo progress, but to help you heal at the root. Dig into your lineage and generational patterns (and trauma) that may be informing your relationship with work and finances.
SEP 17	**RETROGRADE IN ARIES**	Old wounds around identity and self-expression resurface, calling for honest reflection. This inward journey helps you reclaim lost confidence and rewrite the story of your strength—on your own terms.

RETROGRADES IN 2026

When planets go "backward," slowdowns and chaos can ensue

When a planet passes the Earth in its orbit around the Sun, it's said to be going retrograde. From our vantage point on Earth, the planet appears to be on a reverse commute, backing up through the zodiac instead of advancing ahead degree by degree. While these aren't optimal times to start anything new, they can be powerful periods to review our progress and enjoy nostalgia.

Mercury

a time to review	dates	retrograde in
Communication style, social contacts, systems for workflow, short trips and travel plans, contracts and agreements.	FEB 26–MAR 20	PISCES (9°35'–0°00')
	JUN 29–JUL 23	CANCER (29°59'–26°50')
	OCT 24–NOV 13	SCORPIO (15°34'–4°15')

Venus

a time to review	dates	retrograde in
Relationships and love, personal values, self-worth, finances and spending habits, aesthetic and style choices.	OCT 3–25	SCORPIO (10°49'–00°00')
	OCT 25–NOV 13	LIBRA (29°59'–24°39')

Jupiter

a time to review	dates	retrograde in
Long-term goals, beliefs and philosophy, expansion plans, travel and education, opportunities for growth.	NOV 11, 2025–MAR 10	CANCER (25°09'–15°05')
	DEC 12–APR 12, 2027	LEO (27°01'–17°00')

Saturn

a time to review	dates	retrograde in...
Responsibilities, long-term commitments, structures and foundations, career and ambitions, personal discipline.	JUL 26–DEC 10	ARIES (1°56'–00°00')

Neptune

a time to review	dates	retrograde in...
Dreams and intuition, boundaries, spiritual practices, creative projects, escapism tendencies	JUL 7–DEC 12	ARIES (02°11'–00°00')

Pluto

a time to review	dates	retrograde in...
Power dynamics, transformation, control issues, deep-seated fears, emotional intensity	MAY 6–OCT 15	AQUARIUS (3°49'–1°22')

Chiron

a time to review	dates	retrograde in...
Emotional wounds, healing practices, personal vulnerabilities, old traumas, self-empowerment strategies.	JAN 1–2	ARIES (27°10'–22°35')
	AUG 3–SEP 17	TAURUS (0°52'–0°00')
	SEP 17–JAN 6, 2027	ARIES (29°59'–26°16')

All dates and times in Eastern Time Zone

January 2026

Longitude & Retrograde Ephemeris [00:00 UT]

Day	Sid.time	☉	☽	+12h☽	☿	♀	♂	♃	♄	♅	♆	♇	☊	☊	⚸	⚷	Day
1 Th	06:42:39	♑10°34′07	♊06°43′05	♊14°13′32	♐28°39	♑09°12	♑12°41	℞ 21°21	♓26°10	℞ 27°56	♓29°30	♒02°43	℞ 12°10	℞ 10°57	♐01°15	℞ 22°36	**1** Th
2 Fr	06:46:36	♑11°35′15	♊21°45′21	♊29°16′47	♑00°10	♑10°27	♑13°27	♋21°13	♓26°13	♉27°55	♓29°31	♒02°44	♓12°07	♓10°48	♐01°22	♈22°35	**2** Fr
3 Sa	06:50:32	♑12°36′23	♋06°47′06	♋14°14′33	♑01°42	♑11°43	♑14°13	♋21°05	♓26°17	♉27°53	♓29°31	♒02°46	♓12°03	♓10°38	♐01°28	D 22°35	**3** Sa
4 Su	06:54:29	♑13°37′31	♋21°38′29	♋28°57′23	♑03°15	♑12°58	♑14°59	♋20°57	♓26°20	♉27°52	♓29°32	♒02°48	♓12°00	♓10°30	♐01°35	♈22°35	**4** Su
5 Mo	06:58:25	♑14°38′39	♌06°10′54	♌13°17′54	♑04°48	♑14°14	♑15°45	♋20°49	♓26°24	♉27°50	♓29°33	♒02°50	♓11°57	♓10°23	♐01°42	♈22°36	**5** Mo
6 Tu	07:02:22	♑15°39′46	♌20°18′24	♌27°11′41	♑06°21	♑15°29	♑16°31	♋20°41	♓26°28	♉27°49	♓29°34	♒02°52	♓11°54	♓10°19	♐01°48	♈22°36	**6** Tu
7 We	07:06:18	♑16°40′54	♍03°58′08	♍10°37′24	♑07°54	♑16°45	♑17°17	♋20°33	♓26°32	♉27°47	♓29°35	♒02°54	♓11°51	♓10°17	♐01°55	♈22°36	**7** We
8 Th	07:10:15	♑17°42′02	♍17°10′12	♍23°36′28	♑09°28	♑18°00	♑18°04	♋20°25	♓26°36	♉27°46	♓29°36	♒02°56	♓11°48	D 10°17	♐02°02	♈22°36	**8** Th
9 Fr	07:14:11	♑18°43′10	♍29°57′05	♎06°12′11	♑11°02	♑19°16	♑18°50	♋20°17	♓26°40	♉27°45	♓29°37	♒02°57	♓11°44	♓10°18	♐02°09	♈22°37	**9** Fr
10 Sa	07:18:08	♑19°44′18	♎12°22′47	♎18°29′06	♑12°37	♑20°31	♑19°36	♋20°09	♓26°45	♉27°43	♓29°38	♒02°59	♓11°41	♓10°19	♐02°15	♈22°37	**10** Sa
11 Su	07:22:05	♑20°45′26	♎24°32′10	♏00°32′16	♑14°12	♑21°47	♑20°23	♋20°01	♓26°49	♉27°42	♓29°39	♒03°01	♓11°38	℞ 10°19	♐02°22	♈22°37	**11** Su
12 Mo	07:26:01	♑21°46′35	♏06°30′24	♏12°26′49	♑15°48	♑23°02	♑21°09	♋19°53	♓26°53	♉27°41	♓29°40	♒03°03	♓11°35	♓10°18	♐02°29	♈22°38	**12** Mo
13 Tu	07:29:58	♑22°47′43	♏18°22′30	♏24°17′36	♑17°24	♑24°18	♑21°55	♋19°45	♓26°58	♉27°40	♓29°41	♒03°05	♓11°32	♓10°14	♐02°35	♈22°38	**13** Tu
14 We	07:33:54	♑23°48′51	♐00°13′03	♐06°08′53	♑19°00	♑25°33	♑22°42	♋19°37	♓27°03	♉27°39	♓29°42	♒03°07	♓11°28	♓10°09	♐02°42	♈22°39	**14** We
15 Th	07:37:51	♑24°49′59	♐12°05′58	♐18°04′16	♑20°37	♑26°49	♑23°28	♋19°29	♓27°07	♉27°38	♓29°44	♒03°09	♓11°25	♓10°01	♐02°49	♈22°40	**15** Th
16 Fr	07:41:47	♑25°51′06	♐24°04′29	♑00°06′30	♑22°15	♑28°04	♑24°15	♋19°21	♓27°12	♉27°37	♓29°45	♒03°11	♓11°22	♓09°53	♐02°56	♈22°40	**16** Fr
17 Sa	07:45:44	♑26°52′14	♑06°10′56	♑12°17′34	♑23°53	♑29°20	♑25°01	♋19°13	♓27°17	♉27°36	♓29°46	♒03°13	♓11°19	♓09°44	♐03°02	♈22°41	**17** Sa
18 Su	07:49:40	♑27°53′21	♑18°26′55	♑24°38′42	♑25°31	♒00°35	♑25°48	♋19°05	♓27°22	♉27°35	♓29°47	♒03°14	♓11°16	♓09°36	♐03°09	♈22°42	**18** Su
19 Mo	07:53:37	♑28°54′27	♒00°53′22	♒07°10′35	♑27°10	♒01°50	♑26°35	♋18°57	♓27°27	♉27°34	♓29°49	♒03°16	♓11°13	♓09°29	♐03°16	♈22°43	**19** Mo
20 Tu	07:57:34	♑29°55′33	♒13°30′47	♒19°53′33	♑28°50	♒03°06	♑27°21	♋18°49	♓27°32	♉27°33	♓29°50	♒03°18	♓11°09	♓09°24	♐03°23	♈22°44	**20** Tu
21 We	08:01:30	♒00°56′38	♒26°19′23	♓02°47′51	♒00°30	♒04°21	♑28°08	♋18°41	♓27°37	♉27°32	♓29°51	♒03°20	♓11°06	♓09°21	♐03°29	♈22°45	**21** We
22 Th	08:05:27	♒01°57′42	♓09°19′28	♓15°53′51	♒02°11	♒05°37	♑28°55	♋18°33	♓27°42	♉27°32	♓29°53	♒03°22	♓11°03	♓09°20	♐03°36	♈22°46	**22** Th
23 Fr	08:09:23	♒02°58′46	♓22°31′31	♓29°12′06	♒03°52	♒06°52	♑29°41	♋18°26	♓27°47	♉27°31	♓29°54	♒03°24	♓11°00	D 09°21	♐03°43	♈22°47	**23** Fr
24 Sa	08:13:20	♒03°59′48	♈05°56′11	♈12°43′24	♒05°34	♒08°07	♒00°28	♋18°18	♓27°53	♉27°30	♓29°55	♒03°26	♓10°57	♓09°22	♐03°49	♈22°48	**24** Sa
25 Su	08:17:16	♒05°00′50	♈19°34′17	♈26°28′27	♒07°16	♒09°23	♒01°15	♋18°11	♓27°58	♉27°30	♓29°57	♒03°28	♓10°54	♓09°24	♐03°56	♈22°49	**25** Su
26 Mo	08:21:13	♒06°01′50	♉03°26′23	♉10°27′34	♒08°59	♒10°38	♒02°02	♋18°03	♓28°04	♉27°29	♓29°58	♒03°30	♓10°50	♓09°25	♐04°03	♈22°51	**26** Mo
27 Tu	08:25:09	♒07°02′49	♉17°32′23	♉24°40′10	♒10°43	♒11°54	♒02°49	♋17°56	♓28°09	♉27°29	♈00°00	♒03°32	♓10°47	℞ 09°24	♐04°10	♈22°52	**27** Tu
28 We	08:29:06	♒08°03′48	♊01°51′05	♊09°04′15	♒12°27	♒13°09	♒03°36	♋17°49	♓28°15	♉27°28	♈00°01	♒03°34	♓10°44	♓09°22	♐04°16	♈22°53	**28** We
29 Th	08:33:03	♒09°04′45	♊16°19′41	♊23°36′16	♒14°12	♒14°24	♒04°22	♋17°42	♓28°20	♉27°28	♈00°03	♒03°36	♓10°41	♓09°19	♐04°23	♈22°55	**29** Th
30 Fr	08:36:59	♒10°05′41	♋00°53′49	♋08°11′03	♒15°57	♒15°40	♒05°09	♋17°35	♓28°26	♉27°28	♈00°05	♒03°38	♓10°38	♓09°15	♐04°30	♈22°56	**30** Fr
31 Sa	08:40:56	♒11°06′36	♋15°27′40	♋22°42′21	♒17°42	♒16°55	♒05°56	♋17°28	♓28°32	♉27°28	♈00°06	♒03°39	♓10°34	♓09°11	♐04°36	♈22°58	**31** Sa
Δ Delta	01:58:16	30°32′28″	398°44′35″	398°28′49″	49°03′	37°42′	23°15′	-3°53′	2°22′	-0°28′	-0°36′	0°56′	-1°35′	-1°46′	3°21′	0°22′	**Delta**

Ephemeris tables and data provided by **Astro-Seek.com.** All times in UTC.

February 2026

Longitude & Retrograde Ephemeris [00:00 UT]

Day	Sid.time	☉	☽	+12h☽	☿	♀	♂	♃	♄	♅	♆	♇	☊	☊	⚸	⚷	Day
1 Su	08:44:52	♒12°07′29	♋29°54′47	♌07°03′42	♒19°28	♒18°10	♒06°43	℞ 17°21	♓28°38	℞ 27°27	♈00°08	♒03°41	℞ 10°31	℞ 09°07	♐04°43	♈22°59	1 Su
2 Mo	08:48:49	♒13°08′21	♌14°08′54	♌21°09′20	♒21°14	♒19°25	♒07°30	♋17°15	♓28°44	♉27°27	♈00°10	♒03°43	♓10°28	♓09°04	♐04°50	♈23°01	2 Mo
3 Tu	08:52:45	♒14°09′13	♌28°04′57	♍04°54′57	♒23°00	♒20°41	♒08°17	♋17°08	♓28°50	♉27°27	♈00°11	♒03°45	♓10°25	♓09°02	♐04°57	♈23°03	3 Tu
4 We	08:56:42	♒15°10′03	♍11°39′34	♍18°18′15	♒24°47	♒21°56	♒09°04	♋17°02	♓28°56	♉27°27	♈00°13	♒03°47	♓10°22	D 09°02	♐05°03	♈23°04	4 We
5 Th	09:00:38	♒16°10′52	♍24°51′29	♎01°18′57	♒26°33	♒23°11	♒09°51	♋16°55	♓29°02	D 27°27	♈00°15	♒03°49	♓10°19	♓09°02	♐05°10	♈23°06	5 Th
6 Fr	09:04:35	♒17°11′40	♎07°41′20	♎13°58′32	♒28°19	♒24°26	♒10°38	♋16°49	♓29°08	♉27°27	♈00°16	♒03°51	♓10°15	♓09°04	♐05°17	♈23°08	6 Fr
7 Sa	09:08:32	♒18°12′28	♎20°11′25	♎26°19′59	♓00°05	♒25°42	♒11°25	♋16°43	♓29°14	♉27°27	♈00°18	♒03°53	♓10°12	♓09°05	♐05°24	♈23°10	7 Sa
8 Su	09:12:28	♒19°13′14	♏02°25′13	♏08°27′14	♓01°50	♒26°57	♒12°12	♋16°38	♓29°21	♉27°27	♈00°20	♒03°55	♓10°09	♓09°07	♐05°30	♈23°12	8 Su
9 Mo	09:16:25	♒20°13′59	♏14°27′02	♏20°24′48	♓03°34	♒28°12	♒13°00	♋16°32	♓29°27	♉27°28	♈00°22	♒03°56	♓10°06	♓09°08	♐05°37	♈23°14	9 Mo
10 Tu	09:20:21	♒21°14′44	♏26°21′34	♐02°17′32	♓05°16	♒29°27	♒13°47	♋16°26	♓29°33	♉27°28	♈00°24	♒03°58	♓10°03	℞ 09°08	♐05°44	♈23°16	10 Tu
11 We	09:24:18	♒22°15′28	♐08°13′40	♐14°10′09	♓06°57	♓00°42	♒14°34	♋16°21	♓29°40	♉27°28	♈00°26	♒04°00	♓10°00	♓09°07	♐05°50	♈23°18	11 We
12 Th	09:28:14	♒23°16′10	♐20°07′57	♐26°07′10	℞s 08°36	♓01°58	♒15°21	♋16°16	♓29°46	♉27°29	♈00°27	♒04°02	♓09°56	♓09°05	♐05°57	♈23°20	12 Th
13 Fr	09:32:11	♒24°16′51	♑02°08′41	♑08°12′31	♓10°13	♓03°13	♒16°08	♋16°11	♓29°53	♉27°29	♈00°29	♒04°04	♓09°53	♓09°03	♐06°04	♈23°22	13 Fr
14 Sa	09:36:07	♒25°17′31	♑14°19′28	♑20°29′28	♓11°46	♓04°28	♒16°55	♋16°06	♓29°59	♉27°30	♈00°31	♒04°06	♓09°50	♓09°01	♐06°11	♈23°24	14 Sa
15 Su	09:40:04	♒26°18′10	♑26°43′12	♒03°00′26	♓13°15	♓05°43	♒17°43	♋16°01	♈00°06	♉27°30	♈00°33	♒04°07	♓09°47	♓08°59	♐06°17	♈23°27	15 Su
16 Mo	09:44:01	♒27°18′48	♒09°21′46	♒15°46′50	♓14°41	♓06°58	♒18°30	♋15°57	♈00°13	♉27°31	♈00°35	♒04°09	♓09°44	♓08°57	♐06°24	♈23°29	16 Mo
17 Tu	09:47:57	♒28°19′24	♒22°16′06	♒28°49′06	♓16°01	♓08°13	♒19°17	♋15°52	♈00°19	♉27°32	♈00°37	♒04°11	♓09°40	♓08°56	♐06°31	♈23°31	17 Tu
18 We	09:51:54	♒29°19′58	♓05°26′12	♓12°06′46	♓17°16	♓09°28	♒20°04	♋15°48	♈00°26	♉27°32	♈00°39	♒04°13	♓09°37	♓08°56	♐06°38	♈23°34	18 We
19 Th	09:55:50	♓00°20′31	♓18°51′06	♓25°38′33	♓18°24	♓10°43	♒20°51	♋15°44	♈00°33	♉27°33	♈00°41	♒04°15	♓09°34	D 08°56	♐06°44	♈23°36	19 Th
20 Fr	09:59:47	♓01°21′03	♈02°29′17	♈09°22′36	♓19°25	♓11°58	♒21°39	♋15°40	♈00°40	♉27°34	♈00°43	♒04°16	♓09°31	♓08°57	♐06°51	♈23°38	20 Fr
21 Sa	10:03:43	♓02°21′32	♈16°18′41	♈23°16′48	♓20°19	♓13°13	♒22°26	♋15°37	♈00°47	♉27°35	♈00°45	♒04°18	♓09°28	♓08°57	♐06°58	♈23°41	21 Sa
22 Su	10:07:40	♓03°22′00	♉00°17′08	♉07°18′54	♓21°04	♓14°28	♒23°13	♋15°33	♈00°54	♉27°36	♈00°47	♒04°20	♓09°25	♓08°58	♐07°04	♈23°43	22 Su
23 Mo	10:11:36	♓04°22′26	♉14°22′20	♉21°26′40	♓21°41	♓15°43	♒24°00	♋15°30	♈01°01	♉27°37	♈00°49	♒04°22	♓09°21	♓08°58	♐07°11	♈23°46	23 Mo
24 Tu	10:15:33	♓05°22′50	♉28°32′05	♊05°37′51	♓22°08	♓16°58	♒24°48	♋15°27	♈01°08	♉27°38	♈00°51	♒04°23	♓09°18	♓08°58	♐07°18	♈23°49	24 Tu
25 We	10:19:30	♓06°23′13	♊12°44′10	♊19°50′15	♓22°25	♓18°13	♒25°35	♋15°24	♈01°15	♉27°39	♈00°54	♒04°25	♓09°15	℞ 08°58	♐07°25	♈23°51	25 We
26 Th	10:23:26	♓07°23′33	♊26°56′16	♋04°01′27	♓22°33	♓19°28	♒26°22	♋15°22	♈01°22	♉27°40	♈00°56	♒04°27	♓09°12	♓08°58	♐07°31	♈23°54	26 Th
27 Fr	10:27:23	♓08°23′51	♋11°05′57	♋18°08′56	℞ 22°31	♓20°43	♒27°10	♋15°19	♈01°29	♉27°41	♈00°58	♒04°28	♓09°09	♓08°58	♐07°38	♈23°57	27 Fr
28 Sa	10:31:19	♓09°24′07	♋25°10′31	♌02°09′53	♓22°19	♓21°58	♒27°57	♋15°17	♈01°36	♉27°42	♈01°00	♒04°30	♓09°05	D 08°58	♐07°45	♈23°59	28 Sa
Δ Delta	01:46:27	27°16′38″	-355°15′43″	-355°06′10″	32°51′	33°47′	21°13′	-2°04′	-2°57′	0°14′	0°52′	0°48′	-1°25′	-0°08′	3°01′	0°59′	Delta

Ephemeris tables and data provided by **Astro-Seek.com.** All times in UTC.

March 2026

Longitude & Retrograde Ephemeris [00:00 UT]

Day	Sid.time	☉	☽	+12h☽	☿	♀	♂	♃	♄	♅	♆	♇	☊	☊	⚸	⚷	Day
1 Su	10:35:16	♓10°24′22	♌09°07′09	♌16°01′29	℞ 21°58	♓23°12	♒28°44	℞ 15°15	♈01°43	♉27°43	♈01°02	♒04°32	℞ 09°02	♓08°58	♐07°51	♈24°02	**1** Su
2 Mo	10:39:12	♓11°24′34	♌22°53′02	♌29°41′00	♓21°28	♓24°27	♒29°31	♋15°13	♈01°50	♉27°45	♈01°04	♒04°33	♓08°59	♓08°58	♐07°58	♈24°05	**2** Mo
3 Tu	10:43:09	♓12°24′45	♍06°25′36	♍13°06′09	♓20°50	♓25°42	♓00°19	♋15°11	♈01°57	♉27°46	♈01°06	♒04°35	♓08°56	♓08°59	♐08°05	♈24°08	**3** Tu
4 We	10:47:05	♓13°24′53	♍19°42′53	♍26°15′16	♓20°05	♓26°57	♓01°06	♋15°10	♈02°05	♉27°48	♈01°09	♒04°36	♓08°53	℞ 08°58	♐08°12	♈24°11	**4** We
5 Th	10:51:02	♓14°25′00	♎02°43′40	♎09°07′40	♓19°14	♓28°11	♓01°53	♋15°08	♈02°12	♉27°49	♈01°11	♒04°38	♓08°50	♓08°58	♐08°18	♈24°14	**5** Th
6 Fr	10:54:59	♓15°25′05	♎15°27′46	♎21°43′41	♓18°19	♓29°26	♓02°41	♋15°07	♈02°19	♉27°51	♈01°13	♒04°39	♓08°46	♓08°57	♐08°25	♈24°17	**6** Fr
7 Sa	10:58:55	♓16°25′08	♎27°56′04	♏04°04′44	♓17°20	♈00°41	♓03°28	♋15°06	♈02°26	♉27°52	♈01°15	♒04°41	♓08°43	♓08°57	♐08°32	♈24°20	**7** Sa
8 Su	11:02:52	♓17°25′09	♏10°10′28	♏16°13′14	♓16°19	♈01°55	♓04°15	♋15°06	♈02°34	♉27°54	♈01°17	♒04°42	♓08°40	♓08°55	♐08°39	♈24°23	**8** Su
9 Mo	11:06:48	♓18°25′09	♏22°13′51	♏28°12′26	♓15°19	♈03°10	♓05°02	♋15°05	♈02°41	♉27°55	♈01°20	♒04°44	♓08°37	♓08°54	♐08°45	♈24°26	**9** Mo
10 Tu	11:10:45	♓19°25′08	♐04°09′52	♐10°06′19	♓14°19	♈04°25	♓05°50	♋15°05	♈02°48	♉27°57	♈01°22	♒04°45	♓08°34	♓08°53	♐08°52	♈24°29	**10** Tu
11 We	11:14:41	♓20°25′05	♐16°02′44	♐21°59′18	♓13°21	♈05°39	♓06°37	♋15°05	♈02°56	♉27°59	♈01°24	♒04°47	♓08°31	♓08°53	♐08°59	♈24°32	**11** We
12 Th	11:18:38	♓21°25′00	♐27°57′02	♑03°56′06	♓12°27	♈06°54	♓07°24	D 15°05	♈03°03	♉28°01	♈01°26	♒04°48	♓08°27	D 08°53	♐09°05	♈24°35	**12** Th
13 Fr	11:22:34	♓22°24′54	♑09°57′30	♑16°01′24	♓11°38	♈08°08	♓08°11	♋15°05	♈03°10	♉28°02	♈01°29	♒04°50	♓08°24	♓08°54	♐09°12	♈24°38	**13** Fr
14 Sa	11:26:31	♓23°24′45	♑22°08′44	♑28°19′36	♓10°53	♈09°23	♓08°59	♋15°06	♈03°18	♉28°04	♈01°31	♒04°51	♓08°21	♓08°55	♐09°19	♈24°41	**14** Sa
15 Su	11:30:28	♓24°24′36	♒04°34′54	♒10°54′35	♓10°14	♈10°37	♓09°46	♋15°06	♈03°25	♉28°06	♈01°33	♒04°53	♓08°18	♓08°56	♐09°26	♈24°44	**15** Su
16 Mo	11:34:24	♓25°24′24	♒17°19′26	♒23°49′15	♓09°41	♈11°51	♓10°33	♋15°07	♈03°33	♉28°08	♈01°35	♒04°54	♓08°15	♓08°57	♐09°32	♈24°48	**16** Mo
17 Tu	11:38:21	♓26°24′10	♓00°24′38	♓07°05′12	♓09°14	♈13°06	♓11°20	♋15°08	♈03°40	♉28°10	♈01°38	♒04°55	♓08°11	♓08°58	♐09°39	♈24°51	**17** Tu
18 We	11:42:17	♓27°23′55	♓13°51′20	♓20°42′26	♓08°53	♈14°20	♓12°07	♋15°09	♈03°48	♉28°12	♈01°40	♒04°57	♓08°08	℞ 08°58	♐09°46	♈24°54	**18** We
19 Th	11:46:14	♓28°23′38	♓27°38′40	♈04°39′10	♓08°39	♈15°35	♓12°55	♋15°11	♈03°55	♉28°14	♈01°42	♒04°58	♓08°05	♓08°57	♐09°52	♈24°57	**19** Th
20 Fr	11:50:10	♓29°23′18	♈11°43′55	♈18°51′51	♓08°31	♈16°49	♓13°42	♋15°12	♈04°03	♉28°16	♈01°45	♒04°59	♓08°02	♓08°56	♐09°59	♈25°01	**20** Fr
21 Sa	11:54:07	♈00°22′57	♈26°02′48	♉03°15′33	DS 08°29	♈18°03	♓14°29	♋15°14	♈04°10	♉28°19	♈01°47	♒05°00	♓07°59	♓08°53	♐10°06	♈25°04	**21** Sa
22 Su	11:58:03	♈01°22′33	♉10°29′53	♉17°44′35	♓08°33	♈19°17	♓15°16	♋15°16	♈04°18	♉28°21	♈01°49	♒05°02	♓07°56	♓08°50	♐10°13	♈25°07	**22** Su
23 Mo	12:01:60	♈02°22′08	♉24°59′27	♊02°13′19	♓08°43	♈20°32	♓16°03	♋15°18	♈04°25	♉28°23	♈01°51	♒05°03	♓07°52	♓08°47	♐10°19	♈25°11	**23** Mo
24 Tu	12:05:57	♈03°21′40	♊09°26′06	♊16°36′48	♓08°58	♈21°46	♓16°50	♋15°21	♈04°32	♉28°25	♈01°54	♒05°04	♓07°49	♓08°44	♐10°26	♈25°14	**24** Tu
25 We	12:09:53	♈04°21′10	♊23°45′30	♋00°51′23	♓09°18	♈23°00	♓17°37	♋15°23	♈04°40	♉28°28	♈01°56	♒05°05	♓07°46	♓08°43	♐10°33	♈25°18	**25** We
26 Th	12:13:50	♈05°20′37	♋07°54′39	♋14°54′40	♓09°43	♈24°14	♓18°25	♋15°26	♈04°47	♉28°30	♈01°58	♒05°06	♓07°43	D 08°42	♐10°40	♈25°21	**26** Th
27 Fr	12:17:46	♈06°20′03	♋21°51′48	♋28°45′31	♓10°13	♈25°28	♓19°12	♋15°29	♈04°55	♉28°33	♈02°00	♒05°07	♓07°40	♓08°43	♐10°46	♈25°24	**27** Fr
28 Sa	12:21:43	♈07°19′25	♌05°36′16	♌12°23′36	♓10°47	♈26°42	♓19°59	♋15°32	♈05°02	♉28°35	♈02°03	♒05°08	♓07°37	♓08°44	♐10°53	♈25°28	**28** Sa
29 Su	12:25:39	♈08°18′46	♌19°07′59	♌25°49′01	♓11°25	♈27°56	♓20°46	♋15°35	♈05°10	♉28°37	♈02°05	♒05°09	♓07°33	♓08°46	♐11°00	♈25°31	**29** Su
30 Mo	12:29:36	♈09°18′04	♍02°27′12	♍09°02′04	♓12°07	♈29°10	♓21°33	♋15°39	♈05°17	♉28°40	♈02°07	♒05°10	♓07°30	♓08°47	♐11°06	♈25°35	**30** Mo
31 Tu	12:33:32	♈10°17′20	♍15°34′09	♍22°02′59	♓12°52	♉00°24	♓22°20	♋15°43	♈05°25	♉28°43	♈02°09	♒05°12	♓07°27	℞ 08°47	♐11°13	♈25°38	**31** Tu
Δ Delta	01:58:15	-29°52′58″	396°27′00″	396°01′30″	-9°05′	-37°11′	23°35′	0°27′	3°41′	0°59′	1°07′	0°39′	-1°35′	-0°11′	3°21′	1°36′	**Delta**

Ephemeris tables and data provided by **Astro-Seek.com.** All times in UTC.

April 2026

Longitude & Retrograde Ephemeris [00:00 UT]

Day	Sid.time	☉	☽	+12h ☽	☿	♀	♂	♃	♄	♅	♆	♇	☊	☊	⚸	⚷	Day
1 We	12:37:29	♈11°16′33	♍28°29′02	♎04°51′52	Ds 13°41	♉01°38	♓23°07	♋15°46	♈05°32	♉28°45	♈02°12	♒05°12	℞ 07°24	℞ 08°45	♐11°20	♈25°42	**1** We
2 Th	12:41:26	♈12°15′45	♎11°11′58	♎17°28′54	♓14°34	♉02°52	♓23°54	♋15°50	♈05°40	♉28°48	♈02°14	♒05°13	♓07°21	♓08°42	♐11°27	♈25°45	**2** Th
3 Fr	12:45:22	♈13°14′54	♎23°43′10	♎29°54′25	♓15°29	♉04°06	♓24°40	♋15°55	♈05°47	♉28°50	♈02°16	♒05°14	♓07°17	♓08°37	♐11°33	♈25°49	**3** Fr
4 Sa	12:49:19	♈14°14′02	♏06°03′11	♏12°09′11	♓16°27	♉05°19	♓25°27	♋15°59	♈05°55	♉28°53	♈02°18	♒05°15	♓07°14	♓08°31	♐11°40	♈25°52	**4** Sa
5 Su	12:53:15	♈15°13′08	♏18°13′00	♏24°14′29	♓17°28	♉06°33	♓26°14	♋16°03	♈06°02	♉28°56	♈02°21	♒05°16	♓07°11	♓08°25	♐11°47	♈25°56	**5** Su
6 Mo	12:57:12	♈16°12′12	♐00°14′18	♐06°12′22	♓18°32	♉07°47	♓27°01	♋16°08	♈06°10	♉28°59	♈02°23	♒05°17	♓07°08	♓08°18	♐11°54	♈26°00	**6** Mo
7 Tu	13:01:08	♈17°11′14	♐12°09′29	♐18°05′39	♓19°38	♉09°01	♓27°48	♋16°13	♈06°17	♉29°01	♈02°25	♒05°18	♓07°05	♓08°12	♐12°00	♈26°03	**7** Tu
8 We	13:05:05	♈18°10′14	♐24°01′45	♐29°57′52	♓20°47	♉10°14	♓28°35	♋16°18	♈06°24	♉29°04	♈02°27	♒05°19	♓07°02	♓08°08	♐12°07	♈26°07	**8** We
9 Th	13:09:01	♈19°09′13	♑05°54′57	♑11°53′12	♓21°58	♉11°28	♓29°21	♋16°23	♈06°32	♉29°07	♈02°30	♒05°19	♓06°58	♓08°05	♐12°14	♈26°10	**9** Th
10 Fr	13:12:58	♈20°08′09	♑17°53′34	♑23°56′18	23°11	♉12°41	♈00°08	♋16°28	♈06°39	♉29°10	♈02°32	♒05°20	♓06°55	♓08°04	♐12°20	♈26°14	**10** Fr
11 Sa	13:16:55	♈21°07′04	♒00°02′25	♒06°12′07	♓24°26	♉13°55	♈00°55	♋16°34	♈06°46	♉29°13	♈02°34	♒05°21	♓06°52	D 08°04	♐12°27	♈26°18	**11** Sa
12 Su	13:20:51	♈22°05′58	♒12°26′25	♒18°45′27	♓25°44	♉15°08	♈01°41	♋16°39	♈06°54	♉29°16	♈02°36	♒05°22	♓06°49	♓08°05	♐12°34	♈26°21	**12** Su
13 Mo	13:24:48	♈23°04′49	♒25°10′12	♓01°40′39	♓27°03	♉16°22	♈02°28	♋16°45	♈07°01	♉29°19	♈02°38	♒05°22	♓06°46	♓08°07	♐12°41	♈26°25	**13** Mo
14 Tu	13:28:44	♈24°03′39	♓08°17′37	♓15°00′54	♓28°25	♉17°35	♈03°15	♋16°51	♈07°08	♉29°22	♈02°40	♒05°23	♓06°42	℞ 08°07	♐12°47	♈26°28	**14** Tu
15 We	13:32:41	♈25°02′26	♓21°51′04	♓28°47′38	♓29°48	♉18°49	♈04°01	♋16°57	♈07°16	♉29°25	♈02°43	♒05°24	♓06°39	♓08°06	♐12°54	♈26°32	**15** We
16 Th	13:36:37	♈26°01′13	♈05°50′53	♈12°59′56	♈01°13	♉20°02	♈04°48	♋17°04	♈07°23	♉29°28	♈02°45	♒05°24	♓06°36	♓08°03	♐13°01	♈26°36	**16** Th
17 Fr	13:40:34	♈26°59′57	♈20°14′43	♈27°34′00	♈02°40	♉21°15	♈05°34	♋17°10	♈07°30	♉29°31	♈02°47	♒05°25	♓06°33	♓07°58	♐13°07	♈26°39	**17** Fr
18 Sa	13:44:30	♈27°58′39	♉04°57′24	♉12°23′23	♈04°08	♉22°28	♈06°21	♋17°17	♈07°37	♉29°34	♈02°49	♒05°25	♓06°30	♓07°52	♐13°14	♈26°43	**18** Sa
19 Su	13:48:27	♈28°57′20	♉19°51′20	♉27°19′38	♈05°39	♉23°42	♈07°07	♋17°23	♈07°45	♉29°37	♈02°51	♒05°26	♓06°27	♓07°44	♐13°21	♈26°46	**19** Su
20 Mo	13:52:23	♈29°55′58	♊04°47′38	♊12°13′45	♈07°11	♉24°55	♈07°54	♋17°30	♈07°52	♉29°40	♈02°53	♒05°26	♓06°23	♓07°36	♐13°28	♈26°50	**20** Mo
21 Tu	13:56:20	♉00°54′34	♊19°37′31	♊26°57′37	♈08°45	♉26°08	♈08°40	♋17°37	♈07°59	♉29°43	♈02°55	♒05°27	♓06°20	♓07°29	♐13°34	♈26°54	**21** Tu
22 We	14:00:17	♉01°53′09	♋04°13′50	♋11°25′12	♈10°20	♉27°21	♈09°27	♋17°44	♈08°06	♉29°46	♈02°57	♒05°27	♓06°17	♓07°24	♐13°41	♈26°57	**22** We
23 Th	14:04:13	♉02°51′41	♋18°31′51	♋25°33′06	♈11°58	♉28°34	♈10°13	♋17°52	♈08°13	♉29°50	♈02°59	♒05°27	♓06°14	♓07°21	♐13°48	♈27°01	**23** Th
24 Fr	14:08:10	♉03°50′11	♌02°29′24	♌09°20′20	♈13°37	♉29°47	♈10°59	♋17°59	♈08°20	♉29°53	♈03°01	♒05°28	♓06°11	♓07°20	♐13°55	♈27°04	**24** Fr
25 Sa	14:12:06	♉04°48′38	♌16°06′33	♌22°47′47	♈15°17	♊01°00	♈11°45	♋18°06	♈08°27	♉29°56	♈03°03	♒05°28	♓06°08	D 07°20	♐14°01	♈27°08	**25** Sa
26 Su	14:16:03	♉05°47′03	♌29°24′48	♍05°57′27	♈17°00	♊02°13	♈12°32	♋18°14	♈08°34	♉29°59	♈03°05	♒05°29	♓06°04	♓07°21	♐14°08	♈27°12	**26** Su
27 Mo	14:19:59	♉06°45′27	♍12°26′29	♍18°51′46	♈18°44	♊03°26	♈13°18	♋18°22	♈08°41	♊00°03	♈03°07	♒05°29	♓06°01	℞ 07°21	♐14°15	♈27°15	**27** Mo
28 Tu	14:23:56	♉07°43′48	♍25°14′01	♎01°33′06	♈20°30	♊04°39	♈14°04	♋18°30	♈08°48	♊00°06	♈03°09	♒05°29	♓05°58	♓07°20	♐14°21	♈27°19	**28** Tu
29 We	14:27:52	♉08°42′07	♎07°49′39	♎14°03′29	♈22°17	♊05°51	♈14°50	♋18°38	♈08°55	♊00°09	♈03°11	♒05°29	♓05°55	♓07°16	♐14°28	♈27°22	**29** We
30 Th	14:31:49	♉09°40′24	♎20°15′12	♎26°24′31	♈24°07	♊07°04	♈15°36	♋18°46	♈09°01	♊00°13	♈03°13	♒05°29	♓05°52	♓07°09	♐14°35	♈27°26	**30** Th
Δ Delta	01:54:19	28°23′50″	381°46′10″	381°32′38″	-40°25′	35°26′	-22°29′	2°59′	3°29′	1°27′	1°01′	0°16′	-1°32′	-1°36′	3°14′	1°43′	**Delta**

Ephemeris tables and data provided by **Astro-Seek.com.** All times in UTC.

May 2026

Longitude & Retrograde Ephemeris [00:00 UT]

Day	Sid.time	☉	☽	+12h☽	☿	♀	♂	♃	♄	♅	♆	♇	☊	☊	⚸	⚷	Day
1 Fr	14:35:46	♉10°38'39	♏02°32'00	♏08°37'23	♈25°58	♊08°17	♈16°22	♋18°54	♈09°08	♊00°16	♈03°15	♒05°30	℞ 05°48	℞ 07°00	♐14°42	♈27°29	**1** Fr
2 Sa	14:39:42	♉11°36'53	♏14°41'11	♏20°43'06	♈27°51	♊09°29	♈17°08	♋19°03	♈09°15	♊00°19	♈03°17	♒05°30	♓05°45	♓06°49	♐14°48	♈27°33	**2** Sa
3 Su	14:43:39	♉12°35'05	♏26°43'42	♐02°42'42	♈29°45	♊10°42	♈17°54	♋19°11	♈09°22	♊00°23	♈03°19	♒05°30	♓05°42	♓06°37	♐14°55	♈27°36	**3** Su
4 Mo	14:47:35	♉13°33'15	♐08°40'44	♐14°37'33	♉01°42	♊11°55	♈18°40	♋19°20	♈09°28	♊00°26	♈03°21	♒05°30	♓05°39	♓06°25	♐15°02	♈27°40	**4** Mo
5 Tu	14:51:32	♉14°31'24	♐20°33'52	♐26°29'31	♉03°40	♊13°07	♈19°25	♋19°29	♈09°35	♊00°29	♈03°22	♒05°30	♓05°36	♓06°14	♐15°08	♈27°43	**5** Tu
6 We	14:55:28	♉15°29'31	♑02°25'18	♑08°21'10	♉05°39	♊14°19	♈20°11	♋19°38	♈09°42	♊00°33	♈03°24	♒05°30	♓05°33	♓06°04	♐15°15	♈27°47	**6** We
7 Th	14:59:25	♉16°27'37	♑14°17'57	♑20°15'46	♉07°41	♊15°32	♈20°57	♋19°47	♈09°48	♊00°36	♈03°26	℞ 05°30	♓05°29	♓05°57	♐15°22	♈27°50	**7** Th
8 Fr	15:03:21	♉17°25'41	♑26°15'30	♒02°17'21	♉09°44	♊16°44	♈21°43	♋19°56	♈09°55	♊00°40	♈03°28	♒05°30	♓05°26	♓05°53	♐15°29	♈27°54	**8** Fr
9 Sa	15:07:18	♉18°23'43	♒08°22'18	♒14°30'33	♉11°48	♊17°56	♈22°28	♋20°05	♈10°01	♊00°43	♈03°30	♒05°30	♓05°23	♓05°51	♐15°35	♈27°57	**9** Sa
10 Su	15:11:15	♉19°21'45	♒20°43'09	♒27°00'19	♉13°54	♊19°09	♈23°14	♋20°14	♈10°07	♊00°47	♈03°31	♒05°30	♓05°20	D 05°50	♐15°42	♈28°01	**10** Su
11 Mo	15:15:11	♉20°19'45	♓03°23'05	♓09°51'36	♉16°01	♊20°21	♈24°00	♋20°24	♈10°14	♊00°50	♈03°33	♒05°30	♓05°17	♓05°51	♐15°49	♈28°04	**11** Mo
12 Tu	15:19:08	♉21°17'43	♓16°26'49	♓23°08'42	♉18°10	♊21°33	♈24°45	♋20°33	♈10°20	♊00°53	♈03°35	♒05°30	♓05°14	℞ 05°50	♐15°56	♈28°08	**12** Tu
13 We	15:23:04	♉22°15'41	♓29°58'01	♈06°54'29	♉20°19	♊22°45	♈25°31	♋20°43	♈10°26	♊00°57	♈03°36	♒05°30	♓05°10	♓05°48	♐16°02	♈28°11	**13** We
14 Th	15:27:01	♉23°13'37	♈13°58'33	♈21°09'32	♉22°29	♊23°57	♈26°16	♋20°53	♈10°33	♊01°00	♈03°38	♒05°29	♓05°07	♓05°44	♐16°09	♈28°14	**14** Th
15 Fr	15:30:57	♉24°11'32	♈28°27'28	♉05°51'12	♉24°40	♊25°09	♈27°01	♋21°03	♈10°39	♊01°04	♈03°40	♒05°29	♓05°04	♓05°37	♐16°16	♈28°18	**15** Fr
16 Sa	15:34:54	♉25°09'25	♉13°20'21	♉20°53'19	♉26°51	♊26°21	♈27°47	♋21°12	♈10°45	♊01°07	♈03°41	♒05°29	♓05°01	♓05°28	♐16°22	♈28°21	**16** Sa
17 Su	15:38:50	♉26°07'18	♉28°29'22	♊06°06'37	♉29°03	♊27°33	♈28°32	♋21°23	♈10°51	♊01°11	♈03°43	♒05°29	♓04°58	♓05°17	♐16°29	♈28°24	**17** Su
18 Mo	15:42:47	♉27°05'08	♊13°44'11	♊21°20'07	♊01°13	♊28°45	♈29°17	♋21°33	♈10°57	♊01°14	♈03°44	♒05°28	♓04°54	♓05°07	♐16°36	♈28°28	**18** Mo
19 Tu	15:46:44	♉28°02'58	♊28°53'39	♋06°23'05	♊03°24	♊29°56	♉00°02	♋21°43	♈11°03	♊01°18	♈03°46	♒05°28	♓04°51	♓04°57	♐16°43	♈28°31	**19** Tu
20 We	15:50:40	♉29°00'46	♋13°47'59	♋21°07'02	♊05°34	♋01°08	♉00°48	♋21°53	♈11°09	♊01°21	♈03°47	♒05°28	♓04°48	♓04°49	♐16°49	♈28°34	**20** We
21 Th	15:54:37	♉29°58'32	♋28°20'12	♌05°26'40	♊07°42	♋02°20	♉01°33	♋22°04	♈11°14	♊01°25	♈03°49	♒05°27	♓04°45	♓04°44	♐16°56	♈28°37	**21** Th
22 Fr	15:58:33	♊00°56'16	♌12°26'46	♌19°20'03	♊09°50	♋03°31	♉02°18	♋22°14	♈11°20	♊01°28	♈03°50	♒05°27	♓04°42	♓04°42	♐17°03	♈28°40	**22** Fr
23 Sa	16:02:30	♊01°53'59	♌26°07'11	♍02°48'00	♊11°56	♋04°43	♉03°03	♋22°25	♈11°26	♊01°32	♈03°52	♒05°26	♓04°39	♓04°41	♐17°09	♈28°44	**23** Sa
24 Su	16:06:26	♊02°51'40	♍09°23'19	♍15°53'08	♊14°00	♋05°54	♉03°48	♋22°35	♈11°32	♊01°35	♈03°53	♒05°26	♓04°35	♓04°41	♐17°16	♈28°47	**24** Su
25 Mo	16:10:23	♊03°49'19	♍22°18'21	♍28°39'01	♊16°02	♋07°06	♉04°33	♋22°46	♈11°37	♊01°39	♈03°54	♒05°25	♓04°32	♓04°41	♐17°23	♈28°50	**25** Mo
26 Tu	16:14:20	♊04°46'58	♎04°56'01	♎11°09'23	♊18°02	♋08°17	♉05°17	♋22°57	♈11°43	♊01°42	♈03°56	♒05°25	♓04°29	♓04°38	♐17°30	♈28°53	**26** Tu
27 We	16:18:16	♊05°44'34	♎17°19'59	♎23°27'46	♊19°59	♋09°28	♉06°02	♋23°08	♈11°48	♊01°46	♈03°57	♒05°24	♓04°26	♓04°34	♐17°36	♈28°56	**27** We
28 Th	16:22:13	♊06°42'09	♎29°33'31	♏05°37'07	♊21°54	♋10°39	♉06°47	♋23°19	♈11°53	♊01°49	♈03°58	♒05°24	♓04°23	♓04°26	♐17°43	♈28°59	**28** Th
29 Fr	16:26:09	♊07°39'43	♏11°39'17	♏17°39'50	♊23°47	♋11°50	♉07°31	♋23°30	♈11°59	♊01°53	♈04°00	♒05°23	♓04°20	♓04°16	♐17°50	♈29°02	**29** Fr
30 Sa	16:30:06	♊08°37'16	♏23°39'23	♏29°37'44	♊25°37	♋13°01	♉08°16	♋23°41	♈12°04	♊01°56	♈04°01	♒05°23	♓04°16	♓04°03	♐17°57	♈29°05	**30** Sa
31 Su	16:34:02	♊09°34'48	♐05°35'27	♐11°32'17	♊27°24	♋14°12	♉09°01	♋23°52	♈12°09	♊02°00	♈04°02	♒05°22	♓04°13	♓03°50	♐18°03	♈29°08	**31** Su
Δ Delta	01:58:15	28°56'08"	393°03'26"	392°54'54"	61°26'	35°55'	22°38'	4°57'	3°00'	1°43'	0°46'	-0°07'	-1°35'	-3°10'	3°21'	1°38'	**Delta**

Ephemeris tables and data provided by **Astro-Seek.com.** All times in UTC.

June 2026

Longitude & Retrograde Ephemeris [00:00 UT]

Day	Sid.time	☉	☽	+12h☽	☿	♀	♂	♃	♄	♅	♆	♇	☊	☋	⚸	⚷	Day
1 Mo	16:37:59	♊10°32'18	♐17°28'50	♐23°24'51	♊29°09	♋15°23	♉09°45	♋24°04	♈12°14	♊02°03	♈04°03	R 05°21	R 04°10	R 03°36	♐18°10	♈29°11	1 Mo
2 Tu	16:41:55	♊11°29'48	♐29°20'55	♑05°16'52	♋00°50	♋16°34	♉10°30	♋24°15	♈12°19	♊02°07	♈04°04	♒05°21	♓04°07	♓03°23	♐18°17	♈29°14	2 Tu
3 We	16:45:52	♊12°27'16	♑11°13'20	♑17°10'11	♋02°29	♋17°45	♉11°14	♋24°26	♈12°24	♊02°10	♈04°05	♒05°20	♓04°04	♓03°12	♐18°23	♈29°17	3 We
4 Th	16:49:49	♊13°24'44	♑23°08'09	♑29°07'12	♋04°05	♋18°55	♉11°58	♋24°38	♈12°29	♊02°14	♈04°06	♒05°19	♓04°00	♓03°04	♐18°30	♈29°19	4 Th
5 Fr	16:53:45	♊14°22'10	♒05°08'08	♒11°11'00	♋05°38	♋20°06	♉12°43	♋24°49	♈12°34	♊02°17	♈04°08	♒05°19	♓03°57	♓02°59	♐18°37	♈29°22	5 Fr
6 Sa	16:57:42	♊15°19'37	♒17°16'41	♒23°25'19	♋07°09	♋21°17	♉13°27	♋25°01	♈12°39	♊02°21	♈04°09	♒05°18	♓03°54	♓02°56	♐18°44	♈29°25	6 Sa
7 Su	17:01:38	♊16°17'02	♒29°37'52	♓05°54'28	♋08°36	♋22°27	♉14°11	♋25°13	♈12°43	♊02°24	♈04°10	♒05°17	♓03°51	♓02°55	♐18°50	♈29°28	7 Su
8 Mo	17:05:35	♊17°14'26	♓12°16'08	♓18°43'00	♋10°00	♋23°37	♉14°55	♋25°24	♈12°48	♊02°27	♈04°10	♒05°16	♓03°48	D 02°55	♐18°57	♈29°30	8 Mo
9 Tu	17:09:31	♊18°11'51	♓25°16'03	♈01°55'18	♋11°22	♋24°48	♉15°39	♋25°36	♈12°52	♊02°31	♈04°11	♒05°15	♓03°45	R 02°55	♐19°04	♈29°33	9 Tu
10 We	17:13:28	♊19°09'14	♈08°41'37	♈15°34'48	♋12°40	♋25°58	♉16°23	♋25°48	♈12°57	♊02°34	♈04°12	♒05°14	♓03°41	♓02°54	♐19°10	♈29°36	10 We
11 Th	17:17:24	♊20°06'37	♈22°35'29	♈29°43'09	♋13°55	♋27°08	♉17°07	♋26°00	♈13°01	♊02°38	♈04°13	♒05°14	♓03°38	♓02°50	♐19°17	♈29°38	11 Th
12 Fr	17:21:21	♊21°04'00	♉06°58'03	♉14°19'12	♋15°07	♋28°18	♉17°51	♋26°12	♈13°05	♊02°41	♈04°14	♒05°13	♓03°35	♓02°44	♐19°24	♈29°41	12 Fr
13 Sa	17:25:18	♊22°01'22	♉21°46'27	♉29°18'21	♋16°16	♋29°28	♉18°35	♋26°24	♈13°10	♊02°44	♈04°15	♒05°12	♓03°32	♓02°36	♐19°31	♈29°43	13 Sa
14 Su	17:29:14	♊22°58'44	♊06°54'18	♊14°32'29	Rs 17°22	♌00°38	♉19°19	♋26°36	♈13°14	♊02°48	♈04°16	♒05°11	♓03°29	♓02°27	♐19°37	♈29°46	14 Su
15 Mo	17:33:11	♊23°56'05	♊22°12'02	♊29°50'57	♋18°24	♌01°48	♉20°02	♋26°48	♈13°18	♊02°51	♈04°16	♒05°10	♓03°26	♓02°17	♐19°44	♈29°48	15 Mo
16 Tu	17:37:07	♊24°53'25	♋07°28'23	♋15°02'25	♋19°23	♌02°58	♉20°46	♋27°01	♈13°22	♊02°54	♈04°17	♒05°09	♓03°22	♓02°08	♐19°51	♈29°51	16 Tu
17 We	17:41:04	♊25°50'45	♋22°32'26	♋29°56'53	♋20°18	♌04°07	♉21°29	♋27°13	♈13°26	♊02°58	♈04°18	♒05°08	♓03°19	♓02°01	♐19°57	♈29°53	17 We
18 Th	17:45:00	♊26°48'04	♌07°15'30	♌14°27'15	♋21°10	♌05°17	♉22°13	♋27°25	♈13°29	♊03°01	♈04°18	♒05°07	♓03°16	♓01°56	♐20°04	♈29°55	18 Th
19 Fr	17:48:57	♊27°45'22	♌21°32'15	♌28°29'54	♋21°58	♌06°26	♉22°56	♋27°38	♈13°33	♊03°04	♈04°19	♒05°06	♓03°13	♓01°54	♐20°11	♈29°58	19 Fr
20 Sa	17:52:53	♊28°42'40	♍05°20'45	♍12°04'30	♋22°42	♌07°36	♉23°40	♋27°50	♈13°37	♊03°08	♈04°20	♒05°05	♓03°10	D 01°54	♐20°18	♉00°00	20 Sa
21 Su	17:56:50	♊29°39'56	♍18°41'56	♍25°13'02	♋23°23	♌08°45	♉24°23	♋28°02	♈13°40	♊03°11	♈04°20	♒05°04	♓03°06	♓01°54	♐20°24	♉00°02	21 Su
22 Mo	18:00:47	♋00°37'12	♎01°38'42	♎07°59'02	♋23°59	♌09°54	♉25°06	♋28°15	♈13°44	♊03°14	♈04°21	♒05°03	♓03°03	R 01°55	♐20°31	♉00°04	22 Mo
23 Tu	18:04:43	♋01°34'27	♎14°15'00	♎20°26'43	♋24°32	♌11°03	♉25°50	♋28°28	♈13°47	♊03°17	♈04°21	♒05°01	♓03°00	♓01°54	♐20°38	♉00°06	23 Tu
24 We	18:08:40	♋02°31'42	♎26°35'08	♏02°40'22	♋25°00	♌12°12	♉26°33	♋28°40	♈13°50	♊03°20	♈04°22	♒05°00	♓02°57	♓01°51	♐20°44	♉00°08	24 We
25 Th	18:12:36	♋03°28'55	♏08°43'19	♏14°44'01	♋25°23	♌13°21	♉27°16	♋28°53	♈13°54	♊03°24	♈04°22	♒04°59	♓02°54	♓01°46	♐20°51	♉00°10	25 Th
26 Fr	18:16:33	♋04°26'09	♏20°43'18	♏26°41'07	♋25°43	♌14°29	♉27°59	♋29°05	♈13°57	♊03°27	♈04°22	♒04°58	♓02°51	♓01°39	♐20°58	♉00°12	26 Fr
27 Sa	18:20:29	♋05°23'22	♐02°38'15	♐08°34'35	♋25°58	♌15°38	♉28°42	♋29°18	♈14°00	♊03°30	♈04°23	♒04°57	♓02°47	♓01°30	♐21°05	♉00°14	27 Sa
28 Su	18:24:26	♋06°20'34	♐14°30'48	♐20°26'44	♋26°08	♌16°46	♉29°25	♋29°31	♈14°03	♊03°33	♈04°23	♒04°56	♓02°44	♓01°20	♐21°11	♉00°16	28 Su
29 Mo	18:28:23	♋07°17'47	♐26°23'00	♑02°19'26	♋26°14	♌17°55	♊00°08	♋29°44	♈14°05	♊03°36	♈04°23	♒04°55	♓02°41	♓01°09	♐21°18	♉00°18	29 Mo
30 Tu	18:32:19	♋08°14'58	♑08°16'36	♑14°14'18	R 26°15	♌19°03	♊00°50	♋29°56	♈14°08	♊03°39	♈04°24	♒04°53	♓02°38	♓01°00	♐21°25	♉00°20	30 Tu
Δ Delta	01:54:19	27°42'40"	380°47'45"	380°49'27"	27°06'	33°39'	21°05'	5°52'	1°53'	1°35'	0°20'	-0°28'	-1°32'	-2°35'	3°14'	1°08'	Delta

Ephemeris tables and data provided by **Astro-Seek.com.** All times in UTC.

July 2026

Longitude & Retrograde Ephemeris [00:00 UT]

Day	Sid.time	☉	☽	+12h☽	☿	♀	♂	♃	♄	♅	♆	♇	☊	☋	⚸	⚷	Day
1 We	18:36:16	♋09°12′10	♑20°13′10	♑26°12′57	℞ 26°11	♌ 20°11	♊01°33	♌ 00°09	♈14°11	♊03°42	♈04°24	℞ 04°52	℞ 02°35	℞ 00°52	♐21°32	♉00°21	**1** We
2 Th	18:40:12	♋10°09′22	♒02°14′20	♒08°17′08	♋26°03	♌ 21°19	♊02°16	♌ 00°22	♈14°13	♊03°45	♈04°24	♒04°51	♓02°32	♓00°46	♐21°38	♉00°23	**2** Th
3 Fr	18:44:09	♋11°06′34	♒14°22′03	♒20°28′58	♋25°51	♌ 22°27	♊02°58	♌ 00°35	♈14°16	♊03°48	♈04°24	♒04°50	♓02°28	♓00°43	♐21°45	♉00°25	**3** Fr
4 Sa	18:48:05	♋12°03′45	♒26°38′38	♓02°51′01	♋25°34	♌ 23°35	♊03°41	♌ 00°48	♈14°18	♊03°51	♈04°24	♒04°48	♓02°25	♓00°41	♐21°52	♉00°26	**4** Sa
5 Su	18:52:02	♋13°00′57	♓09°06′55	♓15°26′21	♋25°13	♌ 24°42	♊04°23	♌ 01°01	♈14°20	♊03°54	♈04°24	♒04°47	♓02°22	D 00°41	♐21°58	♉00°28	**5** Su
6 Mo	18:55:58	♋13°58′09	♓21°50′09	♓28°18′19	♋24°48	♌ 25°50	♊05°06	♌ 01°14	♈14°22	♊03°57	♈04°25	♒04°46	♓02°19	♓00°43	♐22°05	♉00°30	**6** Mo
7 Tu	18:59:55	♋14°55′21	♈04°51′43	♈11°30′18	♋24°20	♌ 26°57	♊05°48	♌ 01°27	♈14°24	♊03°59	♈04°25	♒04°44	♓02°16	♓00°44	♐22°12	♉00°31	**7** Tu
8 We	19:03:52	♋15°52′34	♈18°14′51	♈25°05′09	♋23°49	♌ 28°04	♊06°30	♌ 01°40	♈14°26	♊04°02	℞ 04°25	♒04°43	♓02°12	℞ 00°44	♐22°19	♉00°32	**8** We
9 Th	19:07:48	♋16°49′47	♉02°01′51	♉09°04′32	♋23°15	♌ 29°11	♊07°12	♌ 01°53	♈14°28	♊04°05	♈04°25	♒04°42	♓02°09	♓00°43	♐22°25	♉00°34	**9** Th
10 Fr	19:11:45	♋17°47′00	♉16°13′32	♉23°28′06	♋22°39	♍00°18	♊07°54	♌ 02°06	♈14°30	♊04°08	♈04°24	♒04°41	♓02°06	♓00°40	♐22°32	♉00°35	**10** Fr
11 Sa	19:15:41	♋18°44′15	♊00°48′18	♊08°12′55	♋22°01	♍01°25	♊08°37	♌ 02°19	♈14°32	♊04°11	♈04°24	♒04°39	♓02°03	♓00°36	♐22°39	♉00°36	**11** Sa
12 Su	19:19:38	♋19°41′29	♊15°41′41	♊23°13′04	♋21°23	♍02°31	♊09°19	♌ 02°32	♈14°33	♊04°13	♈04°24	♒04°38	♓02°00	♓00°30	♐22°45	♉00°38	**12** Su
13 Mo	19:23:34	♋20°38′44	♋00°46′28	♋08°20′09	♋20°44	♍03°38	♊10°00	♌ 02°45	♈14°35	♊04°16	♈04°24	♒04°36	♓01°57	♓00°24	♐22°52	♉00°39	**13** Mo
14 Tu	19:27:31	♋21°35′59	♋15°53′24	♋23°24′28	♋20°06	♍04°44	♊10°42	♌ 02°59	♈14°36	♊04°19	♈04°24	♒04°35	♓01°53	♓00°19	♐22°59	♉00°40	**14** Tu
15 We	19:31:27	♋22°33′15	♌ 00°52′43	♌ 08°16′35	♋19°28	♍05°50	♊11°24	♌ 03°12	♈14°37	♊04°21	♈04°24	♒04°34	♓01°50	♓00°15	♐23°06	♉00°41	**15** We
16 Th	19:35:24	♋23°30′30	♌ 15°35′42	♌ 22°48′49	♋18°53	♍06°56	♊12°06	♌ 03°25	♈14°39	♊04°24	♈04°23	♒04°32	♓01°47	♓00°13	♐23°12	♉00°42	**16** Th
17 Fr	19:39:21	♋24°27′46	♌ 29°55′57	♍06°56′13	♋18°20	♍08°02	♊12°47	♌ 03°38	♈14°40	♊04°26	♈04°23	♒04°31	♓01°44	♓00°12	♐23°19	♉00°43	**17** Fr
18 Sa	19:43:17	♋25°25′02	♍13°49′59	♍20°36′45	♋17°50	♍09°07	♊13°29	♌ 03°51	♈14°41	♊04°29	♈04°23	♒04°30	♓01°41	D 00°12	♐23°26	♉00°44	**18** Sa
19 Su	19:47:14	♋26°22′18	♍27°17′08	♎03°50′56	♋17°23	♍10°13	♊14°11	♌ 04°05	♈14°41	♊04°31	♈04°22	♒04°28	♓01°38	♓00°14	♐23°32	♉00°45	**19** Su
20 Mo	19:51:10	♋27°19′35	♎10°18′59	♎16°41′15	♋17°00	♍11°18	♊14°52	♌ 04°18	♈14°42	♊04°34	♈04°22	♒04°27	♓01°34	♓00°15	♐23°39	♉00°46	**20** Mo
21 Tu	19:55:07	♋28°16′51	♎22°58′40	♎29°11′21	♋16°42	♍12°23	♊15°33	♌ 04°31	♈14°43	♊04°36	♈04°22	♒04°25	♓01°31	♓00°16	♐23°46	♉00°46	**21** Tu
22 We	19:59:03	♋29°14′08	♏05°20′17	♏11°25′34	♋16°29	♍13°28	♊16°15	♌ 04°44	♈14°43	♊04°39	♈04°21	♒04°24	♓01°28	℞ 00°16	♐23°53	♉00°47	**22** We
23 Th	20:02:60	♌ 00°11′25	♏17°28′12	♏23°28′19	♋16°21	♍14°32	♊16°56	♌ 04°58	♈14°44	♊04°41	♈04°21	♒04°23	♓01°25	♓00°15	♐23°59	♉00°48	**23** Th
24 Fr	20:06:56	♌ 01°08′42	♏29°26′51	♐05°23′52	DS 16°18	♍15°37	♊17°37	♌ 05°11	♈14°44	♊04°43	♈04°20	♒04°21	♓01°22	♓00°12	♐24°06	♉00°48	**24** Fr
25 Sa	20:10:53	♌ 02°06′00	♐11°20′17	♐17°16′05	♋16°22	♍16°41	♊18°18	♌ 05°24	♈14°44	♊04°45	♈04°20	♒04°20	♓01°18	♓00°08	♐24°13	♉00°49	**25** Sa
26 Su	20:14:50	♌ 03°03′19	♐23°12′08	♐29°08′21	♋16°31	♍17°45	♊18°59	♌ 05°37	♈14°44	♊04°48	♈04°19	♒04°18	♓01°15	♓00°04	♐24°19	♉00°49	**26** Su
27 Mo	20:18:46	♌ 04°00′37	♑05°05′30	♑11°03′28	♋16°45	♍18°48	♊19°40	♌ 05°51	℞ 14°44	♊04°50	♈04°18	♒04°17	♓01°12	♓00°00	♐24°26	♉00°50	**27** Mo
28 Tu	20:22:43	♌ 04°57′56	♑17°02′56	♑23°03′44	♋17°06	♍19°52	♊20°21	♌ 06°04	♈14°44	♊04°52	♈04°18	♒04°16	♓01°09	♒29°56	♐24°33	♉00°50	**28** Tu
29 We	20:26:39	♌ 05°55′17	♑29°06′30	♒05°11′01	♋17°33	♍20°55	♊21°02	♌ 06°17	♈14°44	♊04°54	♈04°17	♒04°14	♓01°06	♒29°52	♐24°40	♉00°51	**29** We
30 Th	20:30:36	♌ 06°52′37	♒11°17′54	♒17°26′54	♋18°06	♍21°58	♊21°42	♌ 06°31	♈14°44	♊04°56	♈04°17	♒04°13	♓01°03	♒29°50	♐24°46	♉00°51	**30** Th
31 Fr	20:34:32	♌ 07°49′58	♒23°38′36	♒29°52′46	♋18°46	♍23°01	♊22°23	♌ 06°44	♈14°44	♊04°58	♈04°16	♒04°11	♓00°59	♒29°49	♐24°53	♉00°51	**31** Fr
Δ Delta	01:58:15	28°37′48″	393°25′26″	393°39′48″	-7°25′	32°49′	20°50′	6°34′	0°32′	1°16′	-0°08′	-0°40′	-1°35′	-1°03′	3°21′	0°29′	**Delta**

Ephemeris tables and data provided by **Astro-Seek.com.** All times in UTC.

August 2026

Longitude & Retrograde Ephemeris [00:00 UT]

Day	Sid.time	☉	☽	+12h☽	☿	♀	♂	♃	♄	♅	♆	♇	☊	☋	⚸	⚷	Day
1 Sa	20:38:29	♌ 08°47′21	♓ 06°10′01	♓ 12°30′03	DS 19°31	♍ 24°03	♊ 23°04	♌ 06°57	℞ 14°43	♊ 05°00	℞ 04°15	℞ 04°10	℞ 00°56	♒ 29°49	♐ 25°00	♉ 00°51	**1** Sa
2 Su	20:42:25	♌ 09°44′44	♓ 18°53′32	♓ 25°20′11	♋ 20°22	♍ 25°05	♊ 23°44	♌ 07°10	♈ 14°43	♊ 05°02	♈ 04°14	♒ 04°09	♓ 00°53	♒ 29°50	♐ 25°06	♉ 00°51	**2** Su
3 Mo	20:46:22	♌ 10°42′08	♈ 01°50′40	♈ 08°24′43	♋ 21°19	♍ 26°07	♊ 24°25	♌ 07°24	♈ 14°42	♊ 05°04	♈ 04°13	♒ 04°07	♓ 00°50	♒ 29°51	♐ 25°13	♉ 00°51	**3** Mo
4 Tu	20:50:19	♌ 11°39′33	♈ 15°02′58	♈ 21°45′07	♋ 22°21	♍ 27°09	♊ 25°05	♌ 07°37	♈ 14°41	♊ 05°06	♈ 04°13	♒ 04°06	♓ 00°47	♒ 29°52	♐ 25°20	℞ 00°52	**4** Tu
5 We	20:54:15	♌ 12°37′00	♈ 28°31′48	♉ 05°22′36	♋ 23°30	♍ 28°10	♊ 25°45	♌ 07°50	♈ 14°40	♊ 05°08	♈ 04°12	♒ 04°04	♓ 00°44	♒ 29°53	♐ 25°26	♉ 00°51	**5** We
6 Th	20:58:12	♌ 13°34′27	♉ 12°18′06	♉ 19°17′44	♋ 24°44	♍ 29°11	♊ 26°25	♌ 08°04	♈ 14°39	♊ 05°09	♈ 04°11	♒ 04°03	♓ 00°40	♒ 29°54	♐ 25°33	♉ 00°51	**6** Th
7 Fr	21:02:08	♌ 14°31′57	♉ 26°21′56	♊ 03°29′58	♋ 26°03	♎ 00°12	♊ 27°06	♌ 08°17	♈ 14°38	♊ 05°11	♈ 04°10	♒ 04°02	♓ 00°37	℞ 29°53	♐ 25°40	♉ 00°51	**7** Fr
8 Sa	21:06:05	♌ 15°29′27	♊ 10°42′03	♊ 17°57′15	27°27	♎ 01°12	♊ 27°46	♌ 08°30	♈ 14°37	♊ 05°13	♈ 04°09	♒ 04°00	♓ 00°34	♒ 29°53	♐ 25°47	♉ 00°51	**8** Sa
9 Su	21:10:01	♌ 16°26′59	♊ 25°15′32	♋ 02°35′46	♋ 28°56	♎ 02°12	♊ 28°26	♌ 08°43	♈ 14°36	♊ 05°14	♈ 04°08	♒ 03°59	♓ 00°31	♒ 29°51	♐ 25°53	♉ 00°51	**9** Su
10 Mo	21:13:58	♌ 17°24′32	♋ 09°57′44	♋ 17°20′05	♌ 00°29	♎ 03°12	♊ 29°06	♌ 08°56	♈ 14°34	♊ 05°16	♈ 04°07	♒ 03°58	♓ 00°28	♒ 29°50	♐ 26°00	♉ 00°51	**10** Mo
11 Tu	21:17:54	♌ 18°22′06	♋ 24°42′29	♌ 02°03′32	♌ 02°07	♎ 04°11	♊ 29°45	♌ 09°10	♈ 14°33	♊ 05°17	♈ 04°06	♒ 03°56	♓ 00°24	♒ 29°48	♐ 26°07	♉ 00°50	**11** Tu
12 We	21:21:51	♌ 19°19′42	♌ 09°22′51	♌ 16°39′05	♌ 03°49	♎ 05°10	♋ 00°25	♌ 09°23	♈ 14°31	♊ 05°19	♈ 04°05	♒ 03°55	♓ 00°21	♒ 29°47	♐ 26°13	♉ 00°50	**12** We
13 Th	21:25:48	♌ 20°17′19	♌ 23°51′59	♍ 01°00′20	♌ 05°35	♎ 06°09	♋ 01°05	♌ 09°36	♈ 14°30	♊ 05°20	♈ 04°04	♒ 03°54	♓ 00°18	♒ 29°47	♐ 26°20	♉ 00°49	**13** Th
14 Fr	21:29:44	♌ 21°14′57	♍ 08°04′05	♍ 15°02′15	♌ 07°23	♎ 07°07	♋ 01°44	♌ 09°49	♈ 14°28	♊ 05°22	♈ 04°03	♒ 03°52	♓ 00°15	D 29°47	♐ 26°27	♉ 00°49	**14** Fr
15 Sa	21:33:41	♌ 22°12′36	♍ 21°55′02	♍ 28°41′44	♌ 09°15	♎ 08°05	♋ 02°24	♌ 10°02	♈ 14°26	♊ 05°23	♈ 04°02	♒ 03°51	♓ 00°12	♒ 29°47	♐ 26°34	♉ 00°48	**15** Sa
16 Su	21:37:37	♌ 23°10′15	♎ 05°22′48	♎ 11°57′46	♌ 11°09	♎ 09°02	♋ 03°03	♌ 10°15	♈ 14°24	♊ 05°25	♈ 04°01	♒ 03°50	♓ 00°09	♒ 29°48	♐ 26°40	♉ 00°48	**16** Su
17 Mo	21:41:34	♌ 24°07′57	♎ 18°27′18	♎ 24°51′12	♌ 13°05	♎ 09°59	♋ 03°43	♌ 10°29	♈ 14°22	♊ 05°26	♈ 03°59	♒ 03°48	♓ 00°05	♒ 29°49	♐ 26°47	♉ 00°47	**17** Mo
18 Tu	21:45:30	♌ 25°05′39	♏ 01°10′15	♏ 07°24′26	♌ 15°03	♎ 10°56	♋ 04°22	♌ 10°42	♈ 14°20	♊ 05°27	♈ 03°58	♒ 03°47	♓ 00°02	♒ 29°49	♐ 26°54	♉ 00°46	**18** Tu
19 We	21:49:27	♌ 26°03′22	♏ 13°34′39	♏ 19°40′57	♌ 17°02	♎ 11°52	♋ 05°01	♌ 10°55	♈ 14°17	♊ 05°28	♈ 03°57	♒ 03°46	♒ 29°59	♒ 29°49	♐ 27°00	♉ 00°45	**19** We
20 Th	21:53:23	♌ 27°01′06	♏ 25°44′21	♐ 01°44′56	♌ 19°01	♎ 12°47	♋ 05°40	♌ 11°08	♈ 14°15	♊ 05°29	♈ 03°56	♒ 03°44	♒ 29°56	♒ 29°49	♐ 27°07	♉ 00°45	**20** Th
21 Fr	21:57:20	♌ 27°58′51	♐ 07°43′44	♐ 13°40′53	♌ 21°02	♎ 13°42	♋ 06°19	♌ 11°21	♈ 14°13	♊ 05°30	♈ 03°55	♒ 03°43	♒ 29°53	℞ 29°49	♐ 27°14	♉ 00°44	**21** Fr
22 Sa	22:01:17	♌ 28°56′38	♐ 19°37′22	♐ 25°33′19	♌ 23°03	♎ 14°37	♋ 06°58	♌ 11°34	♈ 14°10	♊ 05°31	♈ 03°53	♒ 03°42	♒ 29°50	♒ 29°49	♐ 27°21	♉ 00°43	**22** Sa
23 Su	22:05:13	♌ 29°54′26	♑ 01°29′41	♑ 07°26′32	♌ 25°04	♎ 15°31	♋ 07°37	♌ 11°47	♈ 14°08	♊ 05°32	♈ 03°52	♒ 03°41	♒ 29°46	D 29°49	♐ 27°27	♉ 00°42	**23** Su
24 Mo	22:09:10	♍ 00°52′15	♑ 13°24′47	♑ 19°24′27	♌ 27°04	♎ 16°24	♋ 08°16	♌ 11°59	♈ 14°05	♊ 05°33	♈ 03°51	♒ 03°39	♒ 29°43	♒ 29°49	♐ 27°34	♉ 00°41	**24** Mo
25 Tu	22:13:06	♍ 01°50′05	♑ 25°26′22	♒ 01°30′27	♌ 29°04	♎ 17°17	♋ 08°55	♌ 12°12	♈ 14°02	♊ 05°34	♈ 03°49	♒ 03°38	♒ 29°40	♒ 29°49	♐ 27°41	♉ 00°40	**25** Tu
26 We	22:17:03	♍ 02°47′56	♒ 07°37′27	♒ 13°47′14	♍ 01°04	♎ 18°10	♋ 09°33	♌ 12°25	♈ 13°59	♊ 05°35	♈ 03°48	♒ 03°37	♒ 29°37	♒ 29°50	♐ 27°47	♉ 00°38	**26** We
27 Th	22:20:59	♍ 03°45′49	♒ 20°00′26	♒ 26°16′48	♍ 03°03	♎ 19°01	♋ 10°12	♌ 12°38	♈ 13°56	♊ 05°36	♈ 03°47	♒ 03°36	♒ 29°34	♒ 29°50	♐ 27°54	♉ 00°37	**27** Th
28 Fr	22:24:56	♍ 04°43′43	♓ 02°36′55	♓ 09°00′25	♍ 05°00	♎ 19°52	♋ 10°50	♌ 12°51	♈ 13°53	♊ 05°36	♈ 03°45	♒ 03°35	♒ 29°30	℞ 29°50	♐ 28°01	♉ 00°36	**28** Fr
29 Sa	22:28:52	♍ 05°41′39	♓ 15°27′47	♓ 21°58′34	♍ 06°57	♎ 20°43	♋ 11°29	♌ 13°04	♈ 13°50	♊ 05°37	♈ 03°44	♒ 03°34	♒ 29°27	♒ 29°50	♐ 28°07	♉ 00°35	**29** Sa
30 Su	22:32:49	♍ 06°39′36	♓ 28°33′12	♈ 05°11′09	♍ 08°53	♎ 21°33	♋ 12°07	♌ 13°16	♈ 13°47	♊ 05°38	♈ 03°42	♒ 03°32	♒ 29°24	♒ 29°49	♐ 28°14	♉ 00°33	**30** Su
31 Mo	22:36:46	♍ 07°37′35	♈ 11°52′48	♈ 18°37′31	♍ 10°48	♎ 22°22	♋ 12°45	♌ 13°29	♈ 13°44	♊ 05°38	♈ 03°41	♒ 03°31	♒ 29°21	♒ 29°48	♐ 28°21	♉ 00°32	**31** Mo
Δ Delta	01:58:17	28°50′14″	-395°42′47″	-396°07′28″	51°17′	28°18′	19°41′	6°31′	-0°59′	0°38′	-0°34′	-0°38′	-1°35′	-0°00′	3°21′	-0°19′	**Delta**

Ephemeris tables and data provided by **Astro-Seek.com.** All times in UTC.

September 2026

Longitude & Retrograde Ephemeris [00:00 UT]

Day	Sid.time	☉	☽	+12h☽	☿	♀	♂	♃	♄	♅	♆	♇	☊	☊	⚸	⚷	Day
1 Tu	22:40:42	♍08°35'36	♈25°25'41	♉02°16'37	♍12°42	♎23°10	♋13°23	♌13°41	℞ 13°40	♊05°39	℞ 03°39	℞ 03°30	℞ 29°18	℞ 29°47	♐28°28	℞ 00°31	**1** Tu
2 We	22:44:39	♍09°33'38	♉09°10'39	♉16°07'06	♍14°34	♎23°57	♋14°01	♌13°54	♈13°37	♊05°39	♈03°38	♒03°29	♒29°15	♒29°46	♐28°34	♉00°29	**2** We
3 Th	22:48:35	♍10°31'43	♉23°06'17	♊00°07'28	♍16°25	♎24°44	♋14°39	♌14°07	♈13°33	♊05°40	♈03°37	♒03°28	♒29°11	♒29°46	♐28°41	♉00°28	**3** Th
4 Fr	22:52:32	♍11°29'50	♊07°10'56	♊14°15'56	♍18°15	♎25°30	♋15°17	♌14°19	♈13°30	♊05°40	♈03°35	♒03°27	♒29°08	♒29°45	♐28°48	♉00°26	**4** Fr
5 Sa	22:56:28	♍12°27'58	♊21°22'43	♊28°30'29	♍20°04	♎26°15	♋15°55	♌14°32	♈13°26	♊05°40	♈03°33	♒03°26	♒29°05	D 29°45	♐28°54	♉00°24	**5** Sa
6 Su	23:00:25	♍13°26'09	♋05°39'25	♋12°48'40	♍21°52	♎26°59	♋16°32	♌14°44	♈13°23	♊05°41	♈03°32	♒03°25	♒29°02	♒29°46	♐29°01	♉00°23	**6** Su
7 Mo	23:04:21	♍14°24'21	♋19°58'21	♋27°07'34	♍23°38	♎27°42	♋17°10	♌14°56	♈13°19	♊05°41	♈03°30	♒03°24	♒28°59	♒29°47	♐29°08	♉00°21	**7** Mo
8 Tu	23:08:18	♍15°22'36	♌04°16'22	♌11°23'46	♍25°23	♎28°25	♋17°47	♌15°09	♈13°15	♊05°41	♈03°29	♒03°23	♒28°56	♒29°48	♐29°15	♉00°19	**8** Tu
9 We	23:12:15	♍16°20'53	♌18°29'48	♌25°33'28	♍27°07	♎29°06	♋18°25	♌15°21	♈13°11	♊05°41	♈03°27	♒03°22	♒28°52	♒29°49	♐29°21	♉00°18	**9** We
10 Th	23:16:11	♍17°19'11	♍02°34'47	♍09°32'48	♍28°50	♎29°46	♋19°02	♌15°33	♈13°07	♊05°41	♈03°26	♒03°21	♒28°49	℞ 29°49	♐29°28	♉00°16	**10** Th
11 Fr	23:20:08	♍18°17'31	♍16°27'33	♍23°18'10	♎00°32	♏00°25	♋19°39	♌15°45	♈13°03	℞ 05°41	♈03°24	♒03°20	♒28°46	♒29°48	♐29°35	♉00°14	**11** Fr
12 Sa	23:24:04	♍19°15'53	♎00°04'48	♎06°46'43	♎02°12	♏01°03	♋20°16	♌15°57	♈12°59	♊05°41	♈03°23	♒03°19	♒28°43	♒29°47	♐29°41	♉00°12	**12** Sa
13 Su	23:28:01	♍20°14'17	♎13°24'12	♎19°56'42	♎03°52	♏01°40	♋20°53	♌16°09	♈12°55	♊05°41	♈03°21	♒03°18	♒28°40	♒29°44	♐29°48	♉00°10	**13** Su
14 Mo	23:31:57	♍21°12'42	♎26°24'39	♏02°47'40	♎05°30	♏02°16	♋21°30	♌16°21	♈12°51	♊05°41	♈03°19	♒03°18	♒28°36	♒29°41	♐29°55	♉00°08	**14** Mo
15 Tu	23:35:54	♍22°11'09	♏09°06'23	♏15°20'35	♎07°07	♏02°50	♋22°07	♌16°33	♈12°47	♊05°41	♈03°18	♒03°17	♒28°33	♒29°38	♑00°01	♉00°06	**15** Tu
16 We	23:39:50	♍23°09'38	♏21°31'01	♏27°37'39	♎08°44	♏03°24	♋22°44	♌16°45	♈12°42	♊05°41	♈03°16	♒03°16	♒28°30	♒29°34	♑00°08	♉00°04	**16** We
17 Th	23:43:47	♍24°08'09	♐03°41'19	♐09°42'07	♎10°19	♏03°55	♋23°20	♌16°57	♈12°38	♊05°40	♈03°14	♒03°15	♒28°27	♒29°32	♑00°15	♉00°02	**17** Th
18 Fr	23:47:44	♍25°06'41	♐15°40'59	♐21°38'05	♎11°53	♏04°26	♋23°57	♌17°09	♈12°34	♊05°40	♈03°13	♒03°14	♒28°24	♒29°30	♑00°22	♉00°00	**18** Fr
19 Sa	23:51:40	♍26°05'15	♐27°34'24	♑03°30'08	♎13°26	♏04°54	♋24°33	♌17°20	♈12°29	♊05°40	♈03°11	♒03°14	♒28°21	D 29°30	♑00°28	♈29°57	**19** Sa
20 Su	23:55:37	♍27°03'51	♑09°26'18	♑15°23'07	♎14°58	♏05°22	♋25°09	♌17°32	♈12°25	♊05°39	♈03°09	♒03°13	♒28°17	♒29°31	♑00°35	♈29°55	**20** Su
21 Mo	23:59:33	♍28°02'28	♑21°21'35	♑27°21'52	♎16°29	♏05°47	♋25°45	♌17°44	♈12°20	♊05°39	♈03°08	♒03°12	♒28°14	♒29°32	♑00°42	♈29°53	**21** Mo
22 Tu	00:03:30	♍29°01'07	♒03°24'57	♒09°30'56	♎17°59	♏06°11	♋26°21	♌17°55	♈12°16	♊05°38	♈03°06	♒03°12	♒28°11	♒29°34	♑00°48	♈29°51	**22** Tu
23 We	00:07:26	♍29°59'47	♒15°40'42	♒21°54'15	♎19°28	♏06°34	♋26°57	♌18°06	♈12°11	♊05°38	♈03°05	♒03°11	♒28°08	♒29°35	♑00°55	♈29°48	**23** We
24 Th	00:11:23	♎00°58'30	♒28°12'23	♓04°34'56	♎20°56	♏06°54	♋27°33	♌18°18	♈12°07	♊05°37	♈03°03	♒03°10	♒28°05	♒29°36	♑01°02	♈29°46	**24** Th
25 Fr	00:15:19	♎01°57'14	♓11°02'32	♓17°34'50	♎22°22	♏07°13	♋28°09	♌18°29	♈12°02	♊05°36	♈03°01	♒03°10	♒28°01	℞ 29°36	♑01°08	♈29°44	**25** Fr
26 Sa	00:19:16	♎02°55'59	♓24°12'19	♈00°54'24	♎23°48	♏07°30	♋28°45	♌18°40	♈11°58	♊05°35	♈03°00	♒03°09	♒27°58	♒29°33	♑01°15	♈29°41	**26** Sa
27 Su	00:23:13	♎03°54'47	♈07°41'24	♈14°32'31	♎25°13	♏07°45	♋29°20	♌18°51	♈11°53	♊05°35	♈02°58	♒03°09	♒27°55	♒29°30	♑01°22	♈29°39	**27** Su
28 Mo	00:27:09	♎04°53'37	♈21°27'52	♈28°26'30	♎26°36	♏07°57	♋29°55	♌19°02	♈11°48	♊05°34	♈02°56	♒03°08	♒27°52	♒29°25	♑01°29	♈29°36	**28** Mo
29 Tu	00:31:06	♎05°52'29	♉05°28'25	♉12°32'33	♎27°59	♏08°08	♌00°31	♌19°13	♈11°44	♊05°33	♈02°55	♒03°08	♒27°49	♒29°19	♑01°35	♈29°34	**29** Tu
30 We	00:35:02	♎06°51'23	♉19°38'49	♉26°46'10	♎29°20	♏08°17	♌01°06	♌19°24	♈11°39	♊05°32	♈02°53	♒03°07	♒27°46	♒29°13	♑01°42	♈29°31	**30** We
Δ Delta	01:54:19	28°15'47"	384°13'08"	384°29'32"	46°38'	15°06'	17°42'	5°42'	-2°01'	-0°06'	-0°46'	-0°22'	-1°32'	-0°34'	3°14'	-0°59'	**Delta**

Ephemeris tables and data provided by **Astro-Seek.com.** All times in UTC.

October 2026

Longitude & Retrograde Ephemeris [00:00 UT]

Day	Sid.time	☉	☽	+12h ☽	☿	♀	♂	♃	♄	♅	♆	♇	☊	☊	⚸	⚷	Day
1 Th	00:38:59	♎07°50'20	♊03°54'32	♊11°02'55	♏00°40	♏08°23	♌01°41	♌19°35	℞ 11°34	℞ 05°31	℞ 02°51	℞ 03°07	℞ 27°42	℞ 29°09	♑01°49	℞ 29°29	**1** Th
2 Fr	00:42:55	♎08°49'18	♊18°11'20	♊25°18'54	♏01°59	♏08°27	♌02°16	♌19°46	♈11°30	♊05°30	♈02°50	♒03°06	♒27°39	♒29°05	♑01°55	♈29°26	**2** Fr
3 Sa	00:46:52	♎09°48'20	♋02°25'47	♋09°31'10	♏03°17	♏08°29	♌02°51	♌19°56	♈11°25	♊05°29	♈02°48	♒03°06	♒27°36	♒29°03	♑02°02	♈29°24	**3** Sa
4 Su	00:50:48	♎10°47'23	♋16°35'22	♋23°37'42	♏04°33	℞ 08°28	♌03°25	♌20°07	♈11°20	♊05°28	♈02°46	♒03°06	♒27°33	D 29°03	♑02°09	♈29°21	**4** Su
5 Mo	00:54:45	♎11°46'29	♌00°38'31	♌07°37'12	℞S 05°48	♏08°26	♌04°00	♌20°17	♈11°15	♊05°27	♈02°45	♒03°05	♒27°30	♒29°04	♑02°15	♈29°19	**5** Mo
6 Tu	00:58:42	♎12°45'37	♌14°34'10	♌21°28'50	♏07°01	♏08°20	♌04°34	♌20°28	♈11°11	♊05°25	♈02°43	♒03°05	♒27°27	♒29°06	♑02°22	♈29°16	**6** Tu
7 We	01:02:38	♎13°44'47	♌28°21'33	♍05°11'44	♏08°12	♏08°13	♌05°08	♌20°38	♈11°06	♊05°24	♈02°41	♒03°05	♒27°23	♒29°06	♑02°29	♈29°13	**7** We
8 Th	01:06:35	♎14°43'59	♍11°59'44	♍18°44'54	♏09°22	♏08°03	♌05°43	♌20°48	♈11°01	♊05°23	♈02°40	♒03°05	♒27°20	℞ 29°05	♑02°36	♈29°11	**8** Th
9 Fr	01:10:31	♎15°43'14	♍25°27'33	♎02°07'02	♏10°30	♏07°51	♌06°17	♌20°58	♈10°57	♊05°22	♈02°38	♒03°04	♒27°17	♒29°03	♑02°42	♈29°08	**9** Fr
10 Sa	01:14:28	♎16°42'31	♎08°43'38	♎15°16'43	♏11°36	♏07°36	♌06°50	♌21°08	♈10°52	♊05°20	♈02°37	♒03°04	♒27°14	♒28°57	♑02°49	♈29°05	**10** Sa
11 Su	01:18:24	♎17°41'49	♎21°46'36	♎28°12'42	♏12°40	♏07°19	♌07°24	♌21°18	♈10°47	♊05°19	♈02°35	♒03°04	♒27°11	♒28°50	♑02°56	♈29°02	**11** Su
12 Mo	01:22:21	♎18°41'11	♏04°35'25	♏10°54'14	♏13°41	♏07°00	♌07°58	♌21°28	♈10°42	♊05°17	♈02°33	♒03°04	♒27°07	♒28°41	♑03°02	♈29°00	**12** Mo
13 Tu	01:26:17	♎19°40'33	♏17°09'39	♏23°21'20	♏14°40	♏06°38	♌08°31	♌21°37	♈10°38	♊05°16	♈02°32	♒03°04	♒27°04	♒28°32	♑03°09	♈28°57	**13** Tu
14 We	01:30:14	♎20°39'58	♏29°29'52	♐05°35'03	♏15°35	♏06°14	♌09°05	♌21°47	♈10°33	♊05°14	♈02°30	♒03°04	♒27°01	♒28°22	♑03°16	♈28°54	**14** We
15 Th	01:34:10	♎21°39'25	♐11°37'37	♐17°37'30	♏16°28	♏05°49	♌09°38	♌21°56	♈10°29	♊05°13	♈02°29	♒03°04	♒26°58	♒28°14	♑03°22	♈28°51	**15** Th
16 Fr	01:38:07	♎22°38'53	♐23°35'34	♐29°31'50	♏17°17	♏05°21	♌10°11	♌22°06	♈10°24	♊05°11	♈02°27	♒03°04	♒26°55	♒28°08	♑03°29	♈28°49	**16** Fr
17 Sa	01:42:04	♎23°38'24	♑05°27'18	♑11°22'05	♏18°03	♏04°51	♌10°44	♌22°15	♈10°20	♊05°09	♈02°26	D 03°04	♒26°52	♒28°04	♑03°36	♈28°46	**17** Sa
18 Su	01:46:00	♎24°37'56	♑17°17'15	♑23°12'59	♏18°44	♏04°20	♌11°16	♌22°24	♈10°15	♊05°08	♈02°24	♒03°04	♒26°48	♒28°02	♑03°42	♈28°43	**18** Su
19 Mo	01:49:57	♎25°37'30	♑29°10'23	♒05°09'41	♏19°21	♏03°48	♌11°49	♌22°33	♈10°11	♊05°06	♈02°23	♒03°04	♒26°45	D 28°01	♑03°49	♈28°40	**19** Mo
20 Tu	01:53:53	♎26°37'05	♒11°12'00	♒17°17'31	♏19°52	♏03°14	♌12°21	♌22°42	♈10°06	♊05°04	♈02°21	♒03°04	♒26°42	♒28°02	♑03°56	♈28°37	**20** Tu
21 We	01:57:50	♎27°36'43	♒23°27'21	♒29°41'36	♏20°18	♏02°39	♌12°53	♌22°51	♈10°02	♊05°02	♈02°20	♒03°04	♒26°39	♒28°03	♑04°03	♈28°35	**21** We
22 Th	02:01:46	♎28°36'22	♓06°01'17	♓12°26'24	♏20°38	♏02°03	♌13°26	♌22°59	♈09°57	♊05°00	♈02°18	♒03°04	♒26°36	℞ 28°03	♑04°09	♈28°32	**22** Th
23 Fr	02:05:43	♎29°36'02	♓18°57'44	♓25°35'06	♏20°52	♏01°27	♌13°57	♌23°08	♈09°53	♊04°59	♈02°17	♒03°04	♒26°33	♒28°01	♑04°16	♈28°29	**23** Fr
24 Sa	02:09:39	♏00°35'45	♈02°19'06	♈09°09'11	♏20°58	♏00°50	♌14°29	♌23°16	♈09°49	♊04°57	♈02°15	♒03°05	♒26°29	♒27°56	♑04°23	♈28°26	**24** Sa
25 Su	02:13:36	♏01°35'29	♈16°05'40	♈23°07'42	℞ 20°56	♏00°13	♌15°01	♌23°25	♈09°45	♊04°55	♈02°14	♒03°05	♒26°26	♒27°49	♑04°29	♈28°23	**25** Su
26 Mo	02:17:33	♏02°35'16	♉00°15'15	♉07°27'07	♏20°46	♎29°37	♌15°32	♌23°33	♈09°40	♊04°53	♈02°12	♒03°05	♒26°23	♒27°40	♑04°36	♈28°21	**26** Mo
27 Tu	02:21:29	♏03°35'04	♉14°43'03	♉22°01'33	♏20°28	♎29°01	♌16°03	♌23°41	♈09°36	♊04°51	♈02°11	♒03°05	♒26°20	♒27°30	♑04°43	♈28°18	**27** Tu
28 We	02:25:26	♏04°34'54	♉29°22'13	♊06°43'31	♏20°00	♎28°25	♌16°34	♌23°49	♈09°32	♊04°49	♈02°10	♒03°06	♒26°17	♒27°19	♑04°49	♈28°15	**28** We
29 Th	02:29:22	♏05°34'47	♊14°05'00	♊21°25'13	♏19°23	♎27°51	♌17°05	♌23°56	♈09°28	♊04°46	♈02°08	♒03°06	♒26°13	♒27°10	♑04°56	♈28°12	**29** Th
30 Fr	02:33:19	♏06°34'41	♊28°43'54	♋05°59'50	♏18°37	♎27°17	♌17°36	♌24°04	♈09°24	♊04°44	♈02°07	♒03°06	♒26°10	♒27°03	♑05°03	♈28°09	**30** Fr
31 Sa	02:37:15	♏07°34'38	♋13°12'59	♋20°22'25	♏17°42	♎26°45	♌18°06	♌24°12	♈09°20	♊04°42	♈02°06	♒03°07	♒26°07	♒26°58	♑05°10	♈28°07	**31** Sa
Δ Delta	01:58:16	29°44'18"	399°18'26"	399°19'30"	17°01'	-11°37'	16°25'	4°36'	-2°13'	-0°48'	-0°45'	-0°00'	-1°35'	-2°10'	3°20'	-1°22'	**Delta**

Ephemeris tables and data provided by **Astro-Seek.com.** All times in UTC.

November 2026

Longitude & Retrograde Ephemeris [00:00 UT]

Day	Sid.time	☉	☽	+12h☽	☿	♀	♂	♃	♄	♅	♆	♇	☊	☊	⚸	⚷	Day
1 Su	02:41:12	♏08°34'37	♋27°28'23	♌04°30'12	℞ 16°39	℞ 26°14	♌18°37	♌24°19	℞ 09°17	℞ 04°40	℞ 02°05	♒03°07	℞ 26°04	℞ 26°56	♑05°16	℞ 28°04	**1** Su
2 Mo	02:45:09	♏09°34'38	♌11°28'22	♌18°22'24	♏15°30	♎25°45	♌19°07	♌24°26	♈09°13	♊04°38	♈02°03	♒03°08	♒26°01	D 26°55	♑05°23	♈28°01	**2** Mo
3 Tu	02:49:05	♏10°34'41	♌25°12'55	♍01°59'34	♏14°15	♎25°18	♌19°37	♌24°33	♈09°09	♊04°36	♈02°02	♒03°08	♒25°58	♒26°56	♑05°30	♈27°59	**3** Tu
4 We	02:53:02	♏11°34'46	♍08°42'59	♍15°22'54	♏12°57	♎24°53	♌20°07	♌24°40	♈09°06	♊04°33	♈02°01	♒03°09	♒25°54	℞ 26°55	♑05°36	♈27°56	**4** We
5 Th	02:56:58	♏12°34'54	♍21°59'57	♍28°33'47	♏11°39	♎24°31	♌20°36	♌24°47	♈09°02	♊04°31	♈02°00	♒03°09	♒25°51	♒26°53	♑05°43	♈27°53	**5** Th
6 Fr	03:00:55	♏13°35'03	♎05°05'00	♎11°33'14	♏10°22	♎24°10	♌21°05	♌24°54	♈08°59	♊04°29	♈01°59	♒03°10	♒25°48	♒26°48	♑05°50	♈27°50	**6** Fr
7 Sa	03:04:51	♏14°35'15	♎17°59'00	♎24°21'51	♏09°10	♎23°52	♌21°34	♌25°00	♈08°55	♊04°27	♈01°57	♒03°10	♒25°45	♒26°40	♑05°56	♈27°48	**7** Sa
8 Su	03:08:48	♏15°35'28	♏00°42'16	♏06°59'49	♏08°04	♎23°36	♌22°03	♌25°06	♈08°52	♊04°24	♈01°56	♒03°11	♒25°42	♒26°29	♑06°03	♈27°45	**8** Su
9 Mo	03:12:44	♏16°35'43	♏13°14'54	♏19°27'07	♏07°06	♎23°22	♌22°32	♌25°13	♈08°49	♊04°22	♈01°55	♒03°12	♒25°38	♒26°16	♑06°10	♈27°42	**9** Mo
10 Tu	03:16:41	♏17°36'00	♏25°36'55	♐01°43'53	♏06°19	♎23°11	♌23°00	♌25°19	♈08°46	♊04°19	♈01°54	♒03°12	♒25°35	♒26°01	♑06°16	♈27°40	**10** Tu
11 We	03:20:37	♏18°36'19	♐07°48'35	♐13°50'41	♏05°42	♎23°02	♌23°29	♌25°25	♈08°43	♊04°17	♈01°53	♒03°13	♒25°32	♒25°47	♑06°23	♈27°37	**11** We
12 Th	03:24:34	♏19°36'39	♐19°50'48	♐25°48'46	♏05°17	♎22°56	♌23°56	♌25°30	♈08°40	♊04°15	♈01°52	♒03°14	♒25°29	♒25°34	♑06°30	♈27°35	**12** Th
13 Fr	03:28:31	♏20°37'02	♑01°45'17	♑07°40'17	♏05°04	♎22°53	♌24°24	♌25°36	♈08°37	♊04°12	♈01°51	♒03°15	♒25°26	♒25°24	♑06°36	♈27°32	**13** Fr
14 Sa	03:32:27	♏21°37'25	♑13°34'37	♑19°28'19	D♏05°02	♎22°51	♌24°52	♌25°41	♈08°34	♊04°10	♈01°50	♒03°15	♒25°23	♒25°16	♑06°43	♈27°30	**14** Sa
15 Su	03:36:24	♏22°37'50	♑25°22'20	♒01°16'48	♏05°11	D 22°52	♌25°19	♌25°46	♈08°31	♊04°07	♈01°49	♒03°16	♒25°19	♒25°11	♑06°50	♈27°27	**15** Su
16 Mo	03:40:20	♏23°38'16	♒07°12'47	♒13°10'30	♏05°31	♎22°56	♌25°46	♌25°52	♈08°29	♊04°05	♈01°48	♒03°17	♒25°16	♒25°09	♑06°57	♈27°25	**16** Mo
17 Tu	03:44:17	♏24°38'44	♒19°11'02	♒25°14'39	♏05°59	♎23°02	♌26°12	♌25°56	♈08°26	♊04°02	♈01°48	♒03°18	♒25°13	♒25°08	♑07°03	♈27°22	**17** Tu
18 We	03:48:13	♏25°39'13	♓01°22'30	♓07°34'49	♏06°37	♎23°10	♌26°39	♌26°01	♈08°24	♊04°00	♈01°47	♒03°19	♒25°10	♒25°08	♑07°10	♈27°20	**18** We
19 Th	03:52:10	♏26°39'43	♓13°52'43	♓20°16'21	♏07°22	♎23°20	♌27°05	♌26°06	♈08°21	♊03°57	♈01°46	♒03°20	♒25°07	♒25°07	♑07°17	♈27°18	**19** Th
20 Fr	03:56:07	♏27°40'14	♓26°46'42	♈03°23'47	♏08°14	♎23°33	♌27°31	♌26°10	♈08°19	♊03°55	♈01°45	♒03°21	♒25°04	♒25°05	♑07°23	♈27°15	**20** Fr
21 Sa	04:00:03	♏28°40'47	♈10°08'20	♈17°00'05	♏09°11	♎23°48	♌27°56	♌26°14	♈08°17	♊03°52	♈01°44	♒03°22	♒25°00	♒25°00	♑07°30	♈27°13	**21** Sa
22 Su	04:03:60	♏29°41'21	♈23°59'29	♉01°05'48	♏10°14	♎24°05	♌28°22	♌26°18	♈08°15	♊03°50	♈01°44	♒03°23	♒24°57	♒24°53	♑07°37	♈27°11	**22** Su
23 Mo	04:07:56	♐00°41'56	♉08°19'08	♉15°38'18	♏11°22	♎24°23	♌28°47	♌26°22	♈08°13	♊03°47	♈01°43	♒03°24	♒24°54	♒24°43	♑07°43	♈27°08	**23** Mo
24 Tu	04:11:53	♐01°42'33	♉23°02'57	♊00°31'32	♏12°33	♎24°44	♌29°11	♌26°26	♈08°11	♊03°45	♈01°42	♒03°25	♒24°51	♒24°31	♑07°50	♈27°06	**24** Tu
25 We	04:15:49	♐02°43'11	♊08°03'21	♊15°36'37	♏13°47	♎25°07	♌29°36	♌26°30	♈08°09	♊03°42	♈01°42	♒03°26	♒24°48	♒24°19	♑07°57	♈27°04	**25** We
26 Th	04:19:46	♐03°43'51	♊23°10'31	♋00°43'15	♏15°05	♎25°31	♍00°00	♌26°33	♈08°08	♊03°40	♈01°41	♒03°27	♒24°44	♒24°09	♑08°03	♈27°02	**26** Th
27 Fr	04:23:42	♐04°44'31	♋08°14'09	♋15°41'36	♏16°25	♎25°58	♍00°24	♌26°36	♈08°06	♊03°37	♈01°41	♒03°28	♒24°41	♒24°00	♑08°10	♈27°00	**27** Fr
28 Sa	04:27:39	♐05°45'14	♋23°05'15	♌00°23'52	♏17°47	♎26°26	♍00°47	♌26°39	♈08°05	♊03°35	♈01°40	♒03°29	♒24°38	♒23°54	♑08°17	♈26°58	**28** Sa
29 Su	04:31:36	♐06°45'58	♌07°37'29	♌14°45'15	♏19°11	♎26°55	♍01°10	♌26°42	♈08°03	♊03°32	♈01°40	♒03°31	♒24°35	♒23°52	♑08°24	♈26°56	**29** Su
30 Mo	04:35:32	♐07°46'44	♌21°47'34	♌28°43'54	♏20°36	♎27°27	♍01°33	♌26°44	♈08°02	♊03°30	♈01°39	♒03°32	♒24°32	♒23°51	♑08°30	♈26°54	**30** Mo
Δ Delta	01:54:19	29°12'06"	384°19'11"	384°13'41"	3°56'	1°12'	12°56'	2°25'	-1°14'	-1°10'	-0°25'	0°24'	-1°32'	-3°05'	3°13'	-1°10'	**Delta**

Ephemeris tables and data provided by **Astro-Seek.com.** All times in UTC.

December 2026

Longitude & Retrograde Ephemeris [00:00 UT]

Day	Sid.time	☉	☽	+12h☽	☿	♀	♂	♃	♄	♅	♆	♇	☊	☊	⚸	⚷	Day
1 Tu	04:39:29	♐08°47′30	♍05°34′55	♍12°20′19	♏22°02	♎27°59	♍01°56	♌26°47	℞ 08°01	℞ 03°27	℞ 01°39	♒03°33	℞ 24°29	♒23°51	♑08°37	℞ 26°52	**1** Tu
2 We	04:43:25	♐09°48′19	♍19°00′54	♍25°36′32	♏23°30	♎28°34	♍02°18	♌26°49	♈08°00	♊03°25	♈01°38	♒03°34	♒24°25	℞ 23°51	♑08°44	♈26°50	**2** We
3 Th	04:47:22	♐10°49′09	♎02°08′01	♎08°35′16	♏24°58	♎29°09	♍02°39	♌26°51	♈07°59	♊03°22	♈01°38	♒03°36	♒24°22	♒23°49	♑08°50	♈26°48	**3** Th
4 Fr	04:51:18	♐11°50′00	♎14°59′04	♎21°19′19	♏26°27	♎29°47	♍03°01	♌26°53	♈07°58	♊03°20	♈01°38	♒03°37	♒24°19	♒23°44	♑08°57	♈26°46	**4** Fr
5 Sa	04:55:15	♐12°50′53	♎27°36′45	♏03°51′10	♏27°57	♏00°25	♍03°22	♌26°55	♈07°57	♊03°17	♈01°37	♒03°38	♒24°16	♒23°37	♑09°04	♈26°45	**5** Sa
6 Su	04:59:11	♐13°51′47	♏10°03′16	♏16°12′47	♏29°27	♏01°05	♍03°42	♌26°56	♈07°57	♊03°15	♈01°37	♒03°39	♒24°13	♒23°27	♑09°10	♈26°43	**6** Su
7 Mo	05:03:08	♐14°52′42	♏22°20′21	♏28°25′39	♐00°58	♏01°45	♍04°03	♌26°57	♈07°56	♊03°12	♈01°37	♒03°41	♒24°10	♒23°15	♑09°17	♈26°41	**7** Mo
8 Tu	05:07:05	♐15°53′39	♐04°29′16	♐10°30′52	♐02°29	♏02°27	♍04°22	♌26°58	♈07°56	♊03°10	♈01°37	♒03°42	♒24°06	♒23°02	♑09°24	♈26°40	**8** Tu
9 We	05:11:01	♐16°54′36	♐16°31′03	♐22°29′28	♐04°00	♏03°11	♍04°42	♌26°59	♈07°56	♊03°08	♈01°37	♒03°44	♒24°03	♒22°48	♑09°30	♈26°38	**9** We
10 Th	05:14:58	♐17°55′35	♐28°26′44	♑04°22′36	♐05°32	♏03°55	♍05°01	♌27°00	♈07°55	♊03°05	♈01°36	♒03°45	♒24°00	♒22°36	♑09°37	♈26°36	**10** Th
11 Fr	05:18:54	♐18°56′34	♑10°17′41	♑16°11′49	♐07°04	♏04°40	♍05°19	♌27°01	D 07°55	♊03°03	♈01°36	♒03°46	♒23°57	♒22°26	♑09°44	♈26°35	**11** Fr
12 Sa	05:22:51	♐19°57′34	♑22°05′43	♑27°59′18	♐08°36	♏05°26	♍05°37	♌27°01	♈07°55	♊03°00	♈01°36	♒03°48	♒23°54	♒22°19	♑09°50	♈26°34	**12** Sa
13 Su	05:26:47	♐20°58′35	♒03°53′24	♒09°47′59	♐10°08	♏06°13	♍05°55	♌27°01	♈07°56	♊02°58	D 01°36	♒03°49	♒23°50	♒22°15	♑09°57	♈26°32	**13** Su
14 Mo	05:30:44	♐21°59′36	♒15°44′00	♒21°41′32	♐11°41	♏07°01	♍06°12	℞ 27°01	♈07°56	♊02°56	♈01°36	♒03°51	♒23°47	♒22°13	♑10°04	♈26°31	**14** Mo
15 Tu	05:34:40	♐23°00′38	♒27°41′35	♓03°44′20	♐13°13	♏07°50	♍06°29	♌27°01	♈07°56	♊02°53	♈01°36	♒03°52	♒23°44	D 22°12	♑10°10	♈26°30	**15** Tu
16 We	05:38:37	♐24°01′41	♓09°50′50	♓16°01′18	♐14°46	♏08°40	♍06°45	♌27°00	♈07°57	♊02°51	♈01°36	♒03°54	♒23°41	♒22°13	♑10°17	♈26°28	**16** We
17 Th	05:42:34	♐25°02′43	♓22°16′50	♓28°37′35	♐16°19	♏09°31	♍07°01	♌26°59	♈07°57	♊02°49	♈01°37	♒03°56	♒23°38	♒22°14	♑10°24	♈26°27	**17** Th
18 Fr	05:46:30	♐26°03′47	♈05°04′38	♈11°38′03	♐17°52	♏10°22	♍07°16	♌26°59	♈07°58	♊02°46	♈01°37	♒03°57	♒23°35	℞ 22°14	♑10°31	♈26°26	**18** Fr
19 Sa	05:50:27	♐27°04′50	♈18°18′46	♈25°06′37	♐19°25	♏11°14	♍07°31	♌26°57	♈07°59	♊02°44	♈01°37	♒03°59	♒23°31	♒22°11	♑10°37	♈26°25	**19** Sa
20 Su	05:54:23	♐28°05′54	♉02°02′19	♉09°05′22	♐20°58	♏12°07	♍07°45	♌26°56	♈08°00	♊02°42	♈01°37	♒04°00	♒23°28	♒22°07	♑10°44	♈26°24	**20** Su
21 Mo	05:58:20	♐29°06′59	♉16°16′06	♉23°33′37	♐22°32	♏13°00	♍07°59	♌26°55	♈08°01	♊02°40	♈01°37	♒04°02	♒23°25	♒22°00	♑10°51	♈26°23	**21** Mo
22 Tu	06:02:16	♑00°08′03	♊00°57′46	♊08°27′12	♐24°05	♏13°55	♍08°12	♌26°53	♈08°02	♊02°38	♈01°38	♒04°04	♒23°22	♒21°52	♑10°57	♈26°22	**22** Tu
23 We	06:06:13	♑01°09′08	♊16°01′23	♊23°38′31	♐25°39	♏14°49	♍08°25	♌26°51	♈08°03	♊02°35	♈01°38	♒04°05	♒23°19	♒21°44	♑11°04	♈26°21	**23** We
24 Th	06:10:09	♑02°10′14	♋01°17′48	♋08°57′16	♐27°13	♏15°45	♍08°37	♌26°49	♈08°05	♊02°33	♈01°38	♒04°07	♒23°16	♒21°36	♑11°11	♈26°21	**24** Th
25 Fr	06:14:06	♑03°11′20	♋16°36′03	♋24°12′17	♐28°47	♏16°41	♍08°48	♌26°47	♈08°06	♊02°31	♈01°39	♒04°09	♒23°12	♒21°30	♑11°17	♈26°20	**25** Fr
26 Sa	06:18:03	♑04°12′26	♌01°45′17	♌09°13′27	♑00°22	♏17°38	♍08°59	♌26°45	♈08°08	♊02°29	♈01°39	♒04°10	♒23°09	♒21°27	♑11°24	♈26°19	**26** Sa
27 Su	06:21:59	♑05°13′33	♌16°36′30	♌23°53′15	♑01°56	♏18°35	♍09°09	♌26°42	♈08°09	♊02°27	♈01°40	♒04°12	♒23°06	♒21°25	♑11°31	♈26°19	**27** Su
28 Mo	06:25:56	♑06°14′40	♍01°03′47	♍08°07′22	♑03°31	♏19°33	♍09°19	♌26°39	♈08°11	♊02°25	♈01°40	♒04°14	♒23°03	D 21°25	♑11°37	♈26°18	**28** Mo
29 Tu	06:29:52	♑07°15′47	♍15°04′27	♍21°54′38	♑05°06	♏20°31	♍09°28	♌26°36	♈08°13	♊02°23	♈01°41	♒04°15	♒23°00	♒21°26	♑11°44	♈26°17	**29** Tu
30 We	06:33:49	♑08°16′55	♍28°38′37	♎05°16′15	♑06°42	♏21°30	♍09°37	♌26°33	♈08°15	♊02°21	♈01°41	♒04°17	♒22°57	♒21°28	♑11°51	♈26°17	**30** We
31 Th	06:37:45	♑09°18′04	♎11°48′23	♎18°14′59	♑08°18	♏22°29	♍09°45	♌26°30	♈08°17	♊02°19	♈01°42	♒04°19	♒22°53	℞ 21°28	♑11°57	♈26°17	**31** Th
Δ Delta	01:58:15	30°30′33″	396°13′28″	395°54′39″	46°15′	24°29′	7°49′	-0°17′	0°16′	-1°07′	0°03′	0°45′	-1°35′	-2°22′	3°20′	-0°35′	**Delta**

Ephemeris tables and data provided by **Astro-Seek.com.** All times in UTC.

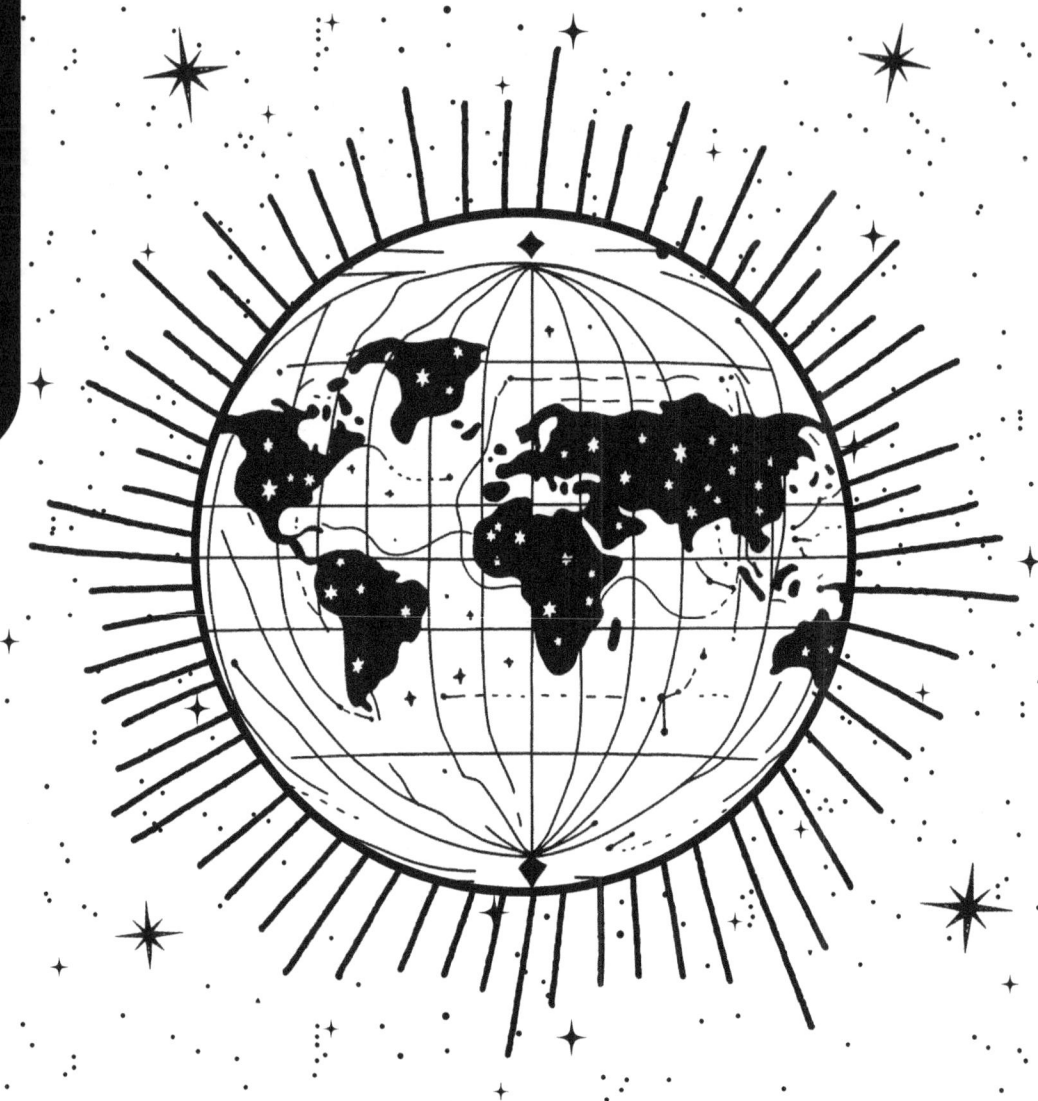

THE ASTROTWINS'
2026
ALMANAC

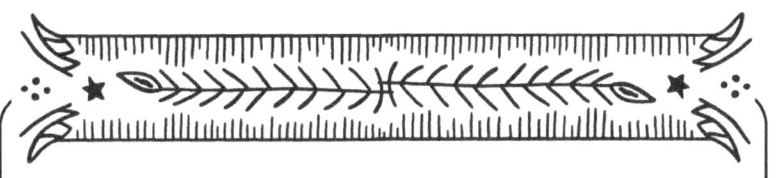

LOVE IN THE AGE OF AQUARIUS

CIVIL WAR 2.0

FINANCIAL CYCLES & ASTROLOGY

BIRTH OF A SPECIES

THE CROSS OF THE SLEEPING PHOENIX

2026 ASTROCARTOGRAPHY

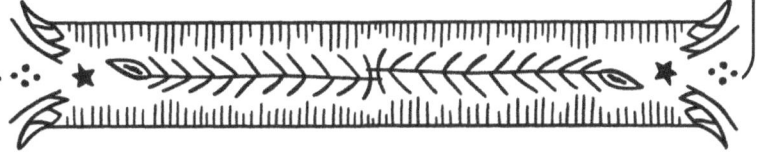

Each year, we take the pulse of the planets and chart out the world's next big chapter. Over the years, many of our forecasts have come true. But before you call us psychic, here's the truth: Astrology isn't a random prediction of fate, it's a system of pattern recognition.

The role of a "mundane" astrologer (one who studies world events through an astrological lens) is more like a statistician, economist or historian. When long-lasting or rare cycles repeat, we look back at what happened in prior times. Then, we compare it to the current social, historical and environmental landscapes. With the extra data point of the planets' astronomical motion, we make our best prognosis for what could occur.

Humans have been doing this for millennia. Long before newsfeeds and TikTok trends, we had almanacs, the original cosmic calendars. The first printed almanac appeared in Europe in 1457, but early versions appeared all over the world for centuries, from Babylonian tablets in the B.C. era to Nostradamus' 16th century prophecies. Medieval almanacs were printed with ephemerides—calendar tables with the exact positions of the Sun, moon and planets.

Almanacs were popular! With the advent of the printing press, they outsold every printed book except the Bible. Benjamin Franklin's Poor Richard's Almanack was in publication for 25 years, from 1732 to 1757. The Old Farmer's Almanac, in continuous publication since 1792, foretells weather patterns, crop cycles and full moons.

Sadly, the Farmer's Almanac, in publication since 1818, will shutter after 208 years in 2026. So this year, we're keeping the tradition alive. The AstroTwins 2026 Almanac is here to help you track the cycles, digest the news and find your rhythm with the planets. We'll look back to look forward, connect the cosmic dots and navigate the year ahead—together.

LOVE IN THE AGE OF AQUARIUS
How to Do Relationships in 2026

2026 ALMANAC

Love has been in the midst of a metaphorical iOS update since this decade began, but the system software is still loading. As 2026 progresses, a new model for relationships may begin to take shape. First, we have to decide which traditions to keep and which ones need to go the way of the floppy disk.

Once upon a time, "love" was a land deed. Marriage began not with Cupid but with crops. When humans transitioned from nomads to farmers over 10,000 years ago, our relationship model shifted, too. As civilization grew, partnership became about property: whose name went on the land, whose lineage inherited it. Monogamy was about management during the Agrarian Age, a social contract meant to secure survival.

Fast-forward to the present-day Aquarian Age, when most people don't need a spouse to eat or a partner to protect the perimeter. We have DoorDash, 401(k)s and social media feeds to fill our loneliness tanks 24/7. Yet many still feel tugged toward a template designed for an earlier era.

It's biological, too, of course. The urge to partner and procreate is wired into every lobe of our brains and our cyclical functions. Humans have been tribal, social beings for as long as we can track our evolution.

our relationship model shifted

10,000

years ago

We have 401(k)s, DoorDash and social media feeds to fill our loneliness tanks 24/7.

For most people wishing to be in relationships and create families in the Aquarian Age, a new and successful model is still at large. Figuring out how to partner in these unprecedented times could offer an exciting design challenge. What would a "smart relationship" look like, and, we have to ask: Is there an app for that?

BACKLASH AND THE RETURN TO THE NUCLEAR IDEAL

Since Jupiter entered Taurus in 2023, we've seen a cultural counter-current: a renaissance of traditionalism. As the planet of expansion transited through this old-school, back-to-basics earth sign, collective attention turned toward stability, legacy and lineage. Cue the "trad-wife" revival, rife with "years I've been pregnant" posts, sourdough starter recipes and scripture quotes in Instagram bios.

By the time Jupiter reached Cancer on June 9, 2025, the pendulum had swung further. Cancer, after all, rules home, family and fertility. Evangelical Christian architects of Project 2025 moved into the White House with an unmistakable pronatalist tone. Billionaire tech moguls warned of "population collapse," while politicians pushed retrograde policies under the guise of protection.

From this Jupiter cycle emerged what we've dubbed The Iron Ladies: women wielding power to enforce submission, like U.S. Homeland Security Secretary Kristi Noem, U.S. Attorney General Pam Bondi and Turning Point CEO Erika Kirk. They've reframed patriarchy as empowerment, marrying the language of leadership to the logic of control. The result is a strange inversion of feminism, where "choice" looks like women volunteering to turn back the clock on progress in the guise of enforcing tropes about femininity, from Eurocentric beauty standards to traditional, gendered household roles.

Meanwhile, reproductive rights remain under siege. Roe v. Wade's reversal has hardened into regional caste systems. The zip code you live in will literally determine your bodily autonomy. Trans and LGBTQ+ communities face escalating legislative attacks. Choosing who to love without government and religious interference has become an act of resistance again.

And yet, even as pundits preach heteronormative roles and stump for procreation, the data tells a different story. According to a MassMutual study, one in four Millennials and Gen Z adults don't want children. The overriding reason? Money. Economic insecurity, housing shortages and rising healthcare costs have reframed parenthood as a luxury lifestyle.

As Jupiter travels through Cancer and Leo (2025-2027)—the zodiac's parenting and fertility signs—there may be attempts to reverse that trend through tokenized tax credits or "family stipends." These incentives, marketed as rewards for "traditional" two-parent households, will likely resemble modernized welfare programs with a moral filter; social safety nets wrapped in sanctimony.

THE GREAT PULLBACK—AND THE REFUSAL

On the other side of the spectrum, some are opting out altogether. The 4B movement, which originated in South Korea, became a global rallying cry for women and nonbinary people rejecting the patriarchal relationship script.

Its name comes from four Korean "no's":
- bihon (no marriage to men)
- bichulsan (no childbirth)
- biyeonae (no dating men)
- bisekseu (no heterosexual sex)

What began as a feminist resistance to South Korea's gender inequality has spread online as a transnational statement of refusal: If the system's broken, stop playing the game.

Gen Z has taken this ethos to heart. Studies show they're having less sex than any prior generation, driven by everything from economic stress to climate anxiety. A world teetering on collapse doesn't exactly set the stage for candlelit commitment. With dating app disappointment leading to coffee date fatigue, opting out can feel like its own form of liberation.

Still, the human desire for connection persists. The male loneliness epidemic is being studied as both a possible cause of depression and radicalization of men across generations.

Therapists, GPTs and astrologers alike field questions about how to love in a world where anxiety and existential fears hover like a constant cloud. The need for partnership hasn't disappeared at all. But it IS changing form.

"A world teetering on collapse doesn't exactly set the stage for candlelit commitment."

LOVE 2.6: THE 2026 RELATIONSHIP UPDATE

This year, the sky's software refreshes again. Jupiter in Cancer (through June 30, 2026) emphasizes emotional security, home life and the desire to nurture. Pronatalist rhetoric is seeping into headlines, encouraging reproduction to counteract declining birth rates. But there's also a quiet movement toward new family structures. Couples are experimenting with hybrid arrangements: co-living collectives, platonic life partnerships, creative and financial unions that prioritize practicality over passion.

Midyear, Jupiter enters Leo (June 30, 2026–July 26, 2027), turning up the theatrical volume. Leo loves a grand gesture and under its rule we could see a resurgence of public declarations, lavish weddings and viral proposals. Celebrity culture will feed the fantasy. Expect the long-teased Taylor Swift and Travis Kelce nuptials to dominate the news cycle, complete with royal symbolism and retro romance.

But astrologically, this isn't the return of the 1950s fairytale.

A mere month later, the lunar South Node will join Jupiter in Leo (July 26, 2026–March 26, 2028), bringing karmic corrections around ego-based love and outdated gender scripts. The North Node in cool-headed Aquarius will demand collaboration and equality. Get ready to see inspiring new examples of partnerships built on shared vision rather than attempts to gain status or draw attention.

BEYOND MONOGAMY AND MARKET VALUE

As the nodes shift into Leo (South Node) and Aquarius (North Node) this July 26, the narrative around love takes a different course. We'll start to move toward relationship models that mirror an interconnected world: fluid, collaborative and honest.

Some people may even prefer to design their romances as constellations rather than pairs. Open relationships and ethical non-monogamy have been embraced more widely in the first half of the decade. Amicable exes are choosing to live in a pod-like community and raise their kids together post-divorce or breakup. As we cross the midpoint of the 2020s, we envision a collective model of families emerging—with both monogamous and non-monogamous couples participating.

This may become ever-more imperative considering the Project 2025 goals of defunding and privatizing everything from schools to social safety nets. To maintain a sense of deregulated sovereignty, citizens could unite to share independent resources, homeschool kids and support each other's daily existence.

These experiments aren't rebellion for rebellion's sake. They're adaptations to a more complex reality. When careers, identities and even genders are no longer fixed, our definitions of partnership can't be either.

In late 2025, The Guardian published a piece "The Lavender Marriage is Back – But Why?" A trend is rising of straight women marrying gay men. Some legally marry a gay male best friend, while others stay married to a partner who's come out years later. These duos may be intimate, or they might live as a platonic couple. In many cases, they have kids and raise them together. The logic is partly economic, allowing the pair to capitalize on benefits not extended to singles, like health insurance and tax breaks. But it's also steeped in a genuine intimacy, love that goes far beyond sexual attraction.

THE HEART'S NEW FRONTIER

Astrologically, 2026 is a bridge year. Jupiter in traditional Cancer nurtures our longing for safety and belonging and we'll feel that immensely in the first half of the year. As the red-spotted planet sashays into Leo on June 30, it reminds us that love still wants to be celebrated. But under the Leo-Aquarius nodal axis, both halves of the zodiac demand balance: heart and intellect, devotion and freedom, the self and the collective.

The big question of 2026 may be this: What does commitment mean when permanence isn't guaranteed?

Some will answer with ceremony, others with conscious uncoupling and others still with creative reinvention. What we need to underscore is this: The Aquarian Age doesn't erase connection; it redefines it. Marriage may no longer be about property, but partnership still shapes destiny. Love, like technology, is iterative. Each version teaches us how to live and how to evolve, together.

CIVIL WAR 2.0
Democracy vs. Technocracy

In 2026, the United States once again stands at an existential crossroads. The nation will encounter the same astrological forces that marked the Civil War of 1861-65, one of America's worst internal ruptures.

This year, two slow-moving outer planets, Uranus and Neptune, assemble in the same signs that housed them nearly two centuries ago. Neptune, planet of ideals and illusion, enters aggressive Aries on January 26, 2026, a cycle that will stretch until 2039.

Meantime, Uranus, the planet of rebellion and invention, charges into Gemini for seven years on April 25. Together, they mirror the skies of the Reform, Civil War and Reconstruction eras of the late 19th century.

Does this mean we're headed for a second Civil War? Are we already there? Astrologers, ourselves included, have speculated about this possibility for several years. We knew that in 2025 and 2026, Neptune would make its once-every-164-years move from Pisces to Aries, repeating a transit that set off the 19th-century Battle of Fort Sumter. Still, the idea seemed like a stretch when we began examining it in earnest back in 2019. Hadn't we come way too far for that?

As astrology has taught us in the 2020s, repeating cosmic cycles tell the real story. Indeed, a second Civil War seems to be brewing. This time, it goes far beyond geographic borders.

On one side stands Democracy: a pluralistic ideal that seeks to redistribute power outward to people, communities and grassroots movements. Democracy's champions are modern-day versions of the 19th-century's abolitionists, spiritualists and suffragists: ordinary citizens banding together to fight for agency and equality. There are also members of the "elite" who echo the wealthy New Englanders who joined the Union Army and fought to preserve the nation.

On the other side rises Technocracy, a concentration of power so extreme it makes the Gilded Age look basic. The new "broligarchs," billionaires wielding bravado and algorithmic prowess, control not only information but infrastructure. They are the spiritual heirs of 1860's robber barons: Vanderbilt, Rockefeller, Carnegie, et al. The difference now is that their empires are built on code instead of coal, and they mine data along with natural resources.

In this age of machines, it's platforms, not plantations, that are the focus of this growing divide. Through data and surveillance—algorithms, AI, drones and facial recognition—we are traceable in untold ways. What's more, the wealth pouring into the companies that produce this technology is enriching only a tiny percentage of the global population. As CEOs like Amazon's Jeff Bezos and Meta's Mark Zuckerberg ruthlessly vie for government contracts, the technocrats of our day are gaining unchecked power.

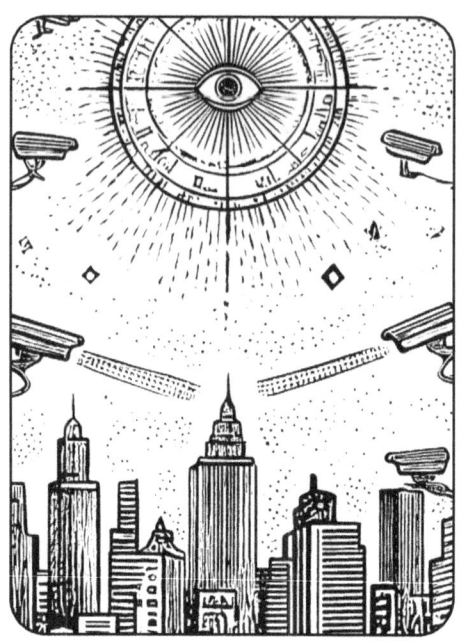

SATURN AND NEPTUNE AT THE ARIES POINT: FEBRUARY 20, 2026

A day that astrologers are eyeing with great concern is February 20, 2026. For the first time in thousands of years, Saturn and Neptune will unite at 0° Aries. Saturn rules the material world and its tangible infrastructures: government, banks, authority figures (and authoritarians). Neptune operates in the quantum realm where boundaries blur, fantasy and escapism reign and time is non-linear. Will the masses wake up or be hypnotized into a Neptunian trance while reality slips from our grasp?

When the U.S. Civil War broke out on April 12, 1861, Neptune hovered

What Is the Aries Point?

(0° Aries)

is where personal and collective worlds collide. Every conjunction here marks a new world era—political upheaval, war, or technological revolution.

The new robber barons mine data instead of coal.

at the final point of the zodiac, 29° Pisces. Two days later, on April 14, Neptune moved into warmongering Aries, where it remained until 1872.

Get ready: Astrological history is about to repeat itself. This January 26, 2026, Neptune will cross from 29° Pisces to 0° Aries, triggering the same "Aries point" that is associated with turbulence and war. Neptune remains in Aries until 2039.

We got a sneak preview of this transit twice in 2025. On March 30, 2025, Neptune briefly crossed the line from Pisces to Aries. That day marked the first time President Trump publicly floated the idea of overturning the 22nd Amendment (the U.S.'s two-term presidency limit) and granting himself a third term. Neptune again crossed from 0° Aries to 29° Pisces during its retrograde on October 22, 2025, just days after Trump began a demolition on the White House East Wing to build a $300 million, 90,000-square foot ballroom set atop a bunker. As Neptune crosses the Aries point again, joining Saturn on February 20, a more aggressive power grab may be coming.

The culture wars are already erupting over the 2026 Super Bowl, which takes place on February 8 while Saturn hovers at the 29° Pisces point. Puerto Rican artist Bad Bunny (himself a Pisces) is slated to perform the halftime show, which is planned as an all-Spanish set. Right-wing backlash has been rampant since Bad Bunny's selection was announced. While the King of Latin Trap lights up Levi's Stadium, the late Charlie Kirk's far-right organization Turning Point USA will air a competing show steeped in xenophobia. The headliner will be (Capricorn) Kid Rock, a vocal MAGA supporter. At this writing, the broadcaster of the show is yet to be disclosed—but given secretive Neptune and heavy-hitting Saturn's fingerprints, prepare for a shockingly large network to make a bid.

TECHNOCRACY: A RISING THREAT

Since volcanic Pluto moved into Aquarius in 2023, science and technology have made quantum leaps in directions that are almost too vast to comprehend. Generative AI has disrupted every industry. Trump's lawless embrace of cryptocurrency enabled dark-money deals to the tune of billions of dollars that he and his family have pocketed.

Little is known about exactly what government data was captured—and who now has access to it—after Elon Musk gained access to Washington D.C.

computer networks during his notorious D.O.G.E. tenure in early 2025. Since then, corporations like Palantir, Meta and major AI defense contractors have woven themselves into the fabric of governance, blurring the line between public good and private gain.

Meanwhile, militarization has entered the picture. Drone fleets patrol the skies, predictive algorithms sort citizens by "risk score," and facial-recognition networks catalog entire populations in real time. Surveillance networks promise efficiency while quietly eroding autonomy.

Does this sound like a bizarre sci-fi movie yet? That's not a far-reaching parallel to draw. One of the biggest flashpoints is money itself. Governments worldwide—including the U.S.—are testing Central Bank Digital Currencies (CBDCs) and digital IDs: cashless systems where every transaction is recorded electronically and tied to a verified identity. With the job market being disrupted by AI, a Universal Basic Income (UBI) is being explored. But instead of cash, citizens would get state-sponsored credits to cover housing, medicine and other needs.

Supporters say these systems will make payments faster and safer. Critics warn they could hand institutions—and the tech firms that build their infrastructure—unprecedented access to citizens' lives. Ironically, this type of system falls closer to communism than to capitalism.

With Pluto in Aquarius from 2024 to 2044, privatized social services could become a huge money grab. The same companies that shape social-media algorithms and store cloud data could soon be the gatekeepers of daily essentials like housing credits, food assistance, health insurance or energy use. Access could be limited—or revoked—at the push of a button.

PRIVATE PRISONS: THE NEW PLANTATIONS?

The fallout from the tariff-fueled "Farmegeddon" crisis of 2025 has left vast swaths of American farmland bankrupt and ready to be bought by investment firms. AcreTrader, an app whose startup funding came from Narya Capital, the investment firm founded by Vice President J.D. Vance, gives private LLCs a platform to purchase farmland in foreclosure. (Vance stepped away from the firm in 2020 but may still retain holdings in AcreTrader.)

Data centers are already rising where crops once grew, pushing the family farm toward obscurity. It's no secret that billionaire investors Warren Buffett and Bill Gates have been buying up farmland for decades. In 2025, Oracle CEO Larry Ellison didn't simply add TikTok and Paramount to his portfolio. He's made his way to Central Texas where he's scooping up acreage to potentially expand his Santa Monica, CA "ag-tech" enterprise, Sensei Farms.

The carceral (prison) economy is part of the story here, too. As vigilante Immigration and Customs Enforcement (ICE) agents disappear both immigrants and legal citizens off the streets, private prison corporations such as CoreCivic expand under the guise of "security infrastructure." Vast detention compounds are being built at alarming rates like the infamous "Alligator Alcatraz"—a swamp-surrounded complex that epitomizes profit-driven punishment.

Fears are already brewing around what this unchecked future could hold. Will the privately-held farmlands become modern-day slave plantations or labor camps? This chilling thought is not out of the scope of what is legal in the United States. ICE detainees could ostensibly be forced into sentences that involve ranching, farming and work once done by migrants.

THE REFORM ERA: PROGRESS BEFORE THE CIVIL WAR

Prior to the U.S. Civil War was a period called the Reform Era. Neptune was in Pisces during this time, fueling both compassion and secrecy. A similar trend has been underway during Neptune's tour of Pisces from April 4, 2011 to January 26, 2026.

The Reform Era of the mid-19th-century was a time when moral idealism and spiritual experimentation intertwined. As Neptune moved through Pisces, the Spiritualist movement—with its séances, trances and claims of communication with the dead—spread rapidly through parlors and town halls. What began as a means to soothe grief after war and epidemic loss evolved into a platform for social change.

Many early Spiritualists were also abolitionists and suffragists. They saw the "spirit world" as a place where all souls were equal, regardless of race or gender and tried to model that equality on earth. Figures like Frederick Douglass, Lucretia Mott and Elizabeth Cady Stanton attended overlapping conventions for women's rights and anti-slavery causes, while Mary Todd Lincoln sought solace through séances in the White House. Faith and reform became interwoven—an early expression of the Neptunian belief that empathy could be the engine of progress.

The digital reformation of the 2010s and 2020s has followed a similar pattern. As Neptune again moved through Pisces, social media became the modern-day parlor. Astrology, tarot and other intuitive mediums entered the mainstream, offering meaning amid instability. At the same time, a wave of activism surged through the collective: #MeToo, #BlackLivesMatter and #FreePalestine galvanized millions to confront injustice and demand systemic reform. Online platforms became gathering spaces for both mysticism and mobilization, echoing the 19th-century circles where political and spiritual debates once intertwined.

As Neptune crosses from Pisces into Aries, ideals are again being tested. The same impulse that once filled parlors and convention halls now drives movements for equality, sustainability and freedom in the digital age. These cycles remind us that every awakening—spiritual or social—eventually reaches its moment of action.

CIVIL WAR: THE TIPPING POINT OF INJUSTICE

When Neptune crossed from Pisces into Aries on April 14, 1861, tensions between the North and South had just exploded into full-on war two days earlier. Confederate cannons fired on Fort Sumter, ending any illusion that moral persuasion alone could heal a divided country.

With innovative Uranus simultaneously transiting through Gemini, technology and communication played a huge part in the battle. Telegraphs, railroads and photography connected the nation even as it fractured. Amid the chaos, Harriet Tubman emerged not only as a conductor of freedom but as a military leader. In 1863, she became the first woman to lead an armed U.S. raid, liberating more than 700 enslaved people in South Carolina. Tubman's heroic work was guided by prophetic visions that came to her in trances and dreams that began after a head injury caused by a cruel overseer.

Now, more than 160 years later, those same transits return. Neptune hovers at 29° Pisces and prepares to enter Aries on January 26, 2026. Uranus plugs back into Gemini on April 25. In eerie resonance, the United States faces a new

kind of internal war. Federal forces have been deployed into major cities like Chicago and Portland under the banner of "national security." Masked ICE officers—many contracted through privatized enforcement agencies—conduct raids that sweep up undocumented immigrants and American citizens alike. Those detained often vanish into a growing network of corporate-run detention centers, where transparency is scarce and accountability scarcer still.

Public outrage has boiled over. The No Kings rallies of 2025 brought nearly seven million people into the streets worldwide—the largest demonstration since the Women's March of 2017. But unlike the 1860s, there is not yet a unified Underground Railroad of resistance. Networks of support exist—mutual-aid groups, encrypted forums, volunteer legal teams—but they remain fragmented, local and vulnerable.

Neptune's return to Aries this January could summon a new cadre of leaders—especially with pivotal midterm elections taking place from April through November of 2026. Political figures such as Gavin Newsom (Libra), Gretchen Whitmer (Virgo), Alexandria Ocasio-Cortez (Libra), Bernie Sanders (Virgo) and Zohran Mamdani (Libra) could become greater forces of influence on the left. Grassroots coalitions like Indivisible and state-level progressive networks could become the connective tissue between outrage and organization. On the right, Uranus' transit could strengthen Tucker Carlson (Taurus) and Marjorie Taylor Green (Gemini).

We are also predicting that Leo Barack Obama could return to the political mainstage in an influential way, especially after Jupiter sweeps back into his sign on June 30, 2026. If Trump presses on toward a third-term, Obama may even announce his own third-term run near August 12, the day of the Total Solar Eclipse in Leo—the first one since the Great American Eclipse that rippled across North America on August 21, 2017.

Obama's lunar nodes are the same as the United States' during its "birth" on July 4, 1976: Leo North Node, Aquarius South Node. Both Obama and the USA will be going through a nodal opposition from July 26, 2026 to March 26, 2028 as the transiting nodes return to these signs in reverse: Aquarius North Node, Leo South Node. The nodal opposition is a period of reckoning where higher purpose cannot be ignored.

Participation from citizens will be essential. Activists talk of "attention strikes"—logging off social platforms to starve disinformation of its oxygen—and of more material refusals: tax boycotts, mass walkouts and coordinated strikes by essential workers whose labor keeps the economy running. These are risky, unglamorous acts of resistance, but under Neptune in Aries, moral courage manifests through direct, embodied action.

RECONSTRUCTION 2.0: BUILDING BACK BETTER?

If the pattern holds, the coming years will bring a new Reconstruction Era—and another Gilded Age beside it. In the post-Civil-War 1870s, wealth pooled in the hands of a few while idealists tried to reform it from within. The same cycle is repeating, now on a digital stage.

Pluto in Aquarius (2024–44) signals a revolution of systems—digital, civic and communal. Power that was once centralized may begin to fracture. In revolt against data control, people may form cooperative networks, mutual-aid economies and transparent frameworks for accountability.

Another counterforce to technocracy? Independent journalists, who will flourish under liberating Uranus' tour through media-savvy Gemini. The late 1800s brought us the muckrackers: Ida Tarbell, Upton Sinclair, Jacob Riis, who used pen and press to expose the corruption hidden beneath Gilded-Age glamour. Their reports on monopolies, child labor violations and political graft seeded the Progressive Era and helped birth modern regulation.

Today's muckrakers (on both the left and right) carry podcasting mics and ring lights. They're the independent journalists, podcasters, whistleblowers and data ethicists who publish outside the corporate media gatekeepers. Their investigations pierce the algorithms, follow digital money trails and expose systems of surveillance, exploitation and environmental harm. In true Pluto-in-Aquarius fashion, truth now spreads through social media leaks and open-source communities.

This movement echoes another chapter of reckoning that unfolded the last time Uranus was in Gemini (1944–52). In the wake of World War II and the atomic bombings of Hiroshima and Nagasaki, humanity confronted the terror of its own inventions. Out of that crisis came an unprecedented global consensus: the creation of the United Nations, the Nuclear Non-Proliferation Treaty and a series of international accords designed to restrain weapons development and regulate uranium enrichment.

Now, under Uranus's return to Gemini, the question is similar but digital: Can the world craft agreements to govern AI, quantum computing and synthetic biology before their consequences outpace ethics? The same planetary archetype that once oversaw the atomic bomb now governs the algorithm. If history repeats, the next generation of "non-proliferation" treaties may focus not on uranium, but on data and intelligence itself.

EPILOGUE

If the 19th century's civil war was fought to end bondage, the 21st century's battle may be to prevent a subtler kind from beginning. The next civil war won't announce itself with cannon fire, but it will seep quietly through code and contracts. As America barrels toward a breaking point, citizens are forced to remember what it claims to stand for. The Civil War made freedom tangible; Reconstruction made equality a law, if not a practice.

This time, the reckoning is digital—and the question is whether liberty can exist inside an algorithm. History isn't repeating itself so much as upgrading its operating system. The download has begun. What installs next depends on us.

"...can the world craft agreements to govern AI, quantum computing and synthetic biology before their consequences outpace ethics?"

FINANCIAL CYCLES & ASTROLOGY
How the Lunar Nodes Could Shape the Economy In 2026

What really moves the markets? Data and algorithms? Human emotion? Or something older—perhaps even cosmic?

Maybe it's all of the above.

As the world races into the second half of the decade, artificial intelligence dominates headlines. Stock valuations for the "Magnificent Seven"— Alphabet, Amazon, Apple, Meta, Microsoft, Nvidia and Tesla—have soared to heights no one could have imagined a decade ago. But underneath the exuberance, the same question lingers: How long can this expansion last?

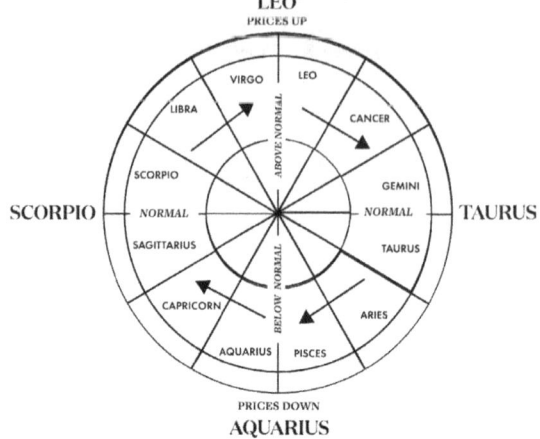

The general economy moves in a 19 year business cycle along with the 18.6-year synodic period of the North Node

Astrologically, that question couldn't be timelier. On July 26, 2026, the lunar North Node shifts into Aquarius for the first time since 2009, repeating an 18.6-year cycle that astrologers have long associated with the rhythm of prosperity and contraction.

In her 1938 book *Astrology and Stock Market Forecasting*, astrologer Louise McWhirter proposed that the North Node—the point where the Moon's orbit crosses the Sun's path—correlates with recurring financial cycles. When the North Node travels through Leo, optimism reigns, confidence inflates and speculative bubbles expand. When it moves into Aquarius, that energy reverses. The market resets, often through crisis or reform.

THE LEO–AQUARIUS PENDULUM

This celestial pendulum between the North Node in Leo and Aquarius has marked nearly every major boom-and-bust moment of the last century. As the North Node approaches Aquarius in 2026, it could bring another round of reckoning—an era of correction and restructuring that lasts until 2028. The question is: What kind of reset will it be this time?

To understand what's ahead, it helps to look back. Each Leo-Aquarius opposition marks one full inhale and exhale of progress: Expansion and exuberance followed by contraction and reform. Over the past century, this rhythm has shown up with uncanny precision.

The Roaring Twenties (Leo) were followed by the Great Depression (Aquarius). The Space Race optimism of the early 1960s (Leo) was followed by Nixon's 1971 "gold shock" (Aquarius). The dot-com mania of the late 1990s (Leo) crashed into the Great Recession of 2007–09 (Aquarius). The crypto bubble of 2017–18 (Leo) now meets the AI boom of 2025, another potential turning point as the North Node swings into Aquarius.

2026 TO 2028: THE COMING AQUARIAN RESET

As we approach the North Node's move into Aquarius on July 26, AI has become the engine of speculative mania. On October 29, 2025, the exact anniversary of the 1929 Wall Street crash, chipmaker Nvidia reached an unprecedented $5 trillion valuation, becoming the most valuable company on Earth. Simultaneously, whispers of an "AI bubble" began to spread. In late 2025, U.S. bank reserves dropped to a $2.8 trillion low, and the Federal Reserve quietly flooded the U.S. banking system with $125 billion over just five days, a move known as "stealth easing."

Meanwhile, the world's monetary system is morphing again. Cryptocurrencies, once fringe, are dividing into two camps: government-backed "stablecoins" and decentralized platforms. One example, Worldcoin (co-founded by OpenAI's Sam Altman), combines digital currency with biometric identity verification. It promises inclusion but raises deep concerns about surveillance and data ownership—issues that feel distinctly Aquarian.

If the 1930s brought social safety nets and the 2000s created the digital economy, this upcoming cycle could deliver what might be called The Great Compression. Everything—information, power and wealth—is being condensed into tighter, faster, more centralized systems.

As the Aquarius North Node returns from July 26, 2026 to March 26, 2028, new forms of regulation are likely to emerge—not for banks this time, but for algorithms, digital currencies and energy use. Governments may impose guardrails around AI ethics, data privacy and the environmental cost of technology. The drive to power vast AI systems may push innovation in nuclear and renewable energy, reviving debates about safety, waste and control.

THE PROPHETS OF PROSPERITY

Astrology's connection to finance isn't new. Long before Louise McWhirter, mystics were mapping the skies for signs of market movement. In 1870, Victoria Woodhull and her sister Tennessee Claflin—both Spiritualists—opened Wall Street's first female-run brokerage, backed by railroad tycoon Cornelius Vanderbilt. Their psychic abilities and boldness made them wealthy and infamous.

A generation later, Evangeline Adams, dubbed "America's first astrological superstar," read charts for financiers including J.P. Morgan. She was tried three times for fortune-telling and acquitted each time, famously impressing a judge by predicting his son's fate through astrology. The apocryphal line "Millionaires don't use astrology; billionaires do" is often attributed to Morgan.

In the early 20th century, trader W.D. Gann merged mathematics and astrology, charting planetary cycles against stock prices. He claimed that "when time and price become equal, the market must reverse." His methods prefigured modern technical analysis and introduced the idea that markets move in natural, geometric rhythms.

Even the U.S. Commerce Department brushed against these ideas. In 1931, Chief Economic Analyst Edward R. Dewey was tasked with finding the cause of the Great Depression. His research led him to the study of cycles—solar, agricultural, social—and their astonishing regularity.

In 1942, under a Leo North Node, Dewey founded the Foundation for the Study of Cycles, documenting thousands of recurring patterns in nature and markets. Among his findings: a 9.2-year rhythm that neatly aligns with half of the lunar nodal period. His book *Cycles: The Science of Prediction* became a cult classic, later republished with bestselling author Og Mandino. Dewey's conclusion was simple: Cycles are the invisible architecture of reality.

THE 1920S LEO NORTH NODE: FROM THE ROAR TO THE FLOOR

In the 1920s, the aptly-named Roaring Twenties brought a Leo North Node cycle from April 23, 1924 to October 26, 1925. True to form, the Big Cat energy inflated the market with jazz-era optimism and opulence. Hope returned after the devastation of World War I, bringing the advent of electricity, radio and motion pictures, appliances and automobiles. Urbanization took hold, as people left farms for industrial jobs, marking the first time in U.S. history that more families lived in cities than in rural areas.

The 1920s also gave birth to consumer credit. With just one household income, the typical family couldn't afford to buy a car or washing machine. In 1919, General Motors offered the first installment plan, allowing autos to be purchased with a 35 percent downpayment. The idea took off. By the time the North Node entered Leo in the mid-1920s, people were buying everything from appliances to stocks on credit. Debt was marketed as

"This celestial pendulum between the North Node in Leo and Aquarius has marked nearly every major boom-and-bust moment of the last century."

an opportunity to gain wealth and be part of America's growth—the land of limitless potential.

In theory, it was inspiring. But as the 1920s stock market bubble inflated, people began buying stocks on "margin," sometimes for as little as a 10 percent downpayment. The catch? At the time, banks didn't have the remaining amount in reserve to cover the 90 percent gap, putting them at risk of failure. When the market dropped, everyday investors would panic, as they had neither the experience nor the extra cash to cover their debts. To pay their loans, they'd sell their shares en masse, sending banks into a spiral.

This volatility set the stage for the October 29, 1929, Wall Street crash, which plunged the United States into the Great Depression, and spread into a multinational economic crisis leading up to World War II.

THE 1930S AQUARIUS NORTH NODE: GREAT DEPRESSION & THE NEW DEAL

The Great Depression lasted from 1929 to 1939, but its low point coincided closely with the bottom of financial astrology's synodic cycle. The North Node entered Aquarius from June 25, 1933 to March 8, 1935, and it was time for repair.

In 1932, the Dow Jones hit rock bottom. One in four people were unemployed and over 9,000 banks had shuttered. Breadlines stretched for blocks as the hungry waited for meals from churches, charities and local businesses. Many Americans lost their homes and moved to self-constructed shantytowns, dubbed Hoovervilles in contempt of then-President Herbert Hoover (a Leo).

The market needed rescuing, and Aquarius Franklin Delano Roosevelt stepped up to do it. In March 1933, three months before the North Node entered Aquarius, Roosevelt was elected U.S. President. He quickly introduced The New Deal, a series of reforms that began to dig America out of its plight.

Recovery began with the Emergency Banking Act on March 9, 1933, which authorized the Federal Reserve to insure bank deposits and offset a potential crash. In June 1933, FDR codified this in the 1933 Banking Act, also known as the Glass-Steagall Act.

Signed just one week before the North Node entered Aquarius, the 1933 Banking Act enforced a strict separation between commercial and investment banking. (This same Act would figure prominently in the Leo/Aquarius synodic cycles of both the late 1990s dot-com boom and the 2008 Great Recession.) Glass-Steagall established the Federal Deposit Insurance Corporation (FDIC), offering government-backed insurance to protect bank deposits. Prior to the FDIC, more than a third of banks failed each year, when panicked customers withdrew all their money at once in "bank runs."

The groundwork for such reform stretched back to earlier nodal swings. The Federal Reserve, founded in late 1913 at the dawn of the 1914-15 Aquarius North Node, had been conceived to prevent the kind of chaos seen during the 1907 Bankers' Panic—a crash that struck while the North Node was in Leo. That episode saw the market plunge 50 percent, forcing financier J.P. Morgan to personally bail out failing banks.

Unfortunately, the Fed was still new when Wall Street crashed in 1929, and was unprepared to mitigate the crisis that led to the Great Depression. Bank deposits were not insured by the Federal Reserve until one full Aquarius Nodal cycle later, when the 1933 Banking Act wrote the FDIC into law.

The 1933 to 1935 Aquarius North Node cycle also produced the Social Security Act of 1935, cementing America's first social safety net—a program now facing its own pressures as the next Aquarius North Node approaches in 2026.

THE 1940S LEO NORTH NODE: WARTIME BOOM & BRETTON WOODS

Franklin Delano Roosevelt was the only U.S. president to serve four terms. His time in office spanned an entire Aquarius–Leo nodal cycle. His first term began in 1933, on the eve of the Aquarius North Node and amid the Great Depression. His fourth ended with his death in 1945, just after the Leo North Node cycle ended, as the nation entered a postwar economic boom.

The North Node was in Leo from November 22, 1942 to May 11, 1944, which were the peak years of World War II. The war, which began on September 1, 1939 and ended on September 2, 1945, mobilized the economy and ended the Great Depression.

Although the government went into debt financing the war, the U.S. employment rate surged as people went to work in factories for wartime production. After the war, the economy continued to boom from consumer demand and the GI Bill (signed right after the North Node left Leo), which funded university educations for many veterans.

At the end of World War II, the world's economies were in chaos—currencies were unstable, trade had collapsed and countries were deep in debt. On July 22, 1944, right after the North Node finished its tour of Leo, leaders from 44 nations came together in Bretton Woods, New Hampshire, to agree on rules for how money and trade would work between countries.

The result was the 1944 Bretton Woods Agreement, which pegged world currencies to the U.S. dollar, which was in turn backed by gold. To keep the peace, Bretton Woods delegates created two institutions: the International Monetary Fund (IMF) to steady currencies and lend to struggling nations, and the World Bank, to fund rebuilding and growth.

Here we see a connection from prior synodic cycles between (Leo-ruled) gold and the United States' position of strength in the gold market. In April 1933, when the North Node was nearing Aquarius, FDR signed an order banning private gold ownership. Americans had to turn in their gold coins, bars and certificates to the Federal Reserve in exchange for paper dollars at about $20 an ounce.

By removing gold from the hands of everyday Americans, FDR centralized the nation's reserves, consolidating power in the U.S. Treasury just as the global economy was preparing for a massive reset.

A decade later, the Bretton Woods Agreement built on that foundation, pegging the world's major currencies to the U.S. dollar, which itself was backed by gold. In effect, gold still anchored the global economy, but now through the dollar rather than direct ownership, and the United States became the world's financial axis, around which other currencies now orbited.

THE 1970S AQUARIUS NORTH NODE: NIXON ENDS BRETTON WOODS AND THE GOLD STANDARD

For almost three decades, the Bretton Woods system held the world economy together, giving postwar nations a stable framework for recovery and trade. But by the late 1960s, the arrangement began to crack. The U.S. had printed more dollars than it had gold to back them, partly to fund the Vietnam War and social programs at home. The Fed's gold reserves were dwindling and other nations started losing faith in the dollar's promise.

In August 1971, with the North Node in Aquarius (November 3, 1970 to April 27, 1972), President Nixon officially ended Bretton Woods. Foreign governments could no longer exchange their U.S. Dollars for gold, silver or other reserves. Overnight and without warning, money became fully "fiat." Rather than being insured by a tangible item like gold, the U.S. Dollar was now backed by something much harder to quantify: the public's trust in its current government and the perceived strength of the market. While the Dow Jones initially shot up and it won Nixon a reelection, his surprise move became known as "Nixon shock."

The biggest change from this nodal reset? Interest rates, which were determined by the current market value of gold, changed from fixed to flexible, determined by fluctuating market forces. To this day, Nixon's 1970s Aquarius North Node policies—and his stunning end of the gold standard—shape how the entire world economy operates.

THE 1980S LEO NORTH NODE: STAGFLATION AND REAGANOMICS

The 1980s Leo North Node began under harsh economic skies—but with optimism puffed up like the decade's signature shoulder pads. During the Leo North Node period that spanned from January 6, 1980 to September 24, 1981, the world experienced another serious recession. It arrived on the heels of the 1979 Iranian Revolution, which caused oil prices to surge and created a global energy crisis. The United States experienced stagflation, a double hit of high inflation and widespread unemployment happening at once.

Despite this turbulence, the cycle was still marked by the Leo North Node's trademark (and sometimes self-deluding) optimism. Ronald Reagan rose to power, elected in November 1980 and inaugurated in January 1981. His charisma and Hollywood roots were quintessential Leo, and his brand of Reaganomics (lower taxes, less regulations on corporations and financial institutions) exuded Leo bravado.

The 1980 Deregulation Act loosened banking rules and expanded financial institutions' lending powers. This fueled more risky speculation, especially in real estate. Gold made a comeback, hitting a record high of $850 per ounce as investors shifted away from fiat currency into tangible assets.

In June 1980, CNN launched, ushering in the 24-hour news cycle and a culture of constant visibility, on brand with showy, dramatic Leo. This was also the dawn of the personal computer revolution. Apple went public in December 1980; the next year, Steve Jobs took over Apple's Macintosh project and IBM released its first PC.

Behind the Leo-era optimism, the reality was far darker. By mid-1982, bank failures reached their highest level since the Great Depression, forcing the FDIC to spend nearly $870 million covering bad loans. It marked the dawn of a new boom-and-bust era—fueled by deregulation and overconfidence—that would echo through future cycles.

THE 1999-2000 LEO NORTH NODE: DOT-COM BUBBLE, BANKING ACT REPEALED

When the North Node returned to Leo in the late 1990s, the world entered another glittering gold rush, this time online. The dot-com boom surged, as tech founders became "paper millionaires," bloated with venture capital financing and overvalued stock options.

In 1999, President Bill Clinton, a Leo, signed the Gramm-Leach-Bliley Act, which repealed key regulations of the 1933 Glass-Steagall Act—the protective 1933 Banking Act signed by FDR during the Aquarius North Node cycle. This move erased the long-standing barriers between commercial and investment banking, and set the stage for the 2008 Great Recession.

By stripping away key safeguards, deregulation fueled reckless risk-taking and birthed the era of "too big to fail" (TBTF) institutions. In 2010, Fed Chair Ben Bernanke defined a TBTF firm as one so large and interconnected that its collapse could trigger severe damage across the entire financial system.

Once again, the speculation and risk-taking of past Leo North Node eras played out on a grand scale. By 2000, the dot-com bubble burst and markets crashed—but the internet remained, permanently transforming how humans connect. Dial-up internet ("You've got Mail!") gave way to broadband, Wi-Fi and the first smartphones, turning the web from a static information source into a living network. In true Leo fashion, everyone suddenly had a stage, and the world was learning how to perform online.

THE GREAT RECESSION OF 2008: AQUARIUS NORTH NODE STRIKES AGAIN

The Aquarius North Node returned from December 2007 to August 2009, ushering in the Great Recession. The U.S. housing collapse triggered a global subprime mortgage crisis, while Bernie Madoff's 2008 Ponzi scheme, exposed under this same transit, erased an estimated $64 billion in client wealth. Few companies mirrored the North Node's Leo-to-Aquarius arc more closely than Lehman Brothers. When the bubble burst under the 2008 Aquarius North Node, Lehman was the world's largest subprime mortgage lender, a position that they'd built up to since the 1999 Leo North Node deregulations.

Because the 1999 Gramm-Leach-Bliley Act removed guardrails between commercial and investment banking, Lehman Brothers was able to pursue riskier ventures like subprime mortgages, and to use complex math that masked their debt-fueled expansion. While the late-90s Leo North Node boosted Lehman's profits, it also left the firm overexposed to risk, setting the stage for its 2008 Aquarius North Node collapse.

In the first half of 2008, Lehman's stock lost half its value. Its $680 billion of assets were supported by only $22.5 billion of firm capital, a huge disparity. Even after receiving over $150 billion of "Federal Reserve-backed advances" from JPMorgan Chase in September 2008, Lehman Brothers ultimately filed for bankruptcy.

As we've seen, Aquarius North Node crashes also bring corrective measures. In November 2008, Barack Obama, a Leo whose birth chart features a Leo

North Node, was elected U.S. President in November 2008, inheriting the worst economic climate since the Great Depression.

In February 2009, right after his inauguration, President Obama signed the American Recovery and Reinvestment Act (ARRA), a nearly $800 billion stimulus package. Much like FDR's 1933 Emergency Banking Act, the ARRA took immediate action, bailing out the Big 3 automakers and creating the Home Affordable Refinancing Program (HARP) to save homeowners from defaulting on their mortgages and losing their properties to foreclosure.

The Aquarius North Node cycle once again brought legislation that could be up for review in 2026 to 2028. In 2010, the Dodd-Frank Wall Street Reform and Consumer Protection Act (known as Dodd-Frank) was signed into federal law. Among its reforms, Dodd-Frank strengthened consumer protections against predatory credit, mortgage and loan practices. It demanded greater transparency from financial institutions, enhanced shareholder oversight and shielded taxpayers from footing the bill for future corporate bailouts.

While the government was protecting U.S. citizens, the last Aquarius North Node cycle paved the way for fintech and decentralized digital currencies such as Bitcoin, which was first minted on January 3, 2009, during this Aquarius North Node cycle.

Amid the 2008-09 Aquarius North Node crash and correction cycle, interest in decentralized finance and digital currency grew. On October 31, 2008, the elusive Satoshi Nakamoto released the Bitcoin white paper, a digital manifesto that introduced cryptocurrency—and a new vision of money—to the world. In the years that followed, a quiet revolution brewed. By 2010, Bitcoin had real-world value (one early user famously traded ten thousand coins for two pizzas, a move they undoubtedly regret). Blockchain technology expanded beyond currency into contracts, art and data systems. As trust in traditional banks waned and smartphones connected the globe, digital assets began to feel inevitable.

2017 TO 2018 LEO NORTH NODE: THE CRYPTOCURRENCY BUBBLE

By the time the Leo North Node returned from May 10, 2017 to November 6, 2018, speculation soared once again. This time, it wasn't over dot-com stocks and IPOs, but rather, crypto coins and ICOs.

These two years marked the first cryptocurrency bubble, as the market exploded from $16 billion to $535 billion. Some investors hailed crypto as the future of finance, while others dismissed it as a fad. As the Leo North Node reached its peak, digital currency entered the mainstream, drawing the attention of regulators and institutional investors alike.

A brief crash came when Bitcoin dropped from almost $20,000 a share in late 2017 to around $3,000 by the end of 2018. Although the market lost $400 billion, it allowed new investors to "buy the dip," and crypto went mainstream. Millions of people first heard of Bitcoin, Ethereum and blockchain, and began buying on crypto exchanges.

On the downside, this era spawned overpriced NFTs and the rise of the "crypto bro." Yet it also offered working people and marginalized communities a rare shot at generational wealth. The high-risk optimism mirrored the Leo North Node cycle of the 1920s—an age of consumer credit and installment dreams. As before, a few struck it rich, but most didn't. Whether buying stocks on margin in the 1920s or overvalued NFTs in the 2020s, many fell prey to the same glittering illusion.

WHERE DO WE GO FROM HERE?

As the North Node enters Aquarius on July 26, 2026, humanity faces another inflection point. What we learn in this next phase could define the century: whether AI becomes an instrument of progress or exploitation; whether currency evolves into a tool for inclusion or control; whether we treat the coming contraction as collapse or as evolution.

History suggests that every downturn is also a dawn. The 1930s birthed modern social systems, the 1970s reshaped global finance and the 2000s gave us digital innovation. As we enter the communal Aquarian Age, and the next Aquarius North Node cycle, perhaps the wisest investment we can make is in humanity's shared survival.

Years	North Node In	Up/Down	Collective Mood or Reset
1905-07	Leo	↑	Stock market high, then three-week plunge in 1907 Panic, corrected by a personal bailout by JP Morgan
1914-16	Aquarius	↓	First years of the Federal Reserve, the official central bank of the U.S., which was formally established December 1913 to mitigate bank failures
1924-25	Leo	↑	The Roaring Twenties: radio, aviation, stock-market euphoria, consumer credit boom
1933-35	Aquarius	↓	Great Depression, the New Deal reforms, Banking Act of 1933 and FDIC creates formal regulations between commercial and investment banking to prevent another Great Depression
1942-44	Leo	↑	Wartime production boom, Bretton Woods Agreement creates "global central bank" World Bank and IMF, makes U.S. dollar the standard international currency, backed by gold
1952-53	Aquarius	↓	Post-war slowdown, Korean War recession
1961-62	Leo	↑	Space-Race optimism
1970-72	Aquarius	↓	Nixon ends Bretton Woods and "the gold standard" by disconnecting the U.S. dollar valuation from gold, reshapes global finance
1980-81	Leo	↑	Deregulation, early tech expansion, first personal computers enter market, stagflation (simultaneous shot of high inflation and high unemployment rates)
1989-90	Aquarius	↓	Black Monday correction, late-'80s savings and loans crisis
1998-2000	Leo	↑	Dot-com mania, repeal of key 1933 Banking Act regulations enables risky moves that lead to 2008 market crash
2007-09	Aquarius	↓	The Great Recession: Global Financial Crisis, U.S. housing market crash, birth of Bitcoin
2017-18	Leo	↑	First cryptocurrency bubble, Bitcoin reaches all-time high then crashes
2026-28	Aquarius	↓	AI gold rush and stock market bubble, tech developments threaten jobs and farming, Big Data tips into possible surveillance with RealID, robots and humans come closer than ever

BIRTH OF A SPECIES
AI & The Transhuman Age

2026 ALMANAC

We're standing on the cusp of an evolutionary turn. Beginning in mid-2026, two of the most transformative outer planets—Uranus and Pluto—form a rare series of exact air trines. Liberated Uranus (in Gemini) and alchemical Pluto (in Aquarius) will make five precise alignments over the next two years: on July 18 and November 29 of 2026, on June 15, 2027 (their energetic peak) and on January 13 and May 9 of 2028.

In astrology, a trine acts like an uninterrupted current of energy—a 120-degree angle of easy flow between two planetary forces. When Uranus, the planet of innovation and surprises, harmonizes with Pluto, the planet of power and metamorphosis, change could arrive at a shocking pace.

These two planets danced in close proximity for most of 2025, which explains the already fast-moving progress of technology. The five Pluto-Uranus trines of 2026-28 could crystallize these developments. If you thought all the talk about AI superintelligence was so next-decade, guess again. This gust of "progress" may blow in much sooner.

American futurist and author Ray Kurzweil, an Aquarius born in 1948 (when Uranus was last in Gemini), predicted the AI phenomenon decades ago. He called it the Singularity, the point where human intelligence merges with machine intelligence and the evolutionary curve takes a completely new trajectory. In his 2006 book, *The Singularity Is Near: When Humans Transcend Biology*, Kurzweil predicted that this human biology-technology fusion would happen in 2045 (interestingly, the year that Pluto is fully done with its 20-year tour of Aquarius).

While this hypothesis felt like a farfetched notion earlier this century, as we cross into 2026, the reality of Singularity feels eerily imminent. Artificial intelligence is no longer a British voice in your car's GPS, a free therapist or an "Alexa, give me the weather" moment. If Kurzweil's imaginings are correct, this technology will soon be embedded into our physical bodies.

Which leads us to transhumanism, the philosophy beneath Kurzweil's vision. Transhumanism proposes that humanity can—and should—use technology to transcend the limitations of biology. The roots of the movement stretch back to the 1940s and 1950s, when computer scientist and cybernetics pioneer Norbert Wiener first conceived of the human body as an information system, with behaviors propelled by feedback patterns that could be replicated by machines. Wiener's book *Cybernetics: Or Control and Communication in the Animal and the Machine* was published in 1948—also while Uranus was last in Gemini.

"We're standing on the cusp of an evolutionary turn."

In the 21st century, the neurotech sector is on the rise, bringing many of these brain-to-computer interface ideas to our imminent reality. Elon Musk's Neuralink promises to restore—and eventually enhance—brain function using threadlike implants that are inserted into the neocortex (the outer layer of the brain) by drilling into the skull. Competitors like Synchron, which is backed by investment from Musk rivals Bill Gates and Jeff Bezos, began implanting test devices in people in 2024.

Then there's CRISPR, a gene-editing technology invented by biochemist Jennifer Doudna and microbiologist Emmanuelle Charpentier. An acronym for Clustered Regularly Interspaced Short Palindromic Repeats, CRISPR essentially acts like a pair of targeted, microscopic scissors that can cut and modify DNA, allowing a cell's natural repair mechanisms to correct mutations, turn off specific genes or even insert new genetic material.

This groundbreaking development has massive potential for curing inherited diseases, but also comes with a huge ethical warning flag. If DNA can be treated like software, humanity could essentially learn to "debug" itself. Aging could be paused or reversed. Humans could expand our sensory limits or even alter DNA to blend with other species.

As quantum computing (a new kind of supercomputer that exceeds the capabilities of current "classical" computers) speeds up pattern recognition, there's no telling where this could go. Could we see humans with wings, centaurs or other mind-boggling hybrids?

As wild as that sounds to our 2026-consciousness, this is not beyond the scope of possibility over the coming decades—especially as Neptune in Aries pushes the boundaries of our imaginations until 2039.

No surprise, major corporations such as Nvidia, Google, Microsoft, Amazon and Palantir are racing to cross the Singularity threshold first. Meta's Superintelligence Lab is reorganizing its AI research toward artificial general intelligence; OpenAI's Sora can already model video and speech with cinematic realism. And that's just the tip of the IT iceberg.

Here's a question we don't want the algorithm to answer: How smoothly will these developments go down with sentient, flesh-and-blood humans? In 2025, the first AI-generated "actress," Tilly Norwood, provoked outrage in Hollywood. Created by Dutch actor and comedian Eline Van der Velden, Tilly was in large part developed as a satiric experiment. But entertainment professionals including Emily Blunt and Natasha Lyonne have been vocal opponents, calling for boycotts of any studio that would work with Tilly. The world, it seems, isn't quite ready to be replaced by avatars.

As the cosmic forces of Uranus and Pluto converge again, the world enters a period that mirrors the early 1920s. Over 100 years ago, these two planets last united in a 120-degree water trine, when Uranus was in Pisces and Pluto was in Cancer. The Roaring Twenties cycle brought a wave of breakthrough inventions that still shape life today, from automobiles to electricity (ruled by Uranus) in the home (governed by Cancer). Einstein's theory of relativity redefined space and time, the discovery of insulin transformed medicine and radio created mass communication.

Along with Uranus' liberation and innovation in the 1920s, however, came domineering Pluto's severe control. All this while Hitler, Mussolini and Stalin began to plant their seeds of power in the wake of World War I. Now, as then, we are witnessing a few key players amass Plutonian power and hoard resources.

Between 1883 and 1886, there were two other Uranus and Pluto trine phases. This was the peak of the Second Industrial Revolution. During the two-year span of each cycle, the Linotype machine revolutionized the printing industry, Thomas Edison launched the first overhead electric lighting system and the Brooklyn Bridge opened after 14 years of construction, connecting Manhattan to its neighboring borough.

Now, as Uranus and Pluto reconnect, a similar surge of both discovery and domination is underway. The late 2020s may become to artificial intelligence and bioengineering what the 1920s were to radio and relativity—a leap that permanently changes how humans see ourselves.

When Neptune in Aries joins Pluto and Uranus in a minor grand trine on June 15, 2027, imagination will collide with science. The same curiosity that once explored atoms is already exploring consciousness. Progress can't be stopped with these energies abuzz, but it can be consciously directed.

What emerges between 2026 and 2028 may not just be a smarter world, but a stranger one. As humans experiment with merging mind and machine, we may have to redefine what consciousness means—and who gets to claim it. Will superintelligent systems evolve as partners, or as competitors?

The Pluto-Uranus trines of 2026-28 will carry both gifts and responsibilities. Left unchecked, the same force that powers invention can also deepen inequalities among humans. The future—and quite possibly, the Singularity—will unfold in breakthrough inventions that force us to decide whether technology becomes an instrument of awakening or another cage of control. The stars have opened the circuit. What flows through it next is up to us.

THE CROSS OF THE SLEEPING PHOENIX

Humanity's Rebirth in 2027 and How to Prepare for It in 2026

As we move through 2026, humanity approaches the close of a four-century cycle known in Human Design as the Cross of Planning. This global configuration has shaped the world since 1615, an era defined by cooperation, infrastructure and shared systems—the building of nations, institutions and networks that supported collective survival.

If you're new to Human Design, it's a system that was introduced in 1987 by its founder, Ra Uru Hu, that combines ancient wisdom (including astrology, the I Ching and the chakra system) with genetics and quantum physics.

On February 15, 2027, the Cross of Planning shifts positions to the Cross of the Sleeping Phoenix, marking the beginning of a new 400-plus year era. The Planning Era organized humanity through contracts and external agreements. The Phoenix Era is about living from your own truth and inner guidance, regardless of what traditions and conventions might dictate.

Astrologically and energetically, 2026 is a bridge year, when our actions leading up to the threshold of this next era will determine how we greet this change.

WHEN ASTROLOGY MET ITS QUANTUM COUNTERPART

For years, Human Design was one of those intriguing "next things" that everyone in trendy spiritual circles seemed to be buzzing about. The jury was out: Was it a passing craze or a rabbit hole worth diving into? We had learned a few basics (6/2 Sacral Generators here!), but never took our curiosity farther than that.

In 2025, we began to pay closer attention to Human Design. Interest in the system, which was founded (more accurately, channeled) in 1987, was surging among our readers and students. Several new books by trusted Human Design experts had landed on our desks.

Human Design might have remained a mere curiosity for us if not for the growing chatter about 2027—the year, according to Human Design, when humanity ends a 412-year cycle and embarks on a new one. That got our attention and we wanted to know more about these cycles.

THE HUMAN DESIGN CHART: ASTROLOGY ON STEROIDS

The Human Design chart, called a Rave Mandala, is essentially an astrology chart on steroids. While we won't get too deep into the details of it here, we'll share a few basics. The Rave Mandala contains a second wheel that wraps around the 12 zodiac sign wheel. This wheel is divided into 64 "gates" based on the 64 hexagrams of I Ching (The Book of Changes), a 3,000-year-old Chinese divination text.

Inside the wheel is the Human Design Bodygraph. Each of the 64 Gates (and the 12 zodiac signs) has a special correspondence with one of the nine "energy centers" that are based on the Hindu-Brahman chakra system, connected by circuitry inspired by the Kabbalah Tree of Life.

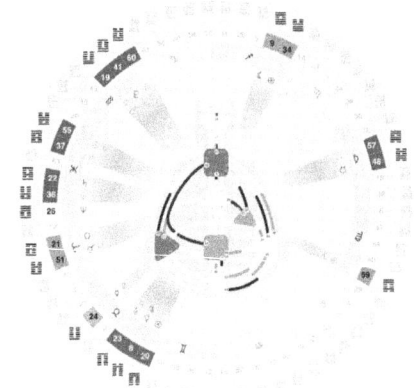

Rave Mandala (mybodygraph.com)

Human Design also gives you two birth charts. The first one is drawn for your actual birthday, which is called your "conscious" or "personality" chart. The second one is drawn for 88 degrees (about 3 months) earlier than your birthday. According to Human Design, this is when the subconscious self begins to form. This is called the "unconscious" or "design" chart.

Just like reading an astrological birth chart, interpreting your Human Design chart is a fascinating study that can last a lifetime. If you're curious to learn more about your Human Design profile from an astrologer's perspective, we've created a special course and platform called Human Design for Astrologers. Geek out with us at humandesignforastrologers.com.

THE INCARNATION CROSS: THE "BIG FOUR" OF HUMAN DESIGN

One of the fundamental components of Human Design is the Incarnation Cross. This is a lot like a Grand Cross in astrology. It's made up of four points in the zodiac/Rave Mandala wheel that form the four corners of a square.

Contained in the Incarnation Cross are:
- The Sun sign in both your Conscious and Design charts
- The Earth sign in both your Conscious and Design charts—which is the zodiac sign opposite the Sun.

If you draw lines between these, they form a cross shape. Human Design does not have a rising sign, but instead, it has an Earth sign (you can learn more about it in our Human Design for Astrologers course, so we'll spare you the mechanics for now).

Every person has an Incarnation Cross in their Human Design chart, which reveals profound information about your life purpose.

That's not all: The Earth also has an Incarnation Cross. Humanity moves through long epochs marked by these Global Crosses. Each one is a roughly 400-year energetic framework that sets the tone for how civilization will evolve.

THE 400-YEAR CYCLES: HUMANITY'S GLOBAL ERAS

In 2027, we reach the end of a 412-year cycle called the Cross of Planning that began in 1615 A.D.

To calculate the Incarnation Cross for the whole planet, Human Design calculates with the precession of the equinoxes, a gravity-induced wobble that shifts the Earth's axis every 26,000 years. Astrologers view this as the reason we moved from the Age of Pisces into the Age of Aquarius, and so forth.

Human Design takes that same astronomical motion and splits it through the 64 Gates of the I Ching. Math moment: When you divide 26,000 by 64, you get cycles of about 405 to 412 years each—the lifespan of a single Global Incarnation Cross.

Toward the end of each cycle, we move into a "shadow phase," when glimmers of the next phase begin to show themselves and the old model starts to dissipate. The past few years have demonstrated that handover, and 2026, the bridge year into the next era, is poised to speed that up.

THE ERA OF PLANNING: 1615 TO 2027

For the past four centuries, humanity has lived under the Cross of Planning, defined by four of the 64 Gates—Gate 9, 16, 37 and 40. These four points align with the mutable signs: Sagittarius, Gemini, Pisces and Virgo.

- *Gate 9* (*Sagittarius*): Focus
- *Gate 16* (*Gemini*): Skills
- *Gate 37* (*Pisces*): Friendship
- *Gate 40* (*Virgo*): Aloneness

Together, these Gates have fueled the rise of alliances, governments and economies.

The Sagittarius-Gemini half of the Cross powered developments in travel, communication, education and global exchange (areas ruled by these signs). Humanity applied its focus (Gate 9) and skill (Gate 16) to tangible innovation, giving rise to Industrial Revolutions, the building of railroads, cars and rockets; and to electricity and computing in the Digital Age, and now, the melding of humans and machines.

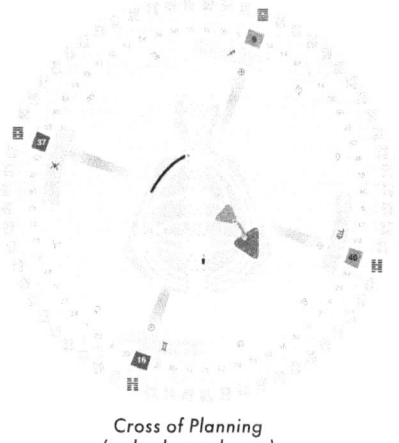

Cross of Planning
(mybodygraph.com)

Meanwhile, the Virgo-Pisces side of the Cross was even more potent. Its two Gates, 40 and 37, form a channel linking the Heart (Gate 40) and Solar Plexus (Gate 37) centers—known as the Channel of Community or Channel of Family. These Gates drew the lines between "us" and "them," defining boundaries, alliances, nations and neighborhoods alike. At their best, the Virgo-Pisces Channel of Community created belonging and mutual support; at their worst, they fueled division, wars and tribalism.

The Era of Planning was about building systems—social contracts, corporations, institutions and communities. Humans planned, produced and organized. In 1785, the introduction of the industrial loom created a huge societal disruption by shifting textile production from the home to massive factories, giving rise to the Industrial Revolution.

What the Human Design Experts Are Saying

We asked a few of our favorite Human Design practitioners how they advise navigating the 2027 shift.

Stacy Cordova, Soul Care Commune (*soulcarecommune.com*)
Transformation or bust! We are being called to evolve and shed the judgments that do not serve us. All Human Design types are being asked to share from our unique experiences and gifts, and most importantly be guided by our Authority. Tapping into our individual strengths we help the collective grow.

Ilona Pamplona - Author, Human Design Made Easy: Understanding the Five Energy Types (*Hachette*), *ilonapamplona.com*
The shift will be from relying on the community for security and belonging to taking ownership of our own security and belonging. So, buh-bye patriarchy! What defined society for centuries (1615 to 2027: wealth, status, and hierarchy) will lose its hold. I feel the recent transits of some non-inner planets/placements in Pisces (Neptune, Saturn, North Node) have given us an amuse-bouche of the kind of fluid, embodied and personal experience of spirituality that Gate 55 of the shift will bring. Those who refuse to evolve will struggle, regardless of their specific Human

Railroads, built throughout the 19th century, put vast sums of wealth in the hands of the "robber barons" like JP Morgan, Andrew Carnegie and Cornelius Vanderbilt. In 1869, the transcontinental railroad connected people from both sides of the United States, accelerating westward development while leaving devastating impacts on indigenous populations.

Once electricity modernized homes in the 20th century, large swaths of the population relocated to cities, reshaping domestic life. The nuclear family model, once an essential unit for surviving on farms and in fields, has outlived its original purpose and continues to struggle.

War and land treaties, though not exclusive to the Planning Era, have also been a huge part of its story. In the West, we saw the American, French and Haitian Revolutions, to the U.S. Civil War and two World Wars. The Planning Era also expressed itself through contracts and alliances, from the Declaration of Independence to the Constitution to the United Nations.

In the final stages of the Planning Era, we are at the brink of the Fourth Industrial Revolution, what many have named the rapid 21st-century race toward automation, AI, data and cloud surveillance and the integration of virtual reality into our daily human lives.

As every planner knows, systems eventually outgrow their purpose. Centralization breeds bureaucracy; belonging often costs individuality. By the 2020s, the collective grid was already overloaded. The old architecture could no longer hold the new frequency. And that's the tremor you may already be feeling.

2026: THE TRANSITIONAL YEAR

Age of Aquarius: incoming? The energy on this planet has shifted in ways that are now impossible to ignore. For many people, life, work and relationships feel faster, more fluid and less defined by old expectations. The rules that once shaped reality no longer seem to apply.

Yet as the Planning Era winds down, some factions of society are clinging tightly to its ways. We see it in the resurgence of ultra-conservative values, in the grueling "9-9-6" work culture (9AM to 9PM, six days a week) glorified by tech companies and in the defense of outdated hierarchies and institutions that exclude entire populations.

From AI data centers devouring farmland and water to the widening gap of billionaire wealth, themes of the Planning Era have accelerated

Design type. Above all, don't panic. This is a 400-plus-year cycle, so we probably will not witness the full shift in our lifetimes. Experiment with your personal design to guide you through this purpose-driven era!

Emma Dunwoody - Author, Human Design Made Simple (Penguin Australia)
Host, The Human Design Podcast (emmadunwoody.com)

2026, to me, is the year of personal responsibility and embodiment. It's the bridge year when we stop waiting for the world to tell us what to do and to start living as the fully expressed, self-sourced beings we came here to be. The era of "the tribe will take care of you" is ending.

The key is to anchor deeply into your Strategy and Authority, to learn how to trust your own internal GPS instead of trying to fit yourself back into old systems that are already crumbling. We're witnessing the breakdown of codependency and the birth of self-trust.

I see the Earth herself shaking off what's not sustainable, literally and energetically. Climate, economy, governance, anything built on extraction or control, is being rewritten. Gaia's moving from being used to being partnered with.

The world's structures are cracking because they're meant to make space for self-led, embodied, purpose-driven beings who create from overflow, not obligation. We'll see people waking up to their true energetic sovereignty, no longer outsourcing truth, leadership or belonging.

Dana Stiles & Shayna Cornelius Co-founders of DayLuna (daylunalife.com) Co-authors, Your Human Design: Discover Your Unique Life Path & How to Navigate it With Purpose (Fair Winds Press) A foundational concept in Human Design is that each individual is meant to make life decisions by following the intuitive wisdom of their body. This is a radical shift from the old paradigm, which taught us to rely on mental strategy, logic and external validation.

For those who have found comfort in following society's rules or outsourcing decisions to experts, it may feel disorienting to navigate a world that's being rebuilt. But those who are attuned to their inner authority will find deep confidence, clarity and spiritual safety through the transitions ahead.

It can be unsettling to watch the world appear to crumble around us. It's natural to feel anxiety or overwhelm when faced with so much uncertainty and change. But remember: These shifts are not a sign of collapse; they're a reorganization toward something more authentic and free. No one person can transform the world alone. But if each of us takes responsibility to reconnect with our inner truth, and embody personal empowerment, the ripple effect will be immense.

beyond our collective capacity and resources.

The message, as governments, traditional media and financial institutions teeter on the brink: Community can no longer come at the cost of personal freedom. But how do we get there? The final years of the Planning Era (2024-26) seem determined to pull us in the opposite direction: toward greater social control, where "family" can look like ideological lockstep, with political, religious or nationalist movements that punish anyone who falls out of line.

Meanwhile, the rapid advance of AI, data surveillance and algorithmic control is intensifying that grip. Across the world, reproductive rights are being rolled back and democratic foundations eroded. In counties like China, citizens live under a "social credit" system that can bar their access to work, commuting, jobs and travel if they fall out of line (e.g., protest or speak against the government). This shadow phase at the end of the 412-year cycle reveals where institutions and administrations are doubling down on their grasp for control.

THE ERA OF THE SLEEPING PHOENIX: 2027 TO 2439

On February 15, 2027, the Planning Era ends and we enter the Cross of the Sleeping Phoenix, a new four-century cycle defined by Gates 20, 34, 59 and 55, also in the mutable signs.

> Never underestimate the power of investing in your own peace, deepening your spiritual connection and learning from teachers who help you expand your compassion and liberation. Every act of personal alignment contributes to the awakening of the collective.

- Gate 34 (*Sagittarius*): Power
- Gate 20 (*Gemini*): Presence/Now
- Gate 55 (*Pisces*): Spirit
- Gate 59 (*Virgo*): Intimacy

During the Cross of Planning, we built the systems of modern civilization. The Sleeping Phoenix Era could dismantle or dissolve many of them, even if it happens over the course of decades, and centuries. While we won't live to see the full expression of the Sleeping Phoenix, we are all alive at this moment to make our contribution.

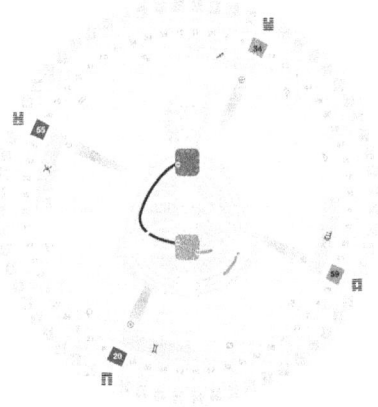

Cross of the Sleeping Phoenix (mybodygraph.com)

Despite its snoozy name, the Sleeping Phoenix may arrive with a jarring wake-up call. We've reached a breaking point, and living within these structures has become unsustainable: Our financial, energetic and environmental resources are stretched to capacity. Who will rise to sound the alarm? Will there be a voice strong enough to drown out the fear and hate that's spread across the planet?

Quite possibly. Two of the Cross of the Sleeping Phoenix's four Gates, Gate 20 (Gemini) and Gate 34 (Sagittarius), form a circuitry that connects the Sacral center (life-force energy) to the Throat center (expression and manifestation) through what's known as the Channel of Charisma. Spiritual Neptune in passionate Aries (2025 to 2039) will amplify this. It's a channel that only Manifesting Generators, one of the five Human Design types, have. (Read more about the types at astrostyle.com/human-design). Collectively, our world may adopt the traits of "Mani-Gens": multi-passionate and self-directed. The magnetism of Manifesting Generators, when used for the greater good, can mobilize the masses. On the negative side, it can be manipulative, entitled and destructive, especially when directed toward selfish gain.

If there was ever a time to learn Human Design and astrology, it's now. Your inner guidance system may be the only trustworthy GPS as we move deeper into this decentralized era and navigate the growing tension between individual and institution.

LIVING IN THE PHOENIX ERA

The transactional approach of the Planning Era has reached a saturation point. The gap between the haves and have-nots has never been wider and it's reaching peak unsustainability.

At the same time, the Information Age has given billions of people access to education and to each other. Networks now exist (though on a tenuous power grid) of people who are resisting the injustice and domination that's spreading throughout the world.

We've seen the glimmers of the Phoenix approach in relationships. Segments of the population have become less interested in traditional roles and contracts, from the "lavender marriage" to "gray divorce" to people opting out of conventional titles altogether. Groups of older women are moving into communal compounds dubbed "birds nests," finding each other's company far more fulfilling and peaceful than growing older with a romantic partner.

Spirituality has become the "new religion" for many, as people are seeking guidance from the temple within. Breathwork, somatic therapy, movement and energy healing carry the same gravitas once reserved for a Sunday service. Astrology, Tarot and other divination systems have gained mainstream popularity.

As we enter 2026, we find ourselves in transition. The overlapping edges of the Planning and Phoenix eras led many of us to want "systems" that liberate and reflect us, rather than stifle our spirits and sovereignty. A call for more choice and less obedience has sounded. Will we be able to move into this era peacefully? That remains to be seen, but we have hope.

2026 ASTROCARTOGRAPHY
Map Your Destiny by Helena Woods

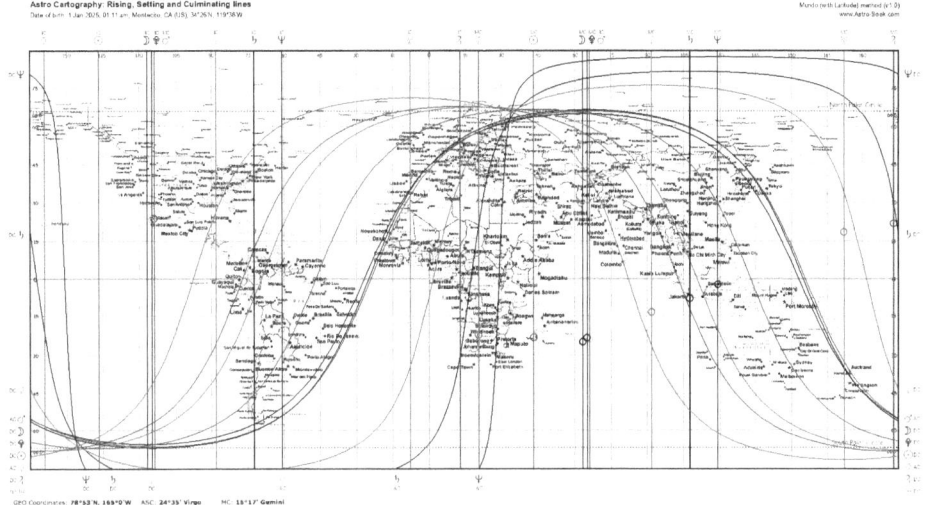

I f "should I move out of the country?" has crossed your mind recently, astrology is here to help! With so much change happening on the planet, many people are exploring where their next home or travel escape might be.

Astrocartography, which is a branch of locational astrology (astrological geography), sets your birth chart to a world map. This helps you find places where you'll feel various planetary influences—known by the technical term "lines"—that can be either helpful or challenging.

HOW TO CAST YOUR FIRST ASTROCARTOGRAPHY MAP

I recommend starting off by going to Astro.com's Astro Click Travel free map calculator or to Astro-Seek's Astrocartography calculator to see where your planetary lines are placed on the map.

Just like with a regular birth chart, enter your time, date and place of birth. The result will be a literal map of the world with the planetary symbols and lines extending out from them. (*Make sure that your birth time is accurate within 15 minutes or there can be a significant change in the lines!)

After generating your map, grab my free Astrocartography cheatsheet at helenawoods.com/cheatsheet, where I've written all the basic meanings of the planetary lines on your map, and included some tips for getting the most out of your Astrocartography planning.

HOW ASTROCARTOGRAPHY WORKS IN REAL LIFE

Before you pack up your whole life and start over, or even plan your next getaway, why not consult the stars? Astrocartography can filter all the options so you choose a place that resonates with your goals.

For example, you might be a fiction writer who wants to complete a draft of your novel. Astrocartography could help you find places where your chart has a Mercury line, since Mercury rules writing. Maybe you'll find love in cities or continents where you have a Venus line, or you could fall for someone who's from that part of the world. There could be places where multiple planets on your chart intersect, allowing you to tap into their combined influence.

Astrocartography is much more than a permission slip to plan a vacation or to move your life to the other side of the world. I map Astrocartography transits in my own life by noting the planets I'd like to receive support from. When I desire more attention for my work, I travel to my Sun lines on the map, because the Sun represents exposure, visibility and creative expression!

By understanding the planets and their meanings, you can travel to specific planetary lines to fulfill your purpose or dream. (**For more advanced Astrocartography that involves transits, check out my courses at helenawoods.com.**)

REMOTE ACTIVATION: WHEN YOU CAN'T ACTUALLY TRAVEL

Sometimes, you just can't leave city limits. Good news: You can still connect with the energy of a fortuitous place! In Astrocartography, there's a technique called remote activation. It allows you to "travel" by simply connecting to the energy of a desired location, right from your own home!

Remote activation essentially brings the energy of any planet to you, no matter where in the world you are. You can tap into a planet's line by learning about the place, studying the language, watching films or listening to music from there. You can explore a job opportunity or Airbnb listings in that location, or collaborate and connect with people based there. But to get the maximum benefit of your "power places" in the world, traveling there physically will enhance your experience even more.

PERSONALIZE IT! BEST ASTROCARTOGRAPHY PLANNING TIPS

Set the intention. One way to pick your Astrocartography line is to ask yourself what you're hoping to receive from that trip. Want to relax, unwind and unplug? Check out Venus and Neptune lines. Planning to launch a business offering from on the road? Check out your ercury, Jupiter or Mars lines.

Time it (**Advanced**). Go to the Astrocartography lines associated with the planets that are currently being transited in your chart. These power lines on your map are being activated by timing! Pay particular note to Jupiter and Venus transits. When Venus or Jupiter transits to your planet, going to that planetary line would be especially advantageous. (Note: My free cheatsheet has advice on the best software for transit maps if you opt to go down this fascinating rabbit hole!)

Bio:
Helena Woods is a full-time world-traveling astrocartographer, author and locational astrology expert. She is on a mission to empower others to find places they most thrive and shine using the power of location and timing. Helena teaches locational astrology and Astrocartography mapping in-depth through her suite of courses at helenawoods.com. *Get your free Astrocartography mapping cheatsheet from Helena at helenawoods.com/cheatsheet*

2026 ASTROCARTOGRAPHY TIPS FOR EVERY SIGN
by The AstroTwins

Here's how to tap into your 2026 Sun or rising sign forecast through Astrocartography and start experimenting with this technique. If any of the places you locate are appealing, consider planning a visit. If they don't feel like bucket-list vacation spots, experiment with remote activation and tune into their frequency through research. Simply connecting to the energy of these lines could deepen your resonance with the 2026 cosmic lineup and the unique gifts it holds for you.

ARIES: In 2026, you're emerging into a whole new version of yourself, thanks to Saturn and Neptune settling into Aries for a long run. Since you'll host both of these planets (and they'll meet at an exact conjunction on February 20), it could be interesting to see where Saturn and Neptune lines fall on your Astrocartography map, if only for some remote-activated enlightenment. Consider visiting a Uranus line to help your radical reinvention, or check out a Jupiter line to keep you inspired to stretch beyond your comfort zone. Mars, your ruling planet, can kick-start your motivation, so check out where your Martian lines are.

TAURUS: Ready to get back to your preferred steady pace? This spring, you finally can. Erratic Uranus finally leaves your sign for good in late April, after a disruptive but highly enlightening eight years. You've discovered parts of yourself that you may never have known. Now, where in the world can you take them? Look for a moon line if you need some emotional restoration, or a Sun line to debut the new and transformed you! (And maybe avoid the Uranus lines for now, since you've had an overload of its destabilizing influence.) Your ruling planet is Venus, so scope out where you have Venus lines to see if any of those spots intrigue you.

GEMINI: Who are you anyway? An unprecedented life chapter is ahead as disruptive and trailblazing Uranus settles into Gemini until 2033. Break free from the old version of yourself by visiting a Uranus line or head to a Jupiter line, which encourages personal growth. Feeling a little too destabilized? A

Saturn line, though challenging, can anchor you back into your core values and priorities. Need to break those big, innovative ideas into smaller steps or put them into words? Seek places where you have lines for your ruling planet, Mercury.

CANCER: Emerge from your comfort zone and head to "parts unknown" (as the late Cancerian Anthony Bourdain would say). With lucky Jupiter in your sign until June 30, and even more favorably, out of retrograde after March 10, the wider world beckons. Suss out where Jupiter lines fall on your Astrocartography map and spread your wings! You've also got planetary permission to have fun, so follow the Sun and Venus lines for unforgettable adventures. For deeper insight into yourself, check out where your ruler, the Moon, activates.

LEO: Take a break from the spotlight, Leo. The first half of the year is internal and reflective, an interesting time to connect to a Neptune, Pluto or moon line—if only for a brief visit. This detour can be healing, helping you release what no longer serves you. Explore these sites before June 30, because after that, it's showtime again. At the end of June, lucky Jupiter enters your sign for the rest of 2026, an ideal time to follow its lines or track down your ruler, the radiant Sun, and see where it takes you.

Astrocartography 101: What the Planet Lines Mean

Here's a quick look at what each planet means in your Astrocartography map.

Sun: Your True Essence & Light
You'll feel most yourself here; ideal spots for visibility and opportunity.

Moon: Your Emotions & Home
Bonding, settling down and family matters can thrive here.

Mercury: Communication & Friends
Great places for writing, speaking, ideas, sales and your social life.

Venus: Love, Beauty & Pleasure
Get a glow-up, fall in love or take a romantic getaway here.

Mars: Drive & Conflict
You'll be driven and courageous, but may also have conflict and stress.

Jupiter: Luck & Growth
A joyful and optimistic place to grow, learn and explore new adventures.

Saturn: Duty & Challenges
May feel isolated or burdened with responsibility. You'll grow through hard work and sacrifice here.

Uranus: Freedom & Individuality
Ready for big changes? Break free of limits and past patterns, find your authentic self.

Neptune: Dreams & Illusions
Good for creativity, spirituality and escape but can bring moodiness and deception for the long-term.

Pluto: Intensity & Power
Power and intrigue are palpable here, as well as a hint of danger. Psychic abilities grow.

VIRGO: You've been through so much internal transformation and while you're much wiser and further along, the journey isn't over. This year brings continued contemplation that will prepare you for a rebirth mid-2027. Scout your Neptune, Pluto and moon lines for places that bring spiritual release, deep transformation and the breaking of old ancestral patterns. Getting lost in the sauce of your soul-searching? Reinvigorate and focus at an energizing Mars line. Follow your ruler Mercury's lines for help processing, even writing about, everything you experience.

LIBRA: Your career and public life are lit up in 2026, making this a great time for career momentum. A Sun or Jupiter line on your personal map could help you realize the percolating potential. Meantime, your relationships are shifting in a more serious but soulful direction. A moon line could help you connect to your heart and true needs if you feel out of touch with them, while lines for your ruler, Venus, can point you to romance. But if you find yourself getting a little clingy, head to a Mars or Uranus line for a confidence boost and a reminder that you're more than enough on your own.

SCORPIO: You've got big dreams to stoke in 2026, so widen your viewfinder! Your appetite for risk and novelty is high in the first half of the year, a great time to check out an expansive Jupiter or courageous Mars line. The second part of 2026 sets your sights on a lofty goal, and you're not afraid to work hard to achieve it. A brief dalliance with a Saturn line can help ground you in discipline or even connect you to a mentor. Avoid Uranus lines, which can destabilize your goals before they gain traction. Connect to your Scorpio depths by exploring lines matched to your complex and powerful ruler, Pluto.

SAGITTARIUS: The first and second half of 2026 will have markedly different energies. Until late June, you could be deeply introspective and intense. Percolating power duos and a fascination with life's mysteries could point you to a Pluto line. Erotic explorations could be stoked in a Mars-ruled location. Fame and adventure call in the later half of the year, the perfect time to visit a Sun or Venus line to amplify your charisma. Stay away from the limiting influence of Saturn lines and move toward your ruling planet, Jupiter, to help you spread your wings.

CAPRICORN: With expansive Jupiter in your relationship houses all year, your closest ties need to be balanced but also challenge you. A Venus line is the obvious choice for bringing back the love (or finding it!). If things have gotten stagnant with a longtime mate, a trip to an authenticity-inspiring Uranus line can jolt you out of stale patterns or roles. To perk up the passion, you might even visit a Mars line. But tread lightly, as these locations can also breed conflict. Your ruling planet Saturn isn't always the best vacation line, but a remote activation can help you better understand yourself.

AQUARIUS: A whole new Aquarius is emerging, and you might barely even recognize yourself these days. You're walking taller, speaking with more certainty and rising into leadership. With powerful, influential Pluto in your sign until 2044, exploring Pluto lines can support your ascent and make sure you have the right puzzle pieces in place. How you present your ideas is key, so head to a Mercury line to craft your pitch and meet allies. Your ruler, Uranus, could help connect you to places where you can be your most colorful self.

PISCES: Reset! Saturn and Neptune complete their long visits to your sign by mid-February and free you from their grips. You've been learning and growing under strict Saturn, but may have felt progress slip through your fingers thanks to ephemeral Neptune. Now, you're ready to shake off the confusion and make a bold move. Head to a Mars line for a shot of courageous motivation, or visit a Uranus line to reclaim your authenticity that may have been suppressed over the past couple years. A romantic influence in the first half of the year can be supported by a moon or Venus line. Your ruler, Neptune, can connect you to places that mirror your soul, but after 13 years of hosting this planet in your sign, you might not be in the mood for places with Neptune's energy

2026

Year of the Fire Horse

FEBRUARY 17, 2026–FEBRUARY 6, 2027

Western Zodiac Equivalent: Gemini
Fire Element: Years ending in 6 or 7
Prior Fire Horse Years: 1906, 1966

Keywords

- Independence
- Drive
- Charisma
- Passion
- Rebellion

Gifts of the Fire Horse

- Trailblazing energy and visionary leadership
- Rapid progress and momentum
- Passion-fueled creativity and charisma
- Collective breakthroughs through teamwork
- Fierce authenticity and independence

Challenges of the Fire Horse

- Burnout from moving too fast
- Restlessness or difficulty committing
- Impulsive decisions and clashing egos
- Overthrowing structure before building new systems
- Learning to balance individuality with teamwork

Giddy Up! 2026 is the Year of the Fire Horse—a once-every-60-years burst of wild independence and trailblazing momentum. From February 17, 2026 to February 6, 2027, this unbridled creature takes the reins.

Fire years—those ending in 6 or 7—already run hot with momentum. When the Horse charges through, its free spirit kicks the pace into overdrive. Saddle up. You'll want to be ready when the starting gate flies open!

In Chinese astrology, the Horse is the zodiac's untamed wanderer—magnetic, determined and happiest with the wind blowing through its tangled mane. The Horse thrives when chasing the horizon, but bristles at fences or rigid routines. Add the Fire element and it's going to be hard to tame anyone's spirit. (And why would you?) Old patterns can burn away in a flash, clearing the field for what feels urgent, alive and true. Take the reins of your own life and steer toward what excites you most. There won't be much time for munching hay in the barnyard stalls in 2026.

The Horse has a kindred spirit in Western astrology. With its quick reflexes, curious mind and appetite for variety, it mirrors Gemini's dual nature. Both are adaptable and socially agile, able to pivot on a dime. Like Gemini, the Fire Horse can turn clever ideas into action at breakneck speed. In 2026, mental agility will keep you ahead of the pack, especially as you train yourself to act more quickly upon your instincts.

During the previous Fire Horse year, 1966, birth rates dipped in Japan and parts of China as families tried to avoid having daughters. Ancient lore painted Fire Horse girls as too fierce, too independent to fit within traditional roles. Some legends even warned that these girls would grow up to kill their husbands!

Seen through today's lens, the myth reads differently—especially in a moment when women's rights face renewed threats in the U.S. and beyond. Further efforts to tame women into submission could turn into an explosive rebellion in 2026. Goodbye, trad-wives, restrictive reproductive laws and voter suppression? We certainly hope so. At very least, systematic oppression will be met with fire and fury this year.

Go back further to 1906—the last Fire Horse year before 1966—when the San Francisco earthquake and fire became a symbol of sudden, sweeping transformation. This mythological creature doesn't just canter through history—its beating hoofprints leave a mark. That unyielding spirit is what 2026 demands of us all. After a year of political gaslighting and cross-industry fealty to authoritarianism, anger could erupt into a full-on conflagration.

Although liberation is a huge theme of the Fire Horse year, isolation is not. It's important to remember that wild horses roam together in herds, protecting one another from predators as they share knowledge and experience. That's a fantastic metaphor for the allyships 2026 requires. To foment change, we need to gallop ahead in a strong-willed stampede.

No matter how unconventional your path may be, if your instincts say, "Hell, yes!" then this is the year to blaze a trail forward against all odds. And yes, you may have to kick up a little dust in order to make your mark. But that's also how you'll become the leader of the pack.

1 Universal Year

By Felicia Bender, the Practical Numerologist

themes
OF A 1 UNIVERSAL YEAR

Releasing
Flow
Completion
Compassion
Collectivism
Humanitarianism
Surrender

challenges
OF A 1 UNIVERSAL YEAR

Stagnation
Control
Resistance
Preservation
Fear
Ignorance

2026 is a 1 Universal Year

$$2 + 0 + 2 + 6 = 10$$
$$10 \rightarrow 1 + 0 = 1$$

In 2025, we weathered a 9 Universal Year, the final phase of each nine-year cycle. It delivered on its promise to be a time marked by chaos, abrupt endings, emotional urgency, angst and fatigue. Collectively, 2025 rattled our cages and pushed us into a place where total reinvention was, and continues to be, the name of the game.

Enter 2026, a 1 Universal Year, which crashes onto the scene like Tom Cruise's Ethan Hunt after a prolonged Mission: Impossible stunt sequence. The promise? A year defined by new beginnings, independence, bravado and panache. The call for mindful leadership is loud in a 1 Universal Year, along with a need for inventive problem-solving. Change is in the air!

HOW TO MAKE THE MOST OUT OF THE
1 Universal Year

DYNAMIC LEADERSHIP
The 1 Universal Year demands bold choices and decisive action as you take charge of your destiny. At its highest expression, this energy calls for intentional, supple leadership. It mirrors Aries—the zodiac's trailblazer—where fortune favors the bold and "failing forward" is part of the process. The key challenge is balancing productive disruption against the risk of ego-fueled megalomania. A wave of entrepreneurial spirit fuels new businesses, passion projects and career reinventions. Collectively, we're at a pivot point, radically redefining everything!

BREAKTHROUGH INNOVATIONS
Technological, cultural and personal innovations thrive under the pioneering energy of the 1. The rising influence of AI is reshaping commerce, communication and nearly every facet of life. True to the adage "necessity is the mother of invention," the 1 Universal Year sparks future-focused solutions and visionary ideas.

PERSONAL POWER
Optimism builds as we shake off the chaotic 9 Universal Year of 2025, replacing uncertainty with renewed purpose and clearer direction. But here's the catch! Any team is only as strong as its individuals. Healing and empowering each person becomes the key to helping the collective thrive.

INCREASED MOTIVATION
New year, new everything! A surge of collective energy pushes us to launch new projects, pivot directions and start fresh. The Age of Aquarius is here, bringing dramatic, sweeping change on a global scale. As political and financial structures dissolve, the call to "go back to the drawing board" grows louder. This isn't about adding to what's already operational—it's about creating entirely new systems to support an evolving global community.

INDIVIDUAL ACTIONS IN ALIGNMENT WITH A

1 Universal Year

BACK UP BOLD TALK WITH ACTION

Kick off the year with clear, empowering goals and stretch beyond your usual limits. Think bigger than ever before. Vision boards, meditations and goal-setting rituals can anchor your focus, with the understanding that your entire mission is likely to evolve as the year unfolds. The key is to begin with concrete steps to channel this initiating energy. Launch the business, write the first chapter of the book, move across country or pivot the career you've been postponing. This is the year to start fresh—not to cling to anything that's long past its expiration date.

INVEST IN SELF-DEVELOPMENT

The 1 Universal Year activates "beginner's mind." Let go of embedded ideas and concepts about yourself, others and the world so that you can approach situations from a different perspective. In 2026, you're invited to learn new skills, develop leadership qualities and take charge of your life. Stop waiting for permission to pursue your dreams—just be sure to make any changes mindfully rather than impulsively.

GET RADICALLY AUTHENTIC

No more apologies for taking up space! The 1 Universal Year is a time for radical authenticity. In places that feel safe (and possibly in some that don't) express your true self unapologetically. In relationships, work and creative pursuits, you won't be able to tamp down your creative expression. Your personal truth will become self-evident this year.

KEEP ON KEEPING ON

Release habits, relationships and careers that no longer support your growth. Start fresh and trust the timing. Every season has its purpose, and life isn't meant to stay comfortable or perfectly clear. We gain strength and evolve when challenges push us beyond the familiar, forcing emotional and spiritual growth.

COLLECTIVE ACTIONS IN ALIGNMENT WITH A
1 Universal Year

INNOVATIVE SYSTEMS AND LEADERSHIP MODELS
New leaders emerge—alongside movements and technologies that champion individual empowerment. Support for entrepreneurs and creators may fuel a surge of startups and independent platforms designed to disrupt traditional systems.

CULTURAL REDEFINITION
Cultural identity, values and social narratives shift toward greater self-expression and individualism. Since this is all happening under the larger umbrella of the Age of Aquarius, there's a "squad goals" vibe to this 1 Universal Year: All for one and one for all. This year's pioneering spirit can fuel visionary social initiatives—ones that serve the many, not just the few.

GLOBAL REBOOTS
Nations and companies may overhaul systems, rewrite policies and reset outdated frameworks. Autonomy and economic independence move to the forefront, while questions of national identity and personal freedom get louder. As old structures crumble, new models start to take shape.

At the crux of the powerful 1 Universal Year is a collective mandate to birth fresh paradigms. In 2026, expect a shift away from ego-driven thinking and toward a more intentional, conscious way of being. We're standing at an existential moment in history where we urgently need to envision new realities. An immense opportunity for lasting transformation lies ahead in 2026. And it's time to lead with courage and plant the seeds for an unscripted future.

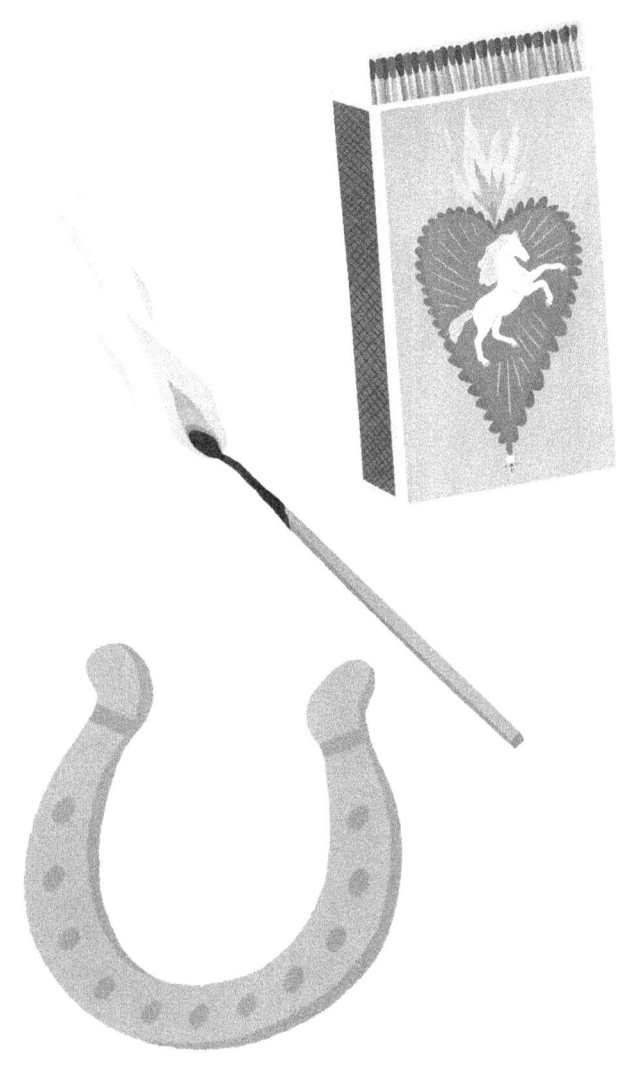

ENJOY MORE FROM
The AstroTwins

Identical twins and co-founders of the leading horoscope platform Astrostyle, Ophira and Tali are the authors of over 22 books, longtime ELLE Magazine columnists and the "secret weapon" consultants for some of the world's most influential people, including top executives, celebrities and impact-driven leaders. They've partnered with top brands, advised luminaries including Beyonce and Dua Lipa, and appeared in major media such as Fast Company, The New York Times and Good Morning America. I*AM is the basis of their national bestselling book, The Astrology Advantage (Simon & Schuster, August 2024).

WEEKLY PODCAST: ASTROTWINS RADIO
Start every week aligned with the stars with a live forecast from Tali and Ophira. **astrostyle.com/podcasts**

JOIN OUR VIP LIST
Join our list for VIP invitations & earlybird access to special events, courses and sales!
astrostyle.com/list-sign-up

www.ingramcontent.com/pod-product-compliance
Lightning Source LLC
Chambersburg PA
CBHW081531300426
44116CB00015B/2592